A BREATH OF FRESH AIR

Birmingham's Open-Air Schools
1911–1970

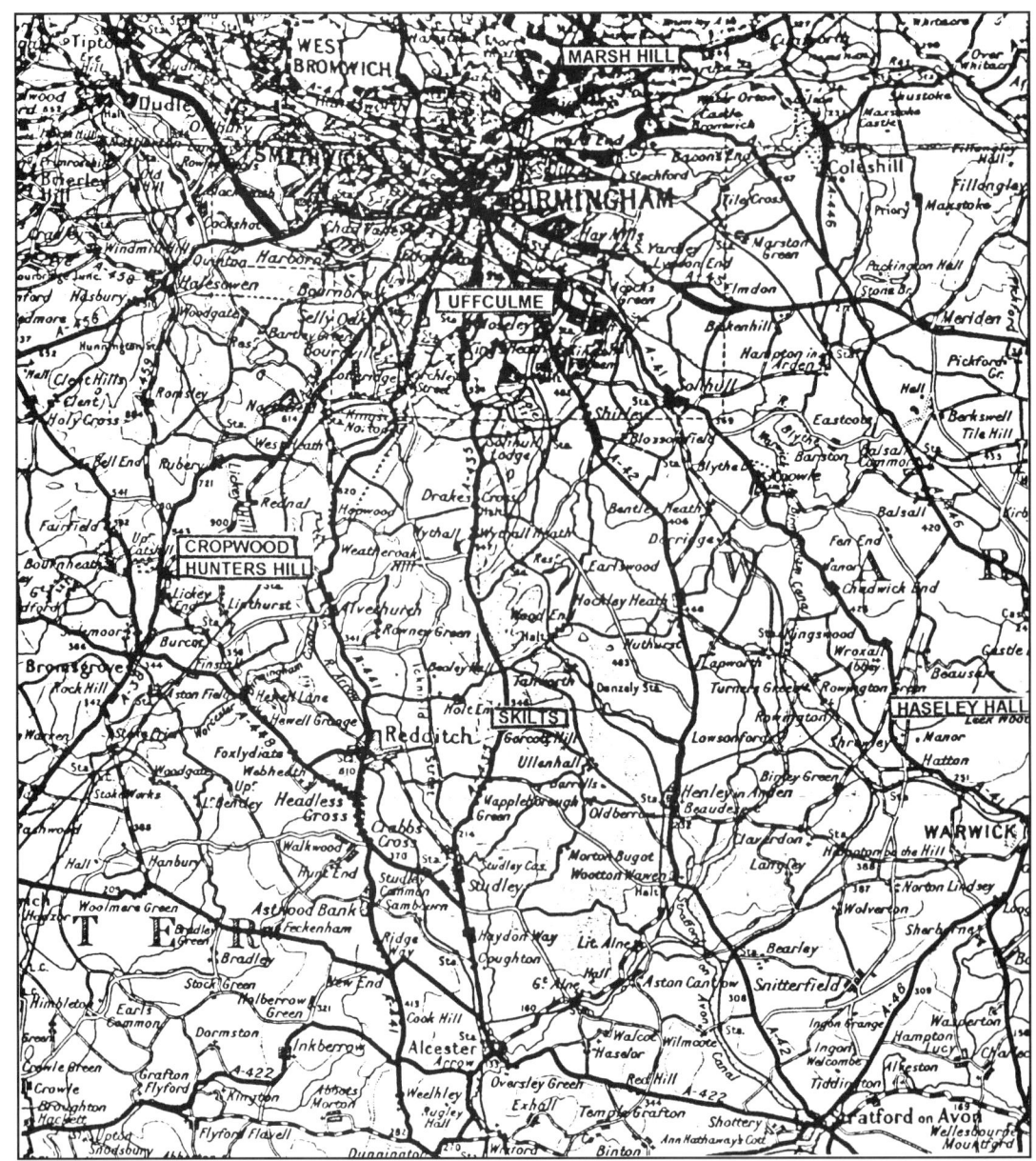

Birmingham's six open-air schools: Uffculme, Marsh Hill, Cropwood, Hunter's Hill, Haseley Hall and Skilts.

A BREATH OF FRESH AIR

Birmingham's Open-Air Schools
1911-1970

Frances Wilmot and Pauline Saul

Phillimore

1998

Published by
PHILLIMORE & CO. LTD.
Shopwyke Manor Barn, Chichester, West Sussex

© Frances Wilmot and Pauline Saul, 1998

ISBN 1 86077 075 4

Printed and bound in Great Britain by
BOOKCRAFT
Midsomer Norton, Somerset

Contents

Acknowledgements vii
Foreword *by Miss Geraldine M. Cadbury* ix
Preface *by Dr. Carl Chinn* xi
Introduction xiii

1 A Matter of Survival 1
2 The Cadbury Gift 12
3 Uffculme: A Breath of Fresh Air (1911–1919) 21
4 The 1920s: Curriculum for Life 50
5 The 1930s: Testament of Health 79
6 The 1940s: The Turning Point 135
7 The 1950s: Widening Horizons 194
8 The 1960s and Beyond: Winds of Change 264

Appendices
I   Head Teachers of Birmingham's Open-Air Schools 337
II School Log Books 338
III Reminiscences: Other Open-Air Schools 340

Bibliography 343
Index 345

Acknowledgements

Our grateful thanks are due to the following people for their invaluable contributions and recollections:

C. Adams, R. Adams, P.W. Allen, M. Armson, G. Bailey, I. Baldwin, C. Barrett, G. Barton, I. Bazire, A. Beasley, D. Bilton, K. Birch, E. Bone, J. Bonner, H. Brant, C. Brinkley, A. Brooke, M. Bullock, J. Burt, G.M. Cadbury, J. Cangy, E. Capper, B. Cartwright, S. Carpenter, G. Cash, N. Cattell, N. Chambers, D. Clarke, J. Claydon, C. Compton, E. Cookson, D. Cooper, L. Cox, N. Crawford, K. Crosby, A. Cross, E. Davies, E.C. Deeble, M. Donnellan, M. Dooling, J. Dwyer, M. Elliott, J. Embury, L. Evans, W. Evans, J. Farmer, G. Fell, P. Fellows, M. Fishley, P. Flannaghan, O. Fox, D. Gartside, F.L. Gladwin, L.M. Goddard, B. Goodby, J. Gould, J. Greaves, J. Green, N. Green, M. Gunn, N. Hall, M.R. Harris, R. Hawkins, P.C.J. Hazel, M. Hewitt, M.C. Hicks, A. Higgins, W. Hill, P. Holmes, F. Homer, J. Hood, G. Hooper, J. Horton, O. Horton, J. Hughes, M. Hughes, A.W. Hunt, Lord Hunt of Llanfair Waterdine, B. James, R. Johnson, J. Jones, M. Jones, R.L. Jones, R.W. Jukes, P. Kenward, P.M. Kidd, J. Kimber, P. King, E.D. Kite, L. Knight, S.J. Knight, V. Knight, C. Laing, H.M. Langdon, O. Lannon, D. Lawrence, V. Layton, H.C. Lowndes, E. Lucas, G. Lunney, R. Mabbett, J. Marshall, J. Marshman, K. Meanwell, I. Mitchell, J. Moore, D.M. Mountford, V. Mullen, J. Murray, C. Musty, R. Newnham, A. Newsome, N. Norris, J. O'Shaugnessy, F. Owen, M. Parker, J. Pegg, O. Phillips, R. Pinner, A. Plowman, I. Radnall, R. Ratcliffe, R. Raybould, P. Reid, M. Rice, L.A. Richardson, B. Roberts, I. Rodell, D. Rolls, G. Royle, D. Smith, G. Smith, R. Smith, D. Sparks, T.M. Stapleton, B.M. Steane, R. Stiles, D.M. Taylor, J. Teece, M. Timmins, W. Tookey, M. Tudor, M.A. Urquhart, M. Wales, M. Wareing, J. Warom, B. Webster, T. Weir, N. Whittall, G. Williams, O. Williams, F. Willis, E. Wilson-Smith.

Grateful acknowledgements are also due to the following persons, periodicals and organisations:

K. Aitken (artwork), Birmingham Archives, Birmingham Education Department, Birmingham Library Services, Birmingham Post and Mail, L. Blennerhassett (photography), Cadbury Ltd., Carl Chinn, R. Cockerham and J. Freakley (photography), A. Crofts, *Good Housekeeping*, C. Hickinbotham, *Housewife*, Hunter's Hill School, *Illustrated London News*, A. Joseph, P.M. Litton, *Moseley and Kings Heath Journal*, *Mother & Home*, National Motor Museum, *Punch*, Skilts School, *Special Education*, *Strand*, *Sunday Pictorial*, Uffculme School, Warwick Record Office, *Woman & Home*, *Womans Outlook*, *Womans Realm*, Nick Wilmot, and Paul Wilmot for his unfailing patience, help and support in the project which has taken over four years.

For reproduction of advertisements we gratefully acknowledge the manufacturers of the following products and many others which we were unable to trace:

Atora, Bassetts Allsorts, Bisto, Blue Band Margarine, Bournvita, Bovril, Cadbury's Cocoa, Dettol, Driway Raincoats, Fennings, Fyffes, Haliborange, Hanovia sunlamps, Horlicks, Lifebouy, Oxo, Philips toothpaste, Ryvita, Scott's Emulsion, Scott's Porage Oats, Spangles, Vaseline, Vitan.

Grateful thanks and acknowledgements to the following people and organisations who have sponsored the publication:

Barrow Cadbury Fund, Geraldine M. Cadbury, GEC Avery Charitable Trust, Lord Mayor of Birmingham's Charity, Catherine R. Hickinbotham, Hugh Kenrick Charitable Trust, John B. Kenrick, A. Denis Martineau, J.F. & E.A. Measures Charity, Quaker Oats Limited, [the late] Francis Winchurch.

Foreword

I understand this book is to be dedicated to my parents, Barrow and Geraldine S. Cadbury, who gave the Open-Air Schools at Uffculme and Cropwood, with the land for Hunter's Hill, to the City of Birmingham.

I have been asked to say something of my connection with the project.

To some extent I think I was a guinea-pig when my mother was making decisions about the planning, treatment and teaching at the schools.

During two years when my family lived at Cropwood, my brother and I slept in the open-air bedrooms later used by the school children. When my older sister was at boarding school she spent her holidays with us, and we all spent much time out of doors. A very health giving experience.

My memories of these years are very happy ones. I was about the same age as Frances Wilmot when she first entered the open-air school as a pupil, and as her health improved, she tells me she, too, was happy there.

I used to wander about the beautiful, peaceful country fields and woods, identifying and studying all the plants and animals I could find. My love of all living things has never left me.

I enjoyed lessons with my mother who was a skilful teacher, until we returned to Birmingham when I was nine and went to school. Perhaps she helped to lay foundations for my career as a teacher?

I was able to return to Cropwood for the official opening of the school in 1922; and it has been good to think of the many children whose health improved while they were there, and to know they enjoyed the same pure air and beautiful surroundings that I did in my childhood.

Geraldine M Cadbury

21 October 1994

Preface

by *Dr. Carl Chinn*
(Community Historian at the University of Birmingham)

History should belong to everyone. Yet too often in the past it has been captured by the wealthy and the powerful so that the lives and deeds of the majority of folk have been largely ignored. For those of us concerned with retrieving the history of the common man and woman, the years since the Second World War have been exhilarating for they have witnessed a shift away from recording the actions and thoughts of the elite. And whilst that move has been welcomed and assisted by many academic historians those at the forefront of this revolution are local and family historians. Through them we have gained a greater knowledge of day-to-day life and a deeper understanding of the importance of neighbourhood and kinship. Such historians have given us valuable insights into urbanisation at a district level, into migration patterns and into the lives of those who have hitherto been neglected—women, children, the poor and ethnic minorities. Frances Wilmot and Pauline Saul are two such historians who have made significant contributions to the wider understanding of the past. Crucially, their current research brings into view another group once hidden from the gaze of historians—those sick children who attended Birmingham's Open-Air Schools. This book is a credit both to the skills and hard work of the authors. They were determined to save from historical oblivion the lives of those hundreds of youngsters who attended special schools in Birmingham, Warwickshire and Worcestershire. They have succeeded in their task.

*Dedicated to our mothers Margaret Headford and Jessie Morgan (formerly Brueton),
who nurtured us through childhood,
and to Barrow and Geraldine Cadbury who founded Birmingham's first Open-Air Schools.*

Introduction

Researching the history of Birmingham's open-air schools has been a privilege and a pleasure, stimulated originally by a nostalgic visit to Uffculme's Open Day in 1989 when old log books and photographs were on display. As two ex-pupils of Uffculme and Cropwood Open-Air Schools, we had met up again through our interest in family history and membership of the Birmingham and Midland Society for Genealogy and Heraldry.

With the help of school records we tracked down Miss Margaret Wales, our Uffculme teacher from the 1950s, who had endured with us the same conditions, winter and summer alike—we all but froze in winter and went barefoot in summer ...

The use of school log books and visitors' books led us to many other past teachers and pupils. After a decision to launch appeals for information in 1993, our project to write the history of Uffculme soon expanded to include all of Birmingham's six Open-Air Schools. These were Uffculme and Marsh Hill Day Schools in Birmingham, and Cropwood, Hunter's Hill, Haseley Hall and Skilts Residential Schools in the surrounding counties of Warwickshire and Worcestershire. The book focuses mainly on Uffculme, Cropwood and Hunter's Hill Schools, which were

The authors at the beginning of their research project in 1993, with their teachers from Uffculme Open-Air School (left to right): Pauline Saul (née Brueton), Moira Armson (née Spence), Arthur Hunt, Isobel Bazire (née Thomas), Margaret Wales, Frances Wilmot (née Headford).

founded as a result of the inspiration of Barrow and Geraldine Cadbury. A chapter is devoted to each decade.

Conditions at some open-air schools were quite severe and unusual. One side of the classroom was always open to the elements: on winter days the ink would freeze in the ink wells! In addition to lessons, a school day included three meals and at least an hour's rest period, outdoors if possible.

It is a testimony to the success of these schools that so many former pupils remember them with such gratitude and affection. Open-air education enabled thousands of city children to recover their health and go on to live relatively normal lives. Without the generosity of Barrow and Geraldine Cadbury many of Birmingham's ailing schoolchildren would never have received any education at all in the first half of this century.

We are indebted to Birmingham Education Department for the use of surviving log books, school photographs and other records to illustrate the success of this innovative movement which lasted just over fifty years.

Appeals to the media and much detective work put us in touch with 161 people who have given us such fascinating reminiscences of a bygone age. Without their memories and photographs the unique history of Birmingham's pioneering Open-Air Schools would probably have been lost forever. Ages, where given, relate to the date of interview or letter. We thank everyone who contributed such entertaining and informative accounts.

While presenting this history of Birmingham's Open-Air Schools we are conscious of the fact that we are not trained teachers. We hope we may be forgiven if any information has been misinterpreted during our research. Some terminology used in the book is pertinent to the language at the time. We recognise that phrases such as 'physically defective', 'feebleminded' and 'educationally subnormal' may not be appropriate today.

Changing conditions dictate different solutions to the health and education of 'delicate' children. Patricia Hazel's thesis on *Education for Delicate Children* concluded with an apt summary of the situation: 'What is today, was not yesterday, and will not be tomorrow'.

We hope that the needs of Birmingham's children will continue to be met in the educational system today, eighty-seven years after the first open-air school opened at Uffculme. Barrow and Geraldine Cadbury set us all an unprecedented example of imagination, foresight and concern for the rising generations of Britain's second city.

FRANCES WILMOT
PAULINE SAUL

Chapter 1

A Matter of Survival

The care and protection of children today is regarded as vitally important to the nation, in stark contrast to the last century when one in every five infants died within the first 12 months of life.

It was not uncommon in the 19th century for whole families of young children to be wiped out by epidemics, especially as they were often weakened by poverty, malnutrition and long hours of labour in factories and workshops. Children had been employed and exploited in ever-increasing numbers in many factories and mills, being subjected to long hours, harsh treatment and inhuman conditions. Although the Earl of Shaftesbury became the champion of these children and was responsible for much factory legislation which limited hours of employment, child slavery took a long time to be abolished. It had been common practice in industry to have gangs of youngsters working day and night, much to the detriment of their health and welfare. It was not until 1918 that child labour was totally banned.

Living conditions in many parts of Birmingham had been unhealthy for most of the 19th century as the city became known as 'the toy shop of Europe', producing wares of all kinds in iron and steel, jewellery, guns, buttons, buckles and trinkets.

A good description of Birmingham at that time is given in Rev. Isaac Taylor's *Scenes in England for the Amusement and Instruction of Little Tarry-At-Home Travellers*, 1822:

Factory children scavenging for food: water porridge and lumps of oaten cake.

> Oh, what a place are we coming to now? It seems as if it were all on fire; what a cloud of smoke rises in the air!
>
> This is Birmingham, where the furnaces, and the glass-houses, and the steam engines, shoot up torrents of sulphureous smoke, where every workshop has its several chimneys, puffing up smoke, smoke, smoke, into the loaded atmosphere. Not only do the coals consumed darken thus the air, but gasses and fumes from metals, oils and varnishes, and every sort of manufacture, help not only to becloud, but almost poison the atmosphere.

Small wonder that generations of children grew up unhealthy, if they survived at all.

At the turn of the century countless children were too ill to take advantage of free education in elementary schools, many suffering from tuberculosis and associated diseases. In 1907 it

Clouds of smoke over Birmingham, 1822

was recorded that over 31,000 children died from the disease in England. Tuberculosis attacked the lungs, glands or bones, and frequently occurred when people lived in densely populated areas with unsanitary housing. By 1882 it was known that the disease was spread by coughing and spitting and the Germans developed the idea of treating patients in sanatoriums with plenty of fresh air and exercise. It was thought that many other children who were ill with anaemia and malnutrition might also benefit from such treatment.

In Britain the *1889 Report of the Royal Commission on the Blind, Deaf and others in the UK* acknowledged that there was a need for 'special boarding schools for pupils who were delicate or neglected' but generally these children were regarded in the same category as those who were blind, deaf, diabetic, epileptic, physically disabled or mentally handicapped.

Children who suffered illnesses which were considered to be the result of malnutrition or poverty were classed as 'physically defective', along with other physically handicapped (but mentally normal) children who by reason of physical defects were unable to attend normal schools. The word 'defective' covered both mental and physical disability and replaced the term 'feebleminded', originally used for educable children who could not be taught in ordinary elementary schools by the usual methods. Thus 'defective' could mean physically handicapped, educationally sub-normal or delicate (the latter term not generally used prior to the 1944 Education Act, when physically defective children were categorised as physically handicapped, diabetic or delicate).

The *1898 Report by the Departmental Committee on Defective and Epileptic Children* revealed that at least one per cent of schoolchildren in London schools were defective, requiring special education, the main defects being caused by malnutrition or chronic illness.

There was very little education for defective children in Britain until the 20th century. Germany took the lead by providing schools in hospitals for the care of the crippled from 1832. In England the education of physically handicapped children dates from 1851 with the opening of the Cripples' Home and Industrial School for Girls in London. Special schools in England developed as a result of the Elementary Education (Blind and Deaf Children) Act 1893 and the Elementary Education (Defective and Epileptic Children) Act 1899.

In 1898 Dr. Alfred Eicholz was appointed as one of Her Majesty's Inspectors in London in the Education Department. He had a tremendous influence on special schools where many pupils who attended were delicate and underfed. Nine years before England's first open-air school he advocated that physically defective children resident in special schools should have plenty of fresh air, dietary supervision and regular medical inspection, together with short lessons and lots of physical exercises and handicrafts. In 1903 he became responsible for the supervision of all the special schools in England and Wales.

The *1898 Report on Defective and Epileptic Children* led to the Elementary Education (Defective and Epileptic Children) Act 1899, which allowed school authorities to make special provision for mentally and physically defective and epileptic children. As it was not compulsory this meant that 10 years later only a third of all authorities had made such provision. One of the inspirations of the 1898 reporting committee had been a school in the German town of Elberfeld which became a model for English special schools. It had been founded in 1867, being a school for the feeble-minded. It was later called a 'help-school', designed with short lessons of 20 minutes' duration, and concentration on manual work or handicrafts, together with lots of 'song and drill'.

A MATTER OF SURVIVAL

At the time when the 1899 Act was passed education was still in its infancy in Britain. Out of 140,000 teachers in ordinary elementary schools only 62,000 were certificated and 26,000 had received no training at all. Children unable to attend ordinary schools because of physical illness were deteriorating at home, very often in crowded, damp and airless homes in city slums where there was little sanitation and an ever-present odour of decay from garbage, sewers or drains.

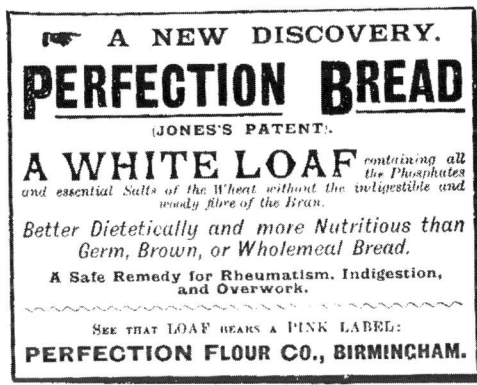

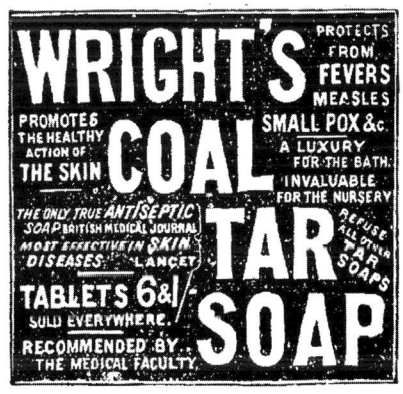
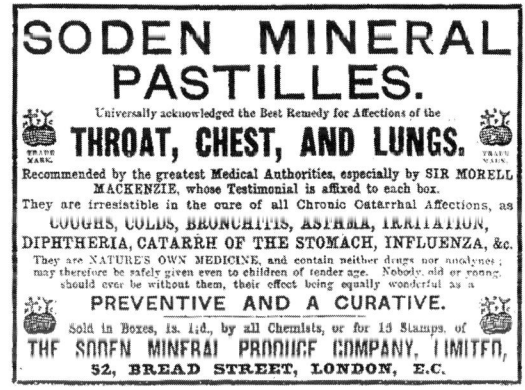

Some patent medical remedies, 1895

Contemporary view of school medical inspections (Punch, 1909).

The birth rate fell at the end of the 19th century and a government report in 1904 revealed that only one in three potential recruits for the army was fit enough for active service. This report shocked the nation which realised it depended on the health of its schoolchildren for its future fighting strength. This lengthy publication by the Local Government Board's Interdepartmental Committee on Physical Deterioration revealed to the public that a childhood of neglect and disease resulted in the physical deterioration of a whole generation. The report was to have a great influence on the future development of medical inspection of schoolchildren. There was also an increase in public opinion that some sort of education should be available for those children who were suffering from physical ailments due to poverty and malnutrition.

Dr. Eicholz gave evidence in the government report of 1904, recommending a system of special schools for semi-invalid children who were attending normal schools. The term 'open-air school' was not used but education in the countryside was advised, where fresh air and regular meals would revitalise and strengthen the children. Dr. Eicholz also considered that regular medical inspection of children in schools was the greatest single need in the school system. This was recommended in the report to be made compulsory for every school authority, together with school meals for malnourished children.

Germany had already appointed their first school doctor in 1883 and soon developed a very thorough system of medical inspection in their schools in the 1890s, much in advance of England. Backward children were treated in special schools and were given baths and hygienic instruction. In Britain the first school doctor was appointed in 1890 by the London School Board, followed by Bradford in 1893. Manchester opened the first local authority school for physically defective children in 1905.

Malnutrition was thought to be the major cause of poor physique, which led to the report by the Board of Education in 1905 on the *Medical Inspection and Feeding of Children attending Public Elementary Schools*. It was disclosed that only a few authorities provided any meals, and some of the meals were produced haphazardly by voluntary bodies. The resultant Education (Provision of Meals) Act was finally passed in 1906.

The need for medical inspection was stimulated in the following year, when the International Congress on School Hygiene met in London. The government took action with a clause in its Education (Administrative Provisions) Act 1907, compelling school authorities to provide medical inspection—but **not** treatment. The Board of Education issued circulars to local authorities on the aims of the school medical service.

The Local Education Authorities (Medical Treatment) Act 1909 led to the establishment of school clinics in the school medical service and the development of open-air schools. Thus the official School Medical Service came into existence, with the Medical Branch (later called the Special Services Branch) of the Board of Education, with Sir George Newman at its head. He was to have great influence on the development of the school health service, and by the time he retired in 1932 nearly 2,000 school clinics had been successfully established to save many children's lives. He was a strong champion of the open-air school movement.

A MATTER OF SURVIVAL

In 1907 Dr. Eicholz became responsible to the Medical Branch of the Board of Education for the supervision of all special schools, including defective children. He was later elected as the Chief Medical Inspector of HM Ministry of Education. Inspections of children revealed many dirty and verminous cases with a great range of diseases and disabilities. Ailments such as swollen adenoids and tonsils, rickets, incipient tuberculosis, ear discharges, and bronchial catarrh were often the result of unhygienic homes and unhealthy environment. Other common ailments were ringworm, measles, scarlet fever and diphtheria.

The only countryside many town children ever saw was on special outings arranged by charitable organisations such as Country Holiday Funds, Fresh Air Funds and Children's Aid Societies which sponsored visits to seaside convalescent homes. The Children's Country Holiday Society sent many children into the countryside for short holidays. In 1909 the Daily Mail Fund provided over 5,000 pairs of boots for Birmingham children and the Police-aided Association for Clothing Destitute Children provided over 3,000 pairs of clogs the following year.

Slum dwellings in 19th-century Birmingham.

Smoke pollution meant many city households sealed their windows at night and children rarely had fresh air. Dr. Caroline O'Connors, one of Birmingham's first Medical Superintendents in Special Schools, reported in 1908: 'one factor that keeps tuberculosis in flourishing condition is the dread of fresh air exhibited by the majority of people. In the houses of the poor, it is the rarest possible thing to find a window open. Yet some medical men certify tuberculous children as 'unfit for school' and one finds them shut up at home in a small airless back room ...'.

Fresh air and sunshine had been recognised as therapeutic for many consumptives since 1840. The open-air school movement was an adaptation of established sanatorium treatment for physically weakened children.

The first pioneer open-air school opened in Germany in 1904 in the pine woods at Charlottenberg, a suburb of Berlin. Pine trees, with their sweet scented vapours, were generally regarded as having a healing effect on throat and lung diseases. The buildings were of a primitive nature: a rest-shed open on the south side, two school barracks of five enclosed classrooms which could be heated in cold weather, two very large sheds open on all sides for lessons and meals, and small sheds dotted over the grounds, each accommodating four to six children. In addition there were slipper and shower baths and children spent their days out of doors.

It was designed as an 'open-air recovery school' for backward and debilitated pupils who were not so mentally deficient as to fit in with subnormal pupils. The children rapidly increased in weight and strength and many who had been seriously ill were entirely cured. Frequent meals amounted to almost forced feeding with five meals a day: soup and a slice of bread on arrival at 8am, milk and bread and butter at 10am, dinner at 12.30, followed by two hours' rest, more milk and bread at 3pm and a final meal of soup and bread and butter at 6.45pm before being sent home.

Chicago's first open-air school: a roof-top site under an asbestos board tent, 1909. Children lived in low temperatures in thick clothing, warm boots and sitting-out bags. (L.M. Ayres: reproduced with permission of Birmingham Central Library)

Not only did children recover physically and educationally but 'moral' improvements were noted with regard to 'cleanliness, self-help, punctuality and good temper, once they were removed from the influence of street life', according to one contemporary source.

Reports on the success of the school stimulated the German school authorities to build open-air schools at Mulhausen (near Cologne) and Elberfeld in 1906 and 1907 respectively. At the time few educational innovations made such an appeal to the popular imagination as did these schools because many seriously ill children were cured.

The open-air movement had spread to England in 1907 when London opened its first school at Bostall Wood, Plumstead. In 20 acres of wooded grounds 108 debilitated children suffering from conditions of crowded city life were at school from 9am to 6pm, with porridge and milk on arrival. Lunch was provided, followed by biscuits and fruit at 3.30pm and tea which consisted of bread and butter and currant buns at 5.30pm. Mackintoshes were provided for wet days and 'steamer chairs' (deck chairs) and blankets for rest. The school was kept open for 13 weeks and all the children improved in health and spirits, as well as intellect. In 1908 the school transferred to a better site at Shooters Hill in Woolwich and two other open-air schools opened in London.

America followed suit in 1908 with open-air schools at Providence (Rhode Island) and Boston. In New York City a moored ferryboat was utilised for tuberculous patients along the same lines. In Chicago a successful open-air school opened in 1909 on a rooftop site where children thrived happily in severe weather conditions, well wrapped up in woollen clothing and 'sitting-out' bags.

Meanwhile, other English schools sprang up at Bradford and Halifax in 1908, followed by Norwich, Sheffield and Barnsley which marked a new chapter in preventative medicine. Margaret McMillan's open-air Camp Schools proved a great success in Deptford, London. Some schools were in large houses with sheds in the grounds whilst others were of the simple 'band stand'

A MATTER OF SURVIVAL

variety, with canvas walls which rolled up in good weather. A typical timetable included breakfast on arrival, with lunch and tea later, interspersed with short lessons, rest periods of up to two hours and several short playtimes.

The contemporary writer, Leonard Ayres, in his book *Open-Air Schools* which was published in America in 1910, wrote:

> It has been said that the two greatest discoveries of recent times are the value of children and the virtues of an open-air life. In the last few years there has been a wonderful public awakening along both these lines. There has been an enthusiastic reception which has been almost universally accorded to the open-air school which is an object lesson in the beneficial results of an outdoor life. It is too soon to prophesy what the future of the open-air school will be ... It seems not improbable that the open-air school will be recognised by future historians of education not merely as a therapeutic agent but rather as marking one long step towards the school of the future where the child will not have to be either feeble-minded, delinquent, tuberculous or truant to enjoy the best and fullest sort of educational opportunity. The keynote of the school work is constant change from work to play, reading, singing and rest, together with constant stimulation of interest.

From the beginning the British Board of Education had been very supportive to the new open-air schools and gave additional grants from 1912 (under the *Medical Treatment Regulations*) for the maintenance of the children. The extra grant of £3 per head was on top of grants made under the Blind, Deaf, Defective and Epileptic Acts for residential and day schools.

TIME TABLE.

	9.0	9.35	9.55	10.5	10.40	10.55	11.25	11.30	12.0	12.45	1.30	3.15	3.30	4.15	5.0	5.30
MONDAY	Breakfast	Assembly for Prayers Scripture or Hymns	Class Talks	Arithmetic	Recreation	Nature Study	Breathing Exercises	Drawing	Prepare beds for mid day rest Personal Hygiene	Dinner	Rest	Recreation	I. Gardening / II. Reading / III. & IV.: Singing	Reading / Gardening / Reading	Pack-up apparatus Assembly for prayers	Tea. Dismissal at 6 p.m
TUESDAY				Modelling		Geography		Reading					Girls — Needlework / Boys — I. Carpentry / II. Gardening / III. Cardboard Work			
WEDNESDAY				Arithmetic		History		Poetry					Drawing	Dictation		
THURSDAY				Arithmetic		Nature Study		Drawing					I. & II.: Singing / III. Gardening / IV. Reading	Reading / Reading / Gardening		
FRIDAY				Arithmetic		Geography		Composition					Girls — Needlework / Boys — I. Gardening / II. Carpentry / III. Cardboard Work			

Typical weekly timetable at Shooters Hill Open-Air School, London, 1914. This made provision for up to two hours' rest time and six hours' manual training as specified by the Board of Education.

Sir George Newman summed up the way of life and the system of treatment in open-air schools with seven cardinal points:

1. Fresh air and sunlight
2. Proper diet
3. Rest
4. The hygienic way of life
5. Individual attention
6. Medical treatment
7. Special educational methods

Contrary to some popular opinions on open-air schools, life did not consist only of eating, sleeping and playing: it was not an everlasting picnic for children. The timetable required dedicated enthusiastic teachers able to carry out a curriculum of study at least three to four hours a day. Only children who were rated strong enough to learn were selected for open-air schools, despite disabilities due to malnutrition, anaemia, mild heart disease, tuberculous glands, nervous diseases such as chorea, adenoids and bronchial catarrh.

In many ways British open-air schools took the lead in modern methods of education, adopting manual instruction (learning by doing) which proved so successful with their pupils. Activities included weather study, paper cutting, metal work, woodwork, clay modelling, drawing, needlework, weaving and practical arithmetic exercises.

The requirements of an open-air school included a situation facing south, on the outskirts of a town which was within walking distance of transport. Trees or land was recommended for protection on the north and east and it was important that large trees provided shade for outdoor lessons. Children spent most of the time in the fresh air and some classrooms were specially

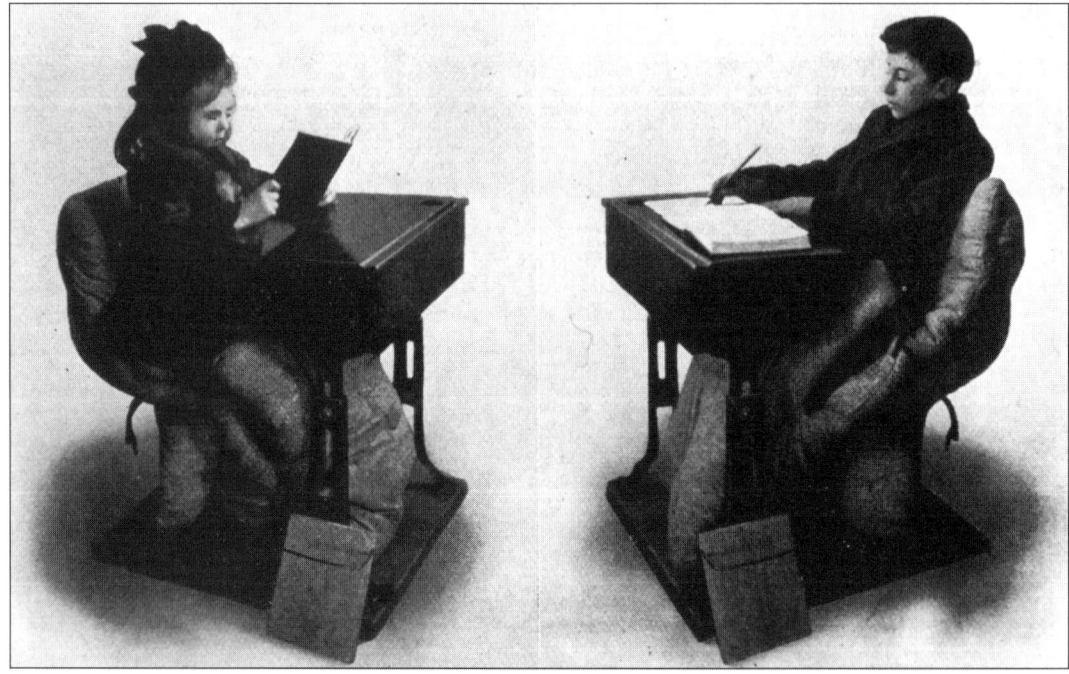

Children at Providence (USA) open-air school, with sitting-out bags, soapstones to warm the feet and heavy outdoor clothing, 1908. (L.M. Ayres: reproduced with permission of Birmingham Central Library)

designed with movable screens on three sides. As the majority of pupils were anaemic, sunlight and fresh air was considered essential for the cure. For this reason most classrooms were detached from the main building which usually included a dining hall, kitchen, medical room, bathroom, and administrative offices. Verandas were often built on three sides of the classroom, intended to be used for teaching in fine weather. In some schools slatted platforms were used outside for classwork.

Artificial heating was not envisaged, unless the temperature fell to 35°F as the theory was that children caught cold passing from warm rooms to the cold outside air. Children became acclimatised to the cold, having a better circulation than adults. Vigorous exercise was recommended before lessons and overcoats and rugs were used to retain heat. Every half hour children had further physical exercises, especially if snow blew in to the classrooms and ink wells froze.

Canvas and wood stretchers were generally used for rest periods and in cold weather extra clothing was worn. All countries providing open-air schools agreed that children had to be kept warm, preferably with woollen underwear and outerwear. In America each child was provided with a heavy overcoat and a 'sitting-out' bag made of blankets and canvas, cut and stitched to conform with the shape of the chair and attached to it by tapes. As these bags were expensive to produce Dr. Carrington of the National Association for the Prevention and Cure of Tuberculosis developed a cheaper product made of flannel, lined with cotton 'batting' and six or seven layers of newspaper. However, one of the main objections to the use of 'sitting-out' bags was that pupils were apt to regard them as ideal places to collect and secrete their childhood treasures—including food supplied which they stored up for future use!

In addition each American child had two blankets, a knitted toboggan hat, warm gloves and 'soapstones' or hot water bottles in the coldest weather to keep feet warm. As the latter created problems with children's footwear (often cracking cheap leather) felt shoes were often provided. Another device was a wooden foot-box lined with padding, into which was placed the soapstone or hot water bottle. Teachers were not forgotten either as they were provided with long wool or fur coats, a fur cap and mittens, felt shoes and a rug to protect their feet.

Pupils at English schools do not appear to have been provided with the luxury of foot warmers or 'sitting-out' bags. A photograph in Ayres' book, which is reproduced here, gives an example of equipment provided for pupils at the open-air school in Providence in America in 1908. It is hard to believe that children were supposed to be educated whilst covered in so many layers of restricting warm clothing.

Regular baths and showers were regarded as most important in those days when few homes had such facilities to combat dirt and disease. The nurse usually regulated the shower baths from the side and they were intended as much for skin tonics as for hygiene. Hugh Broughton's book *The Open-Air School* relates the usual procedure for showers at open-air schools:

> The children strip and take up a position in line just in front of the spray rosettes. The nurse turns on the water ...When ready she blows a whistle and each child steps forward into the shower. After a moment the water is turned off, each child steps back and proceeds to soap the limbs. The water is turned on again and on the sound of a whistle each child steps into the shower. This is repeated twice, for washing of the limbs is followed by the washing of the trunk (the children help each other to wash the back) and finally the face and neck are washed. During the last shower the temperature of the water is reduced to lessen the risk of chills. The children should assist each other to dry themselves properly so that the nurse may give her whole attention to supervision.

Regular weighing sessions were held, together with breathing and physical exercises which strengthened resistance to disease. Breathing exercises formed part of the medical work for which teachers were often responsible. These were usually performed in the fresh air, sometimes as

SPECIMEN DIETARY TABLE FOR ONE WEEK.

	Monday	Tuesday	Wednesday	Thursday	Friday	Saturday
Breakfast	Bread and Milk / Raw Apples	Porridge and Milk / Bread and Dripping	Bread and Milk / Bread and Jam	Porridge and Milk / Raw Apples	Bread and Milk / Bread and Dripping	Porridge and Milk / Bread and Butter
Dinner	Roast Beef Cabbage Potatoes / Boiled Rice and Stewed Fruit	Beef Puddings Potatoes / Custard and Stewed Fruit	Shepherd's Pie / Roly-poly Jam Puddings	Fish Parsley Sauce Potatoes / Currant Puddings	Meat Pies Potatoes / Custard and Stewed Fruit	Soup Potatoes / Boiled Rice and Currants
Tea	Cocoa Bread and Butter / Jam	Cocoa Bread and Butter / Bananas	Tea Bread and Butter / Cakes	Cocoa Bread and Butter / Bananas	Cocoa Bread and Butter / Cakes	

Typical weekly menu at Shooters Hill Open-Air School, London, 1914.

many as four times a day. This was to teach children to breathe properly, to improve blood circulation (which helped to eradicate disease) and to exercise the lungs. Speaking and singing often improved after such exercises. Deep breathing and diaphragmatic breathing were practised for the lower portion of the lungs as children often failed to breathe properly and became prone to diseases.

Spinal curvature was often a result of physical debility and exercises were also given by the nurse to children needing special treatment. Many children were given malt or cod liver oil and received treatment for discharging ears, bad eyes and other ailments.

Rest for two hours in the middle of the day, usually in the open-air, was one of the most curative measures in open-air schools. Many malnourished and anaemic children failed to thrive and to properly digest and absorb their food on account of inadequate sleep in crowded homes and poor living conditions. It became recognised that a good meal frequently generated a feeling of drowsiness, during which time of rest the whole of the available energy in the body could concentrate on the digestive system. Without rest, food often passed through the body without being fully absorbed, especially in anaemic children. Healthy growth was often impossible for many children if their food at home was inadequate or unsuitable and they had insufficient sleep. Deck-chairs were often used in the early open-air schools, although Birmingham was to pioneer the use of specially-made stretchers. To retain body heat blankets, bonnets, caps and mittens were supplied during school rest times.

Food was always a priority in open-air schools as so many children were poorly fed. At home many lived on bread, pastry, jam, fried fish, pickles and anything highly flavoured or filling, without regard to digestibility and nutrition. Plain nourishing food was provided at the schools and most children took full advantage of it, especially as fresh air sharpened the appetite. The result was always an improvement in physique and health at all the open-air schools.

Three meals a day at school was the norm—breakfast, lunch and tea. Porridge or bread and dripping was often served for breakfast and lunch consisted of such filling dishes as beef puddings, roast mutton, jam rolypolys and currant puddings. Beverages were usually cocoa at breakfast and tea at teatime.

There was a great emphasis on outdoor activities such as gardening, nature study, practical geography and dancing. It was, in fact, a completely different way of life and to be selected for an open-air school was considered to be a privilege and a unique experience for any schoolchild.

The British medical profession was generally in favour of open-air schools to combat the dreadful scourge of tuberculosis which affected the whole population. Successful sanatorium treatments had proved that fresh air, food, rest and cleanliness worked wonders. Medical officers were obviously hoping that such schools would more than pay for themselves by creating healthier schoolchildren.

Around this time Birmingham was considering housing reforms and the Open Spaces Association was discussing new recreation grounds for children and the general public. Suddenly the open-air issue had become very important. Birmingham had no open-air school, but the

Education Committee viewed such schools with approval in its 1908/9 Report by the Medical Superintendent:

> … the open-air school, which is the result of a compromise between the state, the parent and the physician, has passed beyond the experimental stage. Their utility has been amply praised by experience and the rapidly increasing number of open-air schools indicates the recognition that they form a necessary part of educational organisation … and it should not be forgotten that fresh air is also necessary to healthy children in schools.

In 1908 Birmingham Education Committee had appointed its first Chief School Medical Officer, Dr. George Auden, a general practitioner from York. He became a leading light in the open-air school movement, referring to the development in Germany in his first annual report. One hundred and twenty applicants were interviewed for the three additional posts of School Medical Officers in the city. The successful applicants were Doctors Agnes Parsons, Lewis Graham and James Fenton whose duties were to examine schoolchildren medically and to advise parents of any treatment needed. They began routine inspections of 5-year-old entrants and 13-year-old leavers. There were no school clinics at this time, nor free medical treatment, and the most frequent defects discovered by the teams were enlarged tonsils and adenoids, dental decay, defective eyesight and malnutrition, in addition to a very high percentage of verminous infestations.

As a result of all these medical examinations Birmingham doctors and hospitals were inundated with requests for treatment and the Education Committee itself took on the responsibility of testing children's eyesight and supplying spectacles. School clinics were soon opened to provide treatment and advice for simple ailments.

Dr. Caroline O'Connors vividly describes the dreaded plague of tuberculosis at that time in her report in 1908 on physically defective children in Birmingham:

> There are 185 defective children in our special schools of which 50% are tuberculosis cases. Complaints are often made of the expense of educating crippled children. The air of a city contains a large number of infectious germs and most of us are only able to resist their infective activity by our strong vitality. Those of low vitality, especially ill-nourished and weakly children, fall victims to the germs scattered broadcast by this most disgusting and unnecessary habit of spitting, which seems to have become second nature to many men. The tops of some trams are in a disgraceful condition and the danger is multiplied by the new trams, which are enclosed above, as well as below, so that sun and fresh air cannot weaken the deadly bacillus of tubercle.

Such was the background to the development of open-air schools in England. Birmingham seems to have been rather backward in the provision of such a school within its special school system, probably lacking the appropriate finance for such a venture. With hindsight, however, the authority was able to draw on the experience and plans of existing open-air schools when the generosity of Barrow and Geraldine Cadbury enabled them to plan for a new open-air school in the city. Birmingham was extremely fortunate to have such enlightened benefactors who provided an establishment which completely changed the lives of so many schoolchildren.

Chapter 2

The Cadbury Gift

Barrow Cadbury was born in 1862, a member of the Birmingham family famous for the manufacture of chocolate. His father was Richard Cadbury who ran Cadbury Brothers Limited with his younger brother George. Richard was a devout Quaker who was always ready to help others financially and was much concerned with his factory workforce, providing educational classes and recreational facilities which contributed to their health and welfare.

Barrow Cadbury was named after his grandmother's family. His mother died after the birth of her third child when he was only six years old and after his father's second marriage he was sent to Germany at the age of 11 to complete his education in a state school. His father firmly believed in giving him a broad education with the opportunity of studying a foreign language. Germany had a profound influence on Barrow and he always admired their educational system. Perhaps it is no coincidence that the first open-air school opened there and that later on Barrow was to adopt their fresh air treatments for his own son.

In 1882 Barrow joined his father in the family firm at Bournville in Birmingham. In the following year all the family moved to Moseley Hall, a beautiful estate of woods and fields near Moseley which in those days was a village with just a handful of shops and houses, a church and a smithy. Moseley Hall was an interesting building with secret doors and passageways, nicknamed 'the Bunny House' by the younger generations of the family on account of the vast number of rabbits on the estate. Richard Cadbury frequently threw open the beautiful grounds for parties of Sunday School children, adult education classes and many other Birmingham people who rarely had the opportunity of a day in the country.

Cocoa was widely advertised at that time as having many nourishing and stimulating properties, serving equally well as a food or drink. Brandon Head's book *The Food of the Gods: a popular account of cocoa,* which was published in 1903, gives a good contemporary account of the product and many details on Cadbury Brothers Limited:

> In health or sickness, infancy or old age, at home or on our travels, nothing is so generally useful, so sustaining and invigorating as cocoa. Far better than the majority of vaunted substitutes for human milk as an infant food, to supplement what other milk may be available; incomparable as a family drink for breakfast or supper ... For the sustenance of invalids nothing is better than a nightly cup of cocoa essence boiled with milk.

It was recommended that cocoa should be made in a jug with cocoa essence, powdered white sugar, milk and water, and whisked vigorously for a few seconds. Cocoa was used increasingly in the British Army and Navy, in hospitals and many other institutions: later on it was provided in Birmingham's first open-air school at Uffculme.

THE CADBURY GIFT

Richard and George Cadbury had developed a model housing estate at Bournville for their workers, as well as offering Bournville Hall for 50 factory girls who had no homes of their own. Tennis courts, playing fields, shrubbery walks lined with rustic seats, cricket grounds, a swimming pool and a dining hall were provided for employees, in addition to a gratuitous sick club which included the services of a doctor and three trained nurses. A woman trained in Swedish athletics was employed to improve the physical culture of factory girls in gymnastics, swimming and games. Every day drill classes were held and girls were entitled to time-off to attend twice a week.

Concern for Cadbury's workforce led to the provision of spacious dressing rooms where women could change into special working clothes. Especially thoughtful were the stools which provided a shelf for heavy boots, and the shelves above hot-water pipes where wet footwear could be dried in rainy weather. There was no doubt that Cadbury's caring attitude produced a healthy happy workforce and Barrow Cadbury was part of it for many years. It must have had a bearing on his future generosity in providing open-air schools for ailing children in Birmingham.

Richard Cadbury's lifestyle probably had a profound influence on Barrow. Richard had always been concerned about the plight of Birmingham's slum children whose health suffered as a result of their environment and he was keen to found a convalescent home on the outskirts of the city. He decided eventually to make a gift of Moseley Hall to the City of Birmingham for this purpose in 1891. Afterwards he continued to take a great interest in the Home and all the children who went there.

Barrow Cadbury's marriage to Geraldine Southall was in 1891 and the reception was the last family event at Moseley Hall. His father and family moved to their new home 'Uffculme', named after their ancestral village in Devon. It was not far from Moseley Hall and on a beautiful hill-top site (now on Queensbridge Road in Moseley). The house was carefully planned by Richard Cadbury, including the enormous great hall full of stuffed birds, butterflies and antiques which were of great fascination to visiting children.

'Uffculme's' grounds were designed personally by Richard Cadbury with rockeries and two ponds at different levels. From the beginning 'Uffculme' was shared by his family with many other people for garden parties and enjoyed especially by his grandchildren, Paul and Dorothy, children of his eldest son Barrow.

After his father's death Barrow Cadbury followed in his footsteps, promoting and financing many worthy causes. He was a devoted member of the Society of Friends, a Justice of the Peace and developed the Adult School Movement which had been started by his father. He taught many boys the skills of writing and reading and became Treasurer and President of the National Adult School Union. In his business life he became Director and Chairman of Cadbury Brothers Limited and pioneered the introduction of office machines and the use of the telephone in the company.

Uffculme House.

With his wife, Geraldine, he became very involved in probation work for 'young offenders'. He was a magistrate from 1906-40, and helped to pioneer children's courts, remand homes and two approved schools for young delinquents.

Barrow Cadbury, drawn by J.E. Southall, 1926. (C. Compton)

His happy marriage to Geraldine Southall marked a turning point in his life. They both gave much time and money to Birmingham and its community in many benevolent and charitable causes. Geraldine Cadbury had many interests apart from her family but especially had great concern for children and their welfare. She was on countless Birmingham committees concerned with sick and underprivileged children and held annual treasure hunts in her garden for them.

One of her main achievements was to campaign for the creation of juvenile courts so that young law breakers could be considered in a more humane way, in more suitable surroundings than the ordinary courts where the public gallery and officials often terrified them. The first Birmingham Juvenile Court was built in 1905, financed and equipped by Geraldine and her husband. It soon became clear to her that prison was no place for children, nor was the Workhouse which was the only alternative before the passing of the Children Act 1908. The Remand Home which was subsequently provided by the Cadburys in 1910 was the first of its type in England and was planned carefully by Geraldine and the architect Barry Peacock (who subsequently also designed Uffculme and Cropwood Open-Air Schools).

She became one of Birmingham's first women magistrates in 1920, after years of voluntary association with the courts, weekly attendances and meticulous record-keeping. As Chairman of the Children's Courts she gained quite a reputation for understanding children, even unmanageable ones brought up before the bench, and was a member of several Home Office Committees on probation.

Geraldine Cadbury also had a great interest in education, being a natural teacher herself, with a love of nature. With Barrow she opened the first of Birmingham's Kindergartens in Greet in 1904. This was equipped with large window boxes for plants, a cage of doves, a rabbit, a cat, a hen, a parrot and some chickens, in addition to little gardens for the children. This successful experiment led to the establishment of others in the city.

During their married life they never used 'Uffculme', acquired after the death of Barrow's stepmother in 1908. With their children Dorothy, Paul and Geraldine (known as Cherry) they lived in a modest house in Edgbaston. 'Uffculme' was used for the Adult School Union and later became a hostel for refugees, then a hospital. It was finally given to Birmingham in 1916, after which it became a convalescent home.

They frequently visited 'Rosemary Cottage', their weekend and holiday home built in 1898 in beautiful countryside beyond the Lickey Hills in Worcestershire. In 1906 they built 'Cropwood', a much larger house nearby, and frequently entertained there many employees from Cadburys who enjoyed the tennis, bowls and the open-air swimming pool, as well as the beautiful grounds.

During this period their son Paul's health deteriorated inexplicably, with suspected tuberculosis or 'delicate glands'. An enlightened Harley Street doctor named Sir Thomas Barlow recommended two years of life in the country, no school, and plenty of fresh air, good food and rest.

The whole family moved to 'Cropwood', following the good doctor's advice, with Barrow commuting to work using the nearby railway. They adapted the children's rooms so that one or two sides could be folded back to admit the fresh air. This was quite revolutionary treatment in England at this time but confirmed Geraldine's passion for the open air as a great cure-all.

Geraldine threw herself wholeheartedly into the new regime. She even slept in an open-air porch herself and endured the same conditions as her children. The treatment proved so successful,

Geraldine and Barrow Cadbury with their children Dorothy, Paul and Geraldine, c.1913. (G.M. Cadbury)

with a tutor for Paul, that his health was fully restored after two years. Consequently, he was able to go away to a normal boarding school, although his father insisted on removing bedroom windows so that the fresh air regime could be continued.

Memories of her happy childhood at Cropwood House are revealed by Miss Geraldine Cadbury, who was 94 at the time this account was given in 1994 and is the youngest daughter of Geraldine and Barrow Cadbury:

> Cropwood was a lovely place for a child as there was plenty of room. I lived there for about two years with the family when my brother Paul, who was five years older than me, had suspected tubercular glands.
>
> Cropwood had been built as a holiday home originally but when Paul became delicate it was adapted so that there were two open air bedrooms—one for Paul and one which I often shared with my older sister Dorothy who was three years older than Paul. I also sometimes slept on the veranda further along, with my mother. My mother crocheted little hoods for us all so we didn't bury our heads under bedclothes to keep warm. I remember rain coming into the room and snow one night. We were also encouraged to take cold baths—in fact my father had one daily until he was nearly 90 years old.
>
> Paul and Dorothy often did things together as they were more of an age but I was very happy at Cropwood and loved it on my own there. I was always an outdoor person and remember once going off on my own and getting on the back of an ancient mare without permission. I fell off but didn't tell anyone.
>
> Paul accepted the fresh air life quite happily. His tutor taught in the house but lived up in the bluebell woods where there was a rather primitive wooden house. The woods were lovely around Cropwood House and I remember that although my mother didn't approve of military things, being a Quaker, she suggested one day that we played 'Robin

Hood' there with a group of visiting children. We made a castle among the tree roots and were given bits of green ribbon—Lincoln green. Mother always had imaginative ideas for children.

My mother had always been keen on the fresh air and had been brought up to go for long walks and look for flowers. She was a keen botanist, as we all were. We all liked to have our own gardens.

We also had fresh air in other rooms in the house—the Loggia which was a new concept was my mother's idea. We always lived with at least one side of the room open. We also had a 'drawing room' at the end which was used on special occasions. We had a pianola there. I remember we had great high jinks up in the attic.

My mother taught me entirely while we lived at Cropwood for two years. She was a born teacher and I was the sort of child who did what I was told. I had a delicate inside, and used to run temperatures, and only went to kindergarten for a short time before going to Cropwood. I didn't go to school until I was nine years old. I remember getting scarlet fever while we were at Cropwood so I was isolated at Rosemary Cottage with someone to look after me until I was out of quarantine.

I often sat in the hay meadow when the hay was being cut and remember Mother reading to us in the orchard as we lay under the cherry trees. In winter we used to toboggan down the hill behind the house in the snow—you went through the hedge if you weren't careful!

Hunter's Hill was near our daffodil field but I wasn't allowed over the road on my own. We often went long walks there together with the family. 'The Shelter' which was

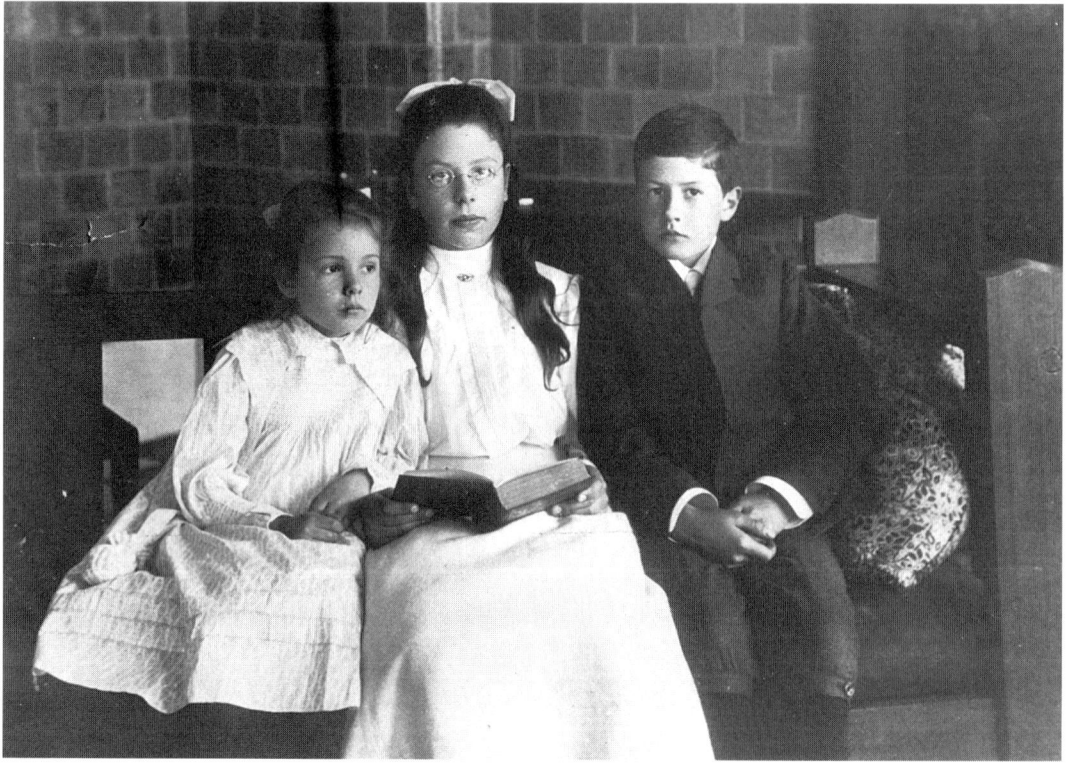

Paul Cadbury at Cropwood during his fresh-air cure, with his sisters Geraldine and Dorothy, 1906/7. (G.M. Cadbury)

over there was like a big empty barn—I think it was used for adult school parties. When we had visitors the older people would go for long walks but I was often left behind as I was too young.

My mother had the most influence on me as she taught me and I suppose we became close because of that. She was often away in Birmingham, concerned with the police courts where she was an unofficial probation officer before there were such people. She was one of the first two women magistrates in Birmingham, with Mrs. Priestman who often spent holidays with us with her family.

My father used to walk to Blackwell Station to catch the train to Bournville each day. He was a great walker. He and my mother worked very closely together and there was seldom disagreement. My mother was involved with many special schools as she was freer than my father who was working. Mother used to take me to some of the schools and she often visited the Maternity Hospital and the Women's Hospital. She was very closely involved with all of them.

My mother was more involved than my father in the planning of the open-air schools and did her own designing with the help of the architect Mr. Peacock who had designed a church near Bromsgrove as well as other buildings in Birmingham. He was in agreement with my mother's ideas but she was the prime mover.

I remember visiting Uffculme House, built by my grandfather Richard Cadbury. It was a thoroughly Victorian mansion with a huge hall and a big stand with bearskins. The parlour maid used to let me see the dining room table which she had arranged with a pretty pool of mirrors surrounded by flowers. We used to skate on the lake which became part of Uffculme Open-Air School. I only visited the open-air school once with my mother.

I was educated at Edgbaston High School and the Mount School in York. In 1922 I was at the opening of Cropwood Open-Air School during my time at Newnham College, Cambridge. I was taking a degree in Natural Sciences—Botany, Zoology and Chemistry but I was a naturalist by heart. Then I spent a year at Birmingham University doing a Teacher's Diploma. After teaching at Warwick and Dudley I became Headmistress of Chelmsford County High School for Girls. Mother was pleased I chose teaching because she could have become a teacher—it was born into me, I suppose.

At the age of 94 I still make myself walk each day and try to carry on some outside interests. Every week I make posies from the garden and take them to the old ladies in hospital. I've been doing that for 30 years. I delivered 'Meals on Wheels' until I was nearly 90. I still visit one of the Old People's Homes. But seeing the architects plan of Cropwood [on page 56] brings back memories of my early life. I was very happy there ...

No doubt the success of Paul's fresh air treatment and the new open-air school opening in London in 1907 had a great influence on Barrow and Geraldine Cadbury. New open-air schools were springing up in other large towns but Birmingham had no plans for such a school in their special school system.

The health of children always concerned Mrs. Barrow Cadbury as two of her own children had more than their fair share of ill health. Encouraged by the success of her own open-air regime she saw the possibilities of such treatment for the thousands of sick children in the city suffering from the effects of malnutrition and poverty. She conceived the idea of building an open-air school in a corner of the garden of their Uffculme estate.

Barrow Cadbury wholeheartedly supported the venture, always keen to use their wealth to meet the needs of Birmingham's young people. He studied the existing open-air schools and on

25 June 1910 many local and national newspapers reported the new revolutionary plans for the Birmingham open-air school, with such headlines as: 'Open-Air School for Birmingham's Weakly Children: Medical Officer Approves the Scheme' (*Daily News*); 'Open-Air School: After Care of Defective Children' (*Birmingham Gazette*); and 'Novel Birmingham Scheme: Gift by Mr. & Mrs. Barrow Cadbury' (*Birmingham Daily Post*).

Barrow and Geraldine Cadbury had generously offered to provide the land and necessary equipment, writing to Councillor Norman Chamberlain of the Birmingham Education Committee:

> For some time my wife and I have been interested in the question of an open-air school and we are anxious that our own city should possess one, planned on the best lines, in a healthy situation and easily accessible from the congested parts of the city.
>
> We have pleasure in offering to the Education Committee the free use of a field of five acres ... opposite Uffculme, which is 500 feet above sea-level with an open view ... The Kings Heath trams pass the gate. We are prepared to provide the simple buildings and furniture required for such a school which we understand will cost about £400.
>
> For the winter months we offer ... a large airy tea-room at Uffculme which was specifically designed with a view to its being used as an open-air school. The Uffculme grounds will be open to the children for study and recreation during the winter months; they will be able to use the grounds in the summertime when they are not required for parties.
>
> Our offer, with Dr. Auden's approval [Birmingham Schools Medical Officer], is made with the understanding that the Education Committee will undertake to keep the school numbers up to the full accommodation of the school; that they will provide for the necessary cleaning, heating and caretaking, and we hope they will also see their way to pay the children's tram fares.

An explanation of the purpose of the open-air school was given by Mr. Norman Chamberlain to the *Birmingham Daily Gazette*: 'An open-air school is for what might be called debilitated and backward children. Consequently the school came halfway between the ordinary elementary schools and the schools for the feeble-minded and physically defective.' He reported that experience of similar schools showed that children's mental alertness and their attention to work increased as their health improved.

The *Birmingham Post* pointed out in its lengthy report on 25 June 1910 that it was:

> ... high time Birmingham follows the good lead given in other cities on the provision of open-air schools. Possibly something of its kind might have been done already, were it not for the fact that the open-air regime requires much land, easily accessible and therefore bound to be expensive. Had Birmingham Education Committee proposed to buy as much land as Mr. & Mrs. Cadbury now place at their disposal, merely for the purpose of putting up a very small school, there would probably have been a good many protests against the lavishness of their expenditure ... The open-air school may be somewhat expensive to establish, and it can never be particularly cheap to manage but there can only be one opinion on the rapid and powerful effects of such healthy surroundings and quiet recreations, reduced hours of work and rational feeding of children.

Finance apart, the physical benefits which Birmingham's children would derive from the new open-air school were incalculable; 70 children would be able to attend the school when it opened and it was planned to accommodate one hundred and twenty. All the children aged between eight and 12 years would be selected by Dr. George Auden, the Schools Medical Officer, and it was hoped to arrest many cases of chronic illness.

Dr. Auden was naturally enthusiastic about the city's acceptance of the Cadbury's generous offer. He was convinced that the school would be invaluable to Birmingham's 'weakly and debilitated' children and especially studied European open-air schools as well as British ones recently opened at Sheffield, Bradford, Manchester and Halifax. Open-air schools had also been discussed at the recent International Congress on School Hygiene he had attended in Paris. Birmingham did not have any school established purely for the recuperative treatment of anaemic and badly nourished children. The system of medical inspection of schoolchildren had revealed an amount of disease, with physical and mental deficiency, that had never previously been suspected. Many of the children's complaints were also associated with mental backwardness where an ordinary school curriculum was totally unsuitable.

Dr Auden proposed to select the children for Uffculme open-air school from the thousands in the city schools, who were, he said, 'unfit for the ordinary strain of school life through poverty, neglect or heredity, suffering from anaemia, malnutrition, enlarged tonsils, adenoids or incipient tuberculosis. They are not radically ill but they are never strong. If they went away to an open-air school for three months they would return fit and strong'.

The plan was to transport children by trams, providing them with cloth capes for the journey, arriving at school at eight o'clock in the morning. There they would remain until six in the evening in summer, five o'clock in winter, with three meals a day, and ample rest and sleep, after the midday meal, on deck chairs or hammocks. A weighing machine, rugs, mugs and plates would be provided, together with teachers 'specially versed in physical drill and nature study'.

Very little formal teaching was originally envisaged as it was intended that the children 'would not be troubled with lessons but what instruction they had would be rather of a physical than a mental character, with particular attention to nature study'. Dr. Auden, continuing his report to the *Daily News*, emphasised that there would be 'as few buildings as possible, only the barely essential shelters, kitchen and sanitary accommodation will be erected ... This scheme would make provision for every youngster whose opening years are blighted by the debilitating environment of 'slumdom'.

Birmingham slums.

It was an ambitious scheme for improving the health of Birmingham's schoolchildren. Fresh air, good food, sufficient rest and suitable exercise, with less formal instruction, were deemed to be the essential requirements. From the results of other open-air schools it seemed that this treatment resulted in 20-25 per cent of children's physical ailments being cured and 45 per cent improved.

There was some doubt concerning conditions at the proposed open-air school in the coldest months of the year but Birmingham Education Committee did not envisage much expenditure on buildings, as much of the instruction was planned to be out of doors. Feeding the children would cost the authority one penny per head—the usual Special School allowance. The initial outlay for the authority would be £205, with an annual expenditure of £700 (£10 per head × 70 children). Most importantly, from Birmingham's point of view, such schools were certified under the Defective and Epileptic Children's Act 1899 which meant that they would get a State Grant of £4 10s. per head instead of £2 10s.

Once the offer had been accepted by Birmingham Education Committee Barrow and Geraldine Cadbury decided to donate the land, rather than offering the free use of it, as originally suggested. An architect was engaged by the Cadburys to design a school which was intended to be the most up-to-date in Europe. Although the Open-Air School had medical approval it was a revolutionary idea for Birmingham at that time and many regarded it as being experimental. Few believed the school would become one of the best examples of its kind and would change the lives of so many sick children. Over the next fifty years thousands of Birmingham's children were enabled to live normal lives, thanks to the benevolence and vision of Barrow and Geraldine Cadbury at the beginning of the century.

Chapter 3

Uffculme: A Breath of Fresh Air (1911-1919)

Uffculme had the distinction of being one of the few purpose-built open-air schools in Britain. Barrow and Geraldine Cadbury instructed the Birmingham architects Cossins, Peacock & Bewlay to design it and to incorporate several new and distinctive features completely different from normal elementary schools. Uffculme had no covered corridors but was designed to take full advantage of light and the circulation of air on its site adjacent to Uffculme House and estate in Moor Green, near Kings Heath and Moseley. The parkland surrounding Uffculme House provided ideal opportunities for school nature study around the ponds and alpine gardens.

The Modern Building Record, 1912, reported that the following firms contributed to the building of Uffculme:

>   Clocks: Swinden & Sons
>   Door, Window and Casement Locks and Fittings: Horrell & Bowman
>   Gas Lighting and Cooking Appliances and Electric Bells: Edward Hill
>   General Furnishing: Chamberlain, King & Jones
>   Green Roofing Slates: J.A. Hesford Ltd.
>   Heating: Henry Hope & Sons Ltd.
>   Landscape Gardening: J. Cheal & Sons.
>   Ornamental Iron Work: Hart, Son, Peard & Co
>   Rainwater Goods: Walter Macfarlane & Co.
>   Sanitary Fittings: Parker, Winder & Achurch Ltd.
>   School Desks and Benches: Midland Educational Co. Ltd.
>   Service Lifts: Smith, Major & Stevens Ltd.
>   Slate Boards and Cloak Room Fittings: North of England School Furnishing Co.
>   Terrazzo Paving: Diespeker Ltd.
>   Wood Block Flooring: Acme Flooring & Paving Co. (1904) Ltd.

The main buildings were unusual as the kitchens were on the first floor, which prevented the smell of cooking pervading the dining room and classroom below. The kitchen was connected to the dining room with a double lift and a serving hatch where a hand-pulley operated. A gas cooker and copper boiler provided the latest in cooking equipment. On the same floor was the Head Teacher's room and a staff room; on the wall outside was a distinctive 24-inch clock dial.

Most meals in the dining room were taken with two sides open to the elements, the glass and wooden screens being pushed back to create a light and airy atmosphere overlooking trees and lawns. Local firms supplying food included groceries/provisions from Messrs. Brown, Hopwood & Gilbert in Vesey St (Birmingham), meat from Charles Adkins (Moseley), bread from E. Harding's Royal Steam Bakery (Yardley) and dairy products from Messrs. Wathes Bros (Moseley).

No expense was spared. A large bathroom with 10 showers was also on the ground floor below the kitchen. When the school first opened these heated showers and the slipper bath must

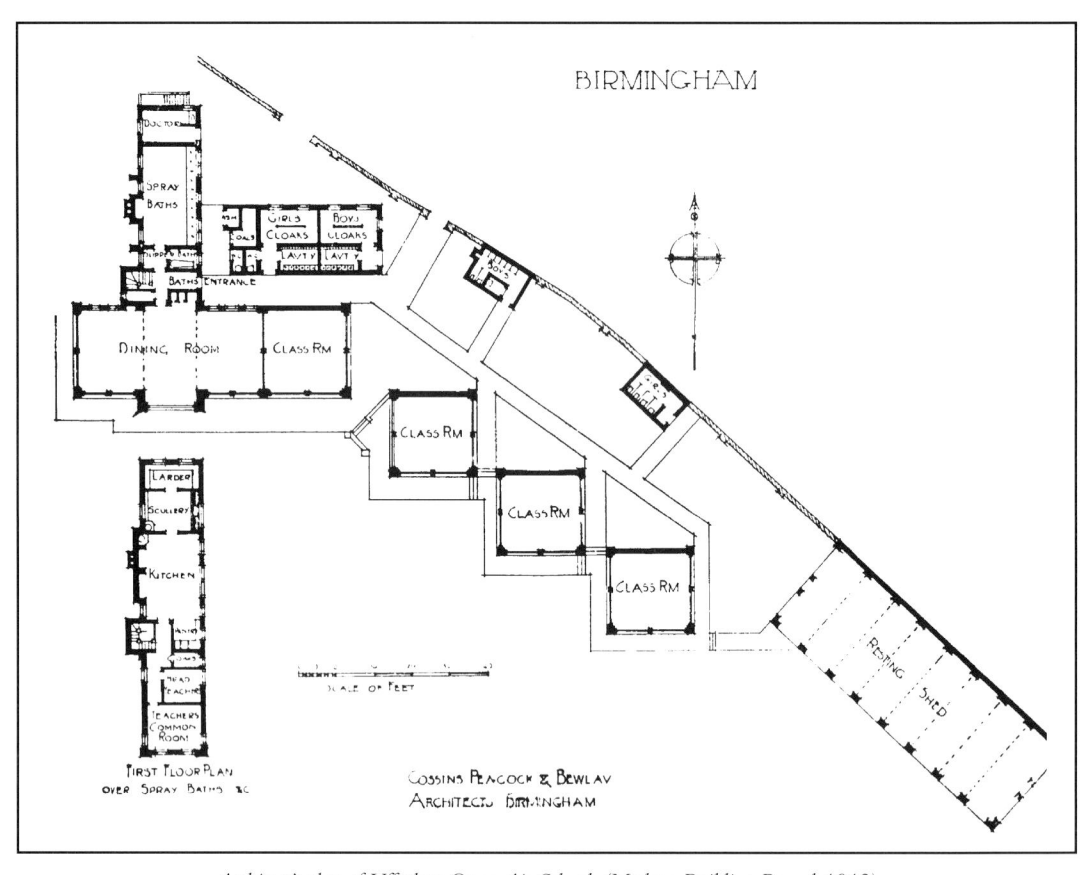

Architect's plan of Uffculme Open-Air School. (Modern Building Record 1912)

have been a source of wonder to the children during their weekly ablutions, as few had experienced such luxuries.

Dr. Auden, Birmingham's School Medical Officer, was quoted in the *Birmingham Daily Mail* as saying, 'This is one of the most important parts of the curriculum designed for the purpose of teaching citizenship. Cleanliness is one of the greatest virtues. Excellent results have attended the bath at Gem St and Floodgate Schools while in Norway no public school can be built without a suite of baths. In Germany a weekly bath is compulsory in every school'.

A room for the medical officer was provided for examinations, weekly blood tests and sputum stainings: in practice it became the domain of the school nurse. There were three separate pavilion-type classrooms, each enclosed only on the north side, the three remaining sides having sliding wood and glass screens. As it was intended to teach children out in the open air, the sliding screens were a concession to bad weather and a feature not seen before in Birmingham. Many wondered how such weakly children would survive during the winter months—and, indeed, the teachers who would endure the same conditions. Geraldine Cadbury is credited with the ingenious idea of the central heating system whereby underfloor hot water pipes ran around the sides of the classroom beneath a grille; the theory being that the cold air entering the room would be tempered by the rising heat. Some pupils may recall it was not totally successful! Each classroom also had awnings for hot weather and protection from the sun.

An important part of the treatment was the 1½ to 2½ hours absolute rest, usually after lunch. For this purpose a large resting-shed was constructed (75 ft. x 25 ft.), enclosed only on the north side. To prevent driving rain or snow drifting over the beds the roof continued as a veranda. Folding stretchers were provided, and each child was given a numbered blanket. The resting-shed, which had a concrete floor, was also used for physical exercises.

The chill of the English climate was of some concern as most of the children were likely to be in a delicate state of health, suffering from anaemia, malnutrition, bronchitis and weakened by acute illnesses. Birmingham Education Committee, however, dismissed the problem quite briefly in the Medical Superintendent's report of 1910:

> There is no reason why the school should not remain open throughout the year. Experience has shown that improvement in physique is most marked in the winter months; the 'flagging' of children in the hot weather is well-known. It is probable that, given an adequate supply of nutritious food and proper clothing, moderate cold is a most valuable natural tonic and one of the most potent remedies for anaemia. An anaemic condition is at the root of much of the debility of childhood.

On the school's opening day, readers of the *Birmingham Daily Mail* may have been reassured after reading that the children would 'be kept warm by rugs and will wear what is known as French capes so that they will be entirely guarded against physical discomfort'. French capes never materialised but jerseys were issued instead.

Dr. Auden had the unenviable task of selecting 80 pupils for the new school from 10,000 ailing children in the elementary schools. Each child was expected to stay an average of three to four months and the main aim of the school was stated to be 'an earnest and effective attempt to counteract the deteriorating influence of slum life'. He declared: 'it cannot be too strongly insisted that improvement in the physical condition of the children is the primary object of an Open-Air School, and that the educational aspect is of secondary importance only. Little more should be attempted than will secure that the education shall be thoroughly practical and based on the lines of nature study and the like. Careful attention must be paid

General view of Uffculme Open-Air School, showing the dining room, classrooms and open rest shed. (Modern Building Record, 1912: reproduced with permission of Birmingham Central Library)

Uffculme's staff (1911): Headmistress Miss Hurst, teachers Miss Burford, Miss Parker, Miss Potter, Miss Edwards, Nurse Wikins, Cook Mrs. Russell, Kitchen Maid Miss Newall. (Uffculme Shool)

to the graduation and performance of the physical exercises for these are an integral part of the curative scheme.'

As Barrow and Geraldine Cadbury requested that there be no formal opening of the new open-air school, Uffculme simply opened its doors without more ado on 18 September 1911, with a full complement of staff—Miss Mabel Hurst, the Headmistress, four assistant teachers, a nurse, a cook, a kitchen maid and a caretaker. Miss Hurst had a salary of £140 a year and had visited open-air schools in London and Bradford before the start of the new term.

Headlines in the *Birmingham Daily Mail* that day reflected the general opinion of the school: 'Open-Air School at Uffculme: inauguration of interesting experiment in Birmingham—baths, meals and sleep'. Despite all the research and positive results of European and British open-air schools, Birmingham still seemed to regard the school as something in the nature of an experiment, even though it was designed as the most up-to-date institution of its kind.

The school logbook, carefully hand-written by the Headmistress, reveals the names of the school staff: Assistant Mistresses (certificated) Miss Harriet M. Burford, Miss Celia Parker, Miss Ellen M. Potter; Miss Ethelwyn Edwards (uncertificated); Nurse Florence Wilkins, Mrs. Russell (cook), Winnie Newall (kitchen maid) and Louis Carr (caretaker).

Additional school records even note where they lived—Miss Hurst (Oakwood Road, Sparkhill), Miss Burford (Small Heath), Miss Potter (Moseley), Miss Edwards (Sparkhill), Nurse Wilkins (Small Heath), Mr. Carr (Small Heath) and Mrs. Russell (Hay Mills). All were fairly local, apart from the cook who had quite a long journey. Research from probate records indicates that Mabel Emma Hurst, the Headmistress, was about thirty-two years of age, and appears to have been a good advertisement for open-air schools (where her career remained for many years) as she lived to be 86 years old. Her first entry in the log book concerned the new intake of children and their activities on that auspicious occasion:

> The Uffculme Open-Air School was today opened by the admission of 28 sickly children, 15 girls and 13 boys. Most of them appear to be backward and of poor intellect. The day was fine and bright and a good one upon which to open.
>
> The morning was occupied by the admissions, medical examination, and advice to parents. The ordinary routine began with the pre-dinner wash and from then the children were in their teachers' charge. They were taken for a walk in the park and talked about their surroundings, and seemed very interested and delighted.
>
> The giving out of the tram tokens needed careful arrangement.

Each child was given a token to cover the tram fares from the city, most coming from within a radius of two miles, arriving at 8.30am. For many children the tram journey was quite a strain on their physical and nervous resources. The fares were paid by Birmingham Education Committee, hence the advantage of 'workman's fares' early in the morning. A few came by train to nearby Kings Heath station. The School Medical Officer's annual report in 1911 described a typical day:

> They receive a breakfast of porridge, milk or cocoa and bread and butter. It has been found necessary to give to some of the children an additional morning meal of hot milk at 11 o'clock. On arrival each child dons a jersey and a pair of clogs, and during the cold weather a knitted cap as well. When sitting at their desks in cold weather the children wrap their legs and feet in a rug. A two-course meal at 12.30 is followed by one-and-a-half hours sleep. At 4.40pm the children have their third meal and leave for home at 5.30pm. Each child is provided with a toothbrush which is used before they leave for home.

Newly opened classrooms, 1911. (Uffculme School)

As dental decay was a major problem at the time a special sum of money which had been donated to the Dental Hospital for the treatment of schoolchildren was earmarked for Uffculme Open-Air School. Children were inspected by Dental Hospital staff and extractions of decayed milk teeth were made at the school or the hospital. In ordinary schools it had been found very difficult to persuade parents to seek dental treatment for their children as they could not be made to understand that decayed teeth were a source of ill health and malnutrition.

Most of the children selected for the school suffered anaemia, debility, malnutrition and chorea (St Vitus's dance, a nervous disorder), with several coming from families where there was a tuberculous parent. They had been recommended for the open-air school by doctors in private practice as well as by those in hospitals and charities. As word spread around parents frequently sent letters to the school seeking admission for their sick children.

By 17 October 1911 a total of 100 children had enrolled at the school. At the beginning of term Miss Hurst recorded the first few days of school life in the log book:

Uffculme log book 1911

19 Sep.   The children thoroughly enjoy their food. Clean plates are the rule. The first serving given is only a moderate one and I insist upon them eating that unless there is a special reason not. They can all have a second serving if they want it. There is one little girl, Alice Piff, who seems too tired and ill to eat. She is given plenty of milk and allowed to rest a good deal. [Alice Piff has the distinction of being Admission No.1 on the School Register which records the dates of admission/leaving, date of birth, address, parents' names and name of last school, and cause of leaving—a wealth of information for family historians! Seven-year-old Alice had come from St John's School in Deritend and stayed at the Open-Air School until November 1912, returning then to an ordinary school. She was re-admitted to Uffculme in May 1913, finally leaving in October that same year. It is to be hoped that the open-air school enabled her to face the trials of life ...]

September 1911. The open-sided dining room on opening day. (Uffculme School)

21 Sep.   Today is a beautiful autumn day. Already the children and staff seem to be settling naturally and happily in their new surroundings. As far as stock and apparatus will permit the time-table is being followed. The children note the atmospheric conditions every morning and are making collections of the leaves of the various forest and fruit trees round them. Part of the clogs and jerseys arrived today and we have fitted each child and found the requisite number of each size. Boys as well as girls are marking the blankets used for rest, which have been temporarily marked with tickets.

22 Sep.   Again a lovely autumn day. Many of the children already show a marked improvement. Miss Dale and Mrs. Pinsent visited the school, mainly for the purpose of considering the question of extra help in the kitchen. Two boys and two girls help every afternoon with the peeling of the potatoes. These they peel in the fresh air in a corner of the dining-hall, and each child's turn comes once a week.

25 Sep.   This morning 24 more children were admitted bringing the number on roll to 87. They were nearly all from Kings Norton and Kings Heath. A boy who had been a little unwell on Friday attended with every symptom of scarlet fever. He was at once sent home again and the Medical Officer of Health notified while his blanket was sent away for disinfection. The Uffculme Open-Air School Sub-Committee met here this morning in the Staff Private Room. There were present Sir George Kenrick, Councillor Sturge, and Mrs. Barrow Cadbury, Miss G. Dale and Mrs. Hume Pinsent. [Mrs Barrow Cadbury was to become a regular visitor to the school and her signature appears often in the visitors' book.]

26 Sep.   The gardening tools arrived yesterday so the gardening begins today with the potting of the bulbs and a talk about the tools and their uses. [Gardening was considered to be an important part of the curriculum in open-air schools. In 1910 the British Association Conference on Open-Air Studies claimed that 'gardening had important intellectual, social, moral, industrial and aesthetic virtues'. It stimulated all branches of study and gave nature study a definite foundation, as well as introducing the skills of growing vegetables and handling tools to children who could continue this hobby into adult life.]

2 Oct.   The weather is much colder with north, north easterly and easterly winds and we have found it necessary to close up on the one or two windy sides. We have today fitted the children with their jerseys and they are proceeding with the task of sewing the names inside ready for wear. The plan of the spring flower beds has been drawn up and the children are going to measure the beds, copy the plan, and proceed to plant. Most of the school work is now being carried out on the intended lines. The two top classes still have no exercise books and so can keep no permanent records yet, and as the basket weaving tools have not yet arrived that cannot begin. Most of the children show a marked improvement physically and mentally. Their pallid, pinched appearance is disappearing and they are much brighter, and more active and alert.

4 Oct.   Bitterly cold with drizzling rain. We therefore used the jerseys for the first time for the children to sleep in. The children are knitting mittens and caps to match their jerseys, for wear in the very cold weather. The boys do knitting also and like it and do it very well.

5 Oct.   John Walker has developed several symptoms of scarlet fever. I have isolated him in the Dr's room, wrapping him up warmly in his blanket and giving him only light nourishment and telephoned for a doctor.

10 Oct.   This afternoon Harold Beecroft has had an epileptic fit of two hours duration. When it was over he sank into a comatose state from which he could not easily be roused, so, after telephoning to the Education Offices for permission, he was taken home in a cab by the nurse.

11 Oct.   Today I have seen Mrs. Beecroft who reports that her boy seems much better, and is sleeping the greater part of the time. The nurse has instructed her how to treat him and to keep him at home until next Monday.

The first 20 pupils listed in Uffculme's Admission Register, listing details of dates of birth, parents, addresses, last school attended and reason for leaving. (Uffculme School)

13 Oct.   The scales came the latter end of last week, so this week all the children have had their second weighing and all but two have gained in weight. Several have gained between 3 and 4lbs in the four weeks. The workmen are still here but the blackboards are not yet fitted and the shower baths cannot yet be used.

17 Oct.   The engineers are putting new valves to the shower baths and we hope to have them in readiness for use by the end of the week. Nurse has today begun testing the eyes. I gave my staff their first lesson in basket weaving during rest-time today so that now they are ready to begin with their children.

18 Oct.   This morning I caned three boys for bad behaviour on the tram car going home. It is the third offence. The two previous occasions they were talked to and warned.

24 Oct.   The workmen completed the fitting of the blackboards this morning, and all teaching can now be carried on as it should. Dr. Auden has given the children two rabbits and some of the elder boys are making a hutch for them. The weather is now much colder and damper and the jerseys and clogs have to be generally worn. The attendance continues to be good and on the whole the children continue to gain in weight, colour and animation. Their lessons show a distinct improvement already.

26 Oct.   The Uffculme Open-Air Sub Committee met here today, when Ald. Sir George Kenrick, Mr. Sturge, Mrs. Pinsent, Mrs. Cadbury, and Miss Dale were present. It was decided that I should act in union with two members of the Committee and decide how much the parents were to contribute for meals when they could not pay the shilling per week, and for how long that reduction should last.

27 Oct.   Now that the colder weather has set in the children do not sleep so well. The attendance is the poorest we have had during the six weeks we have been open being only 87.8%. One child has mumps,

Name of Parent or Guardian.	Name of last School (if any).	Attendances made in this School. (To be inserted if required).				Date of Last Attendance.			CAUSE OF LEAVING.
						Day	Mth	Year	
Walter	St John's, Deritend					24/9	9	1913	Returning to ordinary school 22.11.12. 19.9.13 - 17.10.13
Bertha	St Ann's, Alcester St					16	10	1912	Dr's orders.
Charles Henry	St Asaph's, Bow St					29	7	1914	Dr's Permission, Fourteen years of age
Walter	Upper Highgate St					11	10	1912	To return to ordinary school
Frank	St James, Summer Rd	12 18	7 3	16 17		17 4	5 9	12 1914	Excluded by Dr. Returning to original school Foster Dr's permission
Louisa	Floodgate St					5	7	1912	Returning
Louisa	Montgomery St					"	"	"	"
George	Bristol St					24	4	14	Dr's orders.
Elizabeth	Charles Rd					8	3	12	
Alfred	Montgomery St					17 17	1 5	13 12	Excluded from school 4.11.13. Returning to original school
William	Rae St					16 15	10 9	1912 1914	Returning to ordinary school.
William	Dennis Rd.					16 29	2 7	12 1912	20.9.12. Left, Dr's Orders
Eliza	St Mark's					17	10	13	Foster - Dr's permission.
Richard	Severn St					12	7	1912	Returning to original school
Charles	Hope St					17	5	12	Returning to original school
Samuel	Severn St					23	2	12	Dr's Orders.
Walter	Sherbourne Rd					17 15	5 9	12 1914	Returning to original school
Arthur	Bristol St					8	3	12	Dr's orders.
Thomas	Floodgate St					14	7	12	Returning to original school
Francis	Rae St					19	8	12	Returning to original school

another scarlet fever and seven have been away for the whole week. The children are as enthusiastic as ever about coming to the school.

30 Oct.   When the children had been at rest for an hour today a heavy storm of wind and rain came on, the wind blowing the rain three fourths of the way across the rest shed. It was necessary to get the children up at once and for the blankets to be thoroughly dried afterwards.

31 Oct.   A rainy, windy day like yesterday. Mrs. Cadbury sent some of the gardeners from Uffculme to assist in carrying half of the couches from the rest-shed to the class-room adjoining the dining hall. Immediately dinner was over the caretaker stacked all the tables and forms at one end of the dining hall and placed out fifty six couches. Fifty six children slept in the dining hall and the remainder at the back of the rest-shed. It took twenty minutes to prepare the dining hall and twenty minutes to again arrange it in readiness for tea, this was with all the biggest boys assisting and not reckoning the time taken in carrying the couches to and from the rest-shed; still the children had a clear seventy minutes rest and were not much disturbed from their usual routine, and so it was worth the trouble. Mrs. Cadbury has offered to lend a man for carrying couches whenever the weather is bad during this winter.

1 Nov.   Dr Auden came this afternoon and noted how unsatisfactory the regulating of the temperature of the water in the bathroom was. He declines to take any responsibility if the children are scalded. Nurse and I, however, feel that the bathing is of such inestimable benefit to the children that we purpose continuing it and exercising the greatest care and caution.

9 Nov.   This week has so far passed smoothly and well. The engineers have again been altering the supply of hot and cold water in the bathroom, and this time they seem to have made it satisfactory. The gardeners are

The open rest shed which soon proved impractical in wet weather. (Birmingham Weekly Post: reproduced with permission of Birmingham Central Library)

at work planting trees, shrubs and alpines. The weather for the most part has been fine and cold. The children have to do a good deal of physical exercise, games etc in order to keep warm.

17 Nov.   Since the cold weather set in the children have not shown such a good increase in weight, in fact six were found to have either lost or be at a standstill. We have therefore somewhat changed the menu giving them suet boiled in their milk at breakfast and suet pudding three times a week at dinner, also treacle in place of sugar on the porridge and an apple when there is bread and milk. The result has been most satisfactory. In ten days the children not gaining weight have all gained. There is now no child who is not gaining weight. The children too are eating more pieces of bread and butter and eating those pieces thicker.

27 Nov.   Slight snow fell during the whole of the morning and part of the afternoon, while there were several degrees of frost. The children seemed to feel the cold, and half way through the morning I had the dining hall cleared and allowed the entire school to take part in brisk games. The attendance has been very poor.

20 Dec.   Dr R.H. Crowley, HMI for Open-Air Schools, visited the school this morning. He inspected the whole building and specimens of the children's work, questioning the children in one of the classes. He also inspected registers and the Medical Reports and stated that he had been very pleased with and interested in all he saw. He considered that the rest-shed would be much improved by the addition of some kind of rain or wind screen.

Three months after the school had first opened Dr. O. Robinson, the school doctor, reported that out of 89 children '31 showed great improvement, 45 showed some improvement and 13 appeared to be stationary. Estimation of nutrition and physical vigour is always exceedingly complex ... There is an alertness and smartness of response, with an added interest in life which is quite characteristic. The improvement in the haemoglobin content of the blood was most marked'.

Birmingham Education Committee published in their 1912 report that:

> ... the results achieved by the open-air school have abundantly fulfilled expectations. Since the opening in September 1911, 243 children have been certified for admission. The causes of certification were as follows:
>
> General debility 124, Anaemia 50, General debility and malnutrition 33, Chorea 9, Phthisis contacts (consumption) 9, Tuberculous glands and debility 5, Lupus of old standing (tuberculous of skin) 2, Heart disease 3, Phlyctenular ophthalmia 2, Bronchiectasis 3, Tuberculous peritonitis 2, Rickets and anaemia 1

After discharge from the school, children were examined again after three months at an ordinary school and it was found that out of 77 children 44 maintained their improvement in health while 21 deteriorated again.

One of the problems to emerge after the first year was that many children stayed at the open-air school longer than originally estimated, being termed as 'non-improvable' cases. The authorities had to be more careful in the selection of children and assess home surroundings and intelligence of parents, as without interested co-operation by the families there was 'little likelihood of permanent improvement in the children'. After a year it was found that far more children needed to attend Uffculme for a period of 6 to 9 months, rather than the originally planned 4 months and many stayed 9 to 12 months before being returned to ordinary schools. (Miss Hurst noted in the school log book on 12 September 1913 'I find the average length of stay to be 8.7 months per child' for the year 1911-1912.)

For 'pre-tuberculous' cases it was decided that the day school was not really suitable as they required a much more prolonged course of open-air treatment.

Children in open-air schools also suffered from the general ailments common at the time, including ringworm, eye defects, measles, diphtheria, infestations of fleas and head lice. It was estimated that in all Birmingham schools in 1911 there were 25,070 children with nits and 1,709 were verminous, as discovered by school nurses. School staff had much to contend with, apart from the problems of education!

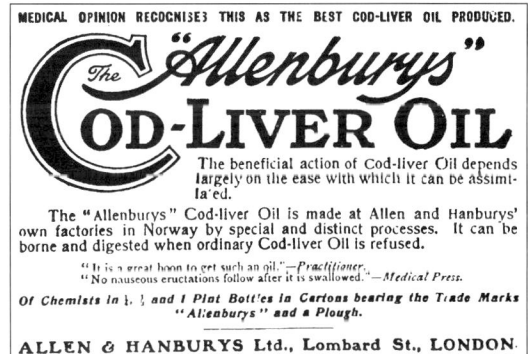

1912

The new term started off badly with many children absent, some suffering scarlet fever or mumps; 41 had lost weight in the Christmas holidays and many children seemed poorly. To make matters worse it was bitterly cold, as the log book records:

Uffculme log book 1912

17 Jan.   *The weather was very bad this morning. Bitterly cold and with snow and sleet falling. Only 67 children were present. Snow continued to fall during the whole of the day. By dinner time it was several inches deep and drifting very deeply in parts. No pains were spared to keep the children warm, but in spite of wrapping them up well and taking plenty of exercise some of the delicate ones seemed to feel the cold keenly. At going home time there were nine inches of snow, and the tram cars were running very badly*

18 Jan.   Snow has continued to fall all through the night and now is extremely deep, knee-deep in some places; 45 children are present. They have arrived very late and very cold. I am keeping them all in the dining room this morning as it is still snowing, and allowing them to play organised games, sing their songs and tell stories. All of them are now dry and warm. Yesterday and today they are all to have hot milk in the middle of the morning.

22 Jan.   This morning the greater part of the snow has gone after a steady thaw during the week-end, which is still continuing, but there has been a thick black fog all day. There are 64 children present, which is very good considering the weather, but many of them have severe coughs.

2 Feb.   The frosty weather has continued through the week, the snow which fell on the 18th & 19th being still on the ground. The percentage of children is 73 and these appear to flourish in the frosty weather. The weighing results this week have been most satisfactory. Most of the children have gained, and gained well, in weight; 14 have lost, but are children who have been absent the greater part of the time since Christmas. All are having lunch during the cold weather, and began last Tuesday to sleep in the Tea Rooms in Uffculme Park. Here the children can have ample ventilation, while they are much warmer and more sheltered during the severest of the weather. They are to continue sleeping there until movable shutters have been fixed to both ends of the rest-shed to enable us to shut out driving rain or snow.

8 Feb.   There is much carelessness in the kitchen in the handling of crockery and glass ware resulting in many breakages. It culminated this morning in the scullery maid slipping and dropping and breaking 19 mugs.

4 Mar.   I have today admitted 14 more children to take the place of those who are leaving on Friday (8 girls and 6 boys). Ernest Langham, admitted this morning, has been very ill all day. I have sent him home this afternoon in nurse's charge. He is suffering from bronchiectasis and very unpleasant to be near anyone else. His sputum is tinged with blood.

22 Mar.   On Monday last we began a revised time-table wherein reading and story-telling are given a more prominent part and the afternoon rest is again extended to two hours.

29 Mar.   A large number of children receive medical treatment at the hospitals and are absent because of that for one day a week.

26 April   Warm summer-like weather this week. The children have been gardening every day because the heavy rains of March have thrown them so behindhand with their gardens. So many children had lost in weight during the holidays that we began to give them all lunch again.

3 May   The second examination for passing out the children who are better was held this morning and Dr. Auden has selected 31 of these to pass out. Councillor Mrs. Hume Pinsent, Miss Dale and Mrs. Beale attended.

20 May   25 new children were admitted this morning. In almost every instance the children are suffering from tubercular or pre-tubercular trouble or there is tuberculosis in the family.

14 June   The week has been marked by a tremendous number of visitors. On the 13th, visiting day, we had at least sixty.

An arithmetic lesson in the school grounds. (Uffculme School)

UFFCULME: A BREATH OF FRESH AIR (1911-1919)

Sowing seeds in school grounds. Gardening was an important part of the curriculum. (Uffculme School)

5 July   Miss A.E. Edwards resigned her post here as assistant mistress, and her time expires on July 31st. She is leaving England to live in the United States.

2 Sep.   Miss E.M. Stockley commenced duty here today as an Uncertificated Assistant Mistress.

20 Sep.   Dr Auden visited the school today with three delegates of the Hospital Conference which is being held here. This morning Miss Mellor was appointed to succeed Miss Stockley as soon as she can be released from her present appointment. Miss Hart was appointed as Cook at £35 per annum.

31 Oct.   Mrs Russell, the cook, ceases duty here today.

9 Dec.   Annual Grant Form in respect of the Uffculme Open-Air School. (For period 18th Sep. 1911 to 31st July 1912.) School year ended July 31st, 1912.

Average attendance	89.5
Average no. of children on books during period	102.7
No. of children on books at end of year	112
% of Attendance, to average no. of children on books	87.1

Schedule of Grants (Bd of Education Regulations 25 & 26)

	£	s.	d.
Grant for instruction other than Manual Instruction	194	10	9
" " Manual " of younger children	37	3	4
" " " " " older "	105	18	0
	£337	12	1

Grant per head per annum on average attendance 1912 £4.6.9¼.

Physical drill: exercises were an integral part of the health cure. (Uffculme School)

In 1912 Birmingham's Medical Officer of Health recorded 521 deaths of schoolchildren aged between five and 15 and 535 children suffering tuberculosis of the lungs which gives some indication of the problems of the era. In fact, tuberculous cases were actually rising. Decayed teeth also continued to be a major problem.

1913-14

The school log book continues to give us a detailed picture of life in those times, sometimes reporting the absences and illnesses of staff who frequently succumbed to influenza, scarlet fever and other ailments. Many entries reported weather conditions in detail as it disrupted school routines in so many ways; weighing results were also mentioned at regular intervals:

Uffculme log book 1913

6 Jan.   *School re-opened this morning after the Christmas Vacation. The attendance is poor, and the weighing results after the holiday are almost disastrous—79 children having lost. The weather during the holidays has been very wet, and no doubt the loss is accounted for by insufficient food, irregular meals and lack of fresh air.*

17 Jan.   *Heavy snow fell last Saturday and Monday, and the weather during the greater part of the week has been unusually severe. Considering this, the attendance (82%) has been excellent and the children seem none the worse for the intense cold.*

21 Feb. *The past week has been intensely cold, 9° of frost being registered one day. The attendance has been excellent being 92.4%. The weighing for the past three weeks shows an average gain of 1.4lbs per child.*

1 April *Miss Mary Jarvis began duty here today as an Uncertificated Mistress. She is taking charge of Class III and Miss Potter, the previous teacher of that class, is taking Class II. A record attendance 94.2%.*

22 April *The weighing today has been a record one showing an average gain of 6lbs per week for each child. School is to be closed tomorrow, the days holiday having been given in honour of the visit of the Duchess of Argyll to B'ham.*

9 May *20 children were admitted on the 5th to take the place of those who left on the 2nd. Their intellectual powers seem to be of the very poorest order, and I am now compelled to put children of only Standard III attainment in my top class.*

23 May *The children are celebrating Empire Day for one hour this afternoon—3.15 to 4.15. The programme is to consist of the singing of The National Anthem and Rule Britannia en masse, the saluting of the flag, a talk upon 'Thoughts for Empire Day', and the rendering of two suitable songs by each class individually.*

30 May *The past week has been extremely hot, and the children seem to feel the sudden change very much. A number have been poorly although everything possible has been done to keep them cool. The kitchen maid, Miss W. Newall, leaves today.*

27 June *The mothers were invited to inspect the school on Monday last. Ninety four came. After the inspection Mrs. Cadbury entertained them to tea and afterwards gave them an address on how they could aid by their treatment of the children when at home.*

26 Sep. *The Special School Sub Committee met at school yesterday to re-consider the children's dietary. It was decided to increase the quantity of butter and dripping and cheese in their diet.*

10 Oct. *The weighing results are still more satisfactory than last time giving an average gain of 4.6lbs per week. 99 children had gained, 10 remained stationary and 3 lost in weight. The children have slept out of doors on three days this week.*

14 Nov. *The attendance is affected, as during last week, by cases of scarlet fever and by attendance at the dental clinic. Mr. Graves, teacher of manual, attended on Thursday morning preparatory to taking the elder boys for a course of woodwork.*

Waiting for the dinner whistle outside Uffculme's dining room (Uffculme School)

24 Nov. *Miss Potter was found to be suffering from scarlet fever and was removed to the Fever Hospital on Saturday last. Miss Line is still in attendance in her place.*

Uffculme log book 1914

12 Jan. *School re-opened this morning after the Christmas vacation. Miss Potter is still absent and has been certified by her Dr to be suffering post-scarlet fever debility and anaemia.*

23 Jan. *There are now 125 children on books. The children seem to thrive well during the clear frosty weather that we are having.*

27 Jan.   *Miss Potter resumed duty this morning.*

17 Feb.   *The meat supplied by the butcher yesterday for roasting was badly tainted and unfit for the children to eat. It could not be returned because the cook failed to notice this before cooking. I have written to Mr. Adkins about the matter. Cook is suffering from a fit of carelessness. The children's dinner was badly burnt on three days of last week, and this week she never read her menu and cooked a wrong dinner necessitating a wholesale revision of the menu.*

13 Mar.   *The Uffculme School Visitors held their meeting here on Wednesday, 11th, to decide the food contracts for the ensuing six months. Miss Bridie is holding a class in Willow weaving here on 12th, 13th & 14th.*

3 April   *Dr Auden held an examination for passing out this morning. Mrs. Cadbury, Mrs. Beale, Miss Martineau, Dr. O'Connor and Miss Bridie were also present. 35 children were certified for leaving.*

8 April   *Nurse Wilkins is absent from school today. Yesterday afternoon she had a severe heart attack at school and today is suffering from the results of it.*

9 April   *Elsie Baker has had a convulsion while under the shower bath this afternoon. Although she has been unwell for several weeks she has never had anything in the nature of a fit before. I wrapped her warmly in blankets, put a spoon between her teeth, chafed her limbs and applied a hot water bottle to her feet. She appeared so ill that I went for the nearest doctor. The fit was then over and he said he thought it was most probably an epileptic seizure. He pronounced her unfit to go home in the tram car so I took her in a cab.*

20 April   *School re-opened today after the Easter Vacation. The entire staff are present with the exception of Nurse Wilkins.*

4 May   *Miss E.M. Jenner commenced duty here today as temporary nurse during the absence of Nurse Wilkins.*

Basket weaving class beneath an apple tree. (Uffculme School)

29 May   The weighing results for the past two weeks are not so good. 73 children have gained, 21 remained stationary and 27 lost. The great changes in the weather and the fact that several children have had teeth extracted is most probably the cause.

17 June   Dr R. Crowley and Dr. Lilian Wilson from Whitehall visited the school yesterday afternoon. Dr. Crowley said everything was developing as he liked. He stated that this was the only open-air school which closed for holidays and that if it continued to do so the grant would have to be curtailed.

8 July   This has been a Red Letter Day for the children. In the morning the Lady Mayoress, accompanied by her niece and sister-in-law visited the school. They stayed two hours and were interested and pleased with all they saw. Each class either sang, recited or acted for their entertainment and the Lady Mayoress spoke to each class and showed them her chain of office.

   In the afternoon more than a hundred mothers visited the school and saw the entire building and the children at work. Mrs. Cadbury entertained them to tea and gave them an address upon how they can co-operate at home in the work done here.

24 Aug.   School re-opened this morning after the mid-summer vacation. The entire staff are present Nurse Wilkins having returned to duty.

13 Oct.   This afternoon the children are celebrating their unique achievement, 100% attendance for the day, by half an hour's play.

29 Oct.   The weighing results for the past three weeks are not quite so excellent as for the previous three, though they are satisfactory. 117 children were weighed and of these 84 have gained, 14 remained stationary and 19 lost in weight. Because the porringer is being re-tinned the children have had to breakfast off bread and milk, the weather too has been less favourable, and there is an epidemic of septic throats in the city, and all these causes have been adverse to gaining.

18 Nov.   Dr O'Connor has this morning excluded ten children from attendance at school on account of septic throats. There are already three away from the same cause. This is first time in the school's history from which it has suffered from any epidemic.

18 Dec.   A medical examination was held here yesterday afternoon when 16 children were certified as fit to attend the ordinary school. Dr. O'Connor sent Nurse Wilkins home to bed, as she believed her to be suffering from tonsilitis or diphtheria, and as there were two fresh cases of septic throats among the children Dr. O'Connor and Mrs. Cadbury decided to close the school this afternoon.

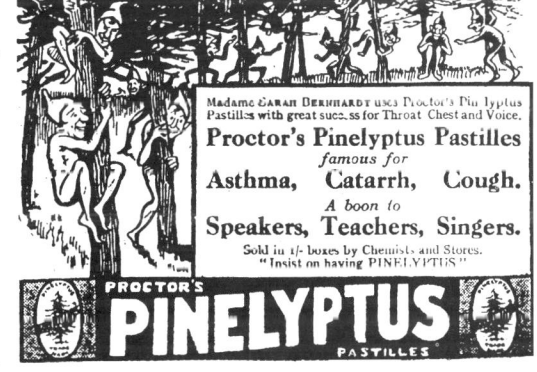

   The annual report of the Assistant Superintendent of Special Schools appeared in the school log book, and is worth quoting:

> **General organisation**. Everything is arranged with great care and thought, and these arrangements are successfully carried out with the hearty co-operation of the entire staff. During the last year a fuller and more complete understanding of the special needs of delicate children has shown itself in various modifications.
>
> **Discipline**. The tone and order of the school are very good, but I think this might be equally good with a freer discipline and more allowance for spontaneous movements of the children.

Instruction. The correlation of manual work and academic work must be especially commended. The instruction generally is on very suitable lines.

I still feel that the lowest class requires much more freedom and self-activity on Kindergarten lines, for in spite of the ages of the children they are small and underdeveloped mentally as well as physically.

Manual work. This merits high praise in all classes, for the quantity and variety of practical, useful and well-finished work is most creditable. Particularly to be noted are the original models made by one class from all sorts of odds and ends of wood, card etc. The weekly woodwork class has proved most successful with the older boys.

Kitchen arrangements are carefully planned and carried out with care and interest. Meals are always well cooked, neatly and punctually served.

General efficiency. Very good.

In 1914 a comprehensive book on open-air schools was published which contained information on Uffculme: Hugh Broughton's *The Open Air School*. The author had been involved in British open-air schools from their creation and Lady St Helier noted in the Foreword of the book:

> The (Open-Air) School is a wonderful example of what an open-air life can achieve. Only those who have seen the puny, undersized, anaemic boys and girls at their entrance into the school, and revisited it after a few months, can realise what Open-Air Schools have done, and will do in the future, for the tuberculous children of England. The improvement in their physical condition is marvellous. In a short time their appetites improve and they grow fatter; the good food, the regular hours and, above all, the enforced rest, have steadied the heart action ... and distressing symptoms have disappeared.
>
> The work of the Open-Air School is almost miraculous ... but one is apt to forget what an amount of labour and anxiety has been expended to ensure its success ...No words are too emphatic to affirm how much children's welfare and happiness are due to their teachers, who are rewarded by the consciousness of the good work they are doing and by the gratitude of many a delicate child that owes its health and future to their care and devotion.

Hugh Broughton had made a special study of Uffculme Open-Air School, rating it as one of the best in the country. The individual classrooms were highly praised, although he made the suggestion that the sliding screens should have 'movable window sashes similar to those in railway carriages. Thus, during a period of strong wind, when the doors to the windward side would be closed, the windows on that side might be open to admit air, but in such a manner that it would pass over the heads of children'. His suggestion was not taken up.

The book mentions Uffculme's bathroom which dispensed with troughs for water, by having 'a sloping floor to obviate the danger of falls when the feet and floors are slippery with soap'.

Uffculme's stretchers for mid-day rest were made by Messrs. Wales Ltd., Atlas Works, Birmingham, being 5 ft. 6 in. long, 2 ft. 3 in. wide, strongly made of canvas on a framework with folding legs—the legs at the head slightly longer than at the foot, so that pillows were unnecessary. These were available in 1914 at 7s. 9d. each, and must have been a great improvement on deck chairs which were provided in many other schools.

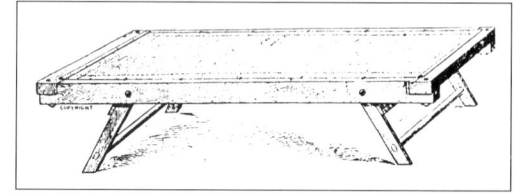

Children were given woollen bonnets/caps and mittens for rest periods in cold weather, in addition to the usual blankets. These were all labelled with children's numbers, to prevent the spread of vermin and skin diseases. It was reported that 'the majority of the children sleep all the time'. Hugh Broughton made the comment that:

> ... nobody expects **every** child to sleep the **whole** of the rest time but the teacher must insist that for the whole time children should lie quite still with eyes closed. The beds should be at least two foot apart, then talking may be easily detected and stopped; a further precaution is to guard against covering the face with the blanket ... Usually it is on days when there is a chilly wind blowing that children sleep most satisfactorily. On such occasions they make full use of their blankets and readily make themselves snug and cosy.

Although standard furniture could be used in open-air schools an alternative arrangement was the provision of individual desks and wooden armchairs which could be carried easily out of doors for lessons. (These individual desks and chairs were still in use at Uffculme in the 1950s.) Most lessons were taken out-of-doors, with no overhead covering apart from the branches of a shady tree. When the ground was wet many schools used raised wooden slatted platforms which could be made in sections in a design easily completed by schoolboys as a woodwork exercise.

Hugh Broughton's book listed in great detail the other requirements of open-air schools: garden tools, carpenter's tools, soldering outfits, bricklayer's trowels, paints and paintbrushes, and clogs for wet weather. The open-air school teacher had to be 'jack-of-all-trades', although many Head Teachers were female, as they were cheaper to employ.

The curriculum recommended many outdoor activities to improve bodily health and make children appreciate a healthy lifestyle. The study of weather was used for lessons, including thermometers, and the making and use of wind/rain gauges and weathercocks. History and geography lessons often took place outside including local studies, making relief maps on the ground and producing dramatic productions of historical events. Nature study and gardening went hand-in-hand and pets such as jackdaws, squirrels, rabbits and tortoises were kept in school. Each pupil was given a garden plot and was responsible for its cultivation, trenching, manuring, seed planting, growing fruit, flowers or vegetables. Cold frames, rockeries and water gardens were tackled, as well as the keeping of poultry, bees and even cows or pigs in one or two schools.

'Handwork' was an important part of the school curriculum. The aim was to present practical exercises of gradually increasing difficulty, as well as introducing an element of utility, with instructions in the use of tools which could be useful later in life.

Paper cutting was one of the simplest handwork exercises: folding, tearing and cutting, which led to picture making by pasting, mounting and colouring. Cardboard work involved making such things as clock faces, draughtboards, mats, cubes and boxes. Woodwork included using saws to make things such as railway signals, pen trays, toothbrush racks, as well as more advanced projects for sledges, garden baskets, beehives, coldframes and fowl houses. Metalwork included using hammers and chisels to make sundials, brackets, flower pot stands and hat pegs. Older boys had instruction in tinsmith's work: repairing watering cans or kitchen utensils, for example.

Basketweaving class, showing the screens which were usually kept open to the elements. (Uffculme School)

In needlework girls learned to use various stitches, in addition to darning, knitting and mending clothes. Weaving, basket making, crochet work, dressmaking, and the use of sewing machines were part of their studies.

Open-air schools followed all the usual subjects which were taught in ordinary schools. Hugh Broughton's book recommended recitations from literature popular at the time: Longfellow's *Hiawatha*, Wordsworth's *To be a Butterfly*, and Tennyson's *Passing of Arthur*. Novels dealing with outdoor life were listed as suitable reading material: *Robinson Crusoe*, *Children of the New Forest*, *Treasure Island*, *Stories of Robin Hood* and *Coral Island*.

By 1914 some architects were being instructed by education authorities to plan school buildings along open-air school lines. For example, Monmouthshire built classrooms in ordinary schools after the style of Uffculme's classrooms. The open-air schools were beginning to influence new trends in mainstream education: no longer were they regarded as experimental institutions.

1915-17

One of the few benefits from the First World War was the improvement in the physical condition of men undergoing army camp training in the open air. The effects of fresh air and sunlight on the human body were finally proven and open-air schools received their final seal of approval, as the Chief Medical Officer's report to the Board of Education stated in 1916:

> During the past three years the nation has had a valuable lesson of the benefit to be derived from open-air life. No one can measure the national gain that will accrue from this increased physical well-being, even as no one can estimate the loss in defective and devitalised man power which the nation has sustained for many years. The open-air school is a simple and economical way of applying a method of natural education to the susceptible body and mind of the child, who is taught under such favourable conditions to recognise and value some of the fundamental principles which underlie a hygienic way of life. **Fresh air, exercise, cleanliness, rest, regular meals, careful supervision** form a series of conditions as certain in their beneficial physical effect as they are conducive to the creation of a mental atmosphere favourable to the opening mind.

Many School Medical Officers had reported that open-air school teachers had observed an increase in physical and mental powers in their pupils. It was urged that new open-air schools should be provided as a matter of some urgency—even temporary huts as provided in military camps were thought sufficient to enable town children to regain their health. After all, the future strength of the nation depended on the vitality, health and education of its children.

In 1916 Dr. Leonard Hill, Professor of Physiology in the Medical School of the London Hospital, wrote a treatise on the physiological advantages of the open air:

> Our people nowadays are generally too sheltered by clothes and confined dwellings and are weakened by over-coddling. The vastly improved health, vigour and manhood of our conscripts taken from desk, shop or factory and put to the open air shows how much ill health arises from sedentary confined occupations. Children should be stimulated by an open-air life to be active, eat and grow ...

The Board of Education recommended that all schools should have baths—'Cleanliness prevents diseases and contributes to the purity of the atmosphere in the classroom as well as assisting physical development'. It even recommended that all ordinary elementary schools should be constructed so as to take advantage of the fresh air. To quote the report: 'most of the children entering an open-air school are dull, listless, anaemic and dejected. A few weeks later we find them bright and alert, quick to perceive a joke, and full of the joy of life that is their birthright. Pure fresh air, rest, cleanliness and wholesome food have performed their usual miracle'.

Dr. Lewis Graham confirmed in the Board's Annual Report that Uffculme Open-Air School continued to be one of the most valuable aids to the medical service and that there was a long waiting list for admissions. He admitted that it had been found that children gained very little from a three month stay at the school and to get real benefit they needed to stay about two years.

We have been able to trace one person who was at Uffculme during the First World War. She was sent to the open-air school on 3 May 1915 from St Patrick's School in Balsall Heath, being Admission No.458 in the Register. Although she left the school 25 July 1916 she was re-admitted 25 June 1917, finally leaving in 1918. She told us of her life at the school:

42   A BREATH OF FRESH AIR

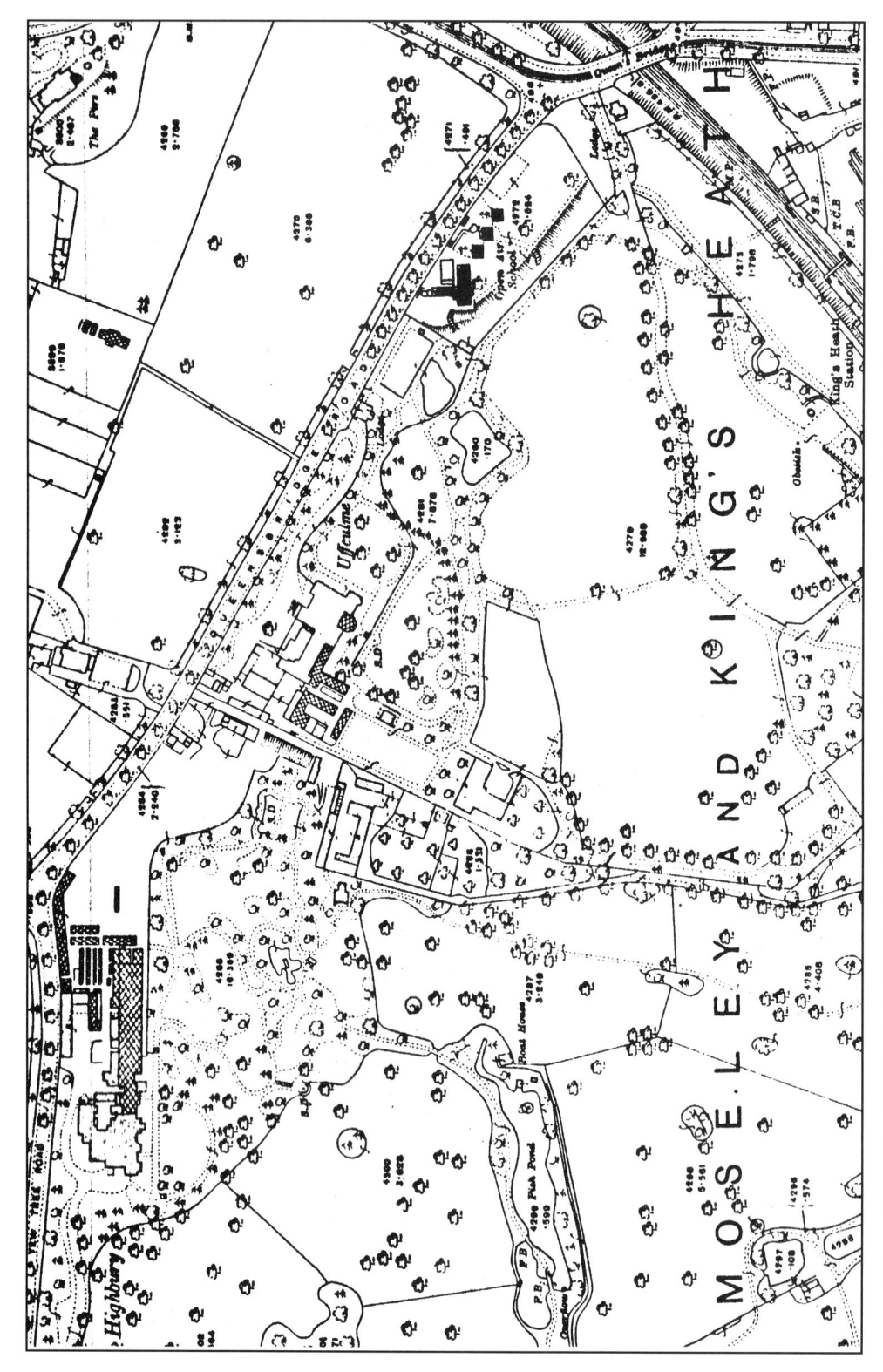

Ordnance Survey Map of 1916, showing Uffculme, its parkland and neighbouring Highbury Hall. Kings Heath Station can be seen in the bottom right-hand corner.

Mrs Ada Elizabeth Newsome (née **King**), 89, Uffculme 1915-18, Birmingham

I was born in December 1907. When I was eight months old my Granny once said: 'You could put Ada in a quart jug, she's so small!' I was the eldest of a family of eight and we only had two bedrooms at home. I was 'farmed out' to live with my Granny in Balsall Heath as there was no room at home. In fact, I never spent more than one Christmas with my parents!

My father was wounded in the First World War, invalided out with mustard gas injuries. He had to sleep in a shed in the garden with a camp bed as my mother stayed in the house with the other children in the two bedrooms. Before the war he had been a carter, working with horses, but afterwards he went to Papworth Hall, near Cambridge, to learn attaché-case making. But he never really recovered and died a few years later, after being in a succession of hospitals.

My mother wasn't strong so when Dad asked his mother to 'have me for a bit' I went to live with my Granny. I stayed there for the rest of my childhood until I married! I suffered from 'chronic catarrh of the chest', and went to Moseley Hall Hospital. From there I went to Uffculme School when I was 7, after I had been examined at Margaret Street.

I travelled to the school on a tram, using red and green tokens. Uffculme was like being in the country, as we'd always lived in a town. I enjoyed painting buttercups and flowers while I was there. At school we wore navy blue jerseys and fleecy lined knickers, black stockings and a skirt. We had special grey/blue linen bonnets in the summer with a flap at the back to protect us from the sun. In summer the boys wore round caps with a button on the top and a flap down the back, as well as shorts. In the winter we were given navy blue mittens and clogs to wear—they were kept by the isolation ward. If you were well-off you could bring your own galoshes to the school. We loved to walk along in the snow in clogs, with the snow sticking on the bottom so that we'd be walking along higher and higher—until the snow fell off one of them! They were quite comfortable to wear. We used to wear clogs when walking around the grounds and the park, on escorted walks.

Miss Hurst was a real Headmistress, quite strict, followed by Mrs. Abbott (a widow whose husband died in the Great War). I remember other teachers—including Miss White (who married Mr. Brown!)—she used to bring lots of apples from her garden to the school. Miss Jarvis was my favourite teacher as she used to write to my Dad for me when he was in the army.

There were four classes of mixed boys and girls. Each class had a great big garden and we had our own little plot to do gardening—there were competitions to grow flowers. They were happy days and the teachers were all very good—they went to a lot of trouble for us. In winter I remember snowballing and dressing up for Christmas plays. We didn't have a long summer holiday, only a week or two. We used to have some lessons then but also lots of nature activities, gardening competitions—and haymaking in the sun! We had to wear our sunbonnets and rake it in—I enjoyed that! Other activities I remember are dancing, physical exercises and basket work. We also had rabbits at the school. We weren't allowed to roam around the grounds without the teachers. There were apple trees on the lawns outside the classrooms. I remember one girl had an enormous pear fall on her head which cut her badly! We weren't allowed to pick the fruit.

Meals were paid according to your income—you didn't have to pay if you didn't have a father. For breakfasts we had bread and milk (always on Mondays) and the rest of the week it was porridge. I disliked porridge and often swapped it with someone else! I've disliked porridge all my life! Ten children sat at a table, with an older boy and girl at each end to serve the food. Mr. Carr worked the food lift which came from the kitchen above—he lived in the house on the edge of the park. I liked mince and sometimes we had fruit— an apple or an orange which was a treat in those days. It was marvellous to see the milk in bottles too—where I lived we had to get milk in a jug from the milkman at the door. There were bottles and bottles of milk at the school!

Every week we were weighed by the nurse who wore a starched head-dress and she also supervised our weekly bath—each class on a different day. About ten at a time went—we each stood in a bowl under a shower. The bowl was emptied afterwards. It was a real luxury as we had no bath at home and we were all given a clean towel too.

Nature study lesson. (Uffculme School)

I remember Mrs. Barrow Cadbury often used to visit the school, dressed in mauve. She'd sit at the teacher's desk with Miss Hurst and was very interested to see what was going on. The apple trees around the school were part of her orchard.

*I was sent back to St Patrick's School in Balsall Heath but I wasn't so good, so after being examined yet again at Margaret Street I was sent back to Uffculme—which I **was** pleased about! I used to be glad of rest time as I got tired of coughing. We had a brown blanket and canvas bed and also had a small rug for the classroom which we kept on the back of our chairs. The rest time blankets were kept in boxes in the rest-shed.*

I remember the wounded soldiers at Highbury Hall convalescing during the war, in their blue and grey uniforms. We used to knit slippers for them. They would buy a leather sole with punched holes all around, and then we would knit the top and stitch the top into the sole to make the slippers. The soldiers used to talk to us as we were taken on walks around the park and through the woods, walking in pairs.

Some children slept at the school if they were extra delicate. My friends May Crampton and Chrissie Collis both slept at the school. May lived to be eighty-five and died only last year [1992] ... and she had always been known as 'the delicate one' as a child in her big family!

I left Uffculme in 1918 and went back to St Patrick's School, finally leaving there at fourteen to work in a sewing factory, where I got a six-month apprenticeship. I stayed there until I married. Many years later I went to Uffculme School's 50th Anniversary in 1961 where I met and was photographed with Miss Hurst, who was then about eighty-two.

They were happy days at the school. For the rest of my life my health has not been bad at all—I owe a lot to the school and the Cadbury family!

In April 1916 Barrow and Geraldine Cadbury donated to the City of Birmingham the whole of their Uffculme estate which included the house, 36 acres of land (partly occupied by the open-air school) and a large field on the opposite side of the road. The house had previously been used for Adult schools and during the war was a home for Belgian refugees and VAD [Voluntary Aid Detachment] nurses from Highbury. The grounds and Tea Rooms had been frequently used by Sunday Schools and Mothers' Meetings as well as Uffculme Open-Air School pupils. In offering the estate the Cadbury's requested as little publicity as possible and additional land for the open-air school.

The difficulties of life during the First World War are barely mentioned in Uffculme's school log book. Children at Uffculme Open-Air School were lucky to receive a full week's schooling and care, in comparison with many of their contemporaries whose schools were taken over by the army or turned into hospitals. Where ordinary schools remained open there were many reduced hours of tuition as conscription had taken most male teachers away to the army. The school log book for 1915-18 records the minutiae of community life at Uffculme Open-Air School during this period:

Uffculme log book 1915

22 Feb.   *Two more children have been notified as suffering from diphtheria, this makes a total of five.*

23 Feb.   *Nurse Wilkins has been found to have diphtheric bacilli in her throat and so cannot attend school.*

4 June   *I met Mrs. Cadbury, Dr. O'Connor and Miss Bridie to confer with them regarding the modifying of the time-table, now that there is such a large number of tubercular children in the school (nearly 100). It was decided that the children should rest or have quiet sitting down games in the organised game time, and also five or ten minutes rest between the last two lessons.*

Uffculme log book 1916

15 Feb.   *Miss Emily White began duty here today as an Uncertificated Mistress.*

28 Feb.   *The resting shed was too cold and damp for the children to rest in today, so I have given them half an hour's rest in their class rooms after dinner, until 1 o'clock and then resumed afternoon lessons.*

2 Mar.   *Snow fell during rest time and the afternoon lessons and appeared likely to continue, so I deemed it wise to send the children home as early as I could after tea. The weather conditions of the last eight days have been the worst conceivable for an open air school.*

28 Mar.   *Heavy snow fell again during the night and continued to fall during the whole morning. 13 children only attended for breakfast. I therefore did not open school, but kept them warm and happy with singing, games etc until dinner time. After dinner I sent them home.*

5 May   *The weighing results for the holiday are not satisfactory. The parents are unusually prosperous and the children have been permitted to attend picture houses and to eat unwholesome delicacies.*

28 June   *I have seen the Dr. this morning and he says I must stay in bed until my feet and ankles are better. They are poisoned with mosquito bites.*

1 Sep.   *The weighing results after the holiday are truly appalling. There is an average loss for the entire school.*
      Mr. Irwin, HMI visited the school this morning, stayed for lunch, and saw the children settle at rest. He saw the gardens, the handwork, the games and nature study and reading lessons.

6 Nov.   *I have this morning refused admission to a child named L... C.... aged 13, until I have consulted with Dr. Graham upon the matter. She is mentally defective, and so far advanced in phthisis as to need a sputum flask. It has, until now, been the rule of the Committee that neither M.D.s nor children in an advanced stage of phthisis should be admitted here, and in the interest of the remaining scholars I have declined to admit this girl for the present.*

6 Dec.   *There is a dense fog this morning and the children who are now all travelling by train arrived an hour late. I have therefore put dinner a little later to give a reasonable interval between breakfast and dinner. On Monday last too, we were obliged, for the first time in the history of the school, to have dinner half an hour late as the supply of gas failed.*

14 Dec.   *Mrs Bott, Supt. of Physical Exs. saw the drill of the two upper classes today, and was very pleased with it.*

Uffculme log book 1917

2 Feb.   *The weighing results are excellent for the last four weeks especially considering the unusually severe weather. The children who lost in weight and most of the staff are suffering from gastric trouble brought about by the intense cold.*

18 May   *On Monday last, 14th, Dr. Graham held a re-examination of the children who had left here*

either six or nine months ago. 29 children attended and Dr. found that 20 of them were maintaining a satisfactory state of health, 3 a fairly satisfactory state and 6 were unsatisfactory and were to return to the school when there was a vacancy.

18 Dec.   *The weighing results are poor. Many of the children are unwell with severe colds and coughs.*

In 1917 Birmingham's School Medical Officer emphasised the benefit of the open-air school in his annual report:

> At the time of the establishment of the Open-Air School the scheme was regarded by some persons as a fad; even now there are to be found some people holding this opinion. The results ... show how erroneous such views are ... it is a boon and a benefit to the community. Furthermore, during the severe epidemic of infectious sickness at the beginning of 1917, when many schools had upwards of 50% of their scholars absent, not 1% of the children of the Open-Air School contracted infectious sickness ... although the children mix at home with children from other schools.

As life in Britain during the First World War became increasingly difficult, with shortages of food and rationing, allotments became a national craze. Gardening and other activities carried on at Uffculme school and the children continued to be well fed, as the log book records:

Uffculme log book 1918

14 Jan.   *Snow has been falling steadily from noon today and as I had to shorten rest twenty minutes on account of it I am sending the children home twenty minutes early.*

26 April   *The weighing results for the past four weeks are again only fair. This is probably due to the extremes of weather we have had and to the War Bread.*

28 June   *The attendance is 85.1%. The City is suffering from severe epidemic of mumps and influenza and the attendance has been somewhat affected by it.*

4 Sep.   *Miss Mellor was absent this morning. Her brother was called away upon military service and it made her mother too unwell to be left.*

6 Sep.   *I leave Uffculme today in order to open a new Open-Air School at Plymouth.*
[Miss Hurst must have returned to Birmingham in her retirement as she was able to attend Uffculme School's 50th Anniversary in 1961. The new Headmistress was to have many new ideas for the school ...]

1 Oct.   *Miss Bridie, the Superintendent of Special Schools, introduced the new Headmistress (Mrs) Elsie A. Abbott.* [written in Mrs. Abbott's script with a note that '*all the classes use the classrooms too much—much more open-air needs to be done*'.]

5 Nov.   *A very fine day. The children had a lesson on the Gunpowder plot in the afternoon and afterwards had games and singing round a bonfire.*

12 Nov.   *On the occasion of an armistice being signed between the Allies and Germany the school was given a day's holiday.*

19 Dec.   *During the fortnight preceding the Xmas holidays an experiment was tried as to the advantage of having a half hour's rest before dinner—this having proved very satisfactory in my former school. Both the staff and myself deeming it to be good for the children this will now continue, an half hour less being taken after dinner. During the winter months therefore rest will be taken from 12-12.30 and 1 to 2 = 1½ hrs per day.*

Rest period in the open-sided rest shed. (Uffculme School)

Uffculme log book 1919

20 Jan.   *Permission was given to keep fowls—I intend to let the top class boys build a fowl-house as soon as a wood-work instructor can be obtained.*

28 Jan.   *Miss White (U.C.T.) [Uncertificated Teacher] who informed me just previous to Xmas that she has been married some years, has been asked by the Committee to send in her resignation this week. This afternoon I have given her permission to visit two other schools with a view to her appointment at one of them. Her married name is Mrs. Brown.*

30 Jan.   *Severe wintry weather has been experienced all week. Special efforts have had to be made by the teacher to keep the children warm. Considering the inclemency of the weather the attendance has been good—the absences have been chiefly amongst the younger children who feel the cold the most.*

11 Feb.   *A deputation of 10 French mistresses at the invitation of the British Govt. visited Uffculme yesterday. The children danced and sang for them. The frost has been intense again, it was very difficult to keep the children warm in the afternoon.*

13 Mar.   *Dr. Ralph Crowley HMI visited the school in company with Dr. Auden, M.O.H. for Birmingham schools. He expressed satisfaction with the general working of the schools and made several suggestions which will be carried out. We discussed my new plans for keeping open during the summer holiday and for making the school residential for certain children. These plans are to be laid before the Committee in due course and have his entire approval.*

2 May   *The Education Committee have passed a resolution that 12 children may stay the night at school on Mon, Tues, Weds and Thurs for 3 months as an experiment. A night attendant being provided.*

5 May   *Mr Lardner took the 2nd Class Boys in Handwork this morning—the work will include woodwork, gardening, organised games, metal work.*

Games on the school field. (Uffculme School)

12 May   Nurse Rogers was appointed on Friday to take the post of night attendant. 12 children are to stay at school commencing tonight. I shall stay at night until the scheme is in working order.

13 May   A fairly good night was passed considering the novelty of the surroundings. Some of the children were rather restless. All had a warm bath and a hot water bottle and were quite warm in bed. They all seemed to have enjoyed the experience and seemed bright and fresh this morning.

23 May   We have commenced keeping fowls by buying 6 white leghorns and 6 black anconas as day-old chicks. The older boys are making a fowl run and will be taught how to rear the chicks.

18 July   Today the Children's Peace Celebrations were held for Special Schools. The official programme of songs and hymns was held after which the children adjourned to the adjacent park for sports. Tea was given to the children on the lawn, prizes were distributed by Miss Smith of Colmore Road Council School and a very happy afternoon was spent.

25 July   As an experiment this afternoon we have let each child in the school choose his or her work for the afternoon. All the classes have responded splendidly—all the children being at work within 5 minutes. The work done includes almost every variety of work taken in the school, painting, raffia work, sewing, bead threading, plasticine modelling, reading, writing and arithmetic and the children all look very happy.

28 July   This is the first time that the children have attended in the ordinary school holidays and there was a very good attendance considering that these children's brothers and sisters will be at home on holiday.

11 Aug.   School re-opened today after Peace Week Holiday granted by the King. The ordinary school curriculum is being adhered to in the morning session and until 2.30 in the afternoon. After this we are running the school on 'play centre lines'; games of all kinds are played in the park, silent reading is encouraged, sewing and story telling are taken. Several parents have expressed their gratification with our holiday school.

6 Oct.   The 'sleeping out' experiment ceased on Friday Oct 3rd.

A taste of country life—apple picking at Uffculme. (Uffculme School)

22 Dec. School closes today for the Christmas vacation. In the afternoon a party was given which the children enjoyed very much. A play was given by the staff. Mrs. Cadbury was present.

School Medical Services emerged from the First World War determined to promote health and hygiene as there were tremendous problems with whole families being infested with lice from soldiers returning from life in the trenches. There were also many outbreaks of scabies which meant that local authorities had to provide special treatment baths as few people had facilities at home. It gradually became much more acceptable for people to ask for advice and treatment as so many families were infected. In an attempt to cope with rampant infection Birmingham had opened a large new school clinic in Great Charles Street. It was equipped with an X-ray room for the treatment of ringworm and specialised in eye cases from all over Birmingham, as well as inspecting and treating over 20,000 pupils from inner city schools.

Medical inspection of five-year-olds entering schools revealed that the commonest defect was still malnutrition which led to rickets and dental disease. Other diseases were probably caused by life in crowded airless homes and a diet of excessive carbohydrates.

There was little development in the provision of open-air schools, as progress had been halted by the war. Despite thousands of recent army recruits being rejected on account of physical defects and many children needing urgent treatment, local education authorities were still very slow to open new open-air schools. Such schools were difficult and expensive to provide but were, to quote the Medical Officer of Health, 'one of the most powerful instruments in our hands for yielding quick returns and enduring value — they spell the ideal mode of education in childhood'.

It had been proven that life in the open air at Uffculme School had strengthened pupils' resistance to infections, as during the 'influenza epidemic' of 1918 the school was the only one to remain open in the city.

After British open-air schools had justified their existence for 10 years, there were still only 20 such schools provided among 318 local education authorities. Birmingham was certainly fortunate to be one of the pioneers and proved the value of its open-air school to the community.

Chapter 4

The 1920s: Curriculum for Life

'Dirt remains our greatest enemy' stated one school medical officer in an official report of 1920. A large number of parents appeared to consider that nits and vermin on their children were simply a natural phenomenon ...

To combat the problem of uncleanliness in children instruction on the basics of hygiene began to take place in all schools. Children were taught that lice and flies spread diseases such as typhoid fever and learned about physical hygiene; by repeated actions they began to form a habit for a more healthy way of life. School hygiene, however, could never be divorced from home hygiene and this was bound up with community conditions.

A new syllabus for physical training replaced the old school drill and included dancing, games, swimming and much emphasis on gymnastics in the open air. Thus school hygiene, physical training and medical care came to be incorporated into the educational system to promote healthy development of children.

Education for defective children became compulsory in 1921. It was realised that the real criterion for education in special schools was to equip the child for life; open-air schools suddenly acquired a new status. The Chief Medical Officer of the Board of Education in 1921 especially emphasised the importance of hygiene and physical training in open-air schools: 'seven things are essential to a child's well-being—food, fresh air, exercise, warmth, cleanliness, rest and regular habits for life. These will give a sound and resistant constitution to the child'.

Many children suffered diseases as a result of insanitary home conditions and unsuitable diets of filling foods such as bread and margarine which made them dull and lethargic. Backwardness came to be associated with malnutrition. Local education authorities began to supply milk to children under a number of different schemes associated with the National Milk Publicity Council from 1923 but parents had to pay 1d. [one penny] for a bottle of one third of a pint of milk. During the 1920s the nutritional value of milk and its beneficial impact on children's growth was emphasised in various reports but it was not until 1934 that schools were supplied with milk at a reduced rate through the Milk Marketing Board's special scheme.

By 1922 there were 60 open-air schools in the country—35 day schools and 25 residential schools, but the slow growth of such schools in England scarcely reflected the urgent need at the time to improve the health of thousands of sick children. Statistics of the death rate of Birmingham's schoolchildren, however, showed that health was gradually improving: 336 children died in 1922, compared with 403 in 1917.

Co-operation between public bodies and voluntary societies had led to Birmingham becoming a pioneer in the provision of schools devoted to the education and health of defective children.

Birmingham gradually developed its school medical services under the inspirational guidance of Dr. Auden. In Court Oak Road in Harborne a residential school for the physically defective had been established at Baskerville House for children suffering from the crippling effects of

A man's man!

Mother—the health doctor in every family—knows that disease germs congregate wherever there is dust or dirt. That is why she keeps a cake of Lifebuoy Soap at every place in her house where hands are washed—and uses it for home cleaning, too.

But they both need mother's care—and Lifebuoy

Yes, he'll grow up a stout fellow like his daddy, one day—thinks his smiling mother, looking on. He *will*—if he keeps his health.

"If?" It is just that "if" that Mother, the health doctor, attends to. She knows the danger of dust and dirt, of contact with other people who may be spreaders of disease. That's why she's taught you both the Lifebuoy habit. For there is in Lifebuoy Soap a wonderful health element which penetrates deep down into the pores of the skin and drives out all impurities. Mother knows.

Lifebuoy Soap
FOR HEALTH

rickets and tuberculosis. By 1926 there were fewer cases of these diseases but an increase in children suffering from heart trouble. The school was extended to specialise in rheumatic children suffering from congenital heart problems and was one of the first of such institutions in the country. Other special schools were also provided for deaf, blind and partially-sighted children, as well as for the mentally defective ('educationally sub-normal', as they were later classified). Open-air schools were an important part of this special school system.

Uffculme 1920-22

Uffculme Open-Air School continued to improve the health of Birmingham's children. The successful two-year experiment whereby a dozen children slept at school four nights a week during the months May to September—combined with the 'Holiday School' which operated instead of the long summer break—had shown highly satisfactory results; the children's height, weight and general health improved dramatically. School log books record this period of change:

Uffculme log book 1920

18 Feb.   *This week there has been an extraordinary spell of fine warm weather. The children have been out in the garden and park all day long revelling in the warm sunshine—all lessons have been taken out-doors and rest hours with stretchers pulled on to the lawn.*

20 Feb.   *Immediately following this fine spell of weather is a heavy fall of snow today.*

5 Mar.   *Miss Lord visited Fashoda Road Infants School and in consequence has become much interested in the Montessori methods employed there. She has now made a start on similar lines with Class IV here with great success. The more individual work can be taken in this school and the better will be the results as these children are all at such different stages.*

7 May   *38 children have been admitted this week. Most of them are very delicate and much below their standard in attainments. 'Sleeping out' commenced on Monday for the 12 boys chosen and a careful record will be kept of their progress. They seem very happy and contented this week. Miss Edwards is again taking charge at nights.*

25 June   *The school dentist has been here all week and has attended to the children's teeth. This was considered preferable to sending the children to the dental clinic at Fashoda Rd.*

23 July   *Miss Jarvis has been presented with a silver dish and vase on the occasion of her leaving school to be married. The ordinary schools close today for the midsummer vacation and we shall commence the summer timetable and syllabus on Monday.*

[Although most of the staff seem to have been dedicated, enduring the same hard conditions in the winter as their pupils, women teachers had to choose between marriage or a career, as a combination of both was not allowed by the education authorities at that time. Log books frequently record the departure of female staff as they left to get married.]

20 Aug.   *In spite of the wet cold weather the children have spent a very happy month and the holiday time-table seems to have answered quite well. The children have much appreciated the toys bought*

for them by Mrs. Cadbury and they have also enjoyed listening to and dancing to the gramophone. Each class has compiled a book of work contributed by all the children consisting of sketches, pressed flowers, essays etc. which are due to be judged by Mrs. Cadbury and class awards are to be given.

23 Aug.   *Miss Tidmus commenced duties here today—25 new children have been admitted.* [Miss Tidmus was an uncertificated teacher but devoted to teaching in open-air schools and remained at Uffculme for many years. She also appears in Cropwood log books as a teacher.]

1 Sep.   *Miss Jackson C.T. [Certificated Teacher] commenced duties this morning. Miss F.Mellor was presented with a silver fruit stand and bowl on the occasion of leaving school to be married.*

30 Sep.   *The mothers of the children were invited to inspect the school and see our exhibition of children's handwork. Songs were sung and a display of dancing was given on the lawn. The Lady Mayoress was present together with Mrs. Barrow Cadbury and members of the Uffculme Special School Committee. A basket of raffia work made by a pupil was filled with garden produce and eggs from our poultry and presented to the Lady Mayoress. By the generosity of Mrs. B. Cadbury all the mothers were subsequently entertained to tea.*

29 Oct.   *The school closes today for the autumn vacation. The children are having a bonfire and fireworks in the park this afternoon to celebrate the completion of the new garden plots. This is the last week for 'sleeping out'.*

13 Dec.   *A very heavy fall of snow, only 80 children present. The temperature registers 22° and it is too cold to allow the children to sit for lessons. Snow games and lessons were taken in the park all day and the children were kept warm and happy and went home early.*

Uffculme log book 1921

14 Jan.   *Miss Checkitts who has been appointed in Miss Tidmus's place is having a month's course of training in special school work previous to taking up her position here. The committee, acting on the urgent representations of the headmistress, have decided that all teachers coming to open-air school work from elementary schools shall in future have some such training.*

3 Feb.   *The weighing results are poor this month owing no doubt to the Christmas holiday. A great number of parents are out of work and the children are both ill-fed and badly clothed. Out of 113 children weighed, 47 had gained in weight, 20 had lost and 46 were stationary.*

23 Feb.   *Owing to the mild sunny weather the boys have taken extra gardening lessons in order to finish double trenching the new garden beds. Rest has been taken in the open and all lessons have been taken out of doors this week. Class IV girls are particularly delicate this term and are eating very little and losing weight in consequence. By Dr. Graham's advice they are all to have a tonic before meals to see if that will give them an appetite.*

8 April   *All classes have seen the remarkably clear annular eclipse of the sun this morning through smoked glass—they have also had interesting lessons on the cause of the phenomenon.*

29 July   *The first week of the ordinary school holidays has been well attended. An average of 108 children present. Each child in the school is making an article costing a definite sum and prizes will be given in each class. The children are showing much skill and ingenuity in their handwork.*

6 Oct.   *Mrs Cadbury kindly entertained the mothers of the children to tea at school this afternoon. More than 100 were present and the children danced and sang on the lawn. After tea Mrs. Cadbury spoke to the mothers of the objects of the school and tried to enlist the active co-operation of the parents in the work of the school.*

23 Dec. School closed this afternoon for the Xmas holidays. The children had a most enjoyable Xmas party, Mrs. Barrow Cadbury and Mrs. Innes being present.

Uffculme log book 1922

20 Jan. The % is 82.8. The low % was caused by absences owing to a very heavy fall of snow during the weekend and inclement weather all week. There are a few cases of influenza, there being an epidemic of this disease in the city.

27 Jan. Very severe frost and inclement weather together with the continuance of the influenza epidemic have led to small numbers during the week. Many of the children who are present are almost too ill to be at school. On two days no bathing was done as it seemed inadvisable to risk the children taking cold.

10 Feb. The children who had returned to school after influenza seem to be suffering from post-influenzal debility. Their appetites are poor and they appear listless and anaemic.

12 May Owing to the continued rainy and cold weather previous to Easter the gardening operations have been much delayed. Extra lessons are therefore being taken whenever the weather permits in place of cane work, needlework etc. for the next few weeks.

26 May The present Headmistress (Mrs E.A.Abbott) will terminate her duties at Uffculme on June 1st. On that day Miss Hibbert will commence duty here as Headmistress, Mrs. Abbott having been appointed Superintendent of the new residential open air school at Blackwell.

1 June Miss Hibbert commenced duties at Uffculme. [Miss Ella Alice Hibbert received a salary of £353 p.a. and remained at the school for 28 years.]

23 Nov. The school was visited by a large number of delegates to the Special Schools Conference. Mrs. Cadbury and Councillor Bartlett also paid a visit.

One ex-pupil of Uffculme recalls her life at the school at this time:

Mrs Doris M. Taylor (née **Edge**), 82, Uffculme 1921-2, Bromsgrove, Worcestershire

I attended Uffculme for 1 year 9 months. We had to get there for 8.30am and have our breakfast. It was lovely hot milk, followed by porridge or ground rice and prunes which was my favourite.

After breakfast would be a bible class followed by lessons which were either outside or in an open classroom. We had to rest on camp beds after lunch under apple trees. Some child was fortunate if an apple fell off! After more lessons, which were fairly simple, there were plenty of breathing exercises. Then home time.

Mrs. Barrow Cadbury had been well aware for some time that many children at Uffculme showed no improvement in their health because they returned each evening to the pollution of the city smoke and their overcrowded and often dirty homes in the slums. The weighing of children at Uffculme proved that children at a day school took much longer to recover from their debilities than those at residential open-air schools in other local authorities.

When Uffculme was fully established Mrs. Cadbury began to formulate some ideas on the further development of open-air treatment for Birmingham's children. Her own children had by now grown up so perhaps the family had less need of their holiday home of 'Cropwood' in Blackwell, Worcestershire. At any rate, the family were united in supporting her idea of offering Cropwood to the authorities.

With the idea of providing a residential home for children who needed recuperation away from home Barrow and Geraldine Cadbury made a gift of Cropwood, together with 65 acres of land, to Birmingham Education Committee in October 1920. The Cadburys planned to make all the necessary alterations to the house, adding open-air classrooms and equipment for 52 children and staff. The house faced south and already had some open-air rooms, with the added advantage of pure bracing air coming from the Malvern Hills and Welsh mountains.

Not only did Barrow and Geraldine Cadbury donate and equip Cropwood but they gave £1,000 per year towards the school expenses for the first three years. Birmingham Education Committee accepted the generous donation without hesitation! It was planned that when children left Cropwood Open-Air School they would be sent to Uffculme Open-Air School for a short while—in order 'to harden them off' before transferring them back to ordinary schools. Rather like hardening off tender plants from the nursery before planting them out, it was hoped to soften the effect of a sudden transfer from the sheltered environment of Cropwood, back to the slum life in the city.

The new headmistress appointed to Cropwood Open-Air School was Mrs. Elsie Abbott, the Headmistress of Uffculme School for the past three and a half years.

1922-25
The Opening of Cropwood

Cropwood was situated on the southern slope of the Lickey Hills, about six hundred feet above sea level and surrounded by 75 acres of woodland and meadows, parts of which were secured as open spaces for posterity. (Later on, Hunter's Hill Open-Air School for boys was built on part of that land.) Situated on a ridge, the house had magnificent views over the countryside as far as the Cotswolds, Malvern and Clee Hills. At that time part of the land was let to a farmer and the rent from it, together with that of nearby Rosemary Cottage on the estate, was intended to provide a small income for the school.

Nowadays, Cropwood House is within a couple of miles of Junction 1 of the M42 (near Bromsgrove), on narrow Spirehouse Lane, near Blackwell village. It was much more isolated in 1922 before the advent of motorways.

Alterations to Cropwood were made by the firm of architects, Peacock and Bewlay, who had built Uffculme school. The building work was carried out by J.A. Brazier Ltd. Geraldine Cadbury is reputed to have added her own womanly touches which made the school easier to clean, insisting on dark polished woodwork instead of white paint, and tile wainscoting round the walls. Two additional pavilion classrooms, identical to those at Uffculme, were built near the main house with its distinctive bell tower and sundial. An extension was built alongside the main building as dormitories.

The very detailed architects' drawing shows the innovative features of the 'sleep-time garden', which was a grassy sunken garden containing a fountain and 'resting shed'. It must have been a pleasant spot for taking a nap to the sound of soothing falling water. Nowadays, the lawns and fountains are long-gone and the resting shed has been converted to classrooms and workshops.

The open air swimming pool lies down the slope, surrounded by a high bank, once the scene of many garden parties given by the Cadbury family. Swimming became a popular feature of the school curriculum; fortunate indeed were the city children attending the school who were also able to use the gardens, the play areas, a tree house, and beautiful grounds. It must have seemed a demi-paradise!

Accommodation was provided for children aged from 9 to 13 years of age and it was envisaged they would stay at least six months. All would be specially chosen by the Special Schools Medical Officer. Debilitated children were mainly from slum areas and in the words of the brochure of the time: 'They will be children who in the city are too tired for lessons, children

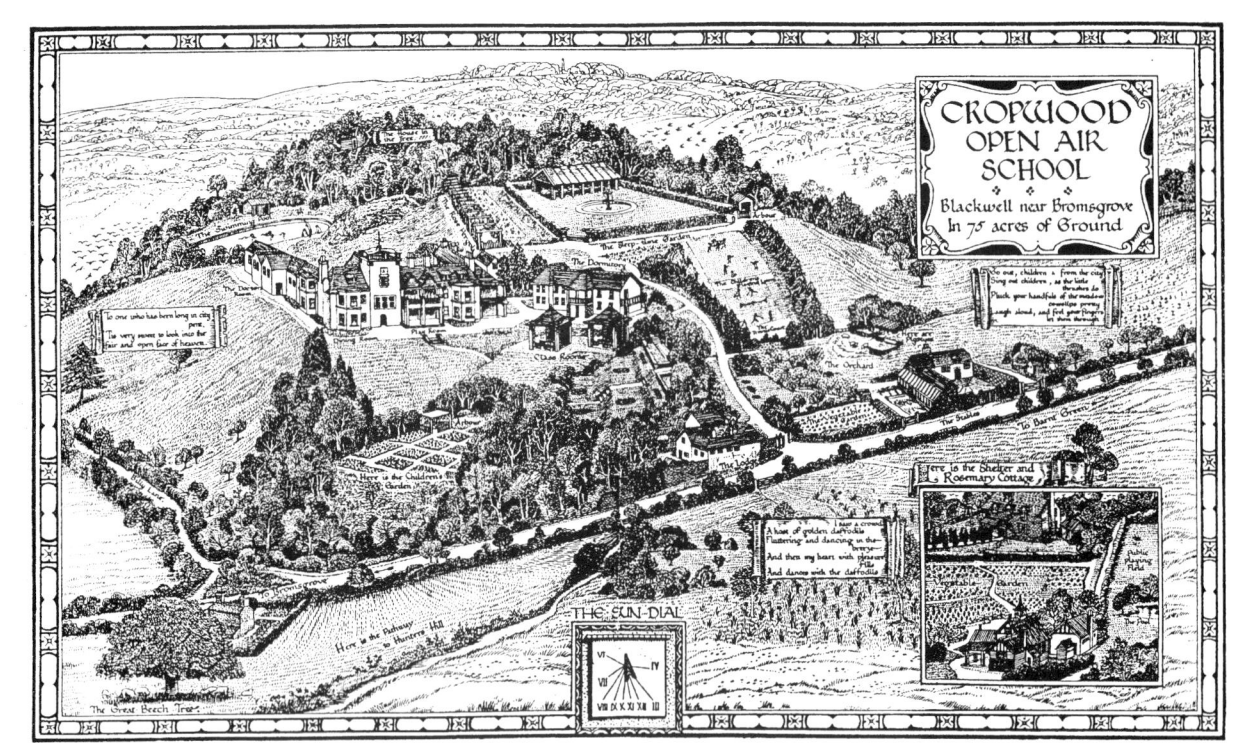

Plan of Cropwood School by architects Peacock and Bewley, 1922. The two separate open-air classrooms can be seen in front of the dormitory extension. In the background are the sleep-time garden and the swimming pool, part of an extensive estate including play areas, gardens and woodland. (Cadbury Archives)

who are under-developed or suffering from anaemia, debility or other troubles, but who may be saved from continued ill-health and become thoroughly healthy boys and girls'. From the beginning it was planned to operate Cropwood on a two year basis, girls alternating with boys: it became a girls school when Hunter's Hill opened in 1933.

The school opened on 6 June 1922 and was the scene of a formal ceremony on 17 June, in complete contrast to Uffculme's quiet beginning. Officially opened by the Lord Mayor of Birmingham, Alderman David Davis, Cropwood was formally handed over to the city's Education Committee by Barrow and Geraldine Cadbury. Also present were the Cadbury's children (Mr. Paul Cadbury with his wife, and the Misses Dorothy and Geraldine Cadbury), together with Mrs. George Cadbury, Miss Martineau (Chairman of the Special Schools Sub-Committee) and various representatives of the Bournville Cadbury works and Birmingham Education Committee.

Barrow Cadbury expressed the hope 'that by God's blessing many generations of delicate city children may gain health of body and mind here. Cropwood will always be associated by us with memories of very happy days here'.

The Lord Mayor, in his speech, made reference to the fact that over 1,000 children had passed through Uffculme since its opening in 1911 and all had improved in health and physique, 'able to take their place equipped for the battle of life'.

Formalities over, tea in a large marquee was served for all officials, before a tour of the school and its magnificent grounds. In addition they were entertained by a display of dancing on the lawn by the first intake of girls, clothed in their Liberty dresses purchased personally by Geraldine Cadbury.

Mrs. Cadbury had, in fact, chosen and purchased every article of furniture and clothing for the school, from the camp beds for rest periods to text and story books. Stock inventories at the school show that blazers, berets, jerseys, pinafores, tunics, wellingtons and liberty bodices were bought. Other items listed are brush and comb bags @ 6d., gingham pinafores @ 1s. 6d., knitted facecloths @ 4d., seagrass and even felt rabbits.

Children usually arrived at the school escorted by a teacher on the train to Blackwell from Birmingham's New Street station, then stayed for an average of eight to nine months. The opening entries in the school log book record the names of staff and life at the school began:

Cropwood log book 1922

6 June   *The staff came into residence at Cropwood Residential Open-Air School this afternoon. This consisted of Mrs. E.A. Abbott in charge, Principal; Miss R.M. Shaw, assistant teacher; Miss C.E. Evans, B.A., assistant teacher; Miss L.E. Layer, Chief Nurse; Mrs. Keen, assistant nurse; Miss Roberts, temporary cook; Miss E. Bradley, parlour maid; Miss K. Hexley, housemaid; Miss F. Cresswell, kitchen maid; and two gardeners.*

Rear view of Cropwood, showing the open 'loggia', the bell tower and extensive views over the countryside. (Hunter's Hill School)

7 June   *26 children were admitted this afternoon. They were re-clothed and bathed, and settled down very happily.* [A further 26 were admitted the following day.]

9 June   *Dr. P.H. Thomson examined 26 of the children today and will examine the rest tomorrow. Several cases for special treatment and medical records have been noted.* [It was soon found that Cropwood was so far away from Birmingham that a local practitioner, Dr. M.I. Dick, was permanently engaged from 1923 for all medical services to children and staff. He visited regularly once a week. The Special Schools Medical Officer continued to make decisions on admissions to the school and conducted 'leaving' examinations in consultation with Dr. Dick.]

7 July   *All the children are remarkably improved by their month's stay at Cropwood. Their weights have increased on an average 2-3lbs and their general appearance is much improved.* [Sister Layer reported that 31 children attended her surgery for treatment in the first month, and she noted gains in weight amongst the girls—from 8oz to a remarkable 13lbs in one case. Sister Layer only remained at the school until August 1923.]

10 Oct.   *One girl has tonsillitis and has been put in isolation.*

30 Nov.   *An examination of children was held today, Mrs. Barrow Cadbury, Miss Martineau, Miss Bridie and Dr. Thomson being present. It was decided that 22 children should return home for a further period after the Xmas holidays.*

6 Dec.   The children had a 'breaking up' party in the Shelter. Mrs. Barrow Cadbury, Miss Bridie and local friends being present. The children sang carols, danced and played games and spent a very enjoyable afternoon and evening.

8 Dec.   The weather has been very mild and dry until today and open air work has been possible on most days this term.

Cropwood log book 1923

14 Jan.   Dr. Dick attended this afternoon and finished the examination of the children; 18 of the children need dental treatment and a great number were found to be very thin and under weight and were put on cod liver oil for a period.

27 Jan.   About 80-90 parents visited here today and witnessed 26 of the older girls being enrolled as Girl Guides as No.2 Blackwell Company. Many parents expressed their pleasure at the improvement in their children in the short time during which they have been in residence here.

1 Feb.   One child has been in bed all week with a high temperature and a bronchial cough.

9 Feb.   The weather is sunny and mild and all lessons are being taken out of doors—the children are already showing signs of improvement.

24 Feb.   The parents again attended in large numbers (95) and were informed of the decision of the committee to have a continuous term of 23 weeks with a fortnight's holiday in June and a month at Xmas as per the scheme drawn up by the Principal. The parents expressed their willingness to cooperate in working this scheme. Several of the rules have been broken by the parents and this was pointed out and they promised a strict adherence in future.

Open-air class at Cropwood, with girls wearing the uniform of gymslips, black stockings and button boots, 1920s. (Hunter's Hill School)

19 Mar.   Brighter weather is being experienced and the children are able to have lessons out of doors. Their vitality seems to increase with the sunshine and drier air.

7 June   Dr. Thomson, Dr. Dick, Miss Martineau (Counc.) and Miss Bridie attended a passing out examination. It was decided to keep 24 girls a further term, one other to be kept after a mental test and of the remainder one is to go to Baskerville now, another when a vacancy occurs, 10 are to be transferred to Uffculme and the remainder pass into ordinary schools. A great improvement in deportment and general intelligence was remarked upon and in spite of dull and cold weather all the girls looked brown and very fit. The average gain in weight is 5lbs and the increases in height vary from 1" to 4".

12 July   Ida Desmond was removed to isolation hospital suffering from Scarlet fever—a mild case.

20 Aug.   Sister Layer left the service of the committee today in order to be married. The children and staff presented her with toilet requisites in ebony and united in wishes for her happiness. Sister Helen Daniels was appointed in her place and takes up duty today.

6 Dec.   A very enjoyable party was held at the Shelter. Mrs. Barrow Cadbury and Dr. & Mrs. Dick were present. The children enjoyed the Father Xmas and Xmas Tree very much.

Cropwood log book 1924

19 Jan.   52 children on roll—all the new children seem to have settled very well at school and are showing signs of improved health and more vitality. Many of the most debilitated are having malt and oil.

8 Mar.   The weather still keeps very cold and the children need to exercise a great deal between lessons in order to keep warm. Great improvement is noticed in the physique and general mentality of the children.

20 Mar.   There has been a spell of beautiful sunny weather. All lessons have been taken out of doors and the children have had two picnic teas.

A collection of old photographic slides at the school reveals life at Cropwood school in the 1920s, with many open-air activities and lessons: nature study, gardening, tobogganing and even naked sunbathing on the lawns. In April 1924 it was the turn of delicate boys to benefit from a spell at the school as the next two years were devoted to the male sex. Teachers Miss Shaw and Miss Evans were replaced by Mr. Dix and Mr. Burbridge and the first intake of 22 boys were admitted on 28 April 1924, 21 one of them from Uffculme school. Eventually, 80 boys were enrolled, extra accommodation being provided by Rosemary Cottage which had been donated, furnished and equipped by Barrow and Geraldine Cadbury. They also provided a new wing to the resting-shed to cope with the increased numbers of children.

It was soon found that there were a few more problems with boys at Cropwood, but they settled in fairly well at first, as the log book relates:

Cropwood log book 1924

3 May   76 boys have been admitted altogether and on the whole have settled down very well. The chief difficulty is getting them to sleep at night as the evenings are now so light.

28 June   A spell of fine weather is being experienced and the children are taking full advantage of it, dining outside, bathing in the pool and lying in the sun for their after-dinner rest.

12 July   The boys have formed a company of Boy Scouts with Mr. Dix as Scoutmaster and Mr. Burbridge as assistant Scoutmaster. Mrs. Abbott is acting as Cubmaster for the smaller boys who form a cub pack. Today the scouts and cubs marched to Bromsgrove and joined a parade … the boys looked very smart in their new uniforms, the poorer boys being fitted out by a donation of £10 from Mrs. Cadbury.

13 Aug.   Four boys left school at rest time unobserved and went home. The leader is a boy of very bad character with a bad home. All the boys were brought back by their parents and on promise of good behaviour were re-admitted. The three smaller boys had been homesick no doubt partly due to the fact that their brothers and sisters were still on holiday.

30 Aug.   Four boys were sent home and to ordinary schools as their behaviour was bad. Three of them were amongst the boys who had run away and they resented being brought back to school and showed this by their behaviour to the staff. The rest of the boys are now settling down and are finding great pleasure in their scout and cub work to which Mr. Dix and Mr. Burbridge are devoting a great deal of their time.

13 Sep.   Mr. Dix and Mr. Burbridge are running a weekend camp in the grounds and each patrol is camping out in turn. The boys are cooking their own food and doing all their own work and are enjoying the experience very much.

25 Oct.   It was decided to give the autumn holiday this year at the close of term and accordingly the school closed for a week on Saturday Oct 25th the boys leaving by train with their parents. The headmistress (Mrs. E.A. Abbott) was the recipient of presents from the staff and boys on the occasion of her leaving on Oct 31st 1924. 19 Boys are being passed out to their ordinary schools.
[Mrs. Abbott left the school after two years. She was replaced by Miss Gertrude Walton who stayed at Cropwood for the next nine years, until the opening of Hunter's Hill School for boys in 1933 when she became the new Headmistress.]

Cropwood log book 1925

16 May   The weather has been much warmer for the last day or two and the boys are going for their first swim in the pool today.

23 May   The weather has continued so sunny and warm that the boys have been for a dip in the bathing pool each day. They have worn nothing but trousers most of the week—taking advantage of the sunshine to have sun baths.

8 June   The boys are sunburnt and wear only shorts. They have been gradually exposed to the sunshine—which has been brilliant—and now spend the day in it with little or no discomfort. They go into the swimming pool daily.

11 June   The boys went to the Lickey Hills for a picnic given by Mrs. Cadbury this afternoon.

29 July   Miss Martineau and Dr. Dick came today and Miss Martineau presented a silver cup as trophy for the 'house' that won the championship for sports throughout the term. This term Mr. Dix's 'House'— The Malverns—has won the championship and Jack Owen as Captain of his house received the cup from Miss Martineau. The cup by the way was specially designed by a student at the School of Art. Dr. Dick gave a prize—The Oxford Book of Ballads—to Hubert Parsons for good work throughout the term.

23 Aug.   One new boy who came in on the 18th went home today. He slipped away unseen just after tea, and before the service began at 6pm. He walked to Rednal and there caught the train, arriving home about 9.30pm. He had not appeared at all unsettled and it was a great surprise to all of us when we discovered what he had done.

11 Sep.   One boy, Bernard Kent, went home after tea. He had shown no sign of being unsettled. His mother said it was an attack of nerves.

21 Oct.   Two boys who decamped yesterday were brought back by their parents today, but they are still very homesick.

THE 1920s: CURRICULUM FOR LIFE

14 Nov.   *The boys seem very happy now. In the evenings they are doing various forms of handwork, country dancing, and are rehearsing for the Christmas play 'Tom and the Water Babies'.*

5 Dec.   *We have had a fortnight's very cold weather with a hard frost. The boys have enjoyed tobogganing very much—but the cold has been too intense to allow of much written work.*

10 Dec.   *The boys had a party, and received presents and chocolates from 'The Old Woman's Shoe'. The staff dressed up as 'The Old Woman and her Children' and the boys were highly entertained.*

Some first-hand accounts of life at Cropwood during its opening years are recorded below:

Mrs. Gladys M. Williams (née **Williams**), 83, Cropwood 1922, Birmingham

I was about 11 years old when I was sent there for six months in 1922. I was a 'delicate child'. I was the youngest of a family of six.

Cropwood was a lovely place, green lawns, trees, flowers, a pool in which we could paddle or swim. About two hours, or perhaps more, we spent in a long open building, on canvas type stretcher beds each afternoon. We could sleep or just rest. Every Sunday, we put on our dresses and we wore straw hats and walked, two by two, to church. These sun dresses had a small flower pattern. In the week they were mostly striped material (cotton), different colours. They were all provided for us.

We were allowed to write home if we wished. I did, of course, get homesick, and used to think of walking back home. The Matron explained that my eldest sister (who was crippled from birth) was quite poorly at the time and that my mother was very worried about her. So, as I loved my mother, I decided I must settle down—after all, it was only for a few months. This is what I did; who knows, perhaps those few months are the reason why I am still around at 83 years!

Off to church in Blackwell, wearing summer uniform and straw hats, 1920s. (Hunter's Hill School)

Mrs. Doris M. Taylor (née **Edge**), 82, Cropwood 1922, Bromsgrove, Worcestershire

I still have the letter which my mother received from the Chief Education Officer, telling her the arrangements for me to go to Cropwood on 8 Jan 1923, together with a number of other children. We had to meet the two teachers on No.6 platform at New Street Station, with a ticket to Blackwell Station, at 1pm. The letter stated that parents would not accompany children to the school but could visit them on the last Saturday of every month.

I went to Cropwood for three months, after being transferred from Uffculme School. My father died when I was a baby so my mother had to go out to work—we lived in Balsall Heath. She did not have to pay for me as she was a widow—other families paid an amount up to 4s.6d.

I travelled to a lovely place in the country—to Blackwell. The weather was very cold and it seemed a good way from Birmingham. We slept in a long dormitory—about eight girls. All the sliding shutters were wide open for fresh air. It was winter time and flurries of snow came through the open shutters. I remember hearing the trains very clearly.

When I first went to Cropwood I came out with boils on my chest. The nurse was a big lady and she put strapping all over my chest and I was extremely sorry for myself. Every morning she gave me a teaspoonful of yeast, followed by a sweet. I eventually recovered and was told it was a change of water—different from Birmingham!

Each Saturday we were given 2d to spend at the village post office. On Sundays we wore a thick woollen jumper and a large felt hat and would walk down the lanes to chapel. It certainly was a very different life for me. On returning from chapel, a cold lunch would be waiting. Hot cocoa at night and in bed for 7 o'clock. Parents would visit once a month, but there was always a crying session when they went.

When I returned home I had rosy cheeks and didn't recognise myself in the mirror.

In *The Annual Report of the Chief Medical Officer of the Board of Education 1923* several pages were devoted to the organisation and conduct of an open-air school for the benefit of the many local authorities who had still failed to make any special provision for delicate children. The report covered the selection of children, buildings and equipment, staff and education, medical supervision, mid-day rest, clothing and finance:

Selection of children: Experience has shown that the following classes of children are likely specially to benefit from attendance at an open-air school:

Children suffering from malnutrition, rickets, anaemia, blepharitis and other chronic infectious eye diseases associated with malnutrition; tuberculous glands in the neck; children convalescent after debilitating diseases such as pneumonia, measles, whooping cough; certain types of crippled children; nervous and highly-strung children.

Site: The site should be of a size sufficient for a playing field and school garden; generally speaking 2 acres must be considered minimum for a school accommodating 100-120 children.

Buildings and Equipment: The classrooms should preferably be so disposed that three sides of the room can be thrown completely open. A spray and shower bath installation should be looked upon as an important part of the equipment of an open-air school. A small room should be provided which can be warmed preferably by an open fire, to serve as a medical examination treatment room and as a rest room for any individual child with symptoms of slight temporary illness.

Furniture: The school furniture should include light individual chairs capable of being moved out of doors as required.

Staff: The Teachers should be chosen for their personal fitness and educational and other experience to serve in a school of this kind. They must have the requisite sympathy and exceptional ability to deal firmly with children (often spoilt at home and difficult to manage owing to irregular attendance, or long absence from school on account of illness). It must be remembered that the long hours and the teaching under open-air conditions constitute a considerable strain.

Education: The health of the child rather than its education must necessarily be the preoccupation of the open-air school. The aim of the curriculum should be primarily to give *life* and *interest* to the child, avoiding at the same time over-stimulation, consideration being given always to the particular needs of each individual child. The teacher may well give special attention to the training of the child in a hygienic way of life.

Lessons: One of the main purposes of open-air education is to encourage observation, to record the results, and thereby to create new channels for expression work whether in written or spoken language.

A feature has been made in several schools of the teaching of *History* by dramatisation. *Arithmetic* can be studied in a thoroughly practical manner, such subjects as the measurement of garden plots, circumference and height of trees, weighing of vegetables, etc., being easily available. In many schools the site and surrounding country afford exceptional opportunities for *Nature Study*. The keeping of pets will also afford subjects for instruction, not only in the study of their habits, but also in kindness to animals and their feeding and general care.

Many schools have made a feature of *Practical Geography,* large contour maps of England, Australia, etc., being cut out on the ground, whilst at one school a model river with source in the hills, waterfall, lake, docks, harbour etc. has been devised.

A special feature should be made of *Gardening*. The school should not be content with a mere allotment garden, but an endeavour should be made gradually to construct, where this does not already exist, a proper English garden with hedges, lawn, shrubs, flower and vegetable and fruit garden. The kitchen garden should provide most of the vegetables required for the school. Individual plots will be necessary, especially for younger children.

Woodwork aims to train children in the use of simple tools. The work should meet so far as possible the requirements of the school e.g. shelves in the class rooms, boot/shoe boxes, seed boxes, duck boards, garden frames, garden fencing.

Care must be taken that participation in *Domestic Work* does not prejudice the open-air life of the child. For this reason cookery and laundry work are not suitable as subjects for regular instruction, though the children may well help in such work as the preparation of vegetables, cleaning, washing up such articles as knives, forks and spoons.

Physical exercises will take on a modified form. Dancing, especially country dancing, forms a prominent feature and provides for these children a particularly healthful and appropriate form of recreation. Singing also, taken informally as well as formally, comes naturally as part of the life of a child at an open-air school.

Medical Supervision: The School Medical Officer should visit the school weekly and the school dentist from time to time. Children should be weighed accurately once a fortnight on a reliable steel yard weighing machine.

Three meals a day, breakfast, dinner and tea, should be provided. Many delicate children are not ready for a meal immediately on rising but make a hearty breakfast on arrival at the open-air school. The dietary should be drawn up and carefully supervised by the School Medical Officer. He should bear in mind that the child's diet is often lacking in protein and fat and in vitamin content, and make a special feature of the provision of milk especially for particular children. He should see, too, that free use is made of vegetables and fruit.

Midday Rest: This is an important part of the cure of the malnourished, delicate child, as there is no doubt that late hours and the necessary disturbed sleep of children living in overcrowded dwellings, is a potential cause of debility. The midday rest should be arranged after dinner for a period of one to two hours, and should always be taken in the open unless weather conditions make this impossible, when the rest-shed should be used. A flat canvas stretcher or trestle bed is recommended; it is comparatively inexpensive and is much more satisfactory than a deck chair.

Each year school medical officers made a report to the Board of Education of all 'exceptional' (delicate) children in their areas. The total national number of children returned under this heading in 1923 was 75,285 and there were only places in the 77 open-air schools (50 Day, 27 Residential) for 6,450 children. The annual cost for each child in a day open-air school was estimated to be £30, compared with £12 in an ordinary elementary school. The increased cost reflected the smaller classes, three meals a day, rest, and the provision of a shower.

Dr. Auden was in no doubt about the benefit children received at Uffculme. During the seven years 1919-1925 he found that 74 per cent of children were discharged as fit to attend ordinary schools. Examining them nine to twelve months later he found no less than 89 per cent were regarded as generally 'satisfactory in health'. The children had gained in health and physique, probably attending school regularly for the first time in their lives. It was hoped they would be able to earn a living in the future and be useful members in the community. As Dr. Auden had been involved in Uffculme School since its inception he could justifiably be proud of its success.

Miss Hibbert, Uffculme's Headmistress, continued to record life during this period:

Uffculme log book 1923

26 April *School closed for the day. General school holiday to celebrate the Duke of York's wedding day.* [The Duke of York became George VI in 1936.]

13 July *The weather has been so abnormally hot this week that gardening had to be abandoned and quiet lessons taken in the shade instead.*

Uffculme log book 1924

28 Mar. *Mr Carr finished duties here, having been transferred to Colmore Road school.* [Mr. Carr had been caretaker since its opening in 1911.]

10 April *The passing out examination took place this afternoon when 21 boys were passed for Cropwood and 36 other children were discharged.*

THE 1920s: CURRICULUM FOR LIFE

Uffculme log book 1925

30 Jan.   *Many children have colds and all 'throats' have been sent home this week because one case of diphtheria was reported on Monday.*

14 May   *School closed at 5pm to allow staff to attend a lecture by Prof. Leonard Hill on 'Sunshine and Open Air'.*

Uffculme's Guide Company, autumn 1929. (Uffculme School)

One ex-pupil of this era recalls her happy memories of Uffculme:

Mrs. Evelyn Cookson (née **Eustace**), 77, Uffculme 1925-8, Birmingham

I was from a large family in a two-bedroomed back to back house in Small Heath. For many years I had my arm in a frame—it was caused by my falling from a baby-walker on wheels at the age of fifteen months. It probably ended up as a TB elbow and I was under the Orthopaedic Hospital for years.

When I was at Uffculme at the age of eight to eleven, I slept there Mondays to Thursdays and loved it. With our pocket money on Monday evenings we were marched from school down to Moseley Village to spend it. Other evenings we were taken on nature walks by Miss Hibbert, the Headmistress, around the grounds. Miss Hibbert knew all the birds and flowers; we used to press flowers and leaves at school and write about them.

Miss Hibbert was a very gentle, kind person although quite strict. She had time for everyone and used to lead the Girl Guides which I loved and we did tracking in the grounds.

I remember doing basketwork and raffia mats in class. Outside the classroom each morning we did exercises. I loved being at the school and felt very privileged to sleep there night times. It was like being in the country to us and we had some happy times. I didn't want to leave the school at the age of eleven but I suppose I must have been a lot better then and also as we had moved to Acocks Green I was considered to be living in the country.

Enjoying the sunshine and fresh air at Uffculme Open-Air School. (Uffculme School)

1926-9

By 1927 it was generally agreed that Day Open-Air Schools were almost a necessity in any educational system in a large urban industrial area. *The 1927 Annual Report of the Chief Medical Officer of the Board of Education* produced more instructions on the planning of such schools, with special reference to efficiency and cost, including such details as:

> **General Planning**: Three types of provision in the main are required—for teaching, dining, and resting ... There must be free access of air all round and protection afforded from wind and driving rain ... The construction of the classroom falls under two main types according to whether provision is made for windows and glazed doors, or these are dispensed with and any necessary protection is provided by a low wall all round with the use of canvas or other material above and with the roof over-hanging.
>
> **Heating**: The mode of heating adopted at an Open-Air School has a close bearing on the considerations of efficiency and cost. There are Open-Air Schools in the country in which no provision is made for heating the classrooms or dining-room ... Generally speaking, experience and records show that in winter the temperature of an Open-Air classroom, provided with any one of the usual methods of heating, is not more than six to eight degrees above that of the outside temperature. Thus, should it be freezing outside, the temperature of the classroom would be as a rule between 30° and 40°F. During the ordinary winter days when the temperature is round about 40°F, the temperature of the classroom will be from 45° to 50°F ... The main purpose of providing heat in an Open-Air classroom is not to secure warmth when the classroom is in use, but to ensure a more congenial and dryer atmosphere ... Moreover, in unpleasant weather, the evidence of some source of warmth has a good psychological effect.

School Medical Officers had more idea which specific medical conditions responded best to open-air schools, as stated in the *1928 Annual Report of the Chief Medical Officer of the Board of Education*:

> The clinical conditions which are most frequently the cause of admission to an open-air school (day or residential) are pre-tubercular, including tuberculous contacts, healed tuberculosis of the lungs, abdomen or bones, anaemia and debility due to infectious disease, and post-operative conditions. Next in order of frequency come children suffering from non-specific disease of the lungs, e.g., asthma or bronchitis, nervous or mental instability, digestive disturbances (acidosis, cyclic vomiting, etc.); suspected rheumatism and glandular enlargements, definite rheumatism, heart disease or chorea; chronic eye diseases such as blepharitis, conjunctivitis, keretitis; non-infectious and chronic skin diseases; minor deformities and after-treatment necessary for children who have been in special orthopaedic hospital schools.

Cropwood 1926–9

Cropwood was another success story. Between 1922 and 1927, 354 children (77 per cent) had been discharged from Cropwood as fit enough to return to ordinary schools, their average length of stay being eight to nine months (much shorter than the average length of stay at Uffculme day school).

It was noticed in the summer holidays that children lost weight—boys more than girls. This was attributed to the loss of regular meals, rest, exercise and an irregular life led in the holidays.

In April 1926 the girls were in residence, as noted in the log books:

Cropwood log book 1926

12 April *The school re-opened. All the staff are present including two new teachers—Miss Perkins and Miss Pratt. 27 girls were admitted this pm and seem to be settling very happily.*

4 May *Dr. Smellie, Dr. Dick, Miss Ross and Miss Fernihough attended Cropwood yesterday with a view to sorting out new girls specially in need of remedial exercises. 26 girls were found with slight curvature and it was arranged that Miss Avery should come to Cropwood every Wednesday and Friday mornings to give remedial exercises to these girls.*

2 June *The registers were not marked as the children went for a picnic (given by Mrs. Cadbury) to the Lickeys.*

3 July *The Midland Section of the Medical Council paid a visit to Cropwood today. They went round the grounds—saw the children at 'rest' and in the bathing pool and went over to the Camp School to tea.*

14 July *We are having very hot weather and the children are making great use of the Bathing Pool. They are going in twice a day and many of the big girls can nearly swim—six can swim.*

18 Aug. *The three children who went off yesterday were sent back by their parents today. They have settled down again quite happily. One girl said she missed the houses, and people and traffic and noise at Cropwood!*

6 Sep. *The Rosemary girls who have been sleeping in the Resting Shed since June 5th are going back tonight to their winter quarters at Rosemary Cottage. This is the first time we have had children sleeping in the Resting Shed at night and it appears to have been a success. The nights are now darker early and it means someone has to sit in the Shed in the dark.*

Rest time at Cropwood, 1920s. (Hunters Hill School)

28 Sep.   Miss Perkins took Class I for a Nature Study expedition to Cofton Woods. They went to study 'mosses'.

1 Oct.   The children had a specially nice tea with home-made sausage rolls and cakes provided by Mrs. Cadbury. In the evening they had charades and the lantern [slide projector] was used for the first time. The children were delighted with it.

6 Dec.   Miss Martineau, Mrs. Cadbury, Miss Ross and Mr. Newsome came to see the concert in the Shelter. The villagers also were invited.

10 Dec.   The children went home today on the 1.10 train. They all looked well and were well.

Cropwood log book 1927

24 Sep.   There have been 7 children with bad throats and high temperatures within the last three weeks. The weather has been extraordinarily wet during this time.

Cropwood log book 1928

19 Mar.   73 children and 5 members of the staff went to Malvern for the day today on the train. The children climbed the Beacon and later the North Hill. (All girls left Cropwood at the end of the month, together with two women teachers.)

14 April   Miss Arnot (the new housekeeper), Mr. Jones and Mr. Goulden came today, ready to begin duty on the arrival of the boys.

26 July   Miss Martineau, Mrs. Cadbury, Mr. Clendon, Miss Barling, Miss Ross came out today to the 'presentation of the cup'. The boys sang and gave a physical exercises demonstration.

Cropwood log book 1929

1 Feb.   Four boys were isolated with mumps today.

13 Feb.   The cold is so intense today that it is almost impossible to continue in school i.e. in the classrooms with open screens. The school work was continued as usual until 11am when the boys went for a walk in charge of Mr. Jones and Mr. Goulden.

22 June   Visiting day. The boys played cricket with a 'fathers' team this afternoon.

3 Oct.   59 boys went off for the day to the Lickeys in the morning and visited the quarries there in connection with the survey work. In the afternoon they went to the Frankley Waterworks to see the Birmingham Water Supply.

   In July 1929 HM Inspector Mr. C.E. Jackson reported on Cropwood school:

   The situation of the school is ideal, not only from the health point of view but also as affording exceptional advantages in the matter of curriculum. The Headmistress has shown herself alive to the possibilities, and with the help of her keen and vigorous assistants she has been at some pains to provide a course of instruction which will make the fullest use of the excellent local material. A recent development in this direction bases most of the work upon a comprehensive study of the immediate vicinity, whereby the teaching of such subjects as History, Geography, Nature Study and Arithmetic acquires a new interest and significance. This work is already producing good results, and its progress should be worth watching.

Careful records are kept of the boys' work from the time when they enter, and these should prove of value when they return to their ordinary schools. This is but one instance of the systematic and business-like way in which the School is directed.

Some ex-pupils of Cropwood have remarkably vivid memories of their schooldays:

Mrs. Marguerite Jones (née **Cooper**), 79, Cropwood 1926, Birmingham

I was a poorly girl with ear aches and was anaemic. My parents were poor, father out of work for 14 years through illness from the First World War. There were eight of us children and my fifth birthday was spent in the Children's Hospital having my tonsils out. When I was nine-and-a-half I was in Moseley Hall Convalescent Home for a month and had to stay in bed. After going to a council school where I fainted nearly every morning my mother took me to see the almoner at the General Hospital and she arranged for me to go to Cropwood Open-Air School. My sister Daisy was already there as she had been in the tuberculosis hospital for three months with my brother David.

Cropwood was a beautiful large house with lovely gardens and scenery. Daisy took me to a dormitory in the extension where it was open to fresh air but there was some underfloor heating. She chose our beds together. Some big girls came in and tried to take them; we had a fight and won. Then all the new girls had to have a shower. These were six bowls in a row with a shower over each, the nurse regulated the water temperature, I thought it was lovely. We had nice white towels.

We were sent into the dining room by a warm fire where we had our tea—bread and butter, two slices and a cup of hot milk. Later we had supper at 7 o'clock, two slices of bread and dripping and a cup of lovely hot cocoa made with milk, then off to bed, lights out at 7.30. One teacher named Miss Pratt kissed us all and tucked us up. I thought she was lovely—my mother didn't do it!

We were each given a locker and part of a boot cupboard for wellington boots, shoes, sandals, and slippers (which we had to wear indoors). We had racks to hang our blazers, overcoats, hats, macs and sou'westers. We all had a number (mine was 58). On the first afternoon we were taken to be fitted with school clothing. I was given a woolly vest, a fleecy lined liberty bodice with four suspenders, black stockings, fleecy lined knickers, a flannelette underskirt and a green dress which was very rough. I complained about that and was told we were soon to get brown uniforms. (We did and it was much better.) The shoes they gave me were worn down at the back and Daisy told me to sneak upstairs to get some new ones so this I did. We had hooks on the walls of the locker room with towel, flannel, soap, tooth mug, toothbrush; I had some Gibbs toothpaste which was solid in a little flat round tin.

The first morning we had to attend assembly, taken by Headmistress Miss Walton. We had prayers and hymns every morning.

We had to strip and make our beds, after breakfast of porridge and bread and butter and milk. We had jobs to do allocated by Miss Walton: shake the bedroom mats, dry mop the floor etc.

One girl brought a little tin wind up gramophone with one record 'I'm an airman come from Norway, Shooting peas up a nanny goat's doorway'. She played it every night in the dorm—we thought it was great! Daisy used to sleep in her clothes with her nightie on top so that she could run to the main building to be first in the queue for a wash! We had to strip to the waist and were not allowed to wear anything other than the nightie in bed. Three times a week we had a shower but when it was time for it I used to climb to the top of a fir tree! I would stay up for hours.

We went scrumping in the gardens for some nice big gooseberries and put them in our beds, together with some slices of bread and dripping I pinched from the kitchen. We ate them after lights out, but one night Miss Walton came in the room, pulled the bed clothes off poor Daisy, smacked her bottom, and revealed our

Gardening lesson at Cropwood, 1920s. (Hunter's Hill School)

nosh up! She parted us, I had to go in the main building and sleep in a bed next to her room.

We didn't learn much with only three classes; Miss Walton took Class 1, Miss Pratt Class 2; Class 3 was the lowest for the youngest, Miss Perkins. The teachers had to give us individual work to suit our age.

We had lessons until 12, then had dinner and pudding, meat and veg and roly poly, spotted dick or apple tart or treacle pudding and custard. We always had a mug of milk. On Sundays we had a special treat, a cup of milky tea and a piece of cake. After dinner we went to the rest-shed where we had to get a stretcher to rest for 1½ hours. The teacher had a deck chair and a blanket and a book to read. She told us to all lie on our right sides and go to sleep.

On Wednesday and Saturday we had threepence each tuck money. Because I was good at reckoning up money I was given the key to the tuck cupboard. I had to put a trellis table on the veranda and place the sweets on it to sell. I locked myself in the tuck cupboard and ate some before I sold them. I was always mischievous.

We used to have to go for a long walk twice a week. They would get us all lined up and I would get at the front while we were being counted, I then got to the back …they had to keep counting as there was always one too many! I didn't like the long distance they made us walk so I delayed them as long as I could.

On Saturday morning we wrote to our parents and darned our stockings. I begged my mother to visit me but she didn't have the train fare. My aunt and my sister came on a motor bike with her boy friend on visiting day, he worked at Cadburys and brought chocolate biscuits. Once after my sister's visit I ate a whole tin of chocolate biscuits. I was very sick.

On my first day gardening I was paired up with a girl who bragged about her marvellous home with a Rolls Royce and a chauffeur, then she said 'I can't bear worms'. As it had been raining I dug up a pile and put them down her back! She became hysterical and had to go to Nurse. I had no tuck money as punishment.

Miss Pratt was our music teacher and she made us practise. In the summer we danced bare foot on the lawn, country dancing in fours and maypole dancing, then danced the other way to unravel the ribbons from the pole.

We were given sandals and short socks in the summer but encouraged to walk about bare foot. We also had some gingham dresses, two each to wear with short white socks as well.

One day the Headmistress was crying and Miss Pratt made up a song as her beloved little Austin 7 had been stolen. 'Miss Walton's lost her Austin, Oh! deary me, Miss Walton's lost her Austin 7, Oh! deary me, I shut the door I'm sure I locked it, Someone's put it in their pocket, Are you sure you haven't got it?

Oh! deary me'... Some days later it was found and she told Daisy and I that if we would be good, she would take us for a ride. I was for two days and she took us out 15 miles an hour for an hour.

We had holidays when we went home Easter, August and Christmas. Not so good, I had to look after my older sisters and three boys and our house was cold—we only got warm cuddling up in bed. Once a year in the summer Miss Walton took us to the tower at the top of the house where we could see the Malverns, the Clent and Clee Hills in the distance.

We had to clean our shoes every morning and we were inspected to make sure we had cleaned the backs and had got our uniforms on properly. Every morning some of us had to queue for medication from Nurse Keen, I had cod liver oil and malt at first, then just cod liver oil. I used to spit it out while rinsing the glass we had to give back to her. Periodically a doctor would visit us, he used to say 'she is not improving'.

After Daisy left Cropwood at the age of 14 I was moved to another bedroom where my room mates became my gang. There was Margaret Tyler, my best friend, Edith Kyte, Edith Shawson and Mary Preece, we were firm friends always together. We each had a mat by our beds and we put them in the middle of the floor and had a feast at midnight, with bread and dripping and some tuck we'd saved.

Margaret told me I would be going to Uffculme so I would have to behave as the Headmistress was strict. She left before me to go to Uffculme but we visited each other during holidays. I gave her my precious Golliwog Man Friday, she said she would never part with it. When I went to Uffculme she was there when I arrived at my new school.

Mr. Bill Tookey, Cropwood 1928-9, Birmingham

I attended Cropwood Open-Air School from April 1928 until March 1929. The outstanding memory for me was the gift of a chocolate bar from Cadbury's to all boys at Cropwood.

One Saturday, pupils put on a display for parents. Because I was good looking, I clicked for Maid Marian's part. I had to fight off the attentions of the sheriff using a quarterstaff. When the practice was over, it was found I had actually whacked him one.

When I started at Cropwood I was placed in the house, sleeping four of us in a small room. I was later quartered in an annexe where a number of us had a bed each night, going back to Cropwood each day. The gardening plots were there and cultivated by us at least once a week. We received marks for the condition of the crops.

Boys from Cropwood gardening in front of Rosemary Cottage. (W. Tookey)

Mr. John Bonner, Cropwood 1928-9, Birmingham

The reason for my stay at Cropwood was a serious illness. I was in hospital for ten days and it was considered that a spell at an open-air school would aid my convalescence. Cropwood was a wonderful place with its pine forest and shrubberies. The Headmistress was Miss Walton, a lady of refinement and infinite kindness.

In front of the dormitory extension where I had a bed and locker were Class-rooms 1 & 2. Each had a brick back wall, the other three sides were glass folding doors which could be adjusted according to weather conditions. Each catered for about twenty four pupils.

Behind the house was the sleep garden, which had a well manicured lawn surrounded by shrubbery. At the far end was the sleep-time shed built like the class-rooms with a back wall and folding doors on the other three sides. It contained stretcher beds on which we took our after-lunch naps.

My parents visited regularly, bringing a bag of sweets, toys, magazines and threepence a week to spend at the tuck counter. My mother also brought a cake to cut, which I shared with my friends, Billy Jones and Leslie Chapman, after lights out in the dormitory. Billy and I sat at the same desk during lessons and he was my special friend.

Life in the dorm was conducted at a fast and furious pace as the linoleum covered floor was highly polished. Everyone preferred socks to slippers in order to skate or slide up and down the long space at the foot of the beds. One night a week this was not possible as the cleaner would have put polish on the flooring but not polished it off, probably relying on us to do the job for her.

Schooling was good and in some respects superior to council schools. We learned to do graph work, keeping accurate graphs of temperature, rainfall and hours of sunshine besides various other graphs. We also learned map making, working from local ordnance survey maps. We also did field work, such as surveying Frankley Water Works and Blackwell village. We frequently went on afternoon rambles, a favourite of mine was to the railway line to see the enormous 'Big Bertha', hauling trains up the Lickey incline: an inspiring sight.

For competitive purposes the inmates were divided into three houses. Malvern (a purple button badge), Clee (a yellow button), and the one which I was assigned to, Clent (a green badge). A shield was competed for every month, decided by totting up points given for sports, schooling and such things as tidiness in lockers and bed making.

Food was good, much better than most of the kids were accustomed to. I remember breakfasts largely consisted of porridge, or in special cases junket, I often wished that I could have junket but I never did. Some boys' parents brought eggs for their sons. It was permissible to write the boy's name on the eggs, hand them in

Some of Cropwood's boys, 1928. (Hunter's Hill School)

to the cookhouse to be boiled daily and handed out to the lucky boy at breakfast. A slice of bread and butter with a boiled egg was more acceptable than jam. I prevailed upon my mother to bring me eggs which she dutifully did on next visiting day. When my parents left for home, I took my paper bag containing six beautiful brown eggs and hurried off to hand them in to the cookhouse. On the way I stumbled and dropped them. Not only was my heart broken by the loss, but I was penalised five points for making a mess on the path.

Another valuable activity during school hours was handicrafts. I made for my mother a leather purse from a single piece. I was taught to punch holes all round it, fold the bottom part up to form the money holder, this was then stitched with a leather lace. The flap had a raised circle tooled on it and inside that a classic M.B. My mother's initials.

I also made her a jotter from two wooden covers hinged together by brass hinges. The wood was stained dark brown, on the front cover was tacked an oblong sheet of pewter, again it had been tooled with the leatherwork press-tool into side by side leaf design with a sapphire inlaid between them.

So the boys' period of tenure came to a close and I was obliged to say a sad farewell to Cropwood.

Uffculme 1926-9

In July 1926 HM Inspector's report on Uffculme school commended highly the efforts of Miss Hibbert and her staff:

> At present there are 135 in attendance, so that full use is being made of the many advantages which the site affords ... and the average length of stay is about 14 months.
>
> On the educational side the school is doing good work, which is all the more creditable considering the conditions of staffing. For the four classes there are only three permanent assistants, the fourth class being taught by the Headmistress on two days of the week and by a part-time teacher on other days. The school remains open during the summer months, and each member of the staff is released in turn for a month's vacation, her place being taken by a supply teacher. When the school was visited, therefore, the Headmistress had only two regular full-time teachers to assist her. Apart from other important duties the Headmistress takes a substantial share in the instruction of the rest of the school.
>
> The children are under wise control, orderly, industrious and keenly interested in all they do. The provision of a suitable curriculum has received very careful attention; this is by no means an easy matter considering the past history of the children, the frequent admissions and the length of stay. In the circumstances the attempts to cultivate a taste for reading and to develop a liberal course of handwork are commendable, and the only point which calls for consideration is the possibility of framing schemes in such subjects as Geography, Nature Study, etc., so as to exploit still further the special advantages of the site and also to suit an organisation which is essentially terminal.

Some of the activities of the school are recorded in the school photograph album; rug making, apple picking, cricket, rounders, sliding on the pond and the Summer Holiday School—clay modelling, picking and shelling beans for lunch, making soft toys. Yearly pageants were also performed, using history in dramatic form. These photographs, probably taken by Miss Hibbert, give a remarkable insight into life at the school, together with entries in the school log book:

Uffculme log book 1926

15 Jan.   *It has snowed continuously for the last two days but there is only a slight falling off in attendance.*

Physical exercises in the open air were an important part of school life, 1928. (Uffculme School)

12 Mar.   Percentage 94.9. We have had 131 children attending school this week. This is the highest number on record for Uffculme.

22 April   A Parents Day was held. Handwork and Dancing were exhibited. About 230 visitors present.

Uffculme log book 1927

4 Feb.   The attendance is very good, and is practically unaffected by the influenza epidemic in the city.

11 Feb.   This has been the coldest day this winter—10° of frost until playtime.

14 Feb.   Miss Hurley commenced duties here today as Physical Training Teacher. She will attend for two mornings per week, giving remedial treatment to deformities and cases of pulmonary fibrosis. She will also take all the classes for drill, leaving games and folk-dancing to the class teacher.

25 Feb.   Percentage 87.5. The attendance has dropped this week owing to an epidemic of bad colds. There is an influenza epidemic in the City, but so far we have only 4 cases from Uffculme.

11 Nov.   The usual timetable was suspended today from 11am to 11.30am for Armistice Day Observance—consisting of 'The Silence', a hymn, prayer, short talk by Mr. Stobart and National Anthem.

Uffculme log book 1928

28 Jan.   Mr. A. Riley was appointed Caretaker in place of Mr. Pearce and commenced duties today.

Uffculme log book 1929

1 Feb.   Mr. E.J. Anderson commenced duties here this morning. (Edward James Anderson remained at the school until 1964, eventually becoming Headmaster.)

Class IV in summer uniform, 1927/8. (Uffculme School)

15 Feb. *Temperature has only been 22° all day. It has been bitterly cold all week and only 83 children came today. It has been impossible to keep to Time Table lessons this week.*

4 Mar. *News was received that Nurse Tippetts died today after one week's illness.*

4 April *School re-opened today—Nurse Bendall commenced duties—newly appointed school nurse.*

17 July *A Pageant of Elizabethan History was held in the school grounds this afternoon, when the children's parents were invited to be present.*

Two ex-pupils of Uffculme relate their schooldays in the 1920s:

Mrs. Marguerite Jones (née **Cooper**), 79, Uffculme 1926-9, Birmingham

My mother's friends said I would not survive beyond the age of eight but I survived because of these two lovely schools. [She also attended Cropwood.]

I had to go to school six miles from Small Heath to Kings Heath. We were given tokens for the bus and tram: tuppence ha'penny each way. I walked it most of the time, and asked the tram conductor to change my tokens for money to buy sweets. I was always late for school after walking. Miss Hibbert, the Headmistress, made me miss my breakfast and stand by her desk. There was usually a nice apple on it and I was so hungry. Miss Hibbert was a real dragon. She made children behave, and also eat up their food, so important for their health. The food was good except on Friday—we had tripe for dinner (I used to give a boy ½d to eat my tripe). We had cheese at tea time. I used to wrap it in my hanky and put it in the waste bin.

I was in top class, the teacher was Mr. Anderson. I was madly in love with him and on my best behaviour, except I used to sneak in the classroom when there was no one about and look at a book of answers to all the sums.

The 'Princely Pleasures of Kenilworth' Pageant, July 1929. Queen Elizabeth (G.Watterson) knights Sir Walter Raleigh (R. Ledbury). (Uffculme School)

We had one-and-a-half hours sleep beneath the apple trees, if one fell off we had to put it on Miss Hibbert's desk. We had classical music from a gramophone to march into the dining room every morning and we said Grace before our meals. I loved the music. When the weather was cold we would have a game of football, I loved that. We danced country and maypole dancing. We had a cloak room where there were pairs of clogs to wear while our shoes dried. They were nice and warm.

There were cherry apple trees past the football field, I was the only one nicking apples. There were cooking apples as well, some in stingers [nettles]; I used to put my wellington boots on to nick them. One night I had six apples down my neck and I bumped into the nurse who saw me putting them in my bag and said she would tell the Headmistress.

I think I was naughty because nobody loved me, only my sisters Daisy and Iris. I left Uffculme at the age of 14 in 1929.

Mrs. Jean Claydon (née **Craythorne**), Uffculme 1928-33, Birmingham

I started at seven years of age, being a delicate child, not exactly ill but in need of building up, according to the school doctor. The Headmistress was Miss Hibbert, and my teacher Miss Gough.

I can't remember being unhappy but remember vividly my mother coming to see Miss Hibbert to say I didn't like the porridge served for breakfast—however it didn't make any difference! I can remember swallowing it down with the mug of hot milk. On the whole I liked the meals—the cheese pie was very good. We were served most peculiar teas: a tomato with two pieces of dripping, one orange or apple, bread and butter (or margarine?). My mother paid 6d a week but most children from the Inner City didn't pay anything.

We were issued with navy blue jumpers to wear over our clothes and a small rug to place over our knees in the winter, as all the screens were open in the classrooms and only closed when raining or snowing. I well remember being sent to the kitchen for hot water to thaw the ink that had frozen in the ink wells overnight. If it was particularly cold we would all go for a run to keep warm.

Summer holidays were limited to two weeks at home. The other four weeks we had to attend school and had lots of games outings to Cannon Hill Park, walking there, of course. My favourite pastime was country dancing (the boys had Morris dancing). I can remember performing country dancing at the Town Hall and I know we came second out of all the schools in Birmingham.

Gardening was also encouraged and I still love my garden, due to the excellent tuition. I seemed to learn the 3Rs working from text books as there were several age groups in each class. Mr. Anderson frightened me to death, a dour Scotsman who shouted a lot. I sat the Entrance Exam for Grammar School and passed for Yardley Grammar School for Girls but didn't want to go—it wasn't deemed so important then.

Pageants were held every year and we made all the costumes in sewing class; one year I sang 'Cherry Ripe' dressed as a cherry seller. Then one year we did the History of Birmingham and I was very grand being the 'Lady-de-Bermingham'—parents were invited and I do remember Mrs. Barrow Cadbury attending.

Christmas time was great and we had a lovely tree, chocolate from Cadbury's and from Kunzles, a well-known firm who also made chocolate.

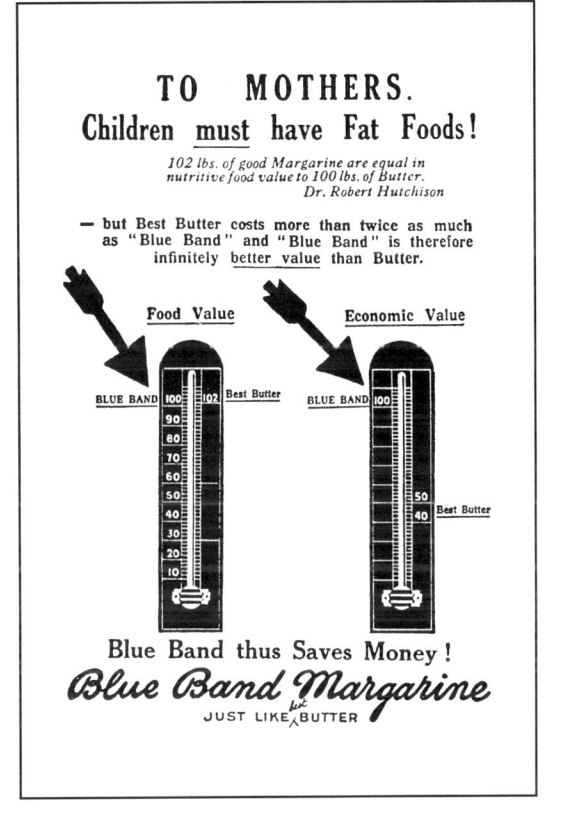

I left Uffculme at the age of 13 years and finished my education at Tindal Street Girls School, Balsall Heath. I was put into the A class so you see our education had been very good at Uffculme.

I look upon those years with great affection and it certainly turned a delicate puny child, as I was then, into a very hearty one. I think Uffculme made me into a healthy adult and will always be grateful.

In 1927 an interesting experiment took place at Uffculme, to test the properties of milk which had been subjected to ultra-violet irradiation. For several months Midland Counties Dairy Ltd. supplied free of charge to Uffculme many gallons of irradiated milk. A similar quantity of untreated milk was also purchased by the school. Children were split into two groups; one group having the special irradiated milk which was reputed to have special 'nutritive and therapeutic properties'. At the end of the test period, however, there was little difference in the physical conditions of the children and the doctor felt unable to recommend the special irradiated milk for children.

Artificial light treatment was also tried in Birmingham School Clinics in 1928 as ultra-violet light was thought to be especially beneficial to debilitated children. Eighty-two cases of anaemia and debility were treated. Dr. Auden reported that debilitated children suffered from lack of energy, fainting, poor appetite, restless sleep and bed wetting, stating: 'Experience shows that all these disabilities tend to improve, some considerably, with radiation. Ultra-violet radiation gives the best result when the diet is adequate and well balanced ... producing Vitamin D in the skin'. Not all Medical Officers were so convinced by ultra-violet radiation.

At the end of the 1920s Birmingham was seeking another site for a new Day Open-Air school to serve the north-west area of the city and was having problems in finding appropriate finance for Marsh Hill Open-Air School. The Education Committee decided to establish instead a second Residential Open-Air school on the Cropwood estate which it already owned; this led to plans for Hunter's Hill School for Boys. It was intended to leave Cropwood permanently for the girls and would solve the current problem every two years of having to discharge all children from Cropwood, when girls replaced boys and vice versa.

By 1928 the Board of Education remained totally convinced of the value of open-air schools: 'Every school in practice should be an open-air school: open-air schools produce a hygienic environment and zest for healthy living which no other school can give ... The schools are an important scheme of preventative medicine'. Lucky indeed were those children selected for this medical therapy which led to new ways of life.

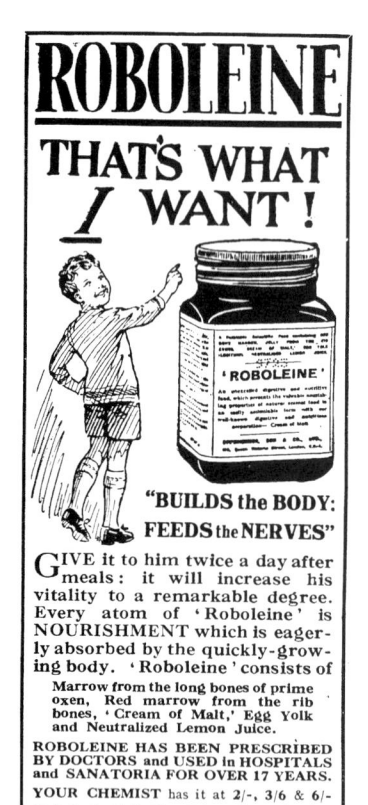

ROBOLEINE — THAT'S WHAT I WANT!

"BUILDS the BODY: FEEDS the NERVES"

GIVE it to him twice a day after meals: it will increase his vitality to a remarkable degree. Every atom of 'Roboleine' is NOURISHMENT which is eagerly absorbed by the quickly-growing body. 'Roboleine' consists of Marrow from the long bones of prime oxen, Red marrow from the rib bones, 'Cream of Malt,' Egg Yolk and Neutralized Lemon Juice.

ROBOLEINE HAS BEEN PRESCRIBED BY DOCTORS and USED in HOSPITALS and SANATORIA FOR OVER 17 YEARS.

YOUR CHEMIST has it at 2/-, 3/6 & 6/-

Write for Booklet to Oppenheimer, Son & Co., Ltd. 179, Queen Victoria Street, London, E.C.4.

Vitamins and fat content— in what other macaroni can you find them?

Only in Milkaroni—formerly called Quaker *MILK* Macaroni —do you get vitamins and adequate fat percentage. The reason is simple, but the result is vital. By a patent process, Milkaroni is manufactured from wheat and milk, not wheat and water.

For the first time in history, therefore, macaroni—when it's Milkaroni—is a *complete* food.

Body-building elements, vitamins, flavour—you get them all in Milkaroni. And you get them pure and uncontaminated because they are locked up in the Milkaroni sealed packet.

Try Milkaroni to-morrow. You will be surprised to find how much more delicious and nourishing it is than you ever considered macaroni could be.

Milkaroni
TRADE MARK

In 1-lb. and ½-lb. sealed packets.

The sealed packet preserves Milkaroni in all its original purity, sweetness and flavour.

Guaranteed by Quaker Oats Ltd.

Chapter 5

The 1930s: Testament of Health

The 1930s was a period when activities such as rambling, camping, swimming and sunbathing gained in popularity. Open-air classes and school camps were developed by education authorities and at the same time the *Hadow Report on Primary Schools* in 1931 took as its model the successful open-air school system.

The significance of vitamins, proteins and minerals in the diet was becoming apparent, although often a meal in industrial working-class homes still consisted mainly of bread, potatoes, tinned food and tea, with very little butter, milk, fruit and vegetables. A series of dietary surveys concluded that the majority of the population had an inadequate diet for the maintenance of good health.

In 1930 the Board of Education reported that there were 135 open-air schools (94 day schools and 41 residential) in Britain. They were hailed as a panacea for all ills.

In his annual report as Chief Medical Officer of the Board of Education in 1932, Sir George Newman emphasised that 'open-air schools were the invention of the school medical service: its effect has been significant for it has been the means not only of benefiting the health of a large number of children but also of introducing the open-air principle to the elementary schools of this century ... Open air schools provide the means of a direct preventative medicine which is unique in its simplicity and effect'.

In the following year he reported that children at open-air schools 'showed astonishing signs of health and vigour, ... freedom from colds, sore throats and respiratory troubles, increase in weight, ruddier complexion, disappearance of eye and ear inflammations, the steadying of the nerves and the general strengthening and health of the body'.

When the latest open-air school opened at Leicester in 1930 the local School Medical Officer declared that 'the aim of the open-air school is so to train the children that they eventually become hardy and handy men and women'. There was much thought given to the problems of combining fresh air principles and the physical well-being of teachers and children. For the first time heating in open-air schools was more carefully considered, as a study at an open-air school in Derbyshire had revealed that children worked best, and absenteeism was at its lowest, when the heating was between 55° and 60°. Many unheated open-air schools in other authorities resulted in the children working (i.e. writing and drawing) at only *half* the average efficiency of children in ordinary heated elementary schools. It seemed, however, as if many open-air schools made a virtue of being out of doors in all weathers, ignoring physiological principles ...

Birmingham's School Medical Officer had reported in 1930 that examination of former pupils of Cropwood Open-Air School showed that their improved general health had not been maintained, due to the depression in industry and the fact that most of the children came from the poorest parts of the city. In view of the urgent need for more open-air schools arrangements were made to open the new day school at Marsh Hill in Erdington in 1931. This provided an extra 200 places for children living on the northern and eastern sides of Birmingham. Plans were also speeded up for Hunter's Hill School for Boys and Cropwood became a girls' school from 1930.

By 1933 there was provision for 14,679 children in open-air schools in Britain. Birmingham had accommodation for 521 children in its two day schools (Uffculme and Marsh Hill) and two residential schools (Cropwood and Hunter's Hill). Only London exceeded this with 2,524 places, whereas all other authorities with open-air schools provided much less accommodation. Birmingham was to remain in the forefront in its pioneering venture.

Barrow and Geraldine Cadbury continued to take an active interest in Birmingham's open-air schools, especially Mrs. Cadbury who frequently visited them. She was a member of the Birmingham Special Schools Sub-Committee for many years. The City of Birmingham officially recognised two of its most energetic citizens with a Gold Medal from the Birmingham Civic Society in 1931. Barrow Cadbury retired from Cadbury's in 1932, just after the company had celebrated its centenary. He was shortly afterwards presented with the Freedom of the City of Birmingham.

Marsh Hill

Sir George Newman formally opened Marsh Hill Open-Air School on 24 June 1931, although it had been in operation since 13 April that year. Emphasising the great importance of the health and education of the nation in his speech he declared

> … it would be the greatest folly for us, even in our present difficult situation, to spend so little on health or education as to put the clock back as a nation …
>
> Debilitated boys and girls were given five things at open-air schools which they were not being given in other schools … fresh air, food and exercise, and it was insisted they must be clean and must rest. Those were the five cardinal tenets of the way of health for everyone of us.
>
> Expenditure on open-air schools would bring back profits hand over fist. It was the very finest and most paying economy of all …

Totally committed to open-air schools from their early beginnings, Sir George Newman watched over the health of the nation like a father over his family. Once described as 'the greatest hygienist since Moses', his obituary in *The Times* on 26 May 1948 titled him 'doctor to the nation'. He had been one of the chief architects of the development of public health administration (as Chief Medical Officer of the Board of Education 1907-35, and also of the Ministry of Health 1919-35). He was a Quaker and great friend of Dame Elizabeth Cadbury (wife of George Cadbury) who was Chairman of Birmingham's School Medical Service Sub-Committee from 1911-30.

A report in the *Birmingham Mail* revealed Marsh Hill Open-Air School had cost £17,900 and that parents paid for the cost of their children's three meals a day according to their circumstances. Designed to accommodate 200 children and to relieve pressure on Uffculme and Cropwood, Marsh Hill was under the direction of Miss Mary Brown, Headmistress.

The Marsh Hill school log book records that teaching staff consisted of Mr. R. Jones and four other teachers. During the first few days 137 children were admitted and Miss Hart, cook at Uffculme School, helped out for a week. In addition there was a nurse, bath attendant, kitchen maid and scullery maid.

The first few weeks must have been rather chaotic as the bath and shower rooms were not ready, very little furniture had been delivered and the water supply was 'unsatisfactory'. Cold, wet and stormy weather created more difficulties as the log book records:

Marsh Hill log book 1931

22 Oct.   *Classrooms too cold to use.*

3 Nov.   *Owing to heavy rain and storms it was again impossible to use flooded classrooms.*

4 Nov.   *Many tiles blew off the roof and several sun blinds broken.*

11 Nov.   *Classrooms flooded—work disorganised.*

Marsh Hill log book 1932

9 Feb.   *Owing to heavy snowstorm during the night it was impossible to take ordinary work.*

19 Feb.   *Thick fog in all classrooms. Work again disorganised.*

Artist's impression of Marsh Hill Open-Air School in 1931, based on a newspaper photograph. (K. Aitken)

Miss Patricia Hazel's thesis *Education for Delicate Children: Day School Provision in the City of Birmingham 1911-1973* comments on the foundation of Marsh Hill School:

Marsh Hill was the first school sited, planned and built for Birmingham without assistance from private donors. It is difficult to understand why, in spite of Britain's unpredictable climate, delicate children were subjected to such bleak Spartan conditions. One must remember, however, that doctors in the 1930's had no x-ray facilities to diagnose tuberculosis nor drugs to treat the disease ...

The log books report frequent nature rambles to Oscott Woods, visits to the theatres, art gallery, Botanical Gardens and other places. Many activities took pupils into the world beyond the school gates and into the company of other children.

The school had extensive grounds five hundred feet above sea level, sloping south. It had a large hall, dining room, rest-shed, five classrooms, staffroom, medical room, bathroom, kitchen, two football pitches and extensive grassy areas, gardens and playgrounds. By 1937 it had an additional large rest-shed equipped and used as a gymnasium. At this time open-air schools had been developed by sixteen nations and three international Congresses had been held in European cities.

Some past pupils of Marsh Hill recall their schooldays:

Ray Mabbett, Marsh Hill 1931-8, Solihull

I started there in 1931 as I had suspected TB. During the summer we were issued with aertex shirts and khaki shorts to wear in all weathers. We changed at the end of the school day.

The collection of buildings were made of wood, all single storey, with a veranda running alongside. Miss Brown was the Headmistress—she was very strict: also Mr. Jones who taught in the top class. One day on a visit to Castle Bromwich aerodrome two of us picked an apple off the ground. Mr. Jones saw us and next day out came the garden cane and we received three of the best on each hand.

After lunch was rest time for an hour, 1.00pm to 2.00pm, on stretchers outside in the summer, under cover in the winter. All lying on our right side and the teacher (mainly Mr. Jones) carried a cane; if a boy was found to be lying on his back or left side he would receive a swipe with the cane.

A group of boys and girls would have a plot of ground to grow various items i.e. potatoes, radishes, leeks etc. A prize would be given for the best plot. The gymnasium was very good, climbing ropes, parallel bars, vaulting horse etc.

Each child had a toothbrush issued and we cleaned our teeth with a powder or salt. A sister and a nurse were on the staff. Football, and hockey for the girls, was played on one afternoon a week. After tea we lined up in the playground in bus lanes to get home. A supervisor came on each bus to look after the children.

I left in 1938—later on I was fit enough to join the RAF.

Mrs. Rose Newnham (née **Turner**), 78, Marsh Hill 1931, Birmingham

I was sent to Marsh Hill when I was 13 because I was frequently unwell and often at the school clinic. At the time I was one of the oldest there. The daily routine consisted of lessons which were all taken outdoors if possible, and regular exercise periods. Or we were occupied by digging and sorting stones out of the ground, preparing the soil for the gardens. For the outdoor lessons, we would take a chair and writing materials outside.

Mr. John Hood, 70, Marsh Hill 1932-3, Bromsgrove, Worcestershire

As a child I suffered from bronchial asthma and was sent to Marsh Hill, which I enjoyed very much. Miss Brown was the Headmistress and Mr. Jones was my teacher. We had to march into the Dining Hall to the sound of piano music played by one of the teachers. We had to sit upright at the tables and were not allowed to talk until our meals were served by a Monitor.

Surprisingly, when I think about it now, corporal punishment was applied in the school. When any boy committed a misdemeanour Miss Brown used to refer them to Mr. Jones who would take the culprit into a store room which held, among other items, a vaulting horse. The culprit would have to bend over the vaulting horse to receive a few good stripes from Mr. Jones' leather belt.

The Report of HM Inspector on Marsh Hill Open-Air School in 1933 paid tribute to the Headmistress and her staff on their achievements, despite the considerable difficulties:

> … lack of screens and absence of heating made the first winter a very trying one to children and staff but the recent improvements will at least provide adequate protection against wind and rain … Experiments are still being tried out to discover what syllabus will best suit the needs of these backward pupils. The cheerfulness, enthusiasm and enterprise of the Headmistress have been equal to the many calls made on them … Most teachers are wisely developing methods which call for initiative on the part of the children.

It would seem that these were still 'pioneering' days for educationalists …

By 1938 the report of HM Inspector on Marsh Hill was moved to record: 'One of the most striking features of the school is the happiness of the children … The immediate problem is the training of staff due to the fact that all but one are unfamiliar with the peculiar demands which a school like this makes upon them … This is a very successful open-air school.' This statement probably could be applied to all of Birmingham's open-air schools and the abundance of happy memories of open-air school days bears testimony to their success.

Uffculme 1930-3

The school's invaluable collection of annotated photographs reveals that in 1930 an old pool had been filled in with builders' rubble. Some of the boys helped to haul 50 loads of soil in wooden boxes to the site! Pupils were involved in planting 1,000 bulbs, making a bird table, levelling the paths and laying crazy paving and constructing drains for pipes going from the stream to the lower pool.

Other activities included weaving with looms, dancing round a maypole and folk dancing. At the Midland Musical Festival in 1931 Uffculme was the sole entrant for Boys Morris dancing.

The annual Pageant at Uffculme involved many aspects of the curriculum and included The Canterbury Tales (1930), Robin Hood and his Merrie Men (1931) and Roundheads and Cavaliers (1932). The official report of HM Inspector in 1932 gives some insight into the value of these events:

> The practice of producing a Pageant in the summer months has succeeded in giving unity and significance to various subjects and has enlisted the lively interest of the children. Advantage is being taken of the practical and concrete experiences afforded by the site to give some help to the teaching of Arithmetic, Geography and Nature Study. The Physical Training is very effective; the children are obviously deriving great benefit from the work of the visiting specialist.
>
> The credit for the satisfactory progress of the school is largely due to the Headmistress [Miss Hibbert].

Elaborate costumes in Uffculme's school pageant 'Roundheads and Cavaliers' in 1932. (N. Whittall)

There was a detailed report on the school in the *Birmingham Post*, 18 March 1931—a chilly spring day when classrooms were open on three sides. The reporter noted that the children did not look delicate:

> They are tanned and vigorous and hardly ever suffer from a cold at all. In the great frost of 1929 pupils and teachers stayed in their open classrooms until the ink froze in the wells and they decided that exercise would be better than sitting still. 75% of pupils go from the school permanently healthy and continue their studies at an ordinary elementary school.

Barefoot country dancing on the lawns in front of Uffculme's dining room on a chilly spring day, March 1931. (Uffculme School)

A love of flowers at the open-air school is encouraged. The school at the moment is full of daffodils and hyacinths in pots, all grown on the premises and right through the year there are flowers in the hall and classrooms. Sometimes daffodils are gathered at Easter and given to the children to take home.

The boys are encouraged to grow vegetables in allotments, working in teams of seven and competing for the honour of sending the largest quantity of vegetables up to the kitchen. The girls concentrate on flower growing.

The standard of achievement in lessons is not very high, as most of the pupils, through ill health, have been forced to miss many days of schooling. But attempts are made to teach the children as much as they would learn in an ordinary elementary school, the morning being the time for greatest concentration. The chief aim is to build up good health. During the twenty years the school has existed it has been the only open-air day school in Birmingham. Now, however, another school is to be opened on the other side of Birmingham [Marsh Hill] ... and will shorten the long waiting list.

Entries in the school log books became much abbreviated, often only stating daily attendance figures, staff sickness and teachers on supply (staff mentioned were Miss Harlow, Miss Plant, Miss Squire, Miss Gough, Miss Webb, Mr. Anderson, Miss Tidmus, Mr. Savage and Nurse Bendall).

The following reminiscences from former pupils record life in the early 1930s:

Mrs. Joyce Turner (née **Hutton**), Uffculme 1930-3, Peterborough, Cambridgeshire

I enjoyed my days at Uffculme, especially the outdoor activities and craft lessons and the food which was just like Mother cooked at home.

Gardening was very much encouraged. There were two ponds in the grounds and it was decided to fill one in and make a sunken garden. Tons of soil were delivered and hundreds of bulbs, and we children had a great time helping to plant these out.

The gardener welcomed any help in sweeping up autumn leaves and putting them into bags, and with all those trees around there were plenty of leaves!

The Guide Company was captained by the Headmistress and we had a lovely time tracking round the grounds and making our camp fires.

Another 'activity' I enjoyed was the yearly Pageant, acted on the lawns for the benefit of parents and school dignitaries. The whole year seemed to be taken up preparing for this occasion, with the making of costumes and scenery. The whole school took part and this is where the country dancing came into its own. I remember quite clearly the last pageant I was in—the Cavaliers and Roundheads. We knitted jumpers in stripes of orange and brown to be worn by Cromwell's Roundhead soldiers. I was very thrilled because I was elevated from a lowly peasant doing country dancing up to a court lady, dancing with a very elegantly dressed Cavalier in coat, breeches, feathered hat and all!

I seemed to get picked for most of the country dancing displays and competitions. I remember being in a display which we performed on the lawns of Cadbury's Bournville Factory. Our team won a competition held at Birmingham Town Hall.

Miss Webb, my class teacher, gave me some coaching lessons (out of school hours) for the Grammar School Entrance Exam. Much to my surprise I passed. But my parents were advised by the school doctors that with the state of my health at that time I would not have stood the strain of all the extra work plus the homework. On their advice, I stayed on at Uffculme.

I can still remember the teachers. Miss Plant and Mr. Anderson took the two senior classes and eventually married each other. My favourite was Miss Webb—she was so disappointed that I couldn't go to the Grammar School after all her help. The staff were dealing with 'delicate' children so the atmosphere was completely different to that found in a normal school—the pace was much slower.

*As I seemed to be getting weaker an extra hour rest period **before** dinner was ordered by the school doctor. I eventually left Uffculme but was shortly to be taken into hospital where the cause of all my problems*

Rest time on stretchers in the open-air, March 1931. (Uffculme School)

was diagnosed. Rotten tonsils! I spent three months in hospital and then went back to ordinary school, part-time, where I was only allowed to do 'sitting-down' lessons.

If my tonsil trouble had been found out in the very early days, there would have been no need for me to go to Uffculme. But I think the experience of being there, with all the facilities and care it afforded, made a lasting impression on me which I have carried through life.

Mrs. Betty Webster (née **Marston**), 73, Uffculme 1931, Birmingham

I had a happy time there. I remember semolina and prunes for breakfast, much better than porridge.

The Headmistress was a large lady with her hair done in plaits and wound round her ears like big earphones. I remember on Friday after lunch the two top classes had to stay in the dining room and polish all the spoons and forks whilst all the younger children had a free afternoon to play. We never seemed to get finished until it was time to go home. I suppose it was one way of showing us life's like that and lots of things are sent to try us.

There was a Marsh Garden with all the different plants which the Headmistress used to explain to us. We had straw hats in the summer and we had to embroider a design on them in coloured raffia so that we would know which was ours. The gardener showed us a nest of hedgehogs. So many things were shown and explained to us. It has made me very observant.

Mr. Bernard William Cartwright, Uffculme 1931-6, Cornwall

I went to Uffculme with my two brothers when I was six years old—we were under Great Charles Street Chest Hospital. We used to go on Monday morning and stop the week, returning home Friday afternoon.

At night we slept in a building with all the sides open. Many a time we went out when it was dark to get some apples from the orchard. At the school the young ones were given a small garden plot to grow flowers and the older ones given plots to grow vegetables. We used to get a prize for the best vegetables grown.'

Mrs. Iris Baldwin (née **Cooper**), 75, Uffculme 1932-3, Scarborough, North Yorkshire

I went to Uffculme from the age of 13 with chronic bronchitis but I didn't see much wrong with anyone who was there and we didn't discuss it. It was the best school I went to.

There was a duck pond; I used to feed the ducks called Billy and Betty. I was 'head gardener of small plots' until I went up the hill to get rid of some rubbish in a tub. On the way back down the tub went rolling down the hill, straight through the best flowerbed of tulips so they were all mown down. I was in disgrace and sent to stand by Miss Hibbert's desk all day, then I was given a good telling off and all my privileges taken away from me.

Uffculme girls happily haymaking in the 1930s—a taste of country life for city children. (Uffculme School)

I remember writing a play with another girl, and the school performed it, our teacher was Mr. Anderson. In the winter every now and then we would run through the grounds and the length of a large field at the bottom.

I liked the school so much, I don't think I lost a day.

Mr. John Bonner, Uffculme 1932-3, Birmingham

Early in 1932 my mother was requested to take me for a physical examination to determine if I was fit enough to withstand the rigours of the workaday world. Apparently I wasn't up to standard as I was instructed to present myself at Uffculme Open-Air School.

When I started at Uffculme I was 13 years old. It was warm enough to adopt summer clothing, which in the boys' case was a pair of khaki shorts and nothing else. It was hard on the feet at first but I soon became accustomed to it and could soon run full pelt over anything. I was big for my age, five feet one, so was one of the few seniors immediately on entrance. I was also a table monitor straight away. This meant I was in charge of one of the long tables, which seated about 14 younger children. I ruled from one end. The other end was in the charge of Grace Barron, a charming and very pretty girl.

Apart from keeping order, our job was to queue up with the other table monitors, a plate in each hand, and pass down the serving line filling the plates for our charges. The serving line always consisted of Mr. Rushton the caretaker, who knew not how to smile, the matron and one or two teachers. The food was generally good and consisted of three meals a day. We monitors were expected to order for each member of our table by proffering the plates to the servers and saying 'small please' for the tinies, 'normal please' for the others and 'large one for me please Mr. Rushton.' Old Stoneface always obliged.

After lunch we all retired to the rest-shed where we were required to collect a blanket and lie on a stretcher bed for an hour. This was an agony to me as I could never sleep and the hour seemed like half a day. I lost count

In Uffculme's open-sided dining room children wear the school's navy blue jerseys. Fresh flowers grown by the pupils were always on the tables. March 1931. (Uffculme School)

of the times that I was caught reading by the duty teacher and had my book confiscated. On dry days, summer or winter, it was outside on the lawn. The only difference during winter was in the mode of dress. The brief summer undress was discarded in favour of our own cold weather clothing, which in the case of some of our less well-off companions meant suffering the vagaries of the English weather at its worst.

I was placed in the senior class. My desk-mate was Leslie Hemming who was a giant of a lad. We rapidly became fast friends and were never far apart.

The senior class was taught mainly by Mr. Anderson, known to the boys, out of his hearing, as 'Jock'. He was a Scot, an excellent teacher and a confirmed athletics fan. He succeeded in introducing rugby in the boys' curriculum.

Lessons were a bit sketchy, some of us were a little more advanced than others, as much as a year older in some cases. My most successful subjects were painting and drawing, English composition and spelling.

'Jock' Anderson had a large wall-map of the world shipping routes and ports. Little flags bearing the names of leading cruise liners were moved around on the map. He brought the 'Daily Mail' and from it he read out the arrivals and departures of these big ships. It was part of our lessons to log these movements and predict where the liner might be heading next.

One lesson which I hated was singing which was always taught by Miss Hibbert the Headmistress. She was quite firm on discipline, but she treated us fairly.

The rest of the teaching staff consisted of Miss Tidmus, and Miss Gough, a young teacher who didn't appear to be much older than us seniors. Mr. Anderson seemed to be the centre of our instructional world.

We played soccer and eleven-a-side rugby around the Kings Heath area and on our own beautiful ground which adjoined Highbury park. On the cricket field, battling against Hunter's Hill I was fortunate enough to establish a record score that was never beaten and the team finished the season without defeat.

Once the warmer weather set in, we were back to the shorts only for the boys, while the girls wore brief knickers and a very short dress, and very fetching they looked too.

Mr. Edward Anderson teaching boys under the trees at Uffculme in 1932. He taught at the school for 35 years, eventually becoming Headteacher. (Uffculme School)

During the summer months, Hemming and I had a special job to do once a week. As the two biggest lads in the school we were chosen to go into town. We were issued with travel tokens for the journey, a sack in which to bring back our purchase and a two shilling piece to buy a block of ice. We set off soon after breakfast and walked up to Alcester Road where we boarded the tram for a leisurely ride to the bottom of the Bull Ring in Digbeth. There we would alight and cross over to the Ice & Refrigeration Company, hand in our two bob piece and receive in return a block of ice to be carried in the sack. It was very heavy and it took the two of us to carry it. I remember the tram conductors would only allow the ice to be carried on the rear platform, so one of us had to stay with it in order to make sure it didn't take off and slide down a side road. On arrival back at Uffculme, it was our job to smash pieces off the ice block and fill the space surrounding the ice-cream mix container and then fasten down the lid. We then took turns to turn the handle, thereby churning the ice-cream ready for sale in cornets at one penny or a ha'penny each. Hemming and I each received a penny cornet as reward for our labours. It doesn't seem like much today, but at that time we were well satisfied. We also had the right to scrape out the drum when the teacher conducting the sales had finished with it.

The annual sports was contested on our ground by us and five other local schools. I worked hard at it as Mr. Anderson expected me to do well in the high jump. Happily, I won it for him along with the Martineau Shield which was for that event only, although I pulled a thigh muscle and Mr. Anderson was compelled to massage it before each jump.

Early in the summer we began planning the school play which was always performed at the end of the school year. It started off with Mr. Anderson telling the English class the story of Sir Edward de Byrmingham and the evil Duke of Northumberland who plotted Sir Edward's demise in order to gain possession of his lands. After the story and a brief description of what was required we settled down to write a composition describing Act One. The following week Mr. Anderson announced that my plot was the best of those submitted, and therefore I would be working on the play alone. I spent a few weeks' English lessons inventing and improving plot and dialogue until 'Jock' was satisfied. He told me that my name would appear in the open day programme as the author, and I was to help him to direct the actors.

On the great day the various entertainments were performed with enthusiasm to a receptive audience of relatives and visitors. The school choir opened the show and was followed by the girls classical dance troupe. There was a display of physical exercise and the boys Morris dance team performed handkerchief and staff dances. The last event was entitled 'The Last of the de Byrminghams.'

It was not until later, when I read through my mother's programme, that I became aware of the deception. The programme simply announced it as written by the seniors. I was very hurt, but I didn't say anything.

Then it was end of term and the end of my year at this wonderful place. On the last day I was summoned to Miss Hibbert's office for the last time. She told me that she was well pleased with the manner in which I had conducted myself throughout the year that I had spent there. In conclusion she gave me the letter of character which she had written for me. It was excellent and I have it still.

I was loath to leave but I had a living to make and I'm sure that Uffculme helped tremendously. I never had one day out of work in fifty years and I was able to serve in the Army for six and a half years in the Western Desert and the European theatre. I owe a lot to Uffculme and 'Jock' Anderson for one of the happiest years of my life.

Mrs. Doris Rolls (née **Freestone**), 75, Uffculme 1932-5, Oxhill, Warwickshire

I was there for a heart problem and boarded in the summer months. Miss Gough was one of my teachers, and Mr. Anderson. Miss Hibbert the Head was strict but fair. I liked her. I remember doing the pageant: Edward de Byrmingham—some pupils had to wear a dress which Miss Hibbert dyed to a certain shade of yellow. She was artistic.

I was in the Guides—we did things like tracking and lighting fires in the grounds, which gave an insight into country life for us townies. Outside the resting shed were some aspen poplar trees where we lay on the beds near them in the open in fine weather. We saw all these leaves coming down just like snow!

We used to take rain water readings and go to cook to get food for the bird tables. We also did a lot of reading—Mrs. Gaskell comes to mind.

School was an experience there; I look back with great pleasure.

The magic of Mayday and the tradition of dancing around the maypole was always celebrated at Uffculme in the 1930s. (Uffculme School)

Cropwood 1930-3

Birmingham's School Medical Officer recorded again in 1933 that the health of some of Cropwood's ex-pupils had deteriorated after leaving the school, largely due to the social environment:

> Housing conditions and poverty are mainly to blame for these relapses; in some cases it is merely the unwisdom of foolish though well-meaning parents; in not a few, however, one feels that the child must be made ill by the mere force of suggestion—so ever-anxious and lugubrious are the mothers about the children's health ... To have these children living a year or two in a promised land of good food and clothes, air and space, and a cheerful freedom from care, and then to send them back to the surroundings from which they came, is little short of tragic.

For the first time a Birmingham teacher was appointed to teach remedial exercises to all children in open-air schools suffering from postural defects and chest complaints. Many of the breathing exercises were to prove invaluable to asthmatic and bronchitic pupils long after they had left open-air schools.

In 1932 the report of HM Inspector on Cropwood had been more than satisfactory:

> The comparative smallness of the numbers and the fact that the school is a residential one have enabled the Headmistress and her staff to study the girls individually, and to give them, in and out of school, the treatment they need.
>
> The girls are well groomed and well cared for in every respect. Outwardly there is little, if any, sign of the devitalising effect of ill-health: their cheerfulness and spontaneity show the happy influences at work here, and their enjoyment of their beautiful home is as noteworthy as their ready speech, their friendly interest and their courteous behaviour.
>
> The curriculum is well balanced. Special advantages are wisely exploited, e.g. the Geography and Nature Study of the top class are based on a detailed study of the neighbourhood, and Mothercraft lessons are given to the oldest girls by the resident nurse. Neat and careful work is demanded and obtained. Initiative is being encouraged: the lecturettes given by some of the senior girls have involved careful research on their part.
>
> The happy inspiration of the Headmistress is to be noted in every detail of the girls' life here: her two assistants give sound and conscientious support.

Headmistress Miss Walton continued to record so fully the activities of the school in the log book that only a few entries can be recorded here:

Cropwood log book 1930

28 April   *Miss Carter and Miss Bolton started work today and all the rest of the staff were present. 27 new girls were admitted this afternoon.*

12 June   *The whole school went to the Clent Hills for the day.*

11 July   *The S.S.Committee had their annual meeting here this afternoon. After the meeting the children sang, danced and performed little plays.*

31 July   *The girls have all gone home today looking well and fit.*

18 Aug.   *The school re-opened today. As the children look—for the most part—as if they are needing extra rest—the rising bell will go half an hour later just for this week.*

30 Aug.   *Class 1 girls in charge of Miss Walton went to Malvern for the day. In the evening three girls decamped. They were discovered to be missing just after 8pm and though every effort to find them was made, no news of them was received until midnight when a police telephone call notified us they had reached home.*

31 Aug.   *The parents of the three children brought them back today. They had been a little homesick.*

1 Sep.   *All three children have settled down happily again.*

Cropwood log book 1931

9 Mar.   *Periodical examination. Dr. Smellie, Dr. Dick, Miss Martineau and Miss Ross present. 63 children seen—22 to be discharged at Easter.*

13 April   *The school re-opened after the Easter holidays and 53 children returned. One girl who went home apparently well has died in the holidays of pneumonia. She was a pulmonary fibrosis case.*

20 June   *Visit of the Education Study Society. 11 people came and saw the grounds and school work as far as possible, had tea and saw the play "Toad of Toad Hall".*

27 June   *Visit of the Special Schools teachers. This was their annual outing and tea was provided by Mrs. Cadbury. Nurse away for weekend.*

Cropwood log book 1932

26 April   *17 girls went to the Town Hall to do Country Dancing at The Midland Festival Competition. They got a 1st class certificate.*

7 May   *11 Uffculme boys came to play rounders with our girls and gave a display of 'Morris' dancing.*

Cropwood log book 1933

23 Jan.   *Children have had 'Cow & Gate' hot drink every day in the middle of the morning since their return.*

25 Jan.   *All children had a teaspoonful of cod-liver oil today and are to have it twice daily as long as the severe frost continues.*

5 April   *Miss Walton finishes at Cropwood as Head Teacher today.* [She moved across the road to take charge of the new Hunter's Hill Open-Air School for Boys where she remained until 1943.]

22 April   *Miss Grant, who has been appointed Headmistress in succession to Miss Walton, arrived at Cropwood today.* [Miss Margaret Emily Grant was to remain at Cropwood for five years until June 1938.]

25 April   *Twenty-two new girls admitted today.*

3 June   *A rounders match with the boys school and a victory for us.*

1 July   *We have had several cases of tonsillitis this week and one slight case of diphtheria.*

31 Oct.   *Elsie H. Gwennie B. and Rose R. ran away this evening but returned at bed-time. They had been punished for letting off fireworks and were not to go to the bonfire on Saturday.*

Three ex-pupils of Cropwood recall their memories of the school between 1930/3:

Mrs. Betty Webster (née **Marston**), 74, Cropwood 1930, Birmingham

I first went to Cropwood at the age of nine. I was a very sickly child weighing only three stone. As you can imagine I was spoilt by my parents and going away from home was an awful wrench for my parents and me.

I can remember the first night; another girl and I were shown into a bedroom with five beds in and told there would be three more girls coming the next day to share it with us. Vera Wrigley and I were both very homesick and couldn't get to sleep. Vera started to cry and I got into bed with her and finally got to sleep. We had pale pink nightdresses in flannelette which we needed as it was cold.

We had been told that we would hear a bell ring in the tower at seven thirty in the morning and this duly happened. A jolly nurse came in and told us to strip the bedclothes back over the chair to air the bed. We were shown by Sister how to make our beds—the corners of the sheets had to be folded just so, like hospital beds; once a week we had to turn the mattresses, it was quite a feat for me! I had to stand on the bed once I had folded the mattress in half and heave it over! Then came breakfast and a large bowl of porridge was put in front of me and it tasted awful. You sometimes were lucky and got a lump of brown sugar in it and then it was quite nice.

We had very nice clothes all in brown and fawn; fawn jumper and brown gymslip, brown woollen ribbed stockings and brown leather boots. We had sandals to wear indoors and brown knickers with white cotton underlinings.

We all had our own hooks for our outside clothes and a cotton toilet bag with our comb and brush. Along the floor ran a wooden bench with space for our boots, then in the middle of the room were the wash basins where we washed morning and night. We had showers once or twice a week. We had to end with a cold shower and if we didn't go under the nurse used to come along with the mop, making sure we backed under.

After lunch every day we had to have an hour's rest. In the warm weather it was out in the playground, we had canvas folding beds and a blanket and we had to lie on our right sides, you weren't allowed to lie on your back or your left side. If it was cold or wet we slept under the covered play area and the front was open to the elements but we were dry.

On Sunday evenings we sang hymns and sea shanties and I loved all that as I heard songs I had never heard before and never forgot. In the winter we had snow and so we had sledges and had a wonderful time.

At Xmas we had a fancy-dress and my mother suggested I went as Amy Johnson as she had just flown to Australia. I went in my blue rubberised mac, my father's leather helmet and goggles (as he had a motor bike and sidecar) and brown leggings. I had a placard on my back saying 'Well done Amy' and won first prize which was a row of pearls in a blue velvet case shaped like an oyster shell. Mr. & Mrs. Barrow Cadbury visited us whilst I was there.

I remember the lovely dolls' house in the hall which we were only allowed to play with if a grown up was there.

After I had been at Cropwood a year they said I could go home and go daily to Uffculme. I cried when I left, I didn't want to go—I had had a wonderful year. I shall always be grateful for those two years of my life. They made me strong in mind and body and I still think of them with such happy memories.

Mrs. Eileen Lucas (née **Dadds**), Cropwood 1930-3, Solihull, West Midlands

I was sent to Cropwood for some months in the period between 1930 and 1933. My eldest sister had been resident at the school for two years before I went there.

Nurse was fair haired, plump and very fastidious—easily fussed, especially when Mrs. Cadbury was visiting the school. As I had long hair at that time, I had special treatment that day and warned to keep tidy! Sister was a small, dark, attractive lady, who not only wore lipstick, but was rumoured to smoke and was known to play golf—she was considered very glamorous by us all.

Mrs. N. Green, 71, Cropwood 1932, Birmingham

I was nine years old and stayed there for about four years. We were rather poor and I was one of six children. The staff at Cropwood were all so kind. I remember many happy times.

We enjoyed swimming, tennis, country dancing and especially Nativity plays around Xmas, entertaining the important people from the Education Committee.

In summer we used to have to rest outside in our next to nothing to get the sun to our bodies. I also remember the long walks every day and coming back to some nice hot drinks. I'm sure this helped to make us stronger.

I still have my bronchitis but I'm sure going to Cropwood helped me to carry on through life. I shall always be grateful and treasure the memories I shall always have.

Mrs. Gladys Cash (née **Coley**), 73, Cropwood 1932-3, Solihull, West Midlands

I suffered with bronchiectasis. Until I was 11 years old I had very little schooling. I attended Birmingham Children's Hospital regularly, and the school clinic, and eventually it was decided that I should go to an Open-Air School. It cost my mother 6s. 6d. per week [32½p].

After the Easter holiday 1932 I was taken to New Street Station in Birmingham. I was met by staff from the school, we had to buy a train ticket (9d.). The train took us to Blackwell; once there we walked in twos to Cropwood situated in lovely countryside. I came from an inner city suburb of Birmingham and to live in the country was so different.

The Headmistress was a very kind lady by the name of Miss Walton. There were two other teachers, Miss Carter and Miss Bottom, and there were also two nurses on the staff. I remember the housekeeper Miss Arnot who told me off for saying 'OK'! She said 'we don't use that sort of talk here'.

There were some children there who came from very poor homes in the Birmingham slums, but we were all equal because clothes were provided for us and we all looked the same.

Most of the children, like me, had not been to school very much, and others had never attended at all. The standard of education was very basic but we were taught a lot of practical things; we learned to sew, knit, darn, also we did craft work e.g. made stools with seagrass seats. We also had a patch of garden to tend.

We led a very simple but happy life, the staff were all very nice. We spent most of the time outdoors, the classrooms were open on two sides, sometimes three, and in the winter we wore our thick overcoats in school. At Christmas we were all given a small box of chocolates from the Cadbury family. Sometimes we had entertainment in the playroom—concerts or pantomimes.

Our parents were allowed to visit us on one Saturday in every month, this was enjoyable for them as well as for us because it was an outing from the big city; such trips were few for the working classes in those days. We came home for two weeks in the summer and two weeks at Christmas.

By Easter 1933 my health had improved so much that it was decided I could return home. I am pleased to say that I have never looked back; that year in the clean country air worked wonders for me and I think for many others.

'The Shelter' on Cropwood's estate was used in the 1930s as a Camp School to provide holidays for Birmingham schoolgirls. (O. Phillips)

'The Shelter' was a building on the Cropwood estate, near Rosemary Cottage, and had been included in the land donated by the Cadbury family in 1922. It was a picturesque single storey building (120 ft. x 54 ft.) with a thatched roof, consisting of one large tiled room (which became a dormitory), one smaller one and a garden. The Juvenile Employment and Welfare Sub-Committee of the Birmingham Education Committee had converted the building into a Camp School after 1923 and it was used during the summer months to accommodate girls and teachers from several Birmingham schools. The dormitory was open-air in design and the Camp School was generally intended to benefit needy children from crowded city homes with a fortnight's holiday in the country. Some of those children can still recall the experience:

Mrs. Margaret (Peggy) Fishley (née **Jones**), The Shelter, two weeks 1931, Bromsgrove, Worcestershire

I will always be grateful for my stay at Cropwood. My childhood was spent in Aston, Birmingham, no green fields, no fresh air.

The memory of the dormitory, open windows, the food and plenty of it, the appetising smells from the kitchen still linger in my mind! I remember walks in the surrounding countryside of Blackwell, the walks up Greenhill and the little Tuck Shop down the lane, in the front room of a cottage, owned by a little lady with white apron and shawl. The counter and shelves were stocked with bottles of pear drops, coloured fishes, acid drops, liquorice laces, sherbet dabs, 'chops, potatoes and peas', not forgetting the sweet heart 'love mottoes', chocolate drops and chewy chocolate nuts. How we pondered over value for money; 6d [2½p] spending money had to go a long way.

The highlight of that holiday was the trip to Bromsgrove to visit the Rialto cinema and to see the sheep and livestock in the cattle market on the opposite side of the road. It was a wonderful experience.

Cropwood was a far distant refuge which gave me the privilege of being so near to nature and a green and pleasant land. I hoped one day to live in Bromsgrove, and in 1964 my wish came true.

During my 30 years here, I have served on the Urban District Council, the District Council and County Council, become involved with Social Services, and many other organisations. All this involvement and activity because of a childhood dream in the 1930s.

Thanks to the foresight of the Cadbury family I have been able to make a small contribution to my town and society.

Mrs. Margaret Timmins (née **Marston**), 73, The Shelter, two weeks 1933, Cannock, Staffs.

I went to Elliot School in Nechells, Birmingham. My teacher asked whose father was out of work and as there were nine children in our family and I had not been well I guess that's why I was sent for two weeks to Blackwell.

We slept in a wooden dormitory in the grounds. It had a veranda going round it where the ladies looking after us slept. I did not get much sleep while I was there, as someone said bats flew in at night and got into your hair! We had good food and walks in fields where we did a lot of our lessons.

It was lovely weather when I was there but I did not enjoy it much. I guess they thought it would do me good.

Miss Olive Phillips, The Shelter, two weeks 1934, Birmingham

My memories of the time spent there are very happy. When we got there we were issued with a cotton dress and knickers to match. We had good food which was served in the Shelter where we also had lessons; it was spotlessly clean. We slept on camp beds which were very comfortable. The teachers and staff were very kind to us.

The dormitory in 'The Shelter', pictured on a postcard sent home in 1934 by a pupil who wrote: 'Today we went to Cofton Woods and saw the wishing tree. I have made a lot of friends here.' (O. Phillips)

I was selected to go there for the two weeks because I'd never had a holiday or seen the sea. My mother was a widow with three of us all young and times were hard.

Hunter's Hill

The long-awaited opening of Hunter's Hill Open-Air School at Blackwell, on a site across the road from Cropwood on Hunter's Hill, took place in May 1933, providing residential accommodation for 120 boys. Classrooms and dormitories were built around a square inner courtyard, with open wooden verandas and sliding screens. The sick bay and administrative parts of the school were more conventionally built but the overall impression which remains with past pupils is of a timber-clad building with open sides.

The annual report by Birmingham's School Medical Officer gives us a good description of Hunter's Hill School:

The school is one of the most cheerful and hopeful places that can be imagined in these times of unemployment and distress. Boys who are described on admission as thin, flabby, anaemic, and so forth, turn in a few weeks into upright, sturdy, brown-skinned specimens. It has been remarked by some who have watched them giving a demonstration of physical training, stripped to the waist, that many of them look very thin, and it is true that in the sun-light their ribs and scapulae stand out in light and shadow, but the same is true of most normal healthy boys round about the age of eleven; if examined close to, they will be found to have firm, well-knit muscles, with no spare flesh, while the skin bears that smooth, satiny quality which constant exposure to sun and wind alone can give.

Miss Gertrude Walton, Headmistress of Cropwood, was appointed to the headship of the new school, after having expressed an interest for some time in the post. For some reason the position was not advertised in the usual manner, leading to some vigorous opposition by the Birmingham and District local branch of the National Association of Schoolmasters who argued that a boys' school should have a Headmaster. As two of the other appointed teaching staff were also women, this led to the Association protesting strongly 'that the constitution of the teaching staff at Hunter's Hill is open to serious criticism on physical, moral and mental grounds. As the majority of the boys are seniors, over eleven years of age, the Association maintains that the teaching staff should consist wholly of men, for otherwise the school cannot produce that virile youth which is surely the main purpose of its existence'.

Despite the fact that 12 Birmingham Members of Parliament were contacted, as well as a carefully worded manifesto being sent to each of Birmingham's Councillors, little could be done as the appointment had been ratified by the city council. Miss Walton went on to complete 10 successful years at the school and was succeeded by another woman! She recorded the year's events in the log book:

Hunter's Hill log book 1933

20 April *The Housekeeper, the Sister, the Nurse, the Head Teacher, Cook, kitchenmaid, housemaid, parlourmaid took up residence here to get the school ready for the boys.*

24 April *Miss Frisby, assistant mistress, began duty here getting the books, clothes etc ready for the boys.*

1 May *Mr. Rogers and Mr. Roberts, the assistant masters, began work here. 23 boys from Marsh Hill Open-Air School admitted.*

15 May *Three new boys admitted. No. on register now 120—full complement.*

27 May *The first visiting day. The parents all pleased with the progress the boys have made. One boy made such a scene that his father took him home.*

5 June *Whit Monday. The boys were bathed and fitted up with summer shorts this morning. The parents came this afternoon and we had sports for the parents which were a success. Since then during the whole of the week we have marked the registers as the boys had ordinary lessons chiefly in the morning and organised games, sports, swimming and gardening in the afternoon.*

2 Sep. *Three boys decamped this evening about 7pm.*

3 Sep. *They were brought back today by their parents.*

12 Sep. *This evening one boy was taken to hospital with acute ear trouble.*

THE 1930s: TESTAMENT OF HEALTH

Hunter's Hill Open-Air School for boys, showing the building with open verandas in the countryside, 1933. (M. Harris)

13 Sep.   Today George P. went to the clinic to have his tonsils removed.

15 Sep.   The Committee came out here today and held their meeting. Later the boys did a play for them 'Robin Hood and the Pedlar' and a PT display.

29 Sep.   Four boys decamped at 7pm and were brought back from the Police Station at Selly Oak at 1am. One boy has done this twice this term. He has been at Cropwood and Marsh Hill Open-Air Schools and as he seemed very fit he was sent home to make room for a more urgent case.

15 Dec.   The boys went home today on the 10.27 train.

Three 'old boys' of Hunter's Hill school's opening years recall their schooldays:

Mr. Arthur Beasley, Hunter's Hill 1933, Tamworth, Staffordshire

I was one of the initial intake when it was first opened in 1933. The school was empty and new when we arrived; we were allowed time to settle in and were sort of 'guinea pigs' for a while. There were 120 boys and my number was 103. Staff I can recall were Sister Daniels, Nurse Ella Kemp, teachers Mr. Jim Rogers and Mr. Jim Roberts, Head Teacher and overall Commander Miss Walton.

Lessons were not so academic as a normal school but we were involved in a lot of activities including handicraft and nature study, gardening, country walks etc. I must admit though, when I returned to my 'normal' school in Birmingham, I quite shone as a pupil, becoming Prefect and Head boy.

Food was good but plain. I particularly remember fish pie, stew, plates of cheese cubes, bread and jam, rice pudding with currants in and fresh fruit on the tables—we also drank quantities of milk. I remember after lunch each day we had to take rest on a foldable stretcher for a one hour period and were not allowed to talk or fidget!

There were four open dormitories each housing thirty boys, with a teacher's bedroom overlooking each one for discipline's sake. We were as cunning as any normal children, many a night after 7 o'clock lights out, we would be out and about in the fields and lanes of Blackwell. We were always cold in bed when the snow and ice was about and usually had most of our clothing on under our pyjamas.

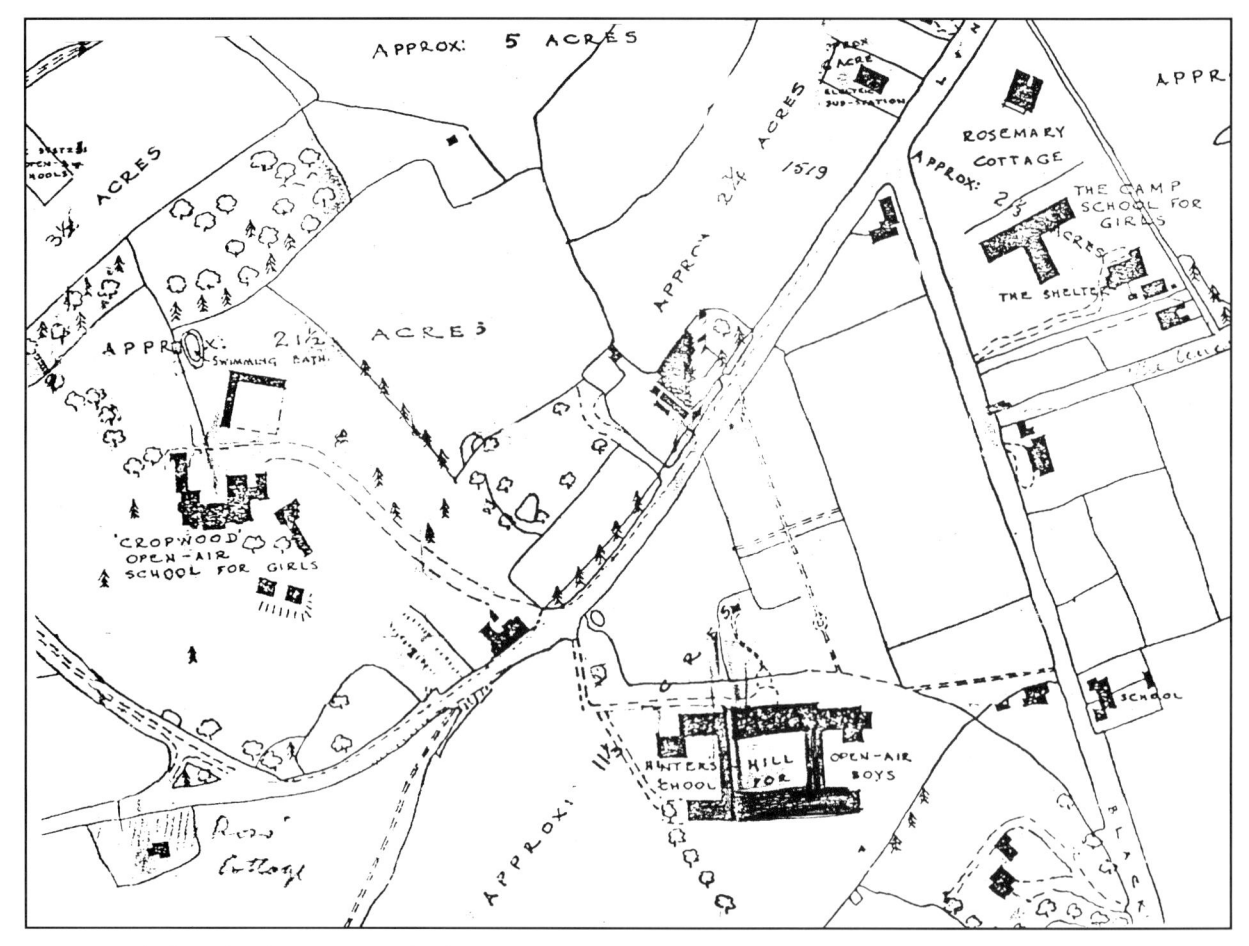

School site plan, showing Cropwood and Hunter's Hill, as well as Rosemary Cottage, the Camp School and the Shelter. (Hunter's Hill School)

    Myself and three friends had a den in the top school field under the hawthorn hedge. Looking back now, this den was quite amazing. We had dug down into the earth about four or five feet, covered this with tree branches and put grass turf on top of this. We had a hidden trap door to enter and for light we had wax tapers stuck into the earth wall! You can imagine the mess we looked after an hour or two in our den!

    Winter clothing consisted of flannel vests and pants, corduroy brown short trousers, grey long-sleeved polo necked jumpers, grey long socks and black leather boots, Sunday best was very nice grey suits, short trousers, grey socks with shoes, grey shirts and tie, coloured according to the 'house' you belonged to. For Sunday in the winter we wore a long grey overcoat, for the visit to the Village Church.

    We engaged in a lot of sporting activities, football, boxing, cricket etc. Athletics was very popular too. Parents visited once a month and left bags of tuck with us. Not that we were allowed to eat it there and then. It was taken away and portions were given back to you on 'Tuck days'.

    I must say that the stay at Hunter's Hill was a very important stage in my life and certainly was a main starter in the building of my character. I am proud to have been a pupil.

THE 1930s: TESTAMENT OF HEALTH

Mr. Bill Tookey, 73, Hunter's Hill 1933, Birmingham.

After leaving Cropwood in 1929 I went to Marsh Hill day open-air school. Hunter's Hill started for me on the day it opened 1 May 1933. I was at the open-air schools because of a bad chest mainly bronchitis.

We all used to attend a church on Sundays, it was in those days a corrugated metal-clad building at the crossroads in Blackwell. After the service the lady organist searched me out and asked if I would be a member of the choir. My reward was to be taken with five others to Worcester Cathedral, trying out the choir stalls during the long service. Afterwards we were given tea and taken back to school.

Parents were allowed to visit us once a month and I know my mother and brother walked the four miles each way to and from the Lickey Hill tram terminus.

The food was excellent, we even had bacon on Sundays. Porridge was a banker at breakfast. Always on Sundays, home-made cakes, cut into about three-inch squares at tea time.

I was chosen to play cricket as wicket keeper, playing against Uffculme and Marsh Hill. Different houses played sports against each other depending on the season, even at cross country races and once only boxing. On Sunday afternoons the school divided and we were taken on a walk by members of staff. A walk as far as the church in Bromsgrove was a possible target.

I believe the schools were beneficial to me in that I enjoyed a good living while I was young, which quite likely stood me in good stead later in life. I count myself fortunate and grateful that I was selected.

The classrooms with their sliding screens and sun blinds at Hunter's Hill, 1930s. (M.R. Harris)

Mr. H.C. Lowndes, 72, Hunter's Hill 1933-6, Birmingham.

I transferred from Uffculme to Hunter's Hill in 1933 and arrived on the second day the school opened at 12 years of age. It was like going on holiday being allocated your own bed in a long dormitory, three rows of beds. Mine was in the first row in front of the windows which I regretted in the winter. The lockers were in a room by the shower unit.

It was fabulous in the summer but different in the winter: waking up in the morning, frost and snow on the beds, washing and getting dressed in the cold and assembling in the large hall.

Meals: Breakfast—porridge, bread and jam and hot milk. Lunch: cooked dinner, semolina or prunes and ground rice. Tea, bread and butter, cheese or apple and milk. Rest period on the veranda in winter, outside in summer. Nature walks were included in the lessons. The school was divided into houses named after the surrounding hills, Clee, Clent, Malvern and Abberley. We all had badges representing the houses and points were awarded on a league system.

There were swimming lessons at Cropwood Girls' School and a few of us went swimming late at night although it was out of bounds. We had Boy Scout meetings in the Old Coaching House. The teachers I remember were Mr. Roberts, Mr. Rogers and Miss Buckley (Mr. Rogers played football for Doncaster Rovers before becoming a teacher). Mr. Roberts held German language classes in his study.

Sunday afternoon walks were a must and it was great fun exploring leafy lanes and woods and fishing for tadpoles and newts. There were days out to visit Bromsgrove Salt works and Blackwell Railway station to see the little bank engines pushing the large trains up the incline, also Blackwell's pumping station to see the great pumps feeding water to Blackwell and surrounding districts.

Like all young boys away from home it was a great experience and if I am honest I missed it when I left, and over the years I have often thought about my schooldays there. I went there with a chest problem and

I would like to think it did me good. But at least for some children in poor health from the back streets of Birmingham it was heaven undreamed of.

1934–6

The health of schoolchildren, especially malnourished ones, became increasingly more important to the government. School medical officers, however, were unable to agree on a system of defining, classifying and measuring nutrition for children. It was difficult to prove that inadequate diet affected the health of children.

A significant event in the history of the school medical service was the provision of subsidised milk to schools, supplied by the Milk Marketing Board, under the Milk in Schools Act 1934. Surplus milk was utilised and a third of a pint of milk was supplied at the cost of a halfpenny, instead of the usual penny (it was not until 1946 that the much needed milk was freely provided). Undernourished children greatly benefited from milk, especially as only a privileged few were eligible for free school meals, if deemed absolutely necessary by the School Medical Officer. Malnourished children in normal schools were lucky if they received more than monotonous soup, occasional stew, bread and jam and a mug of cocoa. Sometimes potato pie replaced the soup but few local authorities provided milk, eggs, green vegetables and fruit, as suggested by the School Medical Board in its 1934 study on the nutrition of schoolchildren. In open-air schools the diet was considerably better.

The government had also passed the Children and Young Persons Act 1933 which stated that no children under 12 years of age could be employed during school hours, nor could children be

Milk and dairy products were well advertised at this time as being nourishing and healthy foods for children.

employed more than two hours out of school hours. This was an important milestone as previously many children had missed schooling while earning much-needed wages for their families, to the detriment of their health, many becoming potential candidates for open-air schools.

A new syllabus on physical training was introduced by the Board of Education in 1933, in an attempt to improve the health and strength of schoolchildren. Birmingham Education Authority soon became known as an expert in this field.

The School Medical Service of local authorities continued to provide an increasing number of school clinics to dispense advice and treatment for all sorts of ailments, in the days before free medical services under the National Health Service. Consultants from the hospital service were employed by some clinics, especially for ear, nose and throat ailments. In open-air schools there was close contact with the school medical service and provision of a nurse on the premises, as well as regular visits by the school doctor.

In an effort to improve the health of children Holiday Camps were developed by local authorities, providing a fortnight's holiday of fresh air and good food to city children who were generally malnourished. Diet was carefully considered and the 1936 report of the School Medical Officer to the Board of Education recommended:

> ... ample quantity of plain wholesome food ... Tinned foods should be banned. Raw vegetables in the form of salads ... fresh fruit such as apples, oranges and bananas should appear in the menu two or three times a week. Roast joints are to be preferred to stews, on account of their higher dietetic value and because their consumption entails the proper use of cutlery, an exercise which is of valuable social training for children. ... The milk allowance should be at least one pint per child a day.

Typical menus for camp schools were given in the report; meals were planned to be filling and nutritious:

Breakfasts: Cocoa, porridge, bread, bacon; cocoa, porridge, bread and sausages.
Dinners: Boiled beef, carrots, potatoes, jam roll; boiled mutton, mixed vegetables, potatoes, currant roll & custard; shepherds pie, peas, potatoes, bread & butter pudding.
Teas: Tea, prunes & custard, bread & butter; tea, bread & butter, jam, fruit.
Suppers: Cocoa, buns; soup, bread; cocoa, bread & butter, cheese.

Birmingham held summer holiday camps for children from Special Schools using Martineau House, Towyn in Wales. The house and grounds had been purchased in 1931 through public subscription and a legacy of Councillor Miss Martineau who had been on Birmingham's Special Schools Sub Committee for many years. It was situated very near the beach, had an open-air shelter for teaching and rest periods and was run by a resident House Mother and Cook. Groups of children with two staff members from their school enjoyed many educational visits to such places as slate quarries, a printing works, a bakery, woollen factory, smithy and farm. Many nature walks formed part of the curriculum.

In 1934 Sir George Newman as the Chief Medical Officer of the Board of Education reported that there were 94 day and 52 residential open-air schools accommodating 14,705 children throughout the country. Further detailed recommendations on ideal open-air schools were itemised:

Clothing In some schools clothing is provided, and jerseys are found to be useful garments for the children. During the winter weather a satisfactory overcoat is essential. The provision of clogs lined with felt is very useful for those engaged in gardening, particularly in bad weather.

Diet The provision of satisfactory meals is most important in the administration of an open-air school. Many of the children suffer from the effects of dietetic deficiencies which have existed for a long time, and come from homes where the standard of living is low. It is advisable that the dietary be planned to supply the total daily requirements of animal protein, fat, minerals and vitamins, for it cannot be assumed that a sufficiency of these will be obtained at home. At least one pint of milk per child should be allowed per day, in addition to an adequate supply of meat or fish. Fruit should be given three times a week and may consist of apples, oranges, tomatoes or fresh salad. In addition, one ounce daily of butter or of vitaminised margarine should be included. In many schools a small regular dose of cod liver oil is included.

Sun-Bathing It is important to acclimatise the children by a process of gradual undressing. It should be realised, of course, that certain children react unfavourably to sunbathing. The clothing during suntreatment worn by the girls consists of a slipgarment and short knickerbockers. Sun hats should be worn, if necessary, and it may also be necessary to provide dark glasses or eye-shades. Whilst children are exposed to the sun or to bright light, written work should be done on grey pastel paper, as by this means the glare of white paper is avoided.

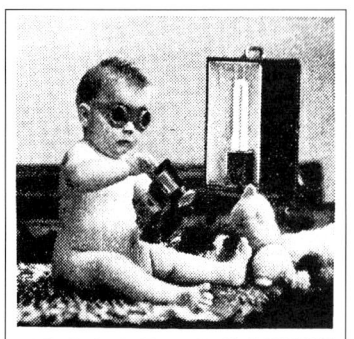

ULTRA-VIOLET RAY TREATMENT IN A COMPACT & PORTABLE UNIT

It is the ultra-violet rays in sunshine that produce the tanned healthy skin. The Vi-Tan Home Unit is a compact self-contained portable unit of robust construction completely enclosed and protected by a neat oak cabinet with cupboard for flex and goggles.
The lamp of fused quartz gives 99% of its radiation in the Ultra-Violet region. It starts on the switch—and no special wiring is required. It can be plugged into any lamp socket or radiator connection and will run for 20 hours on one unit of electricity.

For alternating current only.
Price £12.0.0 *or easy terms.*

VI-TAN
ULTRA-VIOLET HOME UNIT

Ask your usual supplier or write to
The Thermal Syndicate, Ltd., Wallsend-on-Tyne.
Makers of Ultra-Violet Lamps to the Trade for over 25 years.
London Depot: Thermal House, 12-14, Old Pye Street, Westminster, S.W.1.

The Teaching of Personal Hygiene The open-air school affords ample opportunities for the teaching of good habits ... each child, if medically fit, should have a shower at least once a week. It is essential that each child should be provided with a tooth brush or should bring his own from home, a daily tooth brush drill being arranged at a convenient time. Each child should wash his hands before each meal.

When the child comes to the school he should be given a number, and this number should be printed on brush, comb, bag, tooth brush and hand towel, which should hang from a peg also bearing the same number.

Over 13,000 children in the city schools were verminous according to a report by Birmingham's School Medical Officer in 1935. Seventy Birmingham parents were prosecuted for allowing their children to get into a verminous condition. Other ailments were ringworm, which was decreasing, together with scabies. Diphtheria had caused the deaths of 84 children as many had still not been immunised. Acute rheumatic conditions caused heart disease and 198 children suffering from tuberculosis were treated at Yardley Green Sanatorium. Ultra-violet radiation treatment during the winter had proved especially beneficial for children suffering from debility, bronchitis and catarrh. There were long waiting lists for the open-air schools, and at least 30 per cent of cases were victims of bad environment, poverty and malnutrition.

Two children of the 1920s and 1930s suffering from rheumatic heart disease and tuberculosis recall their early lives with all their difficulties:

Mrs. Edna Capper (née **Powell**), 68, Birmingham

I was at Baskerville School when I was seven or eight from 1934 to 36. Rheumatic fever had turned to pneumonia and diphtheria and it left me with a weak heart. I was one of four children in a family and one of my sisters went to Uffculme Open-Air School.

At home we lived in the centre of Birmingham but Baskerville was in the countryside in the Thirties. It was a very large old house along Court Oak Road. I shared a dormitory with several other girls. We had lessons only in the mornings and then rest period after lunch. After that was playtime but not running about: we used to play games sitting down like Ludo or Snakes and Ladders.

My parents could only visit once a month and they had to pay for me to go to there. I eventually left Baskerville to return to a normal school. Later on, when I got married and had my first child, I had to have my heart tested at the General Hospital. It was alright!

Mrs. Florence Willis had poor schooling due to ill health and family tragedies. At her first infants' school she suffered from nervous complaints and then the family suffered the trauma of tuberculosis:

Mrs. Florence Willis (née **Guest**), 73, Uffculme 1932-6, Birmingham

As a family we lived at Penn Street, in the city centre. We were eight children living with my parents in a small house with just one bedroom and an attic room. My four brothers slept in the attic and four girls including me slept in one bed in my parents room, with just a curtain across. I don't remember my Dad ever working. We had no water in the house, just a tap in the yard. The only toilet was a communal one in the yard. We never got much food to eat.

My first infants school was near home but I was frequently away as I suffered with my nerves badly and had migraine. Stress at school was caused by my problems in doing any writing. The teacher used to have me at the back of the class. They didn't bother with me, so I got worse. I could understand the teacher and do sums but was unable to write, and was under the Children's Hospital because of my problems.

Then the family got TB when I was six. My Dad (36 years) and baby sister (18 months old) both died within two weeks of each other. My Dad had refused to go to a sanatorium for treatment and probably was spitting germs out in billions which we all breathed in. For about a week after they died we had a coffin upstairs for my Dad in the room where we slept near my Mum and a tiny coffin downstairs for my baby sister. No-one took them away even though they had died of TB while my mother tried to get money from charities to bury them. I will never forget that terrible time.

All the family had to have tests for TB and X-rays. I was the only one found with actual TB so I went into Yardley Sanatorium (now East Birmingham Hospital) for six months. The others were released after one month's observation, but the disease must have lain dormant as my elder sister who went to Cropwood died seven years later at the age of 16 and my younger brother and sister died sixteen years later, again from TB. My elder sister was sent to Davos in Switzerland for three months, by the Cadburys, but the TB had gone too far.

At Yardley Sanatorium we were in beds out on verandas in the open-air all day—even if there was snow. I had to have injections in each arm, ten a week up each arm, all at once—needles all up the arm. 'Polly Perkins' they called them. It didn't really hurt but I used to hide under the bed clothes when they came to do it. There was a class there which I attended the last six weeks. But I used to get headaches and suffer vomiting again. I was discharged to remain under supervision of the Children's Hospital for nerves and the Chest Unit at Great Charles Street for TB checks.

Back home again I caught diphtheria from my sister and spent six weeks at Little Bromwich Fever Hospital. I went to another elementary school but couldn't do written work. I had worries with PT: I didn't have navy knickers. They tried to get me to do it in what I had—they were full of holes! My teacher tried to help me and got a clothing voucher to take to the local Daily Mail newspaper. I got from them boots, socks, navy knickers and skirt. Everyone knew you were dressed in 'Daily Mail clothes' and you were taunted. Even though a lot wore them in the street I was too sensitive to cope with it. I missed so much schooling as I felt sick and hid at home. Eventually the Children's Hospital sent me to Uffculme Open-Air School in 1932, where I stayed for four years.

My mother had re-married and my stepfather was working so I went to Uffculme daily at a weekly charge of one shilling. Sometimes I didn't go to school if Mum hadn't got the money. When you got there you changed into their uniform which was provided free: navy blue sweater and skirt. We went barefoot in the playing fields in the summer and made yellow summer dresses and knickers to match on sewing machines at school. I thought the sundresses were wonderful!

Miss Hibbert the Headmistress was very good to me. She gave me some dresses to take home for my sisters and she got some other clothes for me, including a bathing costume so I could go swimming. The clothes came from parents who brought in their children's outgrown clothes to the school. Miss Hibbert was very strict but very fair and helped me a lot.

I remember meals at Uffculme: we had egg and bacon and toast at breakfast—more than I'd ever seen before. We also had cocoa and Horlicks which I had never seen in my life. We had good dinners too. I loved the puddings as we never had them at home ... chocolate pudding and jam roly poly with custard. We also had an orange or an apple each day.

Uffculme School helped me as I didn't have to be in the classroom all the time. I could use the rest room when I couldn't cope with written work. I had good treatment there. I overcame my nervous problems, gained confidence and loved the food and clothes. But I never really learned anything. I got healthier and they gave me simpler work for confidence, as opposed to pushing me.

I left at the age of 14 and my mother found me a job in a factory—making wire baskets for fish fryers. At the time I wasn't capable of doing anything else although I can do mental arithmetic and later became chief cashier on the till at a post office.

I stayed at home until I was 17, and then went into the Forces in 1940, in the Auxiliary Territorial Service. I married and had seven children—four went to grammar schools. Doctors tell me that my problems now are probably due to the malnutrition I suffered as a child.

Birmingham's School Medical Officer reported in 1936 that the most useful function of open-air schools was to treat chronic chest conditions:

> It is only the advanced cases of fibrosis or bronchiectasis which are not discharged 'cured'. The cases of asthma are of special interest. It is, of course, a well known fact that many of these children cease to have attacks when removed from home, except in more severe cases, whatever the reason may be. The real test is therefore whether they continue to have attacks at home. It would seem that it takes at least two years to achieve this degree of improvement in moderately severe cases, and longer in the more severe.

Headmistress Miss Ella Hibbert and some of her pupils, 1930s. (Uffculme School)

It was also mentioned that there was an increasing number of 'nervous children' at the day schools:

> While the term may be vague and unscientific it nevertheless has a fairly definite meaning to parents, teachers, and even doctors. It implies mainly timidity, anxiety, fears, lack of confidence on the one hand, and nervous symptoms such as excitability, restlessness, twitching, disturbed sleep etc. on the other. These children are also often backward, or perhaps worried about lessons, as they have probably missed a good deal of school time through illnesses.
>
> It is obvious that both physical and psychological factors play a part in almost every case, and interact upon each other; it is not a case of there being one particular 'cause' for a complex condition.
>
> Some of these cases are sufficiently neurotic or complicated for them to have come through the Child Guidance Clinic, or to be referred there if necessary, and there is, and should be, a close interchange between Open-Air Schools and Clinic.

Uffculme 1934-36

An investigation into the homes of children attending Uffculme was carried out in 1934 by the Headmistress, Miss Hibbert. It was found that 50 per cent of children were chest cases, and many were from homes in back-to-back houses.

In 1935 40 children from poor overcrowded homes slept at Uffculme school during the week in the months May to September. A playleader organised activities in the evenings and two attendants slept with the children in the open-sided rest-shed. Such was the success of the scheme that all improved greatly in health and vitality.

There are few school log book entries of any interest for this period but ex-pupils reveal many facets of school life:

A leaving certificate for a pupil who attended Uffculme for several years, signed by Miss Hibbert, the Headmistress. (N. Whittall)

Mrs. Norah Whittall (née **Adams**), Uffculme 1927-35, Birmingham

I started at Uffculme School when I was seven years of age. I never attended any other school and stayed at Uffculme until I was 16. I enjoyed every minute of my school days. The reason for my being at the school was because I suffered from a complaint called Lupus Vulgaris, a skin disorder and I had to attend hospital three times a week. The nurses at school were Miss Edwards and Miss Bendall.

We had showers two or three days a week. All the girls had to wear summer dresses and pants that we made ourselves.

We had a very nice choir and we used to sing at the Town Hall and some times at Cadburys. We also played netball, sometimes against Cadburys' girls. When we sat by the pool I was very interested in watching the wild life and I saw a kingfisher a few times.

Mrs. Irene Radnall (née **Docker**), Uffculme 1933-6, Birmingham

I went to Uffculme Open-Air School for almost three years as I was underweight and undernourished. Those three years were very happy and I gained two stone in weight. The food was very good. The school sent a note to ask my parents for some money for my meals but they couldn't afford it as my father was out of work for six years.

I remember sitting outside the classroom in the sun to do our lessons wearing a sun hat. In the summer I used to sleep there at night on a stretcher in the big shed. The elderly Night Nurse used to sit with us until we had all dropped off to sleep. Early evening we would play rounders in a big field, there were two swings—one for boys, one for girls.

It was wonderful to get away from the streets and factories.

Mrs. Joyce Pegg (née **Trueman**), 71, Uffculme 1934, Birmingham

I was sent to Uffculme when 11 years old as an experiment, suffering from severe rheumatics—the normal practice being to stay in warm rooms etc. I am more than glad that the doctor concerned did so, for not only was my time there happy but very beneficial.

So many happy memories come flooding back, the visits from the Cadburys who always came bearing gifts, the rest periods, diets and ladling out of medicine by Nurse, and a slap on the spot that you had allowed to become red through sunburn and not wearing your hat—how right she was in view of the present ideas.

Miss Gough taught me the art of embroidery which has been and still is one of the joys of life. I am a busy person and county secretary to the Trefoil Guild, Birmingham. Miss Hibbert, such a wonderful Headmistress, and a member of the Guide Movement, is responsible for the joy I get from this movement.

THE 1930s: TESTAMENT OF HEALTH

Lessons out of doors in the heat of summer at Uffculme, 1930s. (Uffculme School)

Mrs. Florence Gladwin (née **Parker**), Uffculme 1933-7, Birmingham

I was 10 years old. The girls looked after the flower gardens, and some of the flowers were used for the tables in the dining room. I was a monitor and at the end of the week I was allowed to take the flowers home.

Any toast left on the staff table I took down to the duck pond and fed the baby ducks; also the birds in the bird garden

The apple trees and swings were below the classrooms, on the slope. We went down steps through the swings to get to the big field, after tea for one hour, before going home.

The girls in the summer changed into blue linen dresses, underwear to match. We sun-bathed by the flower beds, where we could see the wounded soldiers in the grounds of 'Chamberlain's House' [Highbury Hall].

Christmas time was very good; we made all the trimmings for the dining room. The lanterns were lovely and we had a very good time.

Mr. Robert W. Jukes, Uffculme 1935-7, Blackpool, Lancashire

I attended Uffculme after a period of ill-health when I was 11 years of age.

The school had many activities both indoor and outdoor. Outdoors we did nature study locally, and Morris dancing. We wore clogs and kept our own gardening tools clean.

Our day started at Uffculme with breakfast on arrival—prunes, figs and ground rice were typical. Lessons followed, then dinner about midday. The menu consisted of boiled fish (hated), cheese pie (liked), with vegetables followed by a pudding. More lessons, then our rest period of an hour. After further tuition, tea took place at about 4.00pm—bread and butter and jam with perhaps some cake and tea. Then it was hometime.

The benefits of fresh air, good food and as much outdoor activity as possible helped my health enormously.

Mrs. Gwendoline Joyce Hooper (née **Colin**), 69, Uffculme 1936, Burford, Oxfordshire

On 25 August 1936, I became a pupil at Uffculme. My admission number was 2,589 on the school register and I was 11 years of age. Before this I attended Tindal Street School, but it was recommended that I should be transferred to Uffculme Open-Air School due to continual ill health. Of course the first day at my new school was filled with fear and anxiety for my future. However, it soon became obvious that this was to be a very friendly and happy place. We were treated with great kindness and understanding by the Headmistress and Staff.

On arrival at school (by tram) at 8.30am we were given breakfast. On Mondays this was bread and milk which I hated and any child who refused it had to stay in place until they did eat it. It took me until lunch time to gather the courage to eat this, as I realised at that time there was no way out. As I dreaded this awful bread and milk I came up with a plan and from then on took a clean handkerchief to wrap up the bread from the milk, I was also able to stuff some down the gratings under the pipes, this was my Monday morning ritual!

Grace was always sung before and after meals. At midday we had dinners which were very good; a typical menu would be cottage pie or cheese pie with two vegetables, followed by a pudding. There was only one pudding which I dreaded, resembling frog spawn (like a yellow jelly with black spots). It was usually given once a year which all the children agreed was once too many! Teas, served just before leaving school at 4.30pm, consisted of two slices of brown bread, one slice of white then perhaps water cress, egg, tomato or an apple and with a cup of milky cocoa or tea.

After breakfast we went to our various classrooms for lessons of the day. This usually started with Arithmetic followed by Geography, English or History with an occasional half hour's PT. About two afternoons per week consisted of sewing for girls and gardening for boys. One afternoon a week Miss Gough took a party to Kings Heath swimming baths. Twice a week we had showers at the school supervised by Nurse Edwards.

Outdoor games of netball and rounders were twice a week for girls. In the winter we played indoor hockey and when the pond was frozen the teachers allowed us to skate and slide on the pond.

I can recall a memorable visit to Birmingham Central Hall for the School Choirs Festival. It was here that I saw George Bernard Shaw. When it came to our school's turn to sing, George Bernard Shaw leapt to his feet shouting 'Stop!' With arm upraised he proceeded to instruct our teacher so that we could continue to his satisfaction.

Each Christmas, we had a lovely Christmas party when each child was given a present. After school, a tuck shop was open in the school to use if you had pocket money to spend. Then pupils would assemble in destination groups ready to board trams or buses home.

I look back on my days at Uffculme School as being some of the happiest in my childhood, where I gained so much in health and education.

Children using weaving looms outside a classroom, 1930s. (Uffculme School)

THE BRITISH MEDICAL ASSOCIATION officially recommends larger quantities of

BREAD AND FLOUR

than of any other foods in the family diet

IN its recently-published brochure—FAMILY MEALS AND CATERING—the B.M.A. states that the average family of father, mother, and three children should eat at least from 24 to 28 lb. of BREAD a week with about 5 lb. of other flour-made foods in addition.

Never forget that

BREAD

AND OTHER FLOUR FOODS are the supreme source of ENERGY

Cropwood 1934-6

Many girls had such a poor state of health when first going to Cropwood Open-Air School that the average length of stay was 18 months, reported Birmingham's School Medical Officer in 1934. A large proportion were described as cases of 'debility', a term used to describe a state of poor health in respect of nutrition, posture, energy, appetite and blood condition. Debility was often linked with other conditions, such as rheumatism, anaemia, neurosis, glands and respiratory illnesses. There were 63 girls at Cropwood that year, suffering from the following conditions:

Debility	38
Fibrosis and Bronchiectasis	9
Asthma	6
Bronchitis	6
Bronchitis and TB history	4

Miss Margaret Grant, the Headmistress, recorded life at Cropwood in this period in the log books. The residential nurse was Sister Daniels and other staff mentioned were Nurse Keen, Miss Hardy, Miss Owen, Miss Atkinson, Miss Baldock, Miss Bottom, Miss Arnot, Miss Jay. Some of the entries are related below:

Cropwood log book 1934

21 Jan.   *Pearl & Theresa B. ran away this afternoon. Their father rang up about 8pm to say they had arrived home.*

21 April   *Two new girls ran away this afternoon but were found at Bromsgrove.*

2 July   *Ellen P. taken away by her mother as she had written home saying she was homesick.*

5 Sep.   *Miss Somerwell (gymnastics) came this morning for the first time.*

Cropwood log book 1935

6 May   *Jubilee Day. The whole school went to Malvern for the day.*

9 May   *Three girls ran away last Friday. They were brought back yesterday afternoon and one ran away again during the night.*

Memories of Cropwood 1934-36 are related by several ex-pupils.

Mrs. Rhoda L. Jones (née **Collett**), 69, Cropwood 1933-9, Birmingham

I started at the school at the age of seven after spending two years at the Kunzle home in Davos, Switzerland. My first Headmistress was Miss Grant and later Miss Boothroyd.

A treat would be 'Tuck Day' when we would stand in line outside a big cupboard on the first floor and the boxes of Tuck were brought out. We were able to choose a small amount. As we grew older some of the girls were allowed to go down Hunter's Hill to a cottage-cum-shop which was a great treat.

I left the school at the outbreak of war in 1939 as the school closed. I was then 13 years old, which meant that most of my childhood was spent away from home. At holiday times I remember the great excitement when the train was approaching Birmingham with the girls singing and shouting 'Jolly Good Luck To The Driver' was our usual chorus.

Asthma is still troubling the family. But after all the trials and tribulations of life I still look back at my stay at Cropwood with fond memories of some very happy times.

Schoolgirls on Cropwood's main drive, 1936. (R. Jones)

Mrs. Kathleen Birch (née Booke), Cropwood 1933-5, Birmingham

I spent two happy years at Cropwood from 1933, when I was 12 years old. I was a sickly child who suffered bronchitis and was alwyas having coughs and colds.

The classrooms were situated on a hillside, and three walls were open to the elements. Very often we sat in our overcoats with snow showers blowing in on us. Only very occasionally were the sliding shutters closed.

There was an open-air swimming pool—and no-one wore a swimming costume as it was girls only. It was here I learnt to swim.

Every Saturday morning we assembled in the hall and were each given a duty to do; it could be polishing the lovely wood panelled walls, cleaning light shades, dusting and cleaning staff rooms, cleaning boots, but best of all was the job of cleaning out the games cupboard.

The older girls (about 20 of them) had to sleep out at Rosemary Cottage which was a large house at the end of the lane. We walked in crocodile with one girl carrying a hurricane lamp at the front and another with one at the rear.

We were very well fed but to start the day we all had to line up for a large spoonful of cod liver oil from nurse.

We all had woollen vests, liberty bodices with elastic suspenders to keep up our ribbed wool brown stockings, a jumper, brown gymslip, and lace up brown boots to the knee. In summer we had check dresses, all made by a sewing maid who worked and lived in an attic.

I have always remembered my stay at Cropwood with great affection and I was much healthier when I left.

Mrs. Dorothy Sparks (née Checkley), 70, Cropwood 1936, Cannock, Staffordshire

I remember going on a trip to the Malvern Hills on the Queen Mother's Coronation because we all had a long tin box in silver and blue containing a bar of chocolate from Cadburys.

At breakfast at our table a girl always had a tub of cream. She was very thin and sometimes she would pass it to one of us girls to scrape our finger round. My parents weren't very wealthy but every time I had a

Some of the younger pupils at Cropwood, 1935/6. (R. Jones)

letter, inside were two cigarette cards stuck together with half a crown inside. This was taken to the Headmistress towards tuck money.

In the open-air swimming pool I learnt to swim. The Headmistress promised any girl five shillings to swim the length. I was one of those girls, although there were frogs and leaves in the pool with us.

I shall never forget those days.

Mrs. Alice Higgins (née **Webb**), 70, Cropwood 1930s, Solihull, West Midlands

I was seven years old and slept in the house in a four-bedded room overlooking the hill-side.

My teacher was Miss Alice Bottom from Hall Green, Birmingham; she was a lovely teacher, very artistic. We made lavender bags and then filled them with lavender from the gardens; covered small wooden boxes with egg shells from the kitchen then painted them; collected lambs wool from the fences on our many walks, washed it, dyed it from plants, spun it and then knitted it into small garments.

I have memories of PT every weekday morning in the open-air.

I recall being invited to sit on the lap of Mrs. Cadbury at a pre-Christmas concert, perhaps she liked the poem I recited. Being taught to swim in the open-air pool was good but the water was always cold. Bonfire night was good—a huge bonfire in the meadow, home-made parkin and treacle toffee, a great treat.

Other memories of Cropwood: to be neat and tidy, love of the country, wild flowers, birds, trees and a warm bed at night. My parents often said that the period spent at Cropwood was the making of me healthwise.

Hunter's Hill 1934-6

Birmingham's School Medical Officer recorded in 1934 that more boys suffered from debility than chest problems. In his annual report he made the following observations:

Some cases develop bronchitis, asthma or pneumonia in spite of good environment and adequate nutrition, and the greater number of cases from good homes will be found in this category. It is difficult, therefore, to estimate the value of the different factors which together reduce boys to a condition which renders them suitable subjects for open-air school treatment. A consideration of average weights and heights on admission ... indicate that the majority of cases are considerably below average in these respects and it seems probable that the chief factors have been malnutrition and bad environment.

Miss Walton, the Headmistress, continued to record in the log book daily life at Hunter's Hill from 1934 to '36. Sister Daniels was frequently mentioned and had been appointed when the school first opened. She was the sister of her counterpart at Cropwood. Other staff mentioned were Mr. Roberts, Mr. Rogers, Miss Tearse, Nurse G. Kemp, Miss Frisby, Mr. Parker, Miss Pratt, and Mr. French.

Hunter's Hill log book 1934

8 Jan.   *The school re-opened today. All the staff are present and 105 boys came on the 1.10 train.*

20 Jan.   *No. on roll 116. The children are going to see 'Black Beauty' at the Bromsgrove cinema, partly paid for by the* Birmingham Mail *Christmas contribution of 15/6.* [15s. 6d.]

20 Feb.   *Twenty of the top class boys visited the Longbridge Laundry today. They were taken round the laundry and shown all the processes.*

28 Feb.   *Four boys went to Handsworth Clinic this afternoon to have tonsils removed.*

2 Mar.   *Walter B. to hospital to have his head x-rayed. He is suffering with ringworm in the head.*

10 Mar.   *Parcel of lino-cutting tools and knives delivered.*

27 April   *Visit of Mrs. B. Cadbury and Counc. Loxley.*

14 May   *Miss Buckley has started work today.* [She was eventually to become the Headmistress, until her retirement in 1969.]

27 July   *The meeting of the Education Committee was held at this school today. Members had tea and stayed to see the play 'Hiawatha' and a drill display.*

8 Sep.   *Twelve boys went to camp at the Scouts Camp at Barnes Hill today.*

29 Nov.   *On the occasion of The Royal Wedding* [Duke of Gloucester] *the boys had a holiday today. In the morning they played games. In the afternoon some of the smaller boys went to Cropwood, and the bigger Cropwood girls came here to play.*
   All the Cropwood girls came here for tea so that we had 200 children in our dining room. After tea Mr. Rogers showed them some lantern slides of Devon.

Hunter's Hill log book 1935

12 Jan.   *The children had cakes and jelly for tea with the money from The* Birmingham Mail *Christmas Fund. Afterwards they had a concert.*

1 June   *Visit of Birmingham Women Medical Officers.*

8 July   *Visit of Mrs. Cadbury and Alderman Quinney.*

3 Sep.   *Lawrence T.—a new boy admitted a week ago—went off home at 4 o'clock this morning. He has*

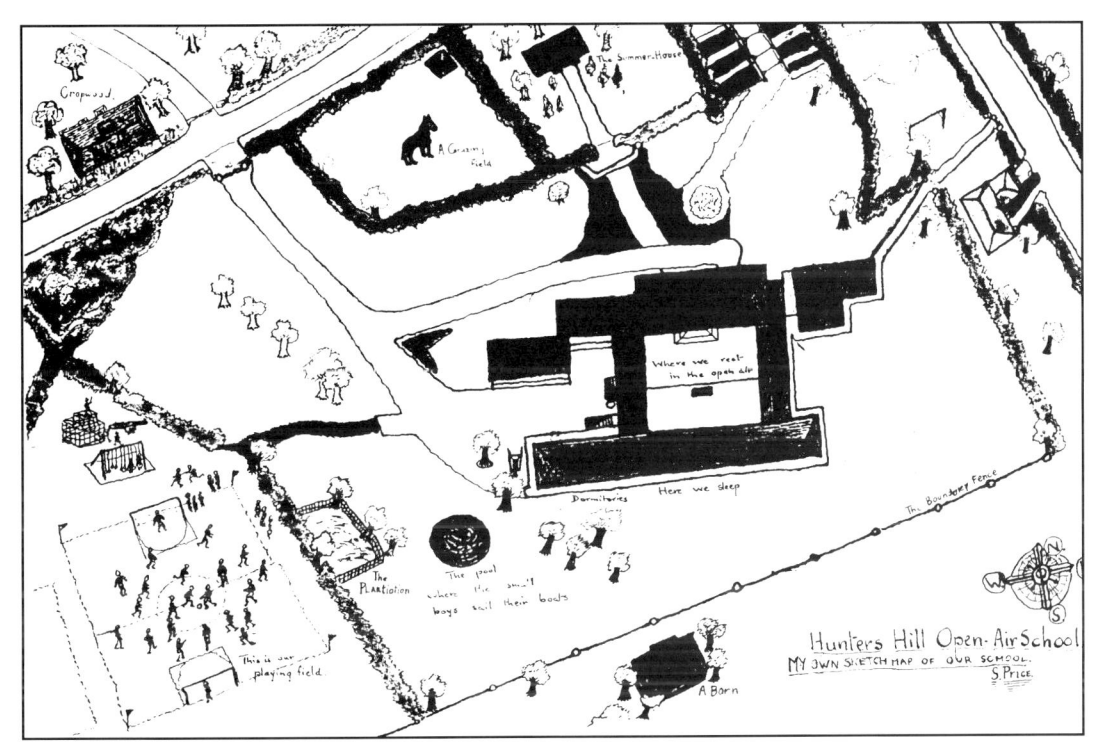

This detailed plan of Hunter's Hill Open-Air School was drawn by S. Price, a pupil in the 1930s. He noted: 'the pool where small boys sail their boats; dormitories where we sleep; where we rest in the open air; our playing field and the summerhouse'. (J. Marshman)

attended the C.G.C. [Child Guidance Clinic] and is reputed to have 'brain storms'. The boy was quite happy during the day if he were kept occupied—but this is the third time he has run away in the middle of the night.

16 Oct.   Two boys have gone to the clinic for ear treatment.

Hunter's Hill log book 1936

18 Jan.   This week the weather has been very trying—frost, extreme cold and snow. On the whole the boys have withstood it splendidly. They have been tobogganing morning and afternoon for a short period every day.

28 Jan.   As this is the day of the funeral of King George V we are not holding any school sessions today. The boys went quietly for a walk in classes. After dinner they listened to the Service at Windsor—on the wireless. Then later in the afternoon they played games quietly in the school grounds.

9 Feb.   Wm A. was taken to Little Bromwich Hospital with diphtheria.

25 Mar.   Team went to Marsh Hill to play football.

2 May   Since our return at Easter the boys have spent a good deal of time in the garden. The weather before the holidays was so cold and wintry that we did not sow any seeds. Since we came back after the first three days the weather has been ideal for gardening. So some part of every day has been spent in the garden.

17 June   The boys went for a picnic to Dodderhill Common this afternoon—the money for fares being provided out of £2 given by a parent.

8 July   This afternoon 21 boys had dental treatment with gas.

11 July After a very wet week it poured all morning so I decided to let the 60 bigger boys go to the Pictures at Bromsgrove for a change.

24 July Presentation of Cup by Mrs. Cadbury.

29 Aug. One boy, Richard D., had haemorrhage Aug. 28th—was isolated and went to Birmingham to be examined by Dr. Dixon—who after examination sent him by ambulance to Yardley Sanatorium.

23 Sep. The top class boys went to Liverpool for the day with Mr. Hughes and Mr. Friend for a visit to the docks in connection with their project on 'Shipping'.

8 Oct.   J.B. who has been isolated for three weeks with chickenpox discharged from isolation today by Dr. Burns.

13 Nov. Miss Walton went to Nottingham for the day to a conference on 'Social Hygiene'.

15 Dec. Children's Christmas Party. Mrs. Cadbury came.

Some reminiscences of life at Hunter's Hill as a housemaid at the school follow, together with two ex-pupils' memories of their schooldays:

Mrs. Nellie Crawford (née **Richardson**), 80, Housemaid at Hunter's Hill 1933-6, Bromsgrove, Worcestershire

I worked there as a housemaid from the age of 17 years; other domestic staff were Mrs. Beth Ross, Margaret Prestage; Elsie Hughes came in everyday to polish the dormitory floors; all the sewing was done by Evelyn Hughes the seamstress, her sister Hetty was Dormitory Maid.

The boys attending the school were full of pranks—one of them put cockroaches in our beds! I remember Billy especially, he was given the princely sum of 6d to be good for one week. After a short time he gave the money back to Miss Walton the Headmistress as he didn't think it was worth it to be a good boy!

They were happy times. After six years of working at the school I left to marry. I can still remember the boys; all for the sum of £3 per month and 7/6 [7s. 6d.] per week, less deductions.

Mr. John Hood, 70, Hunter's Hill 1934-6, Bromsgrove, Worcestershire

As a child I suffered from bronchial asthma and was first sent to Marsh Hill Open-Air School. I was transferred to Hunter's Hill Open-Air School just after it was first opened.

Coming from the built-up area of Aston in Birmingham, I remember how I enjoyed being in the lovely countryside surrounding the school. I enjoyed everything about the school—the meals, the class-rooms, the dormitory and the playing fields. I did have one big problem though; I was very homesick! I used to lie in my bed at night and listen to Big Bertha pushing the trains up the Lickey Incline and thinking how much I would like to be on that train going home! The dormitory windows were never closed; if the rain was blowing in we simply moved our beds back.

In the warm weather at night some of us naughtier lads would put a pillow under our beddothes and, taking our torches with us, would go to the playing field where we had built small dens in the hedge with twigs and grass and thought it a great adventure to stay there for a while before creeping back to our beds! We used to stay in the school playing field at evening time until a whistle summoned us to shower and supper before going to bed.

One day, myself and three other lads decided to do a 'bunk' (i.e. run away from school). Why I agreed to join in this escapade I still don't know today! One night we all scampered down the hill, through the hedge and on to the road and off we went.

We had got as far as Selly Oak, Birmingham, when a policeman on a bicycle stopped us and enquired if we were pupils of Hunter's Hill Open-Air School. We were all dressed in the same school clothing which consisted of khaki shorts, Aertex shirts and pumps. I was the first to answer 'Yes, we are', and was quite relieved because by then I had got no intention of going to my home. My mother would have been very angry and I couldn't face that! We were collected from the police station by a teacher with a car and taken back to school. Of course, the police had been informed of our 'escape' and had visited each of our homes. My mother stopped sending my comics and sweets for a month afterwards as punishment. Miss Walton questioned us as to why we had run away. Probably none of us gave very satisfactory reasons. Anyway, she kept us isolated from the other pupils for a week.

I remember one time in the summer we were told to walk about our own school grounds in the nude. I don't think that was very popular; we didn't know what to do with our hands! The idea was soon dropped.

Well, I think that all that fresh air and good food must have done the trick because the asthma left me! Before reaching the school leaving age of 14 years I was moved back to Marsh Hill where I stayed until I left in 1937. I didn't have any educational qualifications when I left, but I am grateful to remember that I could at least read and write! I am now in my 70th year and, who knows, my good health could be largely due to the good start which I received at Marsh Hill and Hunter's Hill.

Mr. Harry Brant, Hunter's Hill 1936-8, Sutton Coldfield, West Midlands.

I came home from school one day and my mother asked me if I would like to go on a holiday to a place like a farm, where there would be animals, and also other boys to play with. Well, to a lonely little boy of eight its appeal was great.

Came the day of departure my mother took me to town and then to New Street Station and on a huge steam train, to Blackwell. It was very exciting. We then walked up a lane and through a whicker gate. It was at this point that I noticed there were lots of other Mums, all holding boys by the hand, going through this same whicker gate. It was very puzzling.

We assembled eventually in what we came to know as the linen room. I think we were being measured for our uniforms, when suddenly our mothers were seen passing the windows and disappearing back down the path. Pandemonium broke out all around—tears, panic, screaming children, all trying to get out of the room to go with their Mums.

However, the business of getting kitted out for our uniforms got under way. Because I was very small for my age, I was given combinations instead of pyjamas and flannel bib and brace trousers instead of the corduroy trousers, with proper braces. It blighted my life for weeks.

I remember having prunes and bread-dripping for breakfast, but I hated the luke-warm milk with the skin on top. I was never very good with food, and always had to be coaxed to eat. I remember having cod liver oil from Miss Walton and having to say my number (24) after I had swallowed. The food must have been nourishing, as I have had no serious illnesses in my life. Although I'm still only 5ft 3ins on tip toes.

After breakfast, if the weather was good, we went on nature rambles, or to the brickworks and the waterworks. A trip over to Cropwood pool to learn to swim was a time of complete horror. A rope was put round your waist and you were dangled in a dark green slimy pool. It left me with a mental block to swimming and I was 60 years old before I learnt to swim.

Summer and the company of other boys brought consolations, like digging for pignuts and making dens. Games were invented daily, as apart from a few swings we had only comics or small toys brought by visitors once a month.

I have very fond memories of my time at Blackwell: of Miss Walton, who had a house built in the grounds (I remember we were allowed to help and I personally sandpapered the banisters!); of Miss Buckley, she of the black stockings and gymslip (who had a very sharp hand); of Nurse and Sister who saw me safely through chicken pox; and of a young girl in the kitchens who had red hair and freckles (she used to give me extra sugar or puddings). Not forgetting Helen, who was every lonely boy's second Mum. I also remember I was presented with a mug and a bar of chocolate in a flat tin box by a very small lady in a dark fur coat. I believe she was Dame Cadbury and the occasion was the Coronation.

The interruption to serious studies put me way behind when I returned to the new senior school at home. I left school at 14 and became a page boy at the Midland Hotel in Birmingham but after a spell doing war work in a factory I entered the RAF at 18, passing A1, and became a fireman.

1937–9

An article in *The Times* on 9 August 1939 neatly summed up the continual need for improving the health of the nation's children: 'Schools have to do more than merely train the body and the mind—they have to eradicate the results of last century's hectic industrialisation'. Despite improvements and developments of the school medical service, many children continued to suffer from bad health and their poor living environments in city slum areas.

The Chief Medical Officer of the Board of Education had reported in 1937 that there was still a great need for a much larger number of open-air schools and that many local education authorities had failed to make provision for the children unable to attend normal schools on account of their ill health. At that time there were 155 open-air schools (101 day, 22 residential and 32 schools provided by voluntary associations). Selection of children for these schools was the responsibility of the school medical officer who received applications from doctors, hospitals, school nurses, teachers, attendance officers, health visitors and voluntary workers.

EAT SUNSHINE!
HARDING'S BREAD is now impregnated during manufacture with ULTRA-VIOLET (Artificial Sunlight) RAYS. These Rays increase the Vitamines in the Bread, thus greatly improving the Food Value. In fact, you are now eating Sunshine when you eat Harding's Irradiated Bread. *Get Harding's to-day.*
NO INCREASE IN PRICE.
E. HARDING,
Royal Steam Bakery, Yardley.

Many children improved dramatically at open-air schools, especially cases of bronchitis, malnutrition and anaemia. The fresh air and breathing exercises resulted in many cures for bronchitis. Good food, with plenty of milk, and exercises such as dancing, athletics and organised games remarkably improved the health and strength of ailing children.

Birmingham's School Medical Officer, reporting on Hunter's Hill and Cropwood schools in 1937, made the following remarks with regard to asthma:

> ...the cases of asthma sent to residential open-air schools are those with frequent attacks; secondly they are of long standing; and thirdly, they have practically all had some other form of treatment which has failed.
>
> The mere cessation of attacks while at open-air school is nothing surprising, since it is commonly found upon removal of the child from home, but the amount of success can only be measured by the results when the child returns to ordinary school or goes to work.

The average age on admission to Cropwood and Hunter's Hill was about ten and most children had received hospital treatment which had failed, after suffering asthma since early childhood. Many cases had drifted from doctor to doctor, with little communication between them—more co-operation and co-ordination in the treatment of asthma was recommended.

A careful follow-up procedure was regularly carried out on all ex-pupils, with encouraging results.

Over the years some sick children had been sent from Birmingham Children's Hospital to the British Children's Home in Switzerland for treatment. A new scheme to help Birmingham schoolboys suffering from chest diseases was evolved by the Birmingham chocolate manufacturer, Mr. Christian Kunzle, using his chateau in Davos. It was planned as a school rather than a hospital, said Mr. Kunzle to a reporter for the *Birmingham Mail*, 24 February 1937: 'We have been experimenting for some years, as you know, and this is the outcome. To fight tuberculosis it is imperative that we start as early as possible before the child becomes a hospital case. This is what we hope to do at Davos with this scheme, which will obviously allow the boy to continue his education as well as benefit from the dry climate of Switzerland for six months'. The school was run by Mr. F.Y. Witherby, a former Birmingham teacher. Many open-air school pupils were to benefit from Mr. Kunzle's generosity after the war.

The beginning of the Second World War in 1939 marked a period of confusion in education. With the onset of war the school medical service virtually ceased its routine medical work such as inspections and cleanliness surveys. Schools closed when children were evacuated and many staff were recruited for the services.

The mechanics of evacuating a possible 60,000 children from Birmingham was a tremendous feat of organisation, even though only 25,000 took advantage of the scheme. About 4,000 teachers and helpers accompanied children on trains during the evacuation on 31 August 1939, and the whole exercise was accomplished with exemplary behaviour by most of the children.

A few days later, however, there was an outcry from foster parents concerning the unclean state of many of the city's children, most of whom had not been examined prior to their departure as evacuation had taken place at the end of the school holidays. Another 700 children were evacuated from Birmingham between 25 and 27 October, but these were medically examined before being sent off to their new destinations.

Children in special schools were generally treated differently from others, as they were despatched with their teachers to communal billets in camps, hotels and large houses, rather than to ordinary households. Some residential open-air schools even became reception centres for other schoolchildren.

Many children at Uffculme and Marsh Hill Open-Air Day schools were later evacuated to other places in Worcestershire and Gloucestershire. Children from two Birmingham schools for the Physically Defective were evacuated to Cropwood or Hunter's Hill while their open-air school pupils (with the exception of a few very delicate children) were sent back home to be evacuated with children from adjacent elementary schools.

Uffculme 1937-9

Daily life at Uffculme school before the onset of war in 1939 is not revealed in any detail in the log books except that in September 1938 the school had an official visit from HM Inspectors Miss A. Marks and Dr. A. Gale. Their report shows that the school premises were by then considered rather old-fashioned and inadequate, with no large practical room for art and crafts. The large resting shed could not be used for any other purpose on account of its unsuitable floor and poor natural lighting, and some of the senior boys had to attempt woodwork on two extra benches in the dining hall. However, the report commented very favourably on other aspects of the school:

> The children benefit greatly by their life here: their stay averages about 16 months with a minimum of 12 months. Improvement can be seen not only in their increased physical vitality, but also in the transformation from lethargy and self-centredness to ready interest and happy participation in the numerous experiences provided for them.
>
> The Headmistress and her staff have viewed both curriculum and methods from a fresh angle. They have determined to introduce reality into the work, they have made good use of the rich environment and they have been skilful in integrating the various subjects through selected 'projects'. The purposeful character of the efforts required from them appeals strongly to the children who make appropriate progress owing to the individual attention and encouragement they receive.
>
> The teaching and nursing staffs are very ready to co-operate, and take a broad view of their duties. Although the classrooms, being the oldest of the open-air school buildings in Birmingham, are small as judged by modern standards, the resourcefulness of the staff overcomes to a great extent the attendant disadvantages. The general atmosphere of the school is one of happy activity, and is most favourable to the restoration of delicate children to full health and strength.

The Inspectors' General Report on Birmingham's four open-air schools in 1938 recorded that they were now supervised by the School Medical Officer, not as previously by the Special Schools Medical Officer. Interchange of medical records between Medical Officers was deemed essential when children were returned to ordinary schools:

> Very careful medical records of progress are kept in the Open Air Schools and it seems a pity that these full records or copies of them, instead of rather brief summaries, should not accompany the child on his return to the elementary school. The records show that generally speaking progress in these schools is very satisfactory and they constitute a most valuable body of information as to the effects of open air school treatment. The arrangements for admission and discharge of children and for transfer of children from day to residential schools work well and transfers are based on sound medical principles. The nurses attached to the schools are doing good work, and it is pleasing to find that the nursing and teaching staffs work together for the health of the children in perfect harmony.
>
> The diet at all the schools is adequate and appetising, and the provision of three meals per day in the day schools is a satisfactory feature.
>
> The Authority are to be congratulated on the provision which they have made for the care of delicate children. In all the schools there is an atmosphere of happy and healthy activity which is most favourable for the restoration of delicate children to health. Some of the physical training seen would have been creditable for normal children and it did not seem to be overtaxing the strength of these delicate children.
>
> The Head Teachers display a sound conception of the peculiar needs of the children and, in each school, there is evidence of constant care being given to the varied aspects of Open-Air School life. The importance of maintaining a reasonable standard in fundamental work is fully recognised and the wider opportunity for different kinds of activity is thoroughly grasped, with the result that the children enjoy a balanced curriculum carried out in a delightful environment. It is gratifying to find so much thought being

THE 1930s: TESTAMENT OF HEALTH

Children making hay in the sunshine in Uffculme's school field, 1930s. (Uffculme School)

given to the general layout of the surroundings of the schools, for, the more attractive the environment, the more inclined will the children be to spend their time in the open air.

The regular succession of rest and exercise, work and play, coupled with wholesome meals and cultivation of a cleanly open-air habit of life is of immense benefit to the delicate child and in these directions, under the care of enthusiastic teachers, the schools are fulfilling their function extremely well.

Two ex-pupils recall their life at Uffculme in this period:

Mr. John Horton, Uffculme 1937, Kings Heath, Birmingham

I attended Uffculme for a year, then I was sent to Hunter's Hill for a further year. My memories of Uffculme are not so happy: Mother was in hospital, I had impetigo, and parents were not allowed to visit us during the week. (In the summer I slept there during the week, in an open shelter, going home for the weekends.) Dad got around that by walking in Highbury Park and bringing my little sister to stand by the fence which bordered the school. I was able to go and talk to them during playtime.

I recall a huge tree in the grounds, and standing linking hands with several other children, to reach around its enormous trunk. In the winter I fed the birds on the tree near my desk in the open-sided classroom. The robin got tame enough to sit on my desk when we were quiet. Miss Tidmus, our teacher, kept my drawing of 'my' robin for a long time.

I remember a play we did at Uffculme. It was about the children in the sugar plantations in Jamaica, and six of us had to get 'blacked-up' (with cocoa powder) from the waist up.

During this time John Horton wrote letters from the school to his mother who was ill in hospital. His teacher, Miss Tidmus, added comments on them to his mother. Some of his letters relate school activities:

'…We are doing a play and I am a little English boy in the West Indies. Perhaps you will be well enough to come and see the play.'

' … I am getting browner every day. I have 9/10 and 10/10 for Mental Arithmetic.'

'…We are having a competition to see who gets the most grasses.'

Mr. Peter Kidd, Uffculme 1938-9, Whitchurch, Cardiff

At the age of five I was sent to Uffculme because of a heart condition. I was a weekly boarder and a week seemed an eternity! On the whole I have pleasant memories: beautiful grounds adjoining the park, cricket, flowers, trees, gardening (in wooden clogs).

No food was to be left on plates. I did leave some—once—a piece of gristle which I was unable to eat. When the plates were collected up I was identified as the culprit and I had to go to the rostrum and eat the morsel whilst all faces were turned to me. I swallowed it whole as I knew I would not be able to chew it!

I remember with poignancy the moments when beds were made; beds in rows, partitions folded back on all sides, red blankets unfolded—sounds of the evensong of birds, then us singing 'Now the day is ended'. That song always brings back memories. Going home with Mum at the end of the week was always a joy but Monday came all too quickly and it was a wrench to leave home again and go by bus and train to a 'distant' school. It must have done me good though as I had no heart trouble of any description in later life.

Life at the school came to an abrupt halt with evacuation, as the log book reveals:

Uffculme log book 1939

28 Aug.   *Rehearsed for evacuation. 80 children rehearsed on school premises. Breakfast 8.30. All packs ready and children lined up at gate by 10.25 in readiness for bus. No registers marked all day but by 12 noon many new evacuees had arrived for dinner, so we remained here all day.*

31 Aug.   *Order to evacuate. Children sent home 2.30pm.*

There are no further log book entries until 18 March 1940, when Miss Hibbert, Nurse Bendall and the kitchen staff returned to the school to prepare for re-opening. Later on in the war the school evacuated to Kempsey in Worcestershire and school photographs show happy children in sunhats paddling in the river and playing in the fields.

Cropwood 1937-1939

Cropwood Open-Air School had many children suffering from asthma, bronchiectasis and other chronic catarrhal disorders, as the School Medical Officer reported:

> It is common for asthmatical children to respond so rapidly that they never have an attack at all at the school. Both Cropwood and Hunter's Hill are also of immense value in the treatment of maladjusted children who are suffering from the effects of unwholesome mental atmosphere in the home. Many disorders of conduct and nervous symptoms are cleared up completely and we hope permanently.

Miss Grant left her post as Headmistress in June 1938, being replaced by Miss Boothroyd at the beginning of the next term.

The new log book records many items of interest in 1938:

Cropwood log book 1938

22 Aug.   *The school reopened today for the autumn term and Miss Eveline Boothroyd began her duties.*

23 Aug.   *18 more new girls were admitted today. There have not been many tears. It has been decided to revive the Houses at Cropwood. Elsie Annis, Phyllis Williams and Joan Ford appointed temporarily as House Captains of Clent, Clee and Malvern.*

29 Sep.   *Rounders' match against Hunter's Hill resulted in a draw 14-14. This is the first time the boys have not beaten the girls.*

1 Oct.   *The whole school listened-in yesterday evening to the return of Mr. Chamberlain from the Munich Conference and the subsequent scene at Downing Street.*

11 Oct.   *Dr. Gale HMI visited Cropwood today. He brought a colleague Dr. Alford with him. Dr. Mitchell visited today too, and with him a Mr. James, President of the Natal Anti-Tuberculosis Association.*

[In the report of HM Inspectors Miss Marks and Dr. Gale it was noted: 'The Headmistress who took charge six weeks ago, is settling down very well. She has been taking stock of the position and is already alive to the needs of the school. The happy relations existing between staff and girls deserve commendation.

The nursing and housekeeping arrangements of the school are in capable and experienced hands. The medical records, which are carefully kept, show clearly that the children are benefiting greatly and their appearance confirms this impression. The appearance of the children who have been at the school some time is strikingly better than that of those who have recently arrived. A few minor alterations in diet are necessary—notably the provision of at least one pint of milk per head per day, and the inclusion every day of first class protein in the breakfast menu.']

22 Oct.   *Last night Olive H. and Dorothy F. ran away. Dorothy was brought back by her very angry mother this afternoon, but there is no word of Olive, other than information from the police that she has arrived.*

25 Oct.   *Miss Boothroyd received information this morning that as it is the second time Olive H. has absconded, and as Dr. Kemp pronounces her fit to leave, she will not return to Cropwood.*

11 Nov.   *Armistice Day. The school listened to the broadcast from the cenotaph.*

6 Dec.   *Dr. Mitchell visited today to discuss menus with Miss Arnot.*

9 Dec.   *Reading and Speaking Competition held today. Mrs. E. Harris B.A. (Lond.) was the judge and the winners were Juniors—Rita Belsten, Seniors—Lucy Steane.*

12 Dec.   *Christmas party A ciné show followed by a visit from Father Christmas. Everyone worked hard to make this a success and the school looked lovely.*

Four ex-pupils recall their schooldays in 1938/39:

Mrs. Joan Farmer (née **Tomkinson**), 69, Cropwood 1938, Birmingham

I was sent there in 1938. I had a thyroid problem which made me slow in learning. My first three months at Cropwood, however, were sheer hell! The prefects ran the school, while Miss Grant the Headmistress remained aloof in her bed-sitting room. Then Miss Boothroyd came along, with definite ideas regarding staff and prefects.

Miss Hardy was a firm but good teacher. Miss Disney was a younger element to us girls and we used to try her hats on in her room at end of dormitory. Miss Bell helped me to enjoy PT; Sister Daniels looked after our welfare, assisted by Nurse Keen; sun/air bathing (in the nude) for half-hour in better months. There were good basic meals and Quaker-like upbringing which I still retain in my habits.

A children's painting competition for members of the Happy Health Hunters Club (in Midland Counties Dairymaid *1935) includes all the ideals of open-air schools.*

We had three girls at Cropwood who lived apart for some years, because of ringworm. I met my best friend there at 13 years—her parents had both died of TB. I spent most of my schooldays at Cropwood, apart from some months when the war started. I was one of the first children to return and stayed until I left at fourteen.

Mrs. Joan Murray (née **Hughes**), 69, Cropwood 1938, Walsall, West Midlands

I was only there for a short time—but have such happy memories of the place, lovely walks, nature studies and companionship, and our chores shared happily. I wasn't very tall and I suppose they thought it would do me good—it did!

I remember our issue of wellingtons and macs and walking miles among the beautiful countryside—learning about birds and clouds. I remember teachers singing to us at night and making us laugh; the open windows where birds occasionally flew in, sometimes a bat or so they said, I was usually under the bedclothes giggling.

The memory has never faded and I hope it never will; we could do with more places like it.

Mrs. Elsie Kite (née **Annis**), Head Girl, Cropwood 1936-9, Birmingham

I went to Cropwood at 10 or 11 years of age. There were 84 girls at that time. The first Headmistress was Miss Grant and the second one was Miss Boothroyd.

The classrooms had walls that opened wide. In summer we had seats outside near flower beds of Rose of Sharon and we even had the dining room tables outside. Every morning we dressed, opened up our beds to air and had breakfast which was porridge, bread and dripping and sometimes scrambled egg and hot milk. Then we cleaned our teeth and made our beds. For dinner we always had potatoes boiled with the skin on and never any salt. The food was very good and plenty of it, including soup and pudding and homemade cakes. Our cook was Miss Twist. She was sent to Cropwood because she had very bad asthma.

Every Wednesday and Saturday we had to polish our own shoes. Then we went upstairs to our tuck shop for sweets and fruit. We had best clothes for Sundays when we went to church and our Sunday afternoon walk which was very nice. As warmer weather came, we were allowed to leave off our thick socks. Girls had to line up to have their feet bathed in surgical spirits to harden up their skin.

The school grounds were lovely with large cedar trees along the drive. There was an orchard full of apple trees. The fruit was stored in lofts for use during the year. There was a tennis court and a pergola with roses covering the top, and beds of red poppies each side of the path leading to the swimming pool. There were fir trees all round the classrooms. The smell from the trees was supposed to be good for you.

In summer we lay round the pool on blankets with nothing on to get the rays of the early morning sun. No-one ever got sunburnt. I was made Head Girl and helped look after the other children. Not all were happy. One tried to run away as it was getting dark one Sunday. I was worried as she would have to go through Lickey Hills on her own in the dark to get to Birmingham, so as Head Girl I told the Headmistress. None of the girls would speak to me when they found out. Next day the Headmistress called an assembly and told the girls that I had done the right thing.

There was a big indoor playroom with books and toys. Every Saturday the older girls did housework like polishing the floors and wooden panelled walls. I think that was good. I still like housework today and take pride in doing it.

I remember the teachers taking me to the Tower to see the Northern Lights. I shall never forget that. We had our own seamstress, Miss Deakin, who made all our summer dresses, red, green and blue.

Once I was in the isolation ward with a septic throat, and the girl next to me wouldn't eat her rice pudding. She found a hole in the floor and scraped the pudding down it but underneath was the blanket room where the blankets were stored for the afternoon nap. When the girls came to get their blankets, they were covered with rice pudding!

The 'treatment' at Cropwood consisted of plenty of rest, plenty of good plain food with cod liver oil in the winter, lots of fresh air and exercise. When I was old enough to leave school I was given a job in service at Cropwood and I liked it very much.

[Mrs. Kite's 1939 leaving certificate is reproduced here. Her school reports record that subjects studied at the school included Holy Scripture, Reading, Writing, English, Arithmetic, History, Nature Study, Drawing, Handwork, Needlework, Music, Physical Exercises and Swimming.]

Mrs. Lucy Goddard (née Steane), Cropwood 1937-9, Birmingham

I was sent to Cropwood because of frequent, severe attacks of asthma. I remember being quite excited at the idea of going. I had read school stories by Angela Brazil and thought it would be similar, with midnight feasts in the 'dorm' etc. In fact, of course, it was not like that at all; the regime was rather strict and most pupils largely came from under-privileged backgrounds, although I remember one pupil whose parents had a car. We all regarded her with respect.

When I set out for Cropwood, I had to catch a certain train to Blackwell with other pupils at New Street. Our parents could not come with us. When we reached Blackwell, we were told to walk in twos in a crocodile on the long walk to the school.

I was put into a large dormitory and given the school clothes to wear. In summer they were rather attractive—a gingham check dress in mauve and white with a square neck and short sleeves.

I was soon promoted to a higher class and did not find the work difficult the whole time I was there. A lot of time was spent on nature study and craft work. I quite enjoyed the nature study, we spent hours

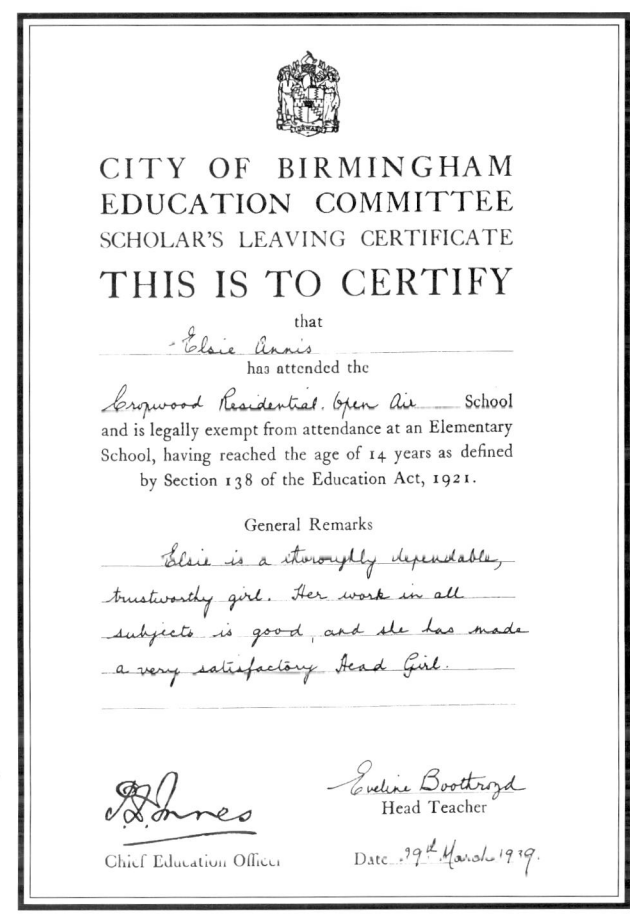

A pupil's leaving certificate signed by the Headmistress of Cropwood, Miss Boothroyd. (E. Kite)

collecting wild flowers, and were particularly thrilled when we found a 'scarlet pimpernel'. We learned the names of trees and were taught to recognise their shapes in the winter. We were taught to recognise all the birds which frequented the area.

Cropwood itself was a most impressive large house with spacious rooms and oak panelling. There were two Dining Rooms; one was called the 'Loggia' modelled on Italian lines with a marble floor and screens open to the air whenever the weather was tolerable. The other was the 'Playroom' which was used for other activities as well as eating. Upstairs were some dormitories, but the main block, where I slept, was apart from the main building and was two storeys high with a large number of beds in each. There was a small room at the end of the row of beds on each storey where a teacher slept. She had a small window on the side of her bedroom covered with a curtain and when she wanted to see if we were going to sleep and not misbehaving she would slide the curtain back. Needless to say, we did often talk and laugh and refuse to settle down so she often had to come in to 'read the Riot Act'.

The main house was set in magnificent grounds, approached by a long curving drive. On each side of the drive were lawns and at the back were tall conifer trees in great profusion. At the back of the house was a vast view stretching into the distance, where we were able to see the Malvern Hills on clear days, and, I think, the Clee Hills.

The food at Cropwood was sufficient but extremely plain, especially at tea time when we would come in hungry to be faced with several plates of wholemeal bread and butter with rarely anything to go with it. We particularly looked forward to Sundays when we would have jam on the bread and plain cake.

We had to spend as much time as possible in the open air; our dormitories and classrooms had open screens, except when it was very cold or wet. In the winter when there was snow or very cold weather, we did not have to play outside but were able to play in the 'Playroom'.

Every afternoon after lunch we had to go down to the rest-shed and spend an hour lying on a canvas bed with a blanket over us. In the middle of the playground, keeping watch over us, was a nursing sister. She was Scottish and a good disciplinarian because I never remember anyone talking or making a nuisance of themselves. One of the domestic staff used to bring her a tray with a teapot, a cup, and a slice of lemon.

On other occasions we had to go and lie on the canvas beds outside the rest-shed for 'sunbathing'. It had been decided by the authorities that sunlight would be good for our health. We wore nothing but our knickers and I remember feeling very resentful because I always felt cold. This was because we were never allowed to lie out in warm sunlight but only when the sun was faint and hidden behind the clouds. It was also usually in Spring before the temperature had really warmed up.

Once a month we had 'Visiting Day' which we looked forward to longingly. The procedure was that the pupils all stood at the top of the drive and waited until the visitors started to arrive. Then girls would detach themselves from the group and run happily down the drive and throw themselves into the arms of their respective family members. After that most families would go down to the 'rest-shed' and partake of tea and other refreshment.

When I first arrived at Cropwood there was a rather authoritarian Headmistress called Miss Grant, whom the children all called 'Piggy-grunt'. Once, I was walking in the grounds and whistling, and she called out to me 'Stop that whistling!'. I did not immediately take any notice because I thought I must have misheard. How could anyone object to a girl whistling, I reasoned. However, she called out again and told me I was disobedient and it was 'unladylike' to whistle.

Not long afterwards we had a new Headmistress, called Miss Boothroyd. Although she would not stand any nonsense she was pleasant and approachable and most children liked her very much. I became a prefect and she used to invite me and all the other prefects into her private sitting room, offer us biscuits, and read to us. She chose Greenmantle and The Three Hostages, by John Buchan, and she read these to us in serial form so after a few chapters she would stop and we would have to wait to the next week to find out the next exciting episode. All of us enjoyed these sessions very much and I remember it with pleasure even now—it was such a high spot in our lives.

My class teacher was Miss Owen. She had a thin face and brown hair which she twined into a bun in her neck. She was kind and humorous. Another pleasant teacher was Miss Hardy who had a mass of fair, curly hair and glasses.

We had a nurse to attend to our minor health problems and supervise our showers; about twice a week we went into the 'shower room' which had eight showers fixed in the ceiling and under each of them was a tin bath. The nurse would turn on the showers and when we had finished washing she would turn them off. We tipped the water from our tin baths into a channel at the back which ran into a drain.

On our birthdays we could have a table to ourselves spread with cakes and any other nice things which our parents were able to provide; and we asked our friends to come to the party. Sometimes, girls who had not been particularly friendly before, suddenly became so!

I remember in 1938 being ushered into the 'Playroom' and listening to a broadcast reporting Neville Chamberlain's return from Munich; when he talked about 'the piece of paper' which he had in his hand, on which was written his own name and that of 'Herr Hitler'. We all felt pleased as we had picked up the relief of the staff, but we had not much idea of the implications of Chamberlain's diplomacy.

While I was at Cropwood my health improved dramatically. I had no more asthma attacks, put on weight, grew taller and developed a healthy appetite. After two years my parents were told I was well enough to leave and I did so with relief; although looking back, it was a good school with a sensible if austere regime. I think it was being separated from home which caused most girls to want to leave.

The results of my education at Cropwood were not so good; I left the school somewhat behind other children of my age and had to obtain educational qualifications by attending a College for Mature Students. However, health is extremely important and that the school certainly delivered.

1939 was to prove a memorable year, with the outbreak of the Second World War, but for the girls at Cropwood the weather was often the focal point of their activities, as the log book records their community life:

Cropwood log book 1939

27 Jan.   The snow is thick and crisp today and all PT lessons have taken the form of sledging on the hillside in 'Sandy's field'. It is a lovely run and the new sledges presented some time ago by Mr. Williams were used for the first time.

31 Jan.   It was so intensely cold in the classroom this morning that we had to send all the children for a good, brisk walk. Their circulation restored they were all warm and happy. This weather is very trying and so far we have had no illness other than one or two colds. Mrs. Abbott, the cook, left today.

1 Feb.   Miss Twist, the new cook, today came and with her, Billy the cat. It is to be hoped that Jim Crow will not resent him.

25 Mar.   Visiting day. The parents were asked to sign Evacuation forms. The Handwork & Art Display was much appreciated.

18 April   Twelve new girls have come and all seem happy. Last night, Florence H. and Elsie J. ran away and Miss Boothroyd did not hear until 2.0am that they were safely home. Florence H. was brought back today—but is very homesick.

22 April   Florence H. was removed by her mother today—a very good thing as she had to be constantly watched and is still very homesick.

30 May   Still glorious weather. This afternoon Miss Boothroyd took the guides for a hike. Fires were successfully lit and 'eggs in orange skins' and dampers cooked. No-one had indigestion!

2 June   *Class picnics today. Class I went to Bakers Hill, Class II to Clodagh, Class III to the Brownie Field. Everyone had a lovely time.*

3 June   *Everyone looking brown and well after extra sun-bathing, and all the gardening and outdoor activities last week.*

5 June   *Dr. Kemp visited today and the list of girls fit for the pool is now complete. Two more new girls admitted—number in residence now 79.*

By August 1939 war was imminent and although many of Cropwood's pupils returned to the school for the autumn term they were soon sent home in groups, ready to be evacuated with other local schoolchildren. Meanwhile, Cropwood prepared to receive an influx of evacuee children from Birmingham's Special Schools—Baskerville, George Street West and Little Green Lane. The log book written by Miss Boothroyd brings to life all the trials and tribulations of life with the evacuees at Cropwood:

25 Aug.   *Sister, Nurse, Miss Boothroyd, Miss Hardy returned after the Broadcast, to be ready to receive evacuated children.*

31 Aug.   *At 1.0pm today we heard the news that the children were to be evacuated. We changed all those who were to go and by 3.6 our groups were ready to get the train; each district group taken by one of the staff of either Cropwood or Hunter's Hill. Miss Walton and I were left behind and got on with the black out. Eleven children were left at Cropwood after Dr. Mitchell's examination yesterday. We were all very sad to see our children go.*

1 Sep.   *This morning was spent in preparation for receiving the expected arrivals. Mr. Wigzell, Mr. Gregory and the firm of contractors' representative from Bromsgrove came to see about our 'black out' arrangements and the Air Raid Shelters. Cropwood is to have three shelters, burrowed into the hillside. This afternoon, almost simultaneously, 17 children from Baskerville, 24 from Little Green Lane and 23 from George Street West arrived. All are now asleep. We have 75 children, and a staff of 11 with one extra maid.*

2 Sep.   *Life here is very busy now. Many of these children are helpless cripples, and a big percentage can do little or no duty. Beds have to be made for them and only the lightest of dusting and sweeping can be done by them. Consequently the staff are very busy indeed and the work of the Nursing Staff is particularly heavy as there are many duties such as bathing, haircombing etc. which cannot be done by the teaching staff. The staff at present is: Heads—Miss Clark—Little Green Lane, Miss Boothroyd—Cropwood, Miss Saxty—George Street West, Miss Davies—Baskerville, Miss Gray—Little Green Lane, Miss Owen—Cropwood, Sister Daniels—Cropwood, Sister Hodgson—Little Green Lane, Nurse Sandy—Baskerville, Nurse Keen—Cropwood.*

3 Sep.   *Another day and the children are settling down very well. A few of them have been a little homesick but the Cropwood girls have been very helpful in making the strangers feel at home. The morale is excellent—everyone is meeting the situation with courage and as cheerful a face as possible.*

4 Sep.   *Miss Clark & Miss Boothroyd have decided that an attendant to help with bathing etc. is necessary—these children need a great deal of care. Duty time-tables are made out, classes formed and we are getting under way but there is so much to be done. A start has been made at changing the children into Cropwood clothes.*

19 Sep.   *A good deal of extra work has been caused by having to separate for meals the 'heart' children, to give them different crockery, and have every piece sterilised after use.*

23 Sep.   *A **very** trying Visiting Day. 15 children were taken home on one pretext or another. Some of the parents, on the other hand, were most appreciative of all that has been done for the children.*

24 Sep.   *The 62 children remaining seem really happy and settled.*

13 Oct.   *Dr. Smallwood visited today and was very pleased with the progress of the 'heart' children. Many of the D's are C's now.*

16 Oct.   *The trenches are now ready and rehearsals of procedure have begun. The children are very orderly on the whole.*

27 Oct.   *Dr. Smallwood came again and several of the B's are now A's and are up for 'Periodical'.*

31 Oct.   *Great activity today   everyone preparing for a Hallow E'en party tomorrow. Miss Clark and Miss Boothroyd have been very busy making ghouls out of turnips and Class I are doing other decorations.*

1 Nov.   *A **most** successful party, everyone enjoyed it. The decorations were really lovely. Everyone had 'fortunes' or apples, and 'bobbing' for apples was very popular; two children got **two** at once.*

3 Nov.   *Mr. Wilson Stuart came today to see the orthopaedic children.*

10 Nov.   *Dr. Smallwood here today. He is still very pleased with the progress of the Baskerville children.*

17 Nov.   *Dr. Austin came today to examine the Open-Air children admitted in the last six weeks or so.*

18 Nov.   *Visiting Day. Miss Boothroyd and Miss Clark talked to the parents about the advisability of leaving their children at Cropwood for Xmas. There was a very good response, and we hope a good many of the children will stay. Miss Boothroyd and Sister Daniels with four other staff will stay for Xmas.*

6 Dec.   *The Fancy Dress Party was held today. Each girl had made her costume out of two packets of crepe paper and some of them were most ingenious and very pretty. There were twelve prizes given by the staff. Mildred Talbot as the Jester was the cleverest costume. She had taken great pains with it and the result was excellent. Buns for tea and jelly and biscuits during the interval added to the fun. It was a **very** happy party.*

17 Dec.   *Visiting Day. A **very** pleasant day. 61 girls out of 78 are staying for Xmas, and all our preparations and hard work seem repaid.*

22 Dec.   *Xmas Party Day. Miss Davies and Miss Disney decked the tree and all the presents were hung on and round it. The prefects helped by looking after the other girls. A lovely tea, followed by a conjuror who was extremely clever, and then a visit from Santa Claus, sent everyone happy to bed.*

24 Dec.   *Christmas Eve. The children enjoyed the Carol Service on the wireless this afternoon. Tonight all the staff worked hard at filling sixty stockings! Parcels were put round the playroom to be opened after breakfast. It was fun filling the stockings, and owing to the generosity of our friends we were able to give every child a well-filled stocking and plenty of parcels.*

25 Dec.   *The communicants and Catholics went to Early Service and some girls also to Matins. Every child was thrilled with her presents and all heartily enjoyed pork etc. and Xmas pudding for dinner. The keynote of the day was a happy atmosphere, and the children were very good.*

29 Dec.   *Another cinematograph—even better than last night's, given by Mr. Rushbrook, the local scout master.*

30 Dec.   *A grand concert tonight with the best items from each of the Class Concerts. Mrs. J. Harris came, and presented the House Cup to the successful House—Clee.*

1940

1 Jan.   *New Year's Day. We had a House Concert. It took all day to prepare and was presented after tea. Clent's show of 'Tom Thumb' was voted the best item and won the prize—a tin of sweets. Also today it was fine for sledging, but our fun was brought to an untimely end when Norma T. broke her leg. She was admitted to the Children's Hospital.*

As the log book marks the end of the Christmas holiday and the beginning of the new decade, Miss Boothroyd, Headmistress, continued to record life at Cropwood during the difficult wartime conditions which demanded complete dedication of all the staff. She remained at the school until her retirement in 1953.

Hunter's Hill 1937-9

Miss Gertrude Walton continued to be the Headmistress until 1943, having had several years' experience as the Head at Cropwood school. Her inspiring influence resulted in many developments in Hunter's Hill school, as the official report of HM Inspector revealed in 1938:

> During the six years the Headmistress has been in charge of the school there have been many pleasing developments. The planning of the curriculum has received considerable thought and the schemes provide for a satisfactory balance between the fundamental work in the 3 R's and the wider aspects of training through varied forms of useful and interesting activity.
>
> In each class care is taken to see that Arithmetic and English reach a satisfactory standard and, at the same time, appropriate activities in connection with the teaching of History and Geography are providing the children with widening interests which not only enter freely into the work of the classroom but also encourage the children to use their spare time profitably. It is good to find that so much care is given to use of tools both in the workshop and in a less formal way through toy-making …
>
> Full use is made of the natural surroundings to develop a love of the countryside— a feature which is worthy of even further development.
>
> It is a pleasure to visit this school and to note the whole-hearted efforts of the Headmistress and her staff to do all they can to make the stay of the children so happy and beneficial. The arrangements for the medical care of the children are admirable in every way.

A very detailed description of the school was given in the *1939 Triennial Report on Hunter's Hill Open-Air School to the Special Schools Sub-Committee*. Miss Walton gave an account of Hunter's Hill during its first six years, when the average length of stay for boys was 12 to 15 months. Staff consisted of the Headmistress, two men and two women teachers, a trained nurse, assistant nurse, housekeeper, cook, sewing maid and five other maids.

The problem of attracting Birmingham teachers to work at Hunter's Hill school was commented upon, as teaching staff were paid on Scale II (as in Worcestershire schools), rather than Scale III (as in Birmingham). Miss Walton's views on the valuable experience teachers would gain from residential work was tempered by 14 years' practice at Cropwood and Hunter's Hill schools:

> … the boys …vary in age from 5 to 14 years and the little boys settle extremely well and take their place easily as the small members of a big family …
>
> I feel that except in very exceptional cases three years is long enough for young teachers in a residential school of this sort. They are more or less isolated from the rest of the world—away in the country and with much less free time than teachers in elementary

schools. The extraneous duties for most of them become rather wearisome after this length of time. It is very good experience for them and for the most part they thoroughly enjoy being here.

The parents of the boys visit the school once a month and though these visiting days mean a good deal of extra work I am convinced that they are very much worth while. The parents see their boys happy and in a new environment—looking better than they've looked before in their lives—well and suitably dressed. These visiting days afford an opportunity for the parents to meet the staff, and the relationship existing between them is a very happy one. Most visiting days we arrange football or cricket matches for fathers and sons—parents' sports—children's sports—a display of the boys' work, or a school concert. We have a great many old boys visiting the school, boys who were at Cropwood more than ten years ago and are now grown up. Without exception they pay a tribute to the good done to them by their stay here …

The day here is a very full one for the boys, and even they often remark how quickly the time goes. Their free half days—Wednesday and Saturday afternoons—are occupied by house-matches, in addition to free play. They are kept out of doors as much as possible all times of the year. In the summer evenings if the older boys are not playing cricket they work in the gardens. In addition to their own plots they are responsible for the care and general neatness of different parts of the grounds. In the winter evenings they have boxing—handwork of all kinds—some woodwork in the woodwork rooms—and also dramatic work. Before school begins each day they have certain domestic duties to perform, e.g. the sweeping and dusting of dormitories and other rooms. These are done by different house teams, working under a leader, and the work is done cheerfully and with zest. Staff and boys alike are kept busy here, and working and living together as we do the staff have a great sense of responsibility to the boys and the boys for their part are very friendly toward the staff, who are looked to for sympathy in any emergency.

An 'isolation' block was under consideration at the time of the report but Miss Walton commented that a fourth classroom was also urgently needed as one class had to work in the dining room, next to the kitchen with all its distracting noises.

Miss E.L. Ross, the Inspector of Residential and Special Schools, added her personal comments to the report:

It is no easy task, this caring for and educating a family of 120 selected delicate boys, many of them nervous and difficult and backward. Yet the most casual visitor is impressed by the atmosphere of strenuous happy activity combined with understanding and friendly individual care.

The Headmistress in rather a remarkable way manages to divide her interest and attention equally with regard to the physical, educational, and social aspects of the work. This interest reacts on the members of the staff and we find them all, teachers, nurses and maids, working enthusiastically as a happy team. One should also, I think, include the Caretaker who in no small measure contributes to the comfort of staff and children, and can always be relied on to give a hand with anything needing to be done …

One feels that the boys will not only be greatly improved in health when the time comes for them to leave, but that they will be the better morally and socially through having shared in the life of such a school and come under the inspiring influence of this Head Teacher.

Hunter's Hill log books fully record life at the school, with teachers and staff frequently mentioned: Miss Pratt, Miss Richards, Miss Buckley, Sister Daniels, Mr. Hughes, Mr. Wainwright and Mr. Wetherall. Some of the more interesting entries are as follows:

Hunter's Hill log book 1937

30 Jan.   *We have had 13 boys in bed with colds and running temperatures this week. After one or two days they are practically well again—but the cold is so intense that we are afraid to get them up until the weather is milder.*

21 April   *60 students from Barry Training College visited the school today.*

11 May   *No. on roll 116. Boys went home today on the 1.8 train for a week's holiday for Coronation.*

20 May   *Three boys decamped in the night.*

21 May   *Two boys were brought back by Miss Buckley and Mr. Wainwright. The other one was brought back by his mother this afternoon but as he has gone off several times on a previous stay—it was decided not to let him return. Half day holiday for Coronation Party.*

1 July   *Nurse took two boys to hospital today for examination on Dr. Burns' advice.*

5 Oct.   *Miss Buckley and Mr. Wainwright away all day at the Training course for teachers of retarded children.*

5 Nov.   *Bonfire in playing field, fine night. All went well.*

28 Nov.   *Miss Walton was taken to the Birmingham General Hospital this afternoon.*

8 Dec.   *We heard that Miss Walton had successfully undergone her final operation.*

Hunter's Hill log book 1938

15 Jan.   *Boys had a party (this was made possible through the* Birmingham Mail *15/6)* [15s. 6d.].

18 Jan.   *Dr. Mitchell (Medical Officer of Health), Dr. Glover, Lieut-Col Caddell, visited the school. Dr. Glover is Senior Medical Officer of Health for Board of Education and Dr. Caddell is Secretary Gen. of Nat. Ass. for the Prevention of Tuberculosis.*

31 Jan.   *Miss Walton back on duty.*

17 Feb.   *R.H. went to the ear clinic this morning. R.K. went to the Orthopaedic Hospital this afternoon.*

2 Mar.   *Nurse took two boys with skin trouble to be examined at the Children's Hospital.*

6 April   *The school closed today. Four boys went to the Little Bromwich Hospital with chickenpox. They were not allowed to go home.*

23 May   *This morning Mr. G. came to fetch his son home. He has been here 1 month and put on 3lbs in weight—tho' only 7 years of age. He had lost the cough he had when he came and was eating and sleeping well and was quite happy. But the parents missed him at home.*

THE 1930s: TESTAMENT OF HEALTH

24 May   *Class 3 with Miss Buckley and Miss Radmore went to see Bromsgrove market this morning in connection with their project on 'markets'.*

31 May   *George C. and Frank H. went to hospital today with diphtheria.*

1 June   *All the staff and boys had their throats swabbed today.*

6 June   *As we could not have visiting day as usual on account of the diphtheria the boys went off to Dodderhill Common leaving at 11.5 by train.*

1 July   *The boys went to Uffculme today on the 1.10 train for the Special Schools' Sports. They won the Senior Boys' Shield.*

11 July   *Miss M. Lowe, assistant mistress, started duty here this morning.*

7 Sep.   *The dentist at Cropwood. 31 boys had gas to have teeth extracted today.*

20 Sep.   *Two boys decamped today and both boys were perfectly happy and did it for an adventure. As they have both done it several times previously I decided in the best interests of the school that they had better not return.*

Hunter's Hill log book 1939

21 Jan.   *Miss J. Fenton came to take up duty as assistant nurse this afternoon.*

1 Mar.   *Mr. Wetherall started duty as assistant master today.*

30 April   *One of our new boys John O. complained of a pain in his throat on Friday though Dr. Kemp had examined him on Thursday. He was put to bed and on Saturday his throat was swollen as in tonsillitis. On*

This postcard sent home by a pupil features the boating pool at Hunter's Hill, with classrooms in the background, 1930s. (J. Hughes)

Sunday his condition became acute and though Dr. Dick was on his way to see him he died of a convulsion before his arrival.

9 June   *Dr. Kemp is immunising 52 boys (whose parents have all given written consent) against diphtheria. He gave these boys their first injection this afternoon.*

28 Aug.   *The school re-opened today.*

31 Aug.   *95 children went home today on the evacuation order.*

1 Sep.   *50 cripples came today. 40 Baskerville children came.*

11 Sep.   *The registers were marked this morning—one for Baskerville—one for George St. West and one for Little Green Lane and one for the Open-Air School children.*

22 Dec.   *All had been encouraged to stay* [for the Christmas holidays] *but as many lived in 'neutral' areas—they were taken home. There were 62 children left.*

29 Dec.   *We had a very full enjoyable week here. Today the other members of staff who have been away returned to take up duty.*

Two 'old boys' of the school recall their experiences and an ex-nurse of the school gives an interesting insight into life at Hunter's Hill, after 32 years' service:

Mr. John Horton, Hunter's Hill 1938, Birmingham

I had attended Uffculme School, then I was sent to Hunter's Hill for a further year. Some of us had arrived at Hunter's Hill without even shoes—but we were all provided with pumps to wear.

My happiest memories are of our walks to the Blackwell Incline—then understood to be the steepest climb for railway engines in the country. We watched the special engine, the 'Lickey Banker', come out of its siding to push the trains up the hill. It waited in a siding where the driver would talk to us boys and although it was strictly forbidden for boys to go up on the footplate, I believe that when no-one was about the occasional boy would be treated to a quick look up there.

My favourite staff member was 'Frisky', the caretaker. I specially recall his helping me with our compulsory boxing which I disliked—he showed me how to protect myself.

We were taken swimming at Cropwood where we 'skinny-dipped'. Most of the time we seemed to run around in khaki shorts and pumps and not much else, though I recall woolly scarves and sweaters were provided for cold days.

There were showers; either Nurse, Matron or one of the four teachers would be there to shoo us all through the showers every night, when we threw our dirty clothes into laundry skips.

I remember one very exciting night when we younger boys were got up out of bed (the older boys had not yet turned in) as the Headmistress wanted us all to see the very rare sight of the Aurora Borealis. We all went outside to look at the great red glow over Clent, with moving rays of light above. Then we were all given a hot drink before going back to bed. Another vivid evening memory is of us boys sitting on the steps having a sing-song watching a beautiful sunset. We finished on the hymn 'Summer suns are glowing' ...

Mr. Maurice C. Hicks, 71, Hunter's Hill 1935-8, Birmingham

I was sent to Hunter's Hill in 1935. The Headmistress was Miss Walton and the teachers were Miss Buckley, Miss Rose, Mr. Hughes, Mr. Friend and Mr. Wainwright. There was also resident Sister Daniels and a nurse.

Mr. Fellows was the caretaker who we nicknamed 'Frisky'. He was very friendly to us and joined in with the games we played in our free time, mainly football and cricket.

In 1938 we competed with other schools for the Sports Shield which we won that year. On a photograph I am pictured holding the shield with Steve Garraway. He made friends with Phyllis Williams of Cropwood Girls School. They were school sweethearts and eventually married.

I remember many mornings, in the winter, waking up to find the bottom of the bed covered in snow. If the snow was deep enough on Hunter's Hill, the teacher would allow us to toboggan down the hill.

When we broke up for the summer holidays, we boarded the train at Blackwell Station for Birmingham. As we went through Bournville we passed right by the Cadbury factory and all the workers would wave to us from the windows. One year Dame Cadbury visited the school and each one of us was introduced to her. I remember being very impressed by her grand style.

The Special Schools Sports Shield was won in 1938 by Hunter's Hill. Pictured holding the shield (from left to right) are John Hall, Maurice Hicks and Steve Garraway. (M. Hicks)

I have very happy memories of the old school and how well we were cared for. When my own children were young we would take them for picnics and bluebell picking at Blackwell. They have since taken their children, and my wife and I still walk the hills of Blackwell for old times' sake.

Miss Claire Barrett, Nurse, Hunter's Hill 1937–69, Blackwell, Worcestershire

I was engaged as assistant nurse at Hunter's Hill Open-Air School in May 1937 and stayed there until my retirement in 1969. I had completed three years' hospital training as a state-enrolled assistant nurse in Birmingham Fever Hospital and Bristol (mental nursing).

There were 120 boys in residence, mostly suffering from asthma, bronchitis and allied chest troubles—generally debilitated boys unable to keep up with ordinary school due to frequent absences, and a few suffering the effects of unsatisfactory homes. There was then a means test in existence and the majority of parents paid some contribution towards their son's keep (never more than 12s.6d.). This was later abolished. All boys were completely equipped with clothes and footgear on entrance—each one having week-day clothing and a special uniform kept only for Sundays and trips outside school.

The boys were divided up into 'houses' named after the four hills visible from the top field, namely Malvern, Clee, Clent and Abberley. Two members of staff were assigned to each house who were responsible for seeing them tidily dressed and shoes cleaned ready for school in the morning, taking an interest generally in their house and encouraging them in inter-house sports matches and so on. Each house was taken on their own special day's outing, senior boys discussing with their staff members where it was to be. Then there was a school outing in summer—Malvern Hills (very popular), Dovedale (often taking in the Well-dressings in Tissington on the way), London Zoo and sometimes the sea-side (namely Rhyl and Aberystwyth). Parents paid for their sons—any child's parents unable to spare the cash was often paid for by a member of staff or else from school funds.

Boys were woken at 7.20am by Sister Daniels and myself and two other staff, beds were stripped, toilets attended to and then breakfast. I saw to boys confined to bed. Whilst Sister Daniels was in charge of the medical side she saw to any pre-breakfast treatments. After 1960 I was left in charge as it was impossible to get a fully trained 'Sister'—not enough money and too much unaccustomed work! The Education Department sent nurses from the School Clinic regularly to Hunter's Hill to check on the boys, which was very helpful to me.

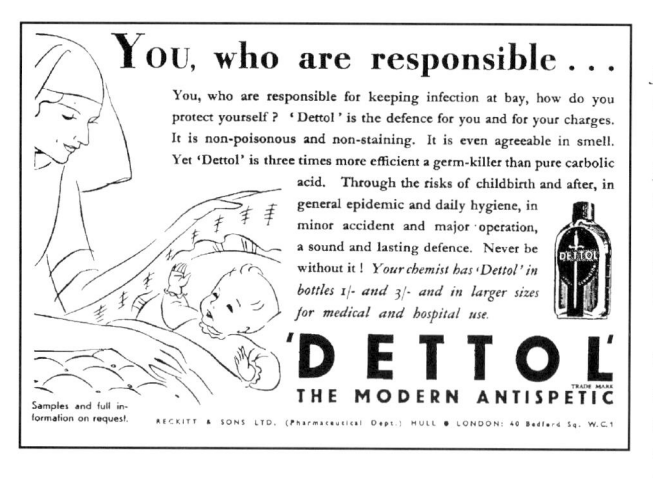

A typical day for me at Hunter's Hill: after breakfast I helped boys make their beds in whichever dormitory I had at the time, which included sweeping and dusting, and then rushed off to see my 'House' prepare for school, shoe-cleaning, hair-brushing, clothes tidied etc. Then I attended to any boys in the sick room, and after that did surgery which usually took me up to morning break at 10.45am. Medical charts had to be kept up to date.

I helped to serve dinner at 12 noon. Once a week I supervised the hour's rest period, when I was excused dinner supervision. If there were no boys to attend hospital clinics in the afternoon I was free until 4pm. I then supervised a group of boys either at indoor games or the stamp club. Once a week I fine-combed all boys' heads and once a fortnight I weighed them all. After tea I did any necessary surgery, dispensed medication and unless I was on my weekly late duty (8.00pm-10.00pm), or it was my half day off, I showered the 60 senior boys whilst a teacher or our 'child-helper' did the juniors. I had alternative Saturdays or Sundays off.

At Hunter's Hill school I 'lived in'. For many years I slept in a very small room next to the little boys dormitory which had a connecting window into the dormitory.

When war was declared in 1939 we were told to send all but the 20 most delicate boys back home, much to their parents' consternation, as it was just about three or four days after we had admitted them. We then received boys from two physically handicapped day schools and 30 boys from the rheumatic heart school—together with various of their respective staffs, so we ended up with two Headmistresses, two 'Sisters', two nurses, two seamstresses and a couple more teachers! We all had to double up in staff bedrooms. We stayed open all the time for the first two years, so that boys did not have to go back into the city at holiday times but we rarely had more than about thirty left.

It was a very happy place to work in; we all worked together and filled in for each other when necessary. We were always faithfully supported by a hardworking domestic staff.

In retrospect, the 1930s was the peak of open-air schools. There were numerous educational reports emphasising the need for such schools as so many children still suffered all sorts of debility due to malnutrition and poverty. Many past pupils of these schools were so completely revitalised by their unique outdoor education that they were able to serve in the armed forces, as **Mrs. Lilian Evans** (née **Vickers**), Uffculme 1936, recalls: 'I was accepted for service during the war to serve in the W.R.N.S. who only took grade A1 fitness, so I think that can be regarded as a testimony of success'.

With the benefit of over twenty years' experience of open-air schools there were many recommended guidelines for local education authorities to follow but fate was to take a hand in preventing further developments with the onset of the Second World War.

Chapter 6

The 1940s: The Turning Point

The Second World War was a period of great turmoil for all school medical services, with the problems of evacuation, the break-up of family life and a lack of continuity in education for several years. The social upheavals and numerous air raids affected the health of many schoolchildren.

Evacuation highlighted many health problems; there were numerous comments made by foster parents on the poor physical condition of the children they received, together with such problems as uncleanliness, anti-social behaviour, nits, skin diseases and bed wetting. School medical service staff rose to the occasion by visiting most pupils in their evacuation areas to sort out difficulties but school populations frequently moved from districts, on account of bombings, or were sent home again. Further development of school medical services was disrupted for a period of several years, even as the need for more psychiatric and psychological services became apparent. There was a great increase in the provision of Child Guidance Clinics after the war.

1940-4

One positive development for the benefit of children was the government's priority in the distribution of food, despite the difficulties of rationing. Children under five had first choice of any available oranges or bananas, with a daily pint of milk and double supply of eggs; children between 5 and 16 years were allowed fruit, a full meat ration and half a pint of milk a day. In 1941 schoolchildren were granted a special daily ration of one-third of a pint of milk at school. The new National Milk Scheme was to prove a boon for poor families who previously had not been able to afford a daily pint of milk for their growing children. Milk was usually 2d. a pint but was free if the joint income of parents was under 40s. (£2) a week.

The importance of nutrition was widely advertised and better school meals began to be provided. Some families were better nourished because women were earning money in the war effort, but scarcity of fruit and rationing of fats produced an increase in skin diseases and lowered resistance to illness. Very often the meat rations in families were reserved for the men and many children would have been undernourished if school dinners and milk had not been available.

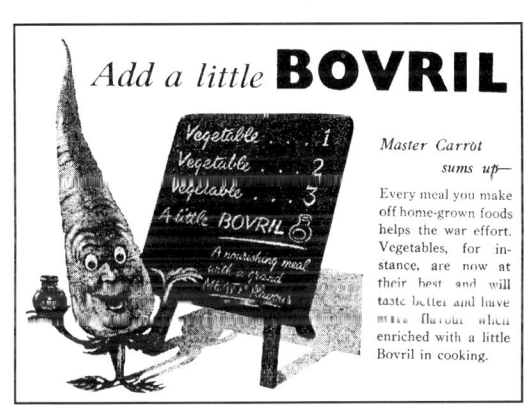

Birmingham school nurses in 1942 noted an increase in the number of children suffering fatigue, anaemia, gum diseases and general lowered resistance to infection, as a result of anxiety and strain, disturbed nights, lack of vitamin C and inadequate ventilation during blackouts. In that year it was reported that generally the city's children had emerged from the fourth year of war 'on a gratifying level of health' but another open-air school opened at Haseley Hall near Warwick. Wartime conditions had brought into prominence the value of open-air schools for the treatment of children suffering from general debility, lowered vitality and nervous ailments. A few cases of 'difficult' children were also being admitted to open-air schools but in general it was thought that, although many would derive much benefit, their behaviour 'might be some menace to the school and its pupils'.

A turning point in the health of schoolchildren was the passing of the government's 1944 Education Act, which made it a requirement for local education authorities to provide free medical treatment, as well as compulsory school medical inspections, for all pupils; previously any treatment had been charged to parents and there had been no obligation for children to submit to inspections. In addition, it was a duty for education authorities to provide free dental inspection and treatment and to supply school meals and milk at all maintained schools. From 1946 the daily third of a pint of milk at school was issued free to children; the government continued to supply free milk to pupils until 1968.

The 1944 Education Act greatly extended the range of children's 'special needs' for which local authorities were obliged to provide special education. In the following year of 1945 *The Handicapped Pupils and School Health Service Regulations* defined 11 categories of pupils, including for the first time 'delicate' children (who had previously been included within the term 'physically handicapped'). Maladjustment and speech defects were also new categories which led to alternative forms of educational provision.

It is a surprising fact that schoolchildren emerged from six years of wartime conditions without any serious decline in health, due to the provision of school meals, improvements in nutritional standards and the school medical services which had now become a legal requirement of every local education authority. By 1945 the School Medical Service was renamed the School Health Service and all local education authorities were required to appoint a senior dental officer.

Uffculme 1940-4

After evacuation of the school in September 1939 there is a gap in the school log book until March 1940, when the school re-opened again for pupils who had not been evacuated to Kempsey. Entries record the difficulties of school life during Birmingham's air raids while teachers took it in turns to go to Kempsey to continue the children's education:

Uffculme log book 1940

18 Mar. *Miss Hibbert, Nurse Bendall and kitchen staff returned to prepare for re-opening.*

1 April *School reopened with 54 children on books.*

27 July *School breaks up for a fortnight summer holiday. Miss Davis goes to Kempsey to release Mr. Anderson.*

12 Aug. *School re-opened. 115 on books. Mr. A. Price appointed as man attendant for night duty.*

13 Aug. *Air raid lasting 4 hours during night. Children very calm, slept in the bathroom and were not unduly upset.*

14 Aug. *Many children absent, many very late in consequence of raid. Rest hour extended to 3pm; all the children sleeping soundly.*

16 Aug. *Rest hour again extended to 3pm. On the whole the children who slept here were much less disturbed by the air raids than those who went home.*

THE 1940s: THE TURNING POINT

30 Aug.   *46%. 6 or 7 hours air raid every night accounts for low attendance.*

6 Oct.   *Miss Hibbert at Kempsey relieving Miss Davis.*

8 Oct.   *Miss Hibbert returned to Uffculme at mid-day.*

16 Oct.   *Severe air raid last night in Balsall Heath. Moseley Road blocked and many children unable to get to school. 40 in attendance.*

4 Nov.   *School was closed today owing to the presence of a delayed action bomb on the games shed.*

8 Nov.   *Low attendance due to raids and difficulty of transport. The Alcester Road is closed along a long portion of the route.*

29 Nov.   *2nd evacuation from Birmingham on the 26th November. 36 children left Uffculme. School had water but no gas—owing to air raids. The school was kept open all the time, the meals being cooked on camp fires.*

6 Dec.   *23%. Low percentage due to evacuation.*

Uffculme children on a country walk while evacuated at Kempsey in Worcestershire. (Uffculme School)

Uffculme log book 1941

24 Jan.   *23.5%. Low attendance due to a very heavy fall of snow—Arctic conditions and consequent dislocation of traffic.*
[Although not recorded in the school log books, Uffculme lost its founder and patron, Mrs Geraldine Cadbury, in January 1941. During the blitz she had undertaken an exhausting schedule of visiting many of the schools and organisations with which she was involved, and was taken ill during a heavy snowfall. She died on 30 January at the age of 75 years, and Birmingham lost 'a real

fairy godmother', to quote the headlines of *The Birmingham Evening Despatch*. Mrs. Cadbury had been a familiar figure to all concerned with child welfare and had always taken a personal interest in the many children she met, whether they were in the magistrate's court or in the open-air schools which she had founded with her husband. She had been Chairman of Birmingham's Open-Air Schools Sub-Committee from 1914-27, and a member of the Special Schools Sub-Committee for many years. The frequent mention of her name in Uffculme's and Cropwood's log books remains a testimony to her constant interest in the education and welfare of delicate children.]

31 Jan. *Very cold and deep snow.*

6 Feb. *Air warning 12.30. Children took dinner into shelter, 'All Clear' 1.30pm. Staff at Kempsey; Miss Hibbert, Mr. Anderson, Miss Pritchard. Staff at Uffculme; Nurse, Miss Tidmus, Miss Gray (2 days), Miss Mitchell PT Specialist (Tues & Thurs morn).*

14 Feb. *Air warning 3.30pm. All children were in gardens. All proceeded to shelter with books. Tea was served in shelter. 'All Clear' 4pm.*

20 Feb. *Air warning 2.15 to 2.25. Children had story. Weather conditions have seriously affected attendance.*

27 Feb. *Air Warning 12.40 to 1.10. Story read.*

7 Mar. *Air Warning 12.30 to 1.10. Children finished dinner in shelter. 2nd Warning at 3.45pm. Story and tea in shelter.*

2 May *Miss Wales appointed Uffculme from May 1st.*

26 Sep. *Miss Hibbert returns to Kempsey.*

16 Dec. *Miss Wales goes to Kempsey to supply in place of Miss Pritchard.*

Uffculme log book 1942

12 Jan. *Miss Hibbert at Kempsey. Staff: Miss Tidmus, Miss Long, Miss Wales, Miss Mitchell Tues. Weather very cold all week.*

19 & 20 Jan. ***Tues.*** *A heavy snowfall—21 children attended. Temp. outdoor 21°. Classrooms 32°. Resting shed snow bound. Transport difficult.*

    Wed. *Still intensely cold 21°. 38 children present. No rest taken on these two days. Gangs of children helped to clear shed and paths for ½hr periods to keep warm and then singing, PT and Folk Dancing and oral lessons of 20 mins duration. Afternoon session 1pm to 3.15pm and the children were given hot milk and bread and butter and dismissed at 3.30pm.*

23 Jan. *Miss Hibbert returned from Kempsey. Weather still very bad.*

19 June *Kempsey dept. closed today for pear-picking.*

6 July *Miss Wales to Kempsey.*

Uffculme log book 1943

12 Mar *Last teacher withdrawn from Kempsey. 6 children left.*

Uffculme log book 1944

27 July *School breaks up for 1 month. Flora Jennings, the last evacuee leaves Kempsey.*

THE 1940s: THE TURNING POINT

For this period of the war we have reminiscences of two ex-pupils and a dedicated teacher:

Mrs. Olive Horton, 64, Uffculme 1941-4, Stourbridge, West Midlands

I went to Uffculme Open-Air School in 1941 and stayed there until I was 14 years old, as did my twin sister. Most of the children at the school had asthma, maybe got from sleeping in the damp, as bedtime was in the Air Raid Shelters.

We enjoyed it there. My Headmistress was named Miss Hibbert who came from Kempsey, Worcester, as did my own mother. It was partly due to Miss Hibbert that many children were sent to Kempsey in the war years.

My classroom was run by Miss Wales who came from Selly Oak. One of the favourite stories for the girls was 'What Katy Did Next'. After PT we always had a shower. Breakfast was usually porridge, a large cup of hot milk, or a boiled egg. My favourite meal was cheese and potato pie plus beetroot and lettuce. The nurse used to line us up for malt and cod liver oil; also Bemax sprinkled on our food, rich in Vitamin B.

We had a good education and lots of reading which helped us to spell. When I left I applied for a Post Office Counter Clerk, passed an entry exam and medical and got employment at Small Heath Post Office.

I would swap my time back at school any day!

Mrs. Jean Dwyer (née **Andrews**), Uffculme 1941-4, Warley, West Midlands

I attended Uffculme during the war for three years but was evacuated to Earlswood, and later to convalescent homes in Southport and Exmouth. I suffered from bronchiectasis.

My most vivid memory of that time was of the navy blue fishermen's jerseys which were issued to us to wear over our own for extra warmth during lessons when the folding sides of the classroom were open to the elements. These outsize jerseys were wool and were very, very itchy!

I hated the rest periods as I could not sleep during the day, so I used to count the wooden planks in the roof area and usually got a different number each time. The rest-shed was also used for country dancing lessons. I seem to remember we danced to one record only which was 'The Honeysuckle and the Bee'.

At the end of term time all the left-over food from the canteen was distributed to the children to take home to Mom, starting with the children from large families downwards. I can remember being very disappointed once when the last joint of meat went to a child with six in family and I was next in line with a family of five.

The teachers I remember were Miss Hibbert, the Headmistress, Miss Wales and Mr. Anderson. Mr. Anderson could be a bit sharp. On one occasion he asked the class what a xylophone was. I put up my hand and said it was like a big table with 'things' on top. 'What sort of things, girl?', he said: 'Cabbages, carrots, potatoes? Explain yourself!' I sank down in my seat with a very red face, to the laughter of my classmates.

I still have the bronchiectasis problem and get chest infections. I try to give myself physiotherapy about once a week to clear my bronchial tubes but on the whole I keep pretty healthy. I think attending Uffculme awakened in me an interest in flowers and nature which I still have to this day, as well as the need to have a constant supply of fresh air with doors and windows open, whatever the weather!

Miss Margaret M. Wales, 82, Teacher and Deputy Head at Uffculme 1941-1958, Northfield, Birmingham

[Margaret Wales, who was born in Montreal in Canada and was the eldest child in a family of five children, came to England as a child. She trained as a teacher at Derby, studying English, History, Art and Crafts and was teaching at St Clements School, Nechells in Birmingham, in 1941 when the school was bombed. During the following weeks she was transferred to a temporary job at the Education Office and applied for the teaching vacancy at Uffculme Open-Air School, which carried the salary of £9 per month at that time. No special qualifications were needed for the post although the interviewers were keen to know her outside interests, she recalls. She was to remain at the school for 17 years, enduring the same freezing conditions in winter as her pupils, and becoming Deputy Head in 1952.]

I was **very** happy at Uffculme. I remember on my first morning there listening to Mr. Anderson telling jokes to the rest of the staff and thought everyone was such fun!

Miss Hibbert, the Headmistress, was a great botany and bird enthusiast and used to get records of bird songs which she would play to us, so we got to recognise most of the usual birds. When a bird was singing she would get us to identify it. She found unusual wild flowers everywhere she went and brought a specimen back to plant in the school grounds. She was a very gifted woman; a silversmith with her own hallmark, often winning prizes, and did marvellous embroidery which was shown all over the country. She was such a dignified and large lady, and never married—you couldn't marry and carry on teaching in those days, of course.

The grounds of Uffculme were a delight—it was quite a nature reserve. We had foxes, moles and many small animals, and all the unusual decorative trees which the Cadbury family had planted—the Norway maple, hornbeam, beech and masses of blossoming trees and bushes such as azaleas, rhododendrons, red hawthorn, pink and white horse chestnuts and laburnum. The water lilies were lovely in spring. The snowdrops in February were a lovely sight and daffodils, narcissus and crocuses were thick on the ground. The apples were picked by the children and stored in the apple storeroom, and lasted until the following March. The boys grew all the soft fruits and vegetables and the girls looked after the flower gardens. We had flowers on the dining room tables nearly all the year round.

We were told that Uffculme was the third open-air school in Europe and many education officers came to see it. Its plan was in our books at Training College and was copied identically in many towns later. The Cadburys had built and stocked the school down to the last knife, fork and spoon, all with the name Uffculme engraved on them. Every Christmas all the children and staff got chocolates sent to them. I met Mrs. Barrow Cadbury, who was a lovely person. Miss Hibbert was very friendly with the Cadburys and used to go for lunch with Mrs. Cadbury.

Miss Tidmus ('Tiddy' we called her) taught the youngest children. She was an uncertificated but very kind and caring teacher, and organised the Morris and maypole dancing in the school.

Edward James Anderson, 'Andy' or 'Jim' as we called him, had been a teacher at Uffculme for quite a few years when I first went to the school and later became the Head Teacher. He tended to be rather sarcastic but always encouraged children to do things despite their health problems.

The four classes were of mixed abilities and each class was more or less split into three: the brighter children who had missed a lot of school but were quite capable of learning and getting on; the ones in the middle who lost a lot of time through illness but still would make good solid citizens; and the very dull children who were the sort usually ignored by ordinary schools. I don't think I was especially strict but I never had any disciplinary problems. I did find if you started with a new class you had to be very firm to let them know what was expected of them. It wasn't easy to teach at Uffculme as if you concentrated on encouraging the bright ones, the rest did nothing, and if you helped the dull ones, the others got bored. There were usually 24 in a class which was smaller than most schools at the time.

THE 1940s: THE TURNING POINT

It was occasionally difficult to enforce rest period but most children were glad of a rest. As children usually came to the school one or two at a time they accepted the rest, as everyone else did. In winter we used to sit in a deck chair with a blanket or hot water bottle while supervising 'rest'. I always felt the children should have more blankets than they did but they seemed alright. They were supposed to lie on their right sides so they could not reach both sides of the bed.

During the war we often got to the school in the morning to find that some children had been out all night picking up 'molotov cocktails'! Teaching carried on in Kempsey when some of the children were evacuated there and were billeted in different houses, while I went to a manor house where I had a huge four poster bed and chaise-longue in my room! The children were well looked after—their health improved with good country food and fresh air.

I suffered from the cold and often had chest problems as a child but was very fit while at Uffculme. When it was very cold we kept on having breaks to exercise ourselves, jumping up and down outside or walking around the classrooms swinging our arms on our chests! Sometimes we could only use pencils to write with, as the ink froze! We skated on the frozen pond in the hard winter of 1947—I remember Mr. Anderson trying out the ice first. Everyone went sliding on it—the rhododendron bushes broke our falls! There were two ponds, one was partly drained and made into a bog garden.

A summer lesson out of doors in sundresses and shorts, 1940s. (M.Wales)

During the 1940's the school didn't close in the long school holidays. Children had a long day, starting at half past eight, and finishing at half past five. Breakfasts of bacon and egg, sausages, toast and porridge were provided for children and teachers alike. I don't remember any great fights to force the children to eat the food—most of them were so much in the open air that they were very hungry and usually wolfed it down ... I didn't agree with forcing children to eat their cold porridge, though, which was often the case.

Children could run anywhere around Uffculme school grounds at playtime, including the field below, but were excluded from the teachers' lawn in front of the dining room. There were lots of apple trees in front of the dining room. When one very big tree was cut down an owl was found to be nesting inside.

Clogs were worn by children when they were doing their gardening so that they didn't get cold feet or damp shoes on the wet soil. We followed a normal curriculum at Uffculme but many lessons were interrupted by children going to the nurse for treatment, inspections or showers. Some children with bad chests had physiotherapy. Others had sunray treatment, carefully timed and recorded by Nurse Bendall (Darkie we called her, because of her dark black hair). There was also an isolation room with three beds. Many children stayed at Uffculme for the duration of their school life.

I enjoyed teaching at Uffculme because of the beautiful surroundings, and there were never many disciplinary problems. Sometimes we were glad if the children could find the energy to be naughty as some were so often ill. I was always pleased in later years to meet ex pupils who had recovered from childhood ills.

Cropwood 1940-4

The school log book begins with Twelfth Night and is a fascinating commentary of life during the war, with evacuees from Birmingham's Special Schools. Most pupils had remained at Cropwood over Christmas 1939 and teachers and staff had worked so hard to provide an enjoyable festive season for the evacuated children.

Cropwood log book 1940

6 Jan.   *Twelfth Night Party—a huge success. Everyone delighted with their 'useful' gift—soap, toothpaste, etc. We have 74 present—76 on roll.*

8 Jan.   *Black Monday with a vengeance! Five Baskerville children, led by one who is nearly fourteen and had engineered the whole affair, ran away before anyone was awake this morning. Miss Boothroyd and Miss Clark went after them with a car, but were unsuccessful in finding them. It was after 6 o'clock in the evening before the police were able to inform us that they were all safe.*

9 Jan.   *Two of the girls have been brought back—one the ringleader—it was abominable behaviour on her part to take younger children into danger. We have heard that one other is to return shortly and there is no further news of the other two.*

15 Jan.   *Dr. Wilson came today—two children have ringworm and have to go to the skin hospital.*

21 Jan.   *Iris J's birthday—every girl had an apple, a cake and a trifle for tea.*

28 Jan.   *Everywhere is thick snow today and it is still falling this evening. The children were unable to go to Church today so Miss Boothroyd took a Service in the playroom.*

29 Jan.   *Today we are completely isolated. The telephone is out of order and we can only walk along the paths cut for us by the gardeners. We have had no milk today.*

30 Jan.   *A bright day, but no improvement in the snow-bound roads. A churn of milk arrived at the station and the big girls helped the gardeners to bring it up on the sledge. The drifts of snow are four or five feet deep, and where it is untrodden we have been able to trace the tracks of birds. Perfect **ice** casts of leaves are to be found on the leaves of evergreens. It is very cold again.*

10 Feb.   *Visiting Day, and the most sunny day this year. It is still very cold and the snow still lies on the ground, thick in many places.*

11 Feb.   *Today Dr. Smallwood came and saw the Baskerville children.*

17 Feb.   *This morning we wakened up to see snow again—really thick again. We are all sorry. The children have had enough of it and it is trying for them to be somewhat restricted in their activities. They were all able to go a good walk again this afternoon. We have had to have walks almost every day during the past week, it was too cold even to **hold** pencils.*

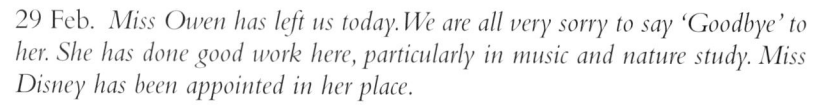

29 Feb.   *Miss Owen has left us today. We are all very sorry to say 'Goodbye' to her. She has done good work here, particularly in music and nature study. Miss Disney has been appointed in her place.*

15 Mar.   *Dr. Smallwood came today. The Baskerville children return to Baskerville on April 1st or after the holidays if they go home.*

20 Mar.   *56 children went home today for the Easter holiday. The children staying were taken to Bromsgrove today to the cinema.*

24 Mar.   *Eggs for breakfast and Easter eggs for all the children today. They have had a very happy time and the weather has enabled them to be out of doors most of the time.*

4 April   *Dr. Wilson came for a routine inspection. Dr. Gale came this morning and seemed pleased with the progress of the orthopaedic children in this environment.*

THE 1940s: THE TURNING POINT

5 April   Mr. Wilson Stuart visited this morning and commented on the greatly improved physical condition of his patients.

6 June   Dr. Wilson came today. It has been decided to accept the nine girls already registered for evacuation from Little Green Lane and George Street West without sending home **any** from here—thus bringing our numbers to **90**.

13 June   Mr. & Mrs. Barrow Cadbury came today. It is their first visit since Mrs. Cadbury retired from our committee—it was delightful to see them. A number of the members of the Camp School Committee, including Dr. Innis, came in after their meeting at the Camp School.

17 June   Mr. Wilson Stuart came today and saw all the orthopaedic children. He remarked on the improvement in their general physical condition.

19 June   Today, for the first time, we have been able to use the pool. It is crystal clear and the filtration plant is working well. The children were very excited and enjoyed their 'dip' very much.

20 June   Today Miss Bell has been married to Mr. Wetherell, a master at the Boys' school. They both have a week's holiday. The Committee have to decide if they will continue to employ Mrs. Wetherell. It is expected that there will be no difficulty about this, at any rate during the war.

25 June   Miss Boothroyd had the first 'yellow' warning at 1.45am this morning. She wakened the staff and 'stood by', however no siren was sounded and the 'All Clear' came through at about 3.50am.

26 June   We were awakened at half-past eleven last night by the siren. Everyone was quickly on duty and the children were in the shelters in about 5 minutes. The yellow warning only came at the end of the siren. The behaviour of the children was excellent; there was no sign of fear or alarm and they carried out in perfect order the movements they had practised.

27 June   We are now working on our new rota for night duty. Only three people are wakened by a yellow—Miss Boothroyd who has the telephone by her bedside—one at the Extension and one at Rosemary. After a fortnight, Sister and Miss Arnot will each relieve Miss Boothroyd for a week. Mr. Groves and Mr. Perrygrove come on duty at once in the event of a siren. Another yellow warning last night, but only half an hour.

28 June   The children are all very well and not showing any signs of strain. The staff are splendid. Mrs. Wetherell is back.

30 June   Siren at 11.35pm last night. The children were so good and slept in the shelters. It was a long wait 2½ hours before the 'All Clear'. Many of them are tired today but quite as usual otherwise—we lengthened 'rest' by half-an-hour.

25 July   Thirty five children are left here for the holiday and the rest went home today.

1 Aug.   The children have had a very enjoyable week and are well and happy. Today was 'Party Day' with swimming in the morning, treasure hunt and party tea. Last night a 'purple' warning lasted 5½ hours. Only one person is 'standing-by' now.

12 Aug.   End of the holiday. The children all say that they have had a lovely time—in the Pool twice a day and several of them can nearly swim. Today six new children were admitted and thirty two girls came back so we are 70 now.

24 Aug.   *Air raid warnings most nights—up to today but for periods not more than three hours.*

31 Aug.   *Air raid warnings every night for eight days—each one five, six or seven hours. The children are very good and sleep very well in the shelters. The staff were feeling the strain—so one shelter is now arranged into beds for any sick children and five staff each night.*

5 Sep.   *Dr. Wilson visited. Mr. & Mrs. Barrow Cadbury called.*

7 Sep.   *For 15 days now we have had long warnings every night—everyone is well except five children with tonsillitis.*

8 Sep.   *One case of diphtheria removed to the isolation hospital today.*

9 Sep.   *The room fumigated and a visit from the sanitary inspector over, we hope we shall have no more diphtheria. Two girls still have tonsillitis.*

23 Sep.   *Visit of Mr. Wilson Stuart for the Orthopaedic children, with the new Masseuse—Miss McIndoe.*

18 Oct.   *Last visit of Dr. Wilson who takes up her new appointment on 1st November. We are all sorry she is leaving us. She has shown such personal interest in the children. Miss Ross came this morning and told us of the resolution passed by the Committee that we should treat all sirens as 'alerts' and go down to the shelters at the discretion of Miss Boothroyd. A rota has therefore been arranged—one member of the staff will patrol each night after an alert has sounded and will call Miss Boothroyd if she considers danger is approaching. The children will thus only be taken to the shelters when danger is imminent. Whoever is up at night on the rota has next morning in bed.*

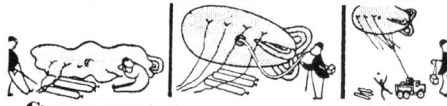

26 Oct.   *A week's working of the plan has proved its worth. Everyone is better in health and life is proceeding fairly normally again. It has been decided also to recommence visiting days and the first was held today. Despite considerable interference to traffic, following the recent bombing of Birmingham, there were a large number of visitors and everything passed very pleasantly.*

20 Nov.   *Last night and last Thursday when Coventry was bombed have been the worst nights we have had—great noise and continuous 'planes—we spent some time in the shelters each night.*

24 Nov.   *A meeting held in Birmingham this morning; nurses and Heads of schools summoned by wireless. Birmingham is largely waterless therefore further evacuation immediately.*

26 Nov.   *Seven evacuated cripples arrived today with Sister Hodgson and Miss McIndoe.*

11 Dec.   *Last night none of the staff slept at all. It was a very bad raid—five bombs fell in this area, one in the field at the rear of Rosemary Cottage. No one was hurt. It was an intensely cold night and the gunfire so heavy it was thought unwise to go to the shelters. The children were all assembled in the safest parts of the ground floor.*

20 Dec.   *Today 33 children have gone home for Xmas. We have five staff and 56 girls left for the holiday.*

Cropwood log book 1941

6 Jan.   *The Xmas holiday has been a good one, and all the children had a thoroughly good time. Owing*

THE 1940s: THE TURNING POINT

to the generosity of our many friends and of the Lord Mayor, we have had enough money to see that all the children had Xmas presents and that plenty of 'treats' were possible too.

7 Jan.   *Mrs. Wetherell has resigned—she is going to have a baby.*

20 Jan.   *Snow has been falling for three days, and once more we are 'snowed up' and the sledges are in use again to bring our provisions up from the station.*

31 Jan.   *Last night we heard with sorrow the announcement of the death of Mrs. Barrow Cadbury.*

3 Feb.   *Miss Boothroyd, Sister Daniels and Nurse Keen attended the Memorial Service for Mrs. Cadbury at the Friends' Institute in Moseley Road.*

4 Jan.   *The girls have collected £1.20 and asked that it be sent to the Red Cross in memory of Mrs. Cadbury. Miss Boothroyd is doing this.*

27 Feb.   *Miss M.A. Clark appointed today as successor to Mrs. Wetherell.*

12 Mar.   *We saw in the distance a bomber being shot down near Droitwich. The flames were discernible with the naked eye.*

17 Mar.   *The picture 'The Shepherd Boy', having been bought with the money collected by the girls in memory of Mrs. Barrow Cadbury, arrived yesterday. It is very attractive. At the suggestion of Mr. Cadbury this is being presented to Long Rede—annex of the Loveday Maternity Hospital and scene of Mrs. Cadbury's last work. The girls took the picture this afternoon and the matron was delighted with it.*

22 Mar.   *Letter received from Maternity Hospital. Mr. Cadbury has also written to say how much he likes the picture.*

10 April   *Last night there was a sudden and very violent raid concentrated for about 3 hours against Blackwell and district, and continuing over Birmingham. Large numbers of flares and incendiaries dropped around us in the fields, so that we appeared to be encircled. Half the children were taken to shelter, but the rest were put under the beds, owing to danger of shrapnel and high explosives which were now falling. Today, members of the Camp School staff took meals with us, since their building was destroyed. No one in any of the schools was hurt.*

16 April   *Children enjoy gardening and walks.*

16 May   *Visit of Mr. Barrow Cadbury and Miss Cadbury. Mr. Cadbury has given £3 for a 'treat'.*

17 May   *Last night Birmingham was attacked by enemy aircraft and in accordance with our new plan we all got up, and at the first appearance of flares, took the children to the shelters. We were there from 1.20 am until 4.0 am.*

3 July   *Visit of Dr. Sainsbury, who passed the list of children to go in the pool. 14 children are to be brought up for Terminal Review. Miss Arnot while on fire-watching at 2.00am, was startled by the sudden appearance of a strange man. He was apparently deranged, as she was unable to make any sense of his references to spiritualism. He was quite calm and not at all aggressive. She succeeded in getting his name and address and informed the Police.*

11 Aug.   *Miss Boothroyd went into hospital. 40 children fetched from town by Miss Disney.*

29 Aug.   *Doctor called in to see Ruth M's ear. Teresa J. has new plaster at Broad St. Miss Boothroyd out of hospital.*

1 Oct.   *Miss Boothroyd returned to duty.*

2 Oct.   The man G. H. was trespassing again tonight having left postcards full of rubbish on the piano stool in the lounge on other evenings. P.C. Hanmer arrested him and took him to Bromsgrove Police Station.

19 Nov.   Visit of HMI Miss Bardsley. Committee meeting at which it has been decided to close Cropwood from 22nd Dec. until 12th January.

Cropwood log book 1942

18 Jan.   Heavy snow. New coats given out and appreciated in bitter weather.

20 Jan.   Another fall of snow—all transport very difficult—tobogganing very popular and taken by Miss Mitchell in 'Sandy's field'. Sledges were also used for bringing goods from the station.

27 Jan.   The coldest day—it was impossible to sit in school—walks and runs taken both morning and afternoon—also wireless programmes heard in playroom.

11 Mar.   Dr. Donovan's first visit as orthopaedic surgeon—he commented on the good general condition of the girls.

14 April   Cropwood is looking lovely, the daffodils are out. It has been decided that the girls should look after all the flower beds and edges, the gardeners being occupied with the vegetables.

20 April   The gardeners having cut the lawns once—the girls are now cutting them regularly for the rest of the summer.

14 May   Dr. Sainsbury visited—he feared it might be his last visit as he is de-reserved on 24th May.

11 June   First visit of Dr. Roberts to replace Dr. Sainsbury—we shall miss him and hope he likes the army.

11 July   Visiting Day sunny today. Class I performed 'King Cophetua and the Beggarmaid' on the lawn and did some country dancing. An exhibition of needlework and handwork was shown. Over thirty girls have made their own summer frocks this year, and each of Class II has made a pinafore. The standard of the needlework is high. From scraps of every kind Class I have made thirty-five animals and dolls and golliwogs. They make an attractive display.

16 July   Miss Ross has asked us to send the toys to Shenley Fields Nursery School.

20 Aug.   Dr. Roberts came today—she saw 10 new children, 6 from Haseley Hall, which has been closed to be re-opened as an Open-Air School for little boys.

28 Aug.   Miss Clark extracted her honey this morning. The girls were able to watch and taste! She had 45lbs of honey, of which we are able to buy 14lbs for the school—Miss Clark has given everyone honey for breakfast tomorrow.

1 Sep.   We have 'lent' Sister Daniels for a week to help open Haseley Hall.

14 Sep.   We have decided to give a Swimming Display on Saturday in aid of the Merchant Navy Comforts Service. We are all working hard for this and are anxious to raise our £10 and get a certificate.

19 Sep.   We held the Swimming Display this afternoon. The visitors enjoyed the programme. Tickets were 6d and included tea which was prepared by Mrs. Perrygrove and handed round by five Class II girls dressed as waitresses. Class II also held a fruit stall—in conjunction with their project and much useful work in practical arithmetic had gone to its preparation. Up to the present we appear to have raised £5.0.1d.

Today's show ends the swimming season, the most successful yet—fifteen girls have learnt to swim, and swim well, some also diving, life-saving etc. Many of the cripple evacuees have benefited very much too.

THE 1940s: THE TURNING POINT

30 Oct.   Mrs. Dallas Warder called for the sack of garments for the Merchant Navy Comforts Service and was delighted to receive our first £10.

14 Dec.   Xmas Party. A very good one with a lovely tea thanks to Miss Arnot's good management—lots of games and competitions. Captain Clayton very kindly was Father Christmas again.

15 Dec.   Merchant Navy Concert. Every girl in the school took some part. Mrs. Warder came to the concert and received the money and a new pile of garments from the girls. She told them that with the £22 raised this term, 22 seamen have been supplied with comforts.

17 Dec.   Cropwood broke up for the holiday—regretfully saying Goodbye to Miss Disney and to Nurse Young, both of whom are returning to Little Green Lane P.D. School.

Cropwood log book 1943

11 Jan.   School re-opened and Miss Wishart replaced Miss Disney as mistress of Class I.

10 Feb.   'The Happy Man' and 'Black Sambo' were performed today at Hunter's Hill for the boys, and were very well received.

11 Mar.   The weather is lovely. Rest is taken out of doors almost every day, and the children are all very well.

4 May   Miss Boothroyd went to Birmingham to fetch the new children—twelve were admitted today, all look thin and grey-faced and very much in need of Open Air treatment.

8 May   One of the new children taken home today; she was **very** homesick.

6 June   Cropwood is 21 years old today.

9 June   Informal 21st birthday held today. Mr. & Mrs. Newsome (neé Wilton), Mrs. Buckley and Sister Dorrie (from Hunter's Hill) came and all our staff—also three old girls. We had a lovely tea—Miss Arnot made a very good war-time birthday cake, and Nurse Keen who has been here since the school opened cut the cake. It was a very successful party and everyone enjoyed it. Everyone had a small composite picture of Cropwood given as a small souvenir—Class I girls did them

Captain Clayton who has been 'Santa Claus' for several years sent a 'wire' herewith affixed ['Congratulations on your coming of age. Santa Claus, Toy Bazaar, Ice Berg, Polar Regions.']

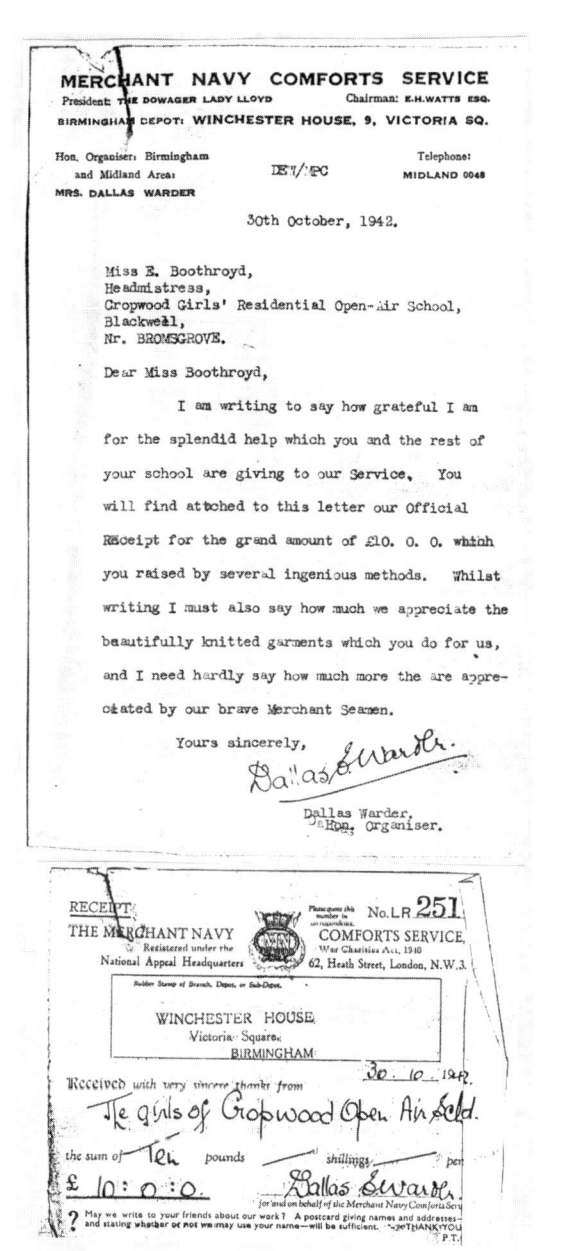

22 June   *Wild flowers and Common Grasses competitions judged. Gwen Birtle and Eunice Clark the winners.*

3 July   *Visiting Day … Our school collection for the Stalingrad Hospital raised £2.15s. We have received our second certificate from the Merchant Navy Comforts Service—six emergency rescue kits provided this time.*

7 July   *The dentist visited today. 20 girl and 20 boy gas cases were successfully treated. Mr. Linn being in the army now, Mr. Baker came, with Mr. Cockburn as anaesthetist.*

20 July   *Mrs. Warder came today. We were able to hand over another £10 and 64 garments for the Merchant Navy Comforts Service. Our total is now £45.*

10 Aug.   *Eleven new girls were admitted today—all very pale and in need of Cropwood. They appeared to settle down at once.*

16 Oct.   *30th October—Holiday school. Games and competitions, needlework and handiwork filled the days. Expeditions to Barnt Green and Bromsgrove made. House Dancing and Entertainments Competitions were held, and a Hallow E'en party ended the festivities. We have now had eleven cases of chicken pox, all told.*

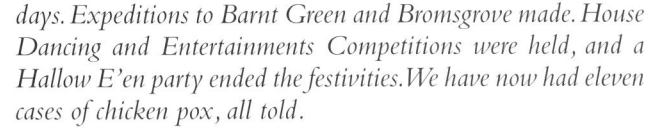

6 Dec.   *Iris J. has won 5/- in the Turog National Handwriting Competition.*

13 Dec.   *Handwork & Needlework were displayed today for Miss Ross to see. She was pleased with what she saw, especially with the Needlework and some Xmas stockings made and filled by Class II for a Nursery School. Miss Clark is in bed today with 'flu. The children are all gargling and having a nasal douche each morning, as a preventative measure.*

22 Dec.   *'Flu broke out in the last weekend and we had ten cases—luckily it was a mild kind. Dr. Mitchell came out both Monday and Tuesday; he arranged for two children to go to hospital and the rest were sent home by ambulance today.*

Cropwood log book 1944

11 Jan.   *Seven new girls were admitted today and seem quite happy. One of them is the school baby—just five years old.*

9 Feb.   *Dr. Mitchell brought Dr. Halliday Sutherland to see the school today. They stayed until after lunch, so were able to make a comprehensive inspection. Dr. Sutherland, an authority on TB as well as an eminent author and the originator of the Open-Air School in Regents Park in 1911, said that Cropwood has full sanatorium conditions and the treatment is complete aero-therapy. It was a most enjoyable day, both Dr. Mitchell and Dr. Sutherland are interesting men to talk to and both staff and children were charmed with their visit.*

19 Feb   *We had a conjuror at Cropwood, his fee was covered by Mr. Cadbury's gift, and he was a great success.*

14 Mar.   *Class II went to Redditch to see over T. Hessin's needle factory. Mr. Clayton (Father Xmas) is the owner, and he gave the girls a most interesting time.*

THE 1940s: THE TURNING POINT

25 Mar.   *It was with regret we learned today of the death of Kathleen S. Head Girl until Xmas 1943. We were able to send a spray of daffodils to the funeral.*

11 May   *Dr. Roberts visited today. Preparations for Sports for the visitors forged ahead. We are sadly missing Miss Hardy who left on 30th April after nine years at Cropwood.*

27 July   *Today Class I produced scenes from 'Little Women'—it was most successfully done and a great credit both to the performers and to Miss Symons who produced it.*

5 Sep.   *Today we had the honour of a visit from the Lady Mayoress of Birmingham, accompanied by Miss Ross. A small show of work was on view and each class did something—games, a dramatised story and country dancing. Class II were making notebooks. Last night we had extracted honey amid great excitement and the evidences were still in Class II. Miss Clark had bottled a small jar for each of our visitors. Miss Arnot had produced a lovely tea and we all enjoyed it.*

22 Nov.   *We have decided to limit the amount of tuck next term and to try to stop 'stuffing' on Visiting Day. Numbers of girls have been sick and ill from over-eating.*

The following reminiscences of ex-pupils of Cropwood in this era provide further insight into the daily life and routine of the open-air school:

Mrs. Betty Roberts (née **Phillips**), Cropwood 2 weeks 1940, Kidderminster, Worcs.

I spent two weeks at Cropwood Open-Air School during the war. We were sent for a break from the bombing and having to spend most nights in the shelter.

Our parents were only allowed one visit. We were allowed to buy sweets in the tuck shop every afternoon as sweets weren't on ration at the time. The food was very good and plenty of it, and everything was very clean.

Mrs. Audrey Plowman (née **Reid**), Cropwood 1941-3, South Australia

I was a pupil at Cropwood then I worked there until I got married in 1951. Miss Boothroyd was Headmistress, I can remember Miss Hardy, Miss Clark, Sister Daniels, Miss Arnot (Housekeeper), Mrs. Bailey, Miss Williams, Miss Soar, Miss Deakin (Sewing Mistress), Mr. & Mrs. Perrygrove (Caretakers), Nurse Keen, Miss Leadbeater, Miss Bloomfield, and Miss Twist (Cook).

We had our own woods and a place called Cloughda which was a hill with trees on and had a cabin up there; it had a fire place and beds up in the roof. I can remember Rosemary Cottage up the road where about 20 of us used to sleep and how scary it was on dark nights during the war when no lights were allowed and we would have to walk up there. Two older girls would have to go to the kitchen to pick up the staff's supper to take up with us and sometimes the girls would have left before the cook had it ready. (The old soup can often got spilt and we would have to fill it up with water.) I can remember the old showers, eight or ten at a time went in and you stood under them in a big tin that looked like a frying pan. I also remember filling tin cans with hot water to get our beds warm in winter.

We had tennis courts, and swings on top of the hill near the air-raid shelters. We also had two sledges, red and blue, which we had great fun with when it snowed on Hunter's Hill. I remember knitting for the Merchant Navy—when you had knitted ten garments you got a badge (I still have the knitting book of patterns we used).

Mrs. Jean Green (née **Nash**), 59, Cropwood 1943-5, Sutton Coldfield, West Midlands

I became a pupil at Cropwood Open-Air School in 1943 when I was eight years old. I had had a lot of 'chest trouble'—probably bronchitis, and was thought to be 'delicate'—a description of me which my family

and friends find very amusing nowadays. When I was six years old I was extremely ill with congestion of the lungs (pneumonia), and though penicillin had been developed by 1941, it was not available to the general public. I was very ill for many weeks and was lucky to survive. This, I believe, was the reason I was sent to Cropwood.

As well as the Headmistress, Miss Boothroyd, and the teaching staff, Cropwood had two nurses, Nurse Comb—small, and round with friendly brown eyes, and Nurse Keen—tall and gingery, with a sharp face and sharp manner. I was given a bed in the 'extension'. After I had been at Cropwood a while, I fancied sleeping at Rosemary, so I asked Miss Boothroyd if I could be moved there. She appeared shocked at my temerity in asking such a thing, but a few weeks later I was moved to Rosemary and very much enjoyed walking there each evening and back to Cropwood each morning. Nurse Comb or Nurse Keen accompanied us and in windy weather I remember Nurse Keen, breasting the wind like the figurehead on a ship, calling 'Forge ahead girls, forge ahead!'.

There were three classes at Cropwood to cover the age range 5 to 14 and when I was nine, I was put into the top class, Class 1, where some of the girls were 14 years of age. It was the custom for all the 'big girls' in the top class to 'adopt' a little girl in the bottom class. The oldest girl in the class always had first choice of little girl, the second eldest had second choice and so on, with the youngest having to wait till last. By the time all the others had made a choice, the only little girl left for me was Rosina Haynes—happy, friendly—but by far the untidiest child in Class 3, with the muddiest shoes (which I had to clean) and always with enormous holes in her stockings (which I had to darn), a raw deal indeed. Miss Symons, the class teacher, did not give me lessons suitable for my age, I just had to do what the older girls did as best I could. Consequently, I missed two years of progressive teaching in maths, which became more obvious as I got older. Classes 1 and 2 were built like bandstands in the grounds—open on three sides, just the blackboard wall being permanent and we did lessons in our coats.

Twice a day, morning and afternoon, we had to have rest periods. In the summer we had to lie on the stretchers early in the morning, without any clothes, and sunbathe for a few minutes. In hot weather we were encouraged to go without clothes all day, though the older girls were allowed to wear knickers and blouses.

After breakfast we all had to do domestic chores. Whether this was genuinely to teach us how to do housework, or a way of saving on domestic help, I don't know. On Wednesday and Saturday afternoons we had no lessons, so after cleaning our shoes and darning our socks, we had some free time. We were allowed to have a few sweets on these days. When our parents sent us sweets they were stored in named shoe boxes (which were called tuck boxes) in a locked cupboard. My mother sent me a letter and a parcel every week, which arrived every Tuesday morning without fail, and it was only when I was older that I appreciated how much time and effort this must have cost her in wartime, when everything was rationed and many things were unobtainable.

The food at Cropwood was very basic. We used to lie in bed and fantasise about the food at home—quite ordinary food like beans on toast, or even just toast.

While we were at Cropwood we had no access to newspapers or radios and we forgot that there was a war on, there being no evidence of it in Blackwell. Five houses in the road where I lived in Birmingham were bombed during this time, but it never occurred to me that while I was away my family could be wiped out.

My two years at Cropwood began my lifetime love of books and reading. We had access to a small library and I walked around most of the time with a book under my arm. On Sunday evenings in the winter, Class I were allowed to sit and sew in the playroom, a lovely room with bay windows on two walls and a polished wooden floor. Miss Boothroyd read 'Jane Eyre' to us. I loved listening to her read and this is one of my happiest memories of Cropwood. We were also taught embroidery and I still have a lined hessian bag on which I embroidered a sample of several different stitches in wool.

Apart from my own circle of friends, two girls I remember very well were Gladys Roberts and Phyllis Staples. Gladys was the leader of 'Gladys' Gang' and Phyllis was her best friend. If you were in 'Gladys' Gang' you were someone, if you weren't you didn't count—at least in the eyes of the gang. I have often wondered what Gladys went on to do in life. I don't know what was the basis of her power—I certainly don't remember her being a bully—but whatever it was it was very strong. Gladys' Gang got up to all sorts of things. They said that Gladys' record said 'Gladys has strong leadership qualities' and I didn't doubt it.

It became the fashion to run away from Cropwood and try to get home. Girls who tried this by various ingenious means were always caught and brought back, usually from the Railway Station—though occasionally someone did get further. I used to listen to their exploits with interest but privately thought them quite mad. After one girl's abortive attempt to run away, we were lectured by Nurse Keen on how ungrateful we were and how lucky we were to be there at all.

I consider myself most fortunate to have been a pupil at Cropwood and I'm sure the experience has enriched my life. Yes, we were cold much of the time, but the regime worked for me as I've never had any chest trouble since I left. I learnt to appreciate many things including books, wild flowers and the countryside. I became independent and resourceful as a result of having to look after myself (and my little girl!) at so young an age, which was to stand me in good stead as my mother died only five years later when I was fifteen.

Mrs. Margaret Hewitt (née **Kite**), 57, Cropwood 1942-5, Solihull, West Midlands

I must have been about four and a half when I became a pupil at Cropwood. My mother had a bad time with me due to my very bad asthma attacks. Many nights she or I did not sleep because I couldn't breathe and had to be propped up in bed, in order to get some air into my lungs. In those days, there was no such thing as inhalers or drugs to eliminate our breathing problems.

I can remember the very first day I arrived. I had no idea, in my childhood mind, that I wouldn't be going home. I was taken by the hand by a big lady, and we began to ascend a large staircase. I can still feel the fear as she let go of my hand and said, 'Now follow me and hurry up'. I was only a dot, and couldn't climb the stairs as quickly as she did, and then to my horror, she disappeared out of sight, so I just kept climbing, getting more and more tearful by the second. I saw an enormous bell and wooden railings looking over fields. I remember I panicked and screamed, which disturbed several bats. Yes, I had gone right up into the belfry. By this time the big lady had wondered where I was, heard me, and brought me down. And so she held my hand now and took me into a dark room with lots of cloth and half sewn dresses. Her name, I remember, was Mrs. Deakin, she was obviously the seamstress. She measured up my tiny frame for my uniform. I remember how kind she was to me and my fears subsided.

I soon began to realise that my mother and father had left me, 'all for your own good, and you will soon be better, and then you can come home for good'. And so my education at Cropwood began. Miss Clark was our teacher—a small lady, wearing always a brown dress and big brown shoes. Miss Clark taught us all the names of the trees, which we recognised by their leaves. We would go on nature walks in the grounds, where we learnt to name wild flowers, to press them, and write their names in a book.

I have memories of lying on sunbeds, always very early in the morning when the rays of the sun were at their lowest, but most beneficial to us all. We were all quite naked but that didn't matter, we were far too young to care.

We had a lot of free time to ourselves when we were allowed to go out to play. In the summer we didn't wear shoes. I had a friend called Barbara. We used to go on to the hillside, and eat anything we could find, like vinegar leaves, pignuts, bread and cheese (hawthorn leaves) and even clover blossoms. One day, after we had been 'feasting', the nurse noticed our mouths, hands and clothes were stained red. Immediately we were taken into the surgery where we were forced to drink salt water to make us sick. I had no ill effects although I wasn't sick but I'll never forget that salt water!

In the short time I had stayed at Cropwood I cannot remember ever having an asthma attack. I began to thrive, being able to breathe properly and put on a bit of weight. I was so thin that I was like a stick. I remember the lovely bacon we had for breakfast, with bread and butter, and also an egg, if our parents were able to bring some from home. My parents kept chickens at home and my mother always wrote my name in pencil on the eggshell. I remember many times for our tea we had raw honey on the beeswax comb, and we were told to chew the wax.

In the evenings, as I got older, we went into a room where we had assemblies and prayers and 'Musical Movement' exercises with Betty Driver on the radio. In the evenings in the winter, we used to sit and knit navy blue scarves for the Merchant Navy men at sea. We used to have games to see who could knit the longest scarf. I often wondered if mine was ever worn, even in spite of some of the holes I'd made when I dropped a stitch or two.

*Us little ones all had what was known as 'A Big Girl' to look after us. But because they were much older than us, we felt in awe of them. When our parents visited us, with sweets or chocolates, or cakes and books, our Big Girls used to hang around until they had gone home, and then they would scrounge everything we had been given. The staff must have found out about this and asked our parents to hand things to them. And so it was 'Tuck Day' came about. We all sat cross-legged at the top of the big staircase in anticipation of what we had in our tuck boxes. Each named box was taken from a small locked cupboard and we were presented with **some** of the goodies in the box. Sweet rationing was still in force and the staff had to be stringent with our rations.*

We had so much fun in the swimming pool, and I really can't ever remember being taught to swim but it just came so naturally to me. We swam up and down that oval shaped pool and splashed and laughed, until the mistress called us out to get dressed, and go and get our hot cocoa.

I left Cropwood with a good bill of health. The doctor said my asthma was certainly cured. I have had one or two attacks as I've become older, but with the help of an inhaler I've managed to cope.

If only I could go back in time and thank the people responsible for my wellbeing it would be wonderful. Miss Boothroyd, the Headmistress, was like a mother to us. Of course, looking back, everything had to be a little regimental, and we got quite homesick at times, but Cropwood left me with some very valuable memories of friendship and togetherness, that I think the average child of today lacks. We were made aware of the wonderful world around us, of trees and birds and insects and the growing of a tiny plant, and above all God's wonderful fresh air.

Hunter's Hill 1940-4

Miss Gertrude Walton, as Headmistress of Hunter's Hill, continued to keep a very detailed school log book until she left at the beginning of 1943. Miss Linda Buckley, an established teacher at the school, originally from Fenny Bentley in Derbyshire, was promoted as Headmistress from that date and remained there for a total of 26 years until her retirement. Some of the more interesting war-time log book entries are detailed below:

Hunter's Hill log book 1940

29 Jan.   *Nurse Fenton away ill. Very heavy snow. As boys cannot go out to play we are having 15 mins extra in bed in the morning while the snow is so thick.*

2 Feb.   *Nine Baskerville boys went home today.*

3 Feb.   *Visiting day postponed on account of the snow.*

16 Feb.   *Sister Nicholls and Sister Daniels in bed with influenza.*

24 Feb.   *Miss Buckley taken to Isolation Hospital with measles.*

1 June   John T. who had been on holiday for three weeks returned today and made such a scene that his parents took him home again.

26 Aug.   As the boys were seven hours in the shelters last night it was not possible to start school until 11am.

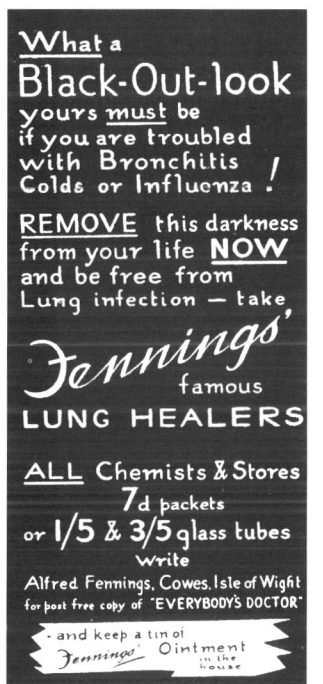

27 Aug.   The boys were again in the shelter for six hours but as they slept most of the time we were able to start school at 10am.

16 Oct.   Committee meeting where it was decided that visiting day should be once a month instead of every week. The children have been in the shelters a great many times during the night lately and it was decided that in the future one member of the staff should remain on duty at night during an 'alert' and that children should be taken to the shelters at the discretion of the Head Teacher when danger might seem imminent.

28 Oct.   Miss Walton on holiday. Ten cases of chicken-pox. Three boys with 'shelter throats'—very high temperatures.

25 Nov.   Notice of 9 cripples to be evacuated here.

26 Nov.   Arrival of 17 cripples.

27 Nov.   Arrival of 5 more cripples. All children but cripples in shelter for two hours.

28 Nov.   Some of our own boys are now sleeping on stretchers in the 'Assembly Room' to make room for 24 P.D. [Physically Defective] children.

20 Dec.   All the boys who were leaving went home by train. There are 62 children left.

Hunter's Hill log book 1941

6 Jan.   The school has had a very peaceful happy fortnight's holiday and re-opens as a school today. 51 boys arrived.

1 Mar.   Three boys decamped today. One was to join his people who are evacuated to the country. One has gone off several times. The other one is to return. Miss Barrett in bed with influenza.

9 April   In the night we had to take in 22 babies (2-5) with 8 members of staff because of fire at the School Camp.

17 April   All the nursery school children except four boys (5 years old) and the staff left for Oxford.

26 April   James H. who had been very ill for four weeks with heart trouble was taken to hospital today.

9 May   James H. died in hospital today.

22 Dec.   94 children went home on the 12.10 train. The school is closed for the first time since July 1939.

Three pupils who were at Hunter's Hill during the early years of the war have vivid memories of the experience:

Mr. Norman Cattell, Hunter's Hill 1939-41, Solihull, West Midlands

I remember the day in 1939 when about ten of us from Little Green Lane school, Small Heath (Birmingham), were taken out of the big city war zone to an open-air school in the country. I was physically disabled and we were a mixture of bad legs, amputees, heart trouble and epileptics. Those boys who stayed were well looked after and enjoyed their stay at Hunter's Hill. Some boys could not come to terms with living away from home and were taken home on the first visiting day.

After breakfast four teams of boys from the four Houses would make the beds and clean the dormitories. The dormitories were very open-air with large windows. In winter you could wake to find snow on the foot end of your bed—especially if you were in the first row.

There were four open-air classrooms which completely opened on two sides. One letter home a week was a must and we wrote it in class time. There was no class work on Wednesday afternoon, Saturday afternoon or Sunday when one could follow one particular hobby or sporting activity, be it football, cricket, roller skating, chess, snooker or model making.

The school had several sledges and in snowy weather teachers and boys would sledge down Hunter's Hill. In winter we each had a polo [neck] jumper and a pair of riding type breeches, long socks and an overcoat. In summer we would wear shorts and an aertex shirt, a belt and a pair of long socks.

I can remember visits from the Cadbury family who always left a large box of chocolate bars which were given out on special tuck nights. We also used to be visited by a Birmingham Councillor who would read a chapter of a book called Honour Bright *to the assembled boys. He provided the school with some silver medallions to be presented yearly to the one who was voted 'The best loved boy in school.' I was chosen one year and I still treasure my medallion which has my name and the name of the school engraved on it. I became the school captain, perhaps because I was the oldest boy.*

Because of my disability I stayed until I was 15 when the Doc. found me fit to leave and seek employment.

Mr. John Hughes, Hunter's Hill 1939-44, Bournville, Birmingham

Soon after starting school in 1936 I had several asthma attacks and was moved to Uffculme Open-Air School. We were evacuated to Kempsey in September 1939. All I can remember of this is being taken to a farm and almost immediately being sat on an enormous shire horse. They thought I would like it, but I just screamed to be lifted down. The only other memory is of waking in the middle of the night unable to breathe with a large farm cat asleep on my chest!

The next memory is of a bewildered arrival at Hunter's Hill, where I stayed for the next five years until 1944. There were 4 dormitories and each had 30 beds in 3 rows of 10; each boy had to make their own bed complete with neat hospital-type tucked-in corners, and then the beds had to be lined up in three perfect lines. The dormitory teacher would squint along the head and foot rails of the metal beds to check if they were perfectly aligned, and all beds were inspected. Any bed not perfectly made would be stripped and you'd be told to start again. This probably happened to me a lot as a new arrival of only eight years old, unused to this sort of discipline.

*The next task in the winter was to polish our boots. We gathered by 'House' at the four corners of the enclosed playground, on the verandas, to perform this task. We were supervised by our house teacher until everybody's boots shone. Then to breakfast. If parents brought their son a real egg on visiting days then his name was written on the egg, and he would get it boiled (instead of dried egg) for his breakfast. I asked my parents **not** to bring me any eggs, as I much preferred dried egg (it was made like a huge omelette and cut into squares).*

The food I hated was tripe. It was like trying to chew Indiarubber and most of us found it inedible, but we were made to sit at table until it was all consumed!

When I arrived Miss Walton was Head Teacher, a kindly and pleasant lady who everyone liked. She retired around 1943 and was replaced by the PT teacher Miss Buckley who was a strict disciplinarian. She was feared, maybe respected, but not liked by anyone! Her idea of a good sporting event was boxing in the main hall on winter evenings. Everyone in turn was forced to don boxing gloves and fight, whether they wanted to or not—I hated it! There was quite a bit of blood, usually from noses.

There was a Surgery in the main quadrangle where cuts, bruises, colds and chilblains were treated. In the cold weather I remember having chilblains on my toes, fingers and ears. I've never been so cold, but it was supposed to be good for us! There was also a hospital room with three or four beds which was mainly used for boys with infectious diseases. As such diseases usually spread to more than three or four boys, this room was used as a staging post on one's way to Little Bromwich Isolation Hospital. I passed through twice—with chicken pox and measles.

Fellow pupils I remember—James Galbraith—my particular friend. Charlie Clements—he had no hands and only one foot, but managed everything wonderfully well and without any help.

I also remember Miss Liquorice, Nurse Barratt and Finky (the domestic help from somewhere in Europe). My particular form teacher was Miss Maguire, an excellent and pleasant teacher. She took several of us through our 12+ year to pass the 13+ exam to go on to a Commercial or Technical School in Birmingham. I think five or six passed; I went on to Sparkhill Commercial School. Before we left an Honours Board was created for those first five or six names and hung in the Dining Room.

Project work out of doors at Hunters Hill, 1940s. (C. Barrett)

Mr. Leslie Knight, Hunter's Hill 1940-1, Great Barr, Birmingham

I was at Hunter's Hill school during the Second World War, when I was aged nine and ten. I hated it. I went there as a disabled child, I have a spinal disability. I am now 62 years of age and in quite good health.

I remember the blackout at night, with no lights visible from the outside. At night, if we wanted to go to the toilet, we had to go along the veranda, into the toilet all in the dark as the lights could not be put on. There was a long underground air raid shelter outside the first dormitory; the floor was always covered with water. I remember doing air raid drill but do not remember going down the shelter during an air raid.

What do I remember about the food? Well, there was never enough of it. I think we were always hungry. When we had breakfast in the morning a teacher would have his sitting on a raised platform. When he had finished he would ask if any boy wanted the crusts left over from his toast, some boy always did. For supper we would have just half a round of bread and dripping. When our parents visited us we would have a boiled egg and a piece of cake, also bread and butter. But during the week it was bread and jam. Food parcels parents sent to boys we rarely saw.

I often saw boys run away at weekends and get a train back to Birmingham if they could. There was an open-air regime; I had frost bite at the back of my knees in the freezing winter weather. It was so strict some boy was always having the cane on the hands or across the backside. I had my hands caned a couple of times—six strokes on each hand.

Whenever we wrote home to our parents we had to give the finished letter to the teacher to read before we put it in the envelope. (This may have been for security reasons as it was during the war.) I hated it at the school and was always begging my parents to have me back home.

Hunter's Hill log book 1942

17 Jan.   *The boys went by bus to Bromsgrove today for their Christmas party which had to be postponed owing to Scarlet Fever.*

14 Sep.   *13 boys went to the Clinic to have their eyes tested.*

17 Dec.   *Since visiting day there has been an epidemic of mild flu. We have had 32 cases—mostly in bed for two or three days with a temperature. Seven boys were not able to go home with the rest today as they were not well enough.*

Hunter's Hill log book 1943

11 Jan.   *School re-opened today. Miss Buckley began her duties as Headmistress.*

Hunter's Hill log book 1944

1 Feb.   *Six new boys were admitted today one of whom John Y. absconded after tea and was later found in the signal box at Blackwell Station.*

2 Feb.   *Miss Maguire took up Duty here today.*

12 Feb.   *John Y. ran away early in the morning before anyone was up and was found by the station master crossing the line in front of a train. He will not promise to settle down.*

2 Mar.   *Three boys took the Secondary Schools Entrance examination Part I this morning.*

13 Mar.   *Visiting Day, boys gave a Pantomime to Parents and also played an exhibition House football match to raise funds for the Fleet Air Arm. A very successful day.*

5 April   *The Lord Mayor & Lady Mayoress of Birmingham visited the school today. The Lord Mayor presented the Honour Bright Cup to the boy chosen for this honour by the rest of the boys.*

14 July   *Peter C. to Anti-Tuberculosis Clinic for examination.*

16 July   *Ivor B. who has had mastoid on left ear had a recurrence of his old trouble today and was examined by Doctor Dick and sent into the Children's Hospital at once.*

10 Dec.   *Following the Visiting Day last Saturday we have had an outbreak of influenza. There are now 15 children in bed.*

20 Dec.   *Boys had their Christmas Party today and had a very good time. We had a conjuror in the afternoon. All boys up today.*

The school nurse gives us an interesting account of life at Hunter's Hill during the Second World War, and a teacher and several ex-pupils contribute their reminiscences.

Miss Claire Barrett, School Nurse, Hunter's Hill 1937-69, Blackwell, Worcestershire

At Christmas 1940 only Miss Buckley and myself were on duty, coping with the thirty to forty physically handicapped evacuated children who had not returned home. We stayed up very late Christmas Eve to fill all those stockings and were exhausted by the time the rest of the staff returned from their Christmas holiday!

I remember we had to get all children to the shelters during wartime air-raids. With so many crippled children it was a nightmare, as we had to carry them to the windows and give them to someone else to carry to shelters. It was not so bad while we still had the men, but when they were all called up it was much more difficult. Eventually we were told unless the raid was in close proximity, we were to put children under their beds with blankets and stay in the dormitories with them. The poor kids used to be terrified, so were we.

We didn't really suffer from basic food shortages, as being so many it was easier to eke things out, and the gardeners grew all our own vegetables. Fruit, of course, was lacking and eggs, and any kind of sweets etc. We did get occasional consignments of sweets from Canada and America.

Keeping the black-out intact in a place consisting of so much glass was another head-ache, and we often got bawled out by the local warden.

Then one night the Camp School, which was full with evacuated nursery school, got blitzed with fire bombs. Everybody got out safely, all the village turned out to help, but the building was burnt out. We got landed with 20 two-five year olds and villagers divided up the rest. It happened during a holiday time so we had room but our place was not scaled down to 'tinies'. We had an hilarious time until another place was found for them.

After the war, when we became an open-air school again, the boys were trained and encouraged to be helpful and courteous, and we were often congratulated on their good behaviour when we were out and about. Many of them were loathe to leave when they were considered fit for ordinary school, and often pleaded with the school's Medical Officer to be allowed to stay a little longer when he came to do terminal review.

Miss Walton retired in 1943 in her fifties and married an education officer. She had originally come from Halifax. When Miss Buckley became Head she relaxed a lot of the rigid rules about never closing windows, and allowed boys to rest on their beds and read at the rest period. She also gave them much more freedom, allowing them to go out walking on their own—to Bromsgrove shopping or to the swimming baths. They went out and about more, to the theatre, circus, museums etc. They were also much better clothed and shod. The boys themselves then were more amenable. Later we began to get more boys with social and psychological problems who were much more difficult, although they were also supposed to have some physical ailment.

Miss Buckley was born and lived in a village in Derbyshire on the doorstep of Dovedale. She won a scholarship to Ashbourne's Queen Elizabeth Grammar School, eventually entering Priestley Teacher Training College in Leeds. She taught in several Derbyshire village schools, before eventually arriving at Hunter's Hill in 1934, as an assistant teacher; she became deputy during the war, and eventually Headmistress. She was a born teacher.

Mr. O. Williams, Teacher, Hunter's Hill 1940-1, Lampeter, Dyfed

I was a teacher at Hunter's Hill for a very short period, before being called up for active service. I was the only male member on the staff—my two younger predecessors had been recruited already.

In general terms, and provided strict discipline was maintained, it was comparatively a 'cushy' number. I was domiciled in an 'en suite' flat adjoining the Senior Boys' dormitory, for which I was responsible. In spite of war time rationing, meals were excellent. Our assistant cook was a dignified and highly intelligent refugee from Austria.

Day-time schooling was fairly normal—regularly interrupted by Sister and/or Nurse for treatment, medication or inspection, but we took it all in our stride. In response to a national request the senior boys in my charge planted about an acre of potatoes!

The imposition of war-time restrictions influenced activities after dark especially, e.g. blackouts, travel

limitations and air-raids in particular. The school was in the direct path of enemy aircraft on their way to Northfield and Coventry. We were able to recognise their 'drone', and the dreaded sirens demanded that we should vacate our cosy beds and dash to the cold shelters in the adjoining fields. It was not unusual for this to happen three times in the long winter nights. The local primary school was severely damaged by incendiary bombs. Naturally one could not expect pupil or teacher to be educationally responsive after such disturbances.

The story would not be complete without reference to some clever attempts at absconding. To quote one instance—two of us (teachers) were on an escapee's trail. We visited his home in Birmingham, but the family had not seen him; we scouted around the area and on our **third** visit to the house, our quarry had been found under a pile of clothes in the bath. He had walked in his school night clothes along a railway line and had crept into the house un-noticed! Another adventurer had thumbed a lift in a Yankee jeep! There were other less spectacular attempts in spite of stringent supervision and some clever deterrent methods on our part.

Eventually the RAF found that they could not carry on without me. I still have some very happy recollections of Hunter's Hill.

Mr. Graham Bailey, Hunter's Hill 1941-3, Great Barr, Birmingham

All my memories of Hunter's Hill are very pleasant ones; I remember my mother and I walking from the railway station to the school, and being greeted by Miss Walton the Headmistress at the time: a visit to the sewing room to be rigged out in corduroy breeches, grey shirt, grey socks and black boots.

Then being allocated a dormitory shared by 30 other boys, with windows which opened from floor to ceiling. These were only closed because of the wartime blackout whilst preparing for bed. Each bed had a chair by it where we kept our overcoat, a blanket and our gas mask in case of air raids or emergencies.

In the mornings we cleaned our teeth with powdered chalk (toothpaste being in short supply), we cleaned our boots with block shoe black and liberal amounts of spit (spit and polish!).

Food was very basic, powdered egg, porridge, stews, bread and butter puddings, cheese and potato pies. We had our sweet ration once a week on Wednesday; however, this privilege was withdrawn for any misdemeanours committed during the week.

Our school subjects were the normal ones e.g. Maths, English, Art, Physical Training, Woodwork and Nature Study. On a Wednesday afternoon we had a free period, our house football games or cricket in the summer. However we went to classes on Saturday mornings to make up the time.

The staff, all female, were totally involved in all our activities. Linda Buckley our form teacher, later to become Headmistress, was our football referee, cricket umpire, boxing referee and for me a lasting influence on my life.

The other members of staff came into their own in the winter evenings, when we had to organise our entertainment. This included pantomimes at Christmas, carol singing around the local area, and several of our boys sang in the choirs of the two village churches on Sundays. On occasions our shows were attended by the girls from Cropwood. All of the female parts in our concerts were played by boys.

I remember Sunday afternoon walks over the Lickeys, Open Days in conjunction with the villagers from Blackwell, the Scout trip, and the naked runs in the snow of winter.

A Birmingham Councillor would visit once a year to present a medal. He had been inspired to make this gesture by reading the book *Honour Bright*, the story of a young man's triumphs over all sorts of difficulties and temptations. The recipient was nominated by the boys of the school and not by members of staff. I have one of these medals.

Through the efforts of all the staff at Hunter's Hill Open-Air School I was able to take part in all sports and never missed a day's schooling. I was school captain in all sports, and Head Boy in my final year.

Whilst I am still an asthmatic I have led a full and eventful career in engineering: all of this would not have been possible without the formative years spent at the open-air school. What a pity that this type of education is not available to young sickly boys and girls today.

THE 1940s: THE TURNING POINT

Mr. Gordon Smith, 63, Hunter's Hill 1941-3, Bromsgrove, Worcestershire

I was recommended to Hunter's Hill by the Birmingham Education Clinic for the treatment of asthma. I spent about two years there.

Memories are of crocodile walks across the Lickeys in smart grey suits. On one such walk I hid in a toilet on the Lickeys and walked home to Weoley Castle because my mother had just had a new baby girl whom I had not seen. Needless to say I was promptly brought back.

After two years I was released, my only complaint being hay fever, after several years of horrendous asthma.

Mr. Leslie Williams, 58, Hunter's Hill 1942-4, Great Barr, Birmingham

I had bronchitis at four years old, pneumonia when I was five and this left me with bronchial asthma. I was sent to Hunter's Hill at around six years old. I was bullied for the first year.

When I was around eight years old I did a bunk (ran away). I walked to the outskirts of Birmingham before I was caught. My Mom and Dad could not afford to visit me very often so I missed them.

I remember the Italian prisoners of war who worked on the nearby farm. We gave them eggs that the chickens laid in our dens; they gave us apples.

We went to dinner at midday; it consisted of potatoes boiled in their jackets, cabbage or sprouts (caterpillars were extra meat!), lamb, beef or pork; sweet was steamed pud or apple tart, sometimes cheese. Tea was egg on toast or bread and jam, sometimes a piece of cake and tea. We then had a play period; one of the teachers would blow a whistle and you ran for your supper, usually bread and dripping and a few sweets or an apple.

Then on the second whistle it was in for showers and bed, sometimes you could read and swap comics, Beano and Dandy etc. After lights out we had 'dares' e.g. shinning up the drain pipe to look in the teacher's room or walking across the field to a crab apple tree and back in deep snow.

It was very cold in the winter even with the radiators on, and we rarely heard a radio or saw a newspaper. Yes, it hardened me up at Blackwell; I became more determined to get well.

Mr. Lawrence Cox, 63, Hunter's Hill 1943-4, Redditch, Worcestershire

I attended Hunter's Hill aged 12 with my brother. We were both anaemic and John was also bronchitic. During my time there, Miss Buckley was the Headmistress, tall, authoritarian, someone not to trifle with, but I came to know that she was a kindly person. Miss Maguire came to the school shortly after I had started, a soft spoken, auburn haired lady from Southern Ireland, she was my favourite.

The things that stand out in my memory are the enforced, but welcome, hour's rest in the early afternoon, with the unforgettable red blanket and folding type beds which were laid along the open veranda.

I joined the local church choir at St Catherine's Church and sang at morning service there and in the evening at the little church opposite the post office. I was also allowed to sing at weddings, for which I was paid 2s.6d.

I will never forget lying in bed at night, in the open sided dormitories, listening to the sound of the Lickey banking engines chugging incessantly up the incline.

Swimming lessons were taken in Cropwood's pool. Little did our teachers know, but we used to go for midnight swims when the weather was warm enough. We used to swim in the nude—no bathing trunks available, except at authorised swimming lessons. We never stopped to think of the consequences if ever we were caught, or worse still, if the girls decided to do the same!

We had our own garden plots. During the daytime we were hoeing, planting and watering. We used to size up the apple and pear trees and at midnight make forays to the orchard. No apple ever tastes so good as a scrumped one!

Whilst at Hunter's Hill I became friends with a lad called Charles Clements. He had been born without hands or feet. He amazed me how he used to be able to lace up his special boots—even thread needles.

My father used to come and visit me whenever he could, my mother occasionally. Father had to catch the tram to Rednal, then walk the rest of the way together with our little mongrel dog Scamp. We used to walk round the little narrow leafy lanes, sometimes down into Bromsgrove.

Overall, I enjoyed my time at Hunter's Hill, and it certainly helped to prepare me for the time when I was conscripted into the army five years later, living away from home and understanding the importance of mixing and being part of a group, enduring the same difficulties and chasing the same pleasures.

Marsh Hill

Logbooks of Marsh Hill school vividly record the traumas of wartime education. Thirty-six per cent of the children were evacuated to billets in Eastington, Gloucestershire, in September 1939, although many had returned home by December that year. Air-raid shelters were provided and the school had re-opened by April 1940 as full-time education again became compulsory. Some children and staff slept at Marsh Hill overnight. In November 1940, 30 children were evacuated to Popplewick in Nottinghamshire, as a time bomb had landed on the school drive in the previous month. In July 1942 the school had to be cleared when an unexploded bomb landed in the rest-shed. Fortunately it was removed without mishap.

Five ex-pupils recall happy years at Marsh Hill Open-Air School:

Mrs. Heather Langdon (née **Brelsford**), 65, Marsh Hill 1942-4, North Harrow, Middlesex

I suffered from asthma as a child. Poor health prevented me playing strenuous children's games and caused frequent absence from school. I attended Marsh Hill Open-Air School, aged 11 to 13 years.

Arriving at school at 7.45am we put on long woollen jumpers—green for girls and grey for boys. Then breakfast: this was porridge (unsweetened and usually lumpy) or cornflakes. Dripping sandwiches every day. Enamel jugs of hot and cold milk. After breakfast we lined up in the playground and played for 10 minutes.

After classes at 9.45am there was a short break for play and toilet. At 10.45am children marched along the veranda to the 'locker room'. This was a large room with gymnasium equipment. Older boys set out camp beds in three rows. The windows were wide open and the outer row could get rain splashed in inclement weather. Children took blankets (boys grey and girls red), made up their beds and laid down for two hours' sleep. They all faced one way, to prevent talk. If a child had a breathing difficulty a pillow was provided. The teacher sat on a chair at the head of the room and read or marked school books.

Lunch was usually jacket potato with meat. Soup was usually onion; Pudding usually rice (which most pupils hated). Other puddings were served—apple or rhubarb or prunes—with custard. Treacle pudding was a favourite.

Afternoon classes were more informal. Sometimes Mr. Jones read tales of the Knights of the Round Table. Children also worked in the gardens, weeding or digging according to their ability. Friday was games afternoon, netball or rounders.

Monday morning children lined up and we were each given two spoonfuls of cod liver oil, and some tablets. The nurse was a plump, jolly woman who joked and laughed away the complaints of the 'nasty' taste of the oil.

After two years my mother received a letter saying that my health had improved and that I could attend a normal school. This was not what I wanted. I had been happy at Marsh Hill. I am sure that the open-air regime improved my health.

THE 1940s: THE TURNING POINT

Mrs. Norma Chambers (née **Goss**), 63, Marsh Hill 1943-5, Walsall, West Midlands

I started at Marsh Hill in 1943 and was there for about two years for anaemia and a weak chest.

The Headmistress was Miss Brown, who always seemed to wear brown clothing and always wore a hat and silk scarf—even without her coat she had those on!

In the classrooms in winter we each had a blanket with tapes which we wrapped around us from waist down. We even wore our gloves and hats in class at times! In the summer we had lessons in the mornings, sometimes outdoors; every afternoon we were outside either gardening or playing games: boys football on lower green, girls played rounders on upper green.

At 4 o'clock lessons finished and we then had tea, bread and jam; occasionally we did have a slice of cake, maybe a home made biscuit. Then the numbers of our buses were called out, and we would be walked up the drive and a bus would take us home.

I enjoyed my time at that school. Afterwards I was sent to Switzerland for about three months in 1946, arranged by Kunzle's and the Health Service.

Mrs. Margaret Bent (née **Leavesley**), Marsh Hill mid-1940s, Jamaica, West Indies

The school lay back from the road surrounded by lawns, the building was low with a veranda right around it. Off the playground was a long building with shutters and camp beds where we took our afternoon rest with blankets in the winter. In the summer we would take our desks and chairs out on the grass and have our lessons there; we had all the fresh air we could get.

I suffered from a nervous problem and I'm sure if I had not gone there, to get the rest and fresh air I needed, I would not have been as fit and well as I am today.

Mr. Owen Lannon, Marsh Hill 1947-8, Builth Wells, Wales

I went to Marsh Hill Open-Air School for two years when I was 12, and they were the best two years of my schooling. I was sent there from Slade Road School Clinic suffering from asthma.

Lunch breaks were unusual there because we had special diet meals, with plenty of salads and green vegetables.

After lunch we had an hour's rest period which simply meant that the pupils had to go out into the playing fields to lie down on two (red) blankets, if the weather was fine; and woe betide any child that misbehaved. If it was raining we went into a big building. After the rest period we had some more lessons, then before we went home we were given afternoon tea, usually salad, such as lettuce or water cress.

*My two teachers were Mr. Jones (deputy head) and Mrs. Browning. For some reason Mr. Jones made me his favourite, probably because I had a good singing voice and he **was** the singing teacher. I was also made the school captain, and I remember very well going to Blackwell Open-Air School, for the sports day against other open-air schools.*

They were happy days spent at Marsh Hill.

Mr. Peter W. Allen, Marsh Hill 1948, Aldridge, Walsall, West Midlands

I went to Marsh Hill after several years at Hunter's Hill and eventually became Head Boy. Headmistress Miss Brown was probably in her fifties, a buxom woman, round and warm. I think in all my school days this was my happiest school. She was a lovely woman, in every way. Most Headmistresses are probably dedicated to the children, but Miss Brown was also friend, mother and very fair. She and the senior teacher, Mr. Jones, were a credit to the system of teaching

1945-9

A sinister by-product of wartime conditions was the increase in tuberculosis cases reported in Birmingham's School Medical Officer's report of 1945. For the first time since 1936 the number of children reported to be suffering from this disease rose from 159 to 175 cases. On the other hand, there were fewer cases of reported diphtheria. Another major problem for the School Health Service was the increase in the number of children suffering from verminous conditions, and school clinics had to provide extra cleansing baths.

Birmingham was at the forefront of developing its school health service when an opportunity arose with the foundation of the Birmingham Institute of Child Health in 1946. This organisation made possible a positive link between the work of the hospitals (who cared for sick children) and the School Health Service (whose main function was to maintain schoolchildren's health as well as to prevent disease). For the first time medical students had the chance to study the work of school doctors and to gain first-hand experience in the clinics—much to the benefit of child health in general.

In 1946 the Swiss authorities and the Swiss Red Cross made the generous offer of a holiday in Switzerland to over 1,200 British schoolchildren whose health had been badly affected by war conditions, preference being given to children of disabled ex-servicemen, children injured during the war and war orphans. Although children suffering from active tuberculosis, asthma or heart disease were excluded, the Swiss Red Cross gave preference in their scheme to delicate children in open-air schools and to children from cities which had suffered severe bombing. Children travelled in parties, staying for three months in the homes of Swiss families who had been carefully selected by the Red Cross. Lucky indeed were the 130 Birmingham children selected by the School Medical Officer for the holiday of a lifetime.

Two hundred children from Birmingham and Coventry open-air schools assembled at New Street Station on 19 September 1946, warmly wrapped in thick winter coats and hats, all bearing a large label for their destination in Switzerland.

All the expense of the accommodation and travel in Europe was borne by the Swiss Government and children set off by train and ferry across the channel on one of the roughest days of the year. Each child had been carefully examined before departure. Dr. Sainsbury, Birmingham's Assistant School Medical Officer, reported that 27 per cent showed 'very great improvement' on their return.

An account of the venture is given by one ex-pupil of Hunter's Hill who thoroughly enjoyed the experience when he was 11 years old.

Mr. Maurice Wareing, Moseley, Birmingham

My destination was St Gallen and the journey was long and tiring for a delicate child suffering from bronchiectasis, travelling overnight on the train via Dover, Calais and Basle. During my three months' stay I enjoyed reading letters from home and The Argos *I regularly received from my mother. I still have one letter I wrote home to her: 'I am billeted in a lovely big house on a hill. I went on a trip to the mountains one day but when I got back I was very tired. The weather here is beautiful'.*

I stayed with a Red Cross Nurse and her civil engineer husband who had three young children. Their chateau was on the outskirts of the town overlooking the Swiss-German speaking part of North East Switzerland. I visited them again in 1955 and corresponded with Mr. & Mrs. Stadelmann for forty-five years. Following my three months' holiday my health was considered to have improved so much that I could attend Uffculme Open-Air School as a day pupil.

That same year in 1946, the government passed the National Health Act which came into force in 1948. This enabled Local Education Authorities to make arrangements with hospitals for

THE 1940s: THE TURNING POINT

Children from Birmingham and Coventry's open-air schools gathered on Birmingham's New Street Station on 19 September 1946 to leave for a three-month holiday in Switzerland arranged by the Swiss Red Cross. Dr. Sainsbury, Birmingham school Medical Officer, can be seen on the left of the photograph at the back. Maurice Wareing from Hunters Hill School was one of these children and supplied the photograph (M.Wareing)

free specialist treatment of schoolchildren at maintained schools: previously Local Education Authorities had had to bear the cost of treatment. At the time it was thought that it would be too great a burden for General Practitioners and the National Health Service to take over all the school health services. In practice this meant that school health services provided treatment for minor ailments, child guidance clinics and speech therapy, also ensuring that all children got free medical treatment from their doctors and hospitals. Over the years a policy of co-operation was gradually developed, and as standards of health and education advanced the school health services began to cover such subjects as sex education, smoking and mental health, aiming to help the developing child within society.

The National Health Service Act also made provision for the specialist services for 'maladjusted' children i.e. pupils showing evidence of emotional disabilities and psychological disturbances, previously classified as 'nervous', 'unstable' or 'difficult'. These children, who were sometimes suffering from the effects of poverty and difficult social conditions, needed special education. Hence many Special Schools were developed and open-air schools (which were part of this special school system) were sometimes thought to be suitable places for such 'difficult and educationally backward children'. The small classes and closer contact with staff were of great benefit to such children, and gradually open-air schools began to take more of these pupils, alongside the other 'delicate' children suffering ailments such as asthma, bronchitis and other conditions.

Birmingham's School Medical Officer reported in 1949 that there were increasing demands for places in open-air schools—mainly children suffering asthma, bronchitis and bronchiectasis. The Medical Officer often visited open-air schools every two weeks and a local practitioner was consulted regularly for any ailments.

For the first time there was considerable mention of the treatment of asthmatic children, for which the main aim was to raise the **whole** health level of the sufferer, together with special attention to diet, vitamins and breathing exercises, as well as the elimination of unhealthy tonsils, infected sinuses and decayed teeth. Of paramount importance was the cultivation of a healthy attitude of mind and the elimination of the fussy and over anxious parent. The results were generally good, with fewer asthma attacks, increase in body weight and a happier mental outlook. However, open-air schools never could **guarantee** a cure, but nearly every case could be **relieved**. Drugs such as Ephedrine, Franol, Neo-Epinine, Nublae, Adrenaline and Atropine Co were used in the treatment. By 1948 it was reported that over a quarter of the pupils attending Uffculme and Marsh Hill Open-Air Schools suffered from asthma.

Uffculme 1945-9

An excellent first-hand account of Uffculme is reported in Janet Whitney's *Geraldine Cadbury*, in which she describes how the Headmistress, Miss Hibbert, reported that the common cold had almost become a thing of the past at her open-air school. Children did not appear to suffer very much from the cold. A few difficult children from the slums were being sent to the school but soon found freedom and peace in the spacious surroundings with the orchards and meadows. The majority of children were still there on the grounds of poor health—malnutrition and debility of various kinds. The daily pint of milk was very important, together with the three good meals a day, supervised by a nurse, dietician and domestic staff.

Miss Hibbert was described as a quiet, serene, vigorous woman with great poise, who loved and understood children. One of Miss Hibbert's nieces recalls visiting her aunt at Uffculme school:

Mrs. Enid Deeble (née **Platt**), St. Ives, Cornwall

Before the war my two brothers, my sister and I used to visit my aunt in Birmingham and also Uffculme school. I must have been about seven and remember feeling cross because I had to lie down after lunch, with everyone else, and try to sleep!

After she retired my aunt renewed her interest in art and did a lot of original design embroidery, much of it for Bournville parish church. She also designed and made silverware, including christening spoons for her great nieces and nephews. She was a wonderful aunt and taught me a lot about natural history, knitting and sewing.

Miss Hibbert continued to keep the school log book although very few details of the curriculum are recorded:

Uffculme log book 1945

26 Jan.   *65.9%. Attendance badly affected by severe weather, 20° all week. Impossible to take 'rest' or to sit for regular lessons. Hot drink at 3pm—dismiss at 3.30.*

29 Jan.   *17° today—gradually rising towards end of day.*

THE 1940s: THE TURNING POINT

Many teachers dedicated their lives to open-air schools, despite severe weather conditions in winter. This group photograph of 1948 shows Uffculme staff (left to right): Miss Margaret Wales (17 years at Uffculme), Edward Anderson (35 years at Uffculme), Nurse Bendall, Miss Betty Tidmus, Head Mistress Miss Ella Hibbert (28 years at Uffculme), Miss Margaret Etherington. (M.Wales)

30 Jan.   *Deep snow—only 44 children came. Then thaw set in.*

10 Sep.   *Miss M. Etherington commenced duties here.*

Uffculme log book 1946

19 Sep.   *Miss Hibbert & 21 children leave for Switzerland.*

16 Dec.   *Miss Hibbert absent. Gone to Calais to meet returning children.*

Uffculme log book 1947

31 Jan.   *Heavy snow. Temperature well below freezing point.*

7 Feb.   *Still very cold. Written work impossible.*

28 Feb.   *Still very cold. Pond frozen sufficiently to bear.*

21 Mar.   *Some improvement. Thaw set in.*

Uffculme log book 1948

8 July   *School closed pm for Special Schools Sports held here.*

19 Oct.   *Class II visiting film **Oliver Twist** am. Miss Wales in charge.*

Uffculme log book 1949

18 Mar.   *Colds and influenza at Uffculme. Nurse Bendall absent.*

29 April   *Miss Etherington left.*

30 Sep.   *Miss L.L. Tidmus retired from teaching.*

6 Dec.   *Visit of Drs. Llewellyn & Henderson from Ministry of Education. 8 boys went to the Alpine School today.*

9 Dec.   *First snow fell this morning.*

Five ex-pupils recall their school days at Uffculme in the late 1940s:

Miss Betty James, Uffculme 1944-7, Brixham, Devon

My life at Uffculme started on a cold winter's day in January 1944. One of the first things I remember was collecting my brush and comb, a navy blue Guernsey, sewing a white square on a blanket for one of the new numbers, also on the Guernsey. Miss Wales, my teacher, gave extra tuition for those wishing to take the Grammar School and Commercial School exams.

Before meals all the children would fall in, in classes, in front of the dining room. I remember the bread and milk, porridge, hot milk, fish, cheese pie and beet-root, the green broccoli that tasted bitter, jam spread on bread and butter, also 'marmite', and pieces of cheese.

If there was a shortage of kitchen staff, the nurse would ask two or three girls to go up and help, doing all the washing-up for the children and staff, and at tea-time spreading the bread with margarine. When the new potatoes were in season, the older children had to help to scrape them.

There were children in need of extra milk; this was drunk during the mid-morning break, in the shower-room. The sick bay was the place for anyone who had to have extra rest between the morning break and lunch-time.

Everyone had to have the rest period after their dinner. The beds were put out by the older boys. If the weather was good, this was outside on the grass; otherwise, undercover. All the children in Classes I and II helped to put the beds away, stacking them up against the wall.

Nurse had two monitors to help each morning: taking messages to the teachers, collecting all the brushes and combs every Friday to be washed, returning them to the classes on a Monday morning, where they were given back to the person whose number was on that particular brush and comb. The monitors also had to clean the shower-room on a Friday, mopping the floors, scrubbing the benches, as during the week every child in the school had a shower.

Every Friday afternoon, all the girls in Classes I and II had to clean the cutlery used by the children and staff. I can see Miss Wales now, inspecting them, particularly the toast-racks. During this time, the boys played football etc. in the field with Mr. Anderson.

There was one special event in the springtime of either 1944 or '45. All the school took part, doing country-dancing, maypole dancing, Morris and sword dancing with a hobby horse. This was held in the field, with all parents and friends invited.

Rest period under the apple blossom, supervised by Nurse at Uffculme, 1940s. (M. Wales)

THE 1940s: THE TURNING POINT

During the warmer months, the boys and girls from Classes I and II went swimming at Kings Heath Baths. We were taught to do the breast stroke action before going to the baths.

In 1946 England, with other countries, was invited by the Red Cross to send children to families in Switzerland for three months. About sixteen children of all ages were chosen from Uffculme. Miss Hibbert was the co-ordinator, arranging for the children to arrive in London at a certain time, and to stay overnight, then travelling with them as far as the French train. She also met the French train on the return journey.

One of the great pleasures of Uffculme was the woods that were in the grounds where we were taken on nature walks looking at the trees and flowers. The great outdoors still holds an attraction for me, appreciating all that I see round about, which started in the woods at Uffculme.

Mrs. Eileen Davies (née **Mullard**),
Uffculme 1945–8, Edgbaston, Birmingham

I had some sort of blood disorder which manifested itself in unsightly sores and blisters and attendance at the school from the age of seven to 10 years was considered to be a last resort, after many years of the illness and periods in hospitals.

School began about 8.00am and ended at 5.00pm in order to take breakfast, lunch and tea there, for which the charge was five shillings per week. The emphasis was on fresh air and nourishing food. Classrooms were open winter and summer and lessons were conducted outside in good weather. I had sun-ray treatment twice-weekly and a daily dose of malt. If necessary teeth were extracted at the school—an event engraved on my memory.

I remember an 'African Lady' bringing cocoa-pods to show the children—we were amazed at the colours. Chocolate was issued twice weekly to everyone—quite an event as rationing was still in force.

The only teacher's name I can remember was Miss Tidmus. She was very kind and very popular. Punishment at Uffculme was picking one hundred dandelions …

Mr. Maurice Wareing, 62, Uffculme
1947–9, Moseley, Birmingham

I was born a healthy 8lb baby in 1934. At the age of three I had a tonsillectomy at the Children's Hospital, Ladywood. I cried a lot and inhaled mucus and blood which damaged my lungs and caused my chest problems.

In the summer of 1945 I had tests in the Queen Elizabeth Hospital and was diagnosed as having bronchiectasis, and was placed on the list for Hunter's Hill

13-year-old Maurice Wareing at Uffculme, wearing the school's navy blue sweater, February 1948. (M. Wareing)

Open-Air School, which I went to in 1946. At the end of that year my health was considered to have improved so that I could attend Uffculme as a day pupil.

January 1947 was the beginning of one of the most severe winters Britain had experienced and I made an inauspicious start by being absent the first week of term with influenza. The Headmistress was Miss Hibbert and Mr. John Anderson (Andy) was my class teacher (Class I); Miss Wales taught Class II, Miss Etherington Class III, Miss Tidmus Class IV—the very young.

The classes were divided into ages so the brighter pupils learned little. When groups visited the school the back row of Class I were asked to stand up and were described as grammar school standard. I recorded the temperature on the thermometer each morning which was pinned to the tree outside the classroom.

Some of the boys, including myself, used to arrive at school at 8.00am and play football until 8.55am when the bell went for breakfast. I remained goalie for the next couple of years in the Friday afternoon games lesson.

Miss Hibbert used to take us for a three-quarters of an hour music lesson and I sang songs of that period—Early One Morning, Greensleeves, John Peel, Lincolnshire Poacher etc. I also had country dancing lessons. One morning a week I travelled by tram to Upper Highgate School and did woodwork. Every week I had a compulsory bath at school to ensure I was clean and free from disease. The toilets were outside and exposed to the elements.

On the few job application forms I filled in during my working life I am afraid I stated that Queensbridge Road School was the name of my school, not Uffculme, because I thought it might have been detrimental to my job prospects. For over thirty years I worked in Local Government with colleagues who had attended grammar schools but having limited education did deter me from seeking promotion due to lack of confidence.

During life I have tried to adopt the attitude that health-wise I am A1 and a living Christian faith has helped to put life in a proper perspective.

Mr. John O'Shaughnessy, Uffculme
1948-50, Aldridge, Walsall, West Midlands

I remember my first day at Uffculme as a very shy 14-year-old lad, who had spent half of his life at home, ill with asthma and wrapped in cotton wool.

I remember a long tram journey from the city centre of Birmingham: the sympathetic conductress, when she learnt which school I was going to, 'Oh dear, you poor thing, they only let you wear a little blue jumper in the winter'. The greeting from Miss Hibbert, Headmistress: coat, scarf and jumper off, on with the infamous blue jumper, weighed in 5ft 9ins, 9 stone weakling. My introduction to my temporary form teacher Mr. Lewis, who later turned out to be a Welsh rugby trialist; my new class mates, who tried to scare me with stories about Mr. Anderson (Andy)—the fearsome Scotsman (our class teacher), due to return soon from Switzerland. The classroom—open to the elements, frozen ink wells ... The afternoon nap after lunch in an outside building where I was first introduced

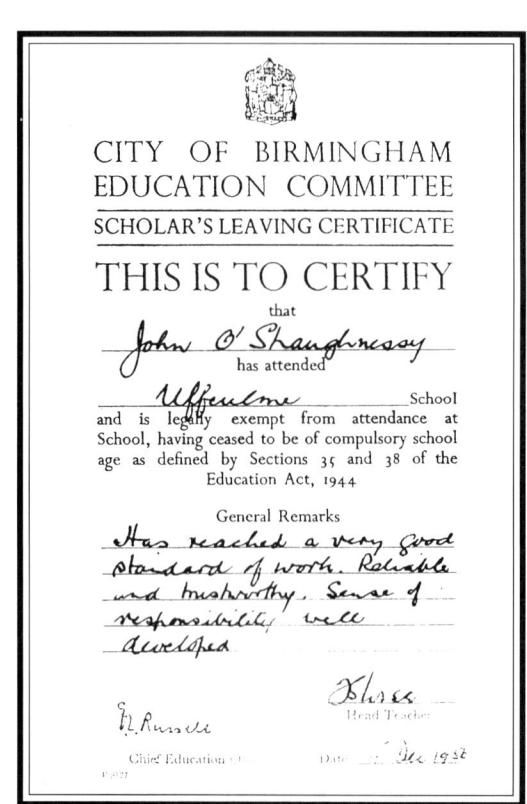

John O'Shaughnessy's leaving certificate from Uffculme Open-Air School.

to English and Scandinavian folk dancing, sometimes with the girls; I was not impressed. My total embarrassment of the communal showers, which I never came to terms with (boys and girls separate I must add).

I also remember my garden plot to grow vegetables, a football and cricket pitch, a running track—all this for a lad who only had a back yard or street to play in.

I left Uffculme two years later, an 11½-stone, self-confident young man ready to face the working world. In later years my thoughts drift back to the happiest two years of my childhood. That pleasant lady teacher Miss Wales, the time I watched her comfort a sick and distressed little boy; that fearsome Scotsman Mr. Anderson, 'Sir' to his face and 'Andy' behind his back, the fairest man I ever met. Most of all I miss Uffculme Open-Air, the school for delicate children.

Mr. Peter Fellows, Uffculme 1948–51, Yeovil, Somerset

Uffculme Open-Air Schooldays were the happiest days of my life and even now I have vivid memories of the time I spent there.

During my time in Class I, I had a lot of duties at the same time; bed monitor, class monitor, sports captain, locker room monitor and Table 4 monitor. Like a lot of boys at the school I got caught eating the crab apples in the staff garden; my punishment, a dose of cod liver oil, 'yuk'!

One thing I do remember of Uffculme was the school uniforms: shorts and plimsolls in summer and a sweater in winter. I didn't wear a tie until I was 18 when I went in the forces.

Cropwood 1945–9

Miss Boothroyd, Cropwood's Headmistress who had experienced so many difficulties during the Blitz, continued to record in the logbook, in meticulous detail, the various events at the school. It demonstrates her devotion to duty and concern for the children in her care:

Cropwood log book 1945

21 Jan.   *The girls sledged this afternoon and loved it.*

24 Jan.   *Doctor anxious about condition of Pat G., a very bad bronchiectasis, in bed with a slight temperature—no pneumonia but lungs very bad. Dr. Mitchell came out himself this afternoon and says Pat is dying. Parents informed.*

25 Jan.   *Dr. Roberts visited. Pat too ill to move. Mr. & Mrs. G. at Cropwood. Pat died at 2.15pm.*

30 Jan.   *A very nice letter received today from Mr. & Mrs. G. The children and staff sent flowers to the funeral.*

3 Feb.   *The mumps epidemic goes on. Miss Broomfield has it now. Miss Boothroyd and Miss Symes have cancelled their weekends.*

26 Feb.   *Still more mumps. Have heard that the school is Highly Commended in last year's Bird and Tree Competition.*

26 April   *Dr. Roberts visited. One of the new girls developed chicken-pox and was taken to Little Bromwich Isolation hospital.*

8 May   *V.E. Day. All the school went to church this morning for Thanksgiving Service. Two Union Jacks put out on the Tower and Loggia and Playroom decorated. Prime Minister's announcement listened to—party tea with Victory Cake specially made and iced by Miss Arnot. Concert in the evening. All big and medium sized girls listened to the King's broadcast.*

5 June   *Miss Boothroyd returned last evening to find that 13 girls had run away for no apparent reason,*

but instigated by the leadership of two girls who have been a source of trouble all the term. Miss Boothroyd has asked that these girls be expelled from Cropwood and sent to ordinary elementary schools.

25 June *Miss Symons' successor appointed today—a Miss Lattimore. Pat Norris has passed into Yardley Grammar School; we are all delighted.*

27 Sep. *Dr. Roberts visited today. Dr. Dick has retired from the school service and Cropwood and Hunter's Hill together sent him a guinea book token and a cheque for £5.*

6 Oct. *Visiting Day ... Mr. Barrow Cadbury, Miss Dorothy & Mrs. Whitney called in the afternoon. This was unexpected but we were delighted to see them. Mrs. Whitney is writing about Mrs. Cadbury's work so wanted to see Cropwood. Mr. Cadbury gave us £1 for the school fund.*

30 Oct. *Hallowe'en Party—very successful with bobbing for apples and other games. Miss Arnot had made special toffee, which was much appreciated.*

2 Nov. *A great musical treat this afternoon when Mr. Davies, Director of Music for Worcestershire, and his wife came to Cropwood. Mr. Davies talked and played, Mrs. Davies sang folk songs. The girls sang to them.*

5 Nov. *Miss Sawdon commenced with us today. The classes are now:*
    I- Miss Lattimore, II—Miss Sawdon, III—Miss Soar; each is taking her own class almost exclusively—none of the three is a specialist in any subject.

22 Nov. *Everyone stirred the Xmas pudding this morning.*

9 Dec. *Christmas pudding for dinner today—many lucky people had charms or 'threepennies'.*

11 Dec. *Christmas Party—a most lovely 'spread' prepared by Miss Arnot; a conjuror and Father Christmas (Capt. Clayton) completed the proceedings.*

Cropwood log book 1946

14 Jan. *Cropwood re-opened today—all the staff were back and a record number of girls. We were distressed to hear the sad news that Iris M. had died during the holiday.*

30 May *A conjuror—H. Lawrence—gave a very good show at 4d per head.*

8 June *Victory Day. The girls listened to the BBC broadcast of the Parade. The loud speaker was at a window and those who were interested stood outside it and listened. Miss Arnot gave them a lovely tea and we had games and competitions in the evening.*

19 June *Five girls ran away and Miss Boothroyd was kept in anxiety all night and until 4pm the following day about one of them. She had spent the night with one of the others and it had not been reported. Miss Boothroyd took a taxi and fetched both of them from Stechford Police Station.*

29 June *Miss Boothroyd in bed with a chill.*

6 July. *Miss Boothroyd has been off school all the week but has conducted school business from her room. Yesterday was the Terminal Review—there are 16 children to leave. In the afternoon Dr. Sainsbury examined 24 girls who are suggested as part of party to go to Switzerland for two months as guests of the Swiss Govt. 21 were passed as fit—now we must wait and see which are chosen.*

13 July   This has been a very hot week and the children are lovely and brown. Visiting today, the parents were delighted to see their children in swim suits or just knickers. Class I presented 'Pastorella' on the lawn, and afterwards there were sports for the visitors. A show of needlework was on view in Class I.

24 July   Nurse Davies appointed to replace Nurse Coan who resigned at the beginning of July.

19 Sep.   Miss Soar left as escort to Switzerland. Miss Lightwood came as supply.

27 Nov.   Nurse Davies admitted to the General Hospital.

2 Dec.   Dr. Kemp made his last visit for the term. Sister is ill in bed with quinsy. Nurse Davies is improving.

10 Dec.   Xmas Party today. Mr. Clayton was again Father Christmas, and had an assistant in Mr. Showell. We had a conjuror and a lovely tea provided by Miss Arnot. The tree was a beauty and a new feature was that each little girl received a doll made by her big girl. 4 girls who ran away ten days ago for no reason had no present from Father Xmas, but partook of the rest of the party. All went very well.

Cropwood log book 1947

25 Jan.   Sledging today for the first time this season—the snow is thick and dry.

29 Jan.   The coldest day—girls have their blankets in school, and go for runs or walks at frequent intervals. Still thick snow.

10 Feb.   Cropwood was visited today by the Lord Mayor and Lady Mayoress—Alderman and Mrs. Bradbeer. It was bitterly cold, but the car managed to get here through the snow. Miss Ross escorted the visitors. Miss Arnot had arranged a nice tea for everyone. Rita Hanley, Head Girl, made a little speech in which she thanked their Worships for the honour they did us, and both the Lord Mayor and Lady Mayoress replied. Both laid stress on the 'atmosphere' of Cropwood which they called delightful. The girls were able to examine both the lovely mayoral chains.

5 Mar.   The blizzard continued all night and all day—there are drifts five and six feet high and nothing can get through to us.

10 Mar.   Until today milk has had to be fetched on sledges. On Friday we had a snow plough up the drive.

24 June   Joyce W. who has been in the Isolation Room for 4 days was removed to the General Hospital today with suspected osteomyelitis. She was in great pain.

25 June   Joyce W. is in a critical condition.

5 July   Visiting Day today … Joyce W. is much better.

12 July   Old Girls Day. The first annual meeting to inaugurate an Old Girls' Association. Fifty-two 'old girls' turned up and had a pleasant afternoon. Miss Boothroyd was elected President, Lucy Steane, Secretary, Joan Ford, Treasurer. Tea was served by Miss Arnot.

15 July   Joyce W. returned to school today; she is looking remarkably well, under the circumstances and is walking, though very slowly.

Cropwood log book 1948

13 Jan.   Cropwood reassembled after the holiday. Fifty-three girls returned and all the staff. The girls look fairly well on the whole and only a few have lost weight.

20 Jan.   We heard the sad news when we returned, that Brenda F. had been admitted to Selly Oak Hospital for observation and died just before Christmas of an inoperable brain tumour.

26 April   Half holiday for the King & Queen's Silver Wedding [George VI & Queen Elizabeth]. Class I and some of Class II went in parties to Barnt Green and Bromsgrove; the little ones enjoyed playing undisturbed.

1 May   A dreadful scene in the village where the latest new girl, S.B., stopped when running away—made a great fuss and had hysterics. Ran away four times in three days. Miss Boothroyd refused to have her back.

9 June   Miss Soar off to Switzerland with the party of boys who are to spend 6 months at Chateau Bruxelles, Davos Dorf. Teaching staff at Cropwood now:
    Miss Rastrick Class I (apptd. May 16th); Mrs. Galtery Class II (apptd. May 23rd); Miss Jones is taking Class III.

27 June   In the last week Audrey O'M. and Barbara P. have run away six times. Barbara has a record of truancy and is a court case—Audrey just seems entirely unsettled. Miss Boothroyd interviewed both mothers and both were most anxious to co-operate.

7 July   Mr. Baker, dentist, with Mr. Finn and anaesthetist, treated 25 cases today. 18 were gas cases—all behaved well, and there were no complications.

29 Oct.   The girls were invited to see the dress rehearsal of 'Treasure Island' given by the boys at Hunter's Hill. It was an excellent show.

5 Nov.   Most of the girls went over to Hunter's Hill to see the Bonfire.

12 Nov.   Miss Soar returned from Switzerland and stayed one night. She is returning to Davos with another party of boys in a fortnight. She gave the children an interesting talk on Davos.

18 Nov.   Dr. Henderson & Dr. Llewellyn from the M of E visited today—they are making a survey of Open Air Schools and Cropwood was their first visit. They stayed all day and had a long questionnaire for Sister and Miss Boothroyd to answer.

7 Dec.   Miss Mann and Miss Moore visited to inspect the needlework. They were very pleased and Miss Mann said that the standard of needlework at Cropwood is now high. She congratulated Diana Rumball, aged 11, on the best piece of embroidery (4 hem stitched handkerchiefs) that she had ever seen done by a girl of Diana's age.

13 Dec.   Christmas Concert was held in the playroom. There were several outside visitors including the mothers of Mary Ewers and Joyce Wallis. These girls had produced a nativity Play by Class III without any adult help. It was very successful.

Cropwood log book 1949

7 Feb.   Dr. Kemp visited today—he immunised 21 girls against diphtheria.

5 May   Mrs. Wilson JP, Mr. Trinder, Clerk of the Court, and Miss Evans, Probation Officer, interested in one of the new girls, came to see Cropwood today. They were very favourably impressed.

12 May   The decorators arrived today. Cropwood is to be painted and re-decorated inside and out.

19 May   Miss Ashby, Superintendent Nurse, brought four Nurse Administrators in connection with UNICEF to see Cropwood.

THE 1940s: THE TURNING POINT

10 June   Dr. Kemp visited. Fifty-six children now able to use pool. Miss Boothroyd at S.S. Committee Meeting today.

25 June   This has been the hottest week of the year and the children are getting very brown. Unfortunately the pool is out of commission owing to some corrosion in one of the pipes. Meals and lessons have been almost entirely out-of-doors all this week owing to the painters' intrusion.

4 July   Dr. Kemp visited—June P. removed to Dudley Road Hospital today with nephritis.

22 July   Cropwood broke up for the holiday. Nurse Keen is retiring at the end of August after 27 years here—ever since the opening of Cropwood. We were able to present her with a little book containing everyone's signatures and a cheque for £12 to which all had contributed.

31 Aug.   Dr. Coker, School Medical Officer, visited Cropwood for the first time today. He seemed very pleased with what he saw, and said how much he preferred the small dormitories in the House to the long Extension ones.

7 Sep.   50 Baskerville children, accompanied by Miss Jenkins, and eleven other staff, came to pick blackberries in our grounds today. The staff all had tea in the lounge, and it was pleasant to renew old acquaintance with Sister Nichol, Miss Constable and Miss Davies who were here in the evacuation at the beginning of the war. Both Cropwood and Baskerville children enjoyed themselves.

4 Oct.   Miss Billing took 16 of Class I to West Bromwich today to Oak House Museum. This is a genuine Tudor building, with some lovely furniture and other interesting exhibits. They were very interested in what they saw, which is all in line with their history period.

31 Oct.   Dr. Kemp visited. A case of ringworm found.

7 Nov.   Mr. Gobin gave an Imperial Institute lecture today. His subject was the West Indies and his lecture very interesting.

21 Nov.   Audrey Reid, admitted to Cropwood when twelve years old—then housemaid now Assistant Cook, is twenty-one today.

24 Nov.   Mr. Barrow Cadbury came to Cropwood today bringing an Australian lady, Headmistress of a school in Western Australia. They were charming visitors—Miss Bowden thoroughly interested in everything she saw. Mr. Cadbury looked well and, though much older, carries his 87 years with dignity and agility.

9 Dec.   Miss Ross, Miss Mann, and Miss Moore visited today to see the Handwork exhibition which has been laid out in readiness for Visiting Day tomorrow. They were all delighted with the work—it really is a very good show. Class I sang four of the lesser-known carols for them.

Cropwood Open-Air School had been visited in October 1945 by Janet Whitney, researching her book on Geraldine Cadbury. She described the school as being full of happiness where rosy-cheeked children were dressed in brown tunics and white blouses. At that time 80 girls from the ages of seven to 14 could be accommodated at the school and parents were allowed to visit only twice a term, as monthly visits had been found to be too disruptive. Handicrafts were an important part of the school curriculum, together with open-air games and swimming in the pool. In many cases the parents visiting the school were so impressed by the improvement in their children by the simple means of fresh air and cleanliness that they attempted to introduce them into their own homes, many of which were in the poorer districts of Birmingham.

For this period we have reminiscences from three pupils, a teacher and a kitchen maid:

Mrs. Jill Embury (née **Halliday**), Cropwood 1947-50, Kings Heath, Birmingham

Cropwood was the happiest time of my life after my troubled and traumatic childhood. That school helped me enormously and probably saved my sanity.

I was there because of a weak chest; every cold turned to bronchitis and also I suffered very badly with my nerves because of emotional and physical abuse by my stepfather and mother.

At last I didn't feel I was the odd one out like I did at home (there were five half sisters and a half brother; I was the oldest and Mom thought I was her personal assistant). Indeed, it seemed to be the only time in my childhood that I was happy, except when I stayed at my grandmother's house.

I was at Cropwood in the severe winter of 1947 and we were able to go sledging on Hunter's Hill. Although it was very cold the screens of the narrow dormitories were nearly always left open except when there was a storm, but for the first time in years I didn't get a chest cold although I got chilblains. I remember one night it snowed unexpectedly in the early hours. When we woke up the next morning the iron bedstead bars of our beds had a layer of snow on them. There were no fires, only pipes to warm your hands on when you came in from school.

Headmistress Miss Boothroyd seemed to have a soft spot for me and I became very fond of her. She was an invalid and walked very slowly with the aid of a stick. The girls said that she had 'creeping paralysis' which, I found out later, was multiple sclerosis. A teacher or pupil always held her arm when she walked. I remember one day she asked me and I had to help her up a flight of steps. She said it was the first time anyone had put her feet correctly on each step because she couldn't bend her knees on her own. She always chose me to help her after that. She made me feel that maybe I was someone, after all.

In the winter after breakfast we had to stand in a long line in the washroom while the nurse gave us all a tablespoon of cod liver oil. We all hated it and I developed a knack of keeping it in my mouth until I got to the toilets and then spat it out, until the cleaner realised that the toilets were greasy as other girls did the same thing!

I thought the food was great because we had porridge and always something fried, like sausage or bacon. I especially liked the deep fried bread, it was no wonder I started to put on weight.

In the summer it was fabulous because we had our own private swimming pool. We went in nearly every day. I still have a feeling of pure joy every time I see an outdoor swimming pool.

On Sunday we always went to the village church, some Methodist and some Catholic. Some went quite a way to the Synagogue with Sister Daniels, who of course was Jewish. I liked going only because there was a boy from Hunter's Hill who used to ogle me and I quite liked the look of him. A note was passed to me one Sunday asking if I would meet him down at the wall—which we all knew to be out of bounds, and was opposite to the boys school. I was a prefect at the time, so I was really taking a risk. I was about 14 at the time but we thought we were very daring just talking to the opposite sex.

Before I went to Cropwood I had absolutely no self-esteem because of my traumatic home life. But Miss Boothroyd took me under her wing and made me feel of some worth. I was very good with younger children and she suggested I would make a good nursery nurse. So besides my leaving certificate, she wrote me a testimonial. I was determined to get out of the inner city back streets and try to make something of myself.

When I left and started my training, I had to leave home. I kept in touch with Miss Boothroyd and arranged to meet her at a 'posh' hotel in town. When I walked into the hotel I felt just like a film star in the pure silk dress Miss Boothroyd had given me before I left. I know she was very proud of me because before I went to Cropwood I was just a downtrodden nervous wreck. That school showed me that there was a better way of life if you were prepared to 'go for it'.

Mrs. T.M. Stapleton (née **Trueman**), Cropwood 1947-9, Corby, Northants.

I have very fond memories of my time at Cropwood School which I attended until I was 16 years old.

I lived in the centre of the city so it was really lovely to move to this big house with its massive grounds; it seemed like a dream come true to me. Staying there opened endless doors to me, like playing hockey and

THE 1940s: THE TURNING POINT

tennis and being close to the wild-life. Living there lifted the emotional pressure of everyday family life and I could now enjoy myself.

There was Miss Jones and Miss Soar (teachers) and Miss Arnot, the House Keeper, who lived in the village and used to take us to her cottage.

Miss Boothroyd was the Headmistress and she was one of the kindest and most considerate people I have ever met. She has made an everlasting impression on my life. She always used to talk to us about the theatre and the ballet, which none of us had ever imagined going to. To my great delight she surprised me and three other girls by getting us tickets and sending us off to Sadlers Wells **Sleeping Beauty**. *I was entranced by it and even now after forty five years I have never forgotten it.*

She also used to let me read her private collection of books. She was a very kind lady and whoever chose her for the job made a wise decision.

Mrs. June Teece (née **Pritchard**), Cropwood 1948-9, Walsall, West Midlands

Miss Boothroyd was the Headmistress. She could barely walk with two sticks but we adored her and found great joy in being able to help her up stairs to her sitting room, which meant lifting one foot up after the other, up each step.

My friend Gwen and I stuck together a lot, so when we got bored we used to run away together. We always knew the end result of our escapade; it was always the same. First we would go to her mothers and have a sandwich and a drink, then we would go to my home and do the same. Mother would then pack us back on our way. We would get from Kingstanding to somewhere along Bristol Road and a friendly police

Schoolgirls at Cropwood, 1949. Back row, left to right: Joyce Brown, Miriam Stokes, Pamela Jackman, Joyce Courill, Gwen Clewer, Doreen Elnell; centre row, left to right: Iris Callow, Joyce Dallow, Joan Carrington, Barbara Duddy, Mary Kinson, Mavis Haliday, Jessie Bradley, Frances Owen, Mary Ewers; (front row, left to right) Ruth Starkey, Diana Rumball, Pat Hall, Rita Brooks, Pat Middleton, Judy Whitehead, Ruby Moss, Margaret Walton, Brenda Copestake. (J. Teece)

patrol would give us a lift back to school. The only reason for absconding was devilment and boredom, never ill treatment.

We used to form small gangs. 'The Wall' was strictly out of bounds but our gang found the shell of an old summer house there. Being very enterprising we sought around for old wood and built a den, thatching the roof with ferns and greenery and holding the walls together with nails we purloined from the gardener's workshop. The door also came from the workshop; we borrowed the furniture from the rest-shed. It was the door that gave the game away but it was a long time before our den was found.

I remember those old brown drawers and knicker linings. One night (on shower night) we all had new linings made by the linen mistress. They were like tents! Two of us decided to prove a point, so one put them on, then the other climbed on the bench and slid in to them as well! But when the joke was over we couldn't get out of them! For punishment we had to stay behind and clean all the showers out.

I left Cropwood after 18 months and went on to Marsh Hill where I finished my school years, becoming head girl in my final year.

Mrs. Freda Owen (née **Belling**), 90, Teacher, Cropwood 1948-9, Trowbridge, Wilts.

I taught for five terms from May 1948 until December 1949. Miss Boothroyd was Headmistress but as she suffered from multiple sclerosis and was in a wheel chair, extra duties devolved on the staff which probably accounted, in part, for teaching staff only staying a short time.

Miss Soar (Deputy) taught the infants, I taught the seniors and Olive Trace the juniors. A few of the children slept in the house where the Headmistress and Senior Nurse were accommodated. Miss Soar and I had our separate bed sitting rooms at the two ends of the dormitory blocks and each one of us was responsible for the pupils who slept in the upper and lower storeys. This entailed getting each up at 11 o'clock at night to take them to the toilet or reporting to the Senior Nurse if any child was taken ill in the night.

'Rosemary' was used as additional sleeping quarters, supervised by Nurse Mort and a member of the teaching staff. Rumour had it that Dick Turpin passed Rosemary Cottage on one of his many legendary nocturnal rides. The girls loved the idea!

During my first term there, there was quite a spate of runaways who were picked up by the police and returned either to the school or to their homes. Olive and I decided these children missed the loving contact of their parents and siblings and decided to treat them more as young sisters and less as pupils. It worked and the running away ceased. As the Headmistress was unwell she tended to postpone the visiting Saturday which should have taken place mid-term. This aggravated the situation.

The children's education was interrupted as they were frequently called out of the classroom for medical inspection etc. The children's feet were rubbed with methylated spirits to harden them and enable them to wear sandals without socks. They did have some jolly times, such as a Hallowe'en Party and a Christmas Party, Treasure Hunts, picnics and even a visit to Stratford-on-Avon in the summer.

Miss Bella Goodby, 84, Kitchen Maid, Cropwood 1944-59, Bromsgrove, Worcestershire

I was Kitchen Maid at Cropwood and this is an example of a typical day at the school:

The day started with a half hour walk to school to be there at 8.00am prompt. On arrival I would go straight to the scullery to the two big sinks, and fill one of soapy water, one of boiling rinsing water to wash up. The plates, cups and cutlery were stacked onto wooden racks and dipped into the very hot soapy water, then into the next sink to be rinsed. This took until about 10.00am when there was a ten-minute break for coffee. Then the preparations for lunch started.

The potatoes were peeled in a machine which was operated manually, and was in the outside blue-brick yard. The potatoes were then laid on racks in a steamer-oven and steam cooked to retain all the vitamins and flavour. The children had lunch at about 12.30pm and staff had a three-quarters of an hour break. Our lunch was taken in the kitchen—payment for this was deducted from wages. A large basin of dripping and leftover bread was kept for any staff not able to buy any lunch, which happened quite often as times were hard.

After lunch all the plates etc. had to be washed, following the same process as at breakfast. Regularly the wooden kitchen tables would have to be scrubbed, also the floors ('right into the corners', said the headmistress). This was a bucket, soap and scrubbing brush job on hands and knees.

At 4.00pm staff had a tea break. Mrs. Perrygrove, the caretaker's wife, sometimes came in to help prepare the children's tea which consisted of brown bread (which had to be sliced) and jam and a cup of tea.

After tea again all the washing up had to be done, and I finished at 6.00pm. Occasionally I had some help from the older girls but this didn't happen very often; I would get through all this work seven days a week with half a day off on Wednesday. I did not find this hard; I was used to this type of work and enjoyed my time at the school.

Hunter's Hill 1945-9

Mr. Christian Kunzle (of the well-known Birmingham firm of Kunzle's who owned a cake-shop and restaurant), had placed his personal chateau in Davos in Switzerland at the disposal of Birmingham Education Committee to be used as an Alpine School. For many years groups of boys were sent from Birmingham's open-air schools for a period of six months at a time to benefit from the pure air. Under the care of Birmingham teachers the boys were educated in the Chateau Dorf, usually improving rapidly in health and strength. The school log books of Uffculme and Hunter's Hill often recorded parties of boys preparing for their trip to Switzerland and there is a personal account of this unique experience narrated in this chapter.

The school log book kept by Miss Buckley is a mine of information and a selection of some of the entries on the daily life of the school is quoted here. It appears that one of the major problems was the regular absconding of boys from Hunter's Hill, despite all the efforts of the staff to make life as interesting as possible:

Hunter's Hill log book 1945

29 Jan.   *4 new boys admitted. John T. has mumps. Isolated in spare teacher's bedroom (Isolation full).*

3 Feb.   *G.W. admitted 29.1.45. was sent home today. He persists in running away and runs down the railway track. I am afraid he may be fatally injured. Boys in isolation making good progress. Dr. Dick has visited them every day this week.*

9 June   *No. on Roll 119. R.B. returned at 1.30pm and absconded again with John G. at 6.30pm, caught wandering through fields by policeman at Barnt Green and returned to school. I caned both boys and they are being kept in bed for a day. This is the sixth time B. has run away.*

17 June   *Ronald B. and J.G. absconded returned 10pm, found wandering on railway line.*

24 Sep.   *Lewis H. admitted to Ear & Throat Hospital for treatment.*

17 Nov.   *G.B. discharged by Doctor Roberts as an unsuitable case for open-air life in the winter. He suffers from frost bite and chilblains.*

8 Dec.   *Parents invited to see an exhibition of Art & Handwork and an entertainment.*

Hunter's Hill log book 1946

4 Feb.   *N.S. returned in a very dirty neglected condition. 5 boys went home today to take the Technical Schools admission examination.*

10 June   R.W. in isolation. Dr. Vollam visited him—severe chill, M&B 3 hourly.

13 June   Boys were taken to Malvern Hills today by special coaches, leaving Hunter's Hill at 10.15am—returning 7.15pm—a very enjoyable day. All staff accompanied children.

28 June   Dentist examined all boys.

30 Aug.   18 boys to clinics to be X-rayed and have passport photographs re. visit to Switzerland.

10 Sep.   Mr. Keen commenced duty as assistant master today. Sent clothing for boys going to Switzerland to clinic today.

14 Sep.   Mr. K.G. Tucker commenced duty as assistant master today.

19 Sep.   Mrs. Whitney went away today accompanying party of Birmingham children to Switzerland.

3 Oct.   William R. absconded at 7pm, returned at 9pm by local police.

7 Oct.   16 backward boys put into small class for specialised teaching, 6 boys went home today to take Grammar Schools entrance examination.

21 Oct.   K.H. still very ill. Dr. Vollam visited him and ordered M&B 4 hourly—he considers boy should be moved to Yardley sanatorium.

5 Nov.   Boys had a party today—special tea, bonfire and fireworks display.

17 Nov.   At 11pm a fire was discovered in the senior cloakroom—boys were removed from dorms III & IV away from fire. Fire kept under control by hydrants manned by staff until the Redditch Fire Brigade took over. Cloakroom burnt out.

Two ex-pupils look back on their time at Hunter's Hill with mixed feelings:

Mr. Maurice Wareing, 57, Hunter's Hill 1946, Moseley, Birmingham

I spent nine months at Hunter's Hill from January to September 1946. They were not very happy times because it was the first occasion I had left home and was homesick.

Miss Buckley the Headmistress was a strict disciplinarian and I stood in awe of her. On one occasion when a boy had something stolen, possibly money, every other boy in the school had two lashes of the cane across the hand because no-one owned up to the crime.

For the first time I played football and cricket which I continued to play and follow in later years.

Parents Day was held on a fine June day and I felt embarrassed having to sing in the choir The Lord's My Shepherd.

On my return to Hunter's Hill from summer holiday in early September I saw a boy reading down a list of boys chosen to go to Switzerland for three months. To my relief I was one of those chosen to spend October to December with a family as guests of the Swiss Red Cross.

Mr. Ronald Hawkins, 49, Hunter's Hill 1946, Warley, West Midlands

Memories of Hunter's Hill when I was 10 years old: my likes were going on organised walks and I always remember a large hill with dozens of rabbits and you could see the warrens. My sister was at Cropwood at the same time and I was allowed to go and see her occasionally.

The dislikes were sleeping after lunch, going to school on Saturday mornings, and forming three lines to go to church. If there were more in one line the teachers levelled the lines up irrespective of your religion, and being Church of England I sometimes ended up going to the Catholic Church.

The highlight of Christmas was a group of carol singers in period costumes singing in the driveway with lanterns on long poles.

THE 1940s: THE TURNING POINT   179

Hunter's Hill log book 1947

4 Feb.   G.R. who went to Anti-T.B. Clinic on Friday returned today, his mother reports that he is to go to Yardley Sanatorium for observation.

3 Mar.   J.J. in isolation, septic chilblains. R.D. in isolation, influenza.

5 Mar.   Boys did not have their half-day today. A blizzard raged all day, roads blocked, milk brought on sledge from farm.

10 Sep. Leslie D. and B.H. absconded during night. B.H. returned and has settled down. D. would not settle and was so hysterical that he was sent home with a teacher.

18 Sep. 5 boys absconded at 6.30am, very wet day and two went off in pyjamas. Found near Barnt Green by local police and returned at 8.30am. All wet and cold, no reason for behaviour, all treated by Sister to prevent colds.

20 Nov. School holiday for wedding of HRH Princess Elizabeth. Lecture by Mr. Murray (Imperial Institute) on West Indies.

10 Dec. Xmas Party—conjuror, Father Christmas with presents and firework display, a very successful party.

Midnight feasts may not be mentioned in the log books but one past Prefect remembers them clearly, among other things:

Mr. Peter W. Allen, Hunters Hill 1943-7, Aldridge, Walsall, West Midlands

Headmistress Miss Buckley: Authoritarian, 5ft. 7ins. tall, severe cropped hair, with a two-inch white stripe going right through it. I found beneath her hard exterior a woman who was very caring and warm.

Memories I have of the school are the sport nearly every day, PE stripped to the waist, even in winter, always outside unless it was raining or snowing. Sunday afternoon walks in the countryside. In the dormitories, the large windows were open day and night, and I have several memories when awakening in the morning in winter for snow to be on the bottom of beds in front row.

Food was excellent, and we used to get seconds. In winter after dinner it was compulsory to have a tablespoon of cod liver oil.

Young children were in dormitory no. 1, aged five to seven; on leaving home at such a young age, they found themselves very bewildered, particularly when they got up in the morning. Many of us prefects were sent down to help them to wash and clean their teeth, to get dressed, fold blankets, and clean shoes. I remember newcomers just standing there helpless, not knowing what to do, so far from their mother and home.

The Midnight Feasts for us older boys were quite good. Miss Buckley and the teachers knew all about them, and kept an eye on them. Just prior to end of term a couple of lads were allowed to leave

---

LOOKING TO THE FUTURE

Children need cod liver oil *every day* for strong, sturdy bones

IT'S in the early years of a child's life that the foundations of his health are laid.

That's why it's so important to make sure that a child's growing body gets everything it needs for its full growth and development.

Cod liver oil supplies a child with the important Vitamins A and D, needed to build strong, sturdy bones, and to strengthen resistance to colds and infections.

Because the Government knows that children may still go short of these vitamins at the present time, they have provided cod liver oil for all children under five.

Every child should have cod liver oil every day all the year round.

For over 70 years Scott's Emulsion has been known as the most digestible form of cod liver oil. We regret that, although more Scott's is being made than ever before, the supply is still insufficient to meet the demand. So, please leave Scott's for the children and invalids—they have first claim to it.

Issued by the makers of **SCOTT'S EMULSION**

school grounds on their own, went into Blackwell, to the Teashop to order cakes and sandwiches for our Feast, also allowed to collect them on eve of Feast—remarkable really!

One year the teacher-in-charge of senior dormitory, asked us if we were having a Midnight Feast because he would like to come, which he did! We had a great time, and I respected him very much.

Hunters Hill log book 1948

15 July   Miss M. Williams (Institute of Educational Research) to give tests to children in all age ranges for purpose of comparison with tests given to blind children in same age ranges.

20 July   School Cricket Team played Staff and won by 30 runs.

13 Nov.   8 boys who were transferred to Davos 5.6.48 were examined by Dr. Kemp today and transferred to normal day schools in the city.

19 Nov.   School visited by Doctors from the Ministry to conduct exhaustive enquiry into the school planning and routine.

29 Nov.   Re-admitted Peter H., John S., two boys who went to Davos in June returned in November and have been ill since returning to Birmingham.

30 Nov.   Mr. Chedgy left today to take charge of party of boys transferred to school in Davos.

15 Dec.   Christmas party—games, competitions, tea, Christmas tree and presents followed by a film show—a very enjoyable party.

Hunters Hill Cricket Team, 1948/9. Back row, left to right: P. Herring, R. Tonks, R. Degg, (unknown), Newman, (unknown); front row, left to right: T. Weir, C. Cully, P. Braker, G. Whitworth, R. Haycock, M. Clair. (T. Weir)

THE 1940s: THE TURNING POINT

Hunter's Hill log book 1949

17 Feb.   *Visiting Day. School team played Fathers at football and won 6-5.*

1 May   *Nurse Atkins commenced duty.*

7 June   *Peter J. sent to Little Bromwich with scarlet fever. D.R. in isolation.*

8 June   *All boys and staff given 2 tablets of Sulphaduazine (this treatment to continue for 14 days).*

9 June   *All the boys taken to Malvern for the day, a very enjoyable day. Dr. Kemp gave permission for the picnic to be taken though we are in quarantine for scarlet fever.*

21 June   *11 boys to Great Charles St for medical examination—remain at home for night and depart for Davos on Wednesday morning.*

18 July   *Dr. Kemp (Routine Visit) saw all boys with ear trouble and boys going to cottage homes. Several boys who got wet on Saturday are in bed today.*

5 & 6 Oct. *Students from Dudley Training College to see the school.*

29 Oct.   *No. on roll 130. D.Lawrence & J.Fowler absconded at 6.15, informed by police at 11.30pm both at former's home.* [There is a first-hand account of this escape by Derek Lawrence later on in this chapter.]

24 Nov.   *School visited by Mr. Barrow Cadbury and a visitor from Australia.*

2 Dec.   *10 boys taken home by parents prior to departure on 6.12.49 for Davos. Ration books sent with them.*

Three 'old boys' of Hunter's Hill, including one who absconded, recall their time at the school:

Mr. G. Barton, Hunter's Hill and Davos, 1948-9, Coleshill, Birmingham

I spent 18 months at Hunter's Hill from the age of eight, and six months at Christian Kunzle's Chateau in Davos Dorf, Switzerland. I was sent to Hunter's Hill from the Chest Clinic in Great Charles Street. I could not even spell 'cat' before I went there because I was forever falling asleep in the class and even walking home from school I frequently bumped into lamp-posts.

I remember my first night at Hunter's Hill when I was homesick and hid behind the laundry basket. I was found by one of the seamstresses who used to look after our clothes, and afterwards I used to frequent their workplace where they mothered me. It was my secret and it continued for my 18 months there.

I did not like it there but we had some good times and the nicest memory was waking up to birds singing at the first light. That was the first time I had ever heard a cuckoo. Considering I lived in Nechells by the Jeyes fluid works, with Saltley gasworks on top of us, we saw or heard very few birds in that area.

We were all dressed the same in grey short trousers, grey red edged collared jerseys; in summer, sandals and white ankle socks outside school premises and no socks around the school. My school number was 48.

Our bedtime was 6.00pm and I think it was lights out at 7.00pm. It was frequent for boys to have 'accidents' because of the noises in the night which could be very frightening and children's imaginations played many tricks on the ears, making them afraid to go to the toilets during the night.

The bath house furniture was six round aluminium six-inch tubs on the floor, filled by a shower above each tub, and the water was only just warm. Then once a week Matron would wash our hair in black soap to keep the nits at bay, after which we would have our height and weight checked and recorded.

We got a visit from our families once a month on Saturday afternoons. We all looked forward to the visitors and the sweets they brought for us which must have been hard on our brothers and sisters because of rationing at that time.

I once had a disagreement with a bigger boy and I was made to put on gloves and fight in the assembly hall, watched by all the school. I ended up in tears.

On hot summer days Class I did PT on the grass area in front of the dorms instead of in the assembly hall and on one of these occasions clothes were not allowed.

Then I was told I was going to Switzerland for six months which cost my parents fifteen shillings (that was my pocket money for six months but we were not allowed to spend it and had to keep it to buy presents prior to coming home). We were all kitted out in short trouser suits, in different colours and patterns, for the journey to and from Switzerland. Over there our dress was similar to Hunter's Hill and we all dressed the same.

Our journey started from Snow Hill station. After a photo call for the **Birmingham Gazette** we set off for London where we were taken on a coach tour of the sights before catching the boat train for Folkestone and our ferry for Calais. I was one of the few children allocated a sleeper on the over night train to Switzerland. Sleepers were allocated to the children they considered to be sickest; the other children had to sleep in the ordinary compartments.

Our routine was much the same but I was made to go straight to bed after tea (which was about 5pm), with lights out and no free time. On Saturdays my bedtime was often earlier. Sunday was letter writing day so I was allowed up till 6.00pm but I went to bed two hours earlier than the other 31 boys, all because I never gained any weight or grew any taller, on our weekly weighing sessions taken by the nurse. The one advantage was that I was the only boy with my own room.

At breakfast we used to have to eat a one-and-a-half-inch square yellow substance called 'plento' which was made out of some kind of wheat and corn enriched with vitamins and the taste was quite pleasant.

We used to have an afternoon nap after lunch on a specially made platform over-looking the valley and most of us never went to sleep. We used to watch for the wild deer which were quite common to see. I was there in the summer months and the flora was beautiful. On Saturday and Sunday afternoons we used to go for walks after our rest. Sometimes into the hills or the lower slopes of the mountains or to Davos or around the lake at Dorf.

The non-teaching staff who looked after us used to come from Kunzle's Five Ways (Birmingham) Factory. I think Kunzle's paid the fares and keep. They used to stay for one month after which we, the pupils, used to give them a party. On these nights I was allowed to stay up, for I was one of the entertainers. I used to dress as a female and sing favourite songs for them (how I do not know because at school prior to Hunter's Hill I used to be told I was tone deaf!). I was always kept to the last act and they always wanted more.

After six months I came home and back to the Chest Clinic. Doctor said I had got to go back to Hunter's Hill but I refused and said I would only run away, so he relented and I was allowed to stay at home.

My education had caught up remarkably and I left school at the top of the B grade of a secondary modern school. Hunter's Hill and Davos had done me a power of good—all due to a wonderful Headmistress from Cromwell Street Junior School who sent me to the Chest Clinic.

Mr. Derek Lawrence, Hunter's Hill 1949-51, Pelsall, nr Walsall, West Midlands

I cannot remember the day I arrived at Hunter's Hill but I can remember Miss Buckley who put the fear of God into us if we did wrong. The food was always plain but never enough of it.

When the weather was nice it was lessons out under the oak trees outside the dormitory. Sport was the main thing, lessons came second.

The open-air was carried to extremes in the winter: we had nowhere to go to warm up, and that was when we missed home a great deal. My mother did not come every visiting day; it was a long way from

Hockley to Blackwell so I and the only real friend I had, John Fowler, decided to run away. This was the middle of winter, snow all over, us in shorts! We got half way from the school to the no. 84 tram terminus when we heard the Prefects coming after us! We hid behind a big gate and when they had gone by an old lady's voice said, 'You can come out now, they have gone!' She asked us where we were going and then gave us 10d so we had the fare for the tram. We waited until a tram was going out, then ran and caught it, thus getting home. Unfortunately the police came after a while and took John back the same night. I stayed at home for a few days but did not settle at Hunter's Hill after that.

I can remember the time I had boils and ulcers in my ears and was very ill for a while. They never even told my mother; not until I tried to join the army did I find it had left me with a perforated ear drum.

The first short holiday of the year we did not go home. They used to take us all by coach to the British Camp on the Malvern Hills. They took a great basket of boiled eggs and loads of bread and butter and orange juice.

Mr. Terry Weir, 60, Hunter's Hill 1948-51, Great Barr, Birmingham

I was sent by Dr. Kemp, the Birmingham Schools Doctor, to Hunter's Hill as I suffered from asthma. I was living at the time at Lozells, Birmingham. On 21 April 1948, at the age of 12, I was put on a bus outside the Hall of Memory; there were about twenty of us. On arriving we bathed and changed into school clothes.

The school was run on the 'house' principle, with four houses being named after the four surrounding hills. Each house had a House Master/Mistress, House Captain/Vice Captain and Prefects plus an overall School Captain. I myself was in Clent which I captained for the last 18 months I was there. I was also School Captain for my last year. The house system ruled all and if someone misbehaved and lost his house some points he was immediately turned on by the boys in his own house. It was a self regulation discipline that certainly worked.

Some of the staff I remember at the school are:

Miss L.M. Buckley, Headmistress, who I feared and respected and on reflection helped to form my views on life, for the better, I hope.

Nursing Staff: Nurse Barrett—rather frightened me at first but to whom I warmed later. Sister Daniels: dear old-fashioned matron type who wore a huge white hat. Nurse Atkins: came with her husband Mr. Atkins, a teacher.

Teachers: Mr. Chedgy: exactly as his name. Mr. K.G. Tucker: wonderful teacher in and out of the classroom. Miss Jones: nice Welsh lady who married Mr. Tucker. Miss Leadbeater: formidable Northerner. Mrs. Whitney: taught infants. Mr. Atkins: nice man married to Nurse Atkins. Mr. Lawrence: interested in mountaineering. Mr. W. Hill 'Bill Hill': Rugger type man's man. Miss Ledger: from Liverpool.

As I was a sports nut the opportunity to play football/cricket at virtually any time of the day, apart from school hours, made my stay at Hunter's Hill very pleasant. I did not suffer, as many children did, from home sickness and at no time ever contemplated doing a 'bunk' or running away from school.

The food at Hunter's Hill was adequate but there was not a lot of it. As I progressed to become School Captain, little bonuses came my way—like taking teachers' trays back, getting to know the kitchen staff, all of which gave us a few extra items to eat. We were not underfed but I think we could have all eaten a bit more.

Visiting day was once a month when our folks came to see us, loaded with goodies, which we should have handed in. But of course we secreted away cakes, sweets etc. to be eaten at a midnight feast which were very popular after visiting day. My Mom and Dad never failed to visit me the whole of my time there and enjoyed it as much as I did: Mom running the raffles and Dad captaining the Dads team to play football or cricket against the lads. But some lads for one reason or other did not have visitors on a regular basis, sometimes not at all.

We wrote home once a week as part of our English lesson. I used to write to lots of people (Aunts, Uncles and Friends etc.) therefore I was always receiving post. Some lads never received any post. Being away

Senior football team at Hunters Hill, 1948/9. Back row, left to right: Terry Weir, Fred George, Ron Emery, Ray Hancock, Colin Bailey, Alan Lee; front row, left to right: Roy Webb, Peter Braker, Brian Robinson, Lawrence White, Lou Henshaw. (T.Weir)

from home could be very cruel for some lads. I personally coped with it very well but found out later that some boys were desperately unhappy at Hunter's Hill.

All in all I enjoyed my time at Blackwell, it taught me to look after myself. I also came across some of the unpleasant things in life; bullying was not rife but it did go on. Stealing was not rife but it did go on; we kept all our belongings in a suitcase at the side of the bed and occasionally something went missing.

There was a meeting of boys and girls in the road that divided Hunter's Hill from Cropwood, down by Billy's Lane. Each boy/girl would be egged on by their friends, a quick kiss, to the roar of approval from both sides, then scurrying back to our own sides and that was that.

It was cold in winter with the emphasis still being on open-air. The dormitory windows were always wide open and I slept in the front row. Many occasions I would put on my day-time clothes and get back into bed to keep warm; this was a punishable offence if caught. When the night teacher was at the other end of the school we used to have the 'steeplechase'. It started at one end, one boy per row, leaping from bed to bed to the other end. A big lad could hit each bed with a single stride; if your stride was short and you hit the bed it slid away from you! Amazingly enough, no one was badly hurt, but I saw some spectacular falls. Pillow and knotted towel fights were a normal way of life, but I do not remember anyone coming to too much harm.

My three years at Blackwell were relatively happy. My big criticism is that no preparation was made for school leavers to get jobs. Within two weeks of leaving Blackwell I was on a building site, because it was an outdoor job: a job which I was physically unable to cope with, and after three years in the dirt, dust and the wet I left the building trade, very much poorer in health than when I left Hunter's Hill. I should have been better advised before leaving school. I had a number of other jobs before becoming a Qualified Photographer at Aston University. My claim to fame is that from 1971 to '95 I was Official Photographer to Aston Villa Football Club, a position that took me to many foreign countries and allowed me to meet many famous people.

Haseley Hall

Birmingham's latest open-air school in this era was Haseley Hall Residential School for Boys which opened in 1942. It was a late 18th-century mansion set in rural Warwickshire and had been occupied from 1891 to 1919 by Sir James Sawyer, an eminent physician. Appointed as Resident Physician and Medical Tutor at Queen's Hospital in Birmingham in 1867, when only 23 years of age, he had been consulting physician to the hospital all his life. He was an authority on practical clinic work and original investigations, writing many medical books, including *Diseases of the Lungs, Heart and Liver; Causes and Cure of Insomnia; Maladies of the Heart;* and *Contributions to Practical Medicine*, which ran to four editions. He was President of the Medical Society and of the Birmingham branch of the British Medical Association. He also had the distinction of becoming Birmingham's first medical man to be knighted by Queen Victoria in 1885 'in recognition of his distinguished position in the medical profession and his long and valued service to the Queen's Hospital'.

Sir James Sawyer

Lady Adelaide Sawyer, his wife, was well known in Birmingham and Warwickshire as she actively supported her husband's many activities outside the medical profession, especially in Birmingham's political scene where he promoted the Conservative cause. In addition, Sir James was Chairman of the Warwickshire Chamber of Agriculture and a Birmingham Justice of the Peace.

In 1889 Sir James Sawyer had purchased Haseley Hall from Sir Edward Antrobus, and completed extensive additions designed by the architects Wood and Kendrick of West Bromwich. The Sawyer family motto features on the side of the Hall, 'Cherche et tu trouveras': Seek and you will find. At that time Haseley was a little rural village with only 150 inhabitants—and still is a very sparsely populated area in rural Warwickshire. He lived there until his death at the age of 74 in 1919. Both Sir James and Lady Sawyer are buried in nearby Haseley churchyard.

From 1919 Haseley Hall was in the care of the Birmingham firm of W & T Avery Ltd who made weighing machines, as a 'Country Home' for senior staff. Sales catalogues in Warwick Record Office show that the Hall boasted four excellent reception rooms, a billiard room, 16 bedrooms, a spacious 42ft.-long gallery and a wide oak staircase with a massive carved balustrade, overlooked by gothic tracery windows. Outbuildings included stables, cowhouse, cart shed, pig sty; and the estate included a croquet lawn, kitchen gardens, farmhouse, several cottages, 14 acres of wood and a lodge. Averys' occupied the premises for nine years and had vacated it by 1928, no doubt having enjoyed what the brochures described as a spacious country residence: 'the charm of Haseley undoubtedly lies in the fact that it is set in thoroughly English countryside, amidst typical Warwickshire scenery, with all the advantages of main road approaches ...'.

By 1930 the Hall had been taken over by the charitable Birmingham Society for the Care of Invalid Children, being run by Matron Miss Moore as a Convalescent Home and Hospital School for girls suffering from rheumatic hearts. The causes of rheumatic diseases were largely unknown, although research had discovered that many of the suffering children had lived around Birmingham's two rivers, the Rea and the Tame. One child with rheumatic fever from a very deprived area discovered Haseley Hall to be a whole new world:

Haseley Hall during the ownership of Sir James Sawyer, c.1906-15. This postcard was sent by kitchenmaid Lucy West to her family when she worked at the hall. (M. Gunn)

Mrs. Ruth Smith (née **James**), Haseley Hall 1934, Kings Norton, Birmingham

On my arrival I was taken down the drive to the meadow, the first I had ever seen, where children were spending the afternoon. My first meal was tea, then I watched with great interest as Nurse Smith went behind every girl, tilted her head back, then with a cloth under her chin poured something down their throats. There was no facial reaction anywhere, so I dutifully held my head back. It was pure cod liver oil and I thought I had been poisoned! The next two shocks on the first day were bedtime at 5.30pm and the nightly strip wash in full view of everyone using a bowl on a bench.

We were not allowed physical exercise and always walked up the lovely staircase backwards, but did do Grecian dancing and daily walks in all weathers: I loved it when it rained as I'd never had a pair of wellingtons before. We also did household tasks on a weekly basis—the worst was cleaning the cutlery and the best folding the serviettes into individual pouchettes. I always liked helping in the kitchen where there was a large bin of sugar cubes. Into the pocket of my knickers were stuffed as many cubes that I could manage for a midnight feast!

All clothing was supplied and clean underwear had to be inspected for repairs which we learned to do. I've never seen stockings with so many darns—money was scarce and the budget tight.

There were two classrooms—Class I: Miss Priestman had bed chairs and bed tables, with very informal lessons; Class II: Miss Boyd in the huge bay windowed room with open fire, reading 'The Secret Garden' which I loved. I also remember sitting outside Miss Moore's french windows by her precious rose garden, listening to Gilbert & Sullivan.

There was an old mulberry tree on the lower lawn and we helped to gather the fruit and blackberries from the meadow.

We also had a girl guide troop and our Lieutenant was the Countess of Warwick. We were once invited to the castle for tea; Lord Brooke was a baby at the time and we were allowed a peep into the nursery.

The pig sties were transformed into little houses where we played and devoured the sweets our mothers brought on their monthly visits. We could buy two pence worth of sweets from the Saturday Tuck Shop but if they weren't eaten by teatime they were handed in and given out again at Sunday tea. I had a celluloid doll whose legs were joined by elastic and by pulling one leg out the stomach made a depository for left-over sweets which we enjoyed after lights out!

Things were never the same for me after Haseley. My expectations were raised and I realised there was a whole new world out there. I am forever grateful for that and for my restored health. I really loved the place.

One of the teachers vividly recalls her time there:

Miss Eileen Wilson Smith, Haseley Hall 1937-42, Rugby, Warwickshire

I was at Haseley Hall Hospital School from September 1937 to March 1942 when it was run by the Birmingham Society for the Care of Invalid Children. The school catered for 40 girls between the ages of about eight and fifteen years. All of them suffered from rheumatism and chorea (St. Vitus' Dance) and they came mainly from very poor housing conditions in Birmingham. Many houses had no indoor bathrooms and the WC's at the end of the backyards were shared by more than one family. The conditions in which the girls lived gave rise to much illness, especially rheumatic conditions.

The girls came to the school usually for nine months—though some stayed longer if they were not fit to return home. They came on the recommendation of doctors in Birmingham, or sometimes direct from hospital following rheumatic fever, in some cases resulting in rheumatic heart condition. Some girls returned to the school as many as three times while I was there. The Headmistress was Miss Marion A. Moore who had trained at Bedford Froebel Training College in Bedford.

Because it was less strain on their hearts, all the girls had to go upstairs backwards, and some of them scuffled upstairs at great speed after a few days! Diet was important and no citrus fruit or other acid fruits were included. Breakfast consisted of a thin porridge (with milk and sugar stirred into it in the kitchen), followed by half a round of fried bread with a blob of Marmite on it.

There was a system of coloured badges, beginning with white and progressing through silver, yellow, orange, light green, dark green, light blue, dark blue, purple to gold, which meant ready to return home. The school doctor, Dr. Mitchell, saw the girls monthly and if they were making normal progress they were promoted to the next coloured badge. Each badge brought with it something extra a girl could do e.g. white, full time in bed; silver, breakfast in bed, up after breakfast but on a chaise longue in school; yellow, up for breakfast and desk and chair in school.

The school had two classes, the younger girls being taught by Miss Priestman and the top class were mine. There were 24 girls in my class and the range of intelligence was very wide. The aim was to try to get each girl up to a standard where she would be able to hold her own in a mainstream school, and the teaching in the three R's was entirely individual. I taught all subjects and took music with each of the two classes. We had singing, bamboo pipe making and playing, and percussion playing.

The nurse who was in charge of the 'home' side of the school was Miss Maud Bigger and there were two housemothers and a housekeeper and the usual kitchen and domestic staff.

The girls were clothed by the school and some of the dresses were distinctly 'orphanage' looking, though gradually more skirts and pullovers were worn in the winter.

In the outbuildings behind the main building the girls had their houses where they played 'families', putting up curtains, cleaning and entertaining in summer evenings and at weekends. There was on the lawn,

Martineau Cottage, a revolving summer-house which was given by the Martineau family of Knowle and which was a lovely place for a child to sit when not well enough to be in school.

There was a music room at the end of the building where we had assembly each morning and a service on Sunday mornings, where I played the piano for hymns, took singing lessons and percussion playing.

Croquet was played on the two lawns as this was a game which put minimum strain on the heart. As girls became better in health they were allowed to play netball. There was a Guide Company of which Miss Moore was the Captain and which I took over when she left; Miss Priestman took Brownies.

We attended Haseley Church on alternate Sunday afternoons for the service at 3pm. Miss Moore brought a small group of less well girls in her car but the rest walked along the Birmingham to Warwick Road for about half a mile, and then turned off across the field beside the Falcon Inn to reach the church. There we were met by the Lady of the Manor who lived at Haseley Manor. Together with us, she and her cook made up the entire congregation, seated in the box pews where the smaller girls could see nothing of what was going on!

During the war, we had to give up going to Church at Haseley as we could have been a good target for German planes as we crocodiled along the main road. At the beginning of the 1939 war, some girls from Harborne, together with a teacher and a nurse, were evacuated to Haseley Hall, but they did not stay long.

We were all supplied with gas masks and were taught how to put them on, and we had gas mask drills. Miss Moore decided that one of the things the girls could do to keep occupied during a gas attack was percussion playing, so we practised playing the instruments while wearing our gas masks! The biggest problem was that one's breath tended to steam up the gas mask, making it difficult to read the music.

After a camp fire one evening the Guide hut was seen to be on fire about midnight, and, in our night clothes we formed a bucket chain to extinguish the fire, terrified that some passing German aeroplane might see us and drop bombs on us.

There was a German plane over about 11.30pm one night and a bomb was dropped in a field near the Falcon Inn. Our blackout in the classrooms was a very heavy, clumsy affair of some black material on wooden frames, which had to be put up at the windows each evening.

As more planes began to come over it was no longer safe to sleep upstairs. As the cellar was not suitable because of damp and frogs, it was decided that the central hall/dining room should be our sleeping place. The teachers had the job of taking out the heavy dining tables and chairs and putting them in the classrooms and then putting down mattresses on the hall floor. As soon as it began to get light, the girls went up to bed for an hour or so, and were served breakfast in bed while the teachers put the dining hall to rights again—up with the mattresses, stacked high under the stairs!

It was thought by the police that German planes were using our artesian type windmill as a guide for turning off to bomb Coventry, and we were asked to have it dismantled. We had long hours of planes droning over us on their way to Coventry for many nights and heard much of the noise of the bombing and firing of the anti-aircraft guns which were mounted on railway trucks for mobility. My job, when the noise was bad, was to put on a gramophone record; the gramophone was on a trolley which always stood beside my mattress at night. When we arose in the mornings we could see from an upstairs window, the glow of the fires in poor, war-torn Coventry.

The Birmingham Society for the Care of Invalid Children ceased to function early in the war, as money was going to the Red Cross and similar organisations rather than to small peacetime societies. The school was taken over by Birmingham Education Authority in 1941 and my salary went from £120 to £180, which in those days was wealth indeed.

THE 1940s: THE TURNING POINT

Miss Moore and Miss Priestman did not wish to work for an education authority and both retired. I left Haseley Hall in March 1942 to take up a teaching post in a private school for backward and delicate boys in Warwick.

An evacuee has happy memories of the school:

Mrs. Patricia King (née **Chiles**), Haseley Hall August 1939-April 1940 (evacuee from Baskerville House School), Castle Bromwich, Birmingham

I was sent to Baskerville in 1938 suffering from St. Vitus Dance. In August 1939 we were evacuated to Haseley Hall.

*I can remember the Matron telling us all that war had been declared. Every morning before they had breakfast the Haseley Hall girls had to put their heads back and have cod liver oil. We, the Baskerville girls, thought it was great we didn't have to have it. My favourite breakfast was **deep fried** bread with Marmite on it.*

I can remember we had to clean all the cutlery with Brasso. We were inspected every week for any holes in the garments we were wearing. We went for lovely walks.

I left Haseley Hall in April 1940 to go home cured. I was one of 12 children, and my mother had to pay 10 shillings a week to the School Board man for my stay at both homes. I don't know how she did it, and will be always grateful to her.

Birmingham Education Committee had taken over the Hall by 1941 and planned to re-open it as a new open-air school. The number of children suffering rheumatic hearts had sharply declined since the end of the 1930s so it was possible to transfer the remaining girls at Haseley Hall to Birmingham's Baskerville School in Harborne which specialised in such cases.

One of these pupils recalls her life at Haseley Hall:

Ms. Rita Stiles, Haseley Hall 1941, Solihull, West Midlands

I had rheumatic fever in 1941, age 10 years, and was nursed at home by my mother. After six months it was found I had a heart murmur so I was sent to Haseley Hall. It was an all girls home; we had to wear clothes provided for us: long white chimmy type night gowns, navy bloomers, different dresses, green blazers and boaters for church on Sunday.

The home was a Manor House: beautiful oak staircase and panelled hall. We had to walk upstairs backwards so we could not run up. Schooling was mostly revision.

The grounds were woods and lawns, the original pig sties were white washed and we used to play 'house' in them. Bed time was 5.30pm, but we could read, knit or talk till 7.00pm, then sleep, if we could. Visits from home once a month on Sundays.

When Haseley Hall was closed down, we were told we could go to Cropwood or Baskerville. Most of us didn't want to go to Cropwood because they wore sleeveless dresses.

Baskerville in Harborne looked very modern after Haseley Hall. We had easy chores to do. I helped Mrs. Goodman the cook. Large trays of bread had to be spread with margarine or dripping for supper. There was a beautiful orchard at the back.

Another of my jobs was to help sister to test urine specimens of the six diabetic children (under supervision). Drop a tablet in the wee, see it fizz up and record the colour. I felt very important. It came in good use, as later in life I became an auxiliary nurse and tested hundreds of pregnant mums' specimens.

Happy days but nicer to come home.

On the opening of Haseley Hall in 1942 Miss Charlton was Headmistress, Mr. Blundel Headmaster, and his wife was the nursing sister. The first intake of 39 boys at Haseley Hall Open-Air School came from Birmingham's elementary schools in the autumn and soon turned from quiet, pale invalids to become 'happy and mischievous imps', reported *The Birmingham Mail* on 24 June 1943:

> One is impressed by the bravery of these little boys aged between 5-9 years. A few tears from a few of them the first night after leaving their mothers, but no more. By the next morning they became engrossed in the activities of the school. There is a farm next door to explore. There is a small outbuilding to be turned into a shop so that money sums and reckoning will soon hold no terrors and be simply fun. There are birds to watch—wagtails, woodpeckers, blue tits, as well as thrushes, blackbirds and starlings. Squirrels fascinate them. There are tame rabbits to feed.
>
> In order that the boys may not feel lonely in a large crowd … they are put together in five small 'families', each watched over by a member of staff. Older and younger boys are mixed together and the older boys take great trouble with the young ones. True, the families have fierce names … Lions, Wolves, Leopards, Tigers and Reindeer and they vie with each other to win a weekly shield which carries with it jelly for tea!
>
> In the sunshine they wear as few clothes as possible. Recently their bodies became very brown except where their braces left a white mark. 'We've got a Victory V on our backs', they announced gleefully!
>
> In their spare time the boys are encouraged to have hobbies. The little ones paint happily or make pictures of coloured paper. The older ones make models of engines, aeroplanes, farms, shops and so on. War time is difficult, however, as there is a pressing need for matchboxes, old but clean cardboard, nails, odd bits of wood, hammers, coloured paper and magazines.
>
> The children benefit from a well balanced diet in which milk and salads form an important part. Green vegetables come in daily from the garden and a two-course meal in the middle of the day is a regular feature.

The following first-hand account of the Haseley Hall Open-Air School comes from a past Headmistress:

Miss Marjory Urquhart, 86, Headmistress Haseley Hall 1947-52, Dunoon, Scotland

Haseley Hall Residential Open-Air School for boys was once an important part of Haseley Manor and the estate which belonged to the Throckmortons.

There were 40 boys, two assistant teachers, a trained nurse, three children's helpers and all the usual domestic and ground staff—but **no housekeeper!** *Here my home training by my highland mother came into play as I had learned how to run a home in a large family. (If I had ever protested my mother always said 'This is knowledge easily carried and may be useful in later life'. How right she proved to be!)*

Miss Charlton had been Head at Haseley Hall from 1942-7. The Hospital School had left behind a wealth of percussion instruments and music stands which I found in the attic. As it was immediately after the war there were also bundles of blackout material! My seamstress and I resurrected percussion and blackout and formed a wonderful little band of boys in black trousers trimmed with red and gold braid! I wrote out the notation scores, repainted the music stands, appointed a conductor and with me at the piano we had lots of fun.

At Haseley Hall my boys were all chest cases: bronchitis, bronchitic-asthma, asthma/eczema, contact TB and the odd epileptic. In healthy Warwickshire, with good home conditions and healthy exercise in the fresh air, success was assured.

I felt very much at home there and found scope for the talents I had. Here my qualifications as Froebel teacher came to fruition. Fortunately I had two young Welsh teachers who were open to my ideas on education. It was considered then that 20 in a class was adequate but I assisted by teaching small groups and individuals, and also bedside teaching if and when needed. Miss Davies and Miss Clarke were my two

Staff at Haseley Hall Open-Air School, c.1948/9. Front row, left to right: Miss Dorothy Baker (children's helper), Miss Julia Hoyle (kitchen maid), Miss M. Clarke (teacher), Miss M. Urquhart (Head Teacher), Miss Davies (teacher, Mrs. Noakes (children's helper), K. Powell (?); back row, left to right: (unknown), Margaret Hoyle (cook), Frank Mortiboys (caretaker), Sister Parry (nurse). (G. Fell)

assistant teachers. Miss Davies later left to take up a post in the newly formed School for Spastics in Birmingham and became Headmistress. She was an excellent teacher.

Housekeeping duties consisted of overall responsibility for creature comforts of boys and staff. I had a good cook who discussed with me menus and special diets and ordered accordingly. I kept all the accounts in order until such time as I was allowed a part-time secretary—three years later!

The trained nurse had charge of health and looked after the boys' welfare, including clothing. She was assisted by three children's helpers, untrained, but with a vocation of looking after children—Sister, as nurse was always called, discussed clothing with me and I ordered. Everything was provided so that there would be no social differences.

Haseley Hall was quite unlike either Cropwood or Hunter's Hill. This was a real solid house with large windows and strong oaken doors. It enveloped us and we felt safe from the outside world. There were no Spartan procedures such as cold baths or showers and open screens. Common sense prevailed! There was no truancy or absconding from Haseley Hall—we were in the heart of the country and the boys were too young to want to leave a place of safety!

Boys remained with us at least three terms or one year so that they could be seen in all weathers in the different seasons. Occasionally a boy had to be transferred to Hunter's Hill on reaching the age of nine. How we hated this procedure, knowing what was in front of him.

All ball games suited to their age were enjoyed—football, rounders and games we invented to improve co-ordination in throwing and catching. Cricket was taught by a very elderly Vicar from Haseley Church. One of his four sons played for Worcestershire—Dodds was the name. There were the usual climbing frames and swings and chutes but we added rope ladders to trees and built a tree house. We tried to inculcate a great love of nature and always had a vase of **wild** flowers on the dining room tables.

Immediately next door was a farm which was a joy and never-ending place of discovery for the city bred youngsters. All the animals children love were there—cats and kittens, dogs and puppies, sheep and lambs, and cattle. I bought my golden cocker spaniel from the farmer and christened him Mac with great ceremony. He was the 'runt' of the litter and the boys helped me to care for him. Of course Mac went with me to Cropwood when I left the school.

All staff with the exception of domestics were resident. Cook and domestics came in daily from nearby cottages. The domestics were nearly all elderly and had spent years in domestic service in the 'big' houses around Warwick. They were excellent and deserved only praise for their work.

The staircase at Haseley Hall was at least five feet wide and rose from the main hall to the gallery above where seven dormitories led off the broad landing. The hall, staircase and gallery were dominated by the huge stained glass window which always seemed to shed a rosy glow on the little boys' faces at morning assembly in the hall below.

I left Haseley Hall somewhat reluctantly but knowing that Birmingham Education Committee only had a short lease on the building I knew I would have to move on sooner or later. (This was the only school building that the committee did not own.) Some years later Haseley Hall closed down.

Miss Urquhart recorded her arrival in the first entry in Haseley Hall's log book on 1 September 1947. The book had apparently been unused during the headship of Miss Charlton from 1942. Boys were transported by a special bus from Birmingham to the school (and returned at the end of term likewise), always with at least two members of school staff in attendance. The log book records life in a rural school, with all its trials and tribulations, as well as its pleasures:

Haseley Hall log book 1947

17 Oct.   *Visit by Miss Ross, Inspector of Special Schools.*

6 Dec.   *Christmas party held. Neighbouring children invited.*

Haseley Hall log book 1948

31 Jan.   *School re-opens. Boys met in Birmingham by Headmistress and the assistant teachers. Only 34 boys returned on opening date. One boy suffering from impetigo on face, head and arms and another from inflammation of the middle ear.*

13 April   *No Sister-in-charge has been appointed to replace Sister Jenkins who retired on 22 March. Responsibility and extra duties taken over by the Headmistress.*

22 May   *Sister Parry takes up temporary duty* [and stayed until 1950].

8 June   *Water not being pumped to top floor, something wrong with mechanism—2½ feet water in well.*

9 July   *Adverse report on water supply submitted to office and to Warwick Borough Engineers.*

18 July   *Parents Visiting Day. Special 'At Home' attended by Chief Education Officer, Councillor Mrs. Smith, Chairman of Special Schools Sub-Committee, Miss Dove, psychologist, Miss Ross, Inspector of Schools, Dr. Kemp, Medical Officer for Special Schools and Vicar Dodds (Vicar of Hatton).*

21 Sep.   *Four boys taken by taxi to Birmingham for removal of adenoids and tonsils.*

Haseley Hall log book 1949

22 June   *Boys and staff outing to Stratford by special bus. A sail on the Avon was greatly enjoyed by everyone.*

21 July   Reunion of Old Boys. Boys who had left Haseley during the past two years were invited; 21 boys attended and all looked fit and well cared for. We all had a very happy afternoon together.

13 Nov.   Parents Visiting Day. We also had a visit from a school photographer who took not only individual photographs of the boys but also group work throughout the school indicative of life in an open-air school. [Unfortunately, these photographs have not been deposited in the archives after the closure of the school so are not preserved for posterity, despite the good idea of the Headmistress.]

Many local people worked at the Hall, including the following:

Mrs. Margaret Gunn (née **Hoyle**), Domestic staff, Haseley Hall 1941-54, Oakham, Leicestershire

I was at Haseley Hall a good number of years, starting off as kitchen maid and ending up doing the cooking. My mother, Miss Lucy West, worked in the kitchens when Sir James Sawyer lived there.

Things were very different in those days as we didn't have a fridge and I remember dragging crates of milk down to the cellar in the hot weather. The porridge was made the day before and put into a hay box overnight to keep warm.

During the war when there were air raids the boys slept downstairs on mattresses in the hall. Most of the staff slept on the top floor so when the sirens sounded we had to drag our mattresses down three flights of stairs.

Mrs. Dorothy Bilton (née **Baker**), Children's Helper, Haseley Hall 1947, Victoria, Australia

I have very happy memories of Haseley Hall having been a pupil there myself before the start of the war. I was later employed as a Children's Helper. I remember Miss Urquhart joining the staff, together with two teachers, a nursing sister and two children's helpers; 40 boys needed quite a lot of supervision with feeding, clothing, bathing, exercising, schooling, resting and being loved.

I remember the evenings and the bathroom which held three baths; it was a case of three undressing, three in the bath and three into pyjamas. The teachers were great with stories on the top landing whilst waiting for the turn in the bathroom.

Most of the times the boys were very active but unfortunately a few had a rough time with asthma attacks but would very quickly get back to the football.

Margaret Gunn, the cook, provided great meals for everyone. The domestic staff were very friendly with the boys and Mr. Hurst, the gardener, was a good friend of the boys.

*I remember taking one boy, Billy, on the bus to Birmingham (there were only two buses per day) to see a Clinic doctor. During the journey he became very sick. I was trying to clean him up when an elderly lady passed me a newspaper for which I was very grateful, but no, it wasn't for cleaning: she told me to **sit** him on it! We had to walk from the Bull Ring to the clinic: a very bedraggled boy but fortunately he got a bath at the clinic. I learnt a lesson—I never did that journey again without a newspaper! Billy and I made quite a few trips to Birmingham. Very strange but sitting on a newspaper really does work for travel sickness.*

In many ways the 1940s era was a watershed in the history of open-air schools as wartime conditions had highlighted the value of such institutions. But the developments after the war set the pattern for a better social environment which was soon to eradicate the very conditions for which open-air schools had been originally founded.

Chapter 7

The 1950s: Widening Horizons

By the 1950s schoolchildren had become considerably taller and heavier than earlier generations. No doubt school milk and meals had played their part, together with increased awareness in nutrition, better social conditions and the development of the School Health Services.

Modern schools were now being designed and built on 'open-air' principles, with maximum light and ventilation—much better, in fact, than some of the existing open-air schools.

In order to evaluate the factors in open-air schools which influenced the health of children, four medical officers from the Ministry of Education carried out a detailed national survey of the 127 open-air schools during 1949 and 1950. The results were published in a lengthy article in the Chief Medical Officer's annual report of 1950/51. Although 11 new open-air schools had recently opened there was actually some doubt about the future expansion of such schools, as most potential pupils seemed to suffer from respiratory disorders or 'maladjustment', rather than debility and malnutrition.

The survey depicted a surprising contrast between schools. Some were very good but far too many were poorly housed in ramshackle, dilapidated buildings which were no longer weatherproof, and often found to be damp and cold. The four inspecting medical officers saw children scraping frost and snow off classroom desks and chairs before they could be used. Rest periods were often on damp canvas beds in unheated leaking rest-sheds. Children seemed to spend much time moving desks and chairs in and out of classrooms and some rooms had no heating at all, with canvas curtains letting in the rain. Some of the comments in the report were quite frank: 'Delicate children were not sent to these schools to become furniture removers'; 'We cannot feel that refrigeration or dampness contributes to health, and therefore we strongly condemn the "band stand" type of classroom', etc ...

In fact, far too many rest-sheds and classrooms were found to be unheated as most schools had been built before Building Regulations standards had been formulated. The report recommended that rest-sheds should be heated multi-purpose rooms and blankets should be stored in dry conditions and that every room should be fairly dry and warm.

Commenting on residential open-air schools the survey dismissed many as 'bare, cheerless and Spartan'. Many had enormous dormitories which were very large and forbidding to young children. Comfortable accommodation was recommended for all residential staff, with the comment: 'It is sometimes forgotten the school is also their home'—a fact which had been neglected over the years.

Active open-air life was advised for delicate pupils and adequate clothing was deemed essential in winter as children could not afford loss of body heat. Facilities and opportunities for outdoor interests were being developed in the grounds of most schools to encourage 'busy and happy lives' for pupils. The planning and making of gardens (including fencing, rockeries and walls), digging, making paths and ponds, beekeeping and work with animals and nature were cited as good examples. The garden was seen literally as a real workshop for learning situations.

Clothing was discussed in detail in the report, varying from wind-cheaters and waterproof capes to two-piece gabardine suits with gloves or mittens. Clogs were still recommended for gardening.

Rest periods of an hour were found to be the norm, with many schools insisting on absolute silence as well as immobility on one side—not a practice really conducive to relaxation. The team of doctors making these comments suggested that rest periods need not be essential and that some alternative solutions could be tried with quiet occupations such as reading and jigsaws. Most of Birmingham's schools did not take up this suggestion, apart from Skilts which solved the rest period with story telling-sessions to children seated in a room.

Respiratory illnesses and debility were cited as the main reasons for admission to the open-air schools—asthma and bronchitis being the most common ailments. Bronchiectasis was also a condition where children improved generally in health at open-air schools where they received regular physiotherapy. Special training for postural drainage of bronchiectic children was given to Birmingham school nurses at the Hill Top Hospital Thoracic Unit in Bromsgrove. Only a few open-air residential schools took in 'maladjusted' children but day schools were beginning to receive a great number of cases.

With regard to medical treatment the report endorsed the practice of ultra-violet light treatment in winter and the use of inhalers and breathing exercises. Full-time nurses were only recommended for residential schools and large day schools of at least 250 children.

Emphasising that there was no justification for providing more open-air schools the report concluded that there was still a place for such institutions in modern society, although the need might diminish in the future. The great advantage of open-air schools was that they were small in size where children were known individually to staff and could thrive in a caring environment.

This critical survey on open-air schools was reported in the national press in December 1952 with such emotive headlines as 'Delicate children work amid the snow' and 'Open-Air Schools condemned by four doctors', causing much concern to Birmingham parents with children at open-air schools. Birmingham education officers were quick to respond with a report in a local newspaper, to reassure worried parents that no children in the city's schools suffered under 'such shocking conditions'.

Mr. P. Hewitt, Senior Administrator for the Special Schools, commented: 'I can assure parents that Birmingham open-air schools all have heating and lighting and all can be fully enclosed from the weather when required. None of the statements in this survey can be applied to our schools ... our open-air schools are under constant medical and administrative observation'.

Miss Mary Brown had been Headmistress at Marsh Hill for over twenty years and was in the news when open-air schools were severely criticised in the 1952 report. After a headline proclaimed 'Birmingham has no ice-box schools', a reporter and photographer were invited by Birmingham Education authority to visit any of their open-air schools. Marsh Hill was chosen for the visit and found to be a carefully supervised and very satisfactory school. Lessons were in 'warm cheerful classrooms and children were well-clad in winter clothing. Rest was in strongly-built open-air shelters with canvas blinds to shut out the rain ... children in comfortable clothes were warm beneath two blankets.' Miss Brown reported that she constantly received letters of thanks from parents' and Birmingham's Medical Officer for Special Schools, Dr. P.R. Kemp, stated firmly: 'Fresh air is important but we don't make a fetish of it'.

This survey seems to have been the last major report on open-air schools by the Ministry of Education. Later annual reports by the Ministry's Medical Officers scarcely mention open air schools amongst all the other special schools. However, Birmingham Education Committee continued to review regularly their own open-air schools in annual reports right through the 1950s and early 1960s, no doubt justifiably proud of the achievement of these Special Schools which continued to improve the health of ailing children in its great industrial city. By 1950 there were three residential open-air schools: Cropwood (80 girls), Hunter's Hill (123 boys) and Haseley Hall (40 boys) and two day schools: Uffculme (169 children) and Marsh Hill (199 children).

By 1951 tuberculosis had ceased to be a major cause of death in children, thanks to the revolutionary drugs such as Streptomycin and Isoniazid. The former had been discovered by 1944 and the latter developed in 1952 to cure tuberculosis sufferers very effectively. Birmingham reported only 8 deaths in 1953 but still 283 cases of the disease.

The treatment of asthmatic children in open-air schools (by then termed Schools for Delicate Children) was mentioned in the 1952/53 report by the Chief Medical Officer of the Ministry of Education. It was advised that every effort should be made to preserve children's links with their home, with frequent visits of families, letters and parcels from home and telephone conversations, in order to prevent emotional upsets.

Dr. H.M. Cohen, Birmingham's principal School Medical Officer, recommended careful selection of asthmatic cases for day or residential schools—depending on the type of illness and home background, as well as the atmospheric pollution of the home environment. Both kinds of open-air schools were needed: day schools for those children whose health would improve there while living at home, and residential schools for those children who would benefit more by leaving the city and spending more time in the purer country air. The building-up of confidence was achieved by special exercises devised by the Asthma Research Council, so that children knew what to do when an attack was imminent.

Asthma is a disease going back to ancient times. The Greeks called it asthma, meaning 'panting attack', and the Ancient Egyptians tried to cure it with crocodile droppings and inhalations. But it was not until the 1950s that fatalities from asthma attacks began to cause concern.

Causes of asthma were various—infective, allergic, climatic or psychological. Educational difficulties were often the result of the asthmatic child's frequent absences from school. When remedial exercises, inhalers or medical treatment failed to cure a child of asthma while attending a normal school, the open-air schools were generally considered a good option.

Some asthmatic children benefited from a stay in Switzerland and Birmingham was particularly lucky to have the unique facility of Christian Kunzle's Alpine School at Davos. Parties of 32 delicate boys were sent from Birmingham's open-air schools at regular intervals, for a six-month stay, nearly all improving in the pure mountain air which seemed to have some specific healing quality. Only boys of a certain height could go as the beds were small and there was a rule that boys should not have reached puberty.

Before being sent out all boys were carefully examined, given chest x-rays and diphtheria immunisation, and academic ability was estimated by the use of school reports. They were taught in Davos in small classes, given plain nourishing food and the confidence and ability to cope with their ailments which usually disappeared with all the exciting organised outdoor activities. Mountain walks, tobogganing, skiing, communal living and regular worship at the English church were part of the life in this alpine open-air school which often resulted in a permanent benefit to health. Subsequent medical examinations on the boys' return estimated that 80 per cent were in better health on their return and 20 per cent were cured permanently of asthma.

Christian Kunzle had opened his home to Birmingham boys in 1948, in return for an annual payment from Birmingham Education Committee of around £5,000 per year on a per capita basis to cover costs. The authority provided the furniture, equipment and teachers, as well as the fares and the medical treatment while Christian Kunzle had personally helped in many ways to make the scheme a great success. Many ex-pupils of open-air schools must surely remember the wonderful experience of Switzerland, as two relate:

Mr. Keith Meanwell, Hunter's Hill 1952-6, Birmingham

I was at Hunter's Hill for two years before I was selected to go to Switzerland. On 15 June 1954, 32 boys aged from 10-14, all from different parts of the Birmingham area, left Snow Hill station for a six-month stay at the Alpine school for boys in Davos. All were asthma sufferers. It did not cost our parents any money as it was paid for by Christian Kunzle of the Kunzle cakes firm at Five Ways [Birmingham].

One of the exciting things on the journey was travelling on the old steam train, the Golden Arrow. On 16 June we reached our destination in Davos: Chateau Bruxelles. It was like a castle, with a quarter of a mile walk up to it from the village. We were amazed to see it snowing at that time of the year.

In charge of us were three teachers, Mr. Yoxall, Miss Aze and Miss Scrivington. Every month Kunzle's would send out a batch of young ladies from the company to serve as waitresses; we had some very fond memories of them!

We used to walk from Davos to Klosters, the next village. Every Sunday we would go to the English speaking church and walk back along the high prom, feeding red squirrels and spotting deer.

Back home again I returned to Hunter's Hill until I left for work in 1956. I outgrew my asthma when I became 21; today I am a 54-year-old granddad!

Mr. John Warom, Marsh Hill 1953-8, Erdington, Birmingham

We left for Davos in Switzerland on 10 November 1954—32 boys, two teachers and a nurse. We were able to go because of the generosity of Mr. Christian Kunzle who owned Chateau Bruxelles. I had chronic bronchitis and was at Marsh Hill Open Air School, when Dr. Kemp asked if I would like to go to Switzerland. Say no more!

We climbed a mountain—with a guide—and it took us a day to climb up and down, but when we got to the top the view took my breath away. It was magnificent; I was 10 years of age and if a view can make an impression on a 10 year old it must have been some view.

On another walk with our teacher, Miss Stewart, we came across a frozen waterfall; it was so beautiful. There were so many different colours, reds, blues and greens; it must have been minerals in the water

We did skiing and tobogganing; we had a fantastic time. I got quite proficient at skiing and Mr. Yoxall (our teacher) with myself and five others went down a mountain ski run. It was great fun. On one boy's birthday he was granted a wish and out of the blue asked if we could go on the Shatz Alps toboggan run—Mr. Yoxall said 'yes'. Alleluia! It was absolutely brilliant: the sound of the wind rushing past your ears (no crash helmets in those days) and the noise of the runners going over the ice—tremendous stuff!

On Christmas Eve we went for a walk and found tracks in the snow so we followed them, keeping very quiet. There in a clearing were two deer, two does and two little ones that looked like Bambi. I can remember it so well because it was so still and silent.

It was my first time away from home and Christmas day we went to Mass; the choir sang Silent Night in German and the tears just fell down my face, I was so homesick.

Sad to say that while we were there Mr. Kunzle died and so did all the good work he started. I thank him from the bottom of my heart for what he did for me, God bless him. The chateau was demolished in 1956, what a shame. It housed a lot of children who were made well again.

By June 1955 Birmingham Education Committee had decided to send no more children to Davos. Under the headlines 'Davos school ban; Birmingham explanation' in the *Birmingham Mail* on 27 June 1955 the Chairman of Birmingham's Education Committee spoke of criticisms of the living conditions at Davos which were not fully accepted by Kunzle's, then being run by 22-year-old George Kunzle, director of the company after the death of his grandfather, Christian Kunzle, in 1954.

Birmingham Education Committee found it impossible to inspect the Alpine School more than once a year and had been concerned about deterioration in the chateau since some damp had been discovered in a dormitory. There was much dispute about the damp by George Kunzle and an expert despatched from England found no great evidence of it.

As the Committee discussed the adverse reports on Davos, advice was sought from a consensus of medical opinion at the Children's Hospital. It was decided that perhaps there was no great advantage in moving sick and chesty children to Switzerland when any area in Britain could be as beneficial if the air was free of smoke and dirt. As supervision of Davos school had become increasingly difficult the scheme was suspended amid much publicity.

The *Evening Despatch* a few months later, in September 1955, revealed that Birmingham Education Committee planned to open another residential open-air school 'in one of the smoke-free zones around Birmingham' in order to compensate for the loss of the school at Davos. Skilts school opened in 1958.

Residential open-air schools were recognised as being 'useful as a means of building up the physical health and nervous strength of anxious or highly-strung children', when the government Report of the Committee on Maladjusted Children was published in 1955. 'The ordered life in special surroundings with rest periods and an abundance of fresh air and good food can in a few months make a considerable difference to children of this type', it emphasised, stressing that all open-air schools were likely to contain some 'maladjusted' children, as well as those officially classified as 'delicate'.

At this time there was no special training required for teachers of 'delicate' and 'maladjusted' children. Teachers needed good health, a sense of humour, a calm disposition and, above all, a capacity to enjoy children's company. Great demands were made on them while they dealt with children's difficult behaviour as well as coping with the common disabilities found in open-air schools—asthma, bronchitis and bronchiectasis. In addition, as children were admitted at all ages and levels of ability, teachers needed to be able to assess educational attainment and remedial teaching skills were essential. Many children needed stimulation to maintain their interest after years of disrupted schooling, and teachers had to appreciate the needs of the 'whole child', in co-operation with social workers, doctors, nurses and physiotherapists.

By the end of the 1950s the school health service was 50 years old and social changes had effected a great improvement in the health and cleanliness of children in general. Fewer children attended school clinics for minor ailments as General Practitioners treated children within the National Health Service. Most school medical officers still carried out three routine medical inspections during the school-years of each child, as practised from the early days of the School Medical Service, but gradually these regulations were relaxed.

Uffculme 1950-4

After 27 years at Uffculme School Miss Hibbert retired in March 1950 to enjoy some well-earned rest until her death at the age of 77 in September 1964. Uffculme's new Headmaster was Mr. F.S. Wise, appointed in the new term beginning in April 1950.

Edward Anderson, teacher for 21 years at the school, had applied for the post of Headmaster but such was his personality that he was not successful. However, within two years Fate was to take a hand and he was to achieve his ambition …

Despite being a healthy young man with a family, Mr. Wise suddenly became ill at the beginning of 1952, and Edward Anderson became Acting Head until the untimely death of the Headmaster in September 1952. In November that same year, Mr. Anderson was appointed Headmaster where he became a driving force for the next 12 years.

THE 1950s: WIDENING HORIZONS

There are few ex-pupils or staff who do not recall Edward Anderson's influence on the school and an HMI's Report bears testimony to his strong leadership, even if many people felt that his loud voice, bullying tactics and frequent sarcasm were not always totally suited to a school for 'delicate' children. However, he did have a sense of humour and a more kindly side to his nature. Many boys in particular have good cause to remember him with gratitude for encouraging them to participate in energetic sports and activities, despite their disabilities and ailments.

The log book records when Mr. Wise became Headmaster at Uffculme but does not record the retirement of Miss Hibbert who holds the record at Uffculme for long service as Head Teacher.

Uffculme log book 1950

18 April *School reopened with good attendance. Mr. Wise commenced duties here.*

10 May *10 students from Coventry Training College visited the school.*

20 Nov. *Nursing Sister Bendall absent from duty.*

Uffculme log book 1951

13 Feb. *Very foggy. Poor attendance.*

11 April *Party of 24 boys to Martineau House School, Towyn. Mr. Anderson in charge of party.*

29 June *Visited by Japanese Civil Servants.*

Uffculme log book 1952

11 Feb. *Mr. Anderson as Acting Head. Mr. Wise absent owing to illness.*

22 April *School reopened for Summer Term. Mr. Cooper appointed.*

23 April *Mrs. Stocker began as supernumerary teacher. Mr. Wise still absent.*

9 Sep. *Announced Death of Mr. Wise the Headmaster.*

11 Sep. *24 girls to Towyn—Miss Wales in charge.*

3 Nov. *Mr. E.J. Anderson appointed Headmaster. The staff is now:*
  1. Mr. R. Cooper CT(E) 2. Miss M. Wales CT
  3. Mrs. Mann Supply 4. Mrs. Stocker Supply
  Nurse Miss E.M. Bendall; Mrs. Hewitt. Visiting Handicraft Teacher (1 day in week).

2 Dec. *Thick fog today—reduced attendance to 90.*

Uffculme log book 1953

6 Jan *School reopened. Miss M. Spence is appointed on permanent staff as teacher of Class II.*

13 Feb. *The attendance is very low, 82.9. This is due to the inclement weather and to a number of mild influenza cases.*

4 May *24 boys with Mr. Cooper went to Martineau House, Towyn, for 2 weeks.*

22 May *Whitsuntide holidays and Coronation Holidays. The Souvenirs from the Education Committee were presented to the children. The Seniors chose and were given a Bible—suitably inscribed. The infants and juniors were given a Coronation mug.*

2 June *The school and grounds were used by the children from a local street for their Coronation party. The school was well used and left in a good condition. A letter of appreciation was sent to the organisers.*

6 June *Mr. E.J. Anderson the Headmaster is away for two weeks attending a Ministry of Education Course on Physically Handicapped Children. Miss M. Wales the Chief Assistant takes charge.*

8 Sep. *Miss I. Thomas has joined the permanent staff in place of Mrs. Stocker the Temporary teacher.*

15 Sep. *The school staff is now:*
1. Mr. E.J. Anderson, Headmaster. 2. Mr. Cooper, Class I.
3. Miss M. Wales, Class II. 4. Miss I. Thomas, Class III.
5. Miss M. Spence, Class IV. 6. Mrs. Southam has been appointed as Nurse in place of Nurse Bendall, retired after 24 years.

12 Oct. *Twenty-four Senior Girls under Miss Spence have gone to Martineau House for two weeks. This is an extra visit.*

Uffculme log book 1954

7 Jan. *The Head attended the funeral of Mr. C. Kunzle who founded the Davos Alpine Home in Switzerland. Many of our children have been to this school for six months.*

1-5 Feb. *Very cold week. Temperature in classroom down to 30°F and 29°F.*

15 Mar. *24 Junior girls to Martineau House Seaside School at Towyn with Miss Thomas and Miss Spence.*

26 Mar. *Children returned from Towyn. All looking very brown and fit.*

Reminiscences of Uffculme in this era include those of several pupils and teachers who all have extremely happy memories of the school:

Mrs. Diane Smith (née **Ball**), Uffculme 1949-55, Hollywood, Birmingham

Looking back at my time at Uffculme as an asthmatic child, they were, without doubt, the happiest days of my school life. The teachers were kind and everyone was so friendly.

We were encouraged to attend school even when we were poorly; there was an isolation room with two or three beds where we rested for the day and were looked after.

The nature walks through the dell are one of my fondest memories, the abundance of snow drops in early spring. Each year when I see these flowers, my mind flashes back to the time spent at the school.

Miss Beryl Steane, Uffculme 1950-2, Shard End, Birmingham

We had an early start to the day and breakfast consisting of porridge or cornflakes, hot or cold milk, bread and honey. Plain wholesome food was always the menu, but I will never forget when curly cabbage was on the

menu with midday meals: it was never washed properly and you had to pick out tiny black mites and place them around the edge of your plate! To this day I have never eaten that species of cabbage again!

Miss Hibbert retired when I was there and a Headmaster took over. Breakfast became eggs and bacon, sausage and beans, toast and jam etc. He wasn't there long because of illness. I was happy at Uffculme.

Mr. Cedric B. Laing, Uffculme 1951-3, Longbridge, Birmingham

There are many people in this world today who owe their lives to Uffculme. Without Uffculme we would have been lost, and perhaps dead long ago. My personal bronchial problems started when I was 17 months old, and the house where I was born was bombed. (I guess brick dust and rubble was no good for a baby in a cot …) It was only after I had been transferred to Uffculme Open-Air School that my asthma and bronchitis became less severe, so I feel it is well after time that those like myself who were helped so much by Uffculme, begin to pay our debts.

It will be my pleasure to help out at Uffculme, if help is ever needed, at any time. Simply walking or driving near the school brings back many nostalgic memories to me, memories that will live as long as I do.

After visiting Uffculme for the 75th celebrations 1986, I left the school, walking slowly along Queensbridge Road, and I could hear the Twenty-Third Psalm being sung to the tune of Crimond. There was no one around singing it, but it came to my mind for some time. That particular Psalm was a favourite of Mr. Anderson's when he was Headmaster, and we often sang it at assembly. It is so strange how things like that come to mind—strange, but beautiful.

Cedric Laing left Uffculme in 1953, starting work as a driver's mate on his 15th birthday. He soon moved on to Bob Wilson's Fairground, as a driver and keeper of a beautiful lion called

Aerial view of Uffculme Open-Air School showing the separate open classrooms and the rest shed in the 1950s. Queensbridge School dominates the photograph. (Uffculme School)

Leno. Later on in life he became Seggy the Clown at Billy Smart's Circus until he formed his own show, Bevan Laing's Circus. In 1986 he sent his biographical details to the school and has subsequently added to his memories thus:

Attending Uffculme Open-Air School was nothing less than a great pleasure in life. My first sight of the four small classrooms and the dining hall with its ornate clock tower sitting among the beautiful grounds, came as a most pleasant surprise to me in January 1951. The Headmaster, Mr. Wise, made me feel very welcome.

My first teacher was Mr. E.J. Anderson, a man who had his own way of teaching what was going to be needed most in the world outside. He was in charge of Class I, Miss Wales took Class II—she was a lovely lady and a friend to all of us.

Having three very good meals a day at school was new to me; it was like being able to go out for a meal each day with sincere friends. The food was very good, and the selection of meals we were given was marvellous. My only dislike was having to take a spoonful of cod liver oil each morning directly after breakfast. We had to stand in line and when our turn came, the Matron would give us the deadly dose! Mr. Anderson stood near to the Matron, watching each child's every move.

With the cooks at each meal time was our caretaker, Mr. Harrison. He used to take the heavy trays or pans of food from the lift, and place them on the serving tables. Mr. Harrison was a good friend to all of the children. He worked hard by keeping the school and the grounds spotless at all times.

When Mr. Wise was taken ill, Mr. Anderson took over as Headmaster, often going from Class I to the office, and back to the classroom. On the days when Mr. Anderson had many other things to do, Miss Wales would take our class in between running her own Class II. The staff really did work together, and they worked very hard.

Mr. Wise came back for a few days, but after another few days when he was away from school, he sadly died. Mr. Anderson was working very hard again with deputising, and interviewing new teachers. There was much talk of there being a new headmaster and Mr. Anderson taking over the class again. But it worked out just as it should have done, Mr. Anderson was our new headmaster, and we had a new teacher, Mr. R. Cooper.

Mr. Cooper was rather tall, had been in Rangoon for some time, and was new to teaching at an open-air school. On his first morning of taking over the class he gave us our maths books to carry on with while he sorted things out. Suddenly, he said, 'Put your pens down, and I'll tell you about my time in Rangoon.' He told us about many of his experiences, including seeing a snake eat a pig. His method of teaching was so very different, yet we did just as much book work as before.

One day during his first week at the school he told us to ask our parents to send a 'signed' note saying we were allowed to go out with him the very next afternoon after school. He did not tell us where we were going, but he said we would all like it. After school that very next day we walked to Cannon Hill Park. There inside the park was an arena in which Toad of Toad Hall was being shown. Mr. Cooper not only paid for us to see the show, but he bought each of us a bar of chocolate and drink of pop.

Mr. Cooper took over from Mr. Anderson in being in charge of the football team. Our strip was red and green; Mr. Anderson explained the green was for nature, and the leaves on the trees and the grass all around us, and the red was for the blood keeping us alive. Some Saturdays we would go over to Marsh Hill and Blackwell. Other weeks they would come to Uffculme for a game.

Late in the year we used to go to Martineau House, Towyn, for two weeks, with Mr. Anderson and Mr. Cooper. We enjoyed walks to Bird Rock, train rides to Harlech, and boat rides on the coast. Most of us had never known a holiday before, so this was really magic for us.

Just before it was time for some of us to leave school we were taken to various factories and other places of work to see how things were made. We visited Cadbury's at Bournville, and Guest Keen and Nettlefold's factory at Smethwick which gave us an insight of life in a big factory. A few days after that we went to the Co-operative Society bakery in Stirchley.

The saddest day at Uffculme for many of us came in July 1953. That was the day we had to see Mr. Anderson to say good-bye, and collect our leaving certificates. Each of us, myself included, was in tears as we shook hands with the staff and the cooks before crying hard at the gate. I was so upset that I did not get on my bike as usual to ride home, I walked with my friends for the very last time, and sat in Highbury Park on a bench overlooking the school until I could cry no more.

I sincerely thank everyone who gave me that wonderful chance of attending Uffculme Open-Air School, I thank our teachers with great sincerity, and really do miss the comradeship of all the children who attended the school.

Miss Margaret M. Wales, 82, Teacher and Deputy Head at Uffculme 1941-58, Northfield, Birmingham

I became Deputy Head in 1952 when Mr. Anderson was appointed Head. Miss Hibbert had retired in 1950 and Mr. Wise had been appointed in her place—much to the disappointment of Mr. Anderson who had been at the school for so long. Mr. Wise was such a nice young man with a wife and three children, but became ill after only two years. He bought a house for his family which seemed to be damp, and he slept there while getting the place ready for occupation, but became ill. He had been a fit man when he came to the school but died of pneumonia.

I often took a party of girls to Towyn Seaside School, where Mr. & Mrs. Morris were in charge. We could watch seabirds and the children did enjoy it. I usually went on my own with 24 girls and we went on several outings during our time there. Later on Birmingham purchased Martineau House at Bognor Regis. All the Special Schools could go there for a fortnight. The house at Towyn was very close to the sea. There were lessons but also a lot of practical work collecting and naming shells, recording birds etc. There was a large schoolroom there, with a balcony all around—it had once been an indoor tennis court.

I remember some of the awful fogs while at Uffculme in the 1950s. On one occasion I had to walk the children all the way home from Kings Heath to Cotteridge and these were delicate chesty children. All buses had been cancelled but I finally found one and pleaded with the driver to make space for my delicate children who were such a responsibility.

In the summer I envied the children walking about barefoot and often did the same! The girls wore very loose and baggy yellow sundresses and sunhats; the boys wore khaki shorts and little else.

Although I enjoyed being at Uffculme I decided eventually that I wanted to go to a Special School and teach retarded children. I felt I wanted to concentrate on children who would benefit more from the extra attention I could give them, and left to become deputy Head of Collingwood School in Northfield. But looking back on my career, I enjoyed Uffculme the most, because of its beautiful surroundings and I was very happy there.

Mrs. Pauline Saul (née **Brueton**), 54, Uffculme 1951-6, Shrewsbury, Shropshire

I was admitted to Uffculme Open-Air School on 9 January 1951 aged nine years. I could have gone to Cropwood but, because I had spent the greater part of my life until then in hospital, it was decided that a residential school would deprive me even further of my loving and caring home environment.

I suffered from chronic asthma and eczema; there was very little then to alleviate the distress of either when they became acute—no instant relief from pocket-sized inhalers for a sudden, frightening asthma attack or soothing creams for weeping, itchy eczema which was socially unacceptable to all but the most compassionate. Both ailments imposed great restrictions on one's lifestyle, inevitably leading to loss of schooling in those early formative years. Not surprisingly, most of us who attended an open-air school felt we had found a safe haven—even heaven on occasion!

I still have some of my exercise books. For Composition on 26 November 1954 we had to write about *Life in an Open-Air School*. I wrote: 'Life in an Open Air-School is very nice. We have lovely meals which

Pupils at Uffculme: (left to right) Pauline Brueton (author) with June Richards and Beryl Cox, 1950s. (P. Saul)

are very cheap. We have breakfast, dinner, and tea five days a week all for 3s. 4d. We have an hour's rest on a camp bed with a blanket each after dinner. In the winter we are supplied with thick navy blue jerseys which keep you very warm. At Christmas we have a school party, concert, and Christmas plays. It is very cold sometimes in the winter but mostly it is my hands and feet which get really cold. In summer the girls are given summer frocks and knickers to wear, and the boys wear shorts which are given them and their own vest, if it is a bit chilly they wear shirts as well. There are four classes and about 130 children altogether. There are four teachers, one headmaster, and a sister.

If you are taken ill in the day you are sent to a room with two beds called 'Isolation room' till you go home. Sister also gives you something like medicine or tablets to help you get well.

The senior boys and girls have their own gardens. The boys grow vegetables and fruit. The girls grow flowers.

Just before we break up for summer holidays we have our own sports day. We also go to the B.S.A. sports ground and compete against other Open-Air Schools.

We have shower baths at least twice a week, the boys one day the girls the next. Each class has a different day. I go to an Open-Air School for asthma and exema [sic]. I have been going for almost four years. I think it is very nice.'

I was awarded nine out of ten marks; my only spelling mistake was eczema—which my teacher corrected as ecxema and I duly copied out five times!

My Composition gives all the facts (and reiterates dozens more reminiscences); what it does not convey, however, are my emotions, experiences and memories.

I would have been in Miss Wales' class at that time—a wonderful teacher who knew how to make lessons interesting, instilling the value of learning tables and the importance of correct spelling. She stood no nonsense but was fair-minded with a sense of fun. Only once did she fail me! During daily rest-periods we had to lie on our right sides (to rest our hearts…) and **rest**—no turning over, no fidgeting or, worse, speaking. One rest period my friend turned over and was whispering at a time when Miss Wales was patrolling the beds. Just as I was saying, 'turn over and be quiet' Miss Wales drew level with my bed, heard me, and without further ado, pulled back my blanket and rapped my hand with her ruler. I was angrier with my friend for not owning up than I was for getting caned but I only forgave Miss Wales for the injustice of it when she cast me as Jo in Little Women, our class play that year.

Mr. Anderson would not have awarded me as many marks for my Composition because I twice used the word 'nice'. He once took our English lesson during which he emphasised that 'nice' was a negative word; he said that the English language had many descriptive words which we should always try to substitute for 'nice'. Even now I think twice before using it—in written work anyway! Whilst he may have been an able Head, Mr. Anderson did not enjoy too good a rapport with many of us children as he was brusque, sarcastic and seemed incapable of taking anyone to task in a quiet confidential manner in the confines of his study, preferring to make a spectacle (he probably thought of it as an example) of a child in front of the class or even the school if the mood took him at assembly time.

I once returned to school after sick leave, still feeling less than well, and was confronted with a bowl of lumpy porridge for breakfast. I was not a fussy eater as a rule but on this occasion I simply could not face it. Mr. Anderson decided that I should and consequently made me sit all alone in the dining room long after the other children had departed to their classrooms, indeed virtually until lunch time. Cook would keep popping in, taking away the porridge to warm it up whilst surreptitiously removing a little each time. Mr. Anderson stopped by occasionally, saw that the bowl contained less and gloated, thinking that his tactics were working. I was over 40 years of age before I could be persuaded to eat porridge again!

Apart from the tea made with boiled milk (ugh!) and Marmite sandwiches, I thoroughly enjoyed the meals the kitchen staff prepared and served us, especially the cheese pie with beetroot and chocolate crunch pudding with butter cream. The recipe for that must be one of the best-kept secrets ever! I have never lost my taste for a cup of cocoa and the daily dose of cod liver oil was acceptable.

None of us minded moving up to Class I whilst Mr. Cooper was in charge. A teacher ahead of his time when it came to implementing the School Curriculum he made school fun and more importantly he had a way of making everybody feel like somebody. Much has been written about his role within the school but he extended that to the school holidays too. Ron Cooper, his wife and five children, lived in a large house in Edgbaston and during school holidays it was often Open House to us. We had permission to visit and we would play games or help look after the babies or just chat to him and Mrs. Cooper, who was not only as delightful as Ron but surely a saint into the bargain! During the summer holidays he would often take us on organised cycle rides or picnics or arrange to meet us at the school for a games afternoon.

Class I Christmas plays became legendary for their off-beat themes and topicality. When The Goon Show *was at the height of its popularity Ron somehow managed to work even this into a Christmas Play. In the mid 1970s I came into contact again with Ron Cooper, then Head of a Birmingham Inner City School. He was standing in the playground surrounded by youngsters all obviously as devoted to him as we had been; he did not appear to have changed at all—including his smile!*

Along with the usual Christmas festivities there was one other tradition at Uffculme concerning the senior boys and girls, beloved by some and hated by others—the Polka Competition. Weeks prior to Christmas rehearsals would begin in the rest-shed which doubled as the gym. Girls would line up at one end of the shed, boys at the other. The boys would come and choose partners; when we were sorted into pairs the music would commence from a scratchy gramophone and we would proceed to be taught or practise (if you were by then an old hand at it!) the Polka. Much tripping over feet, even falling over, and giggling ensued. The same partners were not necessarily chosen each week which was frustrating for those girls who enjoyed dancing and, perhaps, had a crush on someone. The competition took place on the last afternoon of term in the dining room and we were all usually dressed in our best. The Polka was played on the piano instead of the scratchy wind-up gramophone and the staff stood around the perimeter of the hall. As we whirled around, the staff would gradually whittle us down to a few couples

Teacher Ron Cooper (front row) and his wife and baby (back row) during the school holidays, with Uffculme pupils Bruce Ingram, Helen James, Roger Clayton, Beryl Cox, Michael Moore and Bromley Davenport, mid-1950s. (P. Saul)

and eventually to an outright winning couple. One of my finest hours was the year Bromley Davenport and I won … .

In March 1953 I was fortunate enough to go to Martineau House, Towyn, for two weeks' holiday. My diary records that Miss Thomas and Miss Spence were in charge of us 24 girls and I was in charge of Dorm 2; Frances Headford was in Dorm 3 … Our holiday activities and daily timetable are faithfully recorded. That holiday was very special and tucked away in my 'treasures box' I have some pretty shells I collected, along with the brooch which was my prize awarded for the best diary of the holiday. Despite this I always regretted that the girls were denied the opportunity of going to Davos.

Queensbridge School was built opposite Uffculme in the early 1950s and an arrangement was made whereby the senior girls went there for Domestic Science lessons. The school and its equipment were bright and modern but the sheer size of it plus the number of pupils overwhelmed us to begin with. But we benefited from the lessons. There were weeks when I was unable to participate in the cookery lesson because my hands were either sore or bandaged but the teacher gave me interesting project work and always appreciated my tidying the store cupboards!

Where Queensbridge could not compare was in its surroundings. The grounds at Uffculme were beautiful throughout the year. Nature in its purest form was all around us; we learnt about it and grew to love it. Our pond was set in a landscape of varying shrubs and bushes, with a rockery and great flat slabs of stone where one could sit and read, or in springtime watch the ducklings in the water; there was never a spring when we didn't find at least two nests in the bushes. In the winter the pond took on a whole new face but I never remember it being sufficiently frozen to enable us to skate on it though we used to sledge down the steep bank nearby. That same bank would be a-glow with daffodils just a few months later—in fact daffodils to me are synonymous with Uffculme, along with the sound of rustling leaves in the summer sunshine when even now I can recall rest-periods under the enormous horse chestnut trees. I always slept.

Naturally there were spells when nothing in particular happened. Our school day was long (most of us left home before 8.00am), and many of us continued to lose time from school due to illness. But gradually the many benefits of the school, combined with the advent of modern drugs, paid dividends and I was discharged to a mainstream school in March 1956. I started at the local Secondary Modern School for Girls at the beginning of the summer term and after an ability test was assigned to 'A' stream. In the end of year exams I was placed in the top ten of a class of 34, having won two individual prizes.

Shortly after those results I was summoned to the Headmistress who told me that my school records had caught up with me. 'Had these arrived before you I would have placed you in the remedial class', she said. 'But', she added, 'looking at your exam results, whatever an open-air school and its policy stands for, they did a pretty good job with you' … Indeed, for many others too. We are truly grateful.

Mrs. Frances Wilmot (née **Headford**), 53, Uffculme 1952-6, Leamington Spa, Warwickshire

A history of recurrent colds and bronchitis was the main reason for my four years at Uffculme. I arrived there on 9 September 1952, being nine years old. Other health problems included 'flat feet', which meant lots of boring foot exercises, and slight curvature of the spine which necessitated wearing a padded leather T-shaped brace on my back some of the time (a contraption I loathed in hot weather). This had been issued by Birmingham Orthopaedic Hospital. Thanks to Uffculme I was eventually able to attend a normal school for the last three years of my education.

My main recollections of Uffculme are of a happy school in beautiful surroundings where the emphasis was on health rather than education. On arrival we had breakfast in the dining room overlooking lawns and trees. I remember once seeing a green woodpecker on a nearby tree which stimulated a lifelong interest in birds. Meals were designed to be body building and all food had to be eaten up—quite a daunting prospect for me as I didn't have much of an appetite.

Mr. Anderson, the Headmaster, is remembered as a rather terrifying figure with a booming voice. I still possess the swimming certificate he signed and presented to me when I managed to swim my first length at Kings Heath swimming baths. I remember being rather disappointed that it had a picture of a boy on the certificate, but nonetheless I was very proud of my achievement.

Teachers at Uffculme included Miss Wales, Miss Thomas, Miss Spence and Mr. Hunt. Meeting them again after an interval of nearly 40 years has been an interesting experience and I was astonished that one even remembered the clothes I used to wear! Such was their interest in their delicate pupils that I feel privileged to have been at a school where all staff were so kind and caring.

Like most pupils, the open-air classrooms remain vividly in my memory. When it was cold in winter we used to stamp around the classroom on the noisy iron grilles covering the heating pipes, whilst clapping our hands to keep warm and singing songs or chanting our tables. How I survived temperatures of a mere 30° F I shall never know but it is a fact that my health rapidly improved at the school. When it was cold we often had hot Bovril or nourishing cocoa mid-morning. In warmer weather the whole class moved outside, desks and all, to take advantage of the sunshine—not that I recall doing much work on such occasions! Uffculme's surroundings were a delight with all the trees and flowers.

I was one of many children who had remedial exercises for my feet and back, including breathing techniques designed to aid wheezy attacks. Picking up marbles with my toes became a speciality! I hated the regime of having to walk about the grounds barefoot in summer as I couldn't see the sense of getting dirty feet and never liked the sleeveless baggy sundresses we had to wear. I also had sun-ray treatment and a daily dose of cod liver oil most of my childhood.

I was lucky enough to be selected one year for a school holiday in Towyn in Wales, where I remember being fascinated by the flocks of oyster catchers on deserted beaches—their piping calls made a lasting impression on me. Nature study was an important part of schoolwork, especially at Towyn.

It is only now that I realise my passion for fresh air and the great outdoors may well have its roots in Uffculme. I owe so much to the school: my love of nature and the countryside, my enjoyment of arts and crafts and, above all, my health which enabled me to have an interesting career as a librarian. What I owe to the founders of the school—Barrow and Geraldine Cadbury—is inestimable, as good health is beyond price …

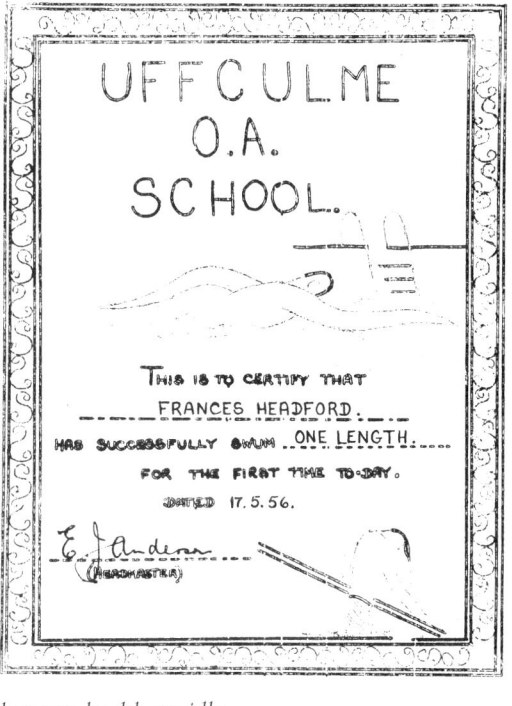

Pupils Frances Headford (author, on the left) and Kathleen Murphy, barefoot at Uffculme in 1955. (F. Wilmot)

Mrs. Isobel Bazire (née Thomas), Teacher, Uffculme 1953-4, Bath, Somerset

I started teaching at Uffculme in September 1953 as Miss Thomas, and left in December 1954, as Mrs. Bazire. On the day of my interview I walked round the grounds, on the paths meandering through the ponds and was told that in the summer the pupils were free to wander at break. 'This is for me' I thought, and that was that!

I remember being set up for the day with a wonderful cooked breakfast. We often played a kind of rugby-netball on the hard pitch. Whenever we got a bit chilly we went out for a bit of exercise.

Each child had a little named towel for handwashing, and a brush and a mug for teeth cleaning. The three meals were 10d a day, and I remember being asked for some change when someone missed tea!

I can vividly recall a Father Christmas walking through the park, and the whole school watching in the dining room. He came with a huge sack of toys, one for each person.

I was quite avant garde as I wore a 'divided skirt' for warmth i.e. culottes, because trousers wouldn't have been allowed. Having survived the cold I got used to it.

I remember the hamsters that got into the underfloor heating round the edges of the room. We retrieved them eventually!

I was there for four terms only, but it was a very happy time of my life.

In their winter uniform of navy blue sweaters Miss Thomas's class pose happily in 1953/4. Pupils pictured here include Anthony Newland, Marlene Sutton, Brenda Hewitt, Ida Worral and Margaret Webb. (M. Armson)

Mrs. Moira Armson (née Spence), Teacher Uffculme 1953-9, Sedgley, West Midlands

After teaching in Hall Green Infants School for two years I saw that Uffculme wanted a teacher for the youngest class. I rang Mr. Anderson for more details and he invited me to go and look round the school and meet the staff before applying for the job. I was invited for breakfast and then stayed most of the morning. It was a lovely Autumn day and I was very impressed with the surroundings and the friendly atmosphere both in the school and in the Staff Room. I had had no training for work with children with special needs and was assured this was not necessary. Seeing the place on a good weather day fooled me into filling in an application form. I never thought what it might be like in the middle of a severe winter. I got the job and started in the January of 1953.

The 30 children in Class IV were aged from five to eight. This meant quite a lot of individual work as they were all at different stages, not just because of their ages but also their disabilities. Some had hardly ever put in a complete week at school. One of the difficulties of teaching at Uffculme was the lack of walls to pin things on in the classroom. Outdoors it was even worse! It was difficult to teach encumbered with coats to combat the cold so I used to wear an extra sweater.

Mr. Anderson was really very kind but he could also be sarcastic. Uffculme was his whole life for years. Arthur Hunt and Isobel Bazire (née Thomas) taught Class III while I was there. Isobel was very popular with the children and always seemed to be laughing. I suppose having meals together every day we got to know each other very well. Margaret Wales was Deputy and taught the top and second class girls needlework and also took them for PE. Ron Cooper taught the Top class and took the boys from Classes I and II for PE and handwork. Mr. Cooper was fun: he was liked by most of the girls and adored by some!

Moira Spence's open-air class at Uffculme on a warm sunny day, 1950s. (Uffculme School)

It was great starting the day with breakfast. We started with cornflakes or porridge and then had something cooked followed by toast and marmalade. It was a very warming meal and fortified us for battling with the elements.

Lessons started anytime after 9.30am and about an hour later was break time. More lessons and before you knew it the Senior boys were out putting those ghastly iron beds down in the rest-shed. It was diabolical! As the shed was open to the wind, rain, and snow it was a very damp place and so was the canvas on the beds. The iron work was going rusty and they were very heavy. In the cold weather the teacher who was on duty sat on a deck chair with about three blankets, two hot water bottles and a pillow. Woe betide anyone who caused us to get up out of our warm snug blankets! Personally I think it was quite wrong to make children, especially the older ones, lie still on beds for an hour. Anyway, time passed slowly and then the beds had to be put away again.

Afternoon school was punctuated, as in the morning, by a constant stream of children going to Nurse for treatment. With no doors to the rooms callers were in before you knew it. There were baths, physiotherapy, medicine, weighing etc. There always seemed to be someone who missed some of the lesson time. When I first went to Uffculme Nurse Bendall reigned in the medical room. She retired whilst I was there and was followed by Sister Crosby. She was very nice and looked after us all but she stood no nonsense!

Before tea time the teachers had to give out the Bus Tokens. Almost always some bright spark dropped one token down the grating. The hot pipes were down there along with tokens, money, counters, pieces of jigsaw, chalk, pencils and anything else that could get through a one inch square.

If we were not on tea or bus duty we were permitted to go home but there was always tea laid in the Staff Room if we wanted it. Down in the Hall the children had a jam sandwich and a cake or an apple or orange and a hot drink. The meals were really very good. After tea the children lined up according to which bus they travelled on and the two teachers marched them round the corner into the main road to get the bus on the bridge. So ended each day at Uffculme.

Apart from the daily routine there were seasonal activities like Christmas when each class had to produce a play to show to the parents. Mr. Cooper wrote his own and there were usually dancing girls in it or an Eastern harem with yashmaks. Miss Wales' play was somewhat more serious but always well produced and enjoyable. Mr. Hunt also did a more serious type of drama but Miss Thomas always made us laugh. I wrote a Nativity Play annually: a Nativity presentation could guarantee tears amongst the mothers and there is nothing like a good cry to get applause!!!

Each year 24 of the oldest children from Uffculme went to Towyn for two weeks holiday. The Warden arranged expeditions and the evening activities. Half the day was spent out at places like Shell Island, the Dollgoch Falls etc. The other half of the day was spent writing about it! The pupils were supposed to keep a log each day which was illustrated with drawings, specimens etc. It was a change from normal routine and it was free. We went by coach and it was with great relief that both times I arrived back at school with the same number of children I set out with two weeks before.

The grounds at Uffculme were beautiful. Each season had its charm. We used to sit by the pond in the summer in our lunch break to recharge our batteries. In winter we did a few sharp circuits to get our circulation going. In the Spring we looked for the wild flowers and the tadpoles. Autumn was beautiful with the changing colours of the trees. I hope the children appreciated it. Many came from very poor homes as in Balsall Heath. Here they had good food and lovely surroundings and as much care as we could give them.

Cropwood 1950-4

After several years of illness which culminated in multiple sclerosis and life in a wheelchair Miss Evelyn Boothroyd, Headmistress of Cropwood, retired in December 1952. Several ex-pupils have remembered her for her great kindness and especially for her story-telling sessions when her love of books gave such pleasure to so many children during the 14 years she spent at Cropwood.

Miss Boothroyd's last two years at Cropwood are faithfully recorded in the school log book with details of life at the school:

Cropwood log book 1950

19 May   *Class I girls are doing a survey of the district. Today the class visited Blackwell Station and acquired much valuable information from the stationmaster who was most helpful.*

1 June   *Class I visited Bromsgrove Church and Library. A number of girls joined the Library.*

16 June   *This afternoon Class I visited the wharf and lock works at Tardebigge.*

19 June   *Terminal Review—Dr. Kemp has pronounced twelve girls fit to leave.*

7 July   *Two further cases of Scarlet fever. Dr. Kemp has prescribed prophylactic treatment for us all—½gr sulphadyazine daily.*

30 Aug.   *11 new girls admitted. Dr. Kemp visited. All the staff present.*

2 Sep.   *Two of the new girls ran away. They are not to be allowed to return as there is such a long waiting list.*

13 Sep.   *Miss Ross visited. She commented upon the very happy atmosphere and said she had never found Cropwood more pleasant. This afternoon the children of Baskerville, accompanied by members of staff and Miss Jenkin, came to pick blackberries and had a picnic tea in the grounds.*

14 Sep.   *Dr. Cohen, School Medical Officer, visited today, discussed the medical care of the children with Miss Boothroyd and Sister and stayed for tea.*

15 Sep.   *Mr. Dellar and Miss Morris HMI visited today. Mr. Dellar was very appreciative of the very long*

service of many of the staff—eg Sister; Miss Arnot; Cook; the Caretaker; Mr. Perrygrove; Miss Soar.

14 Oct.   Visiting Day—a very pleasant day and good weather. The parents of the new girls were all very pleased with them.

31 Oct.   Hallowe'en Party. Miss Arnot made toffee and the girls had 'champit tatties', walnuts and chestnuts. Apple bobbing was much enjoyed as usual, and a mime, 'The Tower' acted by Miss Trace, Miss Haworth and Miss Billing was very well done and much appreciated. It was an excellent party.

6 Nov.   An Imperial Institute lecture on the Antarctic was given today by Mr. Toynbee, one of the party of 11 who were brought back last April from the Antarctic Continent after being marooned there for two years. His talk was very interesting and he had some good photographs to show.

12 Dec.   Christmas party held and, as usual, very much enjoyed. Miss Arnot displayed her usual talent in arranging the 'eats'—a puppet show was given by Mr. Worth and Mr. Showell was the best Father Christmas we have ever had.

15 Dec.   Cropwood broke up for the Christmas holidays. It was remarkable that the girls seemed loath to go and 'prayers' was distinctly damp! Barbara Duddy, Veronica Hughes and Jenny Deathridge won the Needlework Competition having produced very creditable samplers since finishing their term's needlework.

Cropwood log book 1951

16 Jan.   Cropwood reassembled. Miss Taylor has replaced Miss Billing.

6 Feb.   A second case of mumps! Both have been removed to Hayley Green Isolation Hospital.

23 April   All the staff are back. Miss Whipp, newly appointed and Miss Coan, reappointed as Children's Helper to replace Miss Tyler who left at the end of January, both fit in well. Miss Coan was here from 1941-46.

15 May   School in the morning—a Treasure Hunt held in the afternoon—the 'Treasure' tins of toffees.

18 May   Miss Soar admitted to the Q.E. Hospital [Queen Elizabeth] for observation and some tests.

26 May   Visiting Day—a very pleasant one, and good weather. The eighteen new girls have put on an average of 3lbs in weight! All the parents seemed very pleased with their children, and the new ones appeared thoroughly settled.

28 May   Miss Ross is retiring in July. Class I are going to embroider a cushion for her, each girl doing a little piece. Miss Boothroyd has designed it (in Jacobean tradition), so it is entirely 'Cropwood'.

16 June   Audrey Reid, who has been here as girl, maid and assistant cook, since 1941, was married today; after a fortnight's honeymoon, she is returning until September.

23 July   Miss Ross visited today to see the work. She was accompanied by Councillor Mrs. Smallwood and there were also several visitors from Blackwell and Barnt Green. All were delighted with the exhibition and with the school's singing, with the descant, of the 23rd Psalm. Class I presented Miss Ross with a Jacobean cushion which they had **all** helped to embroider and which had then been made up in the Sewing Room. Miss Ross appeared to be very touched by this token of respect and affection on the occasion of her retirement.

25 July   We have learned, with delight, that Miss Dove has been appointed Inspector of Special Schools in succession to Miss Ross.

27 Sep.   Audrey Ploughman (née Reid) Assistant Cook left. She had been consecutively at Cropwood since her admission here nearly 11 years ago as a girl of 12.

1 Nov.   Miss Soar has returned to duty today, looking very much better. Teaching staff now at full strength—domestic staff still 2 short.

19 Nov.   Mr. Perrygrove, Caretaker here for 24 yrs died this evening at The Lodge, having been ill with, apparently, a severe chill and jaundice since last Wednesday (Nov 14th 1951). Sister Daniels was with him when he died.

23 Nov.   Mr. Perrygrove was buried today. Flowers were sent by the children—a sheath of chrysanthemums—the Staff, and Miss Boothroyd—two wreaths. A Service was held in Blackwell Methodist Church and attended by the following representatives of Cropwood: Sister Daniels, Miss Arnot, Mrs. Keen, Nurse Mort, Miss Howarth, Miss Whipp, Miss Hutt (representing Miss Boothroyd).
   Mr. Perrygrove will be sadly missed—he had given devoted and conscientious service, and has been held in affection by everyone.

30 Nov.   Seven members of the Special Schools' Committee, Miss Dove, Mr. Walker and Dr. Cohen visited today. The Prefects showed them around the school and they saw some finished Needlework and a complete set of the girl's clothing for all seasons of the year. Miss Arnot had provided a lovely tea, and Miss Boothroyd, Sister, and Miss Arnot entertained the ten visitors. They seemed to enjoy themselves.

14 Dec.   Cropwood broke up for the Christmas holidays. We are very sorry to be losing Miss Howarth who has done excellent work here and has outstanding ability as a teacher. We all feel that this has been a very happy term.

Cropwood log book 1952

30 Jan.   A new caretaker took up residence in The Lodge on Saturday last—today he is ill and off duty, before he has had time to master any of the duties. We have still no heat during the night and lack of hot water except during middle of afternoon. This state of affairs has been the same for the past week since we have not had any help from the assistant Caretaker at Hunter's Hill—we are now back to relying upon the gardeners, and are very grateful for their help. It is bitterly cold and there has been snow and ice on the ground for 5 or 6 days.

5 Feb.   Miss Twist, Cook here since Feb. 1939, is retiring on Mar. 18th and today the girls in Class I have begun to embroider a tablecloth for her. Each girl will do a little and the cloth is to be known, for secrecy's sake, as 'Operation Muffin'.

5 Mar.   Miss Lake, applicant for the vacancy for Cook, was interviewed today by Miss Boothroyd and seems eminently suitable for the position—she is much younger than any previous Cook. Miss Arnot, Housekeeper, has been ailing and losing weight for some time and really begins to look very ill.

13 Mar.   Miss Arnot collapsed today and has been ordered to bed. Dr. Vollam has said she must have leave of absence until the end of term and get away as soon as possible.

17 Mar.   Mrs. Keen (late Nurse here) has taken Miss Arnot to Weston-super-Mare, where she is staying in a private hotel for some weeks. Sister Hodgson, now retired and resident in Weston, met them and is to arrange medical attention for Miss Arnot during her stay.

22 Mar.   Sister Hodgson reports that Miss Arnot is improving slowly and responding to the treatment of Dr. Stanley, who has taken over her case—he has advised Miss Arnot to resign. Miss Boothroyd has informed the office of her decision and asked that Miss Lake may be appointed Housekeeper as from May 1st and another Cook be found.

26 Mar.   Miss Dove visited today in her capacity as Educational Psychologist and examined 4 girls—Dr. Kemp has passed 12 girls as fit to leave Cropwood this term.

3 June   *A treasure hunt organised by Miss Soar today in which each house hunted its own 'treasure'. Miss Arnot was admitted to hospital in Bromsgrove today. This is a shock to everyone as when we saw her last week she seemed to be feeling better and was talking of returning to work at the beginning of next month.*

5 June   *Miss Arnot died early this morning. Miss Boothroyd has returned from her weekend and efforts are being made to contact Miss Arnot's relatives.*

9 June   *Miss Arnot was cremated today at Lodge Hill Crematorium. Her two cousins and legatees, Miss M. Arnot and Mrs. Jackson, returned to Cropwood, with Sister, Mrs. Keen and other members of the funeral party, after the service. Sister has been invaluable in helping Mrs. Jackson.*

14 June   *Miss Lake, the temporary housekeeper, has been admitted to hospital this week. She has resigned.*

27 June   *The swimming pool is in commission again after three years lapse. The inside has been painted a vivid cerulean blue! It is to be hoped that the paint will keep down any vegetative growth. There is great enthusiasm amongst girls and staff.*

The new cook, who has been here about a month is excellent and we all appreciate her efforts on our behalf—the other day she made 232 rock buns and scones for the children's tea.

5 Nov.   *Dental treatment was given here today by Mr. Linn, he had a lady Dr. as anaesthetist and each had a Nurse with them. All the girls behaved beautifully and no one was too upset to go to see the boys' bonfire and fireworks.*

8 Dec.   *This morning a number of visitors (VIP)! including Mr. Russell, the Chairman of the Education Committee, Chairman of SS Committee, Miss David, Miss Dove, and most welcome of all Mr. Barrow Cadbury himself. No one would believe that a man of ninety could walk, talk or write as he does. The girls excelled themselves in singing their Carols, which were greatly appreciated by all the visitors, who also had much praise for the exhibition of the girls' work.*

9 Dec.   *Christmas party held today with the usual 'spread', Puppet Show by Mr. Worth and the visit of Father Christmas, who came in through the playroom window. Many people said it was the nicest Christmas party we ever had, and much praise is due to cook who produced such delectable food and such marvellous cakes.*

11 Dec.   *A Presentation was made to Miss Boothroyd who is retiring this term. She was given a beautiful brooch and earrings of American paste, a pair of sheets and three pillow cases with two cards.*

Two ex-pupils recall their days at Cropwood as very young children during Miss Boothroyd's time in the early 1950s:

Mrs. Frances Wilmot (née **Headford**), 53, Cropwood 1950-1, Leamington Spa, Warwickshire

I was sent to Cropwood residential open-air school at the tender age of six and three-quarter years in the summer of 1950, on account of the frequent colds and attacks of bronchitis which confined me to bed with regular doses of 'M&B'. I had missed much of my first two years at school, despite the fact that I lived in the pleasant leafy suburb of Acocks Green where we had a lovely garden. My parents were keen on country walks so my illness was not caused by lack of fresh air and exercise and my younger sister was perfectly healthy.

I arrived at Cropwood on 30 August 1950 and remained there until 27 July 1951. It is recorded in the Admission Register that I was one of nine girls who were admitted that day. Only one was younger than myself, just 5 years old; the others were somewhat older. Two ran away a few days later and were not allowed to return as there was such a long waiting list.

I shared a small dormitory known as 'Paul Cadbury's Room' in the main house. One of the 'Big Girls' was designated to look after me but all I can remember is being told to 'mitre' the blanket corners on my

bed—*a difficult task which often left me in tears and to this day is one which I don't practise!*

The first six weeks were probably as traumatic for me as for my parents as they were not allowed to visit until Visiting Day in October. I looked forward to their weekly letters and used to reply every Tuesday, always beginning : 'I am quite well and happy and a good little girl' which we copied off a blackboard. A bundle of letters laboriously written in pencil, always ending with 'lots of love from Frances Headford', remain a testimony to my year at the school. My teacher Miss Soar wrote to my parents a few days after my arrival to say I had settled in remarkably quickly and seemed very happy.

I soon made a special naughty friend who once spurred me on to pick poppy seed-heads in the gardens. Unfortunately, we were caught creeping in the school with our loot scooped up in our gymslips. We were given the punishment of missing our weekly ration of 'tuck' which was always handed out ceremoniously by wheelchair-bound headmistress Miss Boothroyd. Looking back on this episode I cannot recall why we wanted all those poppy seed-heads but I know I badly missed my sweets!

Visiting Days were the high spot of each term when my parents and three-year-old sister would arrive in their recently acquired second-hand Hillman Minx with its sliding sunroof. I was plied with lots of goodies and chocolate Kit Kats and often we went for a picnic in nearby Lickey Woods.

Frances Headford (author, aged seven) at Cropwood Open-Air School, pictured with her younger sister Barbara during a family visit in 1951. Precious letters from home can be seen in the blazer pockets. (F. Wilmot)

After a year at Cropwood my bronchitis miraculously disappeared and I was discharged, the picture of health, to return to a mainstream school. However, after a few months back in Birmingham I gradually became ill again and was transferred a year later to Uffculme Open-Air School as a day pupil.

As a legacy from Cropwood I still have the bundle of letters I sent home, a love of the open-air and an independent nature which was probably fostered by residential life at such a young age.

Mrs. Christine Adams (née **Bartlett**), Cropwood, 1949-55, Solihull, West Midlands

I attended Cropwood with bronchiectasis. Miss Boothroyd was the headmistress who ruled with a rod of iron from her wheelchair as she was disabled.

I have both fond and terrifying memories of these distant times as for one so young to be taken from the family environment was very traumatic and I was only five years old. I can recall vividly my parents pulling me up Broad Street, where all the coaches were lined up by the Hall of Memory to transport us to Cropwood. It was a very strict regime that greeted us upon arrival at the school but on reflection one that was somewhat necessary. I was given a short back and sides as my long flowing locks were quickly cut away. On my parents' first visit they walked straight past me, not recognising their only child!

We were all given a daily rota and after getting up at some unearthly hour, my duty was to pick up all litter around the grounds, a job I did not altogether enjoy, especially during the winter months. Breakfast,

Some of Cropwood's youngest pupils exercising out of doors in the sunshine, 1951. (F. Wilmot)

schooling, lunch and then afternoon nap (invariably outside wrapped in our heavy red hospital blankets), dinner, listening to the radio or joining in evening games and so to bed. That was the basis of our daily routine.

During my long stay girls came and left but old Mac, the white horse in the nearby field, became my friend and confidante and was told all the heartache and fears of one so old for her young years.

I can recall keeping 'cave' for the older girls as they crept out at night to meet the boys from Hunter's Hill across the road, and making up their beds to appear as if they were sleeping in them.

Discipline was at the forefront of this school and the education was excellent so that I came home just in time to sit the 11-plus examination and, much to everyone's surprise, passed.

My main and most important memory is that of my parents saying to me on the day I left, 'That school was the making of you'.

From her post as Head of Haseley Hall Open-Air School for Boys, Miss Marjory Urquhart arrived at Cropwood in January 1953 as the new Headmistress. Like a breath of fresh highland air she brought vigour and vision to Cropwood where she remained for 17 years. To many pupils and staff she was an awe-inspiring figure who imposed strict discipline in the school but underneath that steely exterior was one who could inspire such great affection that even 40 years later she is still in touch with many former pupils who passed through her teaching and care. Now retired in her native Argyllshire she has given a personal account which reveals much of her background, her commitment to Cropwood and her sense of humour:

Miss Marjory Urquhart, 86, Head of Cropwood 1953-70, Dunoon, Scotland

In my formative years I was educated in various schools in Argyll as my father's work took us around the country. Finally I took my Highers in Oban High School, being at that time resident in the school's girls' hostel for country girls as my home was in Tobermory, Isle of Mull. This was my first and very happy experience of residential living—perhaps an early indication of my future in education.

I proceeded to Jordanhill Training College in Glasgow and took a general Primary School Teacher Training Course. Although qualified I decided to return to College to enter the intensive Froebel year's course and duly qualified with a First Class Certificate. I also won a First Class in Music Teaching, having studied piano and pipe-organ music for a number of years. In Scotland at that time to become an Infant teacher you had to play an instrument and sing!

The early thirties was a difficult time for newly qualified teachers as there were at least six applicants for every post vacant. I was one of the lucky few and was immediately appointed to the Infant Department of Dunoon Grammar School. I remained with Argyll as by this time my mother was crippled with arthritis and I lived at home. In the early years of the war I was seconded to the Education Department as an assistant to the Director of Education, my role being to travel the country visiting or advising rural schools and bringing them into closer touch with the department.

After the war, having family ties no longer, I decided to leave Argyll for pastures new! Haseley Hall Residential Open-Air School was advertised in the National Press and I applied and was successful. In January 1953 I moved on to become Head Teacher at Cropwood Residential Open-Air School for 80 girls aged 9-16 years. This was a challenge as my predecessor had retired after a number of years of ill-health and there was much to be done.

The pupils were mostly chest cases, including 14 cases of bronchiectasis who required postural drainage three times per day. We also had the odd epileptic. The local GP was on call and we were visited fortnightly by the Special Schools Doctor, Dr. Mole.

We were reasonably well-staffed with four teachers, one trained Nurse, three or four Children's Helpers, Cook-Housekeeper, all resident plus various categories of daily domestics. Several older domestics dated back to service with the Cadbury family and took great pride in their work. Our parquet floors were a joy to

Cropwood House, showing the Loggia, the open classrooms and dormitories in the 1950s. (Hunter's Hill School)

behold! The Cook-Housekeeper, a Geordie, was at least fifteen stone, round, fat and jolly and Grandma to any homesick bairn! What a cook! We must have been the best fed special school in the country. Cleanliness, good food, fresh air, lots of loving care and understanding I considered to be the basis for a good residential establishment.

About six months after I took up my post at Cropwood I was visited by Mr. Barrow Cadbury who was driven by his daughter. He was 96 years young, he told me, and had just come out to see how the new Headmistress was settling in! We had afternoon tea and I showed him around. He left two hours later reassured, he said, that the old home was in good hands!

In my early teaching years I had taken courses and additional qualifications in Mental Testing and Attainment Testing. Early after admission to Cropwood it was essential to assess potential and attainment and this enabled my teachers to close gaps in education. Most of my girls were of average ability but retarded in attainment owing to ill health and absence from school. Group, individual and bedside teaching was carried out with very good results in most cases. No one was 'pushed' but nurtured according to their individual physical, mental and personality capacity.

At Cropwood I was horrified to find the after dinner rest on camp beds in an open shed. This lasted a week under my regime! Thereafter they rested on their dormitory beds!

We had a wide programme of activities including Girl Guides and Brownies, cycling club, drama, music (choir), dancing (including country dance), camping, swimming (in summer) netball, rounders, croquet and rambling. Typing was also available to senior girls taught by a local lady. Two or three years after my arrival at Cropwood I had persuaded the authorities of the need for a proper dining hall (useful for other purposes!) and a domestic science department. A Home-Economics Teacher was appointed and in no time our social education began. The older girls thrived on their hostess skills and many happy winter evenings were spent in this department. They even entered baking competitions run by the Women's Institute in the village hall and won some prizes.

We had regular contact with the local churches. The respective ministers or priests were encouraged to call at the school and to forge links with home churches.

Volumes could be written on life at Cropwood and its many facets. Good residential schools are the product of staff team work with standards set by Head Teacher.

At Easter 1954 Miss Urquhart and her nephew, two nursing sisters and other staff took a party of 20 girls from Cropwood on a visit to Paris and the Chateaux Country. Despite the fact some girls suffered asthma and bronchiectasis no illness occurred and the event was unusual enough to be mentioned in the School Medical Officer's annual report. Miss Urquhart recalls the trip:

> A bus touring holiday in France was organised for twenty senior girls and staff. We had a weekend in Paris and on Palm Sunday we attended the service in Notre Dame Cathedral— a wonderful experience. Thereafter we journeyed in the wake of R.L. Stevenson south to Tours and finally returned via central France and the Chateaux Country.

Cropwood log books record some of the changes during the years 1953-4:

Cropwood log book 1953

13 Jan.   School reopened after the Xmas Vacation under a new Head Teacher—Miss M.A. Urquhart. The staffing situation had deteriorated over the holiday period. Neither the full-time nor part-time seamstress returned and domestic help had not been replaced. The assistant Nurse left in December to be married and was not replaced.

22 Jan.   Head Teacher has been considering general hygiene situation and has 'stepped up' issue of clean linen to girls.

2 Feb.   Until now girls cleaned their footwear twice weekly in a very indifferent fashion. As from today girls will clean their shoes every morning immediately after breakfast.

12 Feb.   Miss Dove, Inspector of Special Schools, visited and discussed the general situation. The entire premises were thoroughly inspected and notes made on obvious improvements required. Toilet facilities, for example, are quite inadequate for 80 girls. Furthermore there is general overcrowding in day time both with regard to premises and playing areas! Miss Dove undertook to make full report to Committee. Rosemary Cottage requirements were to be specially mentioned in this report.

14 Feb.   Parents Visiting Day. New Headmistress addressed the parents and suggested that a Committee of Parents should be formed. The idea was warmly welcomed and nominations called for. A Committee was formed and a date for their first meeting in Birmingham fixed. Plans for raising funds for a Projection Television were discussed. The support of parents in this matter was surprisingly good.

27 Feb.   Housewifery class to cease meantime as it was felt that girls were being used to make good shortage and short-comings of domestic situation. This class will be resumed at a later date under more suitable conditions. As from this date girls will no longer perform duties in Staff Quarters but will confine their daily activities to their own premises where there is ample scope for their energies! Furthermore girls must in future pay greater attention to their own personal appearance—they must have time for 'running repairs' to their clothing etc.etc.

2 Mar.   Rev. Beatty conducted Morning Assembly. This innovation of inviting members of local clergy to conduct school Assembly is greatly appreciated by all concerned.

13 Mar.   Television installed!

14 Mar.   Parents Visiting Day. Everyone was very delighted that we had installed a Projection TV set. By co-operative effort on the part of the parents and staff £100 has already been raised towards the total cost of the set. The Parents Committee discussed ways and means of raising further funds and on the suggestion of the Headmistress it was agreed to hold a garden fete in the Summer Term.

10 May   Girls are bathed twice weekly. As from tonight girls will have thorough 'strip wash' nightly under strict supervision except on bath nights! Procedure to date has been morning wash only and HM considers this unsatisfactory.

19 May   Visit to school by HMI Mr. Dellar and Dr. Asher. They spent the whole day at Cropwood inspecting premises very thoroughly. Mention was once again made of our overcrowded living conditions.

20 May   All girls take after dinner rest on beds. Rosemary Girls proceed to their own quarters and 'rest' much better than formerly. The old arrangement was that they rested on stretcher beds in Class III. Furthermore experience has shown us that children relax much more readily on their proper beds. Conditions for 'stretcher bed rest' are often too cold in winter and too hot in summer.

1 June   Coronation holiday—all but four girls went home until Wednesday. Special buses were engaged for the double journey.

2 June   Coronation Day! Hunter's Hill staff and boys who didn't go home for celebrations were invited to share our TV set and lunch with us. A very happy day was spent together finishing with our return visit to Hunter's Hill for High Tea at 6pm.

10 June   District Commissioner for Girl Guides came to the school and enrolled 21 Guides and 24 Brownies, this forming a School Guide Company and Brownie Pack.

   The HM (who also was enrolled as a Tenderfoot) is Captain of the Guides ably assisted and instructed by her Co.Lieut. Miss Taylor, and experienced Guider. Miss Whipp is Brown Owl and like the HM had to

THE 1950s: WIDENING HORIZONS

> **SHE WALKS, SITS, LAUGHS, RECITES, SINGS, AND SAYS HER PRAYERS IN A REAL HUMAN VOICE.**
>
> YOUR LAST CHANCE TO BUY YOUR 'DARLING'
>
> **CORONATION DOLL**
>
> **10/-** Deposit and 18 weekly payments of 5/-. Cash £4.15.0. Post/Packing 4/-.
>
> Money Refund Guarantee.
>
> She actually laughs "He, he, he," and says:
>
> *I love my mummy My mummy taught me a Rhyme:*
> Little Bo Peep has lost her sheep
> And doesn't know where to find them.
> Leave them alone, and they'll come home
> Bringing their tails behind them.
>
> **I CAN SING, TOO!**
> Oh dear what can the matter be!
> Oh dear what can the matter be!
> Oh dear what can the matter be!
> Johnny's so long at the fair.
>
> Put me to bed, mummy 'cos I'm tired.
> Now I lay me down to sleep,
> I pray the Lord my soul to keep.
> Goodnight, Mummy.
>
> 27in. tall, combable hair, sleeping eyes, exquisite flowing robe with sash and golden crown. A thrilling present and a wonderful Coronation Souvenir for YOUR little girl. CALLERS WELCOME. Buses: 18B, 67. Trolleybuses: 513, 517, 521, 613, 617, 621, 659. Holborn Hall — 3min. Buses: 14, 38, 170, 171, 172. Trolleybuses: 555, 581, 685
>
> **MORE THAN A DOLL—SHE'S A "DARLING" PLAYMATE**
> Obtainable only from **PETER DARLING LTD.** (Dept. MR), 99, Grays Inn Rd., London, W.C.1.
>
> ---
>
> **CORONATION WALKING GUARDSMAN DOLL YOURS** *for* **5/-** DEPOSIT
>
> plus 2/6d. post & pkg. and 6 fortnightly instalments of 8/-. Scarlet Tunic, Black Trousers, Belt and Bearskin. Overall Height 24".
>
> **CASH PRICE 45/-**
> plus 2/6d. post & pkg.

pass her Tenderfoot test! Mrs. Yates, District Commissioner, will register us as the 2nd Blackwell Company of Girl Guides and the 1st Pack of Brownies.

14 June Rosemary Girls are delighted with a new issue of bed covers. They are the only section of the school which had not been thus provided. Colours vary from dormitory to dormitory.

22 June School visited Bromsgrove to see picture 'A Queen is Crowned'.

11 July A most successful Garden party was held in the school grounds—realising the sum of £100 nett. The final payment on our Projection TV set can now be paid. The Education Committee will then be asked to accept the gift of this TV set (in respect of the Cropwood Girls) from the Parents, Staff and Girls. The raising of the necessary monies was a composite effort.

25 Aug. School reopened after the Summer Vacation. Miss Williams replaced Miss Whipp as teacher of Class II. Sister Daniels retired at the end of July and her successor has not yet arrived.

31 Aug. New Nurse, Miss Genever, took up duty.

23 Sep. School was visited by the Director of Education for Worcestershire, his Deputy County Medical Officer, his Chairman of the Education Committee, accompanied by Mr. Adams, Administrator for Special Schools, Miss Dove, Inspector of Special Schools and Mrs. Wright, Chairman of the Special Services Sub-Committee. They all remained to lunch. The object of their visit was to give the Worcestershire Authorities ideas on Open-Air Residential Schools. They hope to build a model school of this type

24 Sep. Another new girl was admitted direct from the Children's Hospital—Pat W. (Celiac). Arrangements have been made to bake special bread for Pat.

5 Oct.   Class I girls went over to Hunter's Hill School to join the Boys in Country Dancing. The class is being taken by Mr. Richardson and Miss Williams, and will be held every Monday throughout the term.

8 Oct.   Miss Soar held a class in Ballroom Dancing for Class I. Twelve boys came over from Hunter's Hill to join them.

15 Oct.   Ten Hunter's Hill Senior Boys came to tea with the girls and waited for Ballroom Dancing. This was the first occasion on which boys have been invited to tea and it was a great success once the initial bashfulness wore off!

7 Dec.   The older girls and boys of both schools held a dance to mark the end of the term's Dance Classes. Both Country and Ballroom Dances were enjoyed. 'Eats' were provided at the interval by the cook-housekeepers of both schools. This was the first social occasion of its kind held by either school and was thought a tremendous success.

9 Dec.   Four girls were confirmed in the Church of England. The Christmas party was held. Complete with Xmas tree, Father Christmas, tables loaded with Christmas fare.

Cropwood log book 1954

5 Feb.   First visit by Mlle. M.L. Amouret, French student, to take French Conversation with our older girls who are planning an Easter week in France.

5 April   All 21 girls who are to visit France were medically examined by Dr. Kemp.

9 April   Party left for France at 12 noon, travelling to Dover by luxury coaches.

14 May   Patricia F.—new girl age 14—absconded at 12 noon but was overtaken by Headmistress in her car and brought back to school.

26 May   The bathing pool is now ready for use but the weather is so cold that only five girls have bathed as yet this season. These are all strong swimmers but even they did not remain in the pool more than 3 mins!

15 June   Another case of chicken pox. Michele H. removed to Little Bromwich Hospital.

15 Sep.   Miss Dove, Inspector of Special Schools, accompanied by Mr. Lowries, Technical Adviser on School Gardens, visited the school to see whether school gardening would be possible here. It was decided that if any gardening was to be undertaken by my girls it would have to be in the grounds of Rosemary Cottage. Mr. Lowries said he would return at a later date and advise us on lay out of plots etc.

25 Sep.   First Visiting Day of this term. Parents of new girls seemed very satisfied with conditions under which their children live in Cropwood.

5 Nov.   Guy Fawkes Night was celebrated in traditional fashion. Three Fathers came out from the city to assist with the Fireworks.

Hunter's Hill 1950-4

Many changes of staff in the early 1950s added to the difficulties of Headmistress Miss Linda Buckley, according to a report by HM Inspectors and a Medical Officer in 1953. A new Chief Assistant had just been appointed and there were four additional full-time teaching staff—two men and two women, with a vacancy 'for someone good at music'; part-time teachers for woodwork and gymnastics completed the teaching staff.

On the medical side was Sister Daniels, SRN and resident Sister-in-charge since the opening of the school. Her duties included nursing, changing dressings, attending to skin troubles, weighing and measuring pupils as well as supervising one dormitory. Miss Clare Barrett, resident nurse, gave nursing help as well as supervising a dormitory and sharing other general duties with staff. She eventually became the only resident nurse in the school with all the responsibilities it entailed. A non-resident children's helper gave general help to the nurses and took boys into Birmingham or elsewhere, whenever necessary.

Facilities for staff included nine bedrooms, four bathrooms, dining room and lounge and the Headmistress had a separate house in the grounds. In 1953 the school stood in 11 acres of grounds in beautiful countryside, long before the M5 motorway appeared on the horizon. One hundred and twenty boys between the ages of 7 and 16 lived at the school, usually being transferred from day schools or Haseley Hall. Many boys had asthma and bronchial problems: asthma sufferers were taught remedial breathing and postural exercises. None of them needed adrenalin but ephedrine tablets were often used to control attacks. Ten boys had bronchiectasis, several needing postural drainage by medical staff and there was a link-up with the nearby Hill Top Hospital Thoracic Unit for treatment. Other disabilities included general debility, malnutrition, nervous instability, TB contacts, congenital hearts, encopresis, Pott's disease, Perthe's disease, nephritis, post-polio, multiple tics, rheumatism and otitis media.

Four dormitories of 30 beds in each provided the sleeping quarters, with washrooms and a spray bathroom. There was criticism in the report that beds were crowded so close together there was no room for boys to keep their treasured odds and ends and clothing had to be kept in communal stores. Four classrooms, a woodwork room, a gymnasium/playroom and dining room were included on the premises, together with a small collection of books carefully chosen by staff with the totally inadequate fund of £15 a year.

The School Medical Officer visited Hunter's Hill fortnightly, a local doctor weekly, the school dentist yearly and boys were often sent into Birmingham for x-rays or hospital visits. The school isolation ward with three beds, separated by sliding glass partitions, was deemed totally inadequate in size. Enuresis was noted as a particular problem, with 30 boys regularly wetting their beds. In general the report found that the care given to the boys was good.

A typical school timetable records the daily programme. Boys arose at 7.30am, stripped beds and washed under supervision. Breakfast at 7.45am was followed by bed-making and tidying dormitories, with a general 'tidiness inspection'. Assembly took place at 9.15am before the first lesson which lasted 1¼ hours, followed by playtime, which included milk or fruit. Lessons followed for another hour from 11.00am–12noon, followed by playtime and lunch. After lunch an hour's rest was obligatory, followed by playtime, 1 hour's lesson, another playtime and another 1 hour's lesson. Tea from 5.00-5.30pm was followed by 'free play', games, hobbies and clubs for 1½ hours, then bathing, reading in bed at 7.30pm and lights out at 7.45pm for the youngest in Dormitory 1, or 9.00pm in Dormitory 4 where the eldest boys slept. Altogether, the boys were formally taught for only 4¼ hours each day.

Activities at school included organised games, House matches, inter-House concert competitions, nature rambles, film shows with the girls at Cropwood, church or chapel on Sundays, swimming, gardening, and quiet hobbies such as painting, stamp collecting and jigsaws. The boys also had to do domestic chores—cleaning dormitories and washrooms and making beds which often helped to get them warm in the winter.

The average length of stay was just over a year and there was some criticism that the standard of work was too low. It was also felt there should be more opportunities for the boys to follow up their own interests and activities which would be possible when the proposed new Hobbies and Quiet Room was built. The suggestion that boys should have more control of their pocket money and that the more reliable ones should be allowed to have bicycles at school was firmly dismissed by Miss Buckley as being 'unworkable'.

Miss Buckley kept the log books in great detail and some of the more interesting entries are as follows:

Hunter's Hill log book 1950

3 Feb.   P.G., D.B., D.S. absconded at 11am. Mr. Atkins was absent all afternoon and evening searching for them. Informed by police at 6pm that they were at G.'s home.

17 Mar.   Dr. Kemp Terminal review examined 27 boys (15 discharged, 12 to stay).

9 May   James B. absconded and reached home [by the end of the month he had absconded another five times].

12 June   D.S., J.H., D.W. absconded at 10.50am. D.W. brought back by mother at 7.30pm. Police notified me that J.H. was at home 9.00pm. D.S. had not reached home at 1.00am.

13 June   D.S. still missing, Children's Officer informed. J.H. returned 12 noon. D.W. and J.H. caned (severely). D.S. found by police at 9pm, brought back by Miss Jones, put into isolation—to remain there until seen by Dr. Kemp.

14 July   David F. to Cripples Hospital to see Mr. Donovan (ordered raising on boots).

16 July   Cricket team v. Village team, won 100-40.

14 Sep.   Dr. Cohen Chief Medical Officer visited school.

9 Oct.   Dr. Kemp (Routine Inspection). George D. taken home by mother, said to be unhappy and fretting to go home. Boy had gained half a stone in weight since admission and was looking very fit. Patrick D. to Accident Hospital.

18 Nov.   No. on roll 128. School team played Uffculme Open-Air School at football, lost 2-1.

11 Dec.   4 boys to Great Charles St Clinic for Dental Inspection.

Hunter's Hill log book 1951

21 Jan.   Mr. Ross, Mrs. Ross, Mrs. James, E.M. have influenza. Dr. Vollam visited and ordered sulphadiazine tablets 1 daily for all school to check epidemic.

28 Feb.   We have eight cases of dysentery and Dr. Vollam has put the whole school staff and boys on a course of sulphadiazine tablets (2 daily) to minimise the risk of infection. Boys with dysentery on sulphaquanidin.

23 April   Miss Jones, Mr. Weedon attend course in Council House on Treatment of Educationally Subnormal Children. Four boys to Eye Clinic.

1 June   K.C., J.H. absconded, found near Bromsgrove and returned—severely caned.

2 July   B.P., J.B., F.B. to be x-rayed etc. re admission to Davos. E.L. to Accident Hospital. F.F., K.L., J.N. sent to Halesowen Isolation Hospital (chicken pox).

2 Sep.   H.A. and J.L. absconded 5.30pm not home at 10pm. D.M., G.M., B.T. absconded, found on Bristol Rd and brought back at 9pm (taxi).

19 Sep.   Class IV to Dudley Zoo. Mr. Weedon, Miss Leather and 3 prefects with them (Film Show).

29 Oct.   Four boys to Handsworth Clinic for T&A operation. [Tonsils & Adenoids]

8 Dec.   Visiting Day. Pantomime 'Ten Little Niggers' presented to parents, very successful.

12 Dec.   Boys had their Christmas party, three groups in afternoon had games, competitions and presents, followed by tea and a film show which was very much enjoyed.

Hunter's Hill log book 1952

11 Feb.   Miss Howarth for interview for headship of Malvern Open-Air School.

25 Feb.   Miss Howarth left today—we are now one member of teaching staff short so have had to combine Classes IA & IB.

29 Feb.   H.A., H.B., C.H. absconded and were absent all day, found by police at 8pm at one boy's home, brought back by taxi (for which they will pay). Boys caned and put to bed.

5 June   Annual visit to Malvern Hills, all boys, teaching, nursing and domestic staff a very enjoyable day.

11 June   Class I accompanied by Miss Buckley, Miss Ledger, Mr. Ross & Mrs. Ross went to Liverpool to visit the docks in connection with their project work. A most enjoyable and profitable excursion.

26 Aug.   Mr. Chedgy who has been seconded to Davos since 1948 returned today.

28 Aug.   Mr. Aston part-time Handicrafts Instructor started work today

5 Sep.   Mr. Chedgy and Mr. Hardinge took Class I by coach to visit Ford Works at Dagenham. Left at 8am returned 10.30pm, a very enjoyable outing.

15 Sep.   Mr. J.W. Tucker started work as assistant teacher today.

26 Oct.   14 senior boys who had kept fireworks and who were lighting them on the hill amongst the cattle were all severely caned by Mr. Tucker.

1 Nov.   Mr. W. Hill recommenced duty as assistant teacher after absence of 18 months in the RNVR.

10 Dec.   Christmas Party. School in three groups for games and competitions from 3-4pm, Father Christmas visit at 4 with present for each boy. High tea at 4.45 followed by Film Show, The Elusive Pimpernel. Boys had a very good time.

Hunter's Hill log book 1953

25 Feb.   Mr. Hardinge with 20 senior boys to Natural History Museum, Birmingham.

30 May   Mr. Tucker took a party of eight senior boys to the Lake District for a climbing holiday; they left on the 11.30am train carrying their food and equipment with them.

31 May   Boys prepared for Coronation holiday.

1 June   Boys taken to Birmingham by special coaches which left Blackwell at 10am. All boys were given their Coronation Souvenirs (bibles or mugs) before they left

3 June   Party of climbers returned from Lake District looking very fit and well. Mr. Tucker reports that all had thoroughly enjoyed their new experience.

13 June   Visiting day. Class I & II gave demonstrations of PT and games to parents. Mrs. W. insisted that her son Anthony was homesick and would be better off at home in spite of his gain in weight and freedom from asthma attacks since admission.

Exhibition of Everest photographs, maps, models etc. by Class I shown to parents. Collection of £3 towards cost of shelves for new reference library.

24 June   Mr. Tucker aroused at 2.15am, boy had been bitten by a rat. Mr. Tucker informed me and we searched the dormitories and found 2 other boys had been bitten. Nurse washed and treated bites.

25 June   3 boys bitten by rat taken by Mr. Richardson to Bromsgrove Hospital for treatment of bites (cauterisation). Rodent Pest Officer informed and he came out and laid bait and poison for rat.

13 Nov.   School was today visited by Mr. A. Gregory, a member of the 1953 Everest Team. He gave a very interesting talk to the three senior classes and then had lunch with the staff. He was very interested in the Everest Exhibition made by the senior class.

21 Nov.   School was presented with a copy of Col. Sir John Hunt's new book *The Ascent of Everest*, by the Piers Plowman Club Malvern, as a token of their appreciation of the work done on the model of Everest which was borrowed by the club during October when they had a lecture on Everest by Noyce, one of the team.

Visiting Day. Boys played fathers at football and drew 2-2. Raised £22.0.0. for School Party Fund by sale of tickets for pantomime and sale of young rabbits reared by Mr. Richardson and boys.

8 Dec.   Carol Service with the Cropwood Girls who repeated for us the Carol Service they had prepared for their parents. It was very well arranged and presented. Parties, games and competitions. Space Man arrived to present gifts from Mars; tea, film: Bush Christmas shown.

The quoted entries are only a fraction of the total recording the minutiae of life at the school. Entries record boys' illnesses and visits to hospitals, frequent visits of doctors and official visitors as well as details of the many boys who absconded from the school. Despite all efforts of the staff to provide many interesting activities as well as medical care, many youngsters were very homesick and needed a family background in which to thrive although others greatly benefited from the communal life as their health improved. It must also have been difficult for parents to realise that it was in the interest of their sons' health and welfare that children should live at Hunter's Hill.

However, many boys enjoyed life at the school so much that the Headmistress, Miss Buckley, received numerous letters in 1954 from 'old boys' recalling their happy days at Hunter's Hill. The school celebrated its 21st anniversary that year, on 12 June, with a garden party and produced a special souvenir programme which has been carefully preserved by the school nurse, Miss Claire Barrett. In it Miss Buckley wrote a Foreword, looking back over her 20 happy years at Hunter's Hill and commenting that boys had not changed much since 1933: there were still 'the good boys, the naughty boys and the average boys'. Her personal hobbies were still nature study, gardening and the joys of life in the country which she shared with many of her pupils.

Since 1933, 2,031 boys had passed through the school and there had been only two Head Teachers, together with a total of 18 male teachers and 24 female teachers. Since 1942, 14 boys had passed the Grammar School examination, 11 boys the Technical School examination and 3 boys the Junior Art School examination.

To commemorate that special occasion when new extensions were opened there were displays of physical training and country dancing, songs by the choir and a play called 'Here's Magic' written by Miss M. Merriman, a teacher of the school. A copper beech tree was planted by Alderman Mrs. E.V. Smith, Chairman of the Birmingham Education Committee, to celebrate the event. Mrs. Smith's speech referred especially to Miss Buckley and Sister Daniels who had 'mothered' so many boys, now healthy as adults and attending the ceremony.

THE 1950s: WIDENING HORIZONS

Mentioned in the souvenir programme was the model of Mount Everest, made by the boys of Class V, which had been lent to Malvern, Redditch, Bromsgrove and Birmingham when members of the Everest Team gave lectures and the film was shown. This model was made under the direction of Hunter's Hill teacher John (Jack) Tucker, an explorer and mountaineer who was on the reserve team for climbing Everest in 1953.

Lord Hunt, then Colonel John Hunt and leader of the successful Everest Expedition, visited the school with another member of his team and recalls Jack Tucker:

Jack was the last of four reserves whom I invited to be available in the autumn of 1952 for the Everest Expedition of 1953. It was an 'on-the-spot' intuitive decision, taken when I visited Eskdale Outward Bound School where he was an instructor. None of the reserves did, in the event, join the expedition on the mountain.

In 1954 he organised an expedition which attempted to climb Mount Kanchenjunga, in the Himalayas, the third highest mountain in the world. Subsequently, he was chosen by the Outward Bound Trust to set up a school in Singapore, where he married a Chinese girl. He later moved to direct another school in Hong Kong and eventually came back to Britain to settle in his later years. He had a brilliant ballerina daughter.

In his youth and prime, he was a boisterous, cheerful soul with a deep love of the hills.

Claire Barrett, the school nurse, recalls Jack Tucker's expedition:

When Mr. Tucker went on the expedition to the Himalayas all the promotional and advertising material was packed up by the boys of Hunter's Hill and it all arrived intact. Many of the boys corresponded with the team; I kept some letters for many years.

Mr. W. Hill, teacher at Hunter's Hill school, also recalls these events which stimulated much interest in the school:

I found Jack Tucker in post when I returned to the school in November 1952, following an 18 month spell of active service with RN (due to call up of reservists for the Korean war). Jack had already made a considerable impact upon the boys and his colleagues. He had a great deal of charisma, was extremely active in the physical sense and laced all his dealings with the boys with his relish of strong and sometimes quite wicked humour. He was very much a 'man's man'. Although his effect upon the school's curriculum was transitory his influence upon those boys who came within his teaching and supervising orbit was immense. No boy could ever possibly 'forget' Jack. He was a larger than life figure with all the Biggles credentials that boys in their teens admire.

Due to Jack's connections with the Alpine Club he was on familiar terms with a number of the Everest climbers selected for the expedition of 1953. Jack was one of the two reserve climbers for that attempt and kept in close touch by letter with Colonel Hunt and other members of the team.

Jack used this 'entree' into the inner world of mountaineering to the great advantage of his class of boys and other pupils of the school in general. He devised a truly exciting project for his class in which almost every aspect of the expedition was covered. The boys corresponded with the climbers, kept log books of the daily progress of the team, studied the history and regional geography of the area, transport, climate and so on. They also made a quite magnificent model of Everest and its foothills showing each camp and every stage of the progress of the expedition. It was a first class educational project. The Everest model, with pictures, logs and notes was later put on public view in Birmingham.

A few days after Sir John's return to England he visited the school, viewed the model and spoke individually with the boys who had worked so very hard in compiling their log books, designing background information, creating pictures, maps and other detail. He then addressed the whole school before lunching with staff as Linda Buckley's guest. Certainly it was an honour indeed to have the 'man of the moment' amongst us.

In 1954 Jack was invited to join the Kanchenjunga Expedition. The school children were very much involved in the whole affair from the beginning and a wonderfully exciting time they all had of it. Jack and other members of the team wrote to the children during the course of the expedition and a similar type of educational project was established which had almost as much impact upon young and impressionable minds as the Everest project. On his return from India the humdrum daily life of a small boarding school failed to satisfy his newly kindled desires for challenge and adventure. He remained with us long enough to finish the manuscript of his book, accepted a post at an army school in Malaya and sadly left us. But we gave him a hell of a farewell party, believe me!

Jack Tucker's book *Kanchenjunga* gives some insight into his humorous personality as well as the difficulties of organising the Expedition up the south face of one of the highest and most difficult mountains in the world. When he was invited to join the expedition in 1954, whilst a school teacher at Hunter's Hill at the age of thirty-one, his total assets were 'a rather dejected bank balance, a small car, dozens of books and a dog', as well as several seasons of mountain climbing in the Alps. As a teacher at the school he had introduced many boys to the pleasures of walking and climbing British hills on special weekend expeditions.

To be asked to join an expedition, albeit one with scarcely any funds or equipment unlike the famous Everest one, was the realisation of a dream for Jack Tucker. Like many mountaineers, he had fallen under the spell of Kanchenjunga, 80 miles east of Everest, which is a beautiful but deadly mountain with a reputation of terrible weather conditions, ice avalanches, glaciers and crevasses. The name itself means 'the five treasure houses of snow'. Jack was one of five climbers who formed a party under the leadership of John Kempe, Headmaster of Hyderabad Public School in India, their aim being to find a route to the summit.

Thanks to the support and encouragement of Sir John Hunt the Expedition received some funding but most of the resources and finance had to be raised by the team members, with Jack Tucker responsible for equipment and shipping. He recalls how Hunter's Hill school co-operated in the project:

> Miss L.M.Buckley, the Head Teacher of my school, had very kindly given us permission to store and pack our goods on the premises: and about a dozen of my senior pupils were assisting in the work. These boys were in their seventh heaven and I would often catch them surreptitiously trying on climbing boots or wind proof jackets. They did a wonderful piece of work and made such a fine job of the packing that I was not too distressed to find that a slab of Kendal mint cake had unaccountably disappeared. The rations brought forth loud cries of concern for our welfare; schoolboys being what they are paled at the thought of only two and a quarter pounds of food a day. I was told quite seriously by one freckle-faced youth that we were bound to starve to death; and that he, personally, could have eaten the entire porridge ration for the party there and then ...

Despite the reservations of the schoolboys the expedition finally succeeded in its mission to establish that there was a possible route to the summit. It was left for another British expedition, however, to follow in its footsteps the following year and finally conquer the heights of Kanchenjunga. To locals the mountain was considered impossible to conquer but to mountaineers

Kanchenjunga was an enormous challenge, as Sir John Hunt once remarked: 'Those who first climb Kanchenjunga will achieve the greatest feat in mountaineering, with technical climbing problems and objective dangers of an even higher order than those we encountered on Everest'.

There is no doubt that for Hunter's Hill boys it must have been a most exciting period in their schooldays and Jack Tucker must have been a hero-figure to them on his return. After he left the school for Malaya and Hong Kong he published other books: *Safety in the Hills* and *Jungle Handbook*, titles indicative of his adventurous life. Later on he returned to this country with his family, becoming a travelling tutor for the children of the Royal Corps de Ballet—his daughter Rowena has become one of the principal dancers at the Royal Ballet, based at the Birmingham Hippodrome Theatre.

School log book entries for 1954 record many events, together with the numerous problems of running a residential school where boys frequently became ill and the staffing situation was often far from satisfactory:

Hunters Hill log book 1954

28 Jan.   *Gas pressure so bad that cooking cannot be done properly. Hot midday meal sent out for boys from Meals Centre. Boys all feeling the cold—work in classrooms practically impossible—concentrating on keeping boys warm. B.T. very ill temp. rising to 105°. Dr. Vollam came and ordered sulphathiazine three hourly, but temp. at 6pm was 106°. Dr. Rowe (Dr. Vollam's partner) called in. He diagnosed osteomyelitis and sent the boy to the Children's Hospital. Ambulance arrived about 8pm. Parents notified via police at Northfield. C.L. collapsed during prayers—excessive cold always affects him. M.D. to hospital again.*

31 Jan.   *Heavy snow—boys fitted with Wellingtons had snow fights and kept very warm.*

1 Feb.   *Gas all off. Boys meals from Meals dept.—staff cold meal again. D.H. has frost bite and is in bed. New boy David P. had a very severe attack of asthma. P.W. has developed chicken pox and is in isolation.*

28 Feb.   *Mr. J.W. Tucker finished duty tonight—he has leave of absence from March to September to accompany an expedition to Kanchenjunga. The senior boys are assisting him with packing of equipment for transport.*

6 Mar.   *Mr. J.W. Tucker left today at 1.15 to start his journey to India. He was given a send off by the staff and boys. A scrapbook of articles from the press, letters from the members of the expedition and photographs will be made by the senior class.*

3 May   *Dr. Kemp Routine visit (Class I). Several boys in bed with colds—probably due to insufficient heating (and subsequent dampness) of dormitories during the holiday period.*

4 June   *A.W. to Great Charles St for x-ray. J.M. absconded between 4.30-5pm. R. Smith to Dental Hospital.*

12 June   *21st Birthday Celebrations—all parents of present school, approx. 800 old boys, local friends and the following official visitors attended: (Alderman) Mrs. E.V. Smith, Councillor Mrs. Wright, Mrs. Fisher, Mr Rathbone, Mr F.L. Russell, Chief Education Officer, Doctor Cohen, Dr. Kemp, Miss Dove, Mr Adams.*

15/16 July   *Sports held each afternoon. Standard was slightly higher than usual especially in the Athletic events. All teaching staff and Mr. Collins, remedial gymnast and Mr. Aston, Woodwork Instructor, acted as starters or judges and house rivalry was particularly keen. Results Malvern 235, Abberley 229, Clent 191, Clee 190.*

7 Sep.   *Mr. J.W. Tucker gave film show Kanchenjunga 1954 to school. Film made by Dr. Matthews, a*

member of the team, is silent and at present unedited. Mr. Tucker gave a running commentary which the senior boys enjoyed.

25 Sep.   J.P. to Rheumatic Clinic.

5 Oct.   *J.E. to Eye Clinic. Classes 3B and 5C are now working in the Hobbies Block and the Dining Room is at last free from use as a classroom. Lockers supplied for Hobbies Room have proved to be more suitable for use in dormitories.*

13 Dec.   *R.S. to Children's Hospital. Dr. Kemp saw all special cases needing notes to hospitals or clinics.*

15 Dec.   *Children's Parties. Fancy Dress Parade. Tea. Christmas tree and presents. Presentation to Sister Daniels who is retiring after 21 yrs here. Cheque for £60 contributed by Staff and Doctors, Old Boys. Each house also presented Sister with a small gift chosen by the boys. Film Show completed party.*

The Head Teacher's annual report on the school for the period July 1953 to January 1955 gives details of the staffing at the time: Head: L.M. Buckley, Senior Assistant: L.A. Richardson, Teachers: W.F. Hill, J.W. Tucker, Miss D. Blay, Miss J.M. Hardisty and Miss B. Evans. Two had recently completed courses on 'retarded' children and physically handicapped children.

Miss Buckley reported that the provision of the new hobbies room and library had resulted in many out-of-school activities and a noticeable improvement in the standard of work. A visiting remedial gymnast teacher, Mr. Collins, visited Hunter's Hill regularly to give training in postural and breathing exercises. Lack of provision of married quarters was emphasised as several good members of staff had left simply because there was no local accommodation.

On the domestic side, it had been a most difficult time as Mrs. Ross, the cook-housekeeper, had retired after many 'long hours in the badly-planned, ill-equipped kitchen'. Her replacement only stayed a few months, finding conditions too difficult and Miss Buckley had been forced to step into the breach to combine the duties of cook-housekeeper with her own work as Head Teacher. In her report, she commented, 'I now spend time checking groceries and preparing meals, my working day stretches from 7.00am to 10.00 or 11.00pm and each school holiday I have to supervise the cleaning'—a far from ideal situation. Her only help was from the daily cook (Mrs. Wilkins), resident parlour maid, kitchen maid and five daily cleaners.

Miss Buckley noted that on the whole the boys had been happily settled. Physical improvements were marked with increased weight and height, and most of the boys had returned to ordinary schools. This report was one of the first of many she made at regular intervals which give a valuable insight into the organisation of the school.

Reminiscences of Hunter's Hill school of this period include an ex-pupil and two teachers:

Mr. Keith Meanwell, Hunter's Hill 1952-6, Bournville, Birmingham

I was at Hunter's Hill from 1952-6, with a six-month break in Davos, Switzerland. I had four wonderful school years, which I will never forget. Us boys were marched over to Cropwood to swim in the girls' swimming pool. Then one night in the week the girls used to come over to the boys school for dancing lessons with us. We used to play twice a year against Uffculme at football and also Marsh Hill Open-Air School … As they say, Happy Days.

Mrs. Jean Greaves (née **Hardisty**), Teacher Hunter's Hill 1953-5, Sutton Coldfield, W. Midlands

I served my Probationary year at Hunter's Hill having come into teaching as a second career. I had first qualified via a Home Office Course based at Birmingham University for a Certificate in the Residential Care of Children.

The contrast between the lives of pupils at Hunter's Hill and those in Residential Homes was considerable—much less institutionalism at Hunter's Hill. Indeed, the regime was varied and despite the coldness at times of the open-air nature of life there was a warmth and friendship which encouraged 'growth' both in staff developing careers and in children to forget restrictions of health and enjoy pursuits. Credit for this I believe lay with the Head and her relationship with all strands of staff, teaching, medical, domestic and, of course, 'The Office'.

The teaching of reading and Arts and Crafts were my specialities. I enjoyed the use of a 'new classroom' slightly apart from the purpose built, older teaching block. Weaving was enjoyed by many of the older pupils; rug making, bookbinding and, with the younger children, clay modelling.

An entry in my Diary on 14.7.1955 reads: 'Finished Jack's manuscript on Kanchenjunga—took some doing but very pleased with the end result—a well bound job'. This was 'real life' bookbinding and was symptomatic of much of the education—a curriculum for life. Geography was enhanced by contacts with the team members climbing Everest.

Visitors to school included the station master who taught the children about Big Bertha—the engine used on The Lickey Incline. An expert potter, he added a new dimension to craft lessons too and we visited his workrooms after 'baking days' to see his pots.

Open days were held—the biggest and best being the 21st anniversary. My future mother-in-law baked cakes in advance and on the day made sandwiches, sold ice cream and felt a part of the school—this was one of its joys—people were welcome to visit, to share, to enjoy.

Recreation was vigorous—sliding down Hunter's Hill on trays in the snow; football matches; outings to Malvern and, of course, swimming at Cropwood.

Long after leaving to pastures new—I look back with nostalgia on working hard, playing hard and on enjoyment. My period at Hunter's Hill, though brief, set me off on a road on which I stayed throughout my career, that of teaching 'special' children in a remedial department, reading in Primary schools and finally joining a Remedial Teaching Service. My love of reading continued and I was a Committee member of the United Kingdom Reading Association for many years.

Mr. W. (Bill) Hill, Teacher Hunter's Hill 1949-56, Margate, Kent

I joined Hunter's Hill in October 1949, following upon a year of teaching maths and science at one of Birmingham's city centre schools. I was still a bit wet behind the ears as a teacher but possibly compensated for my greenness by having been in the Royal Navy since the beginning of the war at the age of sixteen. Subsequent sea service in many theatres of war and minesweeping and bomb disposal work carried me forward to 1947 when I found myself back once more in a chalk and talk environment. At least I had a fund of real life yarns and adventures to beguile and capture the attentions of the bored and unscholarly, an exciting and true tale to while away the odd moments in lessons.

The boys were certainly frail compared with their more robust contemporaries; many were seriously underweight, a large proportion suffered from respiratory complaints including asthma, many had quite irritating skin conditions brought about by allergies and nervous instability. A few were simply underfed and neglected by incompetent and often harassed mothers of large broods of offspring.

Many of these children were under-functioning physically and educationally through no fault of their own but had simply become overwhelmed by these debilitating conditions at their day schools. Admission to the open-air school rested upon the need of the child for sensible daily routine, removal from too much attention or mild neglect at home, nursing care and physical remediation and an educational regime based upon the co-operation and involvement of the children in the learning process.

Miss L.M. Buckley, the headmistress, was a most talented and forward looking educationalist. Her educational philosophy was a blend of the pragmatic; the Spartan idealism of Gordonstoun minus its accretions of middle and upper class aspirations, a sharp awareness of the needs of boys for purpose and excitement in their lives and a commitment to provide the necessities in educational development to foster self-learning and self-reliance. Linda would have dismissed such views as pretentious but, unexpressed but firmly embedded in her daily work, such aims were put into effect.

Generally speaking the school was staffed by keen and lively teachers. As staff did a full teaching week plus twenty six to twenty eight residential or child care duties, fitness and good health, coupled with an optimistic and balanced temperament were essential prerequisites for survival. The work was exhausting but rewarding as the children responded well to good teaching, firm but sympathetic rules and the occasional grown-up shoulder to cry on when their worries and problems overwhelmed them.

Sister Daniels was an institution in herself, having been in charge of the medical side of the school since it opened. She swept around the school in full sister's uniform, sparkling white and crisp and, whilst now in her fifties, demonstrated all the energy and gusto of a much younger woman. Undoubtedly she was the doyenne of the staff room. As such she always presided with dignity and grace at the head of the table during lunch and dinner times in the absence of Linda Buckley. Miss Daniel's sister occupied a similar post at Cropwood and, as was perfectly natural, there was some degree of professional rivalry between the two medical experts.

The children had great confidence in her judgement. In those days inhalers were unavailable and children undergoing severe asthma attacks just had to be nursed through them the hard way, distressing though this was for the child. Sister spent many a night time hour sitting up with her little patients, offering reassurance, comfort and advice on relaxing. Sister had her own little sanatorium of three to four beds attached to her own quarters where children could be treated and rested away from the hurly burly of the school. Sister, Linda and Nurse Barrett took responsibility for all medical treatments of any kind.

The curriculum for the boys was based upon the approved syllabi for the junior and secondary moderns with much emphasis laid upon the establishment of basic skills in the English language and the fundamentals of arithmetic. Many children had lost a good deal of school through illness and were often working at a less than satisfactory level for their age and innate ability levels. Standards of reading and comprehension of all children over nine were checked by Miss Buckley each term. Moreover she also ran the school library, kept a close and detailed record of the children's completed fictional reading, examined them on the content when they returned the books and guided their choice in the selection of new reading matter.

Teachers had to submit, for her scrutiny on every Monday morning, an outline of all their lessons for the week. Linda was very much in touch with what was going on within and without the classroom. History and geography were taught as a combined study through the medium of topics, centres of interest or by means of local studies when a good deal of very relevant natural history could be included. Art and craft had a large amount of time devoted to it … leather work and tooling, bookbinding, cane work, weaving, simple needlework or

Physical education class in Hunter's Hill courtyard, 1950s. (C. Barrett)

raffia for the younger children, painting, drawing, calligraphy and the usual crayon, stencilling and other pattern work.

Linda felt that religious studies were important and this aspect of the children's moral education was covered by the daily assembly, the BBC schools programme (classrooms were wired for sound) and the formal church service at Blackwell church each Sunday morning when the boys were crocodiled along the road, dressed in their Sunday best which in winter included a smart overcoat. It was all very pre-war and rather remote from the children's usual pattern of behaviour when at home.

Games and physical education were given a high priority. All boys were issued with pumps, football boots, PE shorts and shirts and a bag. Given the degree of asthma, chest complaints and chronic illness amongst many of the boys their standard at PE and Games was extremely high and most were very plucky and determined on the football field and equally tough at games like British Bulldog. Cricket was played but rounders was the preferred summer game. In summer the end of afternoon school would be signalled by a swimming session at the Cropwood open-air pool.

All the boys were placed in one of four 'houses', Abberley, Clee, Clent and Malvern, which held weekly 'Pep' meetings and competed with one another in games, lessons, tidying up the school and in individual conduct. House points were awarded for all kinds of activities as a reward. Conversely they were also used as a means of disapprobation for poor work, minor misdemeanours, loss of kit, untidiness and so forth. Points were added up weekly and the winning house given extra tuck or some other reward of significance to the children. Intense competition, not always of a charitable nature, developed between the members of each house.

After being recalled for active service in the Royal Navy, during the Korean war, I returned to the school at the end of October 1952, to be greeted by many new faces amongst the boys and several members of staff who had taken up posts in my absence. A new art block had been built with a small library room attached. Gardening had developed into small animal husbandry, music was given more attention and the school was sloughing off its pre-war and immediate post-war image of the 'poor relation' in terms of equipment and provision for better teaching at a secondary level. It was to be many years before any semblance of equality with a secondary curriculum could be achieved but a firm and determined start had been made. It is worth noting that the City of Birmingham ran most of its boarding and day special schools on a shoestring budget when compared with other large cities. Capitation allowances were slender and much care had to be shown in ordering new classroom equipment and in the use of consumable stock. During the years 1952 7 a good many small changes took place in the daily routine of the school, most of which were beneficial, helping perhaps to lessen the institutional nature of boarding education.

A canoe and boating club was introduced, on the local canal at Tardebigge. Boys were encouraged to keep rabbits, guinea pigs and birds in the school garden pet shed. This development helped to explode the belief that all 'chesty' children should be debarred from close contact with 'fur and feather', for as far as I can recall, no child suffered adversely from handling these small animals. Bantams were introduced and chicks raised under heaters ...indeed the rural science actively enjoyed by the children would have done credit to very much larger schools. Gardening, of course, had always been a set standby but it is an unusual child who becomes enthusiastic about vegetables and flowers.

At times a visitor to the school might be forgiven for thinking that they had strayed into a sort of super Crufts luxury kennels. It was difficult to walk anywhere without stumbling over a panting, pawing, pathetic pair of pleading canine eyes. Claire and Linda shared a small shaggy animal of uncertain lineage; Beryl Evans was always accompanied by a border collie of high intelligence with an eye to the main chance ... Shep would be at the staff room door at break time, tongue slavering for biscuits, long before any member of staff. Daphne Blay's 'Charlie' was an overfed and pampered animal scorned by the other 'real' dogs ... the Richardsons tossetted a poodle whose lifelong ambition was to take a 'gold' in the canine Olympics high jump whilst Jack Tucker, mountaineer, rock climber and rugged outdoor geographer maintained a large golden retriever whose gentle placid temperament was in sharp contrast to the neurotic frenzy of the rest of the school pack. We later had a housekeeper who added her German 'Sausage' to the menage.

Visiting days were held every month in term time on a Saturday afternoon. These were the highlights of the term as far as the children were concerned. Special buses were always organised from the Birmingham bus station although as time went by and everyone became more affluent more and more parents came by car. I think we were all aware of the intense misery these happy family gatherings had upon the children who had no visitors or who spent all their afternoon waiting forlornly in the driveway for the mum or dad who had promised to come but didn't. But generally these were happy, pleasant afternoons and gave one the opportunity of chatting with a child's family, cracking a joke and building rapport between school and home. Wise and experienced teachers are aware that school cannot replace the love, support and total acceptance of a child by its parents but it can show understanding, care and concern for a child's welfare.

The annual Christmas pantomime was always a hilarious and slapstick occasion. The cast was enormous, the idea being to involve every child in some aspect of stage scenery, costuming, acting, programme printing and selling, ushering, choir etc. There was a tradition of each class teacher selecting a small Christmas present, paid for out of school funds, for each member of their class and also arranging a good old fashioned party with all the old traditional games. As with all schools there was a highly decorated tree with lights, hall lavishly hung with art lesson streamers and decorated with holly, and the customary Christmas themes. Linda always said that the children deserved a 'real' Christmas, including a substantial Christmas dinner and tea as these were the memories on which they must rely throughout their grown-up lives.

In a class by itself for traditional fun and games was 5 November. Always a huge bonfire on the top field was built by the boys with wood and kindling gathered from one end of the village to the other. The older boys made the 'guy'. Mrs. Ross, the cook-housekeeper and the wife of our school caretaker, made up tray upon tray of treacle toffee, baked enormous potatoes and arranged hot drinks. Fireworks, brought by the parents, were always handed in and on the night of the great event were shared out amongst the boys, sparklers and 'safe' ones for the younger boys, larger and more exciting whizz bangs, firecrackers etc. for the older ones. Display rockets and wheels were kept together to be set off on a prepared site by a member of staff. After tea, with the boys all suitably wrapped up, the great procession began. The 'Guy', tied into a chair and placed on poles was carried by four of the older boys, whilst the eight House and Vice Captains surrounded the 'Guy' with huge flaming torches carried on the end of six foot poles. Followed by the mass of wildly excited and screaming children the procession wound its way round the school buildings, weaving in and out until it arrived at the great heap of brushwood and kindling on the top field. The occasion was always a fire officer's nightmare … but in all my years at the school we never had any secondary fires or accidents from this hazardous display.

We did, one year, have an occasion which cleared the top field of staff and boys quicker than rabbits going to earth at the approach of wolves. As I mentioned earlier fireworks for display purposes were kept together in a large laundry basket. A member of staff, trying to close the lid of the basket, only succeeded in upending it … and a drifting spark caused rockets, large Roman candles etc to go here, there and everywhere! Small boys, chased by sizzling rockets whizzing a couple of feet above the ground hurled themselves into bushes, scrambled trees or hurriedly hid behind the nearest big grown-up they could find. It was all over in a few minutes but, as one of the older boys said, it was like a D-day landing.

The summer term was enlivened by class outings for recreation and enlarging the children's experience. There were always whole school outings too, the most popular being a whole day on the Malvern Hills when the boys were turned loose and wandered all over the place. Yet with an erring sense of time and nice judgement they would all be there when the picnic lunch and teas began. Dove valley in Derbyshire was another popular venue. Everyone decanted from the buses at one end and walked through the valley. The buses met us all at the other end and took everyone up to a set tea at one of the local hostels.

The school had a traditional sports day, together with a 'Whitsun Roundabout' in which the children were divided into twelve teams of ten and competed almost on a non-stop basis in games of a fairground and fun nature. This was more equitable for all than the usual competitive track events. Roller skating was a favourite activity of many of the older boys. Younger ones enjoyed the scooters and go-carts. Balls, skipping *ropes and minor games equipment was always available but a nightmare to keep track of. But it kept the boys happily occupied. A coarse fishing club was organised which, in season, was popular, as it meshed in nicely with the canoe and boating club.*

I left the school in July 1956 to take up a science post in a Birmingham school. Beryl (Miss B.Evans) also left at the same time to take up a music post in a primary school. We later became engaged and married in the summer of the following year. We both returned to the school, with our young family of two boys, in January 1963, on my appointment as Deputy Head. It was a delightful environment for young children, plenty of space in which to run, play and explore.

1955-9

By the end of the 1950s many routines in open-air schools were being gradually phased out. Ultra-violet radiation, supplementary vitamins, extra meals and the rest period were either abandoned or gradually reduced to the few children in need of such treatment. Malnutrition scarcely existed and there were, in fact, more obese children than undernourished ones needing medical treatment. At last the strict regime of slavishly following 'open-air' life was relaxed a little and warmth and comfort were no longer regarded as an evil or decadent feature in the schools.

In Birmingham the School Medical Officer reported that only one child in twenty admitted to open-air schools suffered from malnutrition. However, there was a never-ending succession of children suffering from asthma, bronchitis, bronchiectasis, general debility and nervous instability who needed recuperative treatment in these special schools.

'The remedial problem is always medical, educational and social' stated Birmingham's annual report in 1956. It had been found that about a third of the pupils each year were deemed fit enough to return to a normal school after a stay of two to four years at an open-air school. As a point of interest open-air schools were unique among special schools as they aimed to cure children of their ailments rather than educating them to live with their disabilities. Obviously, some severe cases of bronchiectasis or asthma, or other ailments such as eczema and habit spasms, were never completely cured but children who stayed in open-air schools for the greater part of their education were taught how to cope with their problems. For treatment of respiratory illnesses Birmingham had the facility of the Birmingham Chest Clinic and the Asthma Clinic at its disposal.

The continual problem of decayed teeth in children was highlighted by the School Dental Officer at Marsh Hill Open-Air School. Many children were suffering ill health due to decayed teeth poisoning their bodies and some were scarcely able to eat proper food. In an effort to eradicate the problem sweets were banned by the school and by 1961, Birmingham was setting the pace in the fight against tooth decay. Many school tuck shops stocked apples, carrots and nuts instead of sweets and biscuits (but it is not recorded how successful were the sales results!).

Birmingham opened its last residential open-air school in 1958—Skilts at Gorcott Hill near Redditch. In the same year Birmingham's seaside school for the Special Schools was transferred from Towyn to Bognor Regis, Sussex, where many open-air school pupils were to enjoy its facilities.

Tuberculosis continued its decline, and as it was a notifiable disease Birmingham's statistics show that no child had died from it in 1957. Yardley Green Hospital had treated 64 cases of pulmonary tuberculosis in that year. The use of drugs such as Streptomycin, PAS and Isoniazid and improved methods of treatment and diagnosis helped in the decline of the disease in children.

Birmingham's open-air schools still had long waiting lists, even though the character of the schools was changing with the intake of children. More and more cases of children with behaviour problems were being admitted, as lack of regular attendance in schools often led to educational backwardness or even a fear or dislike of school. Many 'delicate', apprehensive, insecure or 'maladjusted' children benefited from the presence of a nursing sister, the midday rest, special attention to diet and, above all, dedicated teachers in small classes.

Doctors, nurses and teachers combined as a team to study the health and education of the whole child and a remedial gymnast also did valuable work helping to estimate the vital capacity of chest cases when asthmatic children were considered at reviews for transfer to normal schools.

Uffculme 1955-9

In 1956 Uffculme's open rest-shed was at long last enclosed, providing some respite from driving winds and rain during rest periods and other activities. Two extra classrooms were also added, together with two extra rooms for practical work.

Edward Anderson, Headmaster at Uffculme, kept the log books neatly and meticulously. Some of the entries are recorded here:

Uffculme log book 1955

Feb. *This month has been very cold with many falls of snow. There were drifts many feet high. Attendance has fallen especially of small children. School continued but the time-table was modified.*

19 April *Mr. A.W. Hunt has been appointed to the staff and will be in charge of Class III. The children now leave at 5.0pm—summer routine.*

4 May *Today we were visited by the brass quintet of the City of Birmingham Symphony Orchestra. We had a concert very suitable for the children of ¾ of an hour. These visits are proving very valuable. We have previously had visits by the strings and woodwind sections.*

7 July *Class II with Miss Wales and Mrs. Hewlett to Stratford-on-Avon.*

13 July *Class IV with Miss Spence, Nurse Bendall, Miss Parks to Dudley Zoo.*

14 July *Class I with Mr. Cooper, Mrs. Hewlett to Warwick.*

Uffculme log book 1956

February *The weather during February has been bitterly cold with many snowfalls. The attendance has fallen to 75%—mainly of the younger children.*

25 Feb. *Today we had a visit from the woodwind section of the City of Birmingham Symphony Orchestra. The sextet played various pieces to explain and show the instruments. The visit was much appreciated by all the children.*

6 Sep. *The rest-shed has now been enclosed. This will enable the shed to be used during wet weather and will also keep the rest beds dry.*

27 Sep. *The Headmaster visited the Seaside School and stayed till October 1st. The boys were very well, happy and interested. The communal life has been of great benefit to the nervous, apprehensive boys.*

Uffculme log book 1957

6 Jan. *School commenced the Spring Term today. Sister Southam is still away. We have a relief nurse in the mornings.*

10 Sep. *Mr. R. Ansell has been appointed as teacher of Class I in place of Mr. R. Cooper.*

25-27 Sep. *This week many children are away with the influenza which is of epidemic proportions in the* city. We have 59 children at school out of 120. 7 children with high temperatures have been taken home from school.

26 Sep.   Sister Mrs. Crosby was appointed School Nurse.

11 Oct.   Influenza shows signs of lessening. Average number this week is 76. At least 4 children have pneumonia following influenza and are in hospital.

21 Oct.   Miss Wales, Miss Grimmet (Supply teacher) and 19 Senior Girls have gone to Martineau House Seaside School, Bognor Regis.

5 Nov.   Girls returned from Bognor after a very happy and instructive fortnight of community life.

Uffculme log book 1958

31 Jan.   Owing to fog the children were sent home at 3.15pm.

10 Mar.   The death was announced today of Mr. Barrow Cadbury aged 96. Although it is not stated, Mr. & Mrs. Barrow Cadbury built this school in 1911. The Headmaster sent a letter on behalf of the many thousands of children who passed through this school expressing sorrow and sympathy.

19 June   Mr. Hunt and Mrs. Hardwick with Class III went to Berkswell to visit the Church and a farm. Mr. Wheatley-Hubbard the squire acted as guide. A very happy time was spent.

25 June   Mr. Anderson and Mrs. Tyner with 29 Class I children made a visit to Coventry. The old and new cathedrals were visited as well as the new planned centre of Coventry. The visit followed a project on the city.

30 June   Miss M. Hurst the first Headmistress of this school—now aged 79 was invited to the school. Some details of the early life of the school were given as this log book gives a meagre account. Miss Hurst thoroughly enjoyed her visit and all were delighted to meet her.

19 Dec.   School closed for the Christmas Vacation. A presentation was made to Miss Wales the Deputy Head who leaves to go to an ESN School as Deputy Head.

Uffculme log book 1959

7 Jan.   Mr. C. Randall has commenced duties as teacher of Class I. This leaves Class II without a teacher as Miss Wales has gone to Collingwood School.

29 Jan.   The weather still remains foggy and cold. Many of the children who have bronchitis are away. Many cases of influenza have been notified.

20 Feb.   School attendance is very low owing to an epidemic of influenza and bronchitis which is due to the fog. The average number this week is 59 out of 120.

14 April   School Staff:
   Headmaster—Mr. E.J. Anderson CT; Deputy Head—Miss Harrison CT
   Class I—Mr. C. Randall CT; Class III—Mr. R. Masters, B.Mus.
   Class IV—Miss Spence CT; Nurse—Mrs. Crosby SRN; Secretary—Mrs. Hardwick.
   Miss E. Harrison has been appointed as Deputy Head in place of Miss Wales. Miss Harrison has come from Baskerville PH School.

8 Sep.   The school has now places for 150 children as the classrooms are in use. Mrs. Joan Moore has been appointed to take the new class of Juniors and started work today.

6 Nov.   *The quintet of the City Orchestra gave an hour's concert to the whole school which was thoroughly enjoyed.*

Reminiscences of Uffculme for this period include two ex-pupils, a teacher and a nurse:

Mr. Roger Adams, 51, Uffculme 1953-9, Stourbridge, West Midlands

I went to Uffculme at the age of 10. I was a very sickly child. I had bronchiectasis and had only been able to attend school in the afternoons.

To come to this school, with its playing fields, woods, gardens and even a pond was wonderful for me. One of my earliest memories is of planting some trees to commemorate the Queen's Coronation, on the left-hand side, between the playing fields and the park.

On my first day at the school I learned that it was school policy that children ate everything that they were given. I was still refusing to eat my stringy beans by playtime in the afternoon! It was the last time I refused to eat anything.

Each day began at quarter to nine with breakfast of porridge (lumpy), bacon and fried bread and tea. In the winter we would all line up for our spoonful of cod liver oil.

Next, came Assembly for the whole school, followed by lessons until playtime. If the weather was really cold we would be given a mug of hot Bovril before the next set of lessons.

We would have a midday meal (at least two courses) and this would be followed by an hour's rest on the beds. We each had our own blanket which was kept in a wire cage, in the blanket locker next to the gym hut.

Afternoon lessons were followed by tea—sandwiches and fruit and more mugs of tea. There would have been about 130 pupils at the school, aged between 4½ and 16, divided into 4 classes. Later on, two new classrooms were built and there were five classes, though still of mixed ages and mixed abilities. The emphasis was always on keeping fit and fresh air!

In the winter the open class rooms were very cold. Miss Wales had the classroom farthest from the boiler and her room was extremely cold. When it got too cold to hold a pencil we would march round the classroom, clapping our hands and stamping our feet, reciting our tables. Miss Wales was my first teacher. At the time I thought she was very severe and strict, but looking back, I realise what a caring person she was.

A lot of children at the school seemed to come from quite poor backgrounds, and I remember, in my first year, a lad who wore clogs. Most children had chest problems. A few had behavioural problems but most of us had long-term illnesses. It wasn't unusual for a child to be away from school for quite a long time, perhaps for a spell in hospital. I must have had my operation to remove part of my lung while I was there. Time was spent each day going to the medical room to do postural drainage.

Mr. Anderson was head teacher all the time I was at the school (I left at the age of 16 and by then I was Head Boy). He took us for reading tests, with advanced maths for the older children and for music when a pianist came in to play.

THE 1950s: WIDENING HORIZONS

Every year a group of children would go, during term-time, to the seaside for a week's holiday. I went twice to Towyn in Wales and once to Bognor Regis. All expenses were paid. On the way down, on the coach, I remember Mr. Cooper asking which children had never been to the seaside before and nearly half of them put up their hands. We had a few lessons while we were there and were taken out a lot. We had a wonderful time and these holidays were very special.

One memory that really stands out is the building of the two new classrooms. They were built in front of the Gym Hut. At the same time glass doors were put on the Gym itself. For the first time we would not be open to the elements!

Looking back, I realise what a very special place Uffculme was. Each classroom stood on its own. There seems to have been grass everywhere—playing fields, a small coppice, a big vegetable garden where we each had our own plot, a greenhouse and a big compost heap.

The school had a long-lasting effect on my life. I have never lost my love of being in the fresh air and spend as much of my leisure time as possible out of doors and in the countryside. I still have bronchiectasis and this love of the outdoors has, I'm sure, helped me to stay fit. Even stamping round reciting tables in a cold classroom has stood me in good stead, as I use mental arithmetic a great deal in my work!

Mrs. Gillian Lunney (née **Peake**), Uffculme 1957-66, Kings Heath, Birmingham

I started Uffculme at the age of five. The school day began early and we started with breakfast, I remember large metal jugs filled with delicious cocoa. I had asthma and was frequently in isolation—the sick room—being looked after by Nurse Crosby and Mrs. Gossage.

Everyone had school dinners and I particularly remember my favourite puddings, chocolate crunch and lemon meringue pie. At Christmas all the pupils lined up to stir the Christmas puddings; if we were lucky we got sixpence when the pudding was shared out. I remember teachers Mrs. Moore, Miss Harrison, Mr. Carr, Miss Kitchen, Mr. Hendrix, Miss Wales and Mr. Anderson the Headmaster.

Mr. Arthur Hunt, 80, Teacher Uffculme 1955-7, Balsall Common, Warwickshire

I had no special training for Special Schools. I was Emergency Trained in 1948 so I had not been out of college very long. I was in charge of Class III, the Junior Class and also took gardening with the boys. While I was there a new nurse was appointed—Nurse Crosby. She came with new ideas of the causes of asthma (eg allergies), much to the disapproval of Mr. Anderson, who was a member of the 'old school' who believed the sufferers should just 'snap out of it'. In fact it was generally held that many of them suffered 'weekend asthma'. Mr. Anderson could not interfere since Nurse Crosby was in sole charge of the medical side of the school. Increasingly, children were entered into the school because of behavioural problems rather than health.

My classroom was open completely on two sides, but teachers had blankets during cold weather, especially

Teachers Moira Spence, Arthur Hunt and Margaret Wales at Uffculme, 1956/7. (M. Armson)

when they were on rest duty. We had a 'full-blown' English breakfast of cereals, bacon, sausage, egg, tomato, toast etc so that morning school started about 9.45am. Lunch was equally sumptuous and then there was afternoon tea before the children went home, which one of us had to supervise. I don't think I have ever been so well-fed in my life!

I live near Berkswell as I did when I taught at Uffculme; Mr. Wheatley-Hubbard, son-in-law of Mrs. Wheatley who lived in Berkswell Hall, very kindly acted as host for the visit of my class in June 1958, who were mainly children from the city centre, so it was a real event for them. They saw the cows, and were shown the electric fence which was their boundary, the stocks on the green, the well from which the village derives its name, and in the church Mr. Wheatley-Hubbard took them up to the bell-tower, and swung one of the bells!

I eventually became headmaster of Lady K. Leveson's CofE School, Temple Balsall. I was not at Uffculme very long for it to have much effect on my health, although I am sure it was beneficial, as I am now 80 years of age!

Mrs. Kathleen Crosby, Uffculme School Nurse 1957–65, Worcester

I was appointed in September 1957 after I was asked to work at the school for a couple of days during the absence of the previous nurse, Sister Southam. I was an SRN, trained at Queen Elizabeth, and had only been in the school health service for a few months, going from one clinic to another to get experience. There was no special training for school nurses—you learned on the job; it was nursing common sense. It was either your métier or not!

Uffculme pupils photographed by Nurse Crosby: (left to right) Theresa Beattie, Philip Jordan, Shirley Morris, Jane Arnott, Linda Frayne, Kenneth Livey. (K. Crosby)

Sister Southam had been away ill on many occasions so that I had a terrific amount to do when I was first appointed. I had one elderly helper, and later Mrs. Gossage who was the nurse's assistant.

I worked full-time, getting to school for the 8.30am breakfast. As I was widowed with two young children at school, and I was living with my mother, I had to engage someone to take my own children to school and collect them as my hours were long. I also worked in the school holidays doing home visits to Uffculme schoolchildren. I had the whole of south Birmingham to cover for home visits as the only other open-air school was Marsh Hill at Erdington on the north side of the city. I had no car so it wasn't easy and I travelled on three buses to work at the school.

I wore full nurse's uniform with a veil at school and had a Medical Room where I treated children every morning for all sorts of things, ranging from runny ears, sore eyes, head lice, inhalers for asthma, postural drainage for bronchiectasis, eczema and various medicines and tablets. Every month we weighed the children, keeping records for the School Doctor.

There were lots of upper respiratory and bronchitis cases and many children suffered what was termed 'general debility'—neglect, in other words. These children came from families who didn't bother to take their children to the doctor and I would chase them up—and take them myself, if necessary. Many children from such families were underweight, poorly, run down, often absent from school. There were also cases of nervous instability and malnutrition and children who didn't fit into ordinary schools, perhaps because of chronic eczema or something like that.

I remember one underweight 13 year old and her little sister who were admitted to the school with dreadful head lice—I'd never seen such an infestation with sores and scabs. Her mother suffered severe depression and couldn't cope.

I used to help supervise breakfast which was available for everyone at first, but gradually it was restricted to the few children who needed it. After breakfast the school day began with assembly, taken in the dining hall by the Headmaster, Mr. Anderson, who often went on for ages in full spate! As I was the only Catholic on the staff he put me in charge of the Catholic children for assembly, which I did for nine years. We had this in the shower room, sitting on the benches there and I often had forty to fifty children of various ages from 5 to 16 years. I had no books or equipment so we used to discuss things and say our prayers.

After assembly everyone lined up for cod liver oil, which I thought was unnecessary as research at the time indicated you could have too much vitamin D. With the help of the Doctor we gradually weeded out children who didn't need it.

After this procedure I used to go to the Medical Rooms, and despatch a message for the teacher to send children for treatment. In the mornings I also used to examine all new admissions and fill in medical forms for the doctor. Each child was examined by the Special Schools Doctor on admission and his/her needs assessed. Thereafter they were examined about once a year, unless I was particularly concerned about a child, when he or she would be seen more often. The records took quite a lot of my time. In the afternoon was the weighing of children and showers once a week. When the whole school had to be weighed it took quite a time as whole classes were done together which must have been frustrating for the teachers. I used to find a lot of the neglected children lost weight during school holidays when they were not fed properly.

One of my duties was to supervise meals and to sit at a table at lunch time but I wouldn't insist on children eating up everything, as Mr. Anderson did. There were two types of children at the school—those who would eat everything in sight as they were neglected at home and didn't get enough to eat, and those who were really fussy eaters. My way of dealing with poor eaters was to give them one teaspoonful of everything they would eat. Gradually they would begin to eat a bit more as I encouraged them, and then I would put them on a table of children who were good eaters.

I would give out medicines and tablets to children, inhalers to asthmatics if needed and often treat the bronchiectasis children again. Some bronchiectasis cases whose lungs were badly affected had to be treated twice a day at school and twice a day at home, with physiotherapy.

Tea time was provided too, at first, but was eventually stopped although some children who had a long journey by bus or taxi would get a hot drink.

It was not really an open-air school when I was there as classrooms were not open but even so they were extremely cold and draughty with no insulation. I sometimes told children to put on coats to keep warm. The rest periods were still in progress when I first arrived but I was horrified as the rest-shed was cold and damp. I insisted the place was properly aired and blankets were not damp. Gradually I put a stop to rest periods, restricting it at first to those who needed it but it was soon abandoned altogether.

*I enjoyed my time at Uffculme School and loved the children. I think you **must** enjoy children and must have fun out of them to do a job like that. If you treated them as though you enjoyed and loved them they responded. It was very rewarding.*

Cropwood 1955-9

Miss Marjory Urquhart, Cropwood's recent Headmistress, had the additional responsibility of running the school without a resident nurse in 1955. 'Much credit is due to the watchful care of the Head' said Birmingham's Chief School Medical Officer in his annual report. A letter inserted in the log book, from the Secretary of Cropwood's newly-formed Parents' Society, formally thanked Miss Urquhart for 'the extreme care and trouble taken in the clothing of the children, an improvement which speaks highly of your personal concern and affection for all the pupils under your charge. We would like you to know how much this was commented upon and appreciated'.

Energetic and enthusiastic pupils used the swimming pool, joined the Girl Guide troop and enjoyed the many activities at Cropwood. Log book entries record many details of residential school life:

Cropwood log book 1955

12 Feb.   Guide Choir competed at Barnt Green in first round of Camp Fire Song Competition. They took first place!

26 Feb   Guide Choir competed in 2nd round of Camp Fire Song Competition at Bromsgrove and again took first place!

21 May   This was the first Visiting Day of the term. The weather was sunny and parents and friends enjoyed their visit to our lovely grounds. Many expressed their appreciation of the care lavished on their children and remarked on the great improvement in their appearance.

11 June   The Guide Captain (Head Teacher), Brown Owl (Miss Shemwell, Assistant Teacher) and four patrol Leaders went on a weekend Guide Camp. This camp was arranged for the training of Patrol Leaders in the Lickey Valley Area and was under the command of the Capt. of the Barnt Green Guides.

13 June   Routine School Medical Inspection by Dr. Kemp. The campers were examined and found fit.

23 June   Mrs. Munroe visited from the Chest Clinic and did Stain Test.

1 July   Dr. Morrison-Smith, Chest Consultant, called and examined all our asthma cases. He recommended Dunlopillo beds and pillows.

16 July   Last visiting afternoon of term. Some time ago the Parents Committee presented our Guide Company with a Union Jack and also the World Guide Flag. These Flags had never been dedicated and on this afternoon a special ceremony took place in the open-air when Rev. Carlisle Patterson conducted a Dedication Service. The Service was most impressive and parents were pleased to see their girls in uniform. Brownies and Guides looked very smart.

8 Dec.   The girls had a special Christmas Dinner—turkey with all the trimmings, Christmas pudding, mince pies etc followed by a special afternoon entertainment then a Christmas tea—tables loaded with Christmas fare, very beautifully decorated by Mrs. Smith. After tea each girl received a gift—value 5s. 0d. The Parents Committee presented us with £20 to defray cost of these gifts. Mrs. Stevenson, a parent, provided crackers for the tea table. The girls had a wonderful time and were waited on throughout Dinner and Tea by **all** the staff.

The staff enjoyed their Christmas Dinner at 9.0pm, when all the girls were fast asleep, exhausted by a day of pleasure.

Cropwood log book 1956

19 Mar.   Patsy D. was admitted to Hayley Green Isolation Hospital with chicken pox. This is the 9th case this term.

1 June   Cycling Club for the 11+ girls started. Enthusiasm is high at the moment.

22 June   Guides are now sleeping on rota of 4 in ridge tent in garden.

6 July   Swimming pool in use for first time this term. Weather not very warm but girls full of enthusiasm.

THE 1950s: WIDENING HORIZONS

15 July   Guide Company cooked their tea out-of-doors. Weather was favourable and everyone enjoyed their meal in the open. Several of us expected the bacon and eggs to be flavoured by smoke but this was not so!

14 Dec.   School closed for the Christmas Vacation. Girls were not conveyed to the City by special buses as usual but had to travel by train to New St Station where they were met by their parents. The girls enjoyed the novelty of a train journey.

Cropwood log book 1957

17 Jan.   The Chief Education Officer decided that in view of the awkward situation created by the building programme the admission of new girls should be postponed meantime. Living conditions at extension and Rosemary Cottage are most difficult. Miss Bromage has replaced Miss Brown as teacher.

Class I learns to swim in Cropwood's outdoor pool, 1955. (Hunter's Hill School)

4 Feb.   Routine Medical examination by Dr. Kemp. His visits will be less frequent this term owing to petrol rationing.

2 May   School should have re-opened today but when Head Teacher arrived back three days previously she found that building operations had reached a chaotic stage and it would be quite impossible to admit children for at least another ten days or a fortnight. It had been discovered that the electrical wiring of the house was unsafe and had to be renewed. Floor boards up all over the main building and it would be a great liability to house children under such conditions.

14 May   School re-opened with 54 girls. It is unlikely that Rosemary Cottage will be habitable this term.

4 June   Sister Southam called and agreed to come to Cropwood daily to do morning surgery. She is really Uffculme's Nurse but has been ill and is still unable to undertake full-time work.

20 June   Mr. Paul Cadbury and Dr. Cohen visited the school and went over all buildings and grounds. Mr. Cadbury was very pleased with the extension of buildings now in progress but regretted the overgrown state of the hillsides. He said he would write to the Chief Education Officer and tell him it would give him very great pleasure to be permitted to defray the cost of clearing the hillsides and restoring them to their former beauty. In addition he would gift a sand garden, paddling pool and lay a hockey pitch.

6 July   Visiting day. Senior girls gave a swimming display which impressed the parents greatly. The swimming pool is a great attraction at Cropwood.

4 Sep.   School re-opened. Everyone was delighted to find our school premises in order: new bathrooms, complete at last. After two terms of builders and all the inconvenience they bring we were relieved to know that we could look forward to an orderly term with additional creature comforts.

5 Sep.   The first batch of new girls arrive: a group of 11 senior girls. One girl is 15½ years of age and contrary to expectations seems delighted to be here. We hope she will settle down for at least one term as she is a bad asthma case.

13 Sep.   Outbreak of 'flu now assuming epidemic proportions—Day and Night nurses sent by School Health Service—six new cases.

Some of Cropwood's older pupils in a physical education class in the 1950s. (Hunter's Hill School)

16 Sep.   *Nine more cases sent to Hayley Green Hospital.*

24 Sep.   *Ann V. died in Hayley Green Hospital.*

Cropwood log book 1958

7 Jan.   *School re-opened. Miss Williams, teacher of Senr. Girls, has left us to take up appointment as Head Teacher of a similar school in Liverpool.*

17 Feb.   *New style uniform introduced—older girls will wear skirts and jumpers in place of pleated gym tunics. Younger girls to wear plain tunics instead of pleated type. The girls, particularly the seniors, are very pleased with the change.*

In March 1958 Cropwood was inspected by one of Her Majesty's Inspectors and a Medical Officer of the Ministry of Education who concluded that great efforts were being made by the school 'to recover the ground the pupils had lost educationally', giving them confidence and poise as well as stimulating an interest in learning. By this time teaching was taking place inside the dining room and the original rest-shed, as well as in the two separate chalet-classrooms. From a total of 80 girls in the school, 36 had respiratory problems, 13 suffered from general debility, 8 from debility due to sociological causes and 11 from nervous debility.

There was no resident nurse at the time of the Inspection although a State Registered Nurse attended the school daily. It was reported that the Head Teacher set high standards and shared teaching with her four qualified assistant teachers, as well as looking after children out of school hours. Much care was given to the skills of reading, writing and arithmetic—a far cry from the original aims of open-air schools where health took precedence over education.

Not until April 1959 could Cropwood have the services of a resident nurse, as the log book records:

Cropwood log book 1959

23 April *Sister Sheldon took up her appointment as resident trained nurse.*

27 April *Routine medical inspection by Dr. Mole. New girls were examined and discussed.*

20 June *Gala Afternoon—a most enjoyable and profitable afternoon was held. Parents' Committee now have enough money on hand to purchase a new school television set.*

7 July *Annual School excursion to Stratford-on-Avon. Weather was perfect and girls enjoyed the cross country coach tour as much as the hours spent in Stratford, sailing on the river, visiting places of historical interest and just lazing by the river in the warm sunshine.*

2 Sep. *School re-opened. Staffing conditions weak: Two assistant teachers left at the end of Summer Term and have not been replaced by resident staff. Teaching position is as follows;*
   Class I Head Teacher   Class IIa Miss Boyd (Daily)
   Class IIb Miss Bromage   Class III Miss Soar
   A new Children's Helper, Miss V. Watts, has taken up duty. Miss Watts is awaiting a place in a Training College.

26 Sep. *First Visiting Day of term. Parents of new girls expressed great satisfaction with the school and surroundings.*

31 Oct. *Miss Soar, Deputy Head, while still on sick leave, has sent in her resignation to take effect as at 31st December 1959.*

16 Nov. *The Annual Meeting of Parents took place in St Thomas' School, Birmingham when the chief speaker was Miss J. Dove, Inspector of Special Schools. At the request of parents she spoke on 'Backwardness and Retardation in our Schools'.*

Past pupils who were at the school as very young children retain vivid memories of Cropwood:

Mrs. Margaret Donnellan (née Okey), 45, Cropwood 1955, Birmingham

My earliest memory of Cropwood is of my mother putting me on the red bus in the old Bull Ring and Miss Urquhart waiting at the top of the steps looking very stern. I was only six years old and it seemed like the end of the world had come.

When we arrived I remember the long drive up to the house and the smell of fresh air and all that green grass and pine trees. I was allocated my number which was no.6; this number was on my locker, all my clothes and the pigeon holes for shoes, toothbrush, beaker etc.

Our day started at 7.00am with the bell. We then went over to the lobby to put on our pinafores and collect our shoes for cleaning; this ritual of standing outside in the courtyard (or under the bike shed if it was wet) happened every day summer and winter. Breakfast came next, followed by the making of our beds, shaking our bedside mat outside, emptying our

Typical exercises for Cropwood's open-air school pupils outside the rest shed which had been converted into classrooms in the 1950s. (Hunter's Hill School)

potties and any other chores we had to do. Then it was time for assembly. This consisted of singing a hymn and saying prayers with Miss Urquhart at the helm. After assembly we all went off to our classrooms for lessons. Part of the day was taken up outdoors, either walking in the countryside or just playing outside in the vast school grounds.

After tea we were allowed to play outdoors in summer. Bedtime was at 7.30pm; we were allowed to read for half an hour, then lights out.

The 'flu epidemic of 1957 was particularly hard on Cropwood as over half the girls came down with it. I was whisked off to Hayley Green Hospital as they couldn't cope with the number of girls falling sick.

Mrs. Vivienne Knight (née Hjelter), Cropwood 1954-6, Solihull, West Midlands

'Cropwood Open-Air School for Girls, Blackwell, near Bromsgrove': that is how we used to address our letters home. Now with the benefit of hindsight, I realise that we were copywriting from the blackboard to practise our handwriting skills. Our teacher was Miss Soar and I was six years old, suffering from asthma.

There were daily routines to be observed. In the mornings we had to get up and stand by our beds so that they could be checked to see if they were dry. They were pulled open to be aired. We lined up for toothpaste which was a pink powder and a small amount was spooned out into each child's cupped hand. A dampened toothbrush dabbed at this until it stuck to the bristles. The idea was to see if the whole amount of powder given could stick to the brush at the first attempt. Then there was the line up for cod liver oil. All pupils had a number—mine was 39—and when each child had swallowed her spoonful of oil her number was crossed off the daily list.

The whole school was cleaned daily by the girls, with the older pupils having more responsibility. Taps in the washrooms had to be gleaming, the floors under beds were swept daily, not a vestige of pink tooth powder was to be seen in the hand basins. All of this was done with the windows wide open so that we could breathe in as much fresh air as possible. Some days it was so cold that chilblains became a problem.

A particular friend of mine suffered very badly from chilblains on her fingers which burst regularly and at such times the school nurse (Nurse Cone) applied a violet liquid to them. Every time my friend tried to write she would leave a purple trail from her fingers across the table and her book.

Class II during a reading lesson in the fresh air at Cropwood, June 1955. (Hunter's Hill School)

The school cook was called Mrs. Miller and I remember her as a fat, jolly woman who sang 'Que Sera, Sera'. Christmas time Mrs. Miller let us go into the kitchen to stir the Christmas pudding mixture and to make a wish. On the day we ate the pudding the staff did their best to make sure that we all had a silver threepenny bit in our portion. I still have a silver threepenny bit from my Cropwood days.

Sundays had a routine of their own. After the usual cleaning tasks had been completed, we had to get dressed in our 'Sunday Best' uniforms. These were a smarter version of our brown gym slips with the addition of an overcoat in winter and a hat. The whole outfit smelled of moth balls and we had to go to the attic rooms and see the two 'sewing ladies' for our Sunday clothes. These two ladies issued us with our clean clothes at regular intervals, and our summer dresses.

We were bathed once a week. The baths were small, circular, tin tubs and were filled by overhead showers. There were about eight tubs in the shower room which was strictly supervised by Nurse Cone.

Behind the shower room there were three swings which gave a lot of pleasure, as there were not many toys available then. During my stay at Cropwood, children were allowed to bring bicycles or scooters if they had them from home to play with.

Visitors came once a month on a Saturday afternoon during term time. After each visit or school holiday, Nurse Cone lined us up and combed our hair with a fine tooth comb dipped in Dettol to combat head lice.

Many an hour was spent standing on the gate to the field where a horse was kept. [This old horse was 'sent out to grass' by Birmingham Corporation and was cared for by the Head Gardener.] Miss Urquhart had a spaniel called Mac who seemed to wander around the premises at will.

We travelled to and from Cropwood by coach, the main pick up point for most of us being at the Hall of Memory in Broad Street. Such occasions were either very tearful or joyful depending on which way we were going.

A member of Birmingham's Dental Service recalls working at Cropwood:

Dr. Mary (Molly) Tudor, School Dentist, Selly Park, Birmingham

I well remember visiting Cropwood Open-Air School in the early 1950s, to administer general anaesthetics to the children there. At that time children's teeth were not in good condition, before the introduction of fluoride in the city's drinking water.

A team of us from the School Dental Clinic went to Cropwood School to do a 'Gas Session'. This involved a preliminary visit by the Dental Surgeon—Mr. Hugh Linn—and his nurse, Miss Norah Brown to inspect the children, dividing them into three categories: ie no treatment required, fillings and extractions. Mr. Linn was an excellent dental surgeon, and could extract a tooth extremely quickly but always with great skill and care.

This is where another dental nurse and myself came in, taking a portable anaesthetic machine cylinders of nitrous oxide 'gas' Oxygen—dental instruments and a resuscitation set, which I am glad to say was never used!

Because of the help given by the resident nurses it was a much easier task than at our school clinics. As patients came round from the anaesthetic in a matter of minutes sometimes seconds—they were looked after by the Cropwood nurses. This meant that the visiting team could proceed immediately with the next patient. I cannot recollect having any really difficult children; being on home ground helped a great deal to calm them, I feel sure.

The hospitality at Cropwood was extremely generous. Morning coffee and biscuits was produced upon arrival—followed by a splendid lunch presided over by the Headmistress—Miss Urquhart—whom I shall always remember as a very charming lady. We were finally entertained to afternoon tea.

The number of cases varied. I remember one memorable day when we had 56 patients on the list—and treated 40 of them before lunch! In spite of this, the procedure was relaxed and unhurried, allowing time to have a little talk to soothe each child to sleep.

The visits took place twice yearly for a number of years. I left the Dental Service after many years service in school clinics to have my second baby, and another anaesthetist took over the task. A task I remember with fond memories of happy days at Cropwood Open-Air School.

Hunter's Hill 1955-9

Continual problems in attracting good teachers and reliable domestic staff to Hunter's Hill in its isolated position made life difficult for Miss Buckley, the Headmistress who set a record for long service. The school was beginning to look out-of-date and ill-equipped for so many boys and staff.

On reading Miss Buckley's regular reports and meticulous entries in the log book one is often overwhelmed by her absolute dedication as a teacher and administrator at the school. On many occasions she took on such extra duties as cook-housekeeper, in addition to her onerous responsibilities as head teacher, and the continual change of staff did not make for an easy life. Teachers who thrived in residential school life, where there was little personal free time, tended to move on to other positions of more responsibility within the special schools system.

During this period there was an increasing trend for boys suffering from behavioural or sociological problems to be sent to Hunter's Hill with 'delicate' children, although boys' physical ailments still dominated most of the entries in the log book until the end of the 1950s.

Hunter's Hill log book 1955

16 Feb.   *M.B. & R.M. absconded early this morning (took bicycle belonging to teacher). Found in Birmingham and detained at Steelhouse Lane Police Station until Mr. Richardson was able to collect them at 10am. M. stated he was bullied by prefect, B. that he was unsettled—both were caned and will pay for the cost of petrol used by Mr. Richardson.*

12 Mar.   *Visiting Day. J.W. in isolation with chill. J.K. and J.I. with broken chilblains on feet.*

30 April   *Boating Club started. Dinghy launched named Cygnet on canal at Tardebigge, all boys over 9 went to watch launching.*

16 May   *Visitor from Asthma Clinic calls to look at children's beds and enquire after boys having treatment at Clinic. T.R. absconded—picked up by Police at Dudley Rd and collected from there by Mr. Tucker at 9.15pm.*

17 June   *Dr. Morrison-Smith and Nurse from Asthma Clinic visited and examined 38 boys, subsequently about half the asthma cases had an attack.*

25 June   *Fishing Club started. 20 boys with rods and licences spent all morning at the Canal.*

10 July   *B. & .B. had a fight and B. became quite hysterical—given cold bath and put to bed.*

17 July   *25 boys took part in a fishing competition at Tardebigge. 8 boys went on a long excursion with the boat through the tunnels and then to Alvechurch and Barnt Green.*

18 July   *Dr. Kemp examined all 30 boys who are to go to Camp on August 5th; passed them as fit.*

10 Sep.   *Boys collected blackberries—103lbs. Some boys rather badly stung by wasps.*

14 Sep.   *Miss Marshall who has been appointed as Sister arrived today.*

30 Sep.   *Dr. Vollam to see boys in isolation with sore throats, ordered all school and staff to have a course of sulphadiazene tablets as a preventative measure.*

27 Oct.   All boys taken to Chipperfields Circus at Redditch at 4.45pm. A good show; hot supper when they returned at 8pm.

28 Oct.   W.T. to Cripples Hospital (must wear back support).

31 Oct.   F.M., R.B. absconded during mid morning break, were not found by police until 11pm—had been in Lickey Woods—taken to Selly Oak police station—parents notified by police, boys brought back to school by taxi (12pm). Hallowe'en Party held, each 'house' presented a short item of entertainment and staff arrived dressed as witches and ghosts etc. Boys enjoyed the fun.

7 Dec.   4 boys to Skin Hospital for treatment. L.B., S.M. kept on fluid diet by Sister Marshall (not in bed).

Hunter's Hill log book 1956

23 Jan.   R.A. to Hill Top Hospital for bronchogram.

13 Feb.   Dr. Kemp to see Carl E. who has 'chorea' and is to go to Hill Top Hospital today for bronchogram. Gas pressure low.

2 May   30 boys went to Villa Ground to see Schoolboy International match England v Germany. Mr. Ross caretaker organised and conducted the outing, accompanied by Mrs. Ross, Miss Buckley and Mr. Luke.

5 May   60 Senior boys to Cropwood to watch the Cup Final on TV.

13 May   8 members of boating club with Mr. Hill and Sister Marshall made a long excursion up the canal, cooked their tea and returned about 8.30pm after a successful trip.

6 July   PT Display by Class V and play *Hiawatha* by Class IV presented to the Girls and Staff of Cropwood.

14 July   Dr. Kemp examined all boys who are going to School Camp.

18 July   R.L. and J.R. to Skin Hospital.

24 Aug.   20 boys arrived from Camp (Exmouth where they have been for a fortnight) with Miss Blay and Miss Evans.

17 Sep.   F.M., D.F. absconded—picked up by police on Bristol Rd and taken to Selly Oak police station from where they had to be collected by taxi for which they will pay.

20 Oct.   Visiting Day. Boating Club organised and ran a Jumble Sale by which they raised £20 1s. 8d. to pay for their new canoe.

23 Nov.   E.P. and E.M. to Cripples Hospital at 10am (did not return until 3pm). Fog very thick.

25 Nov.   A.C. brought back from church by Mr. Rice (asthma attack not very severe but Mr. Rice is not accustomed to seeing a boy with a bad attack).

12 Dec.   Christmas Party—games and competitions all afternoon (in 2 groups)—tea—an entertainment written and presented by the staff.

The school Boating Club was very popular during this period, with boys using the neighbouring Tardebigge Canal, but this was only one of the many varied and interesting outdoor activities organised, as an ex-teacher recalls:

Mr. Leslie Richardson, Teacher and Deputy Head Hunter's Hill 1953-62, York

As Deputy Head from 1956 I was in charge of the school when the Headmistress was off-duty or absent. I taught full-time project work with the senior class, plus gardening throughout the school. In this capacity I was able to initiate certain activities aimed at making the school term more interesting and rewarding for the boys. A putting golf-course around the grounds proved popular—putters and balls supplied by local Golf Clubs. The Blackwell Village blacksmith made some robust scooters for use by the younger boys on the central playground and hard pathways. I also set up a small pets' corner for guinea-pigs, rabbits, pigeons and ducks, which helped with the 'loners' and homesick boys.

Cropwood had a small swimming pool which the boys used regularly in the summer term and there was much passing of notes and whispered messages as we crocodiled across the road to the girls' school on a summer evening.

Ends of terms were occasions for much riotous fun—elaborate midnight feasts were planned and the shadowy walk-ways were alive with the figures scurrying to illicit rendezvous carrying food saved for many weeks. Two occasions spring to mind; one clear summer night at the end of a summer term all was strangely quiet—nobody about yet an air of 'something going on' pervaded the place. It was not until the children had gone home the following day that we discovered that they had found a way into an underground air-raid shelter and had a candle-lit party. There was ample evidence of food consumed and party games having been played.

The other occasion was on a similar evening. We tolerated romps until about midnight, after which we clamped down and disciplined offenders found out of bed. I was making my final rounds of the Hill when a sharp female voice with a Scots accent rang out 'You over there! That tall boy in the red dressing gown! I can see you! Go to bed at once!' It was Miss Urquhart, the Cropwood Headmistress. I obeyed with alacrity and didn't own up for several years!

Visiting Days were highlights of the term. Teachers on duty were redundant—apart from keeping an eye on any boys without visitors. After tea, there was the ceremony of handing in tuck and pocket money. All sweets and food were handed in to be doled out in suitable amounts during the next few weeks. Pocket money was credited and could be spent at the Tuck Shop and could be withdrawn by seniors when they went shopping in Bromsgrove at the week-end.

All the boys admitted to Hunter's Hill were from Birmingham and its environs and amongst them was a high proportion of asthmatics. They did well at Hunter's Hill; it was an open-air regime with the accent on out-of-door activities and healthy food. New boys were cosseted along by friends and teachers.

Four teachers 'put the boys to bed'—one for each dormitory of thirty. The boys were called in from the fields by hand-bell in order, youngest first, and it was a very relaxed time, being inspected (ears, knees, elbows) then sitting on each other's beds, reading, playing board games and finally a story read by the teacher on duty. Then lights out, windows flung wide open, one teacher remaining to patrol the four dormitories until all were asleep. In the three junior dormitories, there was a senior prefect who was present all night to deal with minor emergencies or rouse a teacher if necessary.

One unpopular item of the regime was 'rest' which followed the midday meal, except on Visiting Days. All boys, except the very oldest, went direct from the Dining Hall to their beds where they rested for about an hour—fully clothed, under a blanket if cold—reading, day-dreaming or sleeping as they wished. It was considered an important part of the healthy life-style aimed at restoring them to fit young people by the time they left school at sixteen.

Following a trial trip from Hay-on-Wye to Chepstow by canoe on the River Wye by my wife and myself, I took six senior boys on this self-same journey in six days staying at Youth Hostels en route. It was a remarkable experience for them—the quietness of the countryside, the kingfishers, the hostel life. Out of this grew the Boating Club. The school purchased a rowing dinghy which was moored on the canal at Tardebigge. This was a popular summer term activity. The long tunnel was a thrilling experience especially when a barge panicked us out into the daylight for fear of a collision!

Perhaps the most magical day of the year was the Annual Outing to the Malvern Hills. On this day everybody, staff and boys, departed by coach for the Malvern Heights, equipped with hampers of food and bad weather gear. A kind of mythology had grown up about this day. Descriptions of monsters circulated amongst the younger boys. The ultimate was to reach Pink Cottage, where drinks and crisps and chocolate could be purchased. On arrival the coaches emptied, a time was set for lunch and the final gathering and that was the last we saw of the boys. As we, the staff, strode across the windswept Elgar country, we rarely saw a boy yet never a one was missing, injured or late back. The perfect day out!

Leslie Richardson (Hunter's Hill Deputy Head), with boys on Cygnet, *the school dinghy, on the Tardebigge canal in the 1950s. (C. Barrett)*

The ethos of Hunter's Hill School, during this period, was dominated by the belief of the staff that they were engaged in doing a good job of work. Inspired by Miss Linda Buckley, they set out to educate healthy minds in surroundings which gradually persuaded the bodies to become more healthy. Most boys were reluctant to leave, if fit to return to normal school before sixteen. Leavers kept in touch for long afterwards.

Of my 43 years as a teacher, I consider those spent at Hunter's Hill as the happiest and most formative—because in a Residential School one is aware of the whole child, and these standards I tried to carry into other areas of education. From Hunter's Hill I went on to Headships of Special Schools in Barrow-in-Furness and York.

Mr. Anthony Cross, Hunter's Hill 1954-9, Castle Vale, Birmingham

The kindness, patience and friendship of the teachers is perhaps my abiding memory. While not lacking academic information, education seemed to be based on wide subjects, preparing boys for a life ahead.

The Headmistress was Linda Buckley. She was a very impressive lady, while being somewhat strait-laced and aloof she was very kind and understanding during times of trouble, and did not lack a sense of humour. She was also the strictest football referee I have come across! We used to have inter-house football matches refereed by various teachers, but everyone was on their best behaviour when Miss Buckley was in charge. I was also privileged to play in, and captain, the school team—our colours being dark blue and gold quarters.

Each morning we would rise and wash, go for breakfast and then clean our boots or sandals, perform our cleaning and tidying duties, then have lessons. On Saturday mornings we would clean our 'Sunday Shoes' ready for church or chapel on Sunday morning. We were all given one penny to put on the collection plate.

At weekends we could go on walks if we entered our names in a book. We would walk for miles sometimes. Other times we would just go down to the station and watch the trains struggling up the Lickey Incline. We would also walk to Tardebigge canal where we kept our canoes or kayaks. They were all named after water-birds: Mallard, Teal, the double kayak Heron, and the dinghy Cygnet. Mr. Richardson took us for canoeing lessons.

The teachers were marvellous. Mr. Hill, who married Miss Evans the music teacher; Mr. Rice; Percy Aston; David Lamb; Mr. Tebbit; Miss Dallow; Nurse Hill; Sister Marshall; Mr. Ross the caretaker who lived with his wife in the cottage at the bottom of the hill.

1953/4: There was a warmth and friendship at Hunter's Hill which encouraged boys to forget the restrictions of health and enjoy the many activities. Here some prefects wear the uniform of tweed jackets and shirts in different House colours. (C. Barrett)

Sister Marshall's dog, Susie, a dachshund was pregnant and went missing. She was discovered stuck in a badger sett and couldn't turn around because of her condition. She was first sniffed out by Gunner, a golden labrador owned by Mr. Tucker, an explorer and mountaineer. Most of the teachers had dogs.

We used to pray for snow in the winter so that we could sledge down the Hill. The great feat was to bash through the hedge at the bottom. I remember Torch Chases, similar to paper chases, only at night—the main danger being the cow-pats!

So many memories come flooding back, I could go on forever!

Miss Buckley's report on the work of Hunter's Hill School commented that four new teachers had been appointed in 1956—Miss M. Dallow, Mr. G.A. Rice, Mr. C.T. Dilworth and Mr. W. Bennett. Mrs. Ross, the Cook-Housekeeper, had returned surprisingly on a temporary basis despite her heart condition, but was soon to retire due to ill-health. It was no easy task to produce appetising meals with the poor cooking facilities and staff were often frustrated by a drop in the gas pressure at the crucial moment ...

The increase in asthma attacks was attributed to the changes in nursing and teaching staff who needed 'to adjust themselves to daily living with "delicate" boys, and only time and experience can make them conscious of when to fuss and when to leave alone'—a shrewd comment by Miss Buckley, based on many years at the school.

New activities such as the Boating Club (with its six canoes and rowing boat), summer camp, athletics club and fishing club had widened the interests of the boys: the ultimate goal of the school being, in Miss Buckley's words, 'fitting the child for return to a normal school and

THE 1950s: WIDENING HORIZONS 251

thus preparing him to enter the world of work ready to meet its difficulties without regarding himself as a person needing "special treatment" '.

Her entries in the log book continued to record in great detail the busy life of the school, with the comings and goings of staff and pupils, together with the introduction of new technology:

Hunter's Hill log book 1957

20 July   *Visiting Day. Television set purchased by parents presented to Education Authority by Mr. David Galbraith, a TV star, and accepted on behalf of Education Committee by Councillor Mrs. Smallwood, Chairman of the SS Committee.*

9 Sep.   *L.W., R.H. and B.M. again absconded and were brought back by Mr. & Mrs. Richardson (caned and sent to bed). Letter telling the parents of their refusal to settle down sent tonight.*

23 Sep.   *Dr. Kemp. Routine examination of those boys not in bed with 'flu. 62 boys in bed today.*

28 Sep.   *Visiting Day—boys with slight temperatures kept in bed and parents visited—many parents unable to come because of children ill at home. Fine sunny day and parents were pleased to see the boys so well in spite of the epidemic.*

13 Dec.   *Boys left at 10.30am accompanied by all teaching staff. Mr. Dilworth and Miss Dallow (who are to be married at St Peter's Bromsgrove tomorrow) left today.*

Hunter's Hill log book 1958

7 Jan.   *103 old boys returned. Mrs. Ross (Cook-Housekeeper) is not well and has asked for her resignation to be effective from 31.1.58.*

3 Feb.   *B.P. taken to Bromsgrove to see Mr. Mayfield Chest Specialist—found to have infective TB and is to be admitted to Yardley Green Sanatorium tomorrow. Mr. Mayfield advises that all school be x-rayed.*

20 Mar.   *Mr. Richardson and Sister Marshall took 43 boys for Chest x-rays at Mass Radiography centre.*

8 Sep.   *R.H. absconded (on scooter) reached home. Father brought him back but could not make him stay. M. & F. played truant all afternoon in Lickey Woods. B. & H. absconded after tea but were returned by WVS worker.*

20 Sep.   *D.H. admitted to Children's Hospital (heart condition).*

25 Nov.   *Miss Pedley HMI visited for the day—expressed herself as 'being pleased with her visit—boys friendly and happy and appear to be well cared for'.*

In the annual report of 1958 it was noted that Hunter's Hill school was still lacking replacements for two teachers and to add to Miss Buckley's problems the post of Cook-Housekeeper had been vacant since Mrs. Ross's departure. In particular, early morning breakfasts and evening suppers were being prepared by Miss Buckley as the two daily part-time cooks were not on the premises at that time. That year had also seen the 'flu epidemic with 101 boys succumbing to the illness, some very seriously ill. The new television had been mainly used for schools' programmes and was very strictly rationed to two evenings a week from 5.00-6.00pm during dark, winter evenings.

Birmingham still had long waiting lists for admission to the school, but in its 25th year time had caught up and the accommodation at Hunter's Hill was now proving quite unsuitable for 120 boys and residential staff. Improvements recommended by Miss Buckley included the provision of married quarters, new dormitories and wash rooms, a paddling and boating pool, better staff rooms and a caretaker's cottage. In the following year, when nothing had been done, Miss

Buckley emphasised that new teachers were increasingly reluctant to accept the primitive accommodation at Hunter's Hill and that one parent had even rejected the school because her son would have to share a dormitory with 29 other boys.

The following year, 1959, saw more staff leaving, to be replaced by teachers Mr. M. Tebbutt, Mr. D. Lamb, Mr. T. Trihy, Miss C. Williams and Mrs. Brain, Cook-Housekeeper. The log book records one particularly determined 'absconder' amongst its pupils:

Hunter's Hill log book 1959

21 April   *All teaching staff on duty, Mr. Trihy (new appointment) commenced work today. Admitted 1 new boy John O. who has already attempted to abscond 5 times (by 6pm).*

J.O. absconded again twice during evening and was brought back. He tried again at 10.30pm and was found by Miss Urquhart of Cropwood and returned, clothes removed. He went during the night (about 2pm) taking clothes from older boys and was picked up by the police at Wythall who notified us at 8.30am. Brought back from there by taxi and put to bed in isolation—clothes removed. He got up and found clothes from sewing room and absconded at approx 5pm although Sister Marshall was next door to him, keeping watch on him—he slipped silently through the back window, not found by 6.45pm so reported to police.

18 June   *C.H. to hospital (tonsillectomy).*

16 Dec.   *All boys departed at 9.30am, accompanied by teaching staff and Sister Marshall.*

Sister Marshall has recalled her life and duties at the school for this period:

Miss Jean Marshall, School Nursing Sister, Hunter's Hill, 1955-60, Lytham St Annes, Lancashire

I went to Hunter's Hill School in 1955 as the School Nursing Sister after a period as a SSAFA [Soldiers, Sailors, Airmen's Families Association] Sister with army families in Germany. The reason I chose the job was my little dog; I had permission to take her! I liked working with children and was used to boarding school life and residential positions. I also needed a different life after two years with the army.

There were 120 boys, drawn mostly from the very poor areas of Birmingham. The majority of these boys had a record of poor school attendance due to asthma, eczema, lung diseases, general debility etc. They needed a regime of fresh air, good food and discipline.

Miss Buckley was Headmistress, Mr. Richardson Deputy and six or seven teachers, plus Nurse Barrett and a helper from the village. There was also a daily kitchen staff, one resident maid and Miss Harrison in the Sewing Room and Clothing Store.

The day began with Miss Buckley, Nurse Barrett and myself rousing the boys at 7.30am, sending the 'wet beds' for showers. Enuresis was a great problem. My last job at night at 10pm or later was to rouse the boys concerned, change bedclothes and put linen to soak, but by morning many would be wet again.

Breakfast for the boys was always a good helping of porridge, and at the end, we spooned cod liver oil into them. Then they made their beds, and cleaned the dormitories, before standing on the veranda to polish boots and shoes so all went to assembly spic and span, very much like the army.

As soon as the boys were in the class rooms I opened my surgery and spent the morning collecting boys for their medicines and treatments—various ailments, accidents, verrucas, chilblains etc, and some physiotherapy for the chest complaints. I was helped once a week by a visiting physiotherapist.

I had a little sick bay near my bedroom, but more often the child was happier in his own dormitory. During one severe influenza epidemic when most of the staff and boys were ill our local doctor decided against sending them to hospital. He felt they would lose the will to live, so we nursed quite ill children successfully.

After midday dinner, the boys would rest on their beds for an hour, then there would be lessons and outdoor activities until teatime. The winter evenings were spent indoors, and all staff took small groups for

various activities, depending on their age. In the dormitories the beds nearest the windows were pushed back, and rubber sheets put on them, in case snow or rain blew in. The large windows were opened, but a central heating pipe ran the length of the dormitories. The boys thrived, and were well covered with blankets at night.

The boys were well clad, and Miss Harrison kept the sewing room and clothing store in order. Each boy wore wool vest and pants, grey flannel shirt, pullover, corduroy breeches and long wool socks. In the summer lighter clothes were worn. Each Sunday the boys, smartly dressed in long trousers, jackets, shirts with ties, went to church.

It was quite a revelation to see the boys arrive back after school holidays; dirty grey skin, verminous heads, often a great loss of weight. After a few weeks they soon became rosy cheeked, healthier and with a weight gain. It was a pity our work was undone by holidays.

Visiting Days were traumatic, the boys wild with excitement, the asthmatics wheezed and often verminous heads returned, so a busy evening followed, de-lousing. Boys were sick with too much excitement and sweets, so a busy evening, before calm was restored, although homesickness lasted longer.

One year Mr. Richardson decided the school should go to London by train for a day out, a very noisy, tiring day. We went to London Zoo, where the asthmatics became worse in the camel house. I'm glad that outing wasn't repeated, my headache continued for days afterwards!

The days for me were long and it was a lonely life; early morning to late at night, sometimes a brief afternoon session free, no social life, one and a half days off weekly, only an hourly bus service to Bromsgrove or Birmingham, and it was a lonely walk back from the station at night.

The job didn't have any lasting effects on my life but health-wise was another matter: I had to leave due to illness, brought about by throat infections and stress. I had returned to work too soon after sick leave, due to pressure from Birmingham Special Schools Medical Officer; they needed to have a trained person on the premises, before new boys could be admitted.

After I left I took my Health Visiting examinations at Liverpool University and worked for Lancashire County Council for the next twenty years. I was back looking round Hunter's Hill in 1992. It had not changed very much; the wooden dormitories were still there, and it didn't seem as if 30-odd years had passed.

Marsh Hill

Miss Mary Brown retired as Headmistress of Marsh Hill in 1953, after 22 years at the school. Little is known about her but she was regarded as quite a character, always wearing a hat as she walked around the school. It was reported that she often wore her hat at a particular angle on pay-days and was unapproachable: in the days before equality of pay her salary as Headmistress was considerably less than some of her male teachers who had far less responsibility.

Miss Brown was renowned for the high standard of Marsh Hill School's dramatic productions at Birmingham's Juvenile Dramatic Festivals at the Birmingham and Midland Institute. The school's production in 1949 of *Julius Caesar* Act III, Scene II greatly impressed the theatre critic of the *Times Educational Supplement*: 'one of the best small pieces of school Shakespeare production that a critic is likely to see in a lifetime. This was Shakespeare truly used, not just reverently dusted', reports the newscutting in the school log book. In addition, the school choir was well known for competing with ordinary schools at Music Festivals held at Birmingham Town Hall.

Miss Brown was succeeded by Mr. J. Miles who remained at Marsh Hill for five years. Three past pupils recall their happy schooldays at Marsh Hill during his headship:

Mrs. Margaret Rice (née **Bray**), 49, Marsh Hill 1952-8, Sutton Coldfield, West Midlands

I attended Marsh Hill Open-Air School because I suffered from bouts of bronchitis and pneumonia. When I first attended I had all my meals there—breakfast, dinner and tea. Gradually, it was not thought necessary

to provide breakfast, then tea, so that eventually I only had my dinner there. I was not a very good eater and I hated the prunes they served with the cereals, and also swedes as a dinner vegetable.

As well as nutritious meals, we were also given doses of cod liver oil and malt. I loved the cod liver oil and used to go to the back of the queue for a second dose, but I was not so keen on the brown sticky malt. The health care was excellent as we had our own resident nursing sister, Sister Yelland, who was always very kind and caring. She often called us in for sun-ray treatment and regular check-ups.

Education took second place to our health and well-being, and therefore all the classrooms had opening windows and sliding doors. To keep us warm we were given small red blankets which tied round our waists, and a green knitted woolly jumper. These were worn over our own clothes and provided added protection when we needed to go along the open wooden verandas from the classroom to reach the dining room.

In the summer months we spent a lot of time outdoors as we had two large playing fields at the back of the school and we had country dancing, games and PE out there, as well as playtimes. There were gardening duties too, and looking after the pet rabbits. Summer seemed to go on for months and months.

The teaching staff were very kind and caring and I remember particularly Mr. Miles, Headmaster, Mr. Whitehouse, Mr. Davies, Mrs. Browning, Mrs. Fairburn and Mr. Alflatt. Mrs. Fairburn taught the school choir, and I remember being part of a large choir which sang in Birmingham Town Hall on one occasion.

I was very sad to leave Marsh Hill at aged 11 to go to a secondary modern school, but I shall always be grateful to them for looking after me so well and for giving me what really was an idyllic childhood.

Mr. Edward Bone, Marsh Hill 1954-8, Redditch, Worcestershire

When I was seven I was taken ill with ulcerative colitis and I was in hospital for about four months. I lost twelve months schooling, so they sent me to Marsh Hill. Mr. Miles was the Headmaster.

We started at 8.45am with breakfast and assembly. In the winter at the morning playtime we had a cup of hot chocolate. After dinner we had our rest break. If you were caught talking or playing about in the rest period, you were made to stay in bed, when the other kids went out to play. At the end of the day we had a glass of milk before we caught one of the special buses home.

Mr. John Warom, Marsh Hill 1953-8, Erdington, Birmingham

I was diagnosed as having chronic bronchitis by Doctor Kemp at Great Charles Street Clinic. He suggested to my mother that I should go to Marsh Hill.

Going to Marsh Hill was like going to Butlins Holiday Camp. When arriving in the morning we had breakfast—cornflakes, bacon and eggs or bacon and tomatoes which I enjoyed very much.

The Headmaster was Mr. Miles who was at the school up to the end of summer 1958. He was very good at writing educational books for children and went on to a job in the Education Department doing the same. Teachers were Miss Lambsdown, Mr. Whitehouse, Mr. Hurly, Mrs. Browning, PE teacher Mr. Connors and Mr. Peters. Mr. Peters was very keen on pottery and with some of the older boys built an outside kiln. I enjoyed pottery and had one or two successful firings. We had a Nurse and a Sister Yelland. She would come around the class rooms with vitamin C and iron in drink form—one spoonful per pupil. In the winter it was malt and cod liver oil. I loved it.

We all had our own toothbrush and used horrible tooth powder. We were issued with PE kit which

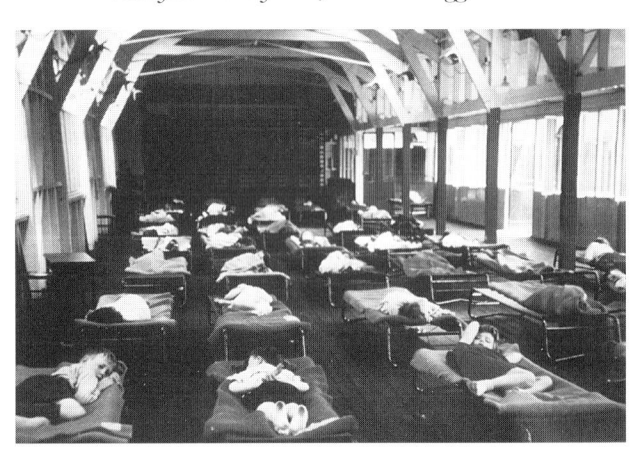

Rest time at Marsh Hill Open-Air School, 1958. (P. Hazel)

consisted of a yellow shirt, navy blue shorts and plimsolls. We used to play cricket and football matches against Blackwell Open-Air School for boys. We had two fields at Marsh Hill—upper and lower—and would play football or cricket. The girls would play netball or rounders.

Rest periods were after dinner for an hour. There were two rest-sheds; upper was for the boys and lower for the girls. The two sheds also were the gymnasiums with ropes hanging down from the beams and wall bars. We had day trips to Dovedale and the Cotswolds: the sun always seemed to shine—hot summer days.

At Marsh Hill the Christmas party was wonderful and the teachers waited on us; I couldn't believe it! Tea, orange squash, lemonade, trifle and jelly, cakes.

In 1958 Miss Patricia Hazel became the last Headmistress of Marsh Hill, having previously taught at several mainstream schools during and after the war, before moving to Birmingham to teach at Waverley Grammar School. Although teaching had been her first choice of career, nursing came a close second, which is perhaps why she had become the Deputy Head Teacher of Baskerville School for Physically Handicapped Children where youngsters with rheumatic hearts and chorea were treated and educated. It was considered that good experience in ordinary schools was essential to teach successfully in these special schools. Applications were invited only from experienced teachers. Marsh Hill Day School for Delicate Children was becoming rather dated by the late 1950s, as Miss Hazel recalls:

Miss Patricia C.J. Hazel, Headmistress Marsh Hill 1958-66, Sutton Coldfield, West Midlands

Marsh Hill was a happy school. We had two huge football fields, lovely lawns and beautiful borders and trees. Ducks used to come and nest in the flower borders. Foxes had their 'earth' in the sandy bank between the football fields.

The school had been purpose built by Birmingham and had incorporated some of the features of other successful open-air schools. But the open corridors with slatted wooden floors used to get terribly wet in the rain. Soon after my arrival at the school I asked for the corridors to be closed in so Mr. Chapman (Chief Administrative Officer of Special Schools) came to visit us on a wet day. One of my rather ungainly girls came along and slipped on the wet floor, landing in a heap at his feet … we couldn't have had a better demonstration if we had tried! The corridors were enclosed shortly after that and the floors were also filled in. But I still have vivid memories of the caretaker on his hands and knees, handling a piece of bent wire and trying to retrieve keys which had dropped through the slats of the corridor floor …! We still kept the sliding doors in the classrooms which we opened in appropriate weather.

School was a structured day which gave a lot of support in small groups on the teaching side and more individual attention. If the weather was nice and there was a special event on somewhere we were able to be flexible enough to take a group to visit it. We often worked out of doors.

Marsh Hill was a school where I was very happy to be so involved with boys and girls of all ages, with their families and with the staff who gave so much of themselves to create a happy family atmosphere. Memories of Christmas activities come to mind—plays and parties when senior pupils prepared all the food, decorated the Hall, set the tables and saw to it that the younger children and guests enjoyed a really festive time. When it came to washing-up, the care-

A group of pupils at Marsh Hill Open-Air School, 1958. (P. Hazel)

taker and his wife, men and women teachers with their wives and husbands, all gave a hand. I recall the snowball battles and building of snowmen while the virgin snow lasted on the football field.

I remember annual visits for groups of children to the seaside residences provided by Birmingham for the use of Special Schools—firstly Towyn in Wales and later Martineau House near Bognor Regis. Stays were generally two weeks and there was the excitement of visiting places of historical interest, exploring seashore and walking in the woods. The garden at Martineau House reached to the beach. The Deputy Headmaster reported the occasion when some boys went in the garden on their first evening, one lad saying 'Please Sir, what's that funny smell?' 'Fresh air' came the reply! …

The rest-sheds were enclosed in 1959 and official rest time was abandoned. Gas panelled heating had been installed in two classrooms and breakfasts ceased in 1961, except for children with special needs. A new housecraft room was built in 1959, as well as woodwork and general craft rooms. A catering course was introduced for all senior boys. Its value was proved by some boys showing ability to cope in a family crisis and a few even went into catering on leaving school.

By the time I left in 1966 when the school closed down we had for some years accepted 'maladjusted' children sent to us via the School Psychiatrist. But many children were sent to Marsh Hill if they were slightly retarded because their health was poor and they didn't flourish in ordinary schools. Marsh Hill as a School for Delicate Children was the making of many children who weren't in robust health and many eventually went on to normal schools. Some were reported by the Head Teachers to achieve higher results than their peers who had followed the normal course of education.

I've known some cases where parents had refused to send their retarded children to an ESN school but it was respectable and acceptable to say that your child was poorly and went to a School for Delicate Children. It was so rewarding to watch the improvement in health, self assurance and educational attainment of so many young people as they worked and played in the company of others who shared their problems.

The school was situated on Marsh Hill in Erdington and was in beautiful surroundings. I can remember many parents coming from Birmingham's inner city areas to Marsh Hill School for their children's medical check-up and often looking around, saying 'I'd give anything to live out here!'

Haseley Hall

Haseley Hall Residential Open-Air School for Boys formed an important part of Birmingham's special schools network. The regime reported in the school log book entries is familiar but despite its isolation in the Warwickshire countryside Haseley Hall formed many links with local schools and the neighbourhood, as well as with other schools in its own education authority. It is, in fact, an interesting social document of the period. Miss Urquhart was in post as Headmistress at the beginning of the 1950s and recorded:

Haseley Hall log book 1950

31 Jan   *Sister Parry retired. No replacement. Headmistress must carry her duties in addition to Miss Cooper's (who left 30.11.49) and her own!*

Haseley Hall log book 1951

26 May   *Festival garden party was held in school grounds to which all the surrounding district was invited. Children from the neighbouring schools joined in Grand Fancy Dress parade and 156 competitions. The Fete was a great success socially and financially.*

1 June   *Nurse Bond took up resident appointment.*

19 July   *Inter-School Sports Day. The following schools took part—Beausale, Wroxall, Hatton, Haseley Hall—and the sports were held in the grounds of Haseley Hall.*

7 Sep.   *Failure of water supply—electric pump burned out. Fire engines from Warwick were called to fill tanks. Seven journeys were necessary to fill tanks to capacity—2,000 gallons!* [The school was not connected to mains water supply until February 1953.]

24 Sep.   *Baskerville School joined us blackberry picking and had tea with us before returning home.*

28 Sep.   *Parents Visiting Day. All parents of new boys expressed their pleasure in our school. Remarks were made on how 'nice' the boys looked.*

13 Oct.   *Visit to school by Senior Administrative Assistant, the Inspector of Special Schools and School Meals Organiser. The purpose of their visit was to discuss improvements in our kitchen premises, special mention being made of limited cooking facilities and ancient wooden sinks or tubs for 'washing-up' purposes.*

6 Dec.   *Christmas party held. All neighbouring children were invited and were remembered equally with our own boys by Santa Claus!*

12 Dec.   *School closed. Miss Urquhart left Haseley Hall to take up new appointment as Headmistress of Cropwood Open-Air School.*

An ex-pupil of the school gives his recollections of a year at Haseley Hall:

Mr. Peter Holmes, 53, Haseley Hall 1950-1, Chelmsley Wood, Birmingham

My first impression at the age of seven or eight years was its vastness. Previously all I had ever seen was factories, terraced houses and bomb-sites. To a child like myself it was magnificent. The countryside and woods were overwhelming and very beautiful and the air so sweet.

I remember we were all issued with identical clothes with our names sewn inside them, and allocated beds in dormitories. One of my happiest memories is the long walks we were taken. We would walk through the woods and visit farms seeing animals and flowers and trees that most of us had only ever seen in books. On these occasions I felt happy and enjoyed the company of the other boys.

The food was very good. We also had indoor toilets and bathrooms, something we didn't have at home, and real toilet paper—not newspaper.

However, although some of the staff were very nice and kind, there were those like Miss Urquhart who were very strict. When we got up of a morning we had to strip our beds and line up for inspection. If a boy had wet the bed he would be stripped and slapped in front of everyone. I had a bed wetting problem and was terrified because I knew what to expect. Many times I was punished and made to stand naked at a sink washing my soiled pants in full view of everyone.

Our dormitories didn't have doors, they had mesh slide-over gates. If, during the night, you wished to go to the toilet or were ill, you had to call out for the member of staff on duty.

I remember how sick some of the boys were and the sadness I felt when a boy died. I remember our classroom lessons and really enjoyed them. On leaving the home and starting normal school I was found to have an above average IQ which says a great deal about the standard of teaching.

I know for a fact that if I hadn't gone to an open-air school, I might not have been around to enjoy a normal, healthy life and write this letter.

Haseley Hall's new Headmistress in 1953 was Miss A. Marjorie Butler-Fleming (from Bramley, Leeds), who stayed at the school until her retirement in 1968. She carried on the log books which very much reflect the homely atmosphere she created in the school.

Haseley Hall log book 1953

2 June   *Everyone watched the Coronation on television. At 2pm went to Hatton for the sports and tea.*

5 Dec.   *Christmas party. Dr. Kemp again Santa Claus.* [Dr. Kemp was the Medical Officer for Special Schools, a frequent visitor to the school, who performed this additional important duty for several years.]

Haseley Hall log book 1954

3 Jan.   *Five hand-bell ringers from Hatton Church came to give a performance and several boys and staff 'had a go'!*

14 Sep.   *Sister and Headmistress went to visit Bromsgrove Hill Top Hospital to see the treatment of bronchiectasis patients. Lunch with Miss Urquhart at Cropwood.*

28 Sep.   *In the evening boys taken to Illuminations in Leamington by special coach. All very excited seeing 'Down The Rabbit Hole', 'Alice in Wonderland' and the Guinness Clock and mountaineer!*

Christmas party at Haseley Hall, 1955, with a well-disguised Dr. Kemp as Father Christmas handing out presents. (M. Bullock)

Haseley Hall log book 1955

4 Nov.   *Bonfire Night Party. Dr. Kemp and Sister Smith came and many other young visitors and parents from around. The boys had a supper after the fireworks display and bonfire. We had turnip lanterns and Hallowe'en pictures up on the wall and candles on the tables, cocoa, parkin pigs, biscuits and sandwiches.*

Haseley Hall log book 1956

16 Dec.   *School Christmas Dinner. Staff served the boys in their dining room prettily decorated. Turkey and Christmas pudding on the menu! The boys had lucky sweet charms from the Witch from the pudding—and a sugar mouse, crackers and balloons.*

Haseley Hall log book 1959

17 July   *'Skilts' younger children over for a play afternoon with our boys and a picnic tea.*

A teacher recalls her three years at Haseley Hall:

Mrs. Mabel Bullock (née **Hancock**), Teacher Haseley Hall 1953–6, Hatton, Warwickshire

I went to Haseley Hall Open-Air School after first working in an ordinary infants school in Handsworth. Although I had no special training I applied for the post at Haseley and was successful.

At Haseley Hall windows were opened as much as possible, although there were no sliding screens as at some other open-air schools. The classrooms were tall airy rooms and looked much like any other school in that era. There was a lovely staircase and stained glass window. It was a happy school under Miss Fleming as Head and we spent a lot of time out of doors, going for walks down the lanes or having picnics. There was a climbing frame in the trees, a sand pit and a paddling pool. The parents raised the money for the paddling pool. In winter the boys wore shorts as usual with their wellingtons and thick winter coats. Feeding the birds was a popular activity.

THE 1950s: WIDENING HORIZONS

A garden party had helped to raise the money for a television which was presented to the school by the parents in 1953 but it broke down on Coronation Day! A tree was planted to commemorate the Coronation.

Wonderful parties were given for the boys on Bonfire Night. There was also a thriving Cub Pack led by Miss Fleming. The Deputy Head was Miss Phyllis Jones who was unfortunately later killed in a car crash. The staff sometimes used to sleep out in a summerhouse in the grounds. I remember we had some great fun!

A Children's Helper at Haseley Hall adds her poignant memories:

Mrs. Gwen Fell, Children's Helper Haseley Hall 1936-40 and 1953-74, Beausale, Warwickshire

I had worked at Haseley Hall from 1936 to '40 as a young girl when I went to help with the children who suffered from rheumatic heart diseases. I lived in the Hall and met my husband while I was there. We married at Hatton as my husband came from there and I left the Home. When my daughter was at school I was asked to help out at Haseley Hall for a few days—and stayed there 21 years! I had worked with children before and had done First Aid with the British Red Cross in the war.

Sister Fisher and some of the boys in the new paddling pool at Haseley Hall, 1955. (M. Bullock)

I helped with the children and took my turn in cooking too. Sometimes I took boys to Birmingham for medical check-ups, going by taxi and train or on the bus. We went to various hospitals—the Children's Hospital, Selly Oak (we had one or two twisted spine cases at the school), the General, Dudley Road Hospital, the Clinic and Chest Clinic in Great Charles Street.

Each evening boys had a bath—we had three baths—you put one boy in to soak and scrub his knees while you did the others! We always had a big fire on the landing where there was a big carpet and this was where they sat after baths in dressing gowns while we read them a story and they had a hot milky drink. It was very homely.

The boys were given good food: there were even one or two celiac cases needing gluten free diets. They had a good breakfast and we had no trouble getting them to eat as many came from very poor homes.

Many boys were asthmatic and the bronchiectasis cases had elevated beds. Some boys came from broken homes and didn't have a decent wash in the school holidays. I remember one little boy's vest had to be soaked off as they hadn't changed it at home and he had eczema. A few boys looked worn out when they returned after the holidays as they had stayed up late to watch television until it closed down! At the school they were in bed by 7.30pm.

The boys all looked the same at Haseley Hall. All the clothing was provided, from wellingtons to toothbrushes. Each boy was given 5 aertex shirts, 3 pairs of trousers, 3 grey pullovers, 6 pairs of socks, 6 hankies, 3 vests, 3 pairs of pants, 5 pairs of pyjamas, indoor and outdoor shoes (bought new from Englands). They also had navy blue macs, royal blue blazers, caps and ties. Each boy had a pigeon hole with their number on (1 to 40) which was in a cupboard where all the clothes were kept.

The dormitories were very cosy with pretty curtains with cars printed on them. They were called Red Deer (8 beds), Squirrels (6 beds), Wolves (9 beds—the 'cougher-ups'), Rabbits (5 beds), Field Mice (5 beds),

Haseley Hall staff and pupils, October 1955. Back row (left to right): Miss Cotton (children's helper), cleaners Mrs. Andrews, Mrs. Cawthorne and Mrs. Hoyle, Miss Butler-Fleming (Head Teacher), Nurse Fisher, Miss Jones (teacher), Miss Hancock (teacher), Mrs. Fell (children's helper), Mr. Plester (gardener). (M. Gunn)

Foxes (5 beds) and the sick bay was Kangaroos! There was a rest period after lunch where boys lay on their beds in special red sleeping blankets we had made up into bags.

Miss Butler-Fleming, the Headmistress, was very particular that the boys didn't get cold but we always took the boys down the field to play for an hour in the afternoons if it was fine. Sometimes we went by the big oak tree at the back which had a big round seat on it. There was also a summerhouse, called Martineau Cottage, which the Martineau family donated to the school. Beatrice Martineau was a member of Birmingham's Special Schools Committee. Sometimes there were outings to the Martineau's home near Knowle or to Coughton Court where we had a tea party. I also took craft school in the afternoons. The boys knitted toys and loved it!

Miss Fleming was a lovely person. She was like a mother hen with her chicks to the boys and it was a very happy school. Dr. Kemp used to visit the school once a month to inspect the boys. He always played Father Christmas at the Christmas parties until he retired. My husband did it once after his retirement—the parties were lovely!

Miss Fleming really was marvellous with the boys—her death was so sad. She often flew off for a holiday abroad with her friend (a Headmistress on the Isle of Wight) and strangely enough didn't really want to go on her final holiday just after her retirement. I received a letter from her two days after she left—but she had died by then in an aircrash. I still have the letter …

One of Haseley Hall's pupils recalls his schooldays:

Mr. David Gartside (known as **Horne**), Haseley Hall 1957-60, Rednal, Birmingham

The first time I went to Haseley Hall I was homesick. This didn't last long as I remember because you were soon made to feel at home.

Being in the country, nature walks and occasionally going on the farm next door were things I liked, plus the big open spaces, the smells of spring and autumn; playing Cowboys and Indians and collecting conkers; sports days with parents watching. I enjoyed walks across the fields and into the big wood; being in the cubs—Miss Fleming was the leader (it also meant staying up late!); visiting Mr. Plester (the gardener) in his greenhouse as he taught me how to grow tomatoes. Bonfire night was held halfway down the drive and nearby was a very large unspoilt area where we could play. I remember stories around the log fire at the top end of the hall; seeing a very large Christmas tree decorated and standing by the side of the staircase—it almost reached the top; listening to pigeons cooing in the summer evenings when trying to go to sleep (when it was still bright day-light).

I disliked being caged in dormitories (I now understand the reason was to prevent sleep walking); emptying chamber pots; being made to eat stewed celery. Any swearing resulted in your mouth being washed out with carbolic soap. Toilets had half-doors so that Miss could 'see' before you flushed it.

In general I thoroughly enjoyed it: when I think back I get a warm feeling about the place (not many people lived in a mansion!). I went on to Hunter's Hill for two terms. It was quite a shock comparing the two schools. There were many more children and it was set out like an army barracks. I have no happy memories at all of Hunter's Hill.

Another pupil recalls that Haseley Hall had a profound effect on him:

Mr. John Moore, Haseley Hall 1957-9, Reading, Berkshire

As I looked apprehensively through the window, I wondered what turns my life would take as a single-decked Birmingham Corporation bus wound its way through suburbs shrouded in snow and into a white and silent countryside towards Haseley Hall.

My memories of the place are joyful on the whole, although I do not know how much middle age causes the imagination to eulogise memories of ordinary childhood happiness. Perhaps it is because, like common sense, happiness is not so commonly found.

Echoes from this period have reoccurred throughout my life. Pictures were important. Sentimental and whimsical Edwardian images of animals hung from dormitory walls to provide a kind of gentle reassurance. A favourite Saturday afternoon haunt for me in later school years was the Birmingham Art Gallery. There, two particular pre-Raphaelite paintings reminded me of the intensity of emotions Haseley Hall provoked. The first was a sad picture of a young couple leaving for Australia by Ford Madox Brown. The other showed a young, contemplative woman in a garden by John Byram Liston entitled 'Boer War'. At the bottom was an inscription by Christina Rossetti: 'Last summer green things were greener, brambles fewer, the blue sky bluer'. The picture laments the unending Boer war. The melancholy it provokes for me was different. Sadness for the loss of something valued and gone forever. Gratitude for the attitudes it had inspired.

The summers at Haseley Hall were glorious. The colours vibrant. Like thick daubs of paint on canvas. The sounds wonderful. Birdsong. Doves hidden in conifers cooing gently and their sound carried with the fragrance of evergreen by warm airs through open dormitory windows. Boys were obliged to rest for one hour after lunch. Those restive hours were agonisingly long.

Incidental experiences still trigger memories that flash through my mind and awaken sleeping senses. The smell of warm cows milk and farm yard manure. The sight of cowslip and primrose and other wild flowers at the field's edge. Hedgerows secreting birds' nests. Prayers. Brown bread sweetened with marmalade. The sound of leather stretching as 40 boys in new shoes march in line to church along the Sunday pavement. Raindrops suspended from spiders' webs. The haughty indifference of posh girls from neighbouring Wroxall Abbey School. Sunday picnics on the lawn and the summer house and paddling pool. Images as vibrant and free as August.

For me, Thomas Hardy's 'Darkling Thrush' will always be perched on the gate to the woods at Haseley Hall. Walter de la Mare's 'Listeners' are there too. These visions are the inspiration for impromptu bedtime stories for my daughters. Always about animals and woods and supernatural presences. But is this all Haseley Hall imparted to its boys? Sentimental recollections?

The function of Haseley Hall was health care. Academic excellence was not sought or expected. Nevertheless, the initial pain I experienced as a young, immature child from the inner city, separated from family and friends, was enough to sharpen my senses and precipitate thinking. This pain was captured for me in Ford Madox Brown's picture 'The Last of England' showing a couple sad at leaving behind forever everything they had known.

Home sickness. The anguish of leaving my mother was particularly sharp, like a hot scalpel lodged and unmoveable at the back of my throat. The pain was made worse by the fear of losing control. It was so unseemly for any boy to show signs of emotional weakness. And I knew how long it would remain there. Two weeks. Mysteriously, it always went after two weeks and then Haseley Hall, in all its richness, could be enjoyed.

Winters were just as vivid. I still remember looking from my desk to see snow flakes furiously flying past the huge gabled window. The classroom was noisy. But this turbulence was so silent and the trees and lawns so white.

I made many friends at Haseley Hall. The teachers, mostly women, were, on the whole considerate and kind to us. Miss Jones was Welsh and very special.

In my final year at Haseley Hall, I befriended the school nurse. She had lived in India. I really liked her and our special friendship was common knowledge. One night there was a crash and the sound of someone groaning. There was a strict rule not to leave our beds and I didn't. One of the boys said he could hear the nurse calling my name. I couldn't hear anything and I was too afraid to climb over the dormitory fence to find out what had happened. He did. An ambulance arrived. The nurse had fallen down a small flight of stairs. I think she had broken her arm and possibly some ribs. Whatever respect I had managed to earn was instantly lost after this incident and the taunts naturally and deservedly followed. I don't remember seeing my friend ever again. Nor do I remember much else about Haseley Hall from this time on. I left, went back to primary school in Small Heath and when I was about seventeen and a factory apprentice went back to visit the place. Miss Fleming was still there as Headmistress.

I went to visit Haseley Hall again some time later in my late twenties. The place was boarded up and its air of neglect was a poignant antithesis to my vibrant memories and to everything it had offered me. In place of Japonica by the entrance door was the rusting remains of a car. Nevertheless, I think part of me will always remain at Haseley Hall because something of Haseley Hall went into the making of me.

Skilts

Skilts had been a country estate, part of the 16th-century manor of Studley, and its opening days in 1958 as an open-air school are recalled by the Deputy Head Teacher who had previously taught at Haseley Hall:

Mrs. Mabel Bullock (née **Hancock**), Deputy Head Teacher Skilts 1958-63, Hatton, Warwickshire

Skilts was owned by Birmingham Corporation and should have opened in September 1958 but was delayed until 5 November as the building wasn't ready. It was a converted house and was the only co-educational residential school in Birmingham. It was officially opened later on by Sir Edward Boyle, the Birmingham MP who was the Education Officer for Special Education. We celebrated the first day of the school with a Bonfire!

A total of 45 boys and girls were sent to Skilts between the ages of 5 to 11. Children were grouped by age into three classes: 5 to 7, 7 to 9 and 9 to 11, although there weren't many of the latter. We followed a normal curriculum as far as possible but the atmosphere was more free and easy than Haseley. It was a very homely place and we tried to run the school like normal schools—we even had a daily register. We often went off for walks if the weather was nice, especially at weekends. Most of the staff lived on the premises, although when Sister James retired we had a nurse who came in daily from Alcester.

I had a nice room in the tower at the top of the house—a bed-sitting room—and the Head, Mr. Ivor Mitchell and his wife who was the secretary, had a flat. The two childcare helpers, Miss Ashfield and Miss Fryers, lived on the same floor as the children. There were two other teachers, Miss Evans (who took the older children) and Miss Helen Furback (who taught the little ones). Sister James lived in with her dog Bruce until she retired. I sometimes went to some of the children's homes with Sister and we were always welcomed—many parents made a special effort when we visited. We also had a daily childcare helper, cook and assistant cook as well as domestic staff.

All clothes were provided for the children. At weekends they wore dungarees and anoraks. It was my job to fit them up with shoes—I learned how to measure their feet for shoes, wellingtons and slippers. They had three good meals a day in the beautiful dining room. Most children were happy although one or two did run away but they didn't do it more than once. The drive was half a mile long down to the road where you could catch a bus to Birmingham. We were surrounded by fields and footpaths—children often walked in fields among the cows. We kept guinea pigs, and a chinchilla in a fireplace!

Many of the children had asthma and bad eczema, and others had chest problems or had some behavioural or social problem. We had a remedial gymnast, Mr. Collins, who visited us, as well as a speech therapist and regular visits from Dr. Kemp. We had to learn the postural exercises to help the children.

The classrooms had some lovely wooden panelling and my room had a French window which was usually open. I always liked to have my children facing me formally, rather than in groups. We did a lot of papier-mâché work, making masks.

We had no Father Christmas at Skilts but we always made something special for the children. One year a train filled with presents, other years a large cracker which split open and a giant snowman filled with surprises. The children had lots of super outings, were taken to church and generally had more freedom at Skilts than at Haseley.

Skilts, 1958. Good use was made of the French windows in the beautiful panelled classroom decorated with papier mache masks. The boxes on the desks were used to store pens and pencils. (M. Bullock)

By the end of the 1950s era Birmingham's six open-air schools were still fulfilling an important function. Malnutrition was now quite rare although overcrowded city homes still caused many health problems, including those of a respiratory nature. 'Delicate' pupils were still listed among the categories of children requiring special educational treatment when the *1959 Handicapped Pupils and Special Schools Regulations* were published.

Lack of regular attendance at ordinary schools often caused 'educational backwardness' and it was reported that some children showing signs of psychosomatic disorders were now often being sent to Birmingham's open-air schools. Waiting lists for admission continued to be long as doctors, hospitals and welfare officials recommended 'delicate' and 'difficult' children to these special schools now functioning under the title of Schools for Delicate Children.

Chapter 8

The 1960s and Beyond: Winds of Change

The decline of many diseases such as rickets, diphtheria, scarlet fever, rheumatic hearts and tuberculosis gave prominence to other conditions affecting children's health, especially emotional and behavioural problems. Birmingham had been the first education authority to open a Child Guidance Clinic in 1932.

In 1960 only 11 children had died of tuberculosis, compared with 4,421 in 1908. The disease had almost been eliminated by the use of x-rays, pasteurisation of milk and modern medicine. By 1971 there were only 4 reported child deaths from tuberculosis, although strains resistant to drugs have since developed.

Despite improvements in modern housing, cleanliness and nutrition the Chief Medical Officer of the Ministry of Education reported in 1960 that 62,000 schoolchildren suffered from lung diseases. It was noted that smoking had become popular with school pupils and that asthma and bronchitis formed the largest category of children's ailments at open-air schools.

A report in the *British Medical Journal* by J. Morrison Smith in 1961 revealed that 1.8 per cent of 10 year olds in Birmingham had missed some schooling because of asthma. In America a study of two schools had recorded some 2 per cent to be asthmatic which proved that the problem was not confined to this country.

Most schoolchildren in Britain were in good health by 1960, with a much improved physique. School milk and free school dinners were being provided, indicating that although malnutrition was no longer a great problem, there was still a need for careful nutrition. Not only were children taller and heavier than their predecessors but they matured earlier and suffered less from infectious maladies. School health clinics had played a major part in detecting health problems at an early stage. The advance of medical science and public health had also contributed to the demise of many diseases. Dirt and poverty had previously caused many disorders such as ringworm, scabies, impetigo and bodylice.

One of the perennial problems of School Medical Officers had been to estimate nutrition needed for healthy development. Although many children were always thin a few were now becoming obese. Good food was considerd to be the basis of good health and was one of the corner stones of the philosophy of open-air schools.

From the beginning, breakfast had been given to all pupils at Birmingham's two open-air day schools, Uffculme and Marsh Hill. In 1960 Birmingham Education Committee experimented with a selective scheme, whereby only needy children received this meal. At the same time, rest after the mid-day meal was modified in a similar manner, with the co-operation and advice of school nurses and teachers.

Demands for places at Birmingham's open-air schools were still pouring in as it was now recognised that children suffering from disabilities other than asthma and bronchitis could improve in such sheltered environments. The small classes were of prime importance to children suffering from such disabilities as 'mild maladjustment', social problems and environmental difficulties. Emotional tangles were frequently unravelled at open-air schools, and symptoms of psychosomatic origin were often eliminated by caring staff who had developed expertise over the years. Birmingham's School Medical Officer paid tribute to the dedication of the team of school nurses and teachers whose knowledge and observation of children had contributed so much to the health and happiness of the pupils in their care.

Dr. P.R. Kemp, Birmingham's Assistant Senior School Medical Officer in 1962, went so far as to say in the annual report: 'It is difficult to know how we could face the manifold paediatric and social problems with which we have to deal if there were no such schools ... Ill health is not a matter of body alone; it involves mind and spirit also ...'. He went on to report that all of Birmingham's open-air schools were producing encouraging results with such children, although there were a few failures when parents removed homesick children too soon from residential schools. Waiting lists were so long that the places were soon taken up, a testimony to the continued value of open-air schools.

The Ministry of Education's annual reports by the Chief Medical Officer ceased to mention open-air schools after 1960, but gave prominence to the problem of asthma that year, as so many schoolchildren in Britain were prevented from living normal lives: 'the asthmatic child lives under a cloud which envelops not only the victim but also his parents ...'.

Asthma, it was reported, was sometimes linked with bronchitis, being an allergic disorder which sometimes involved psychological factors. Emotional disturbances, broken homes and climatic variations all contributed to the disease. Many doctors recommended residential open-air schools in order to remove the over-anxious, over-protective parents but some children did not thrive away from home. At open-air schools children were taught breathing exercises to enable them to control attacks. Common drugs used at the time included Adrenaline, Isoprenaline and Aminophyline. Steroids were still at the experimental stage but inhalers were beginning to be used.

Although asthmatic children sometimes could cope with ordinary schools, if teachers were sympathetic, it was suggested that primary school children would thrive better in the smaller classes at open-air schools where they were less likely to 'become retarded' in school work. By the age of 11 all asthmatic children were more able to cope with ordinary schools.

Since some asthmatics seemed to require drastic changes in climate or environment, the Ministry of Education allowed local education authorities to send children abroad for treatment. The Chest and Heart Association sent several children to Switzerland in 1962/3.

By the end of the 1960s the number of asthmatic children was increasing and about 150,000 children were affected in Britain. The role of the dust mite began to be suspected as one of the allergic causes but the link with atmospheric pollution was not suggested until much later. (In 1994 Dr. K. Calman, the government's Chief Medical Officer, wrote in his annual report that half a million children were now suffering from asthma and that there had been a striking increase in the last decade. As many as one in seven children [15 per cent] were affected with wheeziness.)

Birmingham sent many children to Davos in Switzerland where the air had less grass pollens and mould allergens than London, according to a detailed study mentioned in the 1969/70 annual report of the School Health Service. But a further study by J. Morrison Smith in *Public Health 1970* revealed that most asthmatic children improved dramatically when sent away from home to an institution caring for such cases—even if it was not abroad. In an experiment in Birmingham, two groups of asthmatic children were studied when 110 went to Davos and 60 went to Baskerville School in Harborne, Birmingham. Of the group who went to Switzerland, 77 per cent became symptom free during their stay, although only 13.6 per cent of the children maintained their improvement on their return. Of the children sent to Baskerville 66 per cent became symptom free of asthma, which indicated that remarkable improvements were possible without a radical change in climate.

Open-Air Schools, by then often known as Schools for Delicate Children, continued to function throughout the 1960s but by 1971 only 7,000 out of 8 million schoolchildren in Britain attended such schools. In ordinary schools there were greatly improved facilities, with more emphasis on fresh air, exercise and outdoor sports, as well as cookery and nutrition.

The decline in the number of 'delicate' children since the Second World War had led to the integration of pupils with other handicaps (notably 'educational sub normality' and speech disorders) in Day Schools for Delicate Children. By 1961 the Advisory Committee for Special Education had stressed that these schools had a specific function to perform and 'should not be used as centres for incompatible types of handicapped children'. This led to the *National Union of Teachers* survey of *Day Schools for Delicate Children* in 1963, as there was some opposition on educational grounds to this integration of 'educationally subnormal' pupils with 'delicate' children (the latter now mainly suffering from respiratory problems).

In large classes of 20 to 30 pupils in most of these schools, teachers already faced an exacting test in educating children with a wide range of intelligence and attainments, some pupils suffering from emotional/personal problems and other handicaps which affected their learning abilities. Some Head Teachers were totally opposed to the admission of 'maladjusted' children into these day-schools, although a large number of schools did welcome the opportunity to widen the scope of their work. Generally speaking, schools which welcomed the integration of 'maladjusted' children had generous staffing, smaller classes and good facilities for this type of education. In some schools, many large classes were burdened with 'misfits, chronic irregular attenders and environmental cases so that their function becomes more custodial than educational' stated the National Union of Teachers.

The survey reported a surprising variety of standards and practices:

—not all schools had a nurse or visiting speech therapist.
—rest periods were still applicable in most schools, although not for all pupils.
—there was a great variation in the provision of meals; some still providing breakfast and tea as well as the midday lunch.
—some schools were admitting 'physically handicapped' pupils as there was a marked decrease in conditions such as debility and malnutrition.
—many schools were still termed 'Open-Air Schools' although they were undertaking social and educational work within a wide range of disabilities.
—many schools agreed that 'maladjusted' children thrived in these schools because of the family attitude and small classes. The types of 'maladjusted' children likely to benefit from the open-air school environment were listed as: excessively nervous; anxious; unhappy children with a poor family background; children with physical disabilities caused by emotional disturbance.
—many teachers opposed the integration of 'maladjusted' children because class sizes were still too large to be manageable; such children caused disciplinary problems and a general lowering of standards was the result.

Many of the Head Teachers' comments in the survey reflected the success of open-air schools:

'... open-air way of life benefits and restores to health the hard core of delicates, the bronchial, the asthmatic and the emotionally, intellectually and physically unstable.'

'... there is still a real need for open-air schools in the field of Special Education ... I do not agree with the present policy of closing or greatly reducing numbers in open-air schools. A child has greater security in a small school with more individual attention.'

Most of the Head Teachers favoured the development of open-air schools to meet the needs of 'delicate/nervous' children and those affected by the stress of modern life. Industrial areas in particular were highlighted as producing a large group of children with respiratory weaknesses as well as social/emotional problems. The survey made clear that many of the schools were struggling to cope with 30 pupils in a class. All other types of Special Schools had a maximum of 20 pupils per class.

The overall impression of the report reflected that teachers realised the days of the traditional open-air school were numbered because of the change in social conditions, improved medical care and better nutrition. However, it was felt there would always be some children suffering from asthma/respiratory ailments, as well as social problems. It had become apparent that much of the work carried out in open-air schools restored confidence as much as good health to pupils.

The end of an era was marked in 1974 when the School Health Service was amalgamated into the National Health Service. No longer were education authorities responsible for the service which had originated in 1907. Provision of a school treatment service, with the emphasis on prevention and detection of ill-health in children, was considered no longer necessary as medical facilities had become freely available to all children under the National Health Service. The main aim of the reorganised service was to establish a comprehensive range of integrated health services for children.

Since 1946, with the introduction of the National Health Service Act, a dual system of health care had existed for schoolchildren and gradually became illogical. There was emphasis on the fact that the foundations of physical and mental health are laid in the first five years of life in pre-school care. There was less reliance on regular examination of schoolchildren although many argued that School Doctors had developed special skills and knowledge which General Practitioners lacked. The School Health Service has since developed within the National Health Service, as part of a complex system under the Health Authority, with the provision of Special Needs being arranged by Education Authorities.

'Special Educational Needs' is a relatively new term which arose from *The Warnock Report* (1978) and the subsequent Education Acts. Education and Health authorities work closely with each other to assess children with Special Needs, but there is now more emphasis on the integration, rather than segregation, of children with learning difficulties and special needs. Different strategies are used to enable pupils to overcome their problems, rather than educating them in special schools.

'Delicate' children are no longer one of the categories of pupils requiring special educational and medical treatment, as specified in the 1944 Education Act. One aim of the 1993 Education Act was that most children with Special Educational Needs (SEN) would be in mainstream education and that all pupils would be entitled to the greatest possible access to a broad and balanced curriculum.

Preventative medicine caused continuing improvement in the health of children, with effective vaccination against many diseases. Social conditions had improved greatly since the turn of the century, as had standards of nutrition and hygiene. The expectation of life at birth for a boy in 1910 was 48 years; by 1971 it had increased to 69 years (Registrar General 1973). Health education is now an important and integral part of the school curriculum, with topics including smoking, drugs, sex, alcohol and exercise.

By 1986 Birmingham's open air schools had ceased to exist officially, having either closed or gradually become specialists in educating children with emotional/psychological problems and learning difficulties—the latter formerly categorised as 'educationally subnormal' until 1966. These children often had underlying physical defects or chronic ill health. Many of the children are now socially rather than physically 'delicate', and unable to cope in large schools. They benefit from the small units and by being members of a caring community in Special Schools.

Only half a century after the launch of open-air schools there was no need for such institutions, as social revolutions had eliminated the conditions for which they had been designed. There are many people who look back with nostalgia and affection at these schools and some who believe that there is still a need for such places, especially in view of the fact that asthma is on the increase in today's polluted atmosphere. In fact, there is now one residential school in Britain which is specifically geared to the needs of children suffering from severe asthma and eczema. This is Pilgrims School for secondary school children, run by The Invalid Children's Aid Nationwide. Situated in the bracing air of the East Sussex coast, the pollen-free breezes from the Atlantic contribute to the pupils' recovery. Most children have suffered for years on a dismal cycle of frequent hospitalisation, school failure and isolation, using steroids with all their side-effects. Physical education and outdoor activities are emphasised as well as educational studies, with medical staff on the premises—in many ways following the role model of successful open-air schools.

Three of Birmingham's original open-air schools continue as schools for children with Special Needs—Uffculme, Hunter's Hill and Skilts. Many pupils continue to have physical as well as emotional or behavioural problems. Cropwood amalgamated with Hunter's Hill in 1980, while Haseley Hall and Marsh Hill closed down in 1966 and 1974, victims of the different social climate.

The pioneers of Birmingham's open-air school education would be pleased to know that these schools and their beautiful surroundings are still utilised for the benefit of the rising generation of future citizens.

Uffculme

The official report on Uffculme Open-Air School by the Inspectorate in November 1960 proved to be a watershed in the history of the school when it was suggested that breakfasts and the rest period after lunch could be confined to the children who really needed it. This was rapidly implemented with a radical change of routine at the beginning of the next term in January 1961. Before this change took place, the daily routines of Uffculme were noted by an experienced and qualified teacher who completed three weeks' teaching practice at the school in June 1960, while attending a course on handicapped children. He was teacher of remedial reading and later worked in a Child Guidance Clinic. From his professional notes and observations he recalls his experience:

Mr. John Jones, teacher, Uffculme 13-30 June 1960, Dudley, West Midlands

I was very impressed by the standard of food and the cleanliness of rooms and surroundings. The team work of teaching staff, medical staff, kitchen and dining room staff was excellent and most caring. The most difficult part I found was the rest period between end of dinner and commencement of afternoon school.

I taught mainly in one class consisting of 25 children. There were 16 boys and 9 girls, but frequently only 16 to 21 children were present. Their ages ranged from 10 to 11½, with reading ages from 5 to 12 years. Seven received physiotherapy (for breathing, postural and flat feet), two attended a Child Guidance Clinic or Remedial Reading Centre and one received speech therapy.

My first introduction to the school was the breakfast period which lasted 30 to 40 minutes. I was agreeably surprised at this happy informal atmosphere which made the meal a very sociable and pleasant affair. The children certainly enjoyed their meal as was evident by the very small amount of waste. The children sat in groups of eight, with a senior boy and girl at the end of each table, creating a family atmosphere. The staff remained in the background as much as possible.

Dinner was much the same as breakfast except that staff were absent, apart from the Headmaster. The nursing sister sat at a table which had children with feeding problems. Towards the end of each course Sister walked around seeing that the children had eaten their meal. Children had the option of having small, medium or large portions.

Grace was sung before and after each meal. The children knew many Graces and on my first day each of the three meals started and finished with a different Grace.

On my second morning during Arithmetic period I had the bottom group of eight, including two brain damaged children. One had the knowledge but had poor control over his hands, and his figures were almost illegible at times.

The after play session was taken up writing to penfriends in Kenya. This was a new venture being due to the Headmaster's son who was at a Training College in Kenya. Many children were nervous and had difficulty in knowing what they wanted to put down although the class teacher had given headings on the board. Many of the others were fluent in writing.

In the afternoon the boys of Class I & II were gardening and weeding, earthing up potatoes and planting seeds. Groups of boys worked under Gardening Captains. After break I started a small remedial reading group.

From the timetable notes made, morning classes were mainly of half an hour duration, afternoon sessions slightly longer, finishing at 3.30. Subjects included bible stories, arithmetic, hygiene, handwork, group reading, geography, music, physical education, history, nature study and English. Below are timetables for two days:

Day 1

9.40-10.10	*The Story of Isaac.*
10.10-10.40	*Arithmetic individual work, division.*
11.00-11.30	*Group reading, taken outside under the trees.*
11.30-12.00	*Music—folk songs.*
1.40- 2.20	*History: The Normans.*
2.20- 2.40	*BBC: The Music of Midsummer Night's Dream.*
2.45- 3.25	*Physical education (including various activities, strengthening games, brain stimulating games, team games such as Tip & Run, Cricket).*

Day 2

9.40-10.00	*The Story of Samuel.*
10.10-10.40	*Practical Arithmetic (including Table Lotto, Time Telling and Table Challenge Game).*
11.00-12.00	*English: Completion of Composition (choices included The Circus, The Happiest Day of My Life, A Day in the Life of a Policeman/Cricketer/ Footballer/Dancer.*
1.40- 2.40	*Making a table decoration in a base made of Plaster of Paris. The base was decorated with such things as stones, twigs, grasses and any other materials found around the school grounds.*
2.45- 3.30	*Remedial reading.*

Geography lessons centred on coal and coalfields while Art and Craft lessons used clay for modelling, cut out shapes for pictures and making a book cover. Making pressed flower collections was introduced into the nature lessons with the recognition of flower specimens from the school grounds.

On one of the afternoon sessions it was noted that so many children went along to the Sister for treatment that only nine were left in the classroom.

The school inspection of November 1961 had disclosed that there were quite a few cases of 'maladjusted' children in the school, although the emphasis was still on asthmatic, bronchial and nervous conditions. Still in the administration of the school was the education of children at Moseley Hall Children's Hospital.

The five classes at Uffculme (mostly 25 to 29 children) had wide age ranges, and with the considerable increase in the number of disturbed children it was recommended that smaller groups were needed in future. The chalet-type classrooms were criticised as being 'impossible to ventilate except by opening the door': presumably the sliding screens were being kept closed permanently, in contradiction to the architect's original plan of open-sided class rooms. Other criticisms were made about the old fashioned outdoor toilets, the airing and drying facilities and the remarkably awkward and heavy kitchen hoist from the dining room—the latter once a feature which had been praised when the school first opened, as kitchen smells were avoided by this method.

The rest-shed (often used for musical and physical activities) was in the process of being improved with new underfloor heating, and new classrooms for woodwork, needlework and housecraft were being equipped at the time of the inspection. Gardening activities were still very much part of the school curriculum, together with the three R's (Reading, Writing and Arithmetic) and plenty of music, movement and art.

Edward Anderson, Headmaster of the school since 1952, was much praised in the report for his devoted service, being a good organiser skilled in handling children and parents. Not only did he teach daily but he was willing to accept new ideas. Although he was nearing retirement his 'energy and single-mindedness' were noted particularly as being 'inspiring without being dominating'. His force of character ensured that most of his pupils remembered him with great clarity long after their schooldays!

All the teachers at Uffculme were considered to be making a good contribution to the school—some were 'particularly keen and successful in their approach and warmth of manner', and all were qualified.

Another important member of staff in the school was Nursing Sister (Mrs. Crosby) who was considered to be very competent, exerting a 'bracing yet benign influence on the children': her account appears in Chapter 7. The medical survey reported that 67 children suffered from respiratory ailments (mostly asthma), 9 from debility and 8 from mild maladjustment associated with specific conditions, 12 from nervous instability, 3 from enuresis, 5 from malnutrition (associated with poor social home conditions) and 13 children had other conditions (e.g. school phobias, mild cerebral palsy, psoriasis, eczema, nephritis, migraine and petit-mal).

Uffculme school log book charts the beginning of the 1960s in a period of social change:

Uffculme log book 1960

10 Feb. *Dr. Cohen, the Schools Medical Officer, visited the school today with the architect. They discussed plans and site for the new toilet arrangements to be added to the Isolation Block (Sick Bay).*

7 Mar. *Miss J.C. McCormick has been appointed as Infant School teacher in charge of Class 5 from today.*

6 July *Class III with Mr. Lawson and Mrs. Hardwick visited Stratford-on-Avon.*

13 July *Class II with Mr. Randall and Miss Harrison visited Worcester.*

6 Sep. *Mr. Carr appointed to school. Miss Burt, a domestic science teacher from Follett Oster School, will attend this school for two days a week as our domestic science teacher. The practical rooms are still not ready for use.*

Uffculme log book 1961

The Staff is as follows:

Headmaster   Mr. E.J. Anderson; Class I Mr. C. Randall; Class II Miss E. Harrison, Deputy Head; Class III Mr. Carr; Class IV Mrs. J. Moore; Class V Miss McCormick;

Hospital Miss Franklin; Nurse Mrs. Crosby; Secretary Mrs. Hardwick.

Owing to recommendations from the HMI's there has been a radical change in the regime. Breakfast and tea are now only given to a few children who are in need of extra meals. Rest period is now only for a few children who are in need of rest. The need for rest and extra meals will be determined by the medical authorities. School will now start at 9.15am instead of 8.45am and finish at 3.45pm.

15 Feb.   Miss Wyllie, the new Inspector of Special Schools, visited the school this morning and stayed to lunch.

18 April   Mrs. Hingley has been appointed to take charge of Class V in place of Miss McCormick [who left 29 March].

26 June   24 Senior boys with Mr. Randall and the Headmaster went to Bognor for the two weeks Holiday School at the Martineau House School. [A visit to Bognor was a regular event mentioned in the log book.]

7 July   The boys returned to Birmingham. They had a very busy and interesting two weeks. All are very happy and healthy.

13 July   The Senior Dental Officer visited the school to examine the teeth of the children. He expressed his pleasure at the state of the children's teeth and the supervision.

17 July   Mr. Brooksbank, Deputy Chief Education Officer, Mr. Chapman, Education Officer for Special Schools, Mr. Bugler, Architect, visited the school to discuss the recommendations of the HMI's in their report. They saw the classrooms and toilets.

19 July   Golden Jubilee 1911-1961. The school celebrated its Golden Jubilee today. Displays of dancing, singing, physical exercises and mime were given. The classrooms were open and the children were at work as on an ordinary day. The theme was 'School at work and play'. The visitors included:

Miss Mabel Hurst, the first Headmistress of Uffculme and the first writer in this log book.
Mr. Paul Cadbury—son of the founder of the school.
Alderman Wood. Past Chairman of the Education Committee and a member of the Special Services Committee.
Councillor Powell—Special Services.
Mr. Chapman. An Education Officer Special Schools.
Miss Wyllie. Inspector of Special Schools.
Miss Ramirez. HMI.
Dr. Miller. Deputy Medical Officer for Birmingham.
Dr. Kemp. Special Schools MO.
Miss E. Hibbert. Headmistress. Uffculme 1922-1950.
Mr. E. Anderson. Headmaster OAS.

[The special leaflet produced for this occasion recorded that the school had become a model for other local authorities. Since 1911 over 5,000 children had passed through Uffculme, and about 85 per cent of pupils were able to return fit and well to their ordinary schools.

Miss Mabel Hurst, the first Headmistress of the school, attended the celebrations, together with another past Headmistress, Miss Ella Hibbert. In addition, one of Miss Hurst's former pupils

Uffculme's 50th anniversary, 1961: Miss Mabel Hurst (seated), the first Headmistress, with Mrs. Ada Newsome (on right) who was one of her pupils in 1915. (A. Newsome)

was present, having been at Uffculme School during the First World War: Mrs. Ada Newsome (née King), whose reminiscences appear in chapter 3.]

18 Dec.   *Very foggy. Children sent home 3.30pm.*

[The fog was noted for the next few days.]

21 Dec.   *Foggy. End of Winter term. School closed.*

Uffculme log book 1962

29 Jan.   *A cold spell, 1 classroom is virtually unheated. Temperature before school 39°F and at the end of the day was 43°. Chief engineer was informed.*

12 Feb.   *Miss Lightowler the HMI visited the school and saw the domestic science group at work with Mrs. Burt. Miss Lightowler also inspected the needlework of the Senior and Junior groups with Miss Harrison and Mrs. Moore.*

5 July   *20 girls and a teacher attended a country dance party at Marsh Hill Open-Air School.*

17 Dec.   *The Vicar of Moseley (Rev. Carpenter) today visited the school and took the morning service. He will officiate on alternate Mondays at the school. This is the first time the Vicar of the Parish has taken a service at this school. Four leavers attended the Leavers Service at St. Martins Church.*

Uffculme log book 1963

14 Jan.   *Still very cold—freezing. The temperature is below zero. All toilets are frozen. The classrooms are near freezing. The time table is amended to suit the circumstances.*

28 Jan.   *Still much snow—some thaw but still very cold. This weather does show how necessary it is to remodel the old 1911 classrooms and toilets. Only the co-operation of the staff outside normal duties has kept the school open.*

6 Feb.   *Councillor Mrs. Fisher—Chairman of the Special Services Sub-Committee—and Miss Wyllie—Inspector of Special Schools—came to lunch and stayed for the afternoon. The numbers of children per class was discussed and also the type of children. The Head considered that owing to the change in type from delicate to maladjusted or disturbed children the number per class should be 20.*

16 Mar.   *Miss Wyllie the Inspector and an architect came with proposed plans for the alteration of the old classrooms.*

[The average stay for pupils at Uffculme was only 15 months. About half of the children were medical cases but Uffculme had also helped many 'disturbed' children with psychological troubles. A report in *Birmingham Evening Despatch*, 27 April 1962 quoted an interview with Headmaster E.J. Anderson:

> Many children are two years behind in their school work when they come here. They have been ill and then convalescent. Our job is to get them to mix with one another, to ease them back, as far as we can, into ordinary life again. The children are all sorts; some the sons or daughters of university parents, others come from the city's back streets.
>
> One of the troubles, particularly with the spastic children, is that their families are over-protective. Their Mums try to shield them from life too much. What we have to do is to teach a child that if he falls over he must pick himself up and try again.
>
> I smacked a boy just like his father would and it surprised the life out of him to be treated just like an ordinary naughty boy. It shook him rigid.]

10 Sep.   *Mrs. Burt, the Domestic Science teacher, with Mrs. Bailey, and 15 girls visited the Danish Exhibition in Cannon Hill Park*

21 Oct.   *Mr. Evans the Handcraft Teacher began school today. This is the first term we have had a practical Handcraft teacher working in the Handcraft Room as specialist.*

Uffculme log book 1964

22 Jan.   *A very foggy day. Children sent home early.*

13 May   *Mr. Randall was absent today. He was attending London University to receive his degree of BA, Psychology.*

31 Aug.   *Mr. Anderson completed his service as Head Teacher and retired. Mr. Carr completed his service to take up appointment as Deputy Head at the Victoria PH* [Physically Handicapped] *School.*

[This brief entry does not record that Edward Anderson had completed a remarkable 35 years service at the school, 12 of them as Headmaster. He died in 1983 at the age of 82 years. His detailed entries in the school log books remain a testimony to his dedication and the development and activities of Uffculme.]

The following reminiscences of past pupils and staff chart the development of change in the curriculum as the open-air element of education declined:

July 1964: Edward Anderson's retirement as Headmaster after 35 years at the school. Front row (left to right): Teachers Mrs. J. Burt, Mrs. S. Bailey, Miss M. Harrison, Mr. E. Anderson, Mrs. M. Hingley, Mrs. J. Moore, Miss N. Franklin (Moseley Hall Hospital teacher); middle row (left to right): Mrs. W. Gossage (Sister's Attendant), Ktichen staff Mrs. Watson, Mrs. Millward, Mrs. Atkins, Mrs. Ferkin, Mrs. Megs, Mrs. G. Hardwick (Secretary), Mrs. K. Crosby (Nurse); back row (left to right): Mr. Jones (gardener), Mr. Swift (caretaker), Teachers Mr. D. Carr, Mr. C. Randall, Mr. W. Evans. (J. Burt)

Mrs. Rowena Johnson (née **Churchill**), Pupil, Uffculme 1957-66, Castle Bromwich, Birmingham

My days at Uffculme started in 1957 following a year at an ordinary infants school when it was decided that I could not continue because of my asthma. There followed nine years at Uffculme during which time I saw many changes.

Those first years included breakfast, lunch and tea. However, in my last years the meals changed to just lunch and a glass of milk at tea time before we left school.

I recall the attitude of some of the pupils at the neighbouring Queensbridge School where each year we went to watch a Christmas pantomime; we were considered to be a little simple because we went to Uffculme. We were at first upset by this but as time went by we learned to accept and ignore this.

In my final years I can remember two new classrooms, a woodwork room and a domestic science room, being built.

Mrs. Joyce Burt, Domestic Science Teacher, Uffculme 1960-5, Moseley, Birmingham

Passing Uffculme School regularly on the way to work in 1960 I noticed an extension being built to the school and it soon became evident it was going to be a Domestic Science Room. I was teaching on the other side of the city at the time and applied for the job of part-time Domestic Science Teacher. I had experience of teaching partially sighted and deaf pupils, and was interested in teaching children with special problems.

THE 1960s AND BEYOND: WINDS OF CHANGE

A woodwork Craft Room was also built and Mr. W. Evans was appointed. Having both taught in normal schools, we brought a breath of fresh air and toughness to the school—at least we thought so.

Previously the children had been coddled and treated with kid gloves as 'delicate children'. However, with improved living conditions many of them were not so frail and needed to be stretched and toughened and were capable of much more than was expected of them. School phobia was also very common. Often the taxis would call for children who were still in bed and the parents unconcerned.

Of course, there were genuine cases who needed the special care; anaemic, bronchitic asthmatics, hole in the heart etc. and these benefited greatly. Plenty of fresh air, good food, rest after lunch and a good broad education.

I took my girls to the Ideal Homes Exhibition and the Cattle Show at Bingley Hall, and to Cooking Demonstrations at the Gas Showrooms in Kings Heath. The girls often entertained a member of the staff to dinner (which they had cooked).

In 1961 it was the 50th Anniversary. We had VIP's and one of the Cadburys and a Garden Party, and my girls produced a wonderful tea; savoury sandwiches, cake, and trifle for the important guests in my room.

In Spring 1965 I took a group of boys and girls to Martineau House for a marvellous 10 day holiday by the sea. A male colleague, Mr. Cassell, also came. We visited HMS Victory at Portsmouth, Arundel Castle, Southampton, Beaulieu, Chichester, and Worthing; we walked over the Sussex Downs, had picnics, swam in the sea, played cricket and indoor games and had sing-songs. It was marvellous.

MARTINEAU HOUSE SEASIDE SCHOOL
BOGNOR REGIS

Mr. Evans and I started a gardening club. Cricket and football were played. So with domestic science, needlework and dressmaking, woodwork and metalwork, gardening and games, and a Nurse to look after them, I think the pupils at Uffculme were very lucky. Sister Crosby and her assistant Mrs. Gossage were both very much loved by the children.

Mr. Anderson was a very good, caring Headmaster and there was a happy atmosphere in the school.

I was sorry to leave—we had such a close relationship with the children and my room was very well equipped.

In 1965 I moved to Braidwood Special School as Head of Department and I think that was the beginning of change to autistic specialisation at Uffculme. They didn't appoint another Domestic Science or Woodwork Teacher. Mr. Evans left at the same time to go to Redditch College of Further Education.

Mr. Bill Evans, Woodwork Teacher, Uffculme 1963-5, Kings Norton, Birmingham

I taught woodwork and pottery for two years, and as the workshop was next to Mrs. Burt we became close colleagues.

By 1963 it was not an open-air school but more of a Special School. In 1965 I can remember teaching a young boy who was classed as autistic—the first I had come across. The classrooms were not now open to the four winds but kept closed except during the good summer days.

The school day was 9.30am to 3.30pm with about 1¼ hours for lunch. In fact, it was a series of short periods with longer than usual breaks. At 9.30 every child was given a hot/cold drink before assembly; this usually took until around 10am. Morning break was around 20 minutes and lunch started at 12noon. The last 30 minutes were also given over to a drink before the children left at 3.30pm. It was a very relaxed timetable. I had the boys for woodwork/pottery, usually all morning or all afternoon.

There were certainly children at Uffculme who needed special care, whether physical or emotional, but a high proportion could have easily been assimilated into a normal school.

Mrs. Julia Kimber (née **Godrich**), Pupil, Uffculme 1959-65, Kelmscott, Western Australia

I started at Uffculme Open-Air School in September 1959. I was in Class III and my teacher was Mr. Carr whom I liked very much.

I eventually moved into Class II with Miss Harrison, a strict but kind teacher. She had a little dog called Hamish, a Scottish or Cairn Terrier, and often brought him to the school with her.

I later progressed to Class I with Mr. Randall. He was a big built man with a booming voice that could turn you to jelly if you got on the wrong side of him, although his bark was worse than his bite.

In my last year at the school a new class was formed—1A—for children who were considered a bit brighter than the average. I was among the dozen children in that class. Not having a proper classroom for this new group we had our lessons at one end of the assembly/dining hall. Mr. Randall was our teacher.

My Headmaster at the time of going to Uffculme was Mr. Anderson. He was strict but fair. He retired and a little party was held for him in the evening to which children were invited and I went along. He was replaced by Mr. Alflatt, a lovely fatherly type of man.

Other teachers I remember during my time there were: Mrs. Moore, who taught Class IV; Mr. Evans, the woodwork teacher; and Mrs. Burt, the domestic science teacher. The nurse at the school was Sister Crosby, who was kind and caring. The school secretary was Mrs. Hardwick.

My favourite subjects were domestic science and English. Domestic science for the older girls was a full day each week. The teacher and I had a mutual dislike of each other, but that didn't spoil my enjoyment of the subject. Every week would see me taking my ingredients to school to make something new. Occasionally, some girls would be allowed to cook lunch and invite a teacher over to share it in the domestic science room. The teacher taught me how to make a lovely Christmas cake. I have made this cake nearly every year since then and it receives many compliments.

The subjects I hated were maths and sport. Although I hated sport I did enjoy country dancing which we had in the gym on occasions with Miss Harrison. This was mainly for the girls, although sometimes the boys had to join in too, which I don't think they were too keen on doing!

When I first went to Uffculme everyone had to have breakfast, lunch and tea there. Eventually this was changed to just lunch although children from poorer families still went for breakfast. We all had a hot drink before going home. At lunch time the monitors of the dining room tables had to go and lay the tables before the other children came in. When the others came in, Grace was said, after which the monitors would fetch the meals from the kitchen staff who would serve them out behind a counter. In later years the monitors put the food on the table in serving containers and served it out to the others.

School food is not remembered fondly. Hard cabbage stalks, fatty meat, lumpy rice pudding, salads with caterpillars in them and concrete pudding (which speaks for itself) are just a few of the unpleasant memories

Mr. Carr's pupils in Class III on Uffculme's field. 1960. (J. Kimber)

of school meals. One sweet most people did enjoy was a crunchy chocolate pudding served with a sweet white sauce.

Another thing that was phased out was the rest period after lunch. Camp beds with a blanket were laid out in the gym hall in inclement weather and outside on the grass in fine weather. Everyone had to go to 'rest' for around half an hour each day. I used to love 'rest' outside, you could feel the warmth of the sun and hear the birds whistling and the trees rustling in the breeze. Eventually 'rest' was only for people who had been ill. If you'd been away for a week, you had to have a week's 'rest' and so on.

To replace this rest period hobby classes were introduced to keep children occupied. After lunch on a Friday there was a record session in the dining hall. That was very popular with the children who brought in their records for the teacher to play.

A daily ritual at the school was Sister Crosby contacting each class in turn to see if anyone needed treatment. If you had cuts, bruises, or felt unwell off you went to see Sister. If anyone was really poorly they were put to bed in the two-roomed ward known as 'isolation'. Sister would settle you down with a hot water bottle to rest until it was time to go home. I also had to go to Sister every day for physiotherapy, known as postural drainage, which I have to do even now. This was to help clear my lungs. There were only two or three of us who had to do physiotherapy of this kind. In addition to this a physiotherapist, Mrs. Parsons, came weekly to the school and took a few children for different exercises to improve their breathing. I was among this group and this was held in the gym.

The onset of the cold weather meant that everyone was issued with a navy blue jumper which they wore over the top of their own clothes during school time.

I remember once when Paul Cadbury visited the school to speak to us. Everyone got a little bar of chocolate at the end of the talk.

I was lucky enough to go on three holidays: we were taken to Martineau House in Bognor Regis for a fortnight. I think it cost around £1.10s 0d for the whole holiday. The first time I went I was about 11 years old. The second time two years later, and the last time I celebrated my fifteenth birthday there with the staff baking me a birthday cake. We slept in dormitories of three to six girls. Each morning before breakfast we went for a walk on the beach. When we came in for breakfast we had a great appetite!

We were taken on several interesting trips: Portsmouth to visit Nelson's flagship the 'Victory'; Chichester Cathedral and many other places including a little village called Bosham where we saw the grave of King Canute's daughter. We used to go for long walks over the South Downs. We each had a packed lunch to carry in a knapsack and many interesting places were pointed out to us, such as Goodwood racecourse, and Beachy Head. In the evenings we would gather in the schoolroom and play records or table tennis. I loved my holidays in Bognor although I was very homesick, coming from a close-knit family.

Time for a bottle of milk: Uffculme's pupils enjoying a school holiday at Martineau House in Bognor Regis, 1962. (J. Kimber)

When the time came for me to leave school an interview was arranged for me as a junior in an office. I duly went for the interview and was told that I'd be notified as to whether I'd got the job. Not having heard anything for a while afterwards I mentioned it to Mr. Alflatt who asked Mrs. Hardwick to find out for me. She later came into the classroom and told me that I'd got the job.

Children used to go to a leavers' service at a local church. There were only about four of us leaving at that time and we all went to the service together. I left school in 1965 and although I was glad to be leaving school and starting work, as soon as I got home I was overcome with emotion and burst into tears.

I was glad to have had the opportunity to go to Uffculme. My illness is permanent and, consequently, going to an open-air school could not cure my problem. However, the fresh air and care I received there certainly helped to build up my strength. One thing that always made me smile was when people on learning that you went to an open-air school used to remark 'What do you do when it rains?'

After Mr. Anderson's retirement the next Head Teacher was Mr. Trevor Alflatt (previously a teacher at Marsh Hill Open-Air School) who worked at Uffculme School from 1964-9. Few and brief entries were made in the log book as the emphasis in the school gradually changed from open-air education for all ages to one specialising in autistic and 'maladjusted' children of primary school age:

Uffculme log book 1964

1 Sep.   School opened for Christmas Term. Mr. T.S. Alflatt took up appointment as Headmaster.

Uffculme log book 1965

4 Jan.   School opened. Mr. Cassells appointed from January 1st.

1 April   Marsh Hill girls invited for a dancing party.

2 July   Marsh Hill visited Uffculme, cricket and dancing teams.

9 July   Mrs. Burt and Mr. Evans left due to closing down of craft rooms.

24 Nov.   Inter cities football match—special schools, Midlands v. London held at Uffculme.

THE 1960s AND BEYOND: WINDS OF CHANGE

9 Dec.   *Dr. Smith, Miss Wyllie, Mr. Baugh, Mr. Mata (architects) visited Uffculme to discuss modification of old classrooms for autistic children.*

Uffculme log book 1966

8 Feb.   *Mrs. Crosby terminates her service at Uffculme.*

10 June   *Moseley Hall Hospital closes for repairs and renovation.*

15 July   *Mr. Randall leaves to take up appointment at Westhill Training College. All children over 11 years of age leave, 15 children leave for work, others allocated to various schools, special and ordinary.*

1 Sep.   *School re-opens as a Primary School for 60 Delicate Children. Special coach transport starts.*

11 Dec.   *Birmingham Autistic Society met at Uffculme.*

Uffculme log book 1967

11 April   *School re-opens for Summer Term. Autistic Unit opens with 8 children.*

11 Oct.   *Visit from Rt. Hon. Geoffrey Lloyd MP in his capacity as President of National Society for Autistic Children.*

Uffculme log book 1968

5 Mar.   *Official opening of Charles Burns Clinic by Mr. Paul Cadbury.*

Uffculme log book 1969

28 Mar.   *Mr. Alflatt terminates appointment as Head Teacher. Mr. D.A.F. Wright appointed Head Teacher.*

4 Sep.   *New Impaired Language Unit opened with six children.*

Uffculme School had pioneered an aspect of special education with the new unit for autistic children, who lack the ability to put together messages received by their senses—ears, eyes and touch. By 1970 it was still the only place in the West Midlands where children with this disability could get education tailored to their needs. Without the school many autistic children were unable to develop but there was provision for only 14 pupils at Uffculme and a long waiting list, reported *Express and Star*, 19 October 1970. The unit was integrated into the rest of the school which by then specialised in the physically handicapped and emotionally disturbed or children who failed to communicate.

The school today has seven acres of attractive grounds, including a school farm, and provides education for 116 nursery and primary children with special needs: autism, Asperger Syndrome, learning behaviour and communication impairment.

There are now 11 classrooms with small numbers of pupils, varying from 6 to 16, and a high staff ratio. Each child has an individual programme of learning targets which includes the National Curriculum. The school aims to develop the children's communication, personal and social skills so that they reach their full potential in life.

Cropwood

Throughout the 1960s Miss Marjory Urquhart remained firmly at the helm as dedicated Head Teacher of Cropwood, while social conditions began to affect the intake of children to the school. She had been in post for eight years, living on the premises in accommodation which had become very out-dated. Her reports to the Governing Body had pleaded constantly for improvements at Cropwood, as the place had remained virtually unchanged since it had first opened in 1922, despite the desperate need for new classrooms, improved living conditions for staff and additional rooms for recreational purposes.

One of the greatest difficulties lay in attracting well-qualified and suitable staff due to inadequate accommodation and salaries, as well as isolation in the countryside and the additional duties required from all personnel. It was especially difficult to recruit resident nurses of the right calibre. During staff shortages the Headmistress often stepped into the breach, taking on extra duties and tremendous responsibility for the children's health. The problem of staffing led to the decision to change to 5-day weekly boarding at Cropwood in 1967.

Miss Urquhart has given us an interesting account of her life at Cropwood in the previous chapter and recalls some of her loyal staff who devoted themselves wholeheartedly to life at the school in the 1960s:

> My deputy Miss Bromage ('Brom' as she was known) was a wonderful asset to Cropwood and greatly loved by the girls. In fact, she organised a 'Cropwood reunion' in 1993 when we were given a lavish tea at her home and entertained by a film of activities at Cropwood. The gathering of past members of staff and pupils felt as though we had never been apart—it was one happy family reunion!
>
> Miss Brooke was my deputy after Miss Bromage and was a wonderful organiser, very artistic and never counted the hours she gave to the girls. A lovely memory is of one Christmas when she painted the dining room windows, twelve in all, representing the Twelve Days of Christmas. She drew her subjects in outline in soap, to prevent the paint running, and proceeded to give us the most beautiful stained glass windows. Walking up the drive with the lights full on it was a wondrous sight! I can see it yet!

Writing in 1970 in a school report, Miss Urquhart disclosed:

My kitchen staff and domestics are excellent workers. They are few in number but form a splendid team. We are also fortunate in our caretaker and his wife. A good cook and a good caretaker are, in my opinion, a top priority for a residential school and Cropwood is fortunate.

My Cook/Housekeeper, Mrs. K. Wood, was resident housemaid in Cropwood when the school opened in 1922. She was then Miss Hexley, aged 18, and her name is listed on the first page of the school log book. She told me one of her first duties was to assist Mrs. Geraldine Cadbury to put ribbon on the girls' hats ready for opening day. Her service has not been continuous over 48 years but her love of Cropwood is lasting. She is as active as ever at Cropwood.

One of Miss Urquhart's pupils who remembers vividly her old Headmistress and still writes to her, recalls her schooldays with affection:

Mrs. Maureen Hughes (née **Brennan**), pupil, Cropwood 1957-65, Sutton Coldfield, W. Midlands

The first day on arrival we had a welcoming speech from Miss Urquhart, part of which was:

'Up until now you have had your parents, doctors and nurses to look after you. I am going to show you how to look after yourselves'. She did and I now proudly regard myself as a very independent person.

Miss Urquhart taught us good table manners. Two of her expressions were:

'No uncooked joints (elbows) on the table' and 'Do not hold your knife like a pencil'.

I remember especially the Tuesday lunch; first course was the best home-made soup I have ever tasted—it had leeks in it. Second course was cold brisket of beef, mashed potato and beetroot. Delicious! Pudding was

a juicy green apple. This was the best meal of the week. Cornish Pasties were usually made for our picnic lunch on our annual school outing. I can taste them now and have never tasted better!

We used to do exercises before breakfast. I remember doing 'aeroplanes' on the grassy banks by the swings at the back of the house.

At first we had afternoon naps then they were stopped. I think we went for walks instead. Some walks I remember were The Lickeys (when we got there we had to run up and down the hills two or three times and we still had the walk home to face!); around Barnt Green Golf Course (always peaceful); The Sandpits (an exciting place); and Tardebigge.

The first class I was in (Miss Bromage's) was held in the Loggia—a beautiful room. At the end of lessons, morning and afternoon, we had a mad scramble as we converted it into a dining room. This, along with the playroom, was where we ate before we had the new dining room built. Whilst doing our lessons the call of the wood pigeons would echo around the trees behind us. I still love to hear that sound.

Miss Bromage's class during a reading lesson outside their classroom at Cropwood, 1960s. (N. Hall)

I have wonderful memories of tobogganing in winter—Hunter's Hill had the best run. I once went down too quickly and landed at the bottom in a stream that resembled cow slurry more than water.

Summer Term had the best weather; long days, playing out after tea, and all the time there was a good book waiting to be finished. I did love swimming; we swam at every opportunity.

Autumn Term was the best term in the school year—so many lovely things happened, most of them simple things but probably the more pleasurable because of that. The first 'event' we enjoyed was blackberry picking. This happened in September about a week into the start of term and the weather was always glorious. All the school, staff and girls, spent all of one day picking the fruit. At the end of the day we would have sticky mouths, purple hands, happy hearts and full stomachs. For about two weeks afterwards the puddings we ate would have as their main ingredient—blackberries. Fresh fruit salad, apple and blackberry pie etc. and every one tasted delicious.

Scrumping could be dangerous in more ways than one. First of all there was climbing the apple trees and the hazard of falling but even more dangerous was the fact that one tree in particular was directly in the line of vision of Miss Urquhart. She could be spotted on the landing of the main house looking out and I swear her eyes bored straight into mine as I sat in that tree.

We celebrated Harvest-time at the Methodist Church and at the end of October came Hallowe'en which meant we could dress up as witches and have a party. The recreation room near Rosemary Cottage would be decorated with pumpkin faces and lanterns.

The main celebration in November was Guy Fawkes Night. It actually began a few weeks before when fallen branches would be gathered by the girls. The heavier work was done by the gardeners, carrying bigger branches and old pieces of furniture to make the bonfire. It was quite big when it was all finished. We had the fun of making the Guy. Came the night and it was wonderful. After tea we gathered in the Lobby, wrapped up against the cold. We would each be given a sparkler and a big piece of home made toffee—it was real teeth breaking stuff and tasted delicious. Making our way towards the orchard would give us our first sight of the bonfire as it began to burn—slowly at first and then into a great mountain of flame. Some parents would come along and organise the lighting of the fireworks. Halfway through the evening there would be baked potatoes to eat, hot chocolate to drink. A great way to finish off the evening.

At about this time our evenings would become quite busy, practising for the Christmas carol service which was held at the end of term. As well as traditional favourites we usually learnt at least one modern carol. The senior girls would also learn choral speaking.

Tuesday night was dancing night—the highlight of the week, not so much because we went to Hunter's Hill and actually danced with boys but because it meant being 'allowed out'. It was like being given a little bit of freedom to mix with different people and this was a welcome change.

With December came the preparations for Christmas. First on the list was the stirring of the pudding. All of us had a turn at swirling around the lovely smelling mixture, making a wish and dropping in old silver threepenny bits. I think that little tradition would stay in a child's mind for ever.

At this time we would go round the village one night and sing carols. The houses we visited were those of the kitchen staff so a good welcome was assured. Mrs. Woods (the cook) always gave us sausage rolls and mince pies. She always had a cheery smile.

All our hard work would come to fruition in the carol concert held in the Methodist church. Our families would come to watch, we would feel both proud and apprehensive but usually everything was 'alright on the night'.

There were two other things connected with Christmas that I loved to do and which to me were just as thrilling as the day itself. One was wrapping presents for the younger children (a certain amount of money was set aside to pay for a present for every girl in the school). This really made me get into the spirit of it all. The other was being allowed to stay up late on the night of the staff Christmas party. A few of us older girls would be paired off to mind the dormitories of the little ones while the staff had their celebrations. I used to love to see the teachers dressed up in their finery—they usually showed us their outfits before they went to their party. They seemed like totally different people.

Then the climax of it all—the Christmas party. It seemed to last all day. Lunch time found us sitting at our dining tables—up would go the serving hatch and there would be a neat row of huge, glistening brown turkeys almost standing to attention with their chests swelled out. The afternoon was the time for present giving, games, a film show and all the things that go towards making a happy day. It was a wonderful way to round off a wonderful term and the celebrations continued when we got home and spent the real Christmas with our families.

The school log book remains an invaluable record of this changing era:

Cropwood log book 1960-2

14 Jan.   *Nine new girls admitted. Staffing position difficult—still only two resident teachers—H.T. and Miss Bromage!*

30 Jan.   *Sister Sheldon (now Mrs. Heathcock) resigned from her nursing appointment. No trained nurse appointed to replace Sister Sheldon. Nursing duties being carried out by Head Teacher.*

1 Feb.   *Lynne W.—chickenpox—removed to Hayley Green Hospital. Susan G.—Infective Hepatitis—isolated.*

12 Feb.   *Evelyn T. now has infective hepatitis and on Dr. Vollam's advice has been removed to Hayley Green Hospital.*

13 Feb.   *First Visiting Day of term. Very cold—several inches of snow had fallen in the night. Parents felt the cold keenly.*

18 Feb.   *Miss N. Bromage promoted Deputy Head.*

22 Feb.   *New girl admitted—Teresa L.—verminous head!*

20 Mar.   *Cynthia M. removed to Hayley Green Hospital with chicken pox—**8th case.***

26 April   School reopened after the Easter Vacation. Staffing position quite inadequate—still only two resident teachers, the Head and one assistant.

6 Sep.   School reopened after Summer Vacation. Teaching staff still under strength.

9 Sep.   Three new Children's Helpers took up duty this week.

24 Sep.   Swimming pool was closed down for the winter. Weather during Sept. has been wet and cold and only the hardiest swimmers have ventured into the pool. Senior Girls will continue their swimming at the Northfield Swimming Baths, once weekly.

26 Sep.   Parents Committee Meeting was held in The Temperance Association Office, Temple Street, Birmingham. This was the first meeting of the session and it was well attended. Two new TV sets were gifted to the school, one being installed in Rosemary Cottage for the benefit of the Senior Girls.

1 Oct.   First Visiting Day of Term. Parents of new girls all very anxious and relieved to find their daughters settling down well to boarding school life.

15 Oct.   Miss Dove, Inspector of Special Schools, visited and later in the day interviewed Miss K. Williams for the post of resident assistant teacher who will be appointed in Jan. '61. Among her many interests Miss Williams is a very enthusiastic Brownie Guider and is training as a Brownie Guider Trainer.

5 Nov.   Guy Fawkes Night was celebrated in traditional fashion with a Bonfire and a set Firework Display arranged by the Parents Committee. Mrs. Smith provided baked potatoes and treacle toffee.
   A new caretaker, Mr. Hatfield, took up duty.

17 Nov.   Dental Treatment by Mr. Linn—fillings.

18 Nov.   Dental treatment by Mr. Linn—extractions. Mr. Linn was assisted by Dr. Shewring and two school nurses. 20 girls and 26 boys were treated.

21 Nov.   The Annual General Meeting of Cropwood parents was held in St Thomas' Street School. There was a record attendance of 157 people. The Head Teacher addressed the meeting and answered many questions. A film of school activities was greatly appreciated.

27 Nov.   Six girls were confirmed at a special Confirmation Service held in the afternoon at the Lickey Church, the Bishop of Aston presiding.

28 Nov.   Terminal review by Dr. Kemp and Dr. Mole. Only five girls were examined with a view to transferring them back to City day schools. It is generally considered inadvisable to transfer children from or to residential Schools in mid-winter.

10 Dec.   A Carol Service, attended by parents and friends, was held in the Methodist Church, Blackwell. This has become an annual occasion and is much appreciated by parents. After the service the Head Teacher talked with many mothers concerning the care of their girls during the Christmas holidays. Advice was eagerly asked and, it is to be hoped, will be acted upon!

14 Dec.   The girls enjoyed a Christmas Dinner of Giblet Soup, Turkey with all the trimmings and Christmas Pudding with Rum Sauce. As usual the Staff waited upon the girls. This was followed by a Party afternoon and Christmas tea. Every girl received a gift (value 7s.6d.) made possible by the generosity of the Parents Committee and their money making efforts on our behalf. The Cook-Housekeeper, Mrs. Smith, was responsible as usual for the rich Christmas Fare provided.

15 Dec.   School closed for the Christmas Vacation. The girls were conveyed by special buses to Benacre Street Clinic where they were met by their parents.

Cropwood log book 1961

10 Jan.   *School reopened. Newly appointed assistant teacher, Miss Williams, took up duty.*

8 June   *Mr. Price formally appointed Caretaker and given permission to move into Lodge.*

8 July   *A group of 15 girls and 15 Hunter's Hill boys attended the annual country dance party held at Marsh Hill Day Open-Air School.*

Cropwood log book 1962

10 Jan.   *School reopened except for Rosemary Cottage girls. This residence suffered extensive frost damage at the beginning of January. Head Teacher had to arrange for all beds and bedding to be 'dried out' at local laundry; all floor-coverings to be lifted etc. House quite unfit for children's return.*

16 Jan.   *Rosemary Girls returned to school.*

1 Feb.   *Sister Simfield took up duty.*

4 Sep.   *Reopened after Summer Vacation. No Housekeeper but Miss Costegne, Cook, doing excellent job of work as Acting Housekeeper—Miss V. Brunsden, Ass. Cook appointed. Two new teachers took up resident posts—Miss Burridge and Miss Sharp.*

30 Sep.   *Sister Simfield left Cropwood to take up an appointment in Florence.*

26 Oct.   *School closed for mid-term holiday until 5th Nov. This is a new arrangement made in an attempt to shorten the Autumn term. It can only be hoped that the girls will return on time and in good physical condition.*

5 Nov.   *School reopened after the mid-term break—several girls did not return!*

24 Nov.   *Visiting Day. Caretaker and family vacated cottage and post at Cropwood. His work is to be covered by a temporary caretaker until an appointment can be made.*

17 Dec.   *The new Caretaker, Mr. Thomas, took up duty.*

Thirty years after leaving Cropwood an 'old girl' and her mother are still in touch with Miss Urquhart and recall with great clarity life at the school in this period:

Mrs. Catherine Musty, Active member of Cropwood's Parents Association 1958-62, Ely, Cambs.

It was a very happy school. All the girls who were there benefited from it. It really did my daughter Jenny a lot of good, as she used to have a lot of attacks of asthma.

Miss Urquhart was a good Headmistress and a very fair one. She had a good staff, all of whom were very friendly; the cook, Mrs. Smith, made lovely meals and the girls were all well fed and taken good care of. I used to enjoy going there.

On visiting days I used to take the few girls who didn't have visitors on a country walk which we all enjoyed. When I used to go on my fortnightly visits I used to help bath the little ones and they loved it as I used to tuck them into bed and kiss them Goodnight and God Bless.

Mrs. Jenny Cangy (née **Musty**), pupil Cropwood 1958-62, Ely, Cambs.

I went to Cropwood aged 11 as I had missed a lot of education due to asthma. One year I managed only seven days in a whole year! It was at this stage that Birmingham Education Authorities Medical Officer decided that I should board at Cropwood.

It was a bright sunny day when I got off the bus in Blackwell with my parents and three other new girls, mid-term.

There were 82 girls at the school and my number was 74. This was to identify all my clothing, shoes etc. Even the white sticky tape on my tooth brush, nail brush and tooth mug bore the number.

We were issued with school clothing after being bathed (my second bath that day!) and having our hair checked for nits! My parents left and took my own clothes with them. One surprising thing I do remember is that my school shoes were not new. My Mum had always ensured we had good footwear so I really noticed being issued with shoes that had been worn before.

The uniform was yellow aertex-type shirt, brown tunic gymslip or skirt, green jumper, brown tie (only worn on Sunday or if you had to go to hospital), grey socks, brown blazer, Mac, beret and lace-up shoes, and a Sunday grey wool coat. We had indoor shoes which were classic Clarks type sandals with rubber soles which squeaked on the polished wooden floors. In the summer we wore gingham dresses with much prettier dresses for Sunday.

I was assessed as being bright so I was in Class 1, the class for older girls. The baby class was Class 3 which was in a dipped courtyard with a huge covered play area.

I slept in Rosemary Cottage, about a mile up the lane. We walked there after supper, crocodile fashion, but went back to the main house in the morning in ones and twos as we were ready. We used to race each other to be the first down to Cropwood in the morning. We were awakened by the shout of 'UP GIRLS' at 7.00am, 8.00am on Sunday, and would wash, dress, strip our beds, race downstairs to shake our mats outside the back door, race back to our dorms, make our beds and rush down to the main school. Once there we were out in the courtyard polishing our shoes, this included the instep which I always considered a waste of time and shoe polish. The teacher on duty would inspect that we had done a proper job.

Our children's helper was Miss Pollentine. She lived at Rosemary Cottage and we loved her dearly. She was small and granny-like but much to our surprise, she got married! Miss Bromage also had her room in Rosemary Cottage. She was the teacher we all wanted to be like. Other teachers I recall: Miss Davis my class teacher; Miss Soar, an elderly lady with white hair and very heavy make-up who taught the baby class; a northern woman who played tennis with Miss Bromage and helped her run the Brownies. Miss Bromage and our Headmistress, Miss Urquhart, are to my memory the two most consistent figures throughout my days at Cropwood.

We all had duties to do every day. We swept and dusted dormitories, cleaned sinks and baths (using pink paste cleaner called Chemico) The most prized duties were the kitchen or the sewing room. The sewing room was popular because it was in the attic, lovely and warm, and the sewing lady would give us chocolate.

Kitchen duties were the most prized even though they were the hardest work. You had to get up half an hour earlier to set up for breakfast. You could fill your own cereal bowl really full. You went to the kitchen after each meal to wash up, so you had less time to play, but this did not matter because you got to eat any spare cakes and had the opportunity to eat the fresh crusts when you were buttering the bread. Sometimes Mrs. Smith, the cook, a huge Geordie woman, would send you up to her bedroom to fetch something for her. Her room was in the attic and was luxurious with a pink satin bedspread and a wonderful aroma. If you were very lucky she would invite you to tea in the 'maids room' where you would get to watch TV, mainly horse racing as Mrs. Smith was a great gambler. She would also tell us secrets about members of staff. Mrs. Smith's assistant cook was Ingrinatta Constantina, known as Bella, an Italian lady.

Whilst on the subject of the kitchen, food comes to mind. Breakfast alternated between cereal and porridge followed by bacon or sausage, and occasionally baked egg. We always had an unlimited amount of bread and butter. Tuesdays was my favourite—for tea we had scotch pancakes with golden syrup. Sunday tea included fancy cakes and tea to drink instead of milk. All our drinks were served in thick white mugs. When we had boiled eggs I hated it because they were always hard boiled. I hated heated pork pies too; the jelly melted and when you cut them open water ran out.

The milk came in churns which we dipped scoops into and transferred into jugs or stainless steel buckets. We also skimmed the cream off for the teachers' coffee. There were no fridges, just a tiled basement larder which always felt cold. Sometimes, in the hot weather, the milk would start to go sour but we still had to drink it. The tea was made in a large boiler in the kitchen. The water was boiled and the tea swirled around in a large muslin bag, the milk was added and the large tea bag was left in until the tea came back to the boil. We then transferred it into teapots via a tap on the bottom of the boiler. The same boiler was used to make the porridge, cook the cabbage and boil the eggs!

One year we went to Martineau Seaside School in Bognor Regis for a week. We had a wonderful time. Some of the children had never seen the sea before.

Every year in Summer Term we went on a day trip to Stratford upon Avon. There were two coaches and we parked in a playground by the river where we had a picnic. After collecting our pocket money we were allowed to go off on our own in groups. I knew Stratford like the back of my hand.

On Tuesdays we went to Hunter's Hill boys school for country dancing. How the romances blossomed! I really don't know how because the boys sat on one side of the hall and we on the other! When the next dance was announced the boys would rush over to pick their partners. When a ladies dance was announced it was a different story; we would sit shyly and, slowly and one at a time, ask our favourite boy to dance. Our precious Miss Bromage was the teacher who escorted us. If we saw her talking to a nice-looking teacher our imaginations would run riot and we would have her married off in no time!

The village kids did not like us and gave us a hard time when we went down to the village post office on Saturdays to spend our pocket money. The boys would throw stones and the girls would call us names.

We had both Brownies and Guides; Second Blackwell, and I became a patrol leader. We attended parades and carried the Union Jack at Remembrance Day services. We entered Guide singing concerts and sang 'A Gypsies Life is Free and Gay Oh Fah Re Ah' with great professionalism and excellent conducting from Miss Urquhart. We were always well placed. I think we were super; after all, we were 'delicate children'. Miss Urquhart had a stroke of genius when she decided to send the patrol leaders to the local Girl Guides which were held in the next village, Barnt Green. This move broke down all the hostility between us and the village girls and they became our friends.

My strongest memories involve the dramas; the time myself and another girl were moving tables in the dining room and accidentally caught the leg around the wire of the school radio, breaking the bakelite case. Kathleen had a very serious heart condition and couldn't be upset, so I was the one to take the blame. I fled to the classroom where I was eventually found by some girls sent by Miss Urquhart. By the time I reached her office I was in fear for my life! A mixture of fear and a feeling of injustice made my blood boil. I did not give Miss Urquhart a chance to tell me off; I flew at her, was very rude to her and said I did not care about her school as I was going to run away. I promptly had the only asthma attack I remember having in term time. From then on it seemed that the relationship between Miss Urquhart and me gained a mutual respect.

Other moments of drama occurred when girls ran away. This usually happened at the beginning of term and was usually new girls. My good friend Jeanette usually went with anyone who wanted to as she knew the way. I don't think she had any desire to run home as I believe it was not a happy one. Towards the end of my years at Cropwood more and more girls seemed to have social, rather than health, problems.

During my time at Cropwood I spent eleven months in hospital with a growth problem of my spine. Miss Urquhart visited me several times, on one occasion bringing me a gift of baby doll pyjamas. She stands out in my memory as always encouraging me and supporting me in what I wished to do. I once wrote an essay expressing my desire to be a nurse. When I was 15 she arranged an interview for me for a place on a pre-nursing course and when I was accepted she persuaded the education doctor to let me leave Cropwood. I remember him saying that if I were his daughter he would not let me nurse, with my history of asthma and back problems. However I left at the end of that term and joined the pre-nursing course and gained the necessary 'O' levels to be accepted for SRN training. I qualified with no health problems and to this day my back has never let me down.

My school days were happy and I don't regret a moment of them and feel privileged to have attended a school like Cropwood.

School log books record that at the beginning of 1963 there were problems with the weather and epidemics:

Cropwood log book 1963

8 Jan.   *School reopened. Severe weather. Snow 3′ deep around school premises—trouble with burst tank at Rosemary Cottage. Very cold in Extension Block—below freezing point although heating full on. Two Dimplex Heaters installed pending improvement of heating system.*

21 Jan.   *Nurse Allison took up duty—now resident. Measles cases are being transferred to isolation hospitals—Hayley Green or Little Bromwich.*

24 April   *Nine new girls admitted. New resident teacher appointed to succeed Miss Sharp—Miss Gordon and Mrs. Jordan took up duty in a part-time temporary capacity.*

12 July   *School closed for Summer Vacation. Miss Williams, Teacher, leaving staff to be married.*

3 Sep.   *School reopened after Summer Vacation. Three new teachers took up duty: Miss Newton, Miss Morris, Miss Barrodale. We are now fully staffed on teaching side. A new Children's Helper also took up duty.*

To many pupils Cropwood was more than just a school. It was a way of life and for some girls it was an escape from unhappy home backgrounds. In the era of Beatlemania one person has very sweet memories of her schooldays:

Mrs. Val Mullen (née **Harman**), pupil, Cropwood 1960-4, Woodgate Valley, Birmingham

We had a very special time at Cropwood, a mixture of security and freedom. For security Miss Urquhart ran the school quite strictly—meals on time, everything tidy and rules that had to be followed. This was good for us as children actually need rules to make them feel secure. In the way of freedom we had wonderful grounds to roam round, there were great big rhododendron bushes in which we made dens. The grounds were wonderful and ideal for children to let their minds, as well as their bodies, run free. Miss Urquhart let us roam within the grounds as much as we liked, as long as we kept to the safety rules.

Once a week the senior girls went dancing at the boys school (Hunters Hill). I remember one night coming back to Rosemary Cottage after dancing. We walked along the path and the word spread down the crocodile that President Kennedy had been killed: we were all so shocked and saddened.

We had many things to occupy our minds, including Girl Guide activities; campfire songs led by Miss Urquhart and Miss Williams, team tasks to test our initiative and camping out on the sports field. Lots of giggles and fun accompanying each activity!

The only sad time I remember was the first night back after a holiday. We all missed our families but by the second night we were back in routine. On returning to school after the holiday we all had to have our hair checked (by Nitty Nora as we lovingly called our school nurse), then it was casting off the civvies (our own clothes) and into our uniforms.

When the new canteen was built we were all excited. The first Christmas afterwards the senior girls painted the windows with Christmassy pictures for the little ones. On my window I painted a picture of a big yellow teddy wearing a bow tie and I was proud as punch.

The winter of 1962 was a nightmare to most people but not to the Cropwood girls. It was the only time in my life that I've been able to walk on the top of the hedges (they were so thick with snow). We walked for miles and went sleighing on Hunter's Hill. We all had wonderful thick snowsuits and trundled around like something from another planet but we had a great time.

Summers were a fun time as well, swimming in the outside pool and diving to the bottom to collect rubber rings; fun for the spirit and really healthy for our lungs! I learnt to swim by having a towel round my

Miss Urquhart, Head Mistress of Cropwood 1953-1970, taking tea with her pupils. (N. Hall)

chest and Miss Urquhart or Miss Bromage pulling me while I practised my strokes.

Sunday tea times Miss Urquhart had her tea with us. On her table was a radio and she played 'pick of the pops'. We all thought this was wonderful—cream cakes for tea and the Beatles and Gerry and the Pacemakers to listen to!

There were many evening activities, one of which was the record club. We all put about a penny a week into the club and a latest record was chosen. We then danced to these records. Screaming Lord Sutch was one of my favourites and I did the shake and twist with my friend Pat and thought I was the 'bees knees'!

Saturday afternoon we had a film show and the first time I fell in love was with Dirk Bogarde in 'The Singer Not the Song'. Church on Sundays was important to us as well: we split into three groups according to our faiths, Catholics, Methodists and Church of England. We wore our Sunday best coats and shoes and looked very smart indeed. All the better for eyeing the boys from Hunter's Hill across the aisle …!

The following poem was written by Val Mullen and sent to her old Headmistress in 1992. Miss Urquhart comments: 'As a description of Cropwood it says it all ...!'

CROPWOOD

We came to you, some chubby girls and some were thin and small,
Some of us were tiny girls and some were very tall.

Some of us had lots of love but our health was far from fair,
Then there were the healthy ones but love was never there.

Naughty girls, funny girls, silly girls and good,
We came to nestle in the arms of a school that's called Cropwood.

Our teachers had a burden to make the routine hum,
They had to teach and train us and also be our Mum.

Miss Urquhart had an iron hand held in a velvet glove,
Yet underneath her strictness, her heart was full of love.

Miss Bromage had the older girls, she read us like a book,
She made us laugh, but kept us calm with a 'certain' knowing look.

Our tums were full, our clothes were warm, we breathed in good fresh air,
We always had clean knickers and Derbec for our hair.

We swam like little fishes and walked the countryside,
We danced at our own record club and camped as a girl guide.

We watched our films and played outside and tried to make a den,
Hunter's Hill on Tuesday night for dancing with the 'men'.

THE 1960s AND BEYOND: WINDS OF CHANGE

Our days were full at Cropwood, our evenings lively too,
We learned to cook and sew and type and even clean a shoe.

We learned to love each other and give a helping hand,
We tended smaller children and felt grown up and grand.

Now we're grown up women, we're mothers and we're wives,
Cropwood is a part of us we carry through our lives.

Over the next three years Cropwood experienced severe staffing difficulties, with several changes of teachers and children's helpers, which made supervision of Rosemary and Cropwood extremely difficult, especially at weekends:

Cropwood log book 1965

15 Feb. *Group of seven Senior Guides with their Company Captain and Lieutenant, Mrs. Farr and Miss Bromage went off on weekend visit to London—residing at Olave House.*

7 April *School closed for Easter Vacation. Resignation of Teachers: Miss Bromage—Deputy Head, Miss Newton—Assistant.*

27 April *School re-opened. Two temporary unqualified teachers appointed. There will be* **no** *Deputy Head in Summer Term. Two old girls have been appointed Children's Helpers and registered as disabled persons.*

1 Sep. *New Deputy Head took up duty, Miss E. Hunt. Two new teachers take up duty, Miss Merrick and Miss Mill. Teaching position: Miss E. Hunt, Miss Barrodale, Miss Merrick, Miss Mills.*

Cropwood log book 1966

5 July *Visit by Dr. Lerrin—Chief School Medical Officer—accompanied by six other School Medical Officers. A reappraisal of the Special Schools Medical Service is underway.*

8-11 July *School Brownie Pack Holiday at the Rosemary Social Centre; Brown Owl, Miss Merrick, in charge, assisted by Miss Harper*

1 Sep. *School re-opened. Teaching Staff Position: Miss Hunt, Deputy Head, Miss Barrodale, Mrs Satchwell, Miss Harper, Miss Edwards. Mrs. Satchwell is now resident and will do extraneous duties one evening per week. Miss Edwards is the newly-appointed full-time D.S. Teacher [Domestic Subjects]—also now resident.*

17 Sep. *First Visiting Day of term. Head Teacher admitted to Q.E. Hospital. Miss Hunt will be Acting Head Teacher in Miss Urquhart's absence.*

6 Dec. *Head Teacher resumes duty.*

Cropwood log book 1967

5 Jan. *School re-opened for Spring Term. Miss Cook assistant teacher took up duty in place of Miss Barrodale. New Deputy Head, Miss A. Brooke, took up duty in place of Miss E. Hunt. Miss Brooke and two Children's Helpers reside in Rosemary Cottage: Miss Cook and Miss Harper in Extension Block: Head Teacher and Domestics in House Block.*

11 Feb. *Assistant Teacher Miss Cook repeatedly states that she finds residential work too exhausting.*

5 April *School re-opened but unfortunately* **not** *Rosemary Block. Miss Harper, unqualified assistant teacher, has returned to College to complete her training as a Domestic Subjects Teacher and our Education*

Authority has been unable to replace her. Two Children's Helpers have also left and so far replacements have not been found. Owing to shortage of responsible night supervisors Rosemary Cottage can't be kept open. A full report on the staffing situation has been sent to the Education Office, stressing the following points:
    a) Trained Nurses have long since opted out of residence.
    b) Teachers are also opting out of the weight of residential duties.
    c) Unmarried reliable child-care staff are almost unobtainable.
    d) Schools must have adequate housing accommodation to attract residential staff in all categories.

24 June   The child-care staff who took up duty this term are not very satisfactory. They are very discontented.

30 June   Two helpers leave. Only one left to carry on to end of term.

19 July   School closed for Summer Vacation. A detailed report was made on the serious shortage of residential staff for reopening in September. Unless two resident teachers and two resident child care staff can be appointed it will be quite impossible to remain open at weekends next term.

5 Sep.   School re-opened with roll of 54. The Education Authority has reluctantly agreed to weekend closure until residential staffing problem is resolved. Parents interviewed on opening morning and written details of new arrangements circulated. Parents and children alike seem pleased about weekend closure. The only resident staff meantime is: Head Teacher, Deputy Head and one Children's Helper.

27 Oct.   Observations over weekend closure: 1) asthma cases aren't so well, in particular Barbara A. She appears to spend her weekends in bed, but recovers quickly on return to school. 2) Girls more contented in knowledge that they return home on Fridays. No absconding this term! 3) Teachers all agree that classwork is much improved—more work is accomplished!

6 Nov.   Regular winter evening activities resumed. Monday: Films, Tuesday: Art and/or Craft, Wednesday: Singing, Thursday: Dancing. As staffing situation is little better weekend closure to continue except in the case of illness.

A Deputy Head Teacher at Cropwood reflects that she often wished she had 'the Urquhart training for organisation and co-operation'. She arrived at the school in 1967 and was soon to become involved in the lives of her pupils:

Miss Adrienne Brooke, Deputy Head Teacher, Cropwood 1967-71, Newtown, Powys, Wales

My memories are mostly happy: full of fun and great leaps in my education and appreciation of people. I arrived at Cropwood having been teacher-in-charge of a Country Pursuits Centre in Mid Wales. I woke in a snow storm on the side of Cader Idris one damp November morn and decided that although I was enjoying my job I could not see myself doing the same job in twenty years time. Then I saw a job with Birmingham but in a country setting so applied and began the New Year in Cropwood.

    I remember warmth, cleanliness, good food and a sense of belonging to something rather special. Everybody from the youngest pupil to the elderly housekeeper 'belonged' and was ready to help where possible.

    There were sad moments—watching little faces almost glued to windows on visiting days, waiting for the parent we knew would never come. I hated those days. It was impossible to divert the misery and tears until the last parent had gone and life returned to normal. Weekly boarding stopped those visiting hours and widened my experiences—I was to take most responsibility for the travelling to and from Birmingham on Monday mornings and Friday afternoons. This was an excellent move for nearly all the girls. Return to full health took a little longer but was longer lasting and more willingly accepted.

    I saw a side of life in Birmingham that I did not know existed, squalor, dirt and misery; dreadful 'homes', leaking roofs, dirty streets, broken windows, rat infested homes and gnawed doors—I developed a

respect for the girls who lived these dual lives. I am sure we all gave more freely of our sympathy and understanding when homes were visited regularly. Just occasionally the 'home' had disappeared almost overnight and then it was a visit to the newly formed social service or back to Cropwood and a weekend 'in loco parentis'.

There were strolls in the forest; badger watching at night, swimming before breakfast, a weekend painting the swimming pool (Birmingham refused but would let us have the paint!).

One memory of Kathy, a pupil who was a true Brum, 'Cor, Miss I'm sick of all these flowers and birds. I'd give anything to see a shop and a lamp post'. Our next outing was a bus trip to Bromsgrove and an hour or so in Woolworths. Perhaps as a country lover I should be glad that some are happiest in the bustle and crowds of town and city. Kathy taught me quite a lot and meeting the wishes of others has taken me on outings and into experiences I would never contemplate for myself: films, concerts, darts and pool nights, Bingo!

We spent many happy evenings in the 'Club' house beside Rosemary Cottage: music, drama, disco, toymaking for sales and presents.

There was formal education too and the satisfaction of finding a pupil reading for pleasure; senior girls leaving to take up a place in secondary schools and hearing of their successes in later years. After Miss Clarke was appointed I was made 'acting head' in her absence during one term in her first year.

Teaching, playing, a DipEd in Birmingham, and relevant experience prepared me for the Headship of a 'Save the Children' school in Kent and setting up of my own 'small' school/centre for difficult girls back in Wales some fifteen years later.

One of Cropwood's pupils has vivid memories of her two years at the school:

Miss Pat Reid, pupil, Cropwood 1966-8, Birmingham

I was in Cropwood with my little sister. My Mum said I was sent there for my nerves and my sister was so small and thin. We went there 25 May 1966, I remember the date because it was my 10th birthday.

When we arrived the Headmistress, Miss Urquhart, said we were not due to arrive until the following Monday. I begged my Mum to take us back for the weekend but she wouldn't as it was too expensive and too far.

At first we were put in a three bed dorm next to the Head's living quarters. We were told there were ghosts in the school and one night I couldn't sleep so got up and looked down the corridor. I saw someone standing at the other end of the corridor—it was quite dark and this person was dressed in white.

I also remember one of the girls had been to see 'Sound of Music' and she came back saying the little girl in the film had died. She slept in the next bed to me and one night she suddenly got out of bed and came towards me with her hands and arms stretched in front of her saying 'you killed her'. I jumped out of bed screaming. I woke the whole school and told the teacher the girl was going to strangle me. No-one believed me and I suffered for years after that. I was so frightened. I wouldn't eat for days but still no-one believed me.

Another time I remember having to go to the dentist and we used to have those horrible gas masks. I kept taking it off so they strapped my legs and arms to the chair and stuffed cotton wool down my throat. Those were the worst things that happened to me!

We were there for two years. I hated it for about the first six months then it was just like being at home. I came from a large family of eleven. We used to have family visits once every two weeks. Church every Sunday was our best clothes day and we used to travel by coach to the church, come back and change into our dungarees.

After a while we used to go home at weekends, then all school holidays. Eventually my Dad got fed up with us going back and forth every week. He stopped us going and I was really upset. In all I think it was a good time. We were like a very large family.

The next three years were to be Miss Urquhart's last at Cropwood, but there was certainly no respite from the problems of a residential school, as the log book records:

Cropwood log book 1968

8 Jan.   School re-opened still on weekly basis as no additional **responsible** resident has been recruited. It is regrettable that no trained Child Care Staff can be found. Posts have been widely advertised in National Press with no response. We haven't the accommodation to offer trained House-Parents. This is very obvious to all concerned with present staffing crisis.

9 Feb.   Present two child care staff are so unreliable that they have been told to look out for other posts. Caretaker Mr. Thomas transferred to another school.

26 Feb.   Two Children's Helpers appointed.

22 April   School re-opened after Easter Vacation. Miss Hudson, assistant teacher, took up duty.

26 April   Our new caretakers, Mr. & Mrs. Mountney, took up duty.

24 May   Miss Hudson sent in her resignation to take effect at summer holidays. She finds it impossible to reconcile her extraneous responsibilities with her personal life.

19 July   School closed for summer vacation. Five day boarding has continued throughout session. A great many advantages are to be gained by five day boarding and heavily outweigh the few disadvantages.

   Mrs. Hartman appointed to take up duty on Sept. 9th, replacing Miss Hudson. No replacement appointed as yet for Miss Brooke, Deputy Head, seconded to a Dip.Ed.Course.

9 Sep.   School re-opened. No Nurse! No teacher for Class 3. Mrs. Hartman to take Class 2. Staffing situation very difficult.

20 Sep.   Arrangements have now been made for Nurse Procter to visit Cropwood one day per week—very inadequate arrangement.

30 Sep.   Mrs.Wightman MA took up duty in Class 3. Miss Brooke began her University Course.

28 Nov.   Miss Brooke in motor bike accident—fractured skull—in Bromsgrove Cottage Hospital. Mrs. Stevens, Secretary, appendectomy.

30 Nov.   Miss Brooke regains consciousness.

13 Dec.   Miss Brooke transferred home from hospital.

20 Dec.   This has been a very difficult term from the staffing position but the past three weeks have been most difficult—no nurse, no deputy, no secretary. However, work went on as usual!

Cropwood log book 1969

13 Jan.   School re-opened. 49 girls present. No nurse yet appointed. Miss Brooke, Deputy Head, sufficiently recovered to resume residence and to continue her University Course.

   Two girls, Linda C. and Kathleen D. absconded at 1.30pm. Police informed.

7 Feb.   Head Teacher appeared before Committee for Special Services to give report on Cropwood. She stressed once again the urgent need for suitable residential accommodation to attract resident child care staff and teachers.

10 Feb.   Mrs. Bowen took up duty two afternoons per week as a Physiotherapist. The post has been vacant 10 months.

13 Feb. *Valentine's Supper Dance held—Senior Girls entertained Hunter's Hill Senior Boys.*

8 July *School Outing to London under the control and direction of Miss E.A.Brooke, Deputy Head Teacher.*

8 Sep. *The Deputy Head, Miss Brooke, has been released from class responsibility and will now have time to do more individual testing and teaching in accordance with methods learned in her Dip.Ed.Course just completed.*

28 Sep. *Two new resident Children's Helpers took up duty.*

10 Dec. *Open Day at school. This was a great disappointment to pupils and staff. In view of the continuing five day week boarding and to the fact that few parents had ever visited the school, it was considered advisable and desirable that we should have an Open Day. Invitations were sent out to all Parents and Friends but only 14 people turned up throughout the day—a most disappointing response.*

18 Dec. *Two Children's Helpers resigned. An experiment in 'family grouping' in class has been carried out this term.*

Cropwood log book 1970

22 Jan. *Visit by the Children's Librarian (Birmingham), Mr.Yates to discuss regular deliveries of Library Books to Cropwood.*

13/14 June *Swimming pool repainted by Head, Deputy Head & School Nurse.*

17 July *Two Children's Helpers have been appointed to take up duty on 7 Sep. Both of these young ladies have just completed a two year course in Preliminary Child Care at the Bromsgrove College of Further Education. Mrs. Pearce to succeed Mrs. Hartman, Assistant teacher.*
Miss M.A. Urquhart, Head Teacher at Cropwood since Jan.1953, retires at 31.8.70.

Miss Urquhart's final school report on Cropwood in 1970 stressed yet again the urgent need for better school facilities and especially improved accommodation for residential staff:

> The present accommodation for Head teacher is by official standards 'sub-standard', in recognition of which they have been paying me in the past year an additional £1 a week. The Governors might be interested to know that as Haseley Hall is also in this category I have been living in sub-standard accommodation for 23 years! By comparison my resident colleagues must be sub-sub-standard ...! The day of the dedicated spinster content to exist in a small bed-sitting room is past ...

Miss Urquhart pointed out that although there was a total resident staff of seven, two child care helpers and two domestic staff were under the age of twenty. This meant that the remaining three dedicated members of staff had to bear the brunt of the burden of responsibility — the Head Teacher, the Deputy and Assistant Teacher. Miss Urquhart noted that if each of them had strictly limited their hours of work to the recommended 15 hours a week allowed for 'extraneous duties', the whole of Cropwood school would have ground to a halt.

All the other staff at Cropwood in 1970 were non-resident: three full time teachers, two part-time teachers, two part-time seamstresses and cook/housekeeper, four part-time domestic assistants and caretakers.

Miss Urquhart commented that the word 'delicate' was now inappropriate to describe many of the current intake of Cropwood's children who were victims of social circumstances. Many pupils had serious reading disabilities and other problems, needing skilled individual remedial help and very few teachers with the required skills and knowledge were attracted to residential work. Miss Brooke, Deputy Head Teacher, had recently qualified on a course for 'teachers of the handicapped' and was guiding the rest of the staff in the recommended methods. Parental interest in the school had declined on Open Days in recent years—perhaps as a result of broken homes and many absent fathers in pupils' families.

It was in the field of child care that the greatest difficulties had arisen at Cropwood, as the nurse was no longer resident. As a result resident teaching staff had the responsibility of administering drugs and caring for sick children overnight (between 5.00pm and 8.30am). Many of the teenage child care helpers had proved unreliable and staffing problems were likely to remain acute, so long as there was no suitable accommodation to attract well-qualified staff.

After completing 17 years at Cropwood, Miss Urquhart, the school's longest serving Head Teacher retired in August 1970, concluding in her report:

> Now I am retiring to a small seaside town in Argyll, where daily I will meet pupils of the first ten years of my teaching career—the shy clever boy who is now the architect who planned my retirement bungalow, the solicitor, the bank manager, the shopkeepers and even the laundry van driver whom I failed to teach to read so many years ago. When I hear them say, as I surely will, 'You're back Miss Urquhart,' then I will know I have arrived.

Since her retirement at the age of 60, after serving Birmingham's Special Schools for a total of 23 years, Miss Urquhart returned to her native Scotland, and wrote from Dunoon in 1994 at the age of 84:

> I still do my own housework, drive and potter in the garden. Apart from some arthritis I am a product of a residential open-air school! I am still in touch with at least eight of my old classmates of Oban High School, who sat their 'Highers' with me and proceeded to further education in a variety of professions. They, like me, are octogenarians, and still enjoying life, having returned to Oban from all parts of the world!

Miss Urquhart's retirement was marked by a special presentation to which were invited Mr. Paul Cadbury and Mr. Kenneth Pilling.

Mr. Kenneth Pilling, 86, Head of Birmingham's Special Schools branch (1947-9) and Deputy Chief Education Officer (1968-73) comments:

> What I think is truly remarkable is that the Cadbury family retained their interest in open-air schools for so long. After the ceremony Mr. Cadbury asked me to accompany him on a nostalgic tour of Cropwood. When we came to the open-air swimming pool which was covered in moss and vegetation he stood in horror and wanted to know what had happened to it. I explained that the Education Committee had been obliged to effect economies and could no longer afford to maintain non-essential services. The following morning he rang me at the office and instructed me to get the pool repaired and cleaned and to send the bill to him—which I did.
>
> Birmingham Education Authority was inundated by visitors from all over the country and the world to see our special schools. They commanded respect and approval for the devotion and dedication of the teaching staff. But one person more than anyone was responsible for the efficiency and high standards—Miss Ross, the Inspector of Special Schools. She was so thorough that no inadequacy in teaching or management escaped her attention. She was respected throughout the country and appointed MBE.

Miss Deirdre Clarke became the last Head Teacher of Cropwood's School for Delicate Girls in September 1970, the title of 'delicate' by then being something of a misnomer. The log book records some of the changes she made in her first months at Cropwood:

Cropwood log book 1970

25 Sep.   *We have agreed to hold a weekly staff meeting to discuss general school matters. The Prefects and the Head held a prefects meeting and it is to be held once a fortnight.*

9 Oct.   *The Senior girls have started going for walks on their own after school between 4-5pm.*

16 Oct.   *We have changed the Library into a Classroom for Class 3, and their classroom is now a Remedial, and Practical Room, with the Library taking up one end of the room. The Playroom is coming more and more into its own, thanks to presents of second-hand dolls, books, games etc and with the carpet and chairs from the library it is becoming a much more friendly, homely room.*

20 Nov.   *This week is the first time that we have all met for meals in the school dining room. The staff dining room has been turned into a sitting room for the senior girls, and a coffee room for all the Domestic staff.*

Cropwood log book 1971

29 Jan.   *This week the senior girls have stopped doing housework before and after breakfast, the sweeping and dusting was upsetting the asthma girls. They still lay and clear the tables and keep the dining room clean.*

A school report by Miss Clarke in 1973 disclosed that an analysis of children at Cropwood showed that 55 per cent were admitted for medical reasons (49 per cent asthma), 30 per cent for general debility and sociological problems, 9 per cent for behavioural or personality difficulties and 12 per cent for other ailments. The girls were frequently transferred from Skilts. Out of a total of seven teachers only one was resident. In addition there was a House Mother, three resident Children's Helpers, a part-time secretary and a day nurse.

Miss Clarke relaxed the rules of Cropwood to help the girls to be more independent. The Head Girl had the privilege of her own room—a luxury for girls from deprived families. A House Mother and Children's Helpers looked after children in the hours after school, creating a homely atmosphere, ready to listen and to comfort. This feeling of security was vital as many children had a sense of failure. The House Mother had to be kind but firm, needing endless patience and understanding. Gradually the school changed in the new decade:

Miss Deirdre Clarke, Head Teacher, Cropwood 1970-9, Fordingbridge, Hampshire

I went to Cropwood as Headmistress in 1970, inheriting the post from Miss Urquhart who was a strict disciplinarian. I had worked in Special Schools, with boys and girls. I did have some training in Special Schools as I had been to Reading University for a year after I'd been teaching for fifteen years, but none of my staff had had any special training. I held many discussion sessions with them which I hoped were helpful.

Many of the girls at Cropwood were really poorly and needed help and encouragement as well as plenty of medical help. During my time there the school gradually changed from a school for delicate children to one for children needing special care. The treatment for asthma and diabetes changed and we received very difficult children instead. This caused a lot of hard work for the staff but was a real challenge.

Cropwood was one of nine special schools in Birmingham covering all sorts of handicaps. Cropwood was always known as a school for delicate children—the name never changed, even though the children did. The nine heads of the schools met twice a term to discuss policies, problems etc and we went to each school in turn. It was very interesting and most helpful; we became great friends.

Cropwood was a weekly boarding school. Children were collected by bus on Monday mornings by two teachers who had to be in Birmingham at 9.00am. While Cropwood was an open-air school there was rest time after lunch, open windows in dormitories and no heavy blankets on the beds. In fact, blankets were not allowed to be pulled up higher than the chest. Bedtimes were early and House Mothers supervised daily dormitory routines.

There was a careful regular diet, each day having its own dish. Twice a day there was surgery for diabetic injections, and asthma patients, held by a non-resident State Registered Nurse. Severe asthma cases were sent to Switzerland for six months, with very good results; their swollen faces became normal again. The doctor visited every week and was on call for emergencies.

In the school children worked hard at their lessons. Once a week they had PE or dancing lessons. The games mistress came one morning a week. Music and singing lessons helped asthmatic children. There were Home Economics lessons for older girls. The Seniors had typing lessons on very old fashioned typewriters but good enough to learn on and to practise typing. The teacher was very strict and set a high standard, giving girls plenty of homework to be done after tea.

English was taught throughout the school and there were several visits to Stratford-on-Avon for older girls studying Shakespeare.

We encouraged joint activities with Hunter's Hill—boys came to us for cookery and girls went there for carpentry. We held joint parties, firework night and Christmas parties and best of all the weekly youth club was the highlight of the week. We had activities in the evening—the sweet shop after tea, television and swimming. I was a keen swimmer and felt it was essential for every girl to learn to swim. On warm mornings we even went in before breakfast!

We had a choir which went to Old People's Homes. Many girls did 'work experience'—not an easy thing to organise but it did help them to find jobs before they left school.

I feel very strongly [about the fact] that these schools no longer exist. The children benefited from being in small groups in class, getting much help and encouragement from teachers. It was a healthy life with good food and plenty of fresh air after lessons.

Cropwood 1970. Head Teacher Miss Deirdre Clarke with prefects Colleen Sewell, Janet Wheedon, Joy Brown, Teresa O'Looney, Carol Hall, Pam Davell, Cathy Withy. (Hunter's Hill School)

In the new term of September 1979 Graham Williams, Head Teacher of Hunter's Hill, became temporary Head of Cropwood. By 1981 Cropwood had become part of Hunter's Hill and it was envisaged that it would remain as a boarding school for girls at the school. Then co-educational, the school catered for 125 pupils—84 boys and 41 girls. Not long afterwards, however, the school ceased to take in girls and Cropwood eventually became the living quarters for the senior boys of Hunter's Hill.

Rosemary Cottage has been sold, severing one more link with the Cadbury family in the history of the school.

Some of the staff of Cropwood were absorbed into Hunter's Hill, including one secretary who has very happy memories:

Mrs. Vashti Layton, Secretary, Cropwood/Hunter's Hill 1973-92, Bromsgrove

I started as school secretary in 1973 and finally retired in January 1992. They were the happiest working years of my life. Cropwood House had something about it that was impossible to explain, perhaps it was because it was a family home before it became a residential school. I worked for six Head Teachers: Miss Clarke, Mr. Williams, Mr. Tombs, Mr. Hosegood, Mr. Hardwick and Mr. Lewis. The pupils resident today are very different to when I first started at Cropwood.

Mrs. Carey was cook housekeeper firstly in Miss Clarke's day: very high standards in cleanliness and caring for children. Hot cocoa when they arrived back on Monday mornings, all home cooked cakes and pies; I can almost taste her bread-pudding—it was as good as many a Christmas pudding.

Cropwood House always reminded me of Charles Dickens' time: old oak fireplaces; Doris Goodby (seamstress) played the piano at staff get-togethers at Christmas time etc; everybody had a stir of the Christmas pudding, marvellous days for the children and I am sure many still carry wonderful memories of Cropwood.

These schools offer wonderful opportunities for the children that attend them. The work that all staff put into them is hardly ever praised; endless patience is needed with the children.

Hunter's Hill

Miss Linda Buckley remained Headmistress of Hunter's Hill for the next decade, having a wealth of experience of residential life as she had been at the school since 1934, a year after it first opened.

A series of annual reports and detailed entries in the log books chart the difficulties of modernising the school as well as coping with many children with social problems.

Miss Buckley reported that 1961 was the first year that 'delicate' pupils had been outnumbered by 'problem children' (school phobias, 'maladjusted', sociological/behavioural difficulties. It was found that 'maladjusted' children (especially those regarded as 'educationally subnormal') required far more individual attention from the staff. The ever-changing staff found the extraneous duties at weekends more of a strain than all their work in the week as many children would not conform to the regular routines which 'delicate' children had readily accepted.

Mr. Leslie Richardson, the Deputy Head, was reported by Miss Buckley to 'be full of enthusiasm and zest for the work, and a great help in the organisation and running of the school'. Other teachers at the school included his wife, Mr. M. Tebbutt (who specialised in woodwork and allied crafts), Miss J. MacDonald, Mr. D. George and Mr. M. Roberts.

After the departure of Sister Marshall, earlier in the year, Nurse Barrett had taken over all her duties and was highly praised by Miss Buckley: 'she has been here since 1937 and is very much in touch with the problem of the delicate child and knows just when additional care is needed and when not to fuss'... The Nurse was helped by two Children's Helpers.

School domestic staff included the new cook/housekeeper Mrs. Braithwaite, three assistant cooks, three kitchen workers, parlour maid, five domestic cleaners, two seamstresses and caretaker Mr. Ross who had been there many years.

The school itself was beginning to show its age: original sun blinds needed repairs, the gas cooker was 28 years old and the library needed more space and equipment. A new paddling pool and sandpit had been completed and a new television set installed, but the planned alterations for improvements in accommodation in the 1950's had never been implemented. Dormitories were overcrowded and toilets and cloakrooms were quite inadequate for the usual number of 100 to 120 boys in residence. The school often failed to attract the right type of teacher and there was a rapid turnover in staff as a result of the poor facilities on site and the onerous duties involving the supervision of children.

The school log book, faithfully kept up-to-date by Linda Buckley, continues to record the minutiae of daily life at Hunter's Hill:

Hunter's Hill log book 1960

14 Jan.   Admitted seven new boys. Thick snow, boys out sledging.

21 Jan.   Mrs. K. Richardson (who has been absent from duties since October—maternity leave) was admitted to Bromsgrove Hospital today.

23 Jan.   Miss Buckley in bed with feverish cold.

26 Jan.   Mrs. Richardson had a daughter at 1am today. School visited by students from Worcs T. College and by Mrs. & Mr. Atkins (Methodist Preacher).

18 Feb.   B.O. & M.P. absconded during playtime.

19 Feb.   B.O. returned (accompanied by Mother) made a scene and wanted to go home—very hysterical—put into isolation.

21 Feb.   M.P. brought back by Probation Officer. R.C. & R.H. absconded, were brought back by boys from village who found them on railway lines.

25 Feb.   Several boys kept in bed because of severe chilblains.

29 Feb.   Dr. Kemp routine examination new boys. Miss Lewis handed in her resignation today. Mrs. Brown (Cook/Housekeeper) also resigned.

5 Mar.   Visiting Day … B.O. taken home by parents, said to be homesick.

9 Mar.   K.S. taken to Accident Hospital has slipped epithesis of the right wrist. D.G. taken away by father who stated it was too cold for any child.

6 May   Holiday for Royal Wedding [Princess Margaret]. TV on all morning.

9 June   To Malvern Hills for the day—rather dull at first but a pleasant day until 6.15 when a very heavy rainstorm descended on us. All boys bathed on return and all clothes changed.

20 July   Boys very excited—Miss Buckley and Nurse Barrett on duty from 11pm to 6am to prevent any unruliness and midnight feasting.

21 July   School closes for holidays—boys left at 9.30 accompanied by all teachers, Sister and Miss Tedd. Arrangements at Benacre St are very poor and need to be revised to ensure that boys whose parents happen to be late are not subjected to undue emotional distress.

6 Sep.   All teaching staff and Sister to town to bring boys back. Miss MacDonald new teacher arrived. Very wet all day. T.H. absconded.

9 Sep.   A.R. to Chest Clinic. J.N. brought back by Mother—absconded again after tea—brought back by Miss Williams. Very truculent, caned and put to bed.

20 Sep.   New school TV installed by Radio Rentals; used for Schools Programmes, very satisfactory though we had wanted a model on a stand for easier viewing by a large group of boys.

3 Dec.   Play—King of The Golden River—given for parents—full house. A very wet cold day but parents enjoyed play which went off very smoothly.

5 Dec.   Dr. Kemp and Dr. Mole Terminal Review. 14 boys seen or discussed. Only 8 discharged. M.M. admitted to Bromsgrove All Saints for T&A operation.

10 Dec.   Very cold. Boys played in snow- six boys to party at Mr. & Mrs. Richardson's.

12 Dec.   Dr. Kemp (routine end of term visit). Christmas Dinner—Turkey and Plum Pudding etc. All Choir Boys to Final Rehearsal at chapel (Carol Service and Play).

13 Dec.   Christmas party—staff and boys had tea together (a great success). Film show—presents; a very nice time.

14 Dec.   Choir boys out at 7pm (to Carol Service and Play) to Chapel. Miss Buckley and Nurse Barrett on duty to 2.30am. All boys quietly sleeping.

Hunter's Hill log book 1961

17 Feb.   Sister Marshall gave in her notice today. No. on roll 120.

18 Mar.   Visiting day. Exhibition of model village made by Class V and with a commentary on Tape recorder by same class.

14 May   Paddling pool filled and opened. Swimming pool for swimmers only. Bowling Club re-started.

13 June   Three boys to Eye Clinic. Miss Buckley and Nurse Barrett took Class III to Birmingham Museum in connection with work on Ancient Britain.

14 June   14 boys in bed with influenza.

22 June   House Outings: Malvern to Dovedale, Clent to Clent Hills and Harvington Hall, Clee to Dudley Zoo, Abberley to Drayton Manor Park. 16 boys unable to go, in bed with influenza. Miss Buckley and Sister Marshall remained at school with them.

27 June   B.K and D.B. to Bromsgrove for glasses. Son born to Mrs. Richardson in All Saints Maternity Ward at 4.30pm.

1 July   Marsh Hill to play cricket. School team won by 45 runs to 27 runs (poor game).

8 July   16 boys to Marsh Hill Country Dance party with Cropwood Girls—Miss MacDonald and Miss Williams accompanied them.

Hunter's Hill log book 1962

1 Mar.   School visited by HMI's Miss Pedley, Mr. Holdsworth, Mr. Machin and Dr. Asher. Dr. Asher very dissatisfied with dormitories, toilets and washing facilities.

1 June   School Outing to Dovedale. A full, interesting day. Saw Well Dressing at Tissington.

5 June   Staff Meeting—discussed the general slackness of teaching staff in respect of their extraneous duties.

11 June   Merry Go Round (Potted Sports)—boys in teams of five doing 20 activities for three minutes. All present staff, many old members of staff and some Old Boys to help.

12 July   Mrs. Hughes, assistant cook, who is retiring presented with Electric Toaster. S.W. has developed German Measles. Tennis Tournament finals (T.Harrison). Golf Tournament Finals (T.Harrison).

19 Oct.   Miss Buckley to Education Office re. appointment of Deputy Head. Mr. Hill (former member of staff) appointed. Four boys absconded after breakfast—reported to police but nothing heard of them until 9pm—all at home.

Hunter's Hill log book 1963

12 Jan.   *19 degrees of frost registered—sledging but bitterly cold. Film show.*

29 Jan.   *Architect called to discuss alterations.*

14 Oct.   *Moved 38 seniors to New Block and rest of school (62) to three senior dormitories, leaving Dorm 1 to be used as a playroom and games room.*

11 Nov. *Junior boys fitted with Duffle Coats and Seniors with Macs for everyday wear.*

13 Nov. *Dennis E. brought back from St Cuthberts, Malvern where he refused to settle, looks very ill and had a long list of daily treatments which Nurse Barrett may find difficult to fit in every day.*

15 Nov. *David H. to Children's Hospital. R.B. to All Saints for Physiotherapy. R.D., T.W. and T.J. absconded. Police notified, found at the home of T.W's grandmother at 9.30pm.*

27 Nov. *At some time between 4.15-4.45 a boy or group of boys set fire to a mattress in Dormitory Three. Sheets and blankets ruined and head boards slightly burnt. All boys closely questioned but culprit not traced.*

28 Nov. *Boys again cross questioned but nothing found out—report sent in to S.S. Have decided not to call in police as we have so many disturbed maladjusted boys.*

29 Nov. *14 boys to dentist for extractions (very well behaved).*

30 Nov. *3 boys who had extractions had been bleeding all night and were taken by Nurse Barrett to Mr. Parker, local dentist, who stitched the gums and stopped the bleeding. All three kept in bed.*

After a School Inspection in November 1962, Miss Buckley commented in a report on the urgent need for a washing machine and spin drier, as 22 cases of enuresis were at the school. The responsibility for dealing with wet bed linen fell upon hardworking Nurse Barrett. In addition, the Head Teacher stressed the need for two new classrooms, a day room for pupils and improvements to the Head Teacher's house. The latter was totally unsuitable for families as there was no kitchen, no garage, and only one bedroom. There was a great need for more warmth and comfort in any future plans for the school: 'The days of Spartan endurance in the pursuit of health and strength for the weakling are things of the past. Our present problem is to give warmth, comfort and security to the under privileged whose home circumstances prevent their receiving adequate support during their most impressionable years', stated Miss Buckley firmly.

Despite the high number of sociological cases, the school generally ran smoothly, apart from 'spasms of excessive destructiveness', disclosed Miss Buckley. Often these incidents took place after visiting days, when many parents had failed to visit their boys. Sadly, there were 10 to 15 boys who hardly ever had a visitor or letter from home—some did not even receive parental pocket money. 'Though we try to make up to them for parental rejection, it is often difficult to do so', reported the Headmistress, who made every effort to provide interesting and stimulating out-of-school activities. Apart from the usual sports, canoeing and fishing, there were the collections of ducks, bantams, chickens, rabbits, guinea pigs, hamsters and mice on the premises.

Out of 100 boys on roll (ranging from 7 to 16) 45 were chest cases, 37 had social problems, 'maladjustment' or nervous instability and 18 suffered various debilities and illnesses. The miscellaneous ailments included malnutrition (5), contact TB (2), general debility (6), epilepsy (1), school phobia (1). It was felt that some boys under the age of nine should be sent to Haseley Hall or Skilts, rather than Hunter's Hill. Poor home conditions for many of the boys meant that they were unable to leave Hunter's Hill and attend a day school, even if they were well enough.

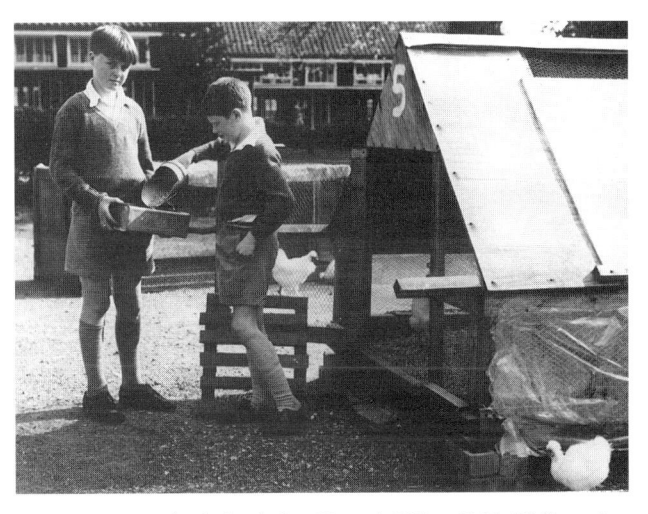

Measuring out the chickenfeed at Hunter's Hill, c.1966. (C. Barrett)

The period 1963-5 was a difficult time at the school while structural alterations took place: a new extension for boys' bedrooms and staff flats in 1963; a new caretaker's house in 1965; painting and decorating throughout the school; and a new kitchen was added to the Head Teacher's house. A large number of adolescent boys were admitted over this period and there were many staffing problems, as experienced members left and were replaced by others who were non-resident. Nurse Barrett supervised the House Mother, and two Children's Helpers cared for the boys in out-of-school hours. The long promised washing machine and spin drier finally arrived to make their routine work more pleasant.

School log books record some of the problems and frequent visits to hospitals and clinics but it is impossible to list more than a few typical entries:

Hunter's Hill log book 1964

22 Jan.   *New set of coloured blankets for New Block given out—very attractive colours.*

2 Feb.   *Another mild day and Mr. Hill took Senior boys for a very long walk. K.F. who has flat feet and should be wearing leg irons had to be brought back by car and was in a state of exhaustion when seen by Nurse Barrett.*

4 Feb.   *Miss Buckley and Nurse Barrett to choose curtain materials, chairs and carpets for Junior Playroom.*

4 May   *T.R. by taxi to Great Charles Street clinic for X ray (unresolved pneumonia), to have treatment and return in 14 days.*

6 May   *K.F. and C.R. to Asthma Clinic.*

29 May   *Miss MacDonald for interview (successful post as Deputy Head in DOAS). This makes our number of teachers leaving in July three so far. We have had no applicants for vacancies. N.D. to Children's Hospital, J.D. to optician, Bromsgrove.*

6 June   *Very wet all day—Visiting Day photographs sold to parents. Parents were not in a very good humour. Two mothers almost came to blows over some silly trifle—the depressing weather was the root cause.*

21 Oct.   *Three boys to Asthma Clinic.*

2 Nov.   *Miss Buckley to a conference of HT's of Special Schools within the Authority to discuss the future of the Special Schools and various alterations that are planned.*

10 Nov.   *F.H. to Children's Hospital to collect new brace for back. Miss Buckley and Nurse Barrett to select curtains for new Isolation Block. First dancing session with Cropwood Girls 6.30-7.30pm.*

13 Nov.   *D.H. brought back to school by Family Service Unit in dirty unkempt condition.*

11 Dec.   *Christmas party—Games in two groups from 2.15-5pm. Staff and Boys together for tea from 5-6.15pm. Presentation to Mr. Ross, Caretaker, who is due to retire. Electric drill from boys, chair and stool from all staff. Conjuror from 6.15-7pm (very good). Giving out of presents, fruit, nuts, chocolate from 7-8.15pm. Seniors cleared up after this and then had supper and to bed late, 9.30pm.*

Hunter's Hill log book 1965

20 Jan.   *Very heavy snow fall—all light and power off from 9am-2pm. Difficulties of keeping flats warm and of cooking precipitated crisis in kitchen—Mrs. Braithwaite threatened to resign. Some Domestic Staff and Mr. Alexander brought from Bromsgrove by Land Rover from local garage. Boys out sledging and snowballing.*

11 Feb.   *Two boys found to have been out of bed from 10-11.30 visiting new maid—she is most unsatisfactory (a liar and pilferer) and is leaving tomorrow.*

15 Feb.   *All school lectured on dirty habits and slovenly appearance and warned that they must smarten up. Walter W. caned by Mr. Hill for insubordination and insolence.*

16 Feb.   *John C. caned by Mr. Hill for climbing through a small top window to enter a locked room.*

19 May   *Three boys to Asthma Clinic re desensitisation treatment.*

16 Sep.   *Peter R. was reproved by Mr. Alexander—ran off and climbed to top of a very tottery oak tree (not at all safe) and refused to come down. Remained there from 3pm to 5.15pm.*

23 Sep.   *12 students from City of Birmingham Training College visited school. An interesting group, but not very well briefed for their visit—they had not realised it was a residential school and thought Special School always meant ESN School.*

5 Nov.   *Five senior boys caught lighting fireworks in classroom jammed into inkwell space of desk—caught before damage was done to desk or room. Punished by being deprived of their senior privileges.*

    Other senior boys were out of the school grounds during the evening and may have been concerned in an incident at a local farm when fireworks were thrown into shed where turkeys were kept and five were killed. All senior boys spoken to about this and also about their general thoughtless behaviour when out for walks or to Bromsgrove resulting in the school having a reputation for hooliganism in the district. All walks and visits to Bromsgrove cancelled except for Prefects and a few conspicuously well behaved boys. (This may also cut down the time spent in smoking which is becoming a problem with the number of senior boys in the school who entered at 13+ and were already smoke addicts on arrival.)

13 Dec.   *Boys had their Christmas Dinner at mid-day (Turkey etc. Plum Pudding). Staff dinner at 8pm.*

    Mr. William Hill, Deputy Head Teacher, had previously worked at the school from 1949-57 (see previous chapter for his reminiscences) and recalls his return to Hunter's Hill at a time of many changes:

Mr. William (Bill) Hill, Deputy Head Teacher, Hunter's Hill 1963-6, Margate, Kent

My wife Beryl and I, with our two small boys, returned to join the staff of the school in January 1963, following Leslie Richardson's appointment to a headship in York.

There had been many changes, largely for the better, in those intervening years; both in the residential accommodation for the children, in the routine of the school and in the range and depth of the education offered. The children now suffered from a wider variety of handicaps and the need for a strict regime of 'open air' policies was no longer a cardinal feature of the children's day.

The school was in an era of rapid change brought about by the transfer of the 30 older teenagers into a newly built residential bedroom block. The boys' bedrooms were made of foursomes, threesomes and a number of twins. There was a small quiet/recreation room on each floor, showers and toilets.

Whilst the senior boys benefited greatly by this change giving them more independence, privacy and room for personal development, the school as a unity suffered. The house system, possibly now outdated, suffered from terminal wastage as the driving force for each house was physically separated from the mass of house members. Also my own policy, which Linda had agreed to upon my appointment as her deputy, was to initiate a large measure of control by the boys themselves in order to break down the 'institutional dependence nourished by most boarding school systems'. This meant creating a climate of self-determination and self control by the boys themselves.

The youngsters coming into the school were no longer purely asthmatic, undernourished and physically below par. Our pupils were, more and more, suffering from psychological disorders brought about by a variety of conditions; bullying at school for instance, family traumas, factors inhibiting learning such as dyslexia or lack of progress in basic study skills, due to inappropriate teaching methods etc. We were, in fact, having to see every child as an individual with specific needs requiring specific remedies. So the old institutional patterns of the past were not only merely unsuitable, they were a positive hindrance to a child's development.

The next three years were years of change, of experiment and hopefully, too, of growth. More and more it became evident that the educational programme would continue to fall below the needs of the children where the totality of the school day required encompassing the needs of little 8 year olds as well as 15 year olds. But change comes slowly in the educational field. At the same time there was a growing body of informed opinion which questioned the value of boarding school education and in particular separating a child from the family culture. My own view inclined to weekly boarding and I was particularly keen to get such a regime established at Hunter's Hill amongst the 15 and 16 year olds but our school inspectors were adamant in their refusal to examine the merits of such a scheme. Boys were encouraged to go home for long weekends whenever a family occasion justified this and all boys were encouraged to go into Bromsgrove or the Lickeys for a few hours every Saturday. Again, one had to positively break the cycle of dependency which boarding encourages.

The boys still enjoyed a good deal of healthy fun. Dark winter evenings were enlivened by 'hunt the whistle' over woodland, meadow and copse. The severe winter of '63 found us all tobogganing by torch and oil lamps down Hunter's Hill itself—one intrepid young man sailed through a gap in the hedge and over the top of an A40 car much to the driver's consternation but the child had thrown himself well clear. We were able to arrange more exciting and more appropriate recreation given the defined age groups. Half an hour of 'British Bulldog' in the hall/gym when the other youngsters were bedded down sapped all the energy of the toughest and wildest child.

I left to take up a similar appointment at Kent's largest boarding school after three years and later opened up a new school at Canterbury from which I retired in 1983.

My assessment of the years 1963-66 would be that the school was at a half way stage in its development towards a secondary boarding school but that was the fault of the administrators, certainly not of Linda Buckley who tried to keep the old verities in place.

Schoolboys mucking out the goatshed, c.1966. (M. Harris)

An exciting event in the school must have been the arrival of the two new goats, as nine-year-old David McLuskey recorded in the school magazine: 'They have nice little horns and they jump on the rabbit hutches. They jump and hop all over the paddock and when people go into the paddock the goats jump all over the people! The goats are white and the boys brush the goats down to keep them clean. The goats are called Candy and Floss.'

Billy Kidgil, goat keeper-in-training, wrote:

> As we trudge towards the goats' pen we can see two little white faces staring at us, then they begin to bleat longingly for us to let them out of their little prison. As we swing the pen door open two sets of horns get ready ... then bingo! Like army horses they charge out to begin another day! The little goats are always on the move. All day long they are teasing the living daylights out of the ducks, chickens and rabbits. But never mind them ... they are beginning to put the wind up us ...!

Sadly, the goats had to be sold in March 1966, in order to make room for some new buildings. Mr. Reginald Harris had looked after them in the school holidays, having taken over the post of caretaker in 1965 when Mr. Ross retired after 25 years at the school. Pupil David Vann described Mr. Ross's retirement in the school magazine:

> Mr. Ross has now retired to live with Mrs. Ross in the little cottage at the bottom of Hunter's Hill. He is very fond of gardening. We all helped to give Mr. Ross a retiring gift of an electric drill and a comfortable chair with a leg rest, because Mr. Ross had a bad leg. Happy Retirement Mr. Ross ...! We like Mr. Harris who lives with his wife and son in the new house just inside the school gates. We hope he will be happy here because he likes the country too.

Reginald Harris died in 1992 but his wife had very happy memories of life at Hunter's Hill when interviewed in 1993. Mrs. Harris died in 1995 but we are indebted to her for the use of her scrapbooks, school magazines and photographs carefully preserved during her time at the school:

Mrs. Margaret R. Harris, wife of Caretaker **Reginald Harris**, Hunter's Hill 1965-85, Bromsgrove, Worcester

We went to Hunter's Hill when my husband was appointed caretaker—or Building Services Supervisor, as he was finally called. We had 20 happy years there before retiring, after my husband had worked for Birmingham Education Committee for 40 years.

I did cleaning in the school. We lived on site in a house specially built in 1965 and were the first caretakers to live on the school premises. The long row of school dormitories was later made into classrooms when new extensions were built in the 1970s.

In the school holidays we looked after the goats, ducks, geese and hens but in term time the boys did that. I remember school scout groups camping in the grounds and making cocoa which we were invited to drink. Somehow we managed to drink it although it was awful! Sometimes the Birmingham Symphony Orchestra used to go to Hunter's Hill to give recitals.

THE 1960s AND BEYOND: WINDS OF CHANGE

We brought up a family at Hunter's Hill, and my daughter worked at both Cropwood and Hunter's Hill. My grandson used to spend his summer holidays with us and was allowed to use Cropwood's swimming pool.

When we retired we received many hand-made cards from the boys, depicting our cleaning activities! They were happy years at the school.

Older boys were allowed to go for walks out of school and many grew to love the countryside, as 14-year-old David Wilson wrote in the school magazine:

> When you reach the age of 13 Miss Buckley gives you a form which your parents sign. This allows you to go for walks out of school ... When I have enough money in my account (about 2/6) I go to Bromsgrove with friends to buy a model or some comics. Often I go for a walk around the wonderful countryside if I have nothing to do. I have been to Tardebigge, down the canal, up to the Lickey monument and many other nice places. It is very interesting going on walks because you may find unusual things. There are certain places where we are not allowed such as Cropwood Wood and Blackwell railway station.

Mr. Reginald Harris, Hunter's Hill caretaker, with the school goats Candy and Floss, 1966. The caretaker's school house is in the background. (M. Harris)

Another boy wrote:

> I have been at this school for a number of years and will be sorry to leave. Living out in the country is like being on top of the world. Blackwell is a small village ... just the right place for a picnic on a nice warm day. We often walk through the village to the small Blackwell station to see trains puffing the longest incline in England. In Blackwell are many interesting things to be seen ...

In January 1967 the new Deputy Head was Mr. W. Powell who arrived at the school with his wife and two children. His family helped to provide a settled atmosphere in the school and his wife taught music and formed a school choir.

Miss Buckley reported later that year that many a newcomer was helped to feel at home by Mr. and Mrs. Powell when boys first arrived at Hunter's Hill—and many of the 'disturbed' adolescents sent to the school had resented being sent away from their families. She commented that coping with disturbed, often socially neglected, children was hard work, but the results rewarding when boys could be returned to ordinary schools in the minimum time possible.

The Duke of Edinburgh Award Scheme was introduced to Hunter's Hill by Mr. Powell, when boys over 14 years of age could prove they had 'grit, perseverance and could be of service to other people', reported Raymond Taylor in the school magazine of 1967. First Aid was learned, hobbies had to be followed for six months, physical fitness was tested and there was the challenge of going on a 15-mile hike, camping out and preparing at least two hot meals. Robert Dunne and David Hunt became the first pupils to receive their Bronze award. Despite being 'delicate', the boys were allowed no special concessions. It was reported that Hunter's Hill was the only Special School in the country to enter the Award Scheme.

Schoolboys from Hunter's Hill collecting honey from the beehives, c.1966. (C. Barrett)

Other popular activities included the Stamp Club, organised by Nurse Barrett: contributions arrived from Old Boys, ex staff, medical officers and local businessmen. Teacher Richard Pinner formed a photographic club and later in this chapter gives us a detailed account of his life at Hunter's Hill.

Mr. Alexander's Art Club produced some good oil paintings for the school. He developed the art and craft work in the school with great success and six boys' paintings were accepted for the National Exhibition of Children's Art in London in 1966. Art activities in the school included weaving with looms, pastels, ink drawing, scraperboards and canework—all exhibited on open days. 'They really are enthusiastic', Mr. Alexander said of his pupils to a newspaper reporter, 'Most of the work has been done at voluntary evening classes. They certainly set a high standard.'

Mr. Idwal Jones had been appointed in 1965, specialising in PT and games, and remained at the school for many years. One of his hobbies was beekeeping which was practised at Hunter's Hill.

Kevin Jones, one of his pupils, wrote in the school magazine in 1966: 'Games are fun at Hunter's Hill. We play rounders and cricket in the summer term. Mr. Jones takes us for games. Sometimes Sparky, his dog, runs off with our ball and we have to chase him to get it back. I like Mr. Jones, he's great'.

Gerard O'Reegan wrote in the magazine of his first day at Hunter's Hill on 12 April 1967:

> When I caught the coach to bring me here I was very lonely and bewildered. I arrived at the school then I had a lovely warm shower, which made me feel better. After the shower I was given my clothes to wear and a pair of shoes. It was now dinner time so I went into the dining hall where I had a lovely dinner and a delicious pudding.
>
> After dinner break I had to see Miss Buckley, the Head Teacher, for a reading test, to find out which class I was to go into. Miss Buckley put me into Class B where I enjoyed it. After school I had a very nice tea and played with some other boys. Soon a bell rang for me to go to bed and I was soon washed and in bed writing a letter to my mother and father.
>
> Soon the lights were put out and I lay down in bed, saying to myself that it was not nice here. Now two months later I have settled down and like it here quite a lot.

Not all new boys liked everything at Hunter's Hill. A survey in the 1966 school magazine revealed some of their views:

Liked: Scouts, dancing, games, football, walks.
Disliked: Domestic duties, going to bed, getting up early, cleaning shoes, no water with dinner, having to rest.

Other candid comments by senior boys were:

THE 1960s AND BEYOND: WINDS OF CHANGE

'I like being here because there is always plenty to do and anyway I keep better and don't get my asthma so much'. (David Vann, 13 years).

'It's good to be back ... there isn't anything to do at home ...' (David Gilbert, 14 years).

'I like the wide open spaces in which you can roam ...' (Richard Gibbs, 14 years).

The last four years of this era at Hunter's Hill saw numerous absconding boys recorded in the log book, together with several changes of staff as boys' health problems continued unabated. Life was as full and demanding as ever for Headmistress Linda Buckley and her nursing colleague, Claire Barrett, who had shared so many experiences in their years working together:

Hunter's Hill log book 1966

5 Jan.   *91 boys returned (84 old boys and 7 new). Mr. R. Pinner commenced duty as assistant teacher.*

8 Jan.   *Sean B. new boy absconded very early in morning—very inadequately dressed for the raw cold morning—police notified as soon as we knew he was missing—no report about him until 12noon when he was said to be at home.*

10 Jan. *Charles T. who has been absent since Easter 1965 returned today. He is to be kept in Isolation Convalescent Room during very cold weather and has to have a daily dressing and Postural Drainage three times daily.*

13 Jan. *Stephen W. brought back to school by Inspector of NSPCC. Charles T. to Hill Top (by taxi)—taken by Nurse Barrett to discuss daily dressings and insertion of drainage tube.*

16 Mar. *Doctor Todman visited to do a Medical Inspection, saw 13 senior boys—very thorough check. Dr. Volam second immunisation (48 boys) today.*

19 Mar. *Fine sunny day. Mr. Pinner took 15 senior boys for long walk from 1 to 5.30pm.*

23 Mar. *All boys weighed—gains very good on the whole.*

26 Mar. *87 boys with 6 members of staff to Billy Smarts Circus at Hay Barns recreation ground, Birmingham—by special coach. Parents of four asthmatical boys (who are allergic to some animals) came to take them out for the afternoon.*

28 Mar. *Eight senior boys found to have been stealing from food store. PC Carey came and cautioned them—parents informed by letter and Dr. Smith notified.*

2 April *Mr. Tebbutt—Rural Science teacher was married today at the local chapel to Sister Allison from Cropwood School.*

3 July   *Seniors canoeing or mapwork with Mr. Pinner. Juniors on Hunter's Hill or Kite Flying.*

13 Sep. *Brian H. to Children's Hospital to see psychiatrist re behavioural problems.*

26 Sep. *Admitted eight new boys. J.B. absconded three times during his first half day.*

24 Nov. *Sunday overcoats fitted.*

5 Dec.   *Candidates for interview for deputy headship brought out by Mr. Tansley to see school. Carol Service arranged by prefects. Miss Buckley in bed with attack of gastric flu but got up to see candidates then retired to bed again.*

6 Dec.   *Miss Buckley to Education Office for appointment of Deputy Head, Mr. W.J. Powell from Standon Bowers ESN School near Stafford. He will take up duties as soon as he can be released by Stafford and as soon as the flat can be cleaned and redecorated.*

10 Dec.   Visiting Day parents delighted with Play, 'Pied Piper', which was produced by Mr. Evershed 'in the round' and was very successful.

Hunter's Hill log book 1967

5 Jan.   Nurse Barrett and four teachers to collect boys from Mowbray St clinic. 86 boys returned, changed, bathed and weighed (most have done quite well during holiday).

22 Feb.   S.C. taken by taxi to Children's Hospital for examination—condition appears to puzzle doctors—no treatment prescribed except continued rest in bed. Probation Officer brought out 13 year old boy who is due for admission next term and who is afraid to come because he thinks it is an approved school.

24 Feb.   Staff meeting held by Mr. Powell to straighten out some errors and misunderstandings about extraneous duties, type written notes to each member of staff.

24 May   Head Teacher to meeting of residential Head teachers at Baskerville School to discuss conditions in these schools leading to poor staffing at the moment (schools mainly affected are Cropwood, Baskerville and Skilts). Resolution taken to ask for a meeting with CEO and head of SS Committee to discuss this grave situation.

27 May   Whit break for day schools but we do not close—Visiting Day held. Summer Fair raised £79.19.6½ for School Funds in spite of very wet weather.

Hunter's Hill log book 1968

26 June   Miss Buckley to Education Office to interview teachers. Mr. Stubbs appointed to take Art & Craft in place of Mr. Alexander.

29 June   11 boys to do walk and overnight camp for Duke of Edinburgh Bronze Award. Two boys attempting walk with equipment, a week end camp for Silver award. Mr. Powell will take heavy equipment for the first group.

30 June   Two boys doing Silver stage of Duke of Edinburgh's Award completed their walking and camping tests.

1 July   Mr. Pinner took three senior boys to Prom Concert in Birmingham Town Hall.

Hunter's Hill log book 1969

8 July   Terminal Review. Dr. Boardman saw 28 boys and discharged 22. All boys have now had a medical examination this term.

9 July   Head Teacher to meeting in Margaret St re new scheme for payment for extraneous duties etc.

12 July   Visiting Day which was an Open Day for parents and old boys and ex members of staff. Miss Buckley and Nurse Barrett who are retiring were presented with gifts from present school, old boys, present and ex staff. All boys took part in a very well arranged PE display. Parents and other friends provided with buffet tea.

16 July   Boys bathed and changed during morning so that all school could watch the TV presentation of the launching of Apollo 10.

17 July   Mr. Tansley to say farewell to Miss Buckley and Nurse Barrett.

The departure of Linda Buckley and Claire Barrett from Hunter's Hill School was not only the end of a long working partnership but marked the end of an era as the school had gradually changed. They had worked side-by-side for 32 years, 26 of them with Miss Buckley as Headmistress. Miss Barrett had nursed generations of boys, latterly taking full responsibility for all the medical care in the absence of a Nursing Sister. After such a remarkable record for long and devoted service to the school they shared their retirement together in Blackwell until Miss Buckley died in 1983. Claire Barrett (whose main reminiscences are included in several earlier chapters) recalls her retirement and happy life at the school:

Miss Claire Barrett, School Nurse, Hunter's Hill 1937-69, Blackwell, Worcs.

So many of them visited Miss Buckley and myself after we retired, and I am still in touch with at least nine of the former staff. We all shared so much fun and laughter together. Boys would find out when your birthday was and you would get a big surprise. It could sometimes be rather embarrassing as when one boy, during a session with the visiting wind section of Birmingham's Symphony Orchestra, on being asked if there were any special requests said 'would they please play Happy Birthday for Miss MacDonald' (on whom he had a crush!). Although a little startled they did so, to much laughter.

In summer all PE lessons were taken outside on the field. Games included soccer, cricket, and rounders for the younger ones. They all had a garden shared between two and grew things like lettuce, radishes, mustard and cress which they could eat with their tea, and some easy flowers which they presented to Mum on visiting days.

Miss Buckley took all boys for nature study when they went many rambles; they knew the common trees and an amazing number of wild flowers. Most of them very much enjoyed these lessons.

One of the teachers who worked during this period gives us a detailed account of everyday life at Hunter's Hill and his efforts to improve cultural standards as the intake of boys changed from 'delicate' to 'maladjusted':

Mr. Richard Pinner, Teacher, Hunter's Hill 1966-73, Edgbaston, Birmingham

I came to Hunter's Hill in 1966. I had come to England as a Jewish refugee at the age of 13 and had entered teaching through the Emergency Training Courses at the end of the war. After years at Secondary Modern and Comprehensive Schools I had applied for a vacant post at Hunter's Hill. Having no family and being more interested in the 'whole person' than in individual subjects, and also having suffered from asthma myself, I thought I could make a bigger contribution at a residential school than at a day school.

Within a few weeks I was thoroughly disillusioned. Hunter's Hill was just about still an Open-Air School, but really in name only. There were a number of sick boys, suffering from asthma and other complaints, but most of them were there for social reasons. Our school title said 'for delicate boys'; 'for maladjusted boys' would have been more correct, but officially that was not allowed. Our 100 boys were there for dozens of reasons, one thing only was common to them: they had not attended school regularly!

There was no self-discipline and I quickly learned kindness on my part was taken to be weakness and I lost all control over them—after having been known as a strict disciplinarian for years. It took me eighteen months to be accepted and to be obeyed—then I started to enjoy life at the school and began to make a positive contribution. I had to learn to come out of my intellectual, Jewish, middle-class background and enter, what were, to me, alien surroundings. But I also decided to try to raise the cultural standards of boys nearer to my own.

The first impression was the 'cold' (I started in January). My first action was to buy a quilted jacket, such as Arctic explorers wore. It became my most valuable property. The heating system was poor, the dormitories and classrooms had only thin, wooden walls and insulation did not exist. We had three dormitories in a long line, each with about twenty-five beds. Between them were two mini-flats, one of which was mine: a small bedroom, a small sitting room, a bathroom and a WC. These 'flats' were warm. Other teachers had rooms in the main building or a flat in the 'Block'—a separate house, used for the senior boys. Deputy head and one married teacher had flats in the 'Block'.

We teachers also had to do all 'child care' work; we had one member of staff as 'child care' assistant. So, our work load was something like this:

Early morning duty: getting boys up—seeing them washed and dressed and to breakfast in time. Breakfast supervision. We could get up later when we were on this duty. Others had their breakfast in a separate staff dining room.

Domestic duties after breakfast: making beds, some cleaning, changing laundry (especially the many bed-wetters). Then school teaching for the morning.

Lunch was always supervised by Miss Buckley and the Nurse, giving us teachers some free time and a meal without stress. Then most of the boys had 'rest'—literally lie on their beds and be quiet! This applied to all Juniors and those Seniors who had lost weight or were considered to need rest for other reasons. This was done in the three dormitories and one of us was on duty there, to enforce the rest and silence. Then back to school.

After school boys changed clothes and we had 'activities'. There was a wide choice, but on any dry day boys were encouraged to get out on to 'the Hill'—the 'Hunter's Hill'—and get rid of their energy there. But there was also football, table tennis and small games. What we did not encourage was television. We had one set—in one room—and boys were allowed once a week to go there and watch for about an hour. We were on duty, supervising, and often I went out on to the hill, watching boys playing there, building dens, chasing etc and trying to take a sympathetic interest in what they were doing. But the positive idea was to let them learn how to occupy themselves on their own—something regretfully abolished years later when every activity had to be organised by an adult.

Then came tea. Like all meals, this was a communal one in the main dining room, and 'tea duty' was the most hated—and feared—duty of the day—and week. If you could keep discipline at this meal, you could rule a prison!

One major problem was lateness. Boys, playing on the hill, did not hear the bell and came in later, often causing havoc with food distribution. Finally, I bought a real alpine cow bell in Switzerland, carried it home and presented it to the school. This bell could be heard from Burford to Barnt Green and excuses for lateness were no longer accepted!

Not enough vegetables and fruit were supplied. 'Tea' was a very poor meal. While going to bed, each boy got half an apple. After breakfast, all boys had to line up to get a spoonful of cod liver oil. Only later, when Mr. Williams had taken over and, I believe, had strongly complained, was our food allowance raised and meals became more varied. The taking of cod liver oil was abolished.

One of our duties was in a dormitory or in the block, supervising, especially making sure the boys had their shower, got undressed and went to bed, where they could read for some time. Finally, one of us was on 'late duty'—patrolling the dormitories or the block until about 10.00pm, getting everybody to shut up and go to sleep. In theory we would be on duty all night, too. I well remember waking up one night and finding a boy sitting on my bed, complaining he could not sleep! After that, I locked my door to the flat!

In this way we worked long hours, and all this without pay! In those days we got free board and lodging plus laundry, for all the work extraneous to teaching. The work continued throughout the weekend. Saturday morning we had 'domestic duties' to supervise; in the afternoon one of us had to go to Bromsgrove. Boys were allowed to go there, and one of us had to take charge. We walked the two miles—there and back (boys had no money for bus fare). Saturday evenings were devoted to film shows. Sunday morning we went to church. Two of us had to be in charge. Afternoons and evenings were given over to games and other activities. As compensation for all this, we had half a day off every week and were free every second weekend. These times were well earned and precious.

Boys coming to Hunter's Hill were met at a clinic in the town. Before boarding the special buses, all were minutely examined and deloused at school later on if necessary. At school, boys had to change into school clothes, their own were collected, fumigated and locked away, to be given back when they went home again. I once asked a boy in the bus whether he felt sorry to come back to school. Not really, he replied, it would be nice to sleep in a bed by himself again! I later found that 'at home' five shared one double bed!

At the end of term, we would take the boys back to the clinic and hand them over to parents, but, if no parent turned up (a frequent occurrence), we would have to get taxis and take the boys home.

We did have boys suffering from asthma, but tried to teach them how to deal with this. Some of it was made worse for psychosomatic reasons e.g. the boy who could promptly start an asthma attack when told off for bad behaviour but whose attack disappeared when told it did not impress.

In 1966 boys had to wear a uniform supplied by the school. While not ugly it was totally inadequate during cold winters—boys constantly felt cold. This was improved later.

Football was played but many boys did not understand the game; they were either too stupid or too maladjusted. It was common to observe boys kicking the ball in either direction. We later got a table-tennis table and became quite successful. One teacher introduced rough games—played in the hall, and here maladjusted boys could get rid of the energies and bad tempers.

Once a year we had our 'Merry-Go-Round'—an obstacle race in teams. Parents came on that day. Parents could come once every three weeks on Saturdays—usually it was rather chaotic and cleaning up in the evening took several hours. It proved quite a shock to see some of the parents and explained only too well why the boys were so disturbed and mixed up.

We suffered a lot from boys running away. The school was wide open and to guard the exits was impossible. Again and again we found boys missing from dormitories. Residents in Blackwell would ring up to say one—or more—boys were walking along the road toward Barnt Green—or the police would ring us. Usually, someone went out by car and found him, or them, walking along, often only too glad to be taken back by car. Only a few ever managed to get home; at first we used to fetch them; later parents were told it was their responsibility to get them back to us.

Mr. Richard Pinner's class in the winter uniform, photographed by their teacher with 'Sparky', the dog. (R. Pinner/M. Harris)

I started to make an attempt to raise standards. Alone among the staff I had spent most of my time in ordinary schools and I could see how disadvantaged our boys would be when they would have to leave and find work. Few of them could count on parental help.

Mr. Jones (who had a car) and I started to take selected boys to the theatre, concerts or opera in Birmingham. We were strongly criticised by some teachers; 'middle-class values, elitism, taking the boys out of their cultural backgrounds', such terms were thrown at us. But we proved even boys from the poorest backgrounds could appreciate real art.

I had run a photographic club at my previous school and had kept my own darkroom equipment. I brought this to Hunter's Hill. We found an unused store room, made it into a darkroom and soon a number of boys became proficient in developing films and making enlargements. We took pictures round the school and made—and sold— picture postcards from these. Of course the main purpose was to develop a worth-while hobby.

For years I had run a Film Club at my previous schools to bring the classics of the cinema to my pupils (TV was unknown to them). At Hunter's Hill we had a contact with one film library who sent one film every week. Invariably they were 'light entertainment' films, devoid of any artistic element. After discussing the matter, I arranged films once every two weeks and raised the cultural levels. I found our boys **could** appreciate great films and there was never a demand to go back to inconsequential rubbish. That even uneducated, maladjusted, disturbed boys could be brought to appreciate great art, I proved to myself with experiments.

I decided to book the film 'Inherit the Wind', a masterwork dealing with the intellectual problem of freedom of thought. I invited six boys from my class to come to my small sitting room and see a preview. They sat on the floor and were completely absorbed in the story. I decided to repeat this two days later with others, though two boys (both very disturbed) begged me to let them see it again. Then came the show. I expected about five or six—over twenty turned up and sat, absorbed, for the two hours. A huge cultural success!

The local parson wanted to bring school and village closer together and we arranged a number of joint functions in the church hall. One such day I booked the film of 'Don Giovanni', Mozart's opera: it was a complete performance, taken in the famous Felsenreitschule in Salzburg, with the finest singers of the time. We arranged to show the film in our hall, invited the whole village, allowed our boys to come if they wished, and tried to turn it into a real festive occasion. We arranged refreshments for the interval (served by volunteers from the boys). Only about twelve people from the village came but it was a cultural success.

But there was something else. I had the film over a week before the show date. I decided to run it through to check for any technical faults in the school hall one Sunday afternoon. Soon I noticed some boys standing outside the hall, young, very maladjusted. I first ignored them, then, I went out and told them they could come in as long as they did not make any noise. They sat there for two hours and thought it was 'great'. Uneducated, maladjusted boys of 11 or 12, never having heard about Mozart, without explanation, being fascinated by one of the supreme operas, somehow said something about our education, our low expectations and what **could** be achieved.

I described some of the above in great detail, as, I believe, these examples show my own dissatisfaction with what we set out to achieve. We were really only meant to contain boys whom nobody else wanted. How much more we could have done …!

Materially, there were improvements after about 1970. Food improved, the heating became more efficient, new facilities appeared (a snooker table, TV sets in all dormitories), but the whole character changed. We were no longer an Open-Air School for the 'delicate'—just a Special Residential School. Child care staff were employed and teachers did not have to live-in any longer, nor share dormitory and child care duties.

Some of us thought that we betrayed the real purpose of a residential special school—we seemed to become more and more aimless. I left in 1973 soon after these changes took place.

Hunter's Hill had re-opened in September 1970 with a new Head Teacher, Graham Williams. By 1975 the school population consisted of 84 boys, of whom 60 per cent were medical cases, 41 per cent asthmatics, 32 per cent 'maladjusted' and 42 per cent socially disadvantaged. Hunter's Hill officially absorbed Cropwood in 1981 and Graham Williams retired in 1985. After a succession of Head Teachers, Kenneth Lewis was appointed to the post in 1989 and still leads the school. A secretary from the school recalls this period of transition:

Mrs. D.M. Mountford, Secretary, Hunter's Hill 1969-90, Bromsgrove

Three new residential units were built in 1976 at a cost of £250,000 and the existing residential block had additions and was modernised. The old dormitories were converted to classrooms and were re-equipped as rooms for specialist subjects.

After Miss Clarke's retirement Mr. Williams ran the two schools separately. The official amalgamation of Cropwood and Hunter's Hill took place in 1981, becoming one co-educational school for secondary pupils aged 11 to 16.

From October 1984, the boys went home every weekend.

The boys currently attending Hunter's Hill are resident during the week and have been identified as having 'moderate learning difficulties with a wide variety of needs'. The school has

70 acres of grounds, fields and woodland, and has a structured sympathetic approach to pupils who are often insecure and lacking in confidence, having failed in mainstream schools.

Boys are encouraged to believe in themselves and are individually assessed to encourage progress and development towards independence when they will live and work within the community. The celebration of achievement is the main philosophy throughout the school, together with the monitoring and fostering of good discipline.

In a very caring community the school nurtures many boys who may have health problems as well as other difficulties, with a large number of child care and teaching staff as well as a Nursing Sister and a Senior Education Social Worker. The older boys in their final years now live in Cropwood House, putting the Cadburys' holiday home to good use after its donation to the authority over 75 years ago.

Marsh Hill

Marsh Hill was the first of Birmingham's six open-air schools to be closed, after having been in existence for 35 years in Erdington for children living in the northern half of the city. The log books have been deposited in Birmingham Central Library (Archives Department): the last few entries record that Birmingham's Special Schools were being re-organised and that 'delicate' pupils would be sent to special units attached to secondary schools. Marsh Hill ceased as a School for Delicate Children on 14 July 1966 and was redeveloped as a Day School for Maladjusted Children. The building was taken over by the Social Services Department as an Assessment Unit on the site of Underwood School but has now been demolished. In its place are flats on Underwood Close. Marsh Hill Open-Air School passed into history ...

The last Head Teacher of Marsh Hill was traced by using the school log book and the telephone directory. Her comments and her 1973 thesis for a Diploma in the Psychology of Childhood at Birmingham University give an invaluable insight into the reorganisation of that period during which Marsh Hill School for Delicate Children came to a close.

Miss Patricia C.J. Hazel, Head Teacher, Marsh Hill 1958-66, and author of *Education for Delicate Children: Day School Provision in the City of Birmingham 1911-1973.*

What is a delicate child? There seemed to be no simple answer to this apparently simple question. Few people were aware of the existence of schools for these children. During the Sixties at Marsh Hill there were fewer references to tuberculosis except to stress that TB cases were excluded from the school, in order to reassure parents that their children were not exposed to this infection.

One of the great problems was the inadequacy and unsuitability of some of the children's clothes. An assortment of rainwear was always kept at Marsh Hill for loan to the needy on wet days.

Birmingham was an area with a high incidence of childhood asthma. It is important to note that many asthmatic children were able to attend normal schools, coping well with the aid of a new drug (Disodium Cromoglycate—Intal) which was often very effective. There was a changing pattern of admissions to Marsh Hill. In the early years children suffered from general debility, malnutrition, anaemia or some form of non-active tuberculosis or were TB contacts. In the middle period asthma, bronchitis or bronchiectasis were very prevalent. Later the most common handicaps were speech and expressive language disorders, physical handicaps, disorders of the central nervous system, respiratory disorders and maladjustment. We had a full time nurse at the school at first until she retired, then we had a series of temporary nurses.

By 1961 breakfast had been discontinued for most children and the school day began at 9.15am and ended at 3.15pm, by shortening the lunch hours. In 1931 a school day had begun at 8.15am with breakfast and ended with tea at 5.30pm, according to log books.

In 1964 Birmingham Education Committee, Special Schools Sub-Committee, announced plans for reorganising education for delicate children, the aim being to make possible easier integration into secondary school life. Marsh Hill would close and re-open after structural alteration as Underwood School for Maladjusted Children. Delicate children of secondary school age from Marsh Hill and Uffculme would transfer to purpose-built units attached to four suitably sited secondary schools. Two more units for primary children would be attached to ordinary schools in the north and west of the city and Uffculme would remain as a primary school. (In point of fact, no purpose-built units were provided.) Two classrooms in each of the four secondary schools were allocated for the use of newly formed classes of delicate children—Dame Cadbury Bilateral School (Bournville), Hartfield Crescent School (Acocks Green), Stockland Green Bilateral School (Erdington), William Murdoch School (Handsworth).

Eventually The Pines (Castle Bromwich) and Shenstone (Bearwood/Winson Green) opened independently as new primary schools for delicate children in 1966—not as units attached to other schools as originally proposed. They opened in adapted buildings intended some years previously to be nursery schools but never used. Another primary unit for delicate children opened in 1973 as Welsh Farm Primary School (Quinton).

I became Head of The Pines when Marsh Hill closed. The new primary schools provided normal primary education with additional special educational treatment. The emphasis was on early detection of specific learning difficulties and any handicaps likely to hinder educational progress. Work needed to be individually tailored to cope with the increasing mixture of multiple handicaps at the schools. There was still an emphasis on outdoor activities even though these schools were not open-air in design.

The four senior units at Dame Cadbury, Hartfield Crescent, Stockland Green and William Murdoch Schools developed along individual lines with highly structured individual timetables. The Senior Units varied in their facilities—not all had a medical room which could be used for physiotherapy or treatment.

The new Units experienced difficulty coping with the pressures of trying to integrate handicapped children into mainstream education. Teachers frequently did not know where to seek advice—whether from the Special Service Department of the Education Authority or the Secondary Education Department. Medical supervision, nurses, speech therapists and physiotherapists were the concern of the School Health Section of the Public Health department. Professional etiquette demanded that no department interfered with the running of another. And the needs of children were great.

There was a greater need for special training courses to help young teachers to cope with children with special needs. More in-service courses for teachers were organised after 1966 which was helpful. The work of rehabilitating delicate children has always depended not only on the teacher's knowledge and understanding of handicap and educational expertise but the availability of supportive services.

The theory was to integrate handicapped children into normal schools but there were vast differences in nursing support in the various units and schools. Each primary school had a visit from one of the Medical Officers once a month and each Senior Unit had two visits a term. Only Uffculme was able to retain a full-time nurse by 1973 as there was a general shortage of nurses and the smaller sizes of the schools did not justify full-time employment. Schools were usually put into the care of their nearest School Clinic, with school nurses regularly visiting the schools. Shenstone had the help of a nurse for only half a day a week and The Pines shared one with another Special School.

Uffculme School became responsible for the primary education of disturbed children in the Charles Burns Psychiatric Unit at Uffculme Clinic and also formed new units for language-impaired and autistic children.

I opened The Pines in 1966 and chose all the furniture and school equipment. We shared a nurse who came from the nearest clinic which was two bus rides and a walk away. I had ten different nurses in one year and started to do the job myself, especially as medication had to be handed out at lunch times when the nurse was not on duty. We had a large number of asthmatics at school. I eventually got a really dedicated nurse from the clinic.

The Pines had its own kitchen where mid-day meals were cooked and 12 out of 60 children were on diets of special kinds, such as low carbohydrate diets for overweight children and fish-free diets for eczema sufferers and meals free of dairy products for a child suffering from Galactocaemia.

Of the 138 children who left The Pines between 1966 and 1973 statistics record:
45 per cent went to normal primary/secondary schools
21 per cent went to Senior Units
3 per cent went to Primary Units for Delicate Children
26 per cent went to other forms of Special Education
3 per cent left Birmingham

Shenstone closed in 1985 but *The Pines* survived as a Special School for children with speech difficulties, communication disorders and autism.

Haseley Hall

Haseley Hall Open-Air School was the next school to close in 1974 as the lease ran out for Birmingham Education Authority. It had been a very happy home for many young boys from the city throughout the 1960s and early 1970s. Unlike some other residential open-air schools, it had never had open-sided dormitories or classrooms, but just a firm emphasis on many outside activities in what was essentially a large country mansion and estate.

Miss Marjorie Butler-Fleming (generally known as Miss Fleming) had run the school as Headmistress since 1953 and devoted her life to the boys at Haseley Hall until her retirement in 1968—a total of 15 years. She brought an unusual atmosphere of maternal warmth to her role so that boys benefited from a homely environment. Some of her school log book entries are recorded below:

Haseley Hall log book 1960

13 Jan.   *32 boys returned.*

14 Feb.   *Seven boys in bed with chicken pox. Visiting Day.*

28 June. *School outing to Whipsnade park Zoo … picnic tea on Dunstable Downs.*

30 Sep.   *Visit to Leamington Lights*

4 Nov.   *Bonfire Night display.*

5 Nov.   *Fireworks and torches at night on the playground—party.*

1 Dec.   *Miss Dainty appointed as school nurse.*

10 Dec.   *Party. Dr. Kemp again Santa Claus. Tea in Dining room. Film show. Punch and Judy Show. Songs to Santa.*

Haseley Hall log book 1961

13 Mar.   *Mr. Thompson, dentist, called to examine teeth*

16 Mar.   *Mrs. Adams came, tested all eyes.*

18 April *Miss G. Royle appointed Deputy head.*

Haseley Hall log book 1962

7 July   *Seven cubs taken to Handsworth Park Rally to take part in March Past and Pageant*

10 July   *Outing on the canal by 'Water Fairy' barge from Knowle Locks to Hatton Lock.*

Boys and staff at Haseley Hall, 1960s. Staff in the middle row (left to right) include: Mrs. Andrews (Helper), Carol McCrea (Helper), Mrs. Gwen Fell (Helper), Shirley Dainty (Nurse), Dr. Kemp (Birmingham's Special Schools Medical Officer), Miss M. Butler-Fleming (Head Teacher), Miss G. Royle (Deputy Head), Mrs. Sharman (Teacher), Mrs. Adams (Birmingham School Clinic Nurse). (G. Fell)

Haseley Hall log book 1963

3 July   *Outing to Royal Show, Stoneleigh.*

12 Dec.   *Xmas party. Dr. Kemp acted as Santa Claus.*

Haseley Hall log book 1964

16 June   *School outing to St Nicholas Park, Warwick. Boys had a lovely time in the playground and on Peter Pan railway. Picnic.*

15 Oct.   *More dry rot discovered in Wolves dormitory.*

23 Oct.   *More dry rot found over staircase—main beam. Parents notified not to bring boys back to school until later date.*

16 Nov.   *Boys returned—only 24 owing to dry rot. The Main Staircase, Top Dormitories and Boys Landing, Hall and Dining Room not in use.*

Haseley Hall log book 1966

22 Feb.   *Pancakes for dinner!*

14 May   *The Headmistress and Mrs. Fell took ten cubs to York Wood 'Jubilee Camp Day'—very good indeed. Picnic tea in the woods. A lovely day.*

THE 1960s AND BEYOND: WINDS OF CHANGE

11 June   *Visiting Day and Fete. Donkey rides and Breaking Crockery Stall. Profit £32.*

29 June   *Dr. Johnstone and seven other Medical Officers came to visit the school. They were impressed and interested in the work done.*

3 July   *Visiting Day. The Midland Red Bus crashed into the Headmistress's Sitting Room window! Otherwise all went well.*

3 Dec.   *Cub party. Shared the cake made with the boys. Cubs had tea in the Headmistress's Sitting Room, 'Uncle H' came … All boys played games.*

Haseley Hall log book 1967

5 June   *Headmistress wakened by smell of fire … newspaper smouldering in kitchen rubbish … used matches later found under boy's bed …*

7 Sep.   *New nurse appointed, Mrs. Puddifoot.*

9 Dec.   *Xmas Party. Mr. Puddifoot acted as Santa.*

Haseley Hall log book 1968

27 April   *Members of Knowle and Dorridge Round Table came over to finish the sand pit they had made in the holidays.*

18 June   *Outing to Twycross Zoo.*

6 July   *Visiting Day and Fete Day … Miss Royle presented Headmistress with a gift (cheque) and lovely oil painting of Haseley Hall from staff, parents and boys, past and present, on her retirement.*

Each year it was the custom of Miss Butler-Fleming to go abroad for a well-earned holiday during the school summer vacation and 1968 was no exception, after being presented with the beautiful painting of Haseley Hall to mark her final departure from a life-time of teaching …

Sadly, she had no time to enjoy her retirement, as the entry in the school log book records in September 1968, at the beginning of the new term—'The staff are all deeply shocked at the death of Miss A.M. Butler-Fleming in an air accident on August 9th'. She was one of the many victims of the British Eagle plane disaster in Germany, together with her life-long teaching friend with whom she had shared so many holidays.

A letter appeared in the *Sunday Mercury* shortly afterwards. It was written by **Mrs. D. Tilley**, mother of one of the boys who spent many years at Haseley Hall School, and was entitled 'The Angel of Haseley Hall':

> Miss Butler-Fleming was one of the most charming and kindly persons I knew. My son was under her care for five years at Haseley Hall Open-Air School and her wonderful attention and kindness helped him through operations he had recently.
>
> Years ago, I stayed at the school one weekend and during the evening I went on the round with Miss Butler-Fleming. She was like the lady with the lamp—looking at each child to see if they were well and offering a goodnight kiss here and there.
>
> I wonder how many mothers realise just how wonderful she was to all those children in her care? I shall never forget her.

One of those children from the 1960s in Miss Butler-Fleming's time recalls his childhood at Haseley Hall in a mist of nostalgia:

Donald R. Cooper, Haseley Hall mid-1960s, Highgate, Birmingham

Transported by coach from the urban sprawl of inner city Birmingham at the age of six years you arrive, deep in the countryside, at a beautiful house nestled midst a forest of trees. Closer now, the driveway approach reveals a sort of ...castle! Momentarily transfixed, you glance toward luscious green lawns that seem to go on forever.

You enter the main hall at Haseley, lined with floor-level lockers at which a number of other boys are playing, sorting toys, arranging possessions. These will be your fellow knights in this castle, undoubtedly. Now you are taken upstairs to your dormitory, but no ordinary stairway this—here is a wide, dark-wood staircase overlooked by a massive floor-to-ceiling stained glass window with crests and designs you cannot wait to copy with paints and crayons in a drawing pad. Reaching the spacious landing reveals a fireplace for gathering around to recount tales of the day's chivalrous deeds, until finally you reach your allotted dormitory and settle your clothes into a chest of drawers and your small belongings to a bedside locker.

Now it's downstairs again at Haseley to view your classroom, then it is onward for an early tea-time. The dinner lady is kind and smiles a great deal, a smile she transfers to the clown face she 'draws' in squeezed tomato sauce on the circle of spam adorning your tea-plate. Looking around you see the other boys have boats or planes, yachts even, for eager consumption in the dining room. This nightly ritual over, you feel a little more welcome as you become vaguely aware of darkness settling itself on the lawns and fields roundabout Haseley.

After washing and teeth-cleaning in a cold-air bathroom, you change into your night-clothes and Rupert dressing gown for a story and song on the open-fire warmed landing before sleepily pacing the upper floor to your dormitory bed and lights-out for this tired first-day knight of Haseley Hall.

Time passes but the homesickness never really disappears. You have ordinary school lessons each weekday just like your primary school back in Birmingham, and you miss your Mum (Dad too, but he is in

Aerial view of Haseley Hall, with the neighbouring farm, 1960s. (G. Royle)

THE 1960s AND BEYOND: WINDS OF CHANGE

Heaven now but still watches over you at night in your dorm as you sleep). You receive, as do all the Haseley boys, regular parcels from home which are opened eagerly in the main hall to invariably reveal a letter, home requested toy, comic or sweets, the latter being pooled for all to share. These treasure-troves become barter at weekends when much 'lending' and 'swopping' is concluded amidst the cacophony of flying planes, and revving Dinky and Corgi toy engines.

You are all 'cubs' at Haseley and the field doubles as your nature reserve wherein foxes, squirrels and badgers appear to exist in relative harmony with running, shouting and leaping boys all trying to get healthier from their ailments. Then one day you succumb to a bad cold and 'flu and must stay in the first-floor sick room overlooking the makeshift wood swings that straddle two trees and make fine Thunderbirds One-Two-Three's. While your friends gambol in delight in the first winter snows you lose your appetite and take to secreting convalescing toast and boiled egg behind a hardboard fireplace cover and pray for non-detection. You pray for a distinct lack of monsters behind the partition, too, especially at nightfall.

The seasons change and you learn evermore about nature on-site, as opposed to picture books back in Birmingham, so that when you return home for holidays to your native City a sense of 'environmental yearning' manifests itself within your mind. This yearning will remain dormant for some considerable time.

Thirty years after the nostalgic-mist events recounted above, that yearning surfaces with a vengeance. The young boy who in effect 'endured' his time at Haseley Hall is now the One-Wife-One-Child Man who finds himself drawn inexorably back to the location of what now seem halcyon days. Winter 1994 found my 'castle' neglected yet still habitable and 'For Sale'! The couple who live at the adjacent Haseley Lodge allow me access to an interior that has always lived in a corner of my mind and we venture tentatively through a trace memory of idyllic days long before. I think of the impending National Lottery in November and ponder silently if 'Camelot' could assist this latter-day knight in his quest for an ever-retreating dream of countryside quality of life.

Donald Cooper wrote home regularly to his mother who kept some of his letters:

'Miss Fleming gave us a cine show on Sunday night. We have been playing in the cubs' field.'

'Went on a picnic on Saturday with a bottle of pop. We saw a baby squirrel down in the field.'

'Jack Frost is about. The pond was frozen. Please will you send me parcel. We went to play in the field.'

'It was nice to see you on Sunday. Thank you for the Thunderbird Two. I played with it in the field.'

Another past pupil **Stephen J. Knight**, Haseley Hall 1961–3, Bournville, Birmingham, writes:

I was six years old when I started at Haseley Hall due to my poor health and constant asthma. We lived at Stirchley, Birmingham, at the time and Warwick seemed the other end of the world to me.

On arriving at the school Miss Fleming the Headmistress greeted us. I remember a large oak panelled entrance hall and staircase, with rooms leading off and dormitories upstairs.

Our school day began early. We used to rise about 7.00am, dress, and then it was breathing exercises, often outside on the lawn regardless of temperature. Breakfast followed and then the normal school curriculum of the day was followed until lunch time. After lunch everyone had to retire to their beds for an hour and lie on the top sheet. This for most of us was particularly difficult and I recall often staring at the ceiling in silence for what seemed an eternity.

More exercises followed outside: deep breathing, jumping on the spot, gambols, relay races, and the very occasional cross country run. There was also a paddling pool in the grounds. Most windows and doors seemed to be open all of the time, day and night, regardless of the weather. Our evening meal was followed by a bath; the water was never more than two inches deep and a starched uniformed 'nurse' used to bath a line of naked boys, all playing up, in about five minutes flat. Pyjamas and bed, lights out was about 7.00pm.

> *I recall two children in particular. One lad was completely bald due to some ailment, but a mischievous likeable soul, and the other was black (this was particularly unusual 35 years ago, especially as I cannot recall any black children at my home school in Stirchley). He suffered from bad eczema as well as asthma. We became particularly good friends.*
>
> *Parents visited the first Sunday in the month, arriving about 1pm with departure about 4.00pm, prior to tea time. Moms and Dads used to bring goodie bags to try and cheer us up, although expensive toys and gifts were discouraged. A fete atmosphere was the usual course of events, bows and arrows, tombola, hoops, tea and scones etc. with the proceeds going towards the school fund. Those three hours passed so quickly, and it was soon time for Mom and Dad to leave. This was a particularly sad time, often with tears, knowing it was another month to wait for those precious hours again.*
>
> *Well, my two years passed and it was time for me to leave. My parents said there was a marked difference in me; my health had improved dramatically, and I was also more independent and could organise myself better than the average eight year old. I returned to Stirchley.*
>
> *My asthma seemed to diminish after this although as a young teenager I still had the occasional bad attack. It is now almost non-existent except for about six weeks in the summer and seems to be hay fever related.*

Although Haseley Hall Open-Air School closed over 20 years ago, it remains firmly in the memories of many local people who worked there. With the help of the caretaker's wife at Haseley Lodge, which guarded the entrance to the deserted Hall in 1994, it was possible to trace some of the staff who worked at the school and some detective work with a telephone directory finally led to the last Headmistress of Haseley Hall.

Some local families had many years' connections with Haseley Hall, before it became a school, as a resident in a nearby cottage recalled in 1994:

Mrs. Mary Elliott (who worked at Haseley Hall 1965-1974), South Cottage, Haseley

I was born and bred in Birmingham and met Reg Elliott, my husband, through family friends. I married during the war but stayed at home with my father as my mother had died. Two years later I came to live in Haseley in South Cottage, near Haseley Hall, where the Elliott family had lived for many years. My son was six weeks old and I brought up my family here.

My father-in-law was the caretaker at the Hall during Sir James Sawyer's time, and my mother-in-law was once the sewing maid to Lady Sawyer. That was how they met. Sir James Sawyer had been a consultant in Birmingham and had rooms in London. He went to London about twice a year and my father-in-law used to take him to Hatton Station in the pony and trap, and meet him off the train on his return.

After Sir James Sawyer's death the Hall became a 'Home' for managers and directors of the Birmingham firm of Averys who made weighing machines. My father-in-law used to work in the bar there and there

were some good times going on there, I was told! Later on the Hall became a charity Convalescent Home for girls who had heart problems.

Haseley Hall had a beautiful staircase and the south window used to be the pride and joy of Sir James Sawyer, according to my mother-in-law. There was also supposed to be a ghost—the Grey Lady—but I never saw her!

My children used to be invited to the Christmas parties at the Hall when it became an open-air school. There were some good bonfire parties too. The two Headmistresses—Miss Butler-Fleming and Miss Royle—were always very friendly.

I went to work at the Hall in 1965 after my husband had died suddenly of a massive heart attack at the age of 51; he'd never had a day's illness before. I worked at the Hall until it closed, under Miss Fleming then Miss Royle. I worked with the caretaker from 8.30-11.30am, sweeping the classrooms and the hall. I also went there at night from 5.00-6.00pm to wash up the boys' tea-things. Many of the little boys came from broken homes and poor backgrounds and many had asthma. Miss Fleming was very keen on the open-air and used to take the boys on walks. By the 1970s there was more emphasis on drugs for the asthmatic boys. After lunch the boys lay on their beds and many Old Boys have come to me over the years to say what a happy place it was. You should have seen the boys' faces at the Christmas parties—they came from such poor homes. My son-in-law was once Father Christmas! In the summer there was a small paddling pool for the boys to sail their little boats.

Miss Fleming, who came from Leeds, gave her life to those boys and was looking forward to a holiday in Austria after her retirement in July ... she was given a beautiful painting of the Hall covered in creeper, when she retired. But she died next month in an aircraft on a flight to Austria.

When the lease ran out in 1974 Birmingham Education Authority wanted to buy the Hall, which was owned, I think, by Warwickshire County Council. Birmingham wanted to expand the school but eventually went on to open Skilts and improve Springfields at Knowle. The Hall was eventually sold to Severn-Trent [Water Authority]. Severn-Trent sold the land off eventually and was only interested in the water. They took all the water from our cottage well and then we had our water round on carts! It took a long time before we got back on to the mains supply. Meanwhile the Hall was sold and turned into twelve flats but is empty at the moment.

In the changing era of the 1960s life carried on at the school for several years, as the log book records in the neat writing of Miss Gillian Royle, who became the final Headmistress of Haseley Hall:

Haseley Hall log book 1968/9

9 Sep 1968   *Mr. Pearce came to look at the teaching staff's residential accommodation before it is assessed by an Estates Valuation Officer. Extraneous duties are to be paid and accommodation charged for.*

9 Feb. 1969   *3 members of Knowle and Dorridge Round Table came in the afternoon to present a film strip projector to the school in memory of the late Miss A.M. Butler-Fleming. A fibre glass slide was also presented for the boys.*

9 Sep. 1969   *Mr. Tansley came out to see me by request to discuss my plans for the internal reorganisation of the school ... he agreed with my idea and gave me permission to go ahead ...*

Decisions to close Haseley Hall were made by Birmingham Education Committee by March 1974, during the reorganisation of the Health Service. Future placements of the boys were eventually noted in the log book and, by the last day of the school on 26 July 1974, 18 boys had been transferred to Skilts, three to Baskerville, one to Astley Hall, one to Springfield, and three to ordinary schools. Staff at the school were also dispersed: Miss Royle and two teachers to

Astley Hall, one teacher to Skilts and children's helpers and domestic staff had to find alternative employment.

It must have been a sad time for all concerned, not least for Miss Royle, the Headmistress. She had become Acting Head on Miss Butler-Fleming's retirement in 1968, as it was never envisaged the school would remain open many more months. Eventually she became permanent Headmistress as the school remained open in an uncertain era. She worked for 13 years at Haseley Hall as a resident teacher, six years of them as Headmistress. Her account of life at the Hall gives us a fascinating insight into a small residential school for boys, very different from Hunter's Hill:

Miss Gillian Royle, Teacher & Headmistress, Haseley Hall 1961-74, Earlswood, W. Midlands

I was born in Salford and went on to Training College to do a three year Froebel training. I wanted to work with handicapped children but was advised to work with normal children for several years before embarking on teaching handicapped ones.

After five years in a Primary School, I went to a Residential School for Physically Handicapped children in Yorkshire. I was responsible for a class of 20 children with a wide range of handicaps and abilities. It was excellent training.

In 1961 I joined the staff at Haseley Hall as Deputy Head. There were 40 boys aged between five and nine years and they were all delicate, in the main suffering from asthma or recurrent bronchitis. I was responsible for a class of ten boys aged eight and nine years.

Miss Butler-Fleming took a day off each week as she worked every weekend, covering Saturday evening and Sunday afternoon and evening. The other teachers—Miss Jones, Miss Ward and I—covered the other three sessions. Not a very satisfactory arrangement as we never got a completely free weekend. At this time teachers received free board and lodgings in return for 15 hours extraneous duty.

If I was on duty Saturday morning, I was responsible for shoe cleaning. I put polish on 40 pairs of sandals and 40 pairs of shoes! The boys then produced the required shine. After this I took the boys out to play at the back of the school. There was a climbing frame, two swings and a sand pit. We gradually built up a collection of second hand bikes and tricycles.

If I was on duty on Saturday afternoon, it was playtime again but this time we went down the drive to play in the field. This became more exciting after a gale blew down a large beech tree. There was the horizontal trunk to walk along, the branches to bounce on, the hole where the roots had been to explore and the exposed roots to clean off their encrusting soil. That tree gave years of pleasure and must have been the cheapest climbing frame on the market!

The short straw of weekend duties was Sunday morning. Miss Butler-Fleming did not wish the boys to play on Sundays, so they put on their best black shoes and best coats, and accompanied by the teacher and two children's helpers (as untrained child care staff were called) we went for a walk. We walked either toward Warwick or Chadwick End and then turned round and returned in time for dinner. As the A41 got busier and the behaviour of some of the boys became more unpredictable, I persuaded Miss Butler-Fleming that these walks really weren't safe. So eventually the boys were allowed to play on Sunday mornings.

Visiting days were once a month on a Sunday afternoon—by special bus from Meriden Street[Birmingham] to the school. The boys were kept in the dining room while the parents congregated in the Hall. After Miss Butler-Fleming had welcomed them and given out any necessary announcements, the boys were brought into the hall to meet their parents. As we never managed to get all the parents to visit there were always a few very disappointed boys to be kept occupied for the afternoon.

Dr. Kemp, the Senior School Medical Officer, paid regular visits and examined every boy at least once a term and more often if it was deemed necessary. When Dr. Kemp retired we had a succession of School Medical Officers visiting and the visits became less frequent. Nurse Adams from Great Charles Street clinic came to visit two or three times a year to test the sight of the boys.

Boys enjoying the fresh air and sunshine in the grounds of Haseley Hall, 1960s. Dave Hammond, Cub Scout leader, is on the right in the back row. (G. Royle)

Mr. Collins, a Remedial Gymnast, came once a week to give exercises to the asthmatic and bronchitic boys. He also gave individual treatment to boys with postural problems. The teachers were instructed how to carry out the programme of exercises. Each morning after assembly the school was divided into three groups: asthmatics, bronchitics and general. One teacher took each group and the morning started with fifteen minutes of exercises. I was responsible for the bronchitic group and the object of the exercises was to increase the capacity of the lungs. The main aim of the asthmatic breathing exercises was to get the boys to empty their lungs. We had a good success rate in preventing wheeziness progressing to a full blown asthma attack, by reassuring the sufferer and encouraging him to do his breathing exercises.

The school nurse was Miss Dainty. She was non-resident, but slept in when Miss Butler-Fleming had her day off. Unless the nurse was on the premises, the teacher on duty was responsible for giving the evening drugs. Miss Butler-Fleming was responsible for dealing with any illness during the night, as she was the only member of staff sleeping on the same landing as the boys. Nurse Dainty eventually married and left, so for a time the school was without a nurse.

During this time we had a small fire. Graham, a hyper-kinetic child, who required very little sleep, had gone walk about at about 5.30am in the morning and set fire to a box of newspapers. Miss Butler-Fleming woke, smelt smoke and went to investigate and put out the fire. Later that day Sgt Puddifoot of Warwick Police came out to get a report of the incident. The unexpected outcome of this incident was that Sgt Puddifoot was a nurse looking for a way back into nursing after bringing up her family. So Nurse Puddifoot joined the staff.

Miss Jones and Miss Ward left and Miss Payne and Mrs. Scrivener joined the staff. Later on, Miss Castle and Mrs. Sharman joined the staff when Mrs. Scrivener and Miss Payne left the school.

In the early days the boys still had a rest after dinner. Each boy had a red blanket bag at the bottom of their beds. They took their shoes off and snuggled into their bags for half an hour. The rest time was stopped shortly after I went to Haseley, as we felt that with an adequate balanced diet and plenty of sleep at night, there was really no need for a rest for the majority of the boys. If nurse considered any boy to be in need of a rest, she supervised it.

During the very cold winter we had some problems with frozen pipes. One night after all the boys were in bed one of the children's helpers reported water dripping through the bathroom ceiling. Miss Butler-Fleming got a mop and bucket and I offered to go up in the roof space to investigate. There were innumerable tanks in the roof and miles of pipes. Some tanks were empty and other full of ice and water. A pipe was leaking and as the ice in the tank melted it was dripping out. The answer seemed to be to empty the one tank. I tied up the ball cock and baled out the tank, lowering the buckets of ice and water to the children's helpers waiting under the hatch in the airing cupboard. What a way to spend an evening! The next morning my little finger was very swollen and black and blue. Down to casualty at Warwick Hospital I went only to be told I had frost bite.

As there was no resident caretaker the last job each evening for the duty teacher was to stoke the hot water boiler and push the damper in.

It was discovered that there was dry rot in the building. The main thing to be affected was the wooden beam on the landing over the top of the stairs. As this beam carried the roof supports we had a major incident on our hands. With hindsight I feel sure that Miss Butler-Fleming should have insisted that the school be closed while the treatment and repair work was carried out. But life at Haseley continued. Half the boys had to be sent home, as three dormitories were out of action. We could only use half the hall and the dining room and toilets were cut off.

The main problem was having access to the toilets for the boys. This I solved by putting the plank of the climbing apparatus onto the window sill. A visit to the toilet involved climbing onto a chair, out of the window, down the plank and off to the toilet. I'm sure more visits to the toilet than were absolutely necessary were taken, but who could blame them!

I always felt that we had a lovely end to the day. The children's helpers took groups of boys for their baths while the teacher on duty supervised the remaining boys. When all were bathed, supper eaten and teeth cleaned, all the boys assembled on the carpet on the landing for their bedtime story. In winter we had an open coal fire on the landing making it very cosy. After the story we had prayers and then off to bed at 7.00pm. The oldest boys were allowed to sit up in bed and read quietly for half an hour. The duty teacher stayed on the landing until the last boys were asleep.

I don't know exactly when the intake of boys to the school altered. It was a very gradual process. We still admitted many asthmatic children, but the bronchitic boys disappeared with the introduction of better antibiotics. There were still boys who failed to thrive at home, but we were increasingly asked to take boys who were emotionally disturbed. It was surprising how quickly they responded to a stable loving environment.

In 1968, when Miss Butler-Fleming retired, I was responsible for organising her present and retirement party. The choice of present was difficult, but in the end we got Mrs. Moore, a local artist, to paint a picture of Haseley Hall. It was beautiful, the house in all its glory with little blue clad boys playing round about.

Miss Butler-Fleming had been abroad every summer since I had known her, but on this occasion she really didn't want to go …

At this time it was already on the cards that Haseley Hall would close, so I was asked to become acting head until the closure. However after 12 months the Education Committee realised that the closure was going to take longer than expected, so they made my appointment permanent.

I had felt for some years that we were wrong in dealing with the boys in a group of 40 for all their out-of-school activities. The more shy, timid boys were getting overlooked and, in some of the things we did, it was like a factory conveyor belt.

There was a spare room on the boys' landing, which was originally the nurse's bedroom, but was no longer required. My idea was to turn this room and two other dormitories into sitting/dining/play rooms for groups of approximately 12 boys. Each group to be the sole responsibility of one children's helper for all their out-of-school activities. This could be achieved by reducing the total number of boys to 35 and by using the obsolete sick bay as a dormitory.

I discussed my idea with Mr. Tansley, the adviser for Special Education, and he approved. The hotplate was moved from the dining room up onto the landing. Now school was downstairs and home was upstairs.

The boys now got up, had breakfast in their own groups, made their beds, and came downstairs for assembly before going into class. At dinner time the children's helpers collected their group and took them upstairs for dinner, after which they played with them until it was time for school again, either in their sitting rooms or outside depending on the weather. At the end of school they were again collected for play and tea. This change had freed the old dining room, which was turned into the third classroom and the very small classroom was turned into a library.

Miss Jones was then appointed Deputy Head, the first non-resident deputy. Mrs. Oliver joined the staff, followed by Mrs. Woodward when Mrs. Sharman retired. They were with me until the school closed.

By this time most parents had cars so I decided to make visiting a much more open affair. Parents were allowed to visit any Sunday afternoon between 2.00pm and 4.00pm and could, if they so wished, have their boy home for the weekend.

In order to broaden their experience, I found two local Cub Scout leaders who were willing to take five boys into their packs. I then spent two evenings a week being a taxi to and from Cub meetings, but it was worth it for the pleasure that the boys got out of it.

As Head I was responsible for writing the menus and ordering the food. This was not as simple as it sounds as there were always about eight boys who couldn't eat certain foods. There were the asthmatics who couldn't eat either fish or eggs. In fact, we had one boy so allergic to fish that he couldn't go into the dining room when fish was on the menu. The coeliacs couldn't have anything with flour. The cook baked special bread for them made with gluten-free flour. We had to read labels very carefully. There was only one make of baked beans we could use. Then, of course, there were the foods denied to certain religions.

Throughout all my time at Haseley Hall the objective was to get as many boys as possible back home and into ordinary Primary Schools. In the early days, if this wasn't possible, the boys transferred to Hunter's Hill. After the opening of Skilts some boys moved on there if it was felt they would be fit to return home at 11 years of age. When the school closed there was little problem about placing the boys, as Skilts had extra residential accommodation built ready to take them.

I was appointed to the headship of Astley Hall Special School, another school that was on the closure list in Birmingham. (Miss Smith, the Head, and two of her teachers had retired.) Mrs. Oliver and Miss Woodward chose to come to Astley with me. Miss Jones opted to move to Skilts, as it was nearer her home in Warwick. It was nice for the boys to have a familiar face when they got there.

Haseley Hall was converted to luxury flats, but eventually stood silent and deserted until 1995, hidden away from the main road in leafy Warwickshire. There was little sign of movement around the Hall, with no hint of the bustle and hustle of school life which had nurtured small 'delicate' boys back to health. The gardens and lawns surrounding the Hall had reverted to nature, overgrown with weeds, whilst the shuttered windows gave a ghostly air ... Today, however, the Hall has taken on a new lease of life with extensions and building developments so that once again it is an exclusive country residence.

Haseley Hall's log book is deposited in Birmingham's Central Library (Archives Department) and remains the only tangible evidence of the city's fifth open-air school, apart from the poignant memories of those who have contributed to our book. There must be many more 'old boys' who could testify to the success of their special education which enabled them to live normal lives.

Skilts

Skilts was the sixth and last of Birmingham's open-air schools, opening in 1958. Birmingham Education Authority probably planned to compensate for the envisaged closure of Haseley Hall, which it leased and never owned. In addition, the loss of the Alpine School at Davos [in Switzerland] must have played some part in its creation, as the number of asthmatic children gradually increased, together with sociological cases.

The school log books recording the opening of Skilts are missing, so it is fortunate that we have been able to trace the first Headmaster, Ivor Mitchell, who kept many notes on his five years at the school.

He had taught in several of Birmingham's special schools, including two for 'Educationally Sub-Normal' children and one for the physically disabled. After leaving Skilts he became Head Teacher of a school for physically disabled pupils, which was one of the first schools to take part in the National Games held by the British Sports Association for the Disabled. He received an OBE in 1988 for his many years service to that Association. His following account gives a detailed description of Skilts, together with the philosophy of the establishment:

Mr. Ivor Mitchell, Headmaster, Skilts 1958-63, Lichfield, Staffordshire

By 1958 the original reason for creating Open-Air Schools had declined but it was recognised that there was a continuing need for residential placement for some children who were not appropriately classifiable under the other categories of Special Education. Some such children were suffering from physical conditions which did not qualify them to be classified as 'Physically Handicapped', but which could reasonably be described as 'Delicate'. Among these there was a range of respiratory conditions, some of which were physical in origin, whereas others were regarded as psychosomatic. Additionally there were children who might be regarded as social or emotional casualties for whom a change of environment on a residential basis was considered to be desirable, or in some cases essential. The traditional Open-Air School for Delicate Children carried no social stigma; it therefore provided a convenient and socially acceptable placement.

The name Skilts is derived from Skyllus Grange which had belonged to the Priory of Studley. The site of the grange was Lower Skilts, situated less than half a mile to the south of Upper Skilts, the house which in 1958 became Skilts School.

Fourteen miles from Birmingham, this three-storeyed country mansion is approached by a half mile long drive from the top of Gorcott Hill on the A435, the main road to Studley and Alcester. From Skilts can be seen the Cotswolds to the south, the distant Malverns and the hills of Shropshire to the west and to the east the fields and farms of leafy Warwickshire. In 1958 the town of Redditch, with a population of under 36,000 and little more than three miles away, was merely a feature in a largely pastoral landscape.

The house had been the home of the titled Jaffray family who lived in gracious oak-panelled style, complete with a home farm at the centre of an extensive estate. Among notable visitors had been Sir Anthony Eden, Member of Parliament for Warwick and Leamington, later Foreign Secretary and Prime Minister before becoming the First Earl of Avon.

When the property was sold the City of Birmingham purchased the house and the home farm. For a period of six years before becoming a school the house had been used by the City of Birmingham Public Health department as a short-stay nursery and with little further adaptation converted successfully to its new function. At the time the school was opened the farm was still occupied by the original tenant Mr. John Pearman. The close proximity of the farm was of considerable advantage to the school for apart from being a very good neighbour Mr. Pearman welcomed the children's interest and readily allowed us to roam freely over his land. This mixed arable and stock farm was an ever-present stimulating visual aid with a herd of pedigree

Herefordshire cattle—including two stock bulls—pigs, sheep and poultry. All with the added interest of tractors and other farm machinery. To complete the rural scene the Hunt occasionally met locally and on one memorable occasion the chase in pink-coated splendour pursued the fox across the field below the school. The educational value of such an event was not to be missed and all the children, perched upon the fence, were so moved by the competition that as one they yelled 'Come on the fox!'.

View of Skilts and grounds at the back, 1958-63. (I. Mitchell)

1958 was towards the end of what might be called 'the country house era of residential special education'. Such establishments were often criticised for being too isolated from the pupil's home environment. In some ways the contrast was a significant advantage. Although fresh air was no longer regarded as the 'cure-all' it was still beneficial, especially when combined with nourishing food, balanced exercise and rest and above all else a planned rhythm of daily routine. In the case of Skilts, its distance from any urban influence and community we saw as an advantage in that its initial development was free from intrusive external influence. It was not necessary to conform to inhibiting behavioural patterns in order to meet the social demands of an established community. This was not regarded as an excuse for undesirable behaviour, rather it was welcomed for the opportunity afforded for acceptable traditions of social conduct to become established free from coercive pressure. That it worked became progressively evident and caused a visiting HMI to remark upon the school being particularly civilised. A more personal testimonial came years later from a self-employed presentable young man, who as a tough eight year old had been admitted for 'non-medical' reasons, who said 'The only time I have ever felt free was when I was at Skilts!'.

At a later stage in the school's development the existence of a nearby compact residential community might have been socially advantageous and could possibly have helped to overcome a practical disadvantage of our isolation—the difficulty of recruiting non-resident child care and domestic staff. However, the advantages clearly outweighed the disadvantages as we roved over fields and farmland and played safely in the three nearby exciting woodlands.

The school opened with a series of bangs on November the Fifth 1958, with 39 children, 4 teachers, 1 nurse, 2 care assistants, domestic staff, a dog, a cat, a Bonfire Party and a lot of optimism! An analysis of diagnoses revealed the majority of the children to be suffering from recurrent respiratory problems, including asthma and bronchitis, while others were variously described as delicate or suffering from debility or other acceptable indicators of a need to be rescued from adverse home conditions.

Detailed records were kept of asthma attacks and it is worthy of note that their frequency was found to be progressively reducing during term time in spite of the fact that many thus diagnosed were recorded as being allergic to pollen and animal dander, both of which there was plenty. Animals were closely observed and fondled. Guinea-pigs eventually played an important role in our community for apart from their therapeutic contribution to the emotional development of individual children, they provided a useful aid in demonstrating the cycle of existence through mating, birth, life and death. Before the days of controversial sex education a regular visitor to the school was greeted one playtime by an eight year old girl inviting him to 'come and see Clara eating her placenta!'

Among the regular visitors was a Remedial Gymnast who spent a morning each week working with the children in groups according to their physical remedial needs. At 9.15am, after Morning Assembly, the children would carry out formal exercises based upon those he had prescribed. In supervising these exercises the teaching staff became very knowledgeable of their pupils' conditions. The groups thus formed were composed of pupils across the age range from five to eleven and in doing so created another social grouping in addition to those of dormitory and dining room.

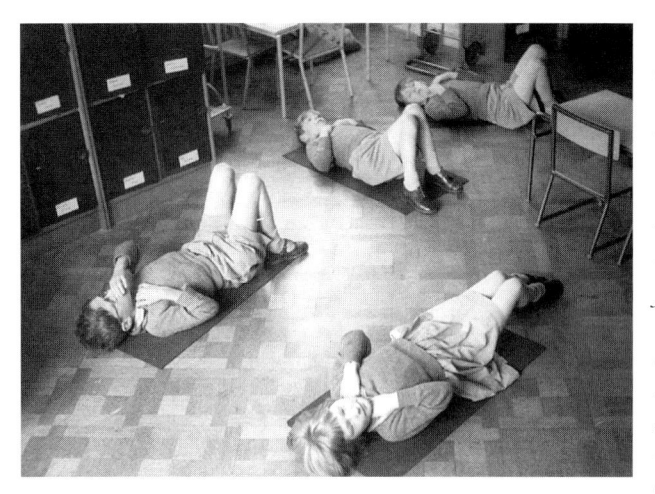

Asthmatic group of children doing remedial exercises at Skilts. (I. Mitchell)

In the dormitory the groups were sex-separated and were broadly age-related, whereas in the dining room the youngest ate with, and were closely supervised by, the care staff, and the older children dined in mixed age group, the whole relaxed procedure being under the discrete supervision of the duty teacher dining with them. Special diets were provided for those for whom they were prescribed and all received a carefully planned diet designed with the assistance of the resident school nurse. Meal times were treated as valuable social occasions, freed from emotion, and where a simple 'we all eat a little of everything' rule was sensitively applied. The oak-panelled dining room decorated with appropriately colourful pictures influenced decorum and the consciously designed relaxed atmosphere established standards which the children soon adopted. Many parents reported upon their children's improved appetites and, in some instances, their children's 'missionary attempts' to change family meal time procedures. Some expressed their regret at their inability to finance what the school was able to provide.

The long-standing Open-Air School tradition of 'bed-rest' after the midday meal was only adopted for the youngest pupils. For those who were older it was decided that physical relaxation should be accompanied by mental stimulation. The multi-purpose Hall/Playroom was furnished with a number of wicker type chairs and a large cushioned window seat and from 1.15 until 2.00pm each day the children listened to readings of quality children's literature. The Puffin Series was a source of much of this and the children became familiar with Lions, Witches and Wardrobes, The Borrowers, Prince Caspian, Emil and the Detectives, Treasure Island, Robin Hood and many other classics. A visiting HMI remarked with some surprise at the literary knowledge of an imaginative, but not academically gifted, young 'toughy'.

This same regular visitor particularly commented upon the school's deliberately planned rhythm, physical activities alternating with spells of quietness and relaxation. He observed that the balanced programme was remarkably effective.

Another regular visitor was the local doctor, Dr. Phillips, who described the school as his hobby, and routinely called once a week, being on call at other times if needed. The School Medical Officer attended for Termly Reviews when pupils were assessed for their readiness to return home (if the home was ready for their return) and the type of school most suited to their needs was considered. These were valuable occasions of multi-discipline consultation when the needs of the whole child were subjected to close scrutiny. Dentistry was carried out by the visiting School Dentist, a skilled friend of the children, who inspired confidence and dispelled fear. Eventually the school also had the services of a Speech Therapist for one morning each week.

The most important visitors were, of course, those who came on Visiting Days—the parents. Before the days of much vaunted accountability these parents were able to learn what the school was doing with their children and at the same time often demonstrated significant factors in their relationship with their children. Two incidents stand out. A six year old boy would hide on these occasions because he was afraid that his mother was going to take him home: their relationship was helped when he was found and she did not take him home. A forthright mother of an older girl brought along her neighbour and the moment of reunion was dominated by the mother lifting the girl's skirt and triumphantly proclaiming 'There! I told you they don't wear navy blue knickers!' The fact that they were bottle green apparently placed the establishment in a class above a blue-knickered institution!

The initial clothing purchases had been arranged centrally before the school opened and seemed to have assumed a regime and life style different from that envisaged by the appointed staff. Pleated flannel skirts soon became unpleated and were replaced by plain worsted. Flannel blazers, bottle green, were rarely worn and the Education Authority was persuaded to purchase anoraks and dungarees. These, and 'wellies', soon became the playtime unisex costume which at weekends promoted a pattern of carefree activity within the school grounds, exploration and wide-games further afield.

Standard playground apparatus supplemented a magnificent and child-tolerant holm-oak tree, designed by nature to be climbed. A number of older children would retreat into the seclusion of its evergreen branches to read their letters from home, or the comics that accompanied them. It afforded a degree of privacy, always hard to find within a residential community.

The maintenance of continued contact with home was of great importance and was served by the Garden Party as well as Visiting Days and the weekly letter writing. The 'long weekend' half term holiday was particularly important, as acknowledged by the father who reported that his son had said 'This has been the best school holiday I've ever had. It wasn't long enough for me to get on your nerves—or you on mine!'

But wasn't this supposed to be a school? What happened to 'Education'? It certainly was a school, and the skilled teaching staff were well qualified for the work they had undertaken in that they did not recognise any artificial distinction between work and play. Stephen Jackson in his 'Special Education in England and Wales' wrote of schools for Delicate children:

'There is no special training for this work, and yet in many ways teaching in this type of school makes greater demands upon a teacher's skill, knowledge and personal qualities than does any other kind of teaching.'

Special educational placement inevitably has an element of therapy, provided in this instance by a total environment for a whole-child approach. The basic ingredient of the 'Three Rs' was not the exclusive province of the classroom, but it was there that they were formalised. Prolonged and often frequent absence from their former day school had caused many pupils to be retarded, unrelated to their alleged intelligence. Small classes with individual attention promoted accelerated learning, assisted by improving physical health in stimulating surroundings.

After the school had been open for four years a report analysing diagnoses, lengths of stay and details of transfer revealed that 69 boys and 48 girls had been admitted. Of these 68 were diagnosed as suffering from respiratory conditions—mainly asthma or recurrent bronchitis—while the others were recorded as having other kinds of problems. The 45 places, 26 boys and 19 girls, were filled for periods of from 1 to 12 terms with 38.4 per cent in school for 3 terms or less, 23.2 per cent for between 3 and 6 terms, 20.5 per cent for from 6 to 9 terms and 6.9 per cent for more than 9. Of the 73 pupils who had left 49 had been returned to mainstream day schools and 11 had continued in residential placement in senior open-air schools; the remaining 13 moving to other day special schools. In the school's fifth year two boys were transferred to residential grammar schools on reaching secondary age. Most pupils remaining at Skilts for short periods reflected causes of admission of a rapidly

Skilts: the holm oak tree was popular for climbing in school dungarees. (I. Mitchell)

remedial nature, usually solved by rehousing. Those staying for longer either suffered from chronic medical conditions or whose home circumstances were not conducive to sustained health and stability.

Success or failure of educational establishments is not always easy to account for, especially when the bases from which the pupils start are so varied, complex and in some cases very disadvantaged. Where are they now, these forty-year-olds? The elective mute girl, the boy whose father had admitted having committed the ultimate crime and was rescued from the pressures of media interest, the girl whose father I visited in prison and the boy who went on to University. Physical, social, emotional and academic development are closely related and are often interdependent. Skilts strove to identify and to nurture positive attributes while largely depending upon the therapeutic regime and environment to reduce those that might be regarded as negative. The most important factor within that environment was the dedication of the professional staff. In such a small three-class school with a less than adequate number of child-care staff, the seven day week demanded good health, and stamina as well as dedication. At times of teaching staff illness the routine twenty-plus hours of 'extraneous duty' per week leapt to the borders of exhaustion.

For me, after five years, family needs and promotion to the attraction of a different challenge, demanded a change. This was achieved with some strong feelings of loss for teachers learn much from their pupils.

Skilts was praised in the school inspection of 1963 as being a good boarding school where staff were aware of the children's needs and skilfully provided conditions where the pupils improved 'satisfactorily in bodily and mental health as well as in educational attainments'. Although more than half the pupils admitted to Skilts were under the age of seven on entry, they were cared for with such affection and understanding that the policy of early admission was regarded 'as a positive advantage to the children concerned'.

It was recognised that the Headmaster, Ivor Mitchell, had made a tremendous contribution to the success of the school, together with his three teachers, all of whom were highly qualified and experienced with children in Special Schools.

It was noted that each day Skilts had a carefully balanced planned rhythm, with physical activities alternating with mental activities, as well as stimulation and relaxation. Any medical treatment was unobtrusive, rarely interrupting classwork and was under the direction of the daily nurse.

The school grounds were mentioned in the report for the imaginative way in which all sorts of leisure opportunities were possible: with a sand pit, hard-surfaced areas and paddling pool, climbing apparatus, pets' corner, garden plots and a craft hut for woodwork and clay modelling. Few children could fail to respond to living in such civilised, interesting and health-restoring surroundings.

Over the years the school has been successfully enlarged and is still part of the network of Birmingham's Special Schools despite its isolation from the city. One member of staff has worked there for a remarkable 37 years and has seen many changes:

Miss Cynthia Brinkley, Bursar, Skilts, 1959 to date, Redditch, Worcs.

I started as an assistant cook in November 1959. For a few years the opening of the school was celebrated by the making of a special birthday cake. I progressed to cook

Even asthmatic children could enjoy boisterous play at Skilts. (I. Mitchell)

Looking towards Lower Skilts on a weekend ramble at Skilts. (I. Mitchell)

then to my present position of Bursar working under five Heads: Mr. Mitchell, Mr. Cameron, Mr. Nye, Mr. Brownsword and Miss Probert. There were 45 resident children here at first all living in what is now the main building. There were three dormitories for the girls, four for boys, three bathrooms, a play room, a dining room, television room, cloakroom, staff room, medical room, two sick bays, three classrooms.

Living accommodation was provided for most of the staff. On the top floor was the Head Teacher's flat, three rooms for teachers and a small sewing room. Second floor: all dormitories, play room, sick bays plus staff accommodation. Ground floor: classrooms, staff room, office, medical room, kitchen, plus accommodation for the housekeeper.

We still have the original fridge in the main kitchen! We did most of the cooking by a big, solid fuel ESSE which was stoked up night and morning by the caretaker. We did all home cooking (frozen food unknown to us then) and grew our own vegetables as there were greenhouses and gardens. We cooked three meals a day, seven days a week. We used the old fashioned thick white china plates, dishes and beakers. These were all washed up by hand, put in trays, and lifted into a sterilizer; it was very hard work.

All staff were very much involved with the children. We always had a Christmas dinner and tea. A Birthday Party was given for every child. Every Saturday and Sunday the children were taken for a walk. This sometimes took the form of a picnic and we often went to a house which had a shop in its front room.

The children wore uniform but this changed over the years. Now all children wear their own clothes. Most washing was done at the school and on the night before the end of term we could be washing until 10pm to get it finished!

The drive has been blocked by snow three or four times since I have been here. I remember the first time, we had to get the children out on sledges going over the fields, and some of us staff were sledging down the drive!

Later on the school was extended. The gardens disappeared and two bungalows were built for Head and Deputy. Three Blocks were built consisting of a kitchen in the middle, dining room, playroom and staff accommodation. More class rooms, gym and office were built and the main front door disappeared along with the gazebo. We eventually had 120 children and the type of child changed from delicate to maladjusted.

As the years went by the number reduced and a block was closed. We now have 45 to 50 children, with quite a few coming in daily. We became a five day week school with children going home at weekends. The children used to be taken into Birmingham by coach, by a teacher. Now it is door to door service with taxis.

At the end of the summer term child care and domestic staff worked for two weeks, doing an annual spring clean. I have seen many staff during my time—some good, some bad, some happy, some sad. But laughter was never very far away. Being out in the country we had to make our own amusements.

A news-cutting gives an account of Skilts in the mid-1960s, as it was run by the second Headmaster, Mr. D. Cameron, who outlined his three main aims in a newspaper interview:

> I want to create a happy and industrious community, to help children obtain their fair measure of health, and to help the maladjusted child fit into ordinary life ...We teach the children to live with a disability, and, if possible, overcome it. We do not fuss over them but treat them as normal children, expecting them to do as much as they are capable of. However, when they are ill, everything is done to assist them to recover ...This entails a tremendous amount of extra work for all the staff ...

There was a family atmosphere at Skilts. The caretaker, Mr. W. Moorehouse, had been there since 1919, first employed as a groom. The Headmaster's wife was the School Secretary, his daughter Jane a physical education specialist who taught the younger children. Mr. Cameron commented:

> The child care staff and nurse feed, bathe, clean and tend the children with continued devotion. Our housekeeper and cook always give them first-class meals. The domestic staff even come in on a Sunday if there is something special to be done. Our three teachers give their time to the children outside school hours by running clubs ... Teaching delicate children is no sinecure, I assure you. Towards the end of term every adult here is exhausted. With happiness, a child can conquer so many problems caused by physical disability.

It was reported that children had 7½ acres of lawns and gardens to play in, as well as access to 100 acres of surrounding farm and woodland. Woods were used at weekends for playing in, building dens and climbing, and the inflatable paddling pool was always popular. These were ideal conditions for children who had missed so much schooling and needed individual medical and educational attention.

A pupil and teacher recall their lives at Skilts:

Mr. Paul Flannagan, Pupil, Skilts 1967-70, Bournville, Birmingham

The Head Teacher was Mr. Cameron who lived in Studley. He was very intimidating but I learnt much later how friendly and caring he was. The Deputy Head Teacher was Mr. O'Riley. He was very jolly, a magician and toffee maker in his spare time. There were two other teachers: one looked after the model railway which was housed in the cellar. There were three female child care staff who had rooms close to the dormitories, plus the usual domestic staff who lived locally.

Skilts dining room with its bay windows had oak panelled walls. There was a central corridor which ran almost the length of the house, with three stairways. The back entrance led into the rear grounds—as you left the building you were confronted with a yew hedge which marked the boundary of a formal garden to your left, and to your right was a large lawn, climbing frame and beyond this a wooded area.

The average term was six to eight weeks long but some were as long as 13. During the term we would only see our parents on Visiting Day; those of us lucky enough to have parents willing and able to get there. If we were really lucky we might get a weekend at home. Unless they had their own transport parents would have to catch a Midland Red bus and then walk up the drive. We would be waiting at the windows looking for that first glimpse of parents or any recognisable relative with great anticipation and excitement but what a let-down if no-one showed.

During the week we would get up at about 8.00am, have breakfast before starting the school day. During break-times we would play outside close to the main building and at the end of the school day we were able to play in the rest of the grounds, including the wooded area until about 7.00pm. There were four dormitories and each was known by a colour (e.g Blue, Orange). There would be between 8 and 12 beds, each with its own pot and side cupboard. Above each door was a red 15 watt light which might be put on if we were good.

Weekend play activities at Skilts. (I. Mitchell)

On Saturdays we would spend most of the day playing in the grounds after cleaning our dorms, shoes etc. and on Sundays we would be taken for a walk around the local area and once a month we would go to the local church.

Mr. Bernard Meer, Teacher, Skilts 1968-86, Rugeley, Staffordshire

I began work at Skilts in January 1968, a bitterly cold month. We were soon cut off from the outside world by heavy snowdrifts. The school milk and other supplies had to be left at the end of the half-mile drive. The caretaker and I set off one noon with sledges to collect the milk, but drifts in the drive were so deep we were forced to detour across fields and into the wood, hauling the crates across fences.

I was totally new to special education, having come from a junior school with classes of 48 children. So it was a pleasant surprise to walk into a class of 18 at Skilts. However, it was not quite as easy as I had first imagined since almost all the children required individual attention. Books and equipment were in very short supply.

However, with the arrival of Spring, lessons could be taken out of doors. We spent some mornings doing surveys of the traffic on the main road, and then returning to school to make all kinds of graphs. Other mornings we measured the water trickling into the pond near the school. There were so many things to do in fine weather, collecting the different kinds of grasses, wild flowers, fungi etc. We bred our own butterflies in spacious gauze cages, watching the caterpillars devouring leaves and changing their forms miraculously.

We had quite a few pets, including two dogs who accompanied us on all our explorations. But the most distinguished pet was a little Rhode Island Red hen who used to run like mad to be picked up when the children emerged at playtimes, and enjoyed being pushed in a doll's pram. There were also quite a few bantams, several goslings, rabbits and guinea pigs.

Terms were long, unrelieved by half-term holidays or weekends at home. But parents were invited to visit once a month, on a Sunday afternoon. Few parents had cars in those days and had the long trek up the drive from the bus, watched from upstairs by tiny, anxious faces.

Winter evenings and weekends were certainly the most difficult and tiring times: hours spent in the playroom with a very old and very defective TV set, snakes and ladders and a gramophone with a few records.

We had a huge craft hut, ideally situated with windows looking down on the wood. There were long sturdy tables with vices and a very primitive solid little kiln. Many hours were spent working with clay on winter evenings. Quite a few older children were skilful at throwing pots. Alas, the craft hut was demolished when the foundations for the new school were laid, and pottery, carpentry and other crafts all went with the wind, never to return.

Finally, one must pay tribute to the wonderful meals the children and staff always had at Skilts. Miss Hilda Simmons was a brilliant cook who provided four-star meals every day throughout the years.

Today Skilts is still a 'very special kind of school', to quote the school brochure. It offers a secure and caring environment for each child to develop and grow. It is a small community where children learn to live together, acquiring new skills to help them cope with their lives. Staff aim to help children to experience success and to feel they are worth something as individuals, whatever their problems in temperament or ability.

Children follow the National Curriculum, as in mainstream schools, but there is a greater emphasis on individual needs, so that classes rarely have more than eight pupils. As in open-air schools, practical activities such as gardening, swimming, art and crafts, music, drama and physical education play an important part in the curriculum. During out-of-school-hours there are choices of activity to encourage the constructive use of personal freedom.

A review of the Educational Needs of each child is completed by school staff each year, with the general aim of returning children to their local schools as soon as parents and school professionals feel it is possible. Staff include seven teachers, 10 residential social workers, two child helpers, two classroom assistants and a nurse.

Conclusion

One of the most surprising elements in the history of open-air schools is that they outlived their usefulness within fifty years of their creation. Uffculme Open-Air School in Birmingham became a role model for others to follow, successfully combating disease, poverty and malnutrition with a healthy educational environment. The other five schools enabled many city children to benefit from this unique blend of medical care and special education.

The demise of open-air schools was due to many causes, including the removal of slums, improved nutritional and living standards, the advancement of medical science and the provision of the welfare state. Three of Birmingham's original school buildings financed by Barrow and Geraldine Cadbury are still in use at Uffculme and Hunter's Hill Special Schools, whilst Skilts has also been adapted to meet the needs of children in a modern world.

Our project grew from one small idea to chart the history of Uffculme Open-Air School. A desire to look back into our childhood education developed into a vast, fascinating topic encompassing much social, local and family history, as well as recording the pioneering spirit and generosity of Barrow and Geraldine Cadbury. Drawing together the threads of Birmingham's innovative educational movement has proved to be no clinical historical account, but one which vibrates with the human element—laughter and tears, joy and tragedy, success and failure.

Our appeals through the media resulted in many affectionate memories as a flood of reminiscences poured in from ex-pupils all over the country, and even from Australia and Jamaica. Staff at the schools had nostalgic memories too, and so many of them had dedicated nearly a lifetime's work to places not renowned for their warmth and comfort. Working and living in Special Schools in such beautiful surroundings had fostered friendships between staff, so that our task of tracing people proved surprisingly easy.

THE 1960s AND BEYOND: WINDS OF CHANGE

The inner courtyard at Hunter's Hill, photographed in 1994 and still retaining some of the original open verandas. (F. Wilmot)

At the beginning of our project we visited our old schools at Uffculme and Cropwood, for the first time since childhood. Uffculme is still an important part of Birmingham's Special School system, a close-knit community behind those high sheltering walls. The disused open-air classrooms at Cropwood still had their original sliding screens in 1993 but these have since been removed as the buildings have been renovated for today's pupils.

On a foggy frosty morning at Hunter's Hill School in 1994 it was bleak and chilly on the original open-wooden veranda surrounding the inner courtyard and it was easy to imagine how cold it must have been for schoolboys in short trousers years ago! The beautiful surroundings, however, continue to be just as enjoyable as they always were to children reared on city streets and playgrounds. On warmer days classes of young pupils on educational visits to the school enjoy the trees and numerous squirrels in the grounds. Geraldine Cadbury would surely have thoroughly approved of these nature lessons in the fresh air and especially of the caring attitude within the school.

Cropwood House is still cherished by Birmingham, providing homely surroundings during the week for the older boys at Hunter's Hill. It is unlikely that Barrow and Geraldine Cadbury had any idea of how many young people would eventually live within the sheltered walls of their treasured country estate and family home. Their generosity enabled so many children to be restored to health and vitality and to live normal lives in society. Perhaps children at these schools today will eventually feel just as fortunate as all those specially chosen in the past to attend open-air schools.

Thousands of Birmingham's open-air school pupils have good cause to be grateful for receiving such understanding and patience from their dedicated teachers, as well as devoted medical care and attention from their school nurses and doctors. On behalf of all those pupils we say a simple but heartfelt thank you.

Two former open-air schools in the 1990s

Cropwood's two deserted open-air classrooms in the spring of 1995. Now renovated for today's pupils they are part of Hunter's Hill School. (F.Wilmot)

Haseley Hall as a private residence recently restored to its former glory, with an additional wing above the Sawyer family's coat of arms, 1997. (F.Wilmot)

Appendix I

Head Teachers of Birmingham's Open-Air Schools

UFFCULME
Miss Mabel Hurst 1911-18
Mrs. Elsie Abbott 1918-22
Miss Ella A. Hibbert 1922-50
Mr. F.S. Wise 1950-2
Mr. Edward J. Anderson 1954-64
Mr. Trevor S. Alflatt 1964-9
Mr. D.A. Wright 1969-80

CROPWOOD
Mrs. Elsie Abbott 1922-4
Miss Gertrude Walton 1924-33
Miss Margaret E. Grant 1933-8
Miss Eveline Boothroyd 1938-52
Miss Marjory A. Urquhart 1953-70
Miss Deirdre M. Clarke 1970-9

MARSH HILL
Miss Mary Brown 1931-53
Mr. J.E. Miles 1953-8
Miss Patricia C.J. Hazel 1958-66

HUNTER'S HILL
Miss Gertrude Walton 1933-43
Miss Linda Buckley 1943-69
Mr. Grahame Williams 1969-85

HASELEY HALL
Miss Charlton 1942-47
Miss Marjory A. Urquhart 1947-52
Miss A.M. Butler-Fleming 1953-68
Miss Gillian Royle 1968-74

SKILTS
Mr. Ivor Mitchell 1958-63
Mr. D.C. Cameron 1963-74
Mr. A.E. Nye 1974-82

Appendix II

School Log Books

As the school log books have proved an invaluable resource for this book, readers may be interested to know the purpose of them. Most school log books date from 1862 when all elementary schools receiving a Government Grant had to keep such records, which were examined annually by the official Inspectors of Schools. Under the revised Code of Regulations 1862, the Head Teacher was required:

> … to daily make into the log book the briefest entry which will suffice to specify either ordinary progress or whatever other fact concerning the school and its teachers, such as the dates of commencement of duty, cautions, illnesses etc., and may require to be referred to at a future time, and may otherwise deserve to be recorded … No reflections or opinions of a general character are to be entered in the log book.

Marsh Hill's log book, which started in 1931, contained a useful summary, according to Education Code Schedule IV. Every school log book was intended to be a bare record of events which constituted the history of the school. It was kept strictly under the care of the Head Teacher who was usually the only person authorised to write in it from time to time. Such events as the introduction of new books and apparatus, courses of instruction and visits by officials were to be recorded. Log books were never intended to be personal opinions on the efficiency of the school. Statements of fact were recorded, together with any deviation from normal school routine. In particular, a school log book had to contain an explanation of the reason for the closing of a school.

In practice, Birmingham log books and admission registers are deposited with Birmingham Archives when schools close down and specific rules exist to restrict their access for fifty years after the date of the last entry. So, generally speaking, keen historians have no chance of seeing these valuable social documents until most of the pupils have died. With regard to schools which are still in existence, log books are usually kept at the schools themselves and are often on display at Open Days.

The quality of hand-written entries in school log books varies enormously as some Head Teachers were more conscientious than others, sometimes recording all names of visitors and pupils, as well as new teaching methods. There is a wealth of social and local history documenting the state of the weather and outbreaks of epidemics (such as whooping cough, diphtheria etc.) as well as details of discipline and the atmosphere of the school. Personal interests often creep into entries, revealing the personality and character of the Head Teacher and the staff, which in our case has helped enormously to portray the life of the school when we have been unable to contact or trace the person involved. It is the unique individualism of these log books which make them so interesting and such an invaluable source of social and educational history.

Our book will demonstrate that these school records contain a vast amount of fascinating material of great interest to local and family historians alike—probably never envisaged by the originators of such documents. Each log book gave a wealth of information not generally available in official educational reports. The log book entries selected for this book are (with a few exceptions) reproduced as originally written. Some children's surnames have been omitted for the period 1930-70 in order to preserve a medical and personal confidentiality.

Some school log books and photographs have been lost over the years as educational administration has taken precedence over the preservation of archival material. It is hoped that Birmingham's school records will be carefully stored and preserved for future generations.

Appendix III

Reminiscences—Other Open-Air Schools

During our many appeals to the media we received numerous accounts about open-air schools in other areas. It is interesting to compare the schools with those of Birmingham. Other education authorities perhaps lacked the inspiration and financial influence of Barrow and Geraldine Cadbury as school buildings ranged from tents to canvas-walled chalets, but the open-air regimes were much the same:

Reedswood Park Open-Air School, Walsall

Ms. Margaret Parker (who has written a book on the school's history): *The school began as an experiment in 1919. An old tent was first provided in a local park. Later, an old army hut replaced the tent.* Log Book entries included: *While I am writing this the ink is freezing in my pen.*

Mrs. Olga Fox, teacher, 1940s: *I had the good fortune to spend four very happy years in Reedswood Park Open-Air School, but froze for two or three months a year. Pupils had luxuries like beef dripping on rounds of thick home baked bread with their milk …*

Malvern Open-Air School

Mr. Fred Homer, Malvern pupil 1931, 75: *At the age of 10 I was sent to West Malvern Open-Air School after a bout of pneumonia. My parents put me on a train at Smethwick Station with my few clothes wrapped in brown paper and I was not to see my family again for six weeks. Only one visit in three months was allowed.*

I was met at the station in Malvern and transported to the school which was set on a wooded hillside, girls in one part, boys in the other.

Children came from all walks of life but every child was treated equally. Any treats brought in by parents were confiscated. Children tried to hide them in all sorts of places but they were always found by the staff. However, every Friday we were lined up and each received either two squares of chocolate or two toffees.

Food was wholesome but plain and you had to eat everything in front of you. Sometimes the staff would hold a child's hands behind his back, pinch his nose to make him swallow the food, such as fat on the meat.

Lessons were basic and we were taught only in the mornings, afternoons we had to sleep for two hours. We did craft work and learned to mend and darn our clothes. We also did light work in the gardens where we had to wear wooden clogs. Saturdays and Sundays we were taken for walks in the countryside. Black Country dialect and 'slang' talk was discouraged and I came home speaking 'posher'.

They were very strict on hygiene. Showers were lukewarm and there was no escaping them. Each week we had to line up for a spoonful of 'physic'. Punishment was administered by the use of a plimsoll.

Even though it was a very strict regime I really enjoyed my time there. For me, coming from the back streets of a dirty Black Country town, it was a holiday and gave me real love of the countryside and country life.

Mrs. D. Saunders, Malvern pupil 1931, 72: *We slept in dormitories, about twenty-four of us; under each bed was an enamel potty. I was 10 years old. Temperatures were taken every morning. Lessons were taken out of doors, weather permitting. There were no windows in the school, just a square frame: if the weather was too rough the shutters went up.*

Breakfast was a bowl of hot porridge with plenty of milk and two rounds of beef dripping, with a mug of hot milk later on. Dinner was always boiled meat and a pudding.

We went lovely long walks into the woods to pick bluebells and primroses, being fitted out first with a pair of Dutch clogs. I loved it all but was still glad to get home to my family.

Mr. Raymond Raybould, Malvern pupil 1935, 67: *At the age of eight I was sent to Malvern School for 3 months. I was tall and thin and underweight. A coach load of us left Dudley to travel to the end of the world. I had never been more than a penny bus ride before. My stomach sank when I saw this strange building, built on the side of a hill, supported on legs. I had never been away from home before.*

The dormitories were open to the elements, the shutters only closed when it rained on us in bed. I never did get used to going to bed in an afternoon. I just lay there hoping that when I opened my eyes it would all have been a bad dream. We were only allowed one visit from our families during our stay.

I did find a lack of warmth about the place. It was rigid and austere. And they didn't seem to realise that we were only eight years old, snatched from our homes and put down in a strange environment.

Bow Road Open-Air School, East London

Mrs. Irene Rodell, pupil 1933-6, 71: *The school had one large wooden hut used for prayers, music lessons and dining room. We also had some wooden huts which were used to store desks, but we were only allowed to take lessons in these if it was raining hard.*

Each morning we had to carry our desks out on to a large area which had wooden slats laid down. It was here we had lessons. In the winter in the snow we were still outside but we had a thin blanket to put round our legs and kept our coats on. We had to use pencils as the ink would be frozen in the ink well.

After dinner we had to carry our desks back to the hut and bring out a canvas stretcher to rest on for an hour. We had showers once a week as none of us had bathrooms at home. I left at the age of 14 as there were five children to care for at home and my father was never in work during the Depression. Although the school was very Spartan I enjoyed it.

Upton House Open-Air School, Hackney, London

Mr. N. Norris, pupil 1936-9: *I was an under nourished eight year old at the time. We had three open-sided classrooms in the playground, two feet off the ground on stilts.*

We spent five and a half days a week there. Breakfast, dinner and tea was provided. Each plate was inspected after each meal to make sure we ate everything on it.

The experience must have helped as when I was 18 I was conscripted to serve in the forces and completed two years service.

Cottingham Road Open-Air School, near Hull, East Yorkshire

Mrs. Muriel Dooling, pupil 1940s: *Our classrooms were open-air huts, like chalets. The sides had wooden shutters which dropped open on good days. The top half was made of canvas blinds which were closed* *and tied down in the winter. Each class overlooked a garden and open fields.*

Each day I had to see the nurse for my horrid black iron medicine. After lunch we had to go to sleep in a large open-air hut on camp beds.

Springwell House Open-Air School, Clapham Common, London

Mrs. Sylvia Carpenter, pupil 1940s–50s: *I was considered underweight when I was admitted. The construction of each classroom was a wooden platform with three open sides and the fourth covered by a green canvas. I only recall having a lesson inside once on a bitterly cold day in December. Our three meals a day were taken indoors. I have very happy memories of my time at the school.*

Mrs. Jean Gould, pupil 1941–50: *I attended Springwell because of chest and nerve problems. It seemed tough being out in all weathers but when I left school to start a career I was given a clean bill of health.*

The classrooms were on platforms with a wooden roof held up by beams, no walls—rather like a roundabout at a fun-fair. We were allowed to wear finger mittens and were provided with a woollen blanket to wind round our legs.

Although the school was in the middle of London it had lovely gardens. We had an hour's rest on stretcher beds outside after lunch. I thought myself very lucky and although times were difficult in the war years my life at the school was a very happy one.

Hazelbury Open-Air School, Edmonton, London

Mrs. Pauline Kenward, pupil 1961–5: *At the age of seven-and-a-half I was sent to the school as I was asthmatic, underweight and suffered from petit mal. We were bussed in from north London areas and had three meals a day.*

Our classrooms had windows on three sides which could concertina back, so that the wall was open to the elements from about two-and-a-half feet above floor level to the ceiling. Only in gales or driving snow would the windward side be shut! There were radiators: the important thing was fresh air not cold. Nonetheless, we often wore coats and fingerless gloves in the classroom in the coldest weather.

We loved the summer; we were taken outdoors as much as possible. Best thing of all was rest hour outside … lying in the sunshine surrounded by flower beds, the hum of insects around you, the scents of flowers wafting on the breeze, was really pleasant and relaxing.

My days at Hazelbury were very happy and benefited me in three obvious ways. Firstly, my health improved. Secondly, I made better progress educationally than I would have in a mainstream primary school. Finally, it was a lesson in compassion and in lack of self-pity—most of us were in the same boat in terms of health and had asthma or eczema. I left at the age of 12 to go to Grammar School, having proved I was fit enough after achieving a year's clean bill of health.

Space does not permit any further reminiscences but those related here are interesting accounts of different types of open-air schools throughout the country. Despite the fact that everyone who attended such schools had a health problem, it is remarkable that most people recall them with pleasure. The experimental nature of the schools which on the surface seemed harsh and severe was more than justified by the fact that so many of their pupils have since lived healthily into old age, with such nostalgic memories.

Bibliography

Alexander, Helen Cadbury, *Richard Cadbury* (1906, Hodder & Stoughton)
Allinson, Helen, 'Open-Air Schools' in *Local History*, June 1988, 11-13
Ayres, Leonard P., *Open-Air Schools* (1910, Doubleday, Page & Co., New York)
Bartlett, Percy W., *Barrow Cadbury: a Memoir* (1960, Bannisdale Press)
Birmingham Education Committee, *Open-Air School Sub-Committee Minutes 1911-1930* (Birmingham Archives)
Birmingham Education Committee, *Reports of the School Medical Superintendent/Officer, 1908-1963* (Accession No.222435 in Birmingham Reference Library)
Birmingham Education Committee, *Special Schools Sub-Committee Minutes 1912-1914* (Birmingham Archives)
Birmingham Education Committee Newscuttings, Vol.1, 1886-1911
Birmingham Evening Despatch, 27 April 1962
Birmingham Gazette, 25 June 1910, 28 June 1955
Birmingham Mail, 18 September 1911, 28 January 1919, 27 June 1955, 28 June 1955
Birmingham Post, 25 June 1910, 18 March 1931, 24 June 1943
Birmingham Reference Library, *Newscuttings on Birmingham Schools and Education*
Bournville Works Magazine, August 1922
British Journal of Tuberculosis, 'Open-Air Life for Children'; 'National Importance of Open Air Schools'; 'The Open-Air School Movement'. Vol.III, No.3, July 1909
Broughton, Hugh, *The Open-Air School* (1914, Pitman)
Cadbury Collection Archives (Birmingham Archives)
Cadbury, Paul, 'Geraldine Cadbury 1865-1941' in *Friends' Quarterly Examiner*, April 1941
Cropwood School Log Books 1922-1970 (Hunter's Hill School)
Cruikshank, M., 'The Open-Air School Movement in English Education' in *Pedagogica Historica*, 1977, 17, No.1, 62-74
Daily News, 25 June 1910, 26 October 1910
Education (Board of), *Annual Reports of the Chief Medical Officer: Parliamentary Papers Sessions 1915-1920* (HMSO)
Education (Board of), *The Health of the School Child: Annual Reports of the Chief Medical Officer, 1910-1938* (HMSO)
Education (Ministry of), *The Health of the School Child: Annual Reports of the Chief Medical Officer, 1939-1972* (HMSO)
Education (Ministry of), *Report of the Committee on Maladjusted Children* (1955, HMSO)
Education (Department of), *The School Health Service 1908-1974* (1975, HMSO)
Harris, Bernard, *The Health of the School Child: a History of the School Medical Services in England and Wales* (1995, Open University Press)
Haseley Hall School Log Books, 1947-1974 (Birmingham Archives)
Hazel, Patricia C.J., *Education for Delicate Children: Day School Provision in the City of Birmingham 1911-1973* (1973, Birmingham University Thesis)

Head, Brandon, *The Food of the Gods: a popular account of cocoa* (1903, R.B. Johnson)
Hunter's Hill School Log Books, 1933-1970 (Hunter's Hill School)
Huss, C.B., 'The Medical Aspects of the Special School' in *Special Schools Journal,* January 1957, 12-18
Jackson, Stephen, *Special Education in England and Wales*, 2nd ed. (1969, OUP)
Leff, S. and V., *The School Health Service* (1959, H.K. Lewis)
Marsh Hill School Log Books, 1931-1966 (Birmingham Archives)
National Union of Teachers, *The Day School for Delicate Children* (1963, NUT)
Parker, Margaret J., *Something Very Special: A History of the Reedswood Open Air School* (1996, Walsall Local History Centre)
Pritchard, D.G., *Education and the Handicapped, 1760-1960* (1963, Routledge & Kegan Paul)
'Sir James Sawyer' in *Warwickshire Lives: Social and Political* 1897
'Sir James Sawyer' in *Edgbastonia, Vol X,* June 1890
Thomas, Ronald, 'Asthma and the School Child' in *Special Education, Vol 60, No.3,* September 1971, 23-25
The Times, 7 September 1910
The Times Educational Supplement, 22 April 1994 ('Breathing Space; Pilgrim School')
Tucker, John, *Kanchenjunga* (1955, Elek Books)
'Uffculme Open-Air School' in *Modern Building Record* 1912, 64-65
Uffculme School Log Books, 1911-1970 (Uffculme School)
Warnock, H.M., *Special Educational Needs: Report of Committee of Enquiry into Education of Handicapped Children and Young People* (1978, HMSO)
Whitney, Janet, *Geraldine Cadbury, 1865-1941* (1948, Harrap)
Yearbook of Open-Air Schools and Children's Sanatoria, Vol.1, 1915 (Accession No.503325 in Birmingham Reference Library)

Index

Page numbers in **bold** are contributors' accounts. Page numbers in *italic* are photographs or illustrations.

Abbott, Mrs. (cook), 125
Abbott, Elsie (headteacher), 43, 55, 60, 337; appointment, 46, 54, 55; in school log books, 46, 54, 57, 59; resignation, 54, 60
ability of pupils, *see* academic ability; educational attainment; educational standards; examinations, academic
absconding (runaways): Cropwood, 60, 67, 91, 92, 109, 121, 122-3, 125, 142, 169, 170, 175-6, 210, 220, 286, 292; Hunter's Hill, 96, 97, 112, 115, 130, 131, 153, 154, 158, 159, 177, 183, 222, 223, 224, 246, 247, 251, 252, 298, 299, 300, 307, 311
academic ability, 196; *see also* educational standards; examinations, academic; leaving certificates; learning abilities
accommodation, *see* dormitories; staff
Acme Flooring & Paving Co. (1904) Ltd., 21
Acocks Green, 65, 213, 214
activities (outdoor), 10, 39, 98, 131, 194, 301, 303, 310, 314, 333; *see also* bicycles; boating club; camping; canoe club; fishing; go-carts; golf; hunt the whistle; roller skating; scooters; skipping; torch chases
Adams, Mrs. (Birmingham School Clinic nurse), 315, *316*, 322
Adams, Christine, **214-15**
Adams, Norah, *see* Whittall, Norah
Adams, Roger, **236-7**
adenoids, 5, 8, 10, 19, 192; *see also* tonsils
Adkins, Charles (butcher), 21
Admissions Registers, 26, 28-9, 338
admissions, 67, 118, 263, 264; Cropwood, 57, 59, 116, 213; Hunter's Hill, 96, 112, 116, 125; Marsh Hill, 80, 83; Skilts, 330; Uffculme, 23, 26, 31, 32, 41, 239; *see also* selection of pupils
Adrenaline, 164, 221, 265
Adult School Movement, 13
advertisements (medicines), *3*, 31, 37, 78, *134*, 148, *153*, *179*
Advisory Committee for Special Education, 266
air raid shelters: Cropwood, 126, 143, 144, 149; Hunter's Hill, 153, 155, 156, 157, 248; Uffculme, 138
air raids, 135; Birmingham, 136, 137, 138, 145; Coventry, 188; Cropwood, 143, 144, 145; Haseley Hall, 188; Hunter's Hill, 152; *see also* bombs
Alexander, Mr. (teacher), 302, 306
Allflatt, Trevor (headteacher), 254, 276, 278, 279, 337
Allen, Peter W., **161**, **179**
allergies, 327; *see also* asthma
Allison (nurse), 287
Alpine School, *see* Davos
America: open-air schools, 6, 9; survey of asthma, 264
Aminophyline, 265
anaemia, 8, 10, 19, 62, 67, 116, 135; Cropwood, 56, 69, 109; Hunter's

Hill, 159; Uffculme, 23, 26, 31, 35
Anderson, Edward J. (teacher/headteacher), 76, 84, 85, 88, 89, 139, 140, 166, 168, 198-9, 201, 202, 204, 205, 207, 208, 236, 237, 270, 337; appointment, 74, 198; in log books, 138, 200, 235, 271; photographs of, 88, *165*, *274*; reports by, 273; retirement, 273, 274, 276
Andrews, Mrs. (cleaner/helper), *260*, 316
Andrews, Jean, *see* Dwyer, Jean
animals, 192, 194, *231*, *257*; *see also* goats; guinea pigs; pets; rabbits
Annis, Elsie, 121; *see also* Kite, Elsie
annual reports of Chief Medical Officer, *see* Chief Medical Officer's annual reports
Ansell, R. (teacher), 234
Antrobus, (Sir) Edward, 185
Apollo 10 launch, 308
apple trees, 43, 44, *49*, 54, 73, 76, 140, 141, 281
architecture (of open-air schools), *see* open-air schools; *see also* bandstand; buildings; huts; platforms; screens; shutters; siting; verandas
Argyll, Duchess of, 35
arithmetic, 8, 63; Cropwood, 242; Hunter's Hill, 128, 230; Uffculme, *32*, 48, 83, 236, 269; *see also* graphwork; tables
armistice, 46; Armistice Day, 74, 121
Armson, Moira (teacher), xiii, **208-10**; *see also* Spence, Moira
army training, influence of, 40-1, 49
Arnot, Miss (cook/housekeeper), 68, 93, 109, 143, 145, 147, 149, 169, 170, 171, 210, 211, 212; death, 213
Arnott, Jane, **238**
arts and crafts, 230, 269, 270, 290, 306; *see also* craftwork; handwork; manual instruction; *individual subjects*: basketmaking; canework; embroidery; knitting; leatherwork; lino-cutting; metalwork; painting; plasticene modelling; pottery; raffia work; rugmaking; weaving; woodwork
Ashby, Miss (nurse), 172
Asher, Dr. (HMI), 299
Ashfield, Miss (children's helper), 263
Asperger Syndrome, 279
assembly, school: Cropwood, 69, 152, 218, 244; Hunter's Hill, 221, 231; Uffculme, 201, 236, 238; *see also* religious education
asthma, 67, 90, 104, 116, 163, 233; causes of, 196, 198, 265, 266, 268, 342; survey of, 264, 265; treatment of 196, 197, 233; Cropwood, 109, 120, 123, 125, 240, 241, 290, 295; Haseley Hall, 190, 193, 259, 319, 321, 322; Hunter's Hill, 112, 114, 115, 133, 154, 158, 159, 221, 223, 227, 229, 230, 247, 248, 252, 307, 309, 311, 312; Marsh Hill, 161, 313; Skilts, 263, 327, 328, 329, 330; Uffculme, 168, 200, 201, 203, 237, 269, 270, 274; *see also* chest conditions; exercises

Asthma Clinic, 233, 246, 301, 302
Asthma Research Council, 196
Astley Hall School, 321, 325
Aston, Percy (teacher), 223, 227, 249
athletics, 98, 116, 227, 250
Atkins, Mr. (teacher), 183, 221
Atkins, Mrs. (kitchen staff), *274*
Atkins (nurse), 181
Atkinson, Miss (teacher), 109
Atropine Co., 164
attainment testing, 216; *see also* educational attainment; testing
attendance, school, 263, 266; *see also* absconding; school log books
Auden, Dr. George (Birmingham's first Chief School Medical Officer), 11, 18, 19, 23, 29, 32, 33, 36, 50, 64; opening of Uffculme, 22
Aurora Borealis, 132
Austin, Dr., 127
autistic children, 276, 278, 279
Avery, Miss, 67
Avery, W. & T. Ltd., 185, 319
Ayres, Leonard, 7, 8
Aze, Miss (teacher), 197

back supports, 206, 247, 302
backward children, 18, 50, 105, 129, 163, 234, 243, 263; Cropwood, 242; Hunter's Hill, 178; Marsh Hill, 82; *see also* retarded children
Bailey, Colin, 184
Bailey, Graham, **158**
Bailey, S. (teacher), 273, *274*
Baker, Mr. (dentist), 148, 172
Baker, Dorothy (children's helper), 191; *see also* Bilton, Dorothy
Baker, Elsie, 36
Baldock, Miss (teacher), 109
Baldwin, Iris, **86-7**
Ball, Diane, *see* Smith, Diane
Balsall Heath, 43, 62, 77, 137, 210
'band-stand' buildings, 6, 194
bank engines, 99, 132, 159; *see also* Big Bertha; Lickey Incline
bantams, 231, 301, 333
Bardsley, Miss (HMI), 146
Barlow, (Sir) Thomas, 14
Barnsley, 6
Barnt Green, 172, 179, 281
Barrett, Claire (nurse), 183, 221, 230, 231, 252, 297, 300, 301, 306, 307; in school log books, 153, 301, 302, 307, 308, personal accounts, **133-4**, **156-7**, **225**, **309**; retirement, 307, 308
Barrodale, Miss (teacher), 207, 209
Barron, Grace, 87
Bartlett, Christine, *see* Adams, Christine
Barton, G., **181-2**
Baskerville House School, 50-1, 103, 126, 132, 142, 173, 189, 235, 257, 265, 321; *see also* rheumatic children
basket-weaving, 36, 40, 65; *see also* canework
baths, 4, 9, 22, 41, 49; Cropwood, 218, 244; Haseley Hall, 193, 259, 319, 324; Marsh Hill, 80; Uffculme, 21, 22, 29, 38; *see also* showers
Bazire, Isobel (teacher), xiii, **208**; *see*

also Thomas, Isobel
BBC schools programmes, 231, 251, 298; *see also* television
Beasley, Arthur, **97-8**
Beattie, Theresa, **238**
Beausale School, 256
bedmaking: Cropwood, 92, 213-14, 243; Hunter's Hill, 221, 310
bedwetting, *see* enuresis
Beecroft, Harold, 27
beekeeping, 39, 146, 194, 306; *see also* honey
behavioural problems, 233, 264, 268; Cropwood, 295; Hunter's Hill, 297; Skilts, 263; Uffculme, 236, 237; *see also* sociological cases
Bell, Miss (teacher), 115, 143
Belling, Freda, *see* Owen, Freda
Belston, Rita, 121
Bemax, 139
Bendall, E.M. (nurse), 75, 84, 106, 120, 136, 141, *164*, 199, 200, 209, 234
Bennett, W. (teacher), 251
Bent, Margaret, **161**
Berkswell, visit to, 235, 238
Bewlay, *see* Cossins, Peacock & Bewlay (architects)
'Big Bertha', 72, 114, 229; *see also* Lickey Incline
Bigger, Maud (nurse), 187
Billing, Miss (teacher), 173, 211
Billy Smart's Circus, 202, 307
Bilton, Dorothy, **193**; *see also* Baker, Dorothy
Bingley Hall, 275
Birch, Kathleen, **110**
bird tables, 83, 90, 107
birds, 124, 140, 181, 206
Birmingham: charities, 5; evacuation of schoolchildren, 117, 137; industry, 19th-century, 1; kindergartens, 14; slums, 5, *19*, 23, 54; smoke pollution, 1, *2*, 5; special schools development, 50-1; *see also* bombs
Birmingham and Midland Institute, 253
Birmingham Central Hall, 108
Birmingham Chest Clinic, *see* Great Charles Street Clinic
Birmingham Children's Courts, 14
Birmingham Children's Hospital, 93, 103, 116, 128, 130, 156, 167, 198, 219, 227, 228, 251, 259, 299, 301, 302, 307, 308
Birmingham Civic Society, 80
Birmingham Daily Mail, 23, 24
Birmingham Daily News, 18
Birmingham Dental Hospital, 26, 227
Birmingham Education Committee, 19, 78, 94, 189, 192, 195, 196, 231, 294; acceptance of Cadbury donation, 18; reorganisations of Schools for delicate Children, 313-15, 321; use of Davos Alpine School, 197-8; *see also* Davos Alpine School
Birmingham Education Committee (School Medical Officers Reports): 1908/9, 11; 1910, 19, 23; 1911, 25-6; 1912, 31; 1914, 37-8; 1917, 49; 1925, 64; 1930s,

79-80, 90, 95-6, 101-2, 104-5, 109, 111-12, 116-17, 120; *1940s*, 135, 162, 164; *1950s*, 220-1, 233-4; *1960s*, 264-5; *1970s*, 312; *see also* Inspectors school reports
Birmingham Evening Despatch, 198, 273
Birmingham Gazette, 18
Birmingham Hippodrome Theatre, 227
Birmingham Institute of Child Health, 162
Birmingham Juvenile Court, 14
Birmingham Mail, 112, 130
Birmingham Natural History Museum, 223
Birmingham Open-Air Schools Sub-Committee, 27, 28, 53, 137, 138
Birmingham Open-Spaces Association, 10
Birmingham Orthopaedic Hospital, 130, 206
Birmingham Post, 18, 83
Birmingham Skin Hospital, 247
Birmingham Society for the Care of Invalid Children, 185, 187, 188
Birmingham Special Schools' Sports, 131, *133*; *see also* sports
Birmingham Special Schools Medical Officer, 118; *see also* Birmingham Education Committee (School Medical Officers Reports)
Birmingham Special Schools Sub-Committee, 35, 56, 80, 91, 97, 101, 128, 138, 313
Birmingham Symphony Orchestra, 234, 304, 309
Birmingham Town Hall, 85, 92, 106
Birmingham's Juvenile Dramatic Festivals, 253
Birmingham's School Medical Service Sub-Committee, 80
birthdays, 125, 142, 147, 331
blackberry picking, 246, 281
blackouts (wartime), 126, 135, 155, 157, 158, 190; *see also* wartime
Blackwell, 62, 72, 97, 158, 180, 248, 305, 311; bombing, 145; church, 99, 283; pumping station 9; station, 17, 57, 62, 93, 99, 123, 133, 210, 229; *see also* Lickey Incline
blankets, 6, 9, 10, 39, 194, 296; Cropwood, 296; Marsh Hill, 161, 254; Uffculme, 23, 27, 29, 141, 236, 237, 239
Blay, Daphne (teacher), 228, 231, 247
blepharitis, 62, 67
blinds, canvas, 7, 341
blood: disorders, 166; tests, 22; *see also* anaemia
boarders, weekly, *see* weekly boarding
Boardman, Dr., 308
boating club, 231, 246, 247, 248, *249*, 250
Bolton, Miss (teacher), 91
bog garden (Uffculme), 86, 141
Bognor Regis, *see* Martineau House (Seaside School)
boils, 183
bombs: in Birmingham, 144, 158; in Coventry, 144, 158, 188; on schools, 137, 140; *see also* air raids
Band, Miss (nurse), 256
Bone, Edward, **254**
bonfire parties: Cropwood, 213, 220,
281, 283; Haseley Hall, 258, 259, 260, 315; Hunter's Hill, 130, 172, 178, 232; Skilts, 327
Bonner, John, **71-3**, **87-9**
bookbinding, 229
Booke, Kathleen, *see* Birch, Kathleen
Boothroyd, Eveline (headteacher), 121, 124, 149, 150, 152, 169, 174, 175, 176, 210, 214, 337; appointment, 120; in school log books, 120, 125, 126, 127, 142, 143, 145, 147, 170, 171, 172, 212; retirement, 213
Bostall Wood (London), 6
Boston, 6
Bottom, Alice (teacher), 94, 109, 111
Bournville, 12, 13, 17, 164, 314
Bovril, 207, 236
Bow Road Open-Air School, London, 341
bowling, 299
boxing, 98, 129, 132
Boyd, Miss (teacher), 186, 243
Boyle, Sir Edward, 262
brace, orthopaedic, *see* back supports
Bradbeer, Alderman/Mrs., 171
Bradford, 6, 19, 24
Bradley, Jessie, *175*
Brain, Mrs. (cook), 252
brain tumour, 172
Braithewaite, Mrs. (cook), 302
Braker, Peter, *180*, *184*
Brant, Harry, **115-16**
Bray, Margaret, *see* Rice, Margaret
Brazier, J.A. Ltd., 55
bread, *3*, 5, 10, 25, 43, 69, 79, 101, *108*, 122, 176, 200; war bread, 46
breakfast, 264, 266, 271, 276; *see also* food; school meals
breathing exercises, *see* exercises
Brelsford, Heather, *see* Langdon, Heather
Brennan, Maureen, *see* Hughes, Maureen
Bridie, Miss, 36, 45, 57, 58, 59
Brinkley, Cynthia, **330-1**
British Association Conference on Open-Air Studies, 27
British Children's Home, 117
British Eagle air disaster, 317
British Medical Association, 185
British Medical Journal, 264
broken homes, 265, 321; *see also* sociological cases
Bromage, Norah (teacher), 241, 243, 280, 281, 282, 285, 286, 288, 289
Bromsgrove, 59, 95, 99, 114, 131, 142, 156, 172, 240, 251, 301, 303, 305, 310; cinema, 219; hospitals, 195, 213, 224, 258, 292, 298; library, 210; salt works, 99
bronchial catarrh, *see* catarrh; *see also* bronchitis; chest conditions
bronchiectasis, 104, 164, 195, 198, 233; Cropwood, 93, 109, 216; Haseley Hall, 258, 259; Hunter's Hill, 221; Uffculme, 31, 32, 139, 162, 236, 238, 239; *see also* physiotherapy; postural drainage
bronchitis, 23, 67, 86, 93, 102, 109, 110, 111, 116, 133, 149, 164, 167, 174, 190, 198; Cropwood, 213; Marsh hill, 253, 254; Skilts, 327, 329; Uffculme, 200, 206, 233, 235, 238, 269, 274; *see also* catarrh; chest conditions
Brooke, Adrienne (teacher), 280, 289, **290-1**, 292, 293, 294
Brooke, Lord, 187
Brooks, Rita, *175*
Brooksbank, Mr., 271
Broughton, Hugh, 9, 38
Brown, Mrs. (cook), 298
Brown, Hopwood & Gilbert (grocers), 21
Brown, Joy, *290*
Brown, Joyce, *175*
Brown, Mary (headteacher), 80, 82, 161, 195, 253, 337
Brown, Norah (dental nurse), 245
Brownies, 217, 218, 286, 289
Browning, Mrs. (teacher), 161, 254
Brueton, Pauline, *204*; *see also* Saul, Pauline
Brunsden, V. (cook), 284
Buckley, Linda (teacher/headteacher), 99, 116, 152, 155, 158, 159, 178, 179, 183, 220, 221, 224, 228, 229-30, 231, 246, 249, 252, 297, 305, 306, 310, 337; appointment, 112, 152, 156; background/training, 157; her philosophy, 229-30; in school log books, 112, 130, 152, 156, 223, 247, 298, 299, 302; retirement, 307, 308, 309; school reports by, 250-1, 251-2, 297, 300-1
Bullock, Mabel (teacher), **258-9**, **262-3**; *see also* Hancock, Mabel
Burbridge, Mr. (teacher), 59, 60
Burford, Harriet M. (teacher), 24
Burns, Dr., 114, 130
Burridge, Miss (teacher), 284
Burt, Joyce (teacher), 270, 272, 273, *274*, **274-5**, 278
buses (transport to schools), 241, 243, 310, 317, 333
Butler-Fleming, Marjorie (headteacher), 257, 258, 259, 260, 315, 316, 319, 322, 323, 337; photographs, *260*, *316*; retirement, 317, 321, 324
butter, 35

Cadbury Bros Ltd., 12, 13, 14, 20, 56, 106; gifts to open-air school pupils, 71; visits to, 202
Cadbury, Barrow, 12-14, 24, 59, 80, 334; early life, 12-14; education, 12; Cadbury Bros Ltd., 12, 13; marriage, 13, 14; portraits, *14*, *15*; move to Cropwood House, 14-15, 17; donation of Uffculme, 18, 20, 24, 44; donation of Cropwood, 54-6; visits to Cropwood School, 143, 144, 145, 170, 173, 213, 217; visits to Hunter's Hill School, 181; death, 235
Cadbury, Geraldine (Mrs.), 14-18, 22, 29, 80, 140, 280, 334; marriage, 13, 14; magistrate, 14; opening of kindergarten, 14; move to Cropwood House, 14-17, *15*; donation of Uffculme, 17-18, 20, 24, 44; on Birmingham's Special Schools Sub-Committee, 80, 137; on Uffculme School Committee, 27, 28, 53, 137; visits to Uffculme School; 35, 37, 44, 45, 59, 53, 54, 77; visits to Cropwood School, 54, 55, 56, 57, 58, 59, 60, 67, 68, 91, 93, 111, 143, 144; visits to Hunter's Hill School, 112, 114, death, 137-8, 145
Cadbury, Dorothy, 13, 14, 15, *15*, *16*, 26, 145, 170
Cadbury, (Dame) Elizabeth, 80, 133
Cadbury, George, 13, 80
Cadbury, Geraldine M. (Miss), ix, 14, 15-17, *15*, *16*, 56
Cadbury, Paul, 13, 14, 15, *15*, *16*, *16*, 56, 241, 271, 277, 279, 294
Cadbury, Richard, 12, 13, 17
Caddell, Dr. (Nat. Ass. for the Prevention of Tuberculosis), 130
calligraphy, 231
Callow, Iris, *175*
Cameron, D.C. (headteacher), 332, 337
Camp School, Cropwood, 67, 94, *98*, 143, 145, 153, 157
camping, 217, 240, 247
canal trips, 315; *see also* boating club
canework, 230, 306; *see also* basket weaving
Cangy, Jenny, **284-6**
caning, of children, 28, 82, 155, 177, 178, 222, 223, 251, 302; *see also* punishment
Cannon Hill Park, 77, 202, 273
canoeing, 231, 248, 301, 307; *see also* boating club
Capper, Edna, **103**
caretakers: Cropwood, 283, 284, 292; Haseley, *191*; Hunter's Hill, 129, 132, 251, 304; Uffculme, 24, 43, 64, 202, *274*
caretakers (names), *see* Carr; Fellows; Harrison; Hatfield; Mortiboys; Mountney; Perrygrove; Price; Riley; Ross; Rushton; Swift; Thomas
Carey, Mrs. (cook), 297
Carey, P.C., 307
carol services, 224, 299
Carpenter, Rev. L., 272
Carpenter, Sylvia, **342**
Carr, D. (teacher), 270, 271, 273, *274*
Carr, Louis (caretaker), 24, 43, 64
Carrington, Dr., 9
Carrington, Joan, *175*
Carter, Miss (teacher), 91, 94
Cartwright, Bernard W., **86**
Cash, Gladys, **93-4**
Cassells, Mr. (teacher), 278
Castle, Miss (teacher), 323
catarrh, 5, 8, 102, 221; *see also* asthma; bronchiectasis; bronchitis; chest conditions
catering courses, 256
Cattell, Norman, **154**
cattle show, 275
Cawthorne, Mrs. (cleaner), *260*
celiac disease, 219
cerebral palsy, 270
chairs, 6, 38
Chamberlain, King & Jones (general furnishers), 21
Chamberlain, Neville, 121, 125
Chamberlain, Norman (councillor), 18
Chambers, Norma, *161*
Chapman, Mr., 255, 271
Chapman, Leslie, 72
Charles Burns Unit, 279, 314
Charlottenberg, 5
Charlton, Miss (headteacher), 189, 190, 337
Chateaux Bruxelles/Dorf, 171, 177, 197, 198; *see also* Davos Alpine School
Cheal, J. & Sons, 21
Checkitts, Miss (teacher), 53
Checkley, Dorothy, *see* Sparkes, Dorothy
Chedgy, Mr. (teacher), *180*, 223
cheese, 35, 76, 99, 101, 166
Chest and Heart Association, 265
chest conditions, 104, 105, 133, 194,

139, 166, 200, 205; *see also* Milk Marketing Board; National Milk Publicity Council; National Milk Scheme
Milk in Schools Act 1934, 100
Milk Marketing Board, 50, 100
Miller, Dr., 271
Miller, Mrs. (cook), 244
Millward, Mrs. (kitchen staff), *274*
Mitchell, Dr. (Medical Officer of Health), 121, 126, 130, 148, 169, 187
Mitchell, Ivor (headteacher), **326-30**, 337
Modern Building Record, 21
Mole, Dr., 243, 283, 298
monitors, 87, 166, 169, 276
Montessori teaching, 52
Moore, Joan (teacher), 235, 271, *274*
Moore, John, **261-2**
Moore, Marian (headteacher), 185, 187, 188, 189
Moore, Michael, 205
Morris, Shirley, *238*
morris dancing, *see* dancing
Morris, Miss (teacher), 287
Morris, Miss (HMI), 210
Morris, Mr. and Mrs. (Martineau House), 203
Morrison-Smith, Dr. J., 240, 246, 264, 265
Mort (nurse), 211
Mortiboys, Frank (caretaker), *191*
Moseley, 12
Moseley Hall, 12, 13; Hospital, 43, 69, 270, 279
Moss, Ruby, *175*
mothercraft lessons, 91
Mountford, D.M., *312*
Mountney, Mr. (caretaker), 292
Mullard, Eileen, *see* Davies, Eileen
Mullen, Val, **287-9**
mumps, 32, 46, 68, 169, 177, 211
Murphy, Kathleen, *207*
Murray, Joan, 122
music, 188, 190, 217, 236, 253, 269, 270, 296; *see also* concerts
Musty, Catherine, **284**
Musty, Jenny, *see* Cangy, Jenny

naked: runs in the snow, 158; walking around, 115; *see also* sunbathing (Cropwood)
Nash, Jean, *see* Green, Jean
National Adult School Union, 13
National Association of Schoolmasters, 96
National Exhibition of Children's Art, 306
National Health Service, 162, 163, 198, 267; *see also* school health services; school medical services
National Health Service Act, 267
National Milk Publicity Council, 50
National Milk Scheme, 135
National Union of Teachers, 266
nature study, 10, 63, 194; Cropwood, 59, 68, 69, 91, 123-4, 151; Haseley Hall, 191; Hunter's Hill, 230, 309; Marsh Hill, 81; Uffculme, 19, 23, 27, 39, 43, *44*, 65, 83, 107, 166, 200, 206, 207, 269
Nechells, 95, 181
needlework, 8; Cropwood, 146, 148, 171, 172, 211; Hunter's Hill, 230; Uffculme, 40, 270, 275
neglected children, 229, 238, 239; *see also* debility
Neo-Epinine, 164
nephritis, 221, 270

nervous children, 163, 198, 233, 234, 267, 342; Cropwood, 242, 291; Hunter's Hill, 129, 221, 229, 301; Uffculme, 103, 105, 238, 269, 270; *see also* maladjusted children
nervous disorders, 8, 62, 67, 136, 229, 313; *see also* backward children; maladjusted children; nervous children
netball, 108, 217, 254
neurosis, 109; *see also* nervous children
New Street station (Birmingham), 62, 115, 162, *163*
New York City, 6
Newall, Winnie, 24, 35
Newland, Anthony, *208*
Newman, 180
Newman, Sir George, 4, 8, 80, 101
Newnham, Rose, **82**
Newsome, Ada E., **43-4**, *272*
Newton, Miss, 287, 289
Nichol, (Sister), 173
nits, 50, 135, 181, 238, 239; *see also* lice
Noakes, Mrs. (children's helper), *191*
Norris, N., *341*
North of England Furnishing Co., 21
Norwich, 6
Nublae, 164
nurses, 101, 118, 135, 172, 195, 234, 266, 314; at Cropwood, 92, 93, 124, 125, 126, 144, 147, 150, 171, 212, 219, 242, 243, 280, 282, 283, 287, 292, 293, 296; at Haseley Hall, 186, 187, *191* 192, 256, *259*, 315, *316*, 322; at Hunter's Hill, 97, 112, 114, 130, 131, 133-4, 156-7, 181; at Marsh Hill, 82, 160, 254, 314; at Skilts, 263, 316, 317, 328, 330; at Uffculme, 24, 36, 37, 45, 48, 75, 84, 106, 108, 166, 208, 234, 235, 237, 238-9, 269
nurses (names), *see* Allison; Ashby; Atkins; Barrett; Bendall; Bigger; Bond; Brown; Coan; Comb; Cone; Crosby; Dainty; Daniels; Davies; Dorrie; Edwards; Fenton; Fisher; Genever; Gossage; Hill; Hodgson; James; Jenkins; Keen; Kemp; Layer; Marshall; Mort; Nichol; Parry; Proctor; Puddifoot; Rogers; Sandy; Sheldon; Shemwell; Simfield; Smith; Southam; Tippetts; Wilkins; Williams; Yelland
nurses (personal accounts): Hunter's Hill, **133-4**, **252-3**; Uffculme, **238-9**
nutrition, 30, 63, 79, 100, 101, 135, 164, 187, 264, 267; *see also* food; school meals
Nye, A.E. (headteacher), 337

obesity, 255
O'Connors, Dr. Caroline, 5, 11, 37, 45
Okey, Margaret, *see* Donnellan, Margaret
Oliver, Mrs. (teacher), 325
O'Looney, Teresa, *296*
open-air schools: aims of, 23, 41, 62-4, 66, 67, 79, 80, 84, 194, 250, 264, 267, 325, changes in, 233, 237, 239, 256, 264-8, 271, 274, 276, 277, 278, 303, 309, 312, 313-15, 325, 334; clothing for, 6, 9, 23, 27, 39, 102, 195; first pioneer schools, 5, 6, 18, 19; requirements of, 8-10, 19, 39, 62-4, 66, 102,

195; survey of, 194-5, 266; treatment, 7, 8, 15, 16, 18, 19, 38, 41, 50, 78, 102, 116, 118, 198, 229; statistics: *1920s*, 50, 56, 64; *1930s*, 79-80, 83, 95, 101, 105, 116; *1950s*, 196, 221, 233, 242; *1960s*, 266, 271, 295, 312, 329; summary of, 334-5, 337; *see also* Appendix III, 340-2
Open-Air Studies, British Association Conference on, 27
Open Days, *see* visiting days
Open-Spaces Association, 10
opera, 311
O'Reegan, Gerard, 306
O'Riley, Mr. (teacher), 332
O'Shaugnessy, John, **168-9**
osteomyelitis, 171, 227
otitis media, 221
outdoor activities, *see* activities, outdoor
outings, *see* school outings
overcoats, 94, 102, 110, 150, 231, 307; *see also* clothing
Owen, Miss (teacher), 109, 125, 126, 142
Owen, Frances, *175*
Owen, Freda, **176**
Owen, Jack, 60

paddling pool, 241, 258, 261, 297, 299, 319
pageants, 75, *76*, 77, 83, *83*, 85, 89
painting, 231, 306
pantomimes, 223, 232
paper cutting, 39; *see also* arts and crafts
parents: over-anxious, 265; parental rejection, 300; *see also* home, links; Parents Committee; visiting days
Parents Committee, Cropwood, 218, 239, 243, 283
Parker, Mr., 112
Parker, Mr. (dentist), 300
Parker, Celia, 24
Parker, Florence, *see* Gladwin, Florence
Parker, Margaret, **540**
Parker, Winder & Achurch Ltd., 21
Parks, Miss (teacher), 254
Parry, Sister (nurse), *191*, 192, 256
Parsons, Mrs. (physiotherapist), 277
Parsons, Dr. Agnes, 11
Parsons, Hubert, 60
paths, making of, 194
Patterson, Rev. Carlisle, 240
Payne, Miss (teacher), 323
Peace Celebrations, 48
Peacock, Barry (architect), 14, 17, 21, 55; *see also* Cossins, Peacock & Bewlay (architects)
Peake, Gillian, *see* Lunney, Gillian
Pearce, Mrs. (teacher), 299
Pearman, John, 326
Pedley, Miss (HMI), 299
Pegg, Joyce, **106**
periodical examinations, *see* medical examinations
Perkins, Miss (teacher), 67, 68, 70
Perrygrove, Mr. (caretaker), 143, 211; death, 212
Perrygrove, Mrs., 146, 177
Perthes disease, 221
Peters, Mr. (teacher), 254
petit-mal, 270, 342
petrol rationing, 241
pets, 39, 231, 247, 330, 333; *see also* animals; bantams; hens

Phillips, Dr., 328
Phillips, Betty, *see* Roberts, Betty
Phillips, Olive, **95**
philosophy of open-air schools, *see* open-air schools (aims)
phlyctenular ophthalmia, 31
phobias: fear/dislike of school, 234, 270, 275, 297, 301
photographic club, 306, 311
Physical Deterioration, Local Government Board's Report (1904), 4
physical drill, 34, 45, 74
physical education, 12, 50, 63, 74, 101, 118; Cropwood, 111, 220, *242*, *243*, 296; Hunter's Hill, 179, 230, 231, 309; Uffculme, 48, 74; *see also* drill; dancing; exercises; sports
physical handicaps, *see* disabled children; physically defective; physically disabled/handicapped children
physically defective, 2, 4, 11; *see also* 'crippled' children
physically disabled/handicapped children, 2, 154, 156, 221, 266, 313; *see also* 'crippled' children; disabled children
physiotherapy, 139, 141, 195, 239, 252, 268, 276, 292
phythisis, 45
picnics, 126
pigeons, 248
Piff, Alice, 26
Pilgrims School (for asthmatics), 268
Pilling, Kenneth, **294**
pine trees, 5, 243
Pines School, 314, 315
Pinner, Richard (teacher), 306, 307, 308, **309-12**
Pinsent, Hume (Mrs.), 27, 28, 32
planned rhythm (timetable), 327, 328, 330; *see also* curriculum
Plant, Miss (teacher), 84, 85
plasticine modelling, 18
platforms, slatted, 39, 341, 342
Platt, Enid, *see* Deeble, Enid
playroom (Cropwood), 123, 124, 125, 295
plays, school: Cropwood, 91, 172; Hunter's Hill, 95, 224, 247, 308; Uffculme, 89, 204, 205, 210; *see also* drama; pantomimes
Plester, Mr. (gardener), *260*, 261
Plowman, Audrey, **149**, 173, 211
pneumonia, 91, 103, 112, 150, 253, 340
pocket money, 248
polio, 221
polka, *see* dancing
Pollentine, Miss, 285
pollution, 1, 2, 5, 54, 196, 265
ponds, making of, 194
pool, Uffculme, 83, 141
porridge, 1, 6, 10, *52*, 101, *236*, 341; Cropwood, 69, 72, 122; Haseley Hall, 187, 193; Hunter's Hill, 187, 193; Uffculme, 25, 30, 43, 54, 76, 139, 166, 200, 204, 208, 236; *see also* school meals
postural defects, 90; *see also* exercises; spine, curvature of
postural drainage, 195, 216, 236, 238, 307
postural exercises, *see* exercises
potatoes, 79, 122, 157; peeling, 27, 166, 176

Potter, Ellen M. (teacher), 24, 35, 36
pottery, 229, 254, 276
Pott's disease, 221
poultry keeping, 39, 47, 53
poverty, 10, 11, 18, 50, 90, 102, 163; *see also* housing conditions; malnutrition
Powell, Councillor, 271
Powell, W.J. (teacher), 305, 307, 308
Pratt, Miss (teacher), 67, 70, 112
Preece, Mary, 71
prefects: Cropwood, 212, 295; Hunter's Hill, 179, 248, *250*, 302; *see also* 'houses'
pre-school care, 267
preventative medicine, 6, 77, 267
Price, Mr. (caretaker), 284
Price, A. (night attendant), 136
Priestman, Miss (teacher), 186, 187, 188, 189
Priestman, Mrs., 17
primary units (for delicate pupils), 314, 315
Pritchard, Miss (teacher), 138
Pritchard, June, *see* Teece, June
probation officers, 172, 298, 308
Proctor (nurse), 292
project work, 248; *see also individual school log book entries*
Providence (America), 6, *8*
prunes, 86, 99, 101, 107, 115
psoriasis, 270
psychological disorders, 267, 303; *see also* emotional problems; learning difficulties; maladjusted children
psychosomatic disorders, 263, 326
public health, 264, 314
Public Health, 265
Puddifoot, Mrs. (nurse), 317, 323
pulmonary fibrosis, *see* fibrosis
punishment, 167, 169, 273, 340; corporal, 82; *see also* caning; discipline

Queen's Hospital, Birmingham, 185
Queensbridge School, 200, 206, 274

rabbits, 28, 224, 231, 247, 301, 333
Radnall, Irene, **106**
raffia work, 48, 65, 86, 231
Raistrick, Miss (teacher), 172
rambles, *see* walks
Ramirez, Miss (HMI), 271
Randall, C. (teacher), 235, 270, 271, 273, *274*, 276, 279
ration books, 181; *see also* food
Raybould, Raymond, **341**
Rea, River, 185
reading: Cropwood, 150, 242, *281*, 293; Hunter's Hill, 128, 229, 230; Uffculme, 32, 48, 236, 268, 269, 306; *see also* remedial reading; storytelling
reading/speaking competitions, 121
records (of pupils), 69; *see also* admission registers
record sessions, 277, 288
Redditch, 148, 178, 247, 326
Reedswood Park Open-Air School, 340
Reid, Audrey, 211; *see also* Plowman, Audrey
Reid, Pat, **291**
religious education, 231, 269; *see also* assembly, school
remedial breathing, *see* exercises
remedial exercises, *see* exercises; physiotherapy
remedial gymnast, 327; *see also* Collins, Mr.

remedial reading, 268, 269, 292
remedial teaching, 198, 229, 269
respiratory disorders, *see* asthma; bronchiectasis; bronchitis; catarrh; chest conditions
rest, 6, 7, 8, 9, 10, 50, 64, 80, 119, 194, 233, 264, 266, 342; Cropwood, 61, 67, *68*, 70, 71, 93, 124, 217, 218; Haseley, 319, 324; Hunter's Hill, 97, 99, 159, 161, 248, 252, 310; Marsh Hill, 82, 160, 254; Skilts, 328; Uffculme, 19, 39, 41, 46, 47, 52, 53, *85* 87, 139, 141, *164*, *166*, 204, 206, 236, 239, 271, 277
rest-sheds: Cropwood, 55, 67, *68*, 71, *243*; Marsh Hill, 81, 195, 254, *255*, 256; Uffculme, 23, 29, *30*, 32, 45, 47, 106, 117, 208, 234, 239, 254, 270
retarded children, 243, 265; Cropwood, 217, 242; Hunter's Hill, 228; Skilts, 329; *see also* backward children
rheumatic children, 52, 67, 185; Cropwood, 109; Haseley Hall, 185-6, 187; Hunter's Hill, 221
Rheumatic Clinic, 228
rheumatic fever, 103, 185, 186, 187, 189
rheumatic hearts, *see* heart diseases
Rice, G.A. (teacher), 247, 249
Rice, Margaret, **253**
rice, ground, 54, 107
rice pudding, 121
Richardson, K. (teacher), 298
Richardson, Leslie (teacher), 220, 224, 228, **248-9**, *249*, 251, 253, 297, 299
Richardson, Nellie, *see* Crawford, Nellie
Richards, June, *204*
rickets, 5, 31, 49, 52, 62, 264
Riley, A. (caretaker), 74
ringworm, 5, 31, 49, 102, 264
Roberts, Dr., 146, 177
Roberts, Betty, **149**
Roberts, Gladys, 150, 151
Roberts, J. (teacher), 96, 99, 111
Roberts, M. (teacher), 297
Robinson, Brian, *184*
Robinson, Dr. O., 30
Rodell, Irene, **341**
Rogers, (nurse), 48
Rogers, J. (teacher), 96, 99, 112
roller skating, 232
Rolls, Doris, **89-90**
Rose, Miss (teacher), 132
Rosemary Cottage, 14, 16, 55, 59, 67, 71, *98*, 110, 144, 149, 176, 218, 219, 220, 241, 283, 284, 289, 290, 296; *see also* Cropwood School
Ross, Mr. (caretaker), 221, 223, 249, 302, 304
Ross, Mrs., 114, 222, 223, 232, 247, 250, 251
Ross, E.L. (Inspector of Special Schools, Birmingham), 67, 68, 91, 129, 144, 146, 148, 149, 171, 173, 192, 210, 211, 294
rounders, 73, 92, 108, 121, 161, 217, 231, 254
Roundheads and Cavaliers Pageant, 83
Rowe, Dr., 227
Royal Commission on the Blind, Deaf (1899), 2
Royle, Gillian (headteacher), 315, *316*, 321, **322-5**, 337
rugby, 88

rugmaking, 73, 229
rugs, 9, 23, 25, 76; *see also* blankets
Rumball, Diana, 172, *175*
runaways, *see* absconding
rural science, 231; *see also* animals; pets
Rushton, Mr. (caretaker), 87
Russell, E.L. (Chief Education Officer), 213, 227
Russell, Mrs. (cook), 24, 33

Sainsbury, Dr., 145, 162, *163*, 170
St Martin's Church, Birmingham, 272
St Vitus's dance, *see* chorea
sandpit, 241, 258, 297, 317, 324
Sandy (nurse), 126
Satchwell, Mrs. (teacher), 289
Saul, Pauline, *xiii*, **203-6**; *see also* Brueton, Pauline
Saunders, D., **342**
Savage, Mr. (teacher), 84
Sawdon, Miss (teacher), 170
Sawyer, Lady Adelaide, 185, 319
Sawyer, Sir James, *185* 185, 193, 319
scabies, 264
scales, 28, 63, 185
scarlet fever, 5, 16, 27, 28, 31, 35, 59, 156, 181, 210; decline of, 264
school attendance, *see* absconding; admissions; school log books
school camps, 79; *see also* camp school (Cropwood)
School Choirs Festival, 108
school clinics, 101, 112, 162, 198, 264, 308, 314; establishment of, 4, 11; eye clinic, 222, 227, 299; *see also* Asthma Clinic; Great Charles St Clinic; Handsworth Clinic; Rheumatic Clinic; school health services; school medical services
School Dental Officers, 233, 245, 271; *see also* dentists
school health services (1945-70) (formerly called school medical services): *1940s*, 136, 142, 162; *1950s*, 194, 196, 198, 241; *1960s*, 264-8, 289, 314; *see also* Birmingham Education Committee (School Officers Reports); Chief Medical Officer's annual reports (Board/Ministry of Education); school medical services (1907-1945)
school inspections, *see* Inspectors school reports
School Inspectors, *see* Inspectors
school leavers, 202, 272, 278; *see also* leaving certificates
school log books, 326, 338-9: **Cropwood**: *1920s*, 57-61, 67-8; *1930s*, 91-2, 109, 120-1, 125-8; *1940s*, 142-9, 169-73; *1950s*, 210-13, 217-20, 240-2; *1960s*, 282-4, 287, 289-90, 292-3, 295; **Haseley Hall**: *1940s*, 192-3; *1950s*, 256-8; *1960s*, 315-17, 321; **Hunter's Hill**: *1930s*, 96-7, 112-14, 130-2; *1940s*, 152-3, 156, 177-81; *1950s*, 222-4, 227-8, 246-7, 251, 252; *1960s*, 298-302, 307-8; **Marsh Hill**: *1930s*, 81; *1960s*, 313; **Uffculme**: *1911-19*, 25, 28-37, 44-9; *1920s*, 52-4, 64-5, 73-5; *1930s*, 120; *1940s*, 136-8, 164-6; *1950s*, 199-200, 234-6; *1960s*, 270-3, 278-9
school meals, 4, 5, 6, 10, 19, 41, 63, 101, 135, 264, 266, 314; payment of, 28, 43, 80, 167, 208;

Cropwood, 72, 92, 122, 124, 174, 280-1, 285; Haseley Hall, 325; Hunter's Hill, 97, 99, 154, 159; Marsh Hill, 82, 160, 161, 254; Uffculme, 21, 25, *26*, 28, 36, 43, 75, 76, 87, 104, 107, 108, 120, 139, 141, 166, 200, 209, 236, 237, 238, 268, 276, 277; *see also* food; nutrition
school medical officers, 11, 63, 79, 100, 112, 118, 164, 173, 194, 195, 196, 221, 239, 243, 264, 289, 314, 317, 328; *see also* Birmingham Education Committee (School Medical Officers Reports); Chief Medical officers annual reports (Board/Ministry of Education); doctors; school health/medical service
school medical services (1907-45): foundation of, 4, 11, 19, 31; First World War, 41, 49; *1920s*, 50, 52, 62-4, 67; *1930s*, 79, 100, 101-2, 117; *1940s*, 135-6; *see also* Birmingham Education Committee (School Medical Officers Reports); Chief Medical officers annual reports (Board/Ministry of Education); school health services (1945-70)
school outings, 133, 222, 232, 290, 299; *see also* Dovedale; France; Leamington; Lickey Hills; Malvern; Stratford
school plays, *see* plays, school
school records, 338; *see also* Admission Registers; school log books
School Registers, *see* Admission Registers
schools, *see individual names*: Astley Hall; Beausale; Bow Rd; Cottingham Rd; Cropwood; Dame Cadbury; Floodgate; Gem St; George St West; Greet Kindergarten; Hartfield Crescent; Haseley Hall; Hatton; Hazlebury; Hunter's Hill; Little Green Lane; Malvern; Marsh Hill; Pines; Reedswood Park; Shenstone; Skilts; Springfield; Springwell Hse; Stockland Green; Uffculme; Upton House; Welsh Farm; William Murdoch; Wroxall; Wroxall Abbey
scooters, 245, 248, 251
Scouts: Cropwood, 59; Hunter's Hill, 99, 112, 304
screens (classroom/dormitory), 9, 21, 22, 38, 68, 76, 82, 124, 270
Scrivener, Mrs. (teacher), 323
Scrivington, Miss (teacher), 197
Seaside School, *see* Martineau House (Seaside School)
Second World War, 117, 126, 134-60, 162, 188, 190; *see also* air raids; wartime
security, 300
selection of pupils, 19, 23, 62, 116; *see also* admissions
selection of staff, *see* staff (selection)
Selly Oak Hospital, 172
semolina, 86, 99
septic throats, 37
Severn Trent Water Authority, 321
Sewell, Colleen, *296*
sewing, 40, 48, 94, 108; *see also* darning; dressmaking
sex education, 267, 327
Shaftesbury, Earl of, 1

Sharman, Mrs. (teacher), 316
Sharp, Miss, 284
Shaw, George B., 108
Shaw, R.M., 57
Shawson, Edith, 71
Sheffield, 6, 19
Sheldon, (Sister), 243, 282
Shelter, The (Cropwood), 16, 17, 58, 59, 68, *94, 95, 98*
Shemwell, Miss (teacher), 240
Shenstone School, 314, 315
Shewring, Dr., 283
shipping routes, 88
shoes, 132, 133, 243, 263, 285; cleaning of, 71, 122, 134, 154, 158, 218, 252, 321; *see also* clogs
Shooter's Hill Open-Air School, 6, 10
Showell, Mr., 211
showers, 5, 9, 102; Cropwood, 69, 92, 244; Hunter's Hill, 132; Uffculme, 21-2, 43, 106, 108, 166, 169; *see also* baths
shutters, 341
Simfield, (Sister), 284
Simmons, Hilda (cook), 334
singing, 63, 88, 106, 108, 161, 217, 290, 296
siting of open-air schools, 8-10, 39, 62
sitting out bags, 6, 8, 9
skiing, 197
Skilts: Lower, 326, 331; Upper, 326
Skilts School: architecture/building, *327*, 331, 332; history of house, 326; opening of, 198, 262, *327*, 330; *1950s*, 258, 262-3, *262*; *1960s*, 268, 295, 321, 325, 326-34; *see also* Inspectors school reports; headteachers
skin diseases, 67, 130, 135, 229; *see also* eczema; impetigo; lupus; psoriasis
skipping, 233
Skyllus Grange, 326
slats, 39, 341
sledging, *see* tobogganing
sleep-time garden, 55, 71
slums, 3, 19, 23, 54, 94; *see also* housing conditions; poverty
Small Heath, 65, 75, 262
Smallwood, Dr., 127, 142
Smallwood, Mrs. (Cllr), 211, 251
Smellie, Dr., 67, 91
Smith, Dr., 279, 307
Smith, Mrs. (cook-housekeeper), 283, 284, 285
Smith (nurse), 186, 258
Smith, Diane, **200**
Smith, E.V. (Chairman of Birmingham Education Committee), 192, 224, 227
Smith, Eileen Wilson, *see* Wilson Smith, Eileen
Smith, Gordon, *159*
Smith, Ruth, **186-7**
Smith, Major & Stevens Ltd., 21
smoking, 267
snow, 194; Cropwood, 62, 125, 142, 145, 146, 171, *287*; Hunter's Hill, 99, 112, 133, 152, 158, 227, 302; Skilts, 331, 333; Uffculme, 30, 31-2, 34, 43, 45, 53, 54, 73, 137, 164, 234; *see also* cold weather; frost
soapstones, 8, 9
Soar, Miss (teacher), 170, 171, 172, 175, 176, 211, 212, 213, 220, 243, 244, 285
soccer, 88
social conditions, better, 267

sociological problems, 264, 265, 267, 295, 297, 301, 305; *see also* 'difficult' children; 'disturbed' children; environment; housing; maladjusted children; phobias
soldiers, 40-1, 44, 49
Southam, (Sister), 234, 238, 240
Sparks, Dorothy, **110-11**
speaking/reading competitions, 121
Special Education, Advisory Committee, for, 266
'special needs', 136, 267, 334
special schools, development of, 4, 163, 268; Birmingham, 50-1, 195-6, 203, 233
Special Schools Sub-Committee, *see* Birmingham Special Schools Sub-Committee
speech disorders, 266, 313
speech therapy, 266, 268, 328
Spence, Moira (teacher), 199, 200, 206, 207, *209*, 234, 235, *236*; *see also* Armson, Moira
spine, curvature of, 10, 67; *see also* exercises; postural defects
spitting, 11
sports: annual sports contests, 89, 164; sports days: at Cropwood, 60; at Hunter's Hill, 96, 158, 183, 299; *see also* activities (outdoor); athletics; cricket; football; hockey; merry-go-round; rounders; rugby; soccer; table tennis; tennis
Springfield School, 321
Springwell House Open-Air School, London, 342
Squire, Miss (teacher), 84
staff: accommodation, 194, 228, 251, 252, 279-80, 290, 292, 309, 331; dedication of, 265, 330, 332, 334; extraneous duties of, 129, 134, 176, 256, 292, 297, 308, 309, 321, 322, 330; problems in staffing, 290, 292, 308, 327; selection of, 62-3, 96, 128-9, 280; *see also* caretakers; children's helpers; cooks; doctors; kitchen (staff); nurses; school medical officers; teachers; teamwork
stamp club, 134, 306
standards, educational, *see* educational standards
Staples, Phyllis, 150
Stapleton, T.M., **174-5**
Starkey, Ruth, *175*
stay, average length of, 233; Cropwood, 55, 57, 67, 109; Hunter's Hill, 128, 221; Skilts, 329; Uffculme, 31, 118, 273
steamer chairs, 6
Steane, Beryl, **200**
Steane, Lucy, *see* Goddard, Lucy
steroids, 265, 268
Stewart, Miss (teacher), 197
Stiles, Rita, *189*
Stocker, Mrs. (teacher), 199
Stockland Green School, 314
Stockley, E.M., 33
Stokes, Miriam, *175*
story-telling, 195; Cropwood, 124, 150, 210; Hunter's Hill, 248; Marsh Hill, 160; Skilts, 195, 328; Uffculme, 32, 39; *see also* literature; reading
Stratford, 192, 234, 243, 270, 286
Streptomycin, 196, 233
stretchers, 9, 23, *38*, 64, 82; *see also* rest
Stubbs, Mr. (teacher), 308
Studley, 326

suet, 30
Sulphadiazene, 181, 210, 222, 246
Sulphaquanidin, 222
Sulphathiazine, 227
sun, 8, 22, 40, 52
sunbathing, 79, 102; Cropwood, 59, 60, 93, 121, 122, 124, 126, 150, 151; Uffculme, 106, *107*
Sunday Mercury, 317
Sundays: Cropwood, *61*, 62, 122, 124, 174, 244; Hunter's Hill, 99, 178, 179; *see also* churchgoing
sunray treatment, 141, 167, 207, 254
surgery, 134, 155, 238, 252
surgical spirits, 122
Sutherland, Dr. H., 148
Sutton, Marlene, *208*
sweaters, *see* jerseys; *see also* clothing
sweets, 94, 122, 150, *170*, 200, 233, 248; *see also* tuck
Swift, Mr. (caretaker), *274*
swimming, 50, 79; Cropwood, 55, 66, 67, 93, 110, 111, 122, 143, 146, 152, 174, 213; Hunter's Hill, 96, 99, 115, 132, 159; Uffculme, 108, 207
Swinden & Sons, 21
swings, 245, 322
Swiss Red Cross, 162, 166
Switzerland, 162, 165, 166, 170, 171, 172, 178, 181, 182, 196, 197, 198, 265; *see also* Davos Alpine School
sword dancing, *see* dancing
Symons, Miss (teacher), 149, 150

table tennis, 310
tables (arithmetic), 207, 236
Tame, River, 185
Tansley, Mr. C., 321
Tardebigge: canal, 210, 305; canoe/boating club, 231, 246, 248
Taylor, Miss (teacher), 211, 218
Taylor, Doris, M., **54**, 62
Taylor, Rev. Isaac, 1
Taylor, Raymond, 305
teachers (names), *see* Alexander; Alflatt; Anderson; Ansell; Armson; Aston; Atkins; Atkinson; Aze; Bailey; Baldock; Barrodale; Bazire; Bell; Belling; Bennet; Billing; Blay; Bolton; Bottom; Boyd; Bromage; Brooke; Browning; Bullock; Burridge; Burt; Carr; Cartes; Cassells; Castle; Chedgy; Clark; Clarke; Cook; Cooper; Dallow; Davies; Davis; Dilworth; Disney; Dix; Edwards; Etherington; Evans; Evershed; Franklin; French; Frisby; Furback; Galtery; George; Gorden; Gough; Goulden; Hardinge; Hardy; Harlow; Hartman; Haworth; Hill; Hingley; Hudeson; Hughes; Hunt; Hurley; Hurly; Jarvis; Jay; Jones; Keen; Lamb; Lambaderwn; Lattimore; Lawrence; Lawson; Leadbeater; Ledger; Lewis; Long; Lowe; McCormick; McDonald; Maguire; Mann; Meer; Mellor; Merrick; Merriman; Moore; Morris; Newton; Oliver; O'Riley; Owen; Parks; Payne; Pearce; Perkins; Peters; Pinner; Plant; Potter; Powell; Pratt; Priestman; Pritchard; Raistrick; Randall; Rice; Richardson; Roberts; Robinson; Rogers; Rose; Satchwell; Savage; Sawden; Scrivener; Scrivington; Sharman; Sharp; Soar; Stewart; Stocker; Stubbs; Symons; Taylor; Tearse;

Tebbutt; Tedd; Trace; Trihy; Tucker; Wainwright; Wales; Ward; Webb; Weedon; Wetherall; Whipp; White; Whitehouse; Wightman; Wishart; Woodward; Yoxall; *see also* headteachers
teachers: difficulties in open-air schools, 140, 208, 266, 280, 314; remedial teaching skills, 198; requirements of, 198, 230, 330; residential duties, 290, 292, 310, 332; training of, 3, 53, 82, 198, 216, 228, 314, 329; *see also* classes; headteachers; Froebel training; staff; teamwork; 'whole child' (approach to teaching)
teachers (personal accounts): Cropwood, **176**, **215-17**, **280**, **288**, **292**, **294**, **295-6**; Haseley Hall, **187-9**, **190-1**; Hunter's Hill, **157-8**, **225**, **228-9**, **229-33**, **248-9**, **303**, **309-12**; Marsh Hill, **255-6**, **313-15**; Skilts, **262-3**, **326-30**; Uffculme, **140-1**, **203**, **208-10**, **237-8**, **268-9**
teamwork, 129, 134, 265; *see also* staff; teachers; 'whole child'
Tearse, Miss (teacher), 112
Tebbutt, M. (teacher), 249, 251, 297, 307
Tedd, Miss (teacher), *298*
Teece, June, **175-6**
teeth, *see* dental decay; dental treatment; toothbrushes
television, 218, 231, 247, 251, 257, 283, 296, 298, 308, 310; *see also* BBC schools programmes
temperature (body), 341
tennis, 93, 122, 175, 299
termly reviews, *see* medical examinations
testing: attainment testing, 217; mental testing, 217; *see also* academic ability; educational attainment; examinations, academic
theatres, 81, 175, 311
Thomas, Mr. (caretaker), 284, 292
Thomas, Isobel (teacher), 200, 206, 207, 208; *see also* Bazire, Isobel
Thomson, Dr. P.H., 57, 59
throat infections, 246, *see also* septic throats
Throckmorton family, 190
thyroid problems, 121
tics, multiple, 221
Tidmus, (Betty) L. (teacher), 53, 88, 138, 140, *164*, 166
Tilley, D., 317
Times, The, 118
timetables, 7, 8, 10, 221, 269, 327, 328, 330; *see also* curriculum
Timmins, Margaret, *95*
Tippetts (nurse), 75
Todman, Dr., 307
tobogganing, 59, 61, 113, 125, 128, 133, 146, 149, 154, 171, 174, 197, 281, *187*, 298
toilets, 270
tokens (for trams/buses), 25, 43, 209
Tomkinson, Joan, *see* Farmer, Joan
tonics, 53; *see also* medication
Tonks, R., *180*
tonsils, 5, 11, 19, 86, 97, 112, 164, 192, 222, 298; tonsilitis, 92, 131, 144; tonsilectomy, 252; *see also* adenoids
Tookey, Bill, **71**, **99**
tools, 27, 128
toothbrushes, 25, 69, 82, 102, 244,

254; *see also* dental decay
torch chases, 250
tower, the (Cropwood), 123
Towyn, 101, 199, 202, 203, 206, 207, 210, 233; *see also* Martineau House
Trace, Olive (teacher), 176, 211
training courses, *see* teachers
trains, 25, 57, 68, 72, 93, 97, 109, 114, 121, 132, 159, 249; *see also* bank engines; 'Big Bertha'; Blackwell; Lickey Incline
trams, 11, 18, 19, 43, 89, 99, 183
transfers to normal schools, 234; *see also* medical examinations
treatment, medical, *see* medical treatment; National Health Service; open-air schools; school health services; school medical services
trees, 8, 124, 140, 151, 257, *329*; *see also* pine trees
Trihy, T. (teacher), 252
tripe, 155
truancy, *see* absconding
Trueman, Joyce, *see* Pegg, Joyce
Trueman, T.M., *see* Stapleton, T.M.
tuberculosis, 1, 2, 5, 6, 19, 67, 104, 121, 148; Birmingham schoolchildren, 11, 52, 102, 116, 162; contact TB, 190, 221, 301; death rate from, 196, 233, 264; decline of, 264; tubercular glands, 8, 14, 31, 62; Hunter's Hill, 156, 179, 251; Uffculme, 31, 32, 45, 65, 103
tuck: tuckshops, 94, 233; Cropwood, 70, 72, 111, 122, 149, 150, 151, 214; Hunter's Hill, 98, 248; Uffculme, 108; *see also* sweets
Tucker, John (Jack) W. (teacher), 223, 224, 225, **226**, 227, 228, 231, 250
Tucker, K.G. (teacher), 178, 183
Tucker, Rowena, 227
Tudor, Mary (dentist), 245-6
Turner, Jayne, **84-5**
Turner, Rose, *see* Newnham, Rose
Twist, Miss (cook), 122, 125, 211
Tyler, Miss (children's helper), 211
Tyler, Margaret, 71
typing classes, 217, 296

Uffculme House, 13, *13*, 14, 17, 18, 21, 44
Uffculme Park, 32
Uffculme School, 228, 335, 337; architecture/building, 21-3, *23, 25, 26, 30, 35,* 38, *66, 107, 201, 202*; Cadbury donation of, 18; map, 42; opening of, 21-49; selection of first pupils, 19; *1920s*, 52-5, 56, 64-6, 73-7; *1930s*, 83-90, 104, 105-8, 117-20, 131; *1940s*, 136-41, 164-9; *1950s*, 198-210, 222, 234-9; *1960s*, 264, 268-79; *see also* Inspectors school reports; pool; school log books
Uffculme School Committee, 27, 28, 53
ultra-violet radiation treatment, 77, 102, 233

underweight children, 341, 342; *see also* debility; malnutrition
Underwood School, 313, 314
uniform, *see* clothing
Upton House Open-Air School, London, 341
Urquhart, Marjory A. (headteacher), 193, 215, 239, 243, 245, 248, 256, 279-80, 281, 284, 286, 287, 288, 291, 292, 294, 295, 337; appointments, to Haseley and Cropwood, 190, 215, 217, 257; in school log books, 217, 252, 257, 258, 289, 293; personal accounts, **190-2**, **215-17**, **280**, **294**; photographs of, *191, 288*; reports by, 280, 293-4; retirement, 293
USA, *see* America

vaccination, 267
Vann, David, 307
vegetables, 27, 63, 84, 86, 157, 331
verandas, 9, 95, 97, 103, 159, *335*
verminous children, 5; *see also* dirty children; fleas; lice; nits
verminous infestations, 31, 50, 102, 162, 282; *see also* dirty children; fleas; lice; nits
verrucas, 252
V.E. Day, 169
Victory Day, 170
visiting days, 196; Cropwood, 58, 62, 68, 72, 94, 124, 125, 126, 142, 146, 148, 211, 220, 240, 241, 243, 283, 292, 293, 294; Haseley Hall, 192, 193, 257, 315, 317, 319, 322; Hunter's Hill, 96, 99, 129, 153, 156, 159, 181, 182, 183, 231, 247, 248, 253, 298, 299, 300, 301, 308; Skilts, 328, 333; Uffculme, 35, 74
visitors, to open-air schools, 294
vitamin supplements, 233, 254; *see also* Bemax; cod liver oil; iron; malt; tonics
Vollam, Dr., 178, 222, 227, 246, 282

Wainwright, Mr. (teacher), 130, 132
waiting lists, 265; *see also* admissions; selection of pupils
Wales, Margaret (teacher), *xiii*, 139, 166, 168, 202, 204, 207, 208, 210, 236; appointment, 138; in log books, 138, 199, 200, 234, 235; personal account, **140-1**, **203**; photographs of, *165, 237*; resignation, 235
Wales Ltd., 38
Walker, John, 27
walking barefoot, 70, 87, 104, 122, 151, 203, 207
walks (rambles), 79; Cropwood, 70, 72, 93, 94, 122, 125, 142, 281; Davos Alpine School, 197; Haseley Hall, 258, 321; Hunter's Hill, 99, 132, 158, 178, 221, 226, 249, 301; Marsh Hill, 81; Skilts, 263, *331*
Wallis, Joyce, 172
Walsall, 340
Walton, Gertrude (headteacher), 69,

70, 71, 91, 94, 96, 114, 115, 116, 128, 152, 155, 158, 337; appointments, 60, 96; in school log books, 130, 147; retirement, 157; school reports by, 128-9
Walton, Margaret, 175
Ward, Miss (teacher), 321, 323
Warder, Dallas, 146
Wareing, Maurice, **162**, *163*, 167, **167-8**, **178**
warmth, 300; *see also* comfort; heating
Warnock Report, 267
Warom, John, **197**, **254-5**
wartime, 117, 126-7, 134-60, 162, 188, 190; *see also* air raids; air raid shelters; bombs
Warwick, Countess of, 187
Warwickshire Chamber of Agriculture, 185
washing machine, 300, 301
washing up, 176; *see also* domestic duties
water, measurement of, 333
water supply (Haseley Hall), 192, 257
Wathes Bros, 21
Watson, Mrs. (kitchen staff), *274*
weather, conditions of, *see* cold weather; fog; frost; hot weather; school log books; snow
weather study, 8, 39, 72, 90, 168
weaving, 8, 40, 83, *108*, 229, 230, 306
Webb, Miss (teacher), 84, 85
Webb, Alice, *see* Higgins, Alice
Webb, Margaret, *208*
Webb, Ray, *184*
Webster, Betty, **86**, **92-3**
Weedon, Mr. (teacher), 222
weekend closure (Cropwood), 290
weekly boarding: Cropwood, 290, 296; Skilts, 332; Uffculme, 47, 48, 52, 65, 86, 105, 106
weighing sessions, 9, 54, 63; Cropwood, 57, 211; Hunter's Hill, 181, 221, 307; Uffculme, 19, 28, 30, 35, 37, 45, 46, 53, 239
Weir, Terry, *180*, **183-4**, *184*
Welsh Farm School, 314
West, Lucy, 193
Wetherall, Mr. (teacher), 131, 143
Wetherall, Mrs., 143, 144
Wheatley-Hubbard, Mr., 235, 238
Wheedon, Janet, *296*
wheeziness, 265; *see also* asthma; bronchiectasis; bronchitis; chest conditions
Whipp, Miss (teacher), 211, 212, 218
White, Emily (teacher), 43, 45, 47
White, Lawrence, *184*
Whitehead, Judy, 175
Whitehouse, Mr. (teacher), 254
Whitney, Mrs., 178, 183
Whitney, Janet, 170, 173
Whittall, Norah, **106**
Whitworth, G., *180*
'whole child' (approach to teaching and health), 198, 233, 249, 309,

328, 329
Wightman, Mrs. (teacher), 292
Wilkins, Florence (nurse), 24, 36, 37, 45
William Murdoch School, 314
Williams, Miss (teacher), 219, 220, 242
Williams, Miss, 298, 299
Williams, C. (teacher), 252
Williams, Gladys, M., **61**
Williams, Graham (headteacher), 296, 312, 337
Williams, K. (teacher), 283, 284, 287
Williams, O., **157-8**
Williams, Phyllis, 121, 133
Willis, Florence, **103-4**
Wilmot, Frances, *xiii*, **206-7**, **213-14**; *see also* Headford, Frances
Wilson, David, 305
Wilson, Dr., 142, 143
Wilson, Dr. L., 37
Wilson, Mrs., 172
Wilson Smith, Eileen (teacher), **187-9**
Wilson Stuart, Mr., 127, 143, 144
Wise, F.S. (headteacher), 198, 199, 202, 203, 337
Wishart, Miss (teacher), 147
Witherby, F.Y. (teacher at Davos), 116
Withy, Cathy, *296*
Wood, Mr. (Chairman of Birmingham Education Committee), 271
Wood, K. (cook), *see* Hexley, K.
Wood & Kendrick, architects, 185
Woodward, Mrs. (teacher), 325
woodwork, 8, 39, 63; Cropwood, 296; Hunter's Hill, 129, 220, 221, 296; Skilts, 330; Uffculme, 35, 38, 47, 168, 270, 275, 276
World War I, *see* First World War
World War II, *see* air raids; Second World War; wartime
Worrall, Ida, *208*
Wright, Mrs. (Cllr), 227
Wright, Mrs. (Chairman of Special Services Sub-Committee), 219
Wright, Mr. D.A. (headteacher), 279, 337
Wrigley, Vera, 92
writing, 214, 244; Cropwood, 242; Hunter's Hill, 306; Skilts, 329; Uffculme, 269
Wroxall Abbey School, 261
Wroxall School, 256
Wyllie, Miss (Inspector of Special Schools), 271, 273

x-rays, chest, *see* chest conditions

Yardley Green Sanatorium/Hospital, 102, 103, 114, 233
Yelland, Sister, 254
York, Duke of, 64
York Woods, 316
Yorkshire, East, 341
youth hostelling, 248
Yoxall, Mr. (teacher), 197